MANAGING FOODSERVICE OPERATIONS:

A systems approach for healthcare and institutions

Third Edition

John B. Knight, Ph.D.

DMA

Dietary Managers Association

KENDALL/HUNT PUBLISHING COMPANY
4050 Westmark Drive Dubuque, Iowa 52002

ISBN 7872-3374-9

Printed in the United States of America
10 9 8 7 6 5 4

DEDICATION

To the students and dietary managers who will read this text, benefit from it, and apply its principles to their working lives to better serve their fellow human beings. May God richly bless each of them!

Dr. John B. Knight, CFBE
Director
Hotel, Restaurant and
Tourism Management
Indiana University
Purdue University
Fort Wayne, Indiana

CONTENTS

Preface vii
Acknowledgment ix

1. INTRODUCTION TO FOODSERVICE AND MANAGEMENT 1

FOOD PROCUREMENT, PRODUCTION AND SERVICE

2. MENU PLANNING AND RECIPES 43
3. SANITATION AND SAFETY 73
4. PURCHASING, RECEIVING AND INVENTORY MANAGEMENT 115
5. FACILITY LAYOUT, DESIGN AND EQUIPMENT 167
6. FOOD PRODUCTION AND SERVICE 197
7. EVALUATION OF FOOD AND NUTRITION SERVICES 235

ADMINISTRATIVE AND HUMAN RESOURCE MANAGEMENT

8. STAFFING AND SCHEDULING 279
9. HUMAN RESOURCE DEVELOPMENT 337
10. SUPERVISOR AS MANAGER OF CHANGE 383
11. LEADERSHIP 399
12. COMMUNICATION: INTERNAL AND EXTERNAL RELATIONS 427
13. FINANCIAL MANAGEMENT 453
14. MARKETING MANAGEMENT 483
15. PROFESSIONAL DEVELOPMENT 493

Appendix A 507
Appendix B 509
Appendix C 511
Appendix D 517

Index 527

PREFACE

This third edition of *Managing Foodservice Operations* has been reorganized and rewritten with the student and dietary manager in mind. Chapter outlines have been added, as have end-of-chapter summaries, key terms, questions, and case studies. The reader will appreciate the new figures and pictures that have been added, and will benefit from the margin captions which have been retained from previous editions.

This book has been written to assist (a) students to gain skills necessary to meet their goal of becoming dietary managers; (b) those persons who desire to take the certification examination and use this book as a review manual; (c) practicing managers who need more up-to-date information to perform their jobs more effectively and efficiently; and (d) those wishing to develop training programs for employees and staff and improve current operations and practices. This text provides information on the major areas of responsibility as defined by the Dietary Managers Association. Questions regarding certification exams, professional development, and other matters of self-improvement should be directed to the association.

Dietary Managers Association
One Pierce Place
Suite 1220 W
Itasca, Illinois 60143

ACKNOWLEDGMENTS

Recognition of the previous authors' excellent contribution in establishing this popular foodservice management text is given to Jack Ninemeier, and Ruby Puckett.

In consideration of their time, effort and assistance in completing this text, the author wishes to acknowedge the following professionals:

Beth Johnson, Louise Pruse, Ken Jordan and Jan Goshert for their untiring dedication to the goals set before them;

Elaine Fisher, Director of Education, Dietary Managers Association for the time she spent in consultation with the author;

The Book Review Committee established by the Dietary Managers Association: Louise Conway, Columbus State Community College; Linda Eck, Northampton Community College; Nancy Hinman, Wichita Area Technical College; and Janet Raytek, Pennsylvania State University.

All others whose assistance helped in the preparation of this book including the author's family Whitney, Brad, David and Jackie Knight; Herb and Ellie Knight; Paul and Lauren Knight; and Leonard and Joan Jones for their unselfishness in allowing the author time away from them to complete this project.

1

INTRODUCTION TO FOODSERVICE AND MANAGEMENT

Chapter Outline

- Overview of Institutional Foodservices
- Foodservice Operations
- Proprietary, Philanthropic, and Governmental Facilities
- Self-operated and Contracted Foodservices
- Goals of Institutional Foodservice
- Management Principles in Non-Commercial Foodservices
  - A Simple Definition of Management
  - Management Practices: Are they Old or New?
  - The Management Loop
- Organization
  - Organization of Institutional Foodservices
  - Important Organizing Concepts
  - Steps in the Organizing Process
  - Flow of Communication and Organization
  - Power in Organizations
- Organizing Dietary Services
  - Some Common Mistakes
  - Basic Principles
  - Systems Approach
- The Dietary Manager as Part of the Healthcare Team
- Types of Nursing Care
  - Skilled Care
  - Acute Care
  - Subacute Care
  - Mental Health and Rehabilitation Care
  - Assisted Living
  - Institutional Living
  - Long-term Care for the Chronically Ill
- Medicare and Medicaid Programs

Overview of Institutional Foodservices

People must eat to maintain their health and well-being. While this statement is correct, it does not do justice to the wide range of dietary alternatives available today. Lifestyles are changing, and these changes have a dramatic impact on the eating habits of all of us. For the majority of persons in the United States, and many other areas of the world, who are responsible for their own care, the traditional "meal at home" has been replaced with a wide variety of dining alternatives. By some estimates, nearly 44 percent of the food dollar eaten in the United States is consumed away from home.

Institutional (non-commercial) foodservice is defined as an organization that operates its own foodservice, not necessarily to make money, but to provide a service to its customers or clients. An institutional foodservice operation may be part of some larger package, such as meals served to patients in hospitals or low-cost meals served in elementary and secondary schools. The key is to distinguish these operations from commercial foodservice.

In contrast, then, to commercial foodservice operations, these institutional foodservices are a necessity in facilities that exist for reasons other than to provide foodservice. An emphasis on cost minimization, (without reducing quality requirements), rather than profit maximization is a primary financial concern of many institutional foodservices.

An overview of the hospitality industry indicates where institutional foodservices fit into the industry of which they are a part. As shown in Figure 1.1, there are three major segments in the hospitality industry: lodging operations, food and beverage services, and travel and tourism. This book will focus on the food and beverage services segment. Each segment has foodservice as an integral part of the primary task or activity for which the facility exists. For example, healthcare facilities operate primarily to care for clients; schools, colleges, universities, and other educational institutions provide knowledge to students; business and industry

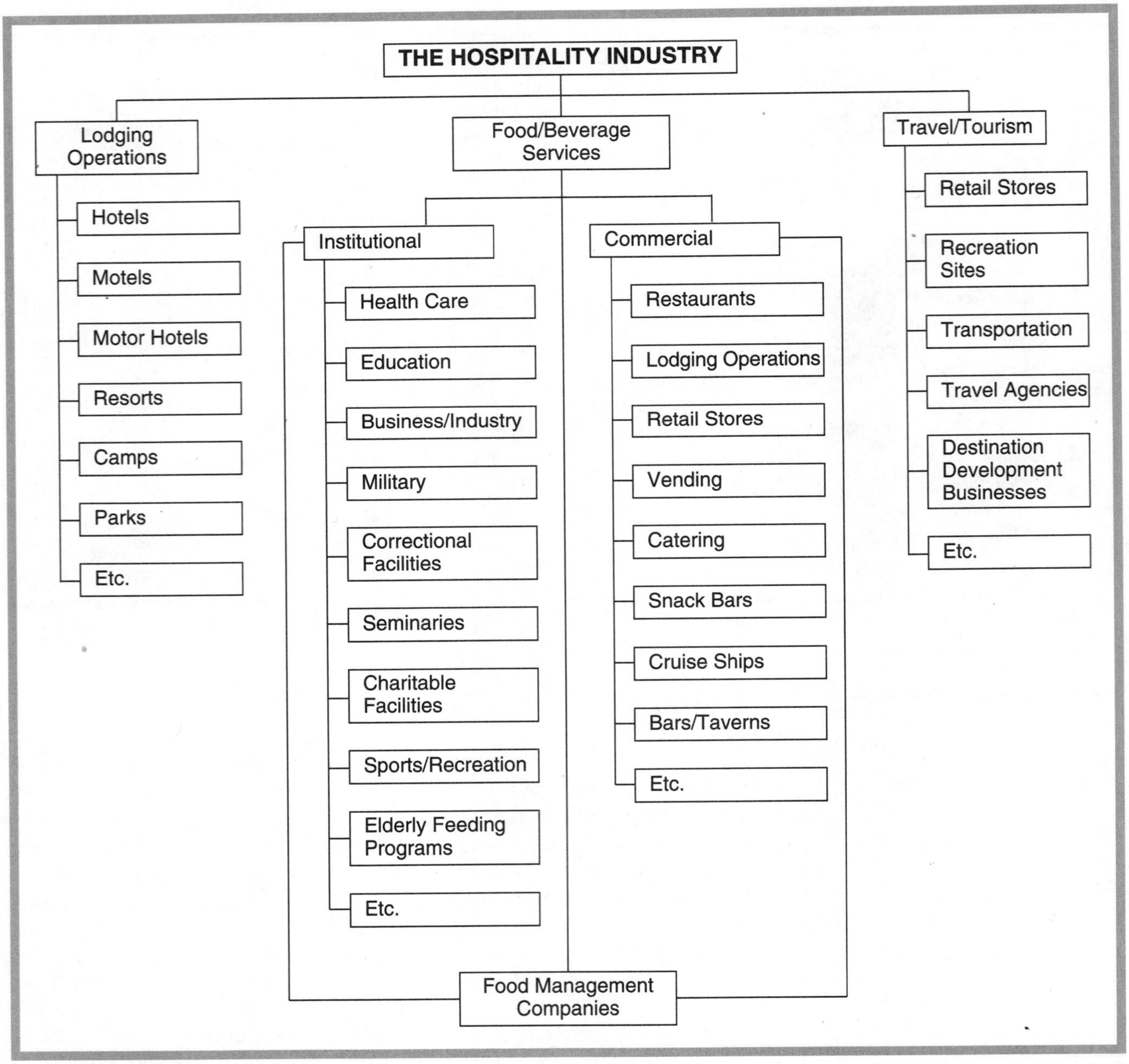

FIGURE 1.1 OVERVIEW OF HOSPITALITY INDUSTRY

operations exist to manufacture products and/or to provide services; the military must defend the country; correctional facilities, seminaries, charitable facilities, and sports/recreation units all exist for specialized purposes. Each of these organizations must provide food and beverage as it undertakes its primary activities; thus, the health and well-being of the individuals being served demand that quality dietary services be an integral part of the organization. This point will be addressed later in this chapter as specific objectives of institutional foodservice operations are discussed, but one should begin now to recognize the important role dietary services play in institutional feeding.

A clear-cut distinction between institutional (non-commercial) and commercial dietary services is not always possible. Figure 1.1 suggests the role of food management companies which can be responsible for foodservices in any type of operation. For example, a hospital or school may "contract out" food and beverage services to a food management company. Food management companies may also operate restaurants and provide foodservices in snack bars, on cruise ships, and so on. In the institutional domain, the role of food management companies is increasing; a later section of this chapter will be devoted to the topic.

It may be easier to think about the segments of food and beverage services by considering the approach taken by the National Restaurant Association's categorization of foodservice operations (Figure 1.2). In this figure, after commercial foodservice, the institutional segment is recognized as the second category, and military the third largest category of foodservice industry.

Statistics are also available for the student and healthcare markets, which comprise the largest segments of institutional foodservices. Figure 1.3, an economic overview of the student market, reviews the foodservice sales and purchases in both self-operated and contract-managed schools and colleges/universities. Note that sales in this market approximated $16.5 billion in 1991 (with projected 1996 sales of $20.1 billion). The total dollar value of food purchases was, for that year, more than $7.7 billion. Internally-operated programs spent more than $5.6 billion for food products in 1991; contract-managed operations spent almost $2.2 billion. Self-operated programs comprise the dominant operational structure for this segment.

Figure 1.4 shows the other significant foodservice specialty involving institutional operations, the heathcare market. Contract services represent $2.8 billion and $1.4 billion, respectively, in sales and purchases in the total healthcare market of approximately $11.6 billion in sales and $5.8 billion in purchases. With today's federal and state emphases relating to reimbursement and other concerns, the role of contract management companies in health care is likely to continue to increase.

Looking at recent overall foodservice sales growth figures, the industry grew 2.5 percent in 1996. The institutional share of the market was 26 percent, which was only a slight decrease from the previous year. In the institutional category, as shown in Figure 1.5, the largest amount of sales is education (primary/secondary schools and colleges), second is health care (hospitals, nursing homes, and elder care), followed by correctional institutions.

FOODSERVICE OPERATIONS

Foodservices offered by educational and healthcare facilities comprise the two largest segments of the institutional foodservice market. Hospitals provide dietary services, not only to clients and employees but to visitors and others, in cash operations in manual and vended dining services. Some hospitals are generating additional revenues by marketing their dietary services to the community for special functions. Elderly feeding programs (on- and/or off-site), outpatient foodservices, nutrition counseling, provision of meals to government or charitable group-operated programs, serve as other examples of foodservices in hospitals.

I. **Commercial foodservices**
   a. Eating places
      1. Restaurants, lunchrooms
      2. Limited-menu restaurants, refreshment places
      3. Commercial cafeterias
      4. Social caterers
      5. Ice Cream, frozen-custard stands
      6. Bars and taverns
   b. Food contractors
      1. Manufacturing and industrial plants
      2. Commercial and office buildings
      3. Hospitals and nursing homes
      4. College and universities
      5. Primary and secondary schools
      6. In-transit foodservice (airlines)
      7. Recreation and sports centers
   c. Lodging places
      1. Hotel restaurants
      2. Motor-hotel restaurants
      3. Motel restaurants
   d. Other
      1. Retail-host restaurants, such as restaurants or delis in grocery stores or gas stations
      2. Recreation and sports
      3. Mobile caterers
      4. Vending and nonstore retailers

II. **Institutional foodservice** (organizations that operate their own foodservice)
   a. Employee foodservice
   b. Public and parochial elementary/secondary schools
   c. Colleges and universities
   d. Transportation
   e. Hospitals
   f. Nursing homes, homes for the aged, visually impaired, orphans and the mentally and physically disabled
   g. Clubs, sporting and recreation camps
   h. Community centers

III. **Military foodservice**
   a. Officers and noncommissioned officers (NCO) clubs ("Open Mess")
   b. Foodservice—military exchanges
   c. Defense personnel

FIGURE 1.2 CATEGORIES OF FOODSERVICE OPERATIONS ***Source:*** National Restaurant Association

Today many hospitals offer clients "restaurant style" menus, which allow choices from among a variety of different menu items. The need to prepare a variety of special diets to meet medical needs of clients dictates special concerns in many facilities. Dietary services in hospitals also offer special catered events, such as banquets for governing boards, departmental administrative staff, and physicians. Indeed, hospital dietary services are complex, requiring personnel with a wide variety of management, dietetic services, and other skills.

Nursing homes comprise the other major segment of the healthcare industry. Traditional long-term care, often requiring skilled nursing services, is the most common example. However, comprehensive retirement communities, foster care pro-

	1982 Sales ($000,000)	1982 Purchases** ($000,000)	1982 vs 1981 % Sales Growth	1983 Sales ($000,000)	1983 Purchases ($000,000)	1983 vs 1982 % Sales Growth	1988 Sales Growth ($000,000)	1983–1988 % Compound Annual Growth: Nominal	1983–1988 % Compound Annual Growth: Real
School—Internal *(public, parochial, elementary & secondary)**	2,464	2,814	4.2	2,496	2,690	1.3	2,564	0.5	−3.8
School—Contract	720	295	9.5	723	287	0.4	953	5.7	1.1
Colleges, Universities—Internal	2,783	1,243	9.7	3,061	1,268	10.0	3,874	4.8	0.3
Colleges, Universities—Contract	1,407	451	10.7	1,556	460	10.6	2,019	5.3	0.8
TOTAL	7,374	4,803	8.0	7,836	4,705	6.3	9,410	3.7	−0.8

1982: $7,374,000,000 + 8.0% Sales Growth
1983: $7,836,000,000 + 6.3% Sales Growth
1988: $9,410,000,000 + 3.7% Compound Annual Sales Growth

* Actual cash receipts from children plus parochial and other private schools.
** Not including $841 million worth of commodities and milk—a 13.7% decrease from 1981.

FIGURE 1.3 Economic Overview of Student Market Foodservice Sales
Source: *Restaurant Business.* September 20, 1991. (pg 110). Reprinted with permission of *Restaurant Business.*

grams, and temporary care facilities, with or without skilled nursing services, provide other examples of nursing home operations—all of which require the services of skilled dietary managers, dietetic and other personnel to assure that dietetic goals are fully attained.

	1982 Sales ($000,000)	1982 Purchases ($000,000)	1982 vs 1981 % Sales Growth	1983 Sales ($000,000)	1983 Purchases ($000,000)	1983 vs 1982 % Sales Growth	1988 Sales Growth ($000,000)	1983–1988 % Compound Annual Growth: Nominal	1983–1988 % Compound Annual Growth: Real
Hospital—Internal	7,641	3,439	6.4	8,038	3,618	5.2	10,534	5.6	1.0
Hospital/Nursing Home—Contract	989	396	9.6	1,082	433	9.4	1,690	9.3	4.6
Other Institutions—Internal *(For specialized care including nursing and old age homes, orphanages, etc.)*	2,705	1,662	6.1	2,843	1,747	5.1	3,933	6.7	2.1
TOTAL	11,335	5,497	6.6	11,963	5,798	5.5	16,157	6.2	1.6

1982: $11,335,000,000 + 6.6% Sales Growth
1983: $11,963,000,000 + 5.5% Sales Growth
1988: $16,157,000,000 + 6.2% Compound Annual Sales Growth

FIGURE 1.4 Economic Overview of Healthcare Market Foodservice Sales
Source: *Restaurant Business.* September 20, 1991. (pg 110). Reprinted with permission of *Restaurant Business.*

Total Foodservice Growth

The industry will grow 2.5% this year, adding $14.3 billion in sales.

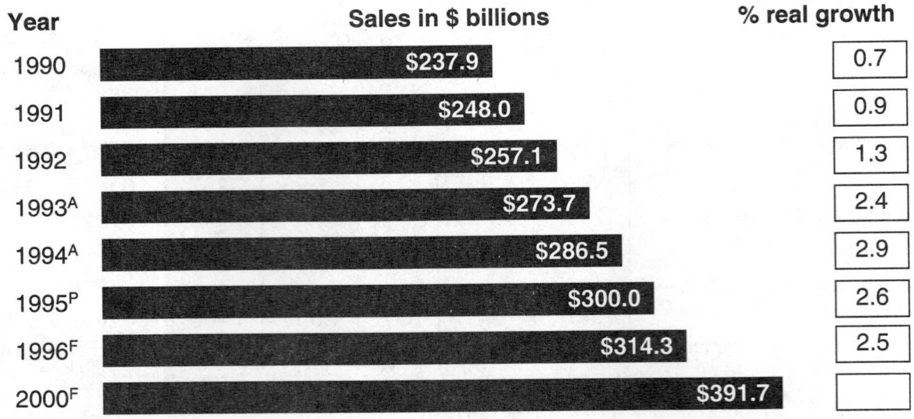

Source: Cahners Bureau of Foodservice Research; (A) adjusted; (P) preliminary; (F) forecast

Commercial vs. Institutional Share

Although the commercial segments continue their encroachment on institutional market share, the pace is slowing. Commercial foodservice will account for 74.3% of all sales this year, only a slight increase over 1995.

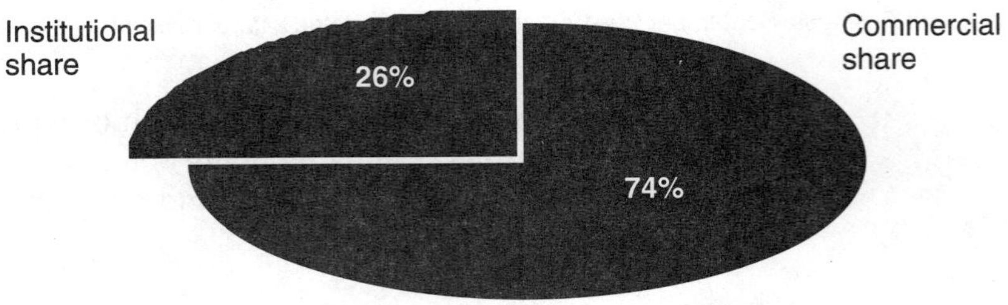

The Year's Top Gainers

Here's a summary of how this year's $14.314 billion growth is divided among major segments.

Segment	Projected sales growth ($ millions)
Quick service	5,806
Full service	4,754
Lodging	636
Health care*	484
Corrections	390
Education**	813
Retail†	443
Business and industry	435
Recreation	163
Social caterers	134
Child care	103
Military	38
Transportation	11
Other foodservice‡	103

Source: Cahners Bureau of Foodservice Research; *includes hospitals, nursing homes and life care/elder care; **includes primary/secondary schools and colleges; †includes supermarkets, department/discount stores and c-stores; ‡includes fraternal organizations, city and country clubs, conference centers, religious organizations and other residential homes.

Figure 1.5 Total Foodservice Growth

Today, a wide variety of other healthcare facilities require dietary services: wellness/fitness clinics, mental health facilities, ambulatory services, and so on. Many other institutions may offer healthcare services to residents, students, and others who consume the institutions' products and services. To the extent that this occurs, healthcare dietary services are an integral part of many facilities with primary goals other than health care.

The second largest employer of institutional foodservice personnel are schools, colleges, and universities. Feeding programs are offered in many public and private elementary and secondary schools. A wide range of post-secondary schools, including one- and two-year community colleges, vocational schools, four-year undergraduate and graduate universities, must also provide foodservices. These services can range from basic foodservices available for commuting students at the facility during weekdays, to a vast array of often very creative programs featuring up to twenty-one meals per week for residents of housing programs and others. Likewise, a wide variety of specialized schools providing educational services to handicapped children and clients, government-sponsored vocational preparation services, and, of course, pre-school programs, frequently offer foodservices for attendees.

Extensive dietary programs are operated by correctional facilities, charitable organizations, sports and recreation entities, and the like. Elderly feeding programs, ranging from Meals on Wheels (in which meals are delivered to homebound recipients) to congregate-site feeding programs, often feeding hundreds of people, are other examples of institutional foodservice operations. With the growth in correctional institutional feeding and the fact that their clients are aging, special dietary services are in greater demand today than ever before in these facilities.

While the list of examples can continue, the point is that a wide range of institutional foodservice programs are available for recipients of all ages, ranging from very basic to highly specialized, extensive, and complex feeding operations. Just a few—or many thousands—of meals can be prepared. Institutional dietary managers must use the same basic principles of management necessary for any business to assure that all resources available to the foodservice operation are used to meet organizational goals most effectively.

Proprietary, Philanthropic, and Governmental Facilities

Institutions offering dietary services are generally organized into one of three different types of structures. Many are proprietary (self-owned), for-profit facilities: nursing homes owned and operated by individuals or corporations, facilities offering foster care services, some specialized schools teaching vocational skills, and so on. While some of these operations are small, they can also be very large. Privately owned nursing homes, for example, can range in size from fewer than five beds to several hundred beds. Likewise, privately held corporations own and/or operate multi-unit chains of nursing homes or hospitals, which can have only a few or very many units within the chain.

Another category of facility organization includes voluntary, not-for-profit (philanthropic) facilities. Many hospitals, nursing homes, and schools, for example, are owned and operated on a not-for-profit basis by charitable organizations. Again, they can range in size from very small operations to very large facilities, and from one unit to a multi-unit chain.

Governments at all levels also own and/or operate institutional facilities. State governments may run special schools for the handicapped; local governments operate elementary and secondary schools; states run colleges, universities, and correctional facilities. The wide range of federal government facilities includes hospitals and educational institutions. County and city governments operate jails, homes for the indigent, hospitals, and so on.

Fortunately for the institutional foodservice operator and dietary manager, the basic principles of organizing and managing foodservices do not vary by the type of organization operating the facility. While budgeting, record-keeping, policies and procedures will be different, the basic management principles and procedures used to meet dietary goals will not change.

Self-Operated and Contracted Foodservices

Institutional foodservice programs can be operated by the facility itself (self-operated programs) or by a for-profit management company. While there are potential advantages and disadvantages to each type of operation, each facility must determine for itself the best management plan for operation of its dietary services. Traditionally, institutions have operated their own programs; however, there has been a significant growth in the use of management companies over the past decade. Today institutional administrators are facing increased pressure to operate within cost containment and other restraints that received less emphasis in the past. Therefore, many facilities desire to reconsider traditional methods of operation to assure that, in the process, the best alternative is being used.

Details about the many considerations important in making these decisions about management companies are beyond the scope of this book. However, the need to consider this alternative carefully is easily justified:

- A significant part of the operating expense of every facility is consumed in the purchase of resources needed for dietary services;
- Resources needed for capital costs involved in construction of space and purchases of equipment are expensive;
- Dietary services have a direct impact upon the quality of care and other services provided to patients and residents of the facility and other consumers;
- Management of dietary services is a specific discipline for which many institutional administrators are unprepared;
- Dietary services are frequently used as the basis for personal evaluation (by patients, residents, and others) and by objective evaluation (by governmental agencies, accreditation/licensure commissions, etc.); and
- Frequently, institutional dietary services can be operated more effectively so that costs can be reduced without sacrificing dietary services goals.

When considering the usefulness of a management company, it is important to assess—for the specific facility—advantages and disadvantages. Review Figure 1.6, which lists advantages and disadvantages.

Considerations in Use of a Management Company	
Advantages	**Disadvantages**
Staff specialists are available	Loss of local decision making control
Lower product and supply cost	Negative image of profit making
Experienced staff as consultants	Support services shared with other units
Operating costs may be less	May have higher operating costs
Less time/work for administrator although responsibility is retained	Standards may differ or need monitoring
	Dependence on external company

Figure 1.6 Considerations in Use of a Management Company

The ultimate responsibility for operation of dietary services will still rest with top-level administrators; they cannot delegate important matters, such as establishing dietary goals and evaluating performance of the dietary department, to a management company.

The procedures used by some institutional facilities to consider use of a management company for dietary services really involve little more than "calling around, getting prices, and making a decision." A more formalized process should be used and should include the following steps:

1. Representatives of the facility must first define objectively the goals of the dietary services for the facility;
2. The existing dietary operation should be analyzed to determine where improvements can be made. This process will yield the foundation of the basic program which will need to be implemented—or improved upon—if a management company is to be utilized;
3. All concerns for operation of dietary services, such as menu, quality of food to be purchased, operating costs, and responsibilities of each party, must be assessed and incorporated into a series of dietary specifications;
4. Dietary specifications should be incorporated into a formalized request for proposal. Additional information relating to the proposal responses, criteria to be used to determine eligibility of companies for providing dietary services for the facility, should also be included in the request for proposals;
5. Requests for proposals should be sent to all management companies deemed eligible for potential operation of the facility's foodservice program;
6. Proposal responses returned must be analyzed objectively to assess the extent to which each meets the standards cited in the specifications. Also, references are checked and visits are made to sites managed by contract company.
7. A contract may then be awarded to the management company whose proposal response is judged to be most useful in attaining dietary goals. Frequently, a series of negotiation sessions to discuss concerns in a "give-and-take" atmosphere must take place between the management company and the facility. This procedure is better than a more traditional approach, which involves the facility "taking or leaving" the contract offered by the management company.

As a result of the negotiation process, an agreement for dietary services may evolve. To the extent possible, the dietary specifications originally incorporated into the request for proposal should become part of the contract itself. These specifications, along with general provisions, agreements about the responsibilities of the facility and the contractor, a wide range of legal and financial provisions and related concerns, will typically constitute the finalized agreement for dietary services.

After the agreement has been negotiated and signed, it must be monitored. A wide variety of intentional or unintentional problems can arise because of procedures which have been used by either the facility or the management company. Problems can involve economic or non-economic concerns and could be one-time or continual. In any event, a process to monitor and correct operating problems as they arise should be an integral part of any agreement for management company operation of institutional dietary services.

Typically, the contract will specify that a committee made up of representatives of both the facility and the management company participate in regularly scheduled meetings and special sessions as necessary to assure that operating problems do not arise. Formalized checklists are also frequently used by both parties to assure that, over time, important provisions of the contract are not neglected.

As you can see from the above discussion, the use of management companies in institutional foodservices must be carefully studied and will be affected by a wide range of factors specific to the individual facility. It is always better, however, when decisions about the use or non-use of management companies are made on the basis of objective facts and identified concerns as opposed to attitudinal or subjective factors which may not take the best interests of the facility and its clients into account.

Goals of Institutional Foodservices

Why exactly do institutional foodservice operations exist? The answer may be obvious, but there is a need for the question to be asked and sufficiently answered in every institutional facility. Goal statements must be measurable so that evaluation of the extent to which they are attained can be done. Likewise, there must be agreement between top-level administrators and the dietary managers about these goals and the priorities for attainment. Following are some of the basic objectives of institutional foodservices which are likely to be shared by operations in all types of facilities:

GOAL 1: *Nutritional Concerns.* Many patients in hospitals depend upon therapeutic nutritional intake as an integral part of their recuperation. Residents in nursing homes and other facilities offering long-term care may depend upon dietary services for 100 percent of their total nutritional intake.

These concerns begin when menus are planned by a registered dietitian; care must be taken to assure that the proper nutrients or dietary restrictions in the required amounts are contained in the menu items being offered to the consumer. Concern about nutrition continues as food purchase specifications are developed and as products are purchased and received, so that items of proper quality which will yield maximum nutritional benefit are brought into the operation. Increasingly, dietary managers and others must have an extensive understanding about nutrition so that their input to decisions affecting the quality of meals can help with the attainment of nutritional goals.

GOAL 2: *Educational Goals.* Many institutions are concerned that nutritional principles be understood and practiced by participants in the dietary program. In hospitals, nursing homes, and other health-related facilities, nutrition education concerns are evident when registered dietitians or trained dietetic personnel visit with clients to explain special diet requirements. In schools, especially elementary and secondary programs, foodservice officials attempt to correlate nutrition education activities in the classroom with dining experiences offered through the foodservice program. Today, concerns about wellness, health, and nutrition have done much to change the eating habits of many Americans. For example, concerns about the ingestion of salt, fats, and carcinogenic agents have had a real impact upon the consumer's eating patterns—in the home and when dining out.

GOAL 3: *Social/Personal Concerns.* For many consumers of institutional foodservices, meal service is a high point of the day. For example, the hospital patient's many physical and psychological concerns can be offset, at least temporarily, by the enjoyment of a meal. Offering variety and choice in menus for hospital patients, students, or residents is an example of how this concern is implemented in operating plans and procedures.

GOAL 4: *Economic Goals.* Traditionally, economic goals have taken a "back seat" to several of the concerns addressed above. Today, however, concerns about cost containment and/or cost minimization are at the top of the list in many facilities. Concerns about high operating costs (including those incurred for dietary services) and government, consumer, and societal concerns about increasing charges have placed a real bind on the institutional administrator. Areas where costs are excessive are being closely analyzed today. Goals themselves are being reviewed, and the end result will probably be dramatic changes in the way health care and educational programs are delivered. These changes will impact all areas of the institution, including dietary services. Concern about economics must be given a higher priority, so that dietary services and the facility itself can remain viable and competitive in a fast-changing external environment

Fortunately for the foodservice operation, the basic principles of managing resources—including food, labor, energy, and operating supplies—are the same regardless of whether the program being managed is a commercial or an institutional facility. This means that many of the operating procedures successfully used by profit-seeking operations can be used, with modification as necessary, to meet the goals of the institutional facility.

GOAL 5: *Community Service.* Many institutional facilities are concerned about providing community services, from providing space and meals for disaster feeding plans, to promoting nutrition education and health awareness, to sponsoring a wide range of educational and other activities. Institutions, especially those which are government operated and those which are managed by charitable facilities, have a need to be an integral part of the community. (In this sense, the term "community" may extend to state and national borders.) Many dietary professionals attempt to quantify how their facility, including dietary services, can "fit into" the community and provide service to it.

GOAL 6: *Personal Goals.* Dietary professionals must attempt to recognize the goals of individuals as dietary plans are developed, including the patients and residents being served by the institutional operation as well as the employees of the facility itself, whether or not they are employed by the dietary service. The development of training and continuing-education programs, the development of career ladder and "promotion from within" programs, and so on provide examples of the way that dietary services address personal goals of employees.

Clearly, personal goals of recipients of the foodservice must receive high-priority attention at all times and in all phases of the dietary services. This "marketing concern" (looking at foodservices from the perspective of the consumer) is, in many facilities, a relatively recent management activity; it can be a most effective strategy to assure success of foodservices.

GOAL 7: *Professional Goals.* Foodservice professionals who have, over the years, learned much and benefited from institutional foodservices have an obligation to "put something back" through involvement in professional activities. A wide range of professional associations, including the Dietary Managers Association, American School Food Service Association, American Dietetic Association, American Correctional Food Service Association, National Association of College and University Food Services, American Society of Healthcare Food Service Administrators, and others, provide a forum for this involvement. Helping to teach young people entering the profession, providing professional growth experiences for currently employed staff, and learning and growing in one's own career are additional ways that these concerns about professional goals can be met on the job.

GOAL 8: *Societal Goals.* Closely aligned with community service goals (see Goal 5), many societal goals can be addressed in institutional foodservices. What, for example, are the dietary manager's concerns about equal employment opportunities, the provision of dietary services for everyone regardless of race, creed, national origin, and so on? How do government-operated institutional foodservices make certain that tax dollars are spent most effectively? How are wastes from the foodservice operation disposed of? The answers to these and related questions all point to societal concerns which can be addressed in the strategic planning for the everyday operation of institutional foodservice programs.

As illustrated in this discussion, institutional foodservices must attain both broad goals and specific objectives. This can only be done if, first, facility administrators are aware of the need to establish goals and, second, if "action plans" to attain them are addressed, as operating procedures are developed for the dietary operation.

Management Principles in Non-Commercial Foodservices

The principles of management are to be practiced at all levels in the organization. Many people commonly—and incorrectly—think that only professionals at higher levels in the facility are responsible for attaining organizational goals. However, the work done by staff members (both administrative and non-administrative) at all organizational levels is critical. At its most basic level, the process of management is the same regardless of whether the organization is concerned about health care, defending the country (the military), or education. Yes, the goals and the environment in which people work differ among organizations. However, the process by which people work together and the ways that resources are used to attain goals have many more similarities than differences.

Dietary managers are critical to the success of their department. They serve as "linking pins" to represent non-management employees in the department to professionals at higher organizational levels. At the same time, they present the organizational policies, procedures, regulations, and so on, to the entry-level staff members they supervise.

Dietary managers need to not only be familiar with a wide range of very technical skills, but also possess and be able to appropriately apply a wide range of "people" (human relations) skills as they interact with employees above and below them in the organization. The dietary manager must be an expert in "people" management duties.

It is unfortunately true that some entry-level employees who can do their work well (that is, they possess a high level of technical skill) are often promoted to supervisory positions in which they must manage people. The principles used to develop and organize work procedures (technical skills) are vastly different from those required to direct the work of people. While many employees may perform very well in supervisory positions, the types of skills and responsibilities change—and different principles must be used—as one manages people rather than "things."

A Simple Definition of Management

Management can be defined as the process of using resources to accomplish what needs to be done. A supervisor has resources and uses them to attain organizational goals. There are seven basic types of resources the supervisor must manage:

1. Employees
2. Money
3. Time
4. Work procedures/methods
5. Energy
6. Materials (food and beverage products)
7. Equipment and tools

Each of the above resources are in limited supply; no supervisor has all of the resources that he or she would like to have available. The job of the supervisor then becomes, in part, trying to decide how best to use the limited resources to attain goals. As part of the ongoing job, the dietary manager must ask—and react to—questions such as:

- How do we find and retain the best staff members?
- How can we operate dietary services most effectively given the operating budget?
- Are there ways to perform work more efficiently without reducing quality requirements?
- Are the current work procedures/methods being used best, from the perspectives of the department, the staff, and (of course) the consumers being served?
- Are we using effective energy management procedures so that this resource is not being wasted?
- Are we properly controlling the food and beverage products and supplies?
- Do we have adequate inventory control and evaluation procedures?

The list of questions can continue (seemingly forever!) . However, the point is that resources are limited and managers must use them as effectively as possible—by practicing basic management principles.

The second element in the definition of management stresses the need to attain goals. Goals, as discussed at length in the preceding section, indicate what the dietary department wants to accomplish, in other words, why the department exists.

Management Practices: Are They Old or New?

The study of management has been complicated by the widespread belief that it is an art—not a science. Many observers believed that there was no need to study management—one either knew about it or one didn't.

Today, however, management thinkers have contributed to a vast foundation of information we can use to improve the way we manage dietary services. The principles discussed in this book have evolved through a process of study and examination, tempered by the insights and experiences of many people.

Management thinkers developed a broad range of theories about the management process. Classical approaches looked at the work environment and the people within it. Other models, which focused on behavior, looked at the employee alone and/or as a member of a group, and at the relationship between employees and management staff. Over time, these and other approaches have been developed into a "systems approach" to management. It suggests that the organization is made up of interrelated parts (subsystems). The organization, then, becomes the focal point of study rather than just isolated work tasks, employees, and/or environmental concerns.

Today's management thinkers look at the organization as a whole. They recognize that an activity going on in one part of the organization is likely to affect the activity of the other parts. In the hospital, for example, we cannot look at dietary services and make decisions without considering the relationship with and potential impact upon other departments within the facility.

The Management Loop

The management process can be divided into separate components or tasks, developed as a result of asking the question "What exactly does a manager do—to some greater or lesser extent—as part of his or her work?" Figure 1.7 identifies each of the components in the management process and illustrates their relationship. As illustrated in the figure, the management process starts at the beginning: planning.

Planning: Planning is used to determine the broad goals which will help managers in the institution to focus specifically on what is to be accomplished. After these broad goals are developed, specific operating objectives can be established.

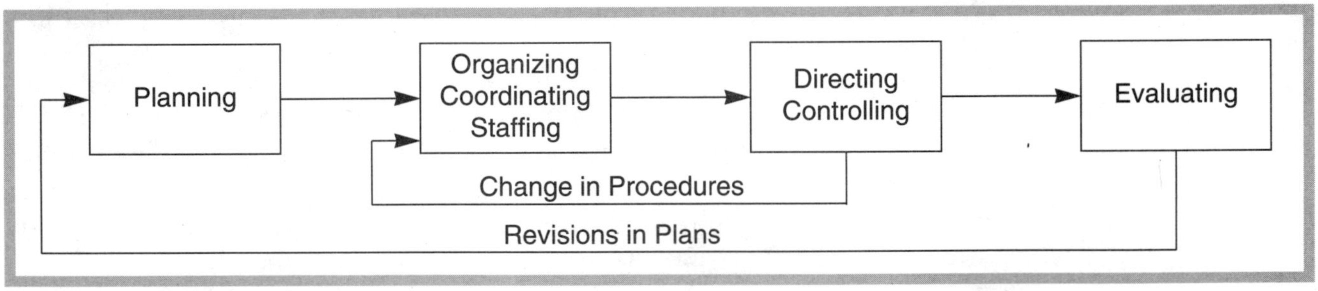

FIGURE 1.7 THE MANAGEMENT LOOP

For example, finance administrators may work with the director of dietary service to establish an operating budget that specifies the economic goals for the department for the upcoming budget period. The director may then develop more specific objectives about the amount of funds to be spent on each category of allowable expense charged to the department.

A different level of planning occurs when standard operating procedures are developed. Recurring situations (the need to order food products, to stock carts to par inventory levels, etc.) necessitate the use of exact procedures each time the situation arises. Standard operating plans, then, dictate exactly how personnel are to do the required work.

Daily activities are a third example of planning. For example, staff members must be scheduled, equipment schedules developed, and policies regulating employee actions incorporated into action plans. Planning for special events, for new orientation and training programs, and so on, are still other examples of planning activities performed by the dietary manager.

Effective planning requires use of the following principles:

- Goals must be established before plans can be developed.
- Managers must regularly set aside time to plan. It should be done as an important part of one's job, not only when time permits.
- All the necessary information should be gathered before plans are developed.
- Planning should be done at the appropriate organizational level. It's not good use of a top manager's time to write employee schedules, for example. On the other hand, only top managers can develop strategic, long-range plan.
- Employees should be allowed to contribute to plans that affect their work.
- You should be flexible when planning. Managers should recognize that situations change and that plans may need revision.
- Plans must be implemented. At the appropriate time, managers must act with the best plan available.

Organizing: After goals, objectives, and procedures to attain them have been established, the management task of organizing becomes important. This is the process by which authority and communication flow within the organization. As a result of organizing, managers know how communication flows up, down, and through the organization, and (as importantly) between and among departments within the institution. Likewise, organizing yields specific relationships between and among different positions in the facility.

Coordinating: The third management task is that of coordinating. As this step is undertaken, personal and group goals are brought together in a meaningful way to achieve organizational goals. It is necessary to coordinate both the type and the amount of resources made available to attain goals. Decisions are made about the number of employees one person supervises. Likewise, as plans for interacting with formal and informal groups are developed, and as authority is delegated as necessary, coordinating tasks are being undertaken.

In many ways the task of coordinating means the same as communicating. It is necessary for communication to flow up, down, and horizontally within the organization. Communication devices such as memos, conversation, meetings, and so on are coordinating tools.

Staffing: The next management task is that of staffing, which involves recruiting and selecting the best-qualified persons for the job. Most hospitals have a human resources department involved in helping dietary services obtain qualified staff; however, it is clearly the responsibility of dietary professionals to make the final selection decisions. Many other aspects of human resource administration, including orientation, training, evaluation, employee development programs, and so on, are additional examples of staffing activities.

Directing: The four management tasks discussed to this point—planning, organizing, coordinating and staffing—each involve activities required to "get the operation going." The next activity—directing—is required to keep it going! Directing, for all practical purposes, means the same as supervising. Directing involves all those activities supervisor does to "manage" employees. The tasks of supervising work, motivating, disciplining, communicating, and so on, are examples of the directing activity.

Controlling: Another management activity involved in "keeping the operation going" is that of control. Controlling is simply a process that helps to ensure that activities are contributing to established goals and objectives. The management process of control first involves establishing performance standards to quantify plans. For example, an operating budget specifies how much money should be spent for various categories of expenses.

A second step in the control process involves assessing actual performance. Departmental operating statements quantify actual costs, while work-analysis procedures help to determine the time a worker actually spends on specific duties.

A third step in the control process requires the dietary manager to compare and search for differences between the standard (expected) and actual performance. If the difference exceeds a predetermined variance, corrective action is necessary.

The final step in the control process requires a performance assessment of the extent to which corrective action plans have reduced the variance between standard and actual operating results. [*Note:* Evaluation as a final step in the control process yields changes in procedures; goal evaluation as a separate component in the management process yields revised plans (this difference is noted in Figure 1.7)].

Evaluation: The final management task—evaluation—is undertaken to determine the extent to which organizational goals that were developed as part of the initial planning process were in fact met. Unfortunately, the evaluation component in management is frequently overlooked, or done only haphazardly. A "spin-off" effect of evaluation is the provision of input for revision of departmental plans for subsequent periods. If one does not know how well the department is doing, it is not possible to know whether strategies and procedures should be continued in an attempt to meet objectives or, alternatively, whether they should be revised to meet the needs and challenges of new plans.

By contrast, the dietary manager, his or her boss, and also subordinates (line personnel) make the operating decisions with information supplied as necessary from the staff or advisory specialists. For example, dietary managers can accept or reject the applicants referred from the human resources department, or the proposed purchase specification from the purchasing department.

An additional principle of organizing suggests that it is unwise for a department such as dietary services to be responsible for evaluating its own performance. Yes, the dietary manager can play a role in determining how well, for example, dietary goals are being attained. However, the boss of the dietary manager, the entire top-level administration, and the board of directors or other governing group would likewise be involved in this task.

Finally, routine and simple tasks are best managed through centralized organizational structures. By contrast, complex and creative tasks are best managed through decentralized organizational systems. Since much of the work of dietary services is routine, there is a benefit in centralizing the decision-making responsibility in one or several positions. It will not then be necessary for specific employees performing different jobs to make a wide range of important decisions that will impact the work of others in their department or other departments.

ORGANIZATION

The basic principles of the management process in dietary services have been discussed. Now the organization of dietary services must be considered.

ORGANIZATION OF INSTITUTIONAL FOODSERVICES

What do you think of when you hear the term "organization"? Do you think about the facility in which dietary services are located, the dietary services system itself, or everything that must be done to get ready to deliver quality services and products to the patients/residents? Actually, any of the above definitions is correct, and the dietary manager must know how to "organize" within the context of each of these definitions. In today's highly complex dietary operation, the dietary manager must know how to best assemble limited resources to attain goals of dietary services. Someone must, of course, be responsible for undertaking every task necessary to meet the goals. What tasks are the responsibility of dietary services? Who exactly should do them? What should be the relationship among positions and work sections within the dietary services? How should the dietary department interact with other departments within the facility? These and related questions are answered as the dietary manager organizes his or her department.

As an important first step in organizing the dietary department, the manager should obtain a copy of the facility's current mission statement, talk with the administrator having overall responsibility for dietary services, and consider exactly how the dietary department "fits into" the mission of the facility. Then, with this as background information, it is possible to develop the specific purposes for which the dietary department exists, and, in turn, influence the planning of strategies and the development of procedures used to attain dietary goals. Figure 1.8 illustrates the relationship between the facility's mission statement and the purpose of dietary services. Simply stated, the facility's mission statement must be determined first; it tells what the facility wants to do. Then dietary department purposes can be developed. The mission statement shapes dietary department goals, which, once attained, help the facility in turn to accomplish its mission.

Note that since the mission statement is a broad statement of purpose, it allows for alternative action strategies to accomplish the mission. You can see how the goals for dietary services could be modified to fall within the facility's mission and, at the same time, to provide rather specific guidance to the dietary manager as strategies and action plans are developed.

IMPORTANT ORGANIZING CONCEPTS

The task of organizing relates to how work within dietary services will be divided up to better assure that department goals and the facility's mission will be attained. Someone must be given the responsibility and authority necessary to do all required work. *Authority,* defined as the right to give orders to others, comes to a per-

A. Facility Mission Statement

The purposes of this corporation, in keeping with principles established by The United Methodist Church, are charitable, and are to create and maintain a community primarily for older persons and to provide them with suitable accommodations destined to meet their spiritual, mental, physical, social, and psychological needs. Some of these facilities and services will be available to out-resident persons. The corporation will also sponsor and encourage education and research in the field of gerontology; gather and disseminate facts and information concerning retirement planning; share methods of caring for aged persons; cooperate with community organizations with like purpose; as resources permit, provide assistance for persons who are unable to pay for the cost of services; and serve persons regardless of their race, creed or national origin.

B. Purpose of Dietary Service Department

It shall be the policy of the Dietary Service Dpeartment to serve a variety of foods in a pleasing and attractive form which will supply all the essential nutrients the body needs for optimum nutrition of the Residents.

Meal planning and service shall consider the nutritional needs, as well as the social, cultural and psychological needs, of the Resident and the role of food in geriatrics to conserve the health of the individual and delay the onset of chronic degenerative diseases.

The Dietary Department shall encourage and participate in the educational needs and responsibilities of the local community of residents and employees, as well as the general public.

Figure 1.8 Facility Mission Statement and Purpose of Dietary Department
Adapted from Statement of Purpose, Otterbein Home, Lebanon, Ohio; courtesy of Jerrold E. Blackmore

son because of the position which he or she occupies within the dietary department. For example, a dietary manager must have authority in order to get work done. He or she must be able to make a decision or do specific work that affects the department. Typically, a job description defines the authority of someone holding a position.

While managers have the authority vested in their position, they may not be able to carry out orders successfully. (Most everyone recognizes that giving orders and having them followed are two different things!) Authority should be defined, then, as "power to influence others so that they will do assignments as required by the manager." *Power* is the ability to get others to do what one wants them to do, when one wants them to do it, and in the proper way.

Personnel occupying positions in the dietary department have some power that "comes with the position." It is called *formal authority*. By contrast, many managers have *informal authority*, a power available because of one's personality, background, and reputation. In other words, skills, knowledge, and abilities are a significant influence in getting work done. An effective dietary manager has both formal authority (that which comes with the position) and informal authority (the ability to influence). While formal authority enables one to punish and reward employees, the motivation and inspiration provided by effective managers using informal power are often a greater influence on whether, and how, work is done.

In addition to authority (power), the dietary manager must also understand the concept of *responsibility*, which refers to the need to answer to someone as to how authority is used. The dietary manager must, for example, answer to his or her own supervisor how formal authority is used. At the same time, it is necessary to answer to friends and subordinates for the way in which informal authority is used.

Delegation is another integral part of the organizing task. It refers to the process of giving away some formal authority that rests in a manager's position. It is simply not possible for a dietary manager to perform all of the work required in dietary services. Therefore, the manager must determine what work must be done by whom. Some of the formal authority and responsibility initially given to the dietary manager is delegated to other positions. For example, the dietary manager may be responsible to the facility's business administrator for the attainment of all dietary goals. However, since the dietary manager cannot possibly do all of the work alone, other personnel are hired and given specific tasks, along with the necessary authority (power) and responsibility (requirement to answer for use of the power).

The delegation process described above does not relieve the dietary manager of ultimate *accountability* for the dietary department. In other words, he or she must still account to his or her own boss for the use of the power and delegated responsibility. For example, the business manager may ask the dietary manager to undertake a special project. The dietary manager may delegate this assignment to someone else. However, if the work is not done correctly and/or on time, the dietary manager is still accountable to the business administrator for these problems. Therefore, during the time of the project, it is important that the dietary manager work with the employee assigned to the task so that both can assure the work will be done correctly and on time. [*Note:* It is ironic but true that, in dietary services, the dietary manager with an excellent department "owes it all to the employees." By contrast, the dietary manager with problems must take full accountability for those problems and cannot "blame it on the employees."]

Understanding and applying the concepts of authority, responsibility, accountability, and delegation are absolutely critical to the successful performance of the dietary manager's job. These are the forces which make dietary services "work." It is not possible to manage activities without defining authority relationships among people. At the same time, the relationships of all staff members are affected by the way work is defined and allocated among positions. Figure 1.9, a close look at important organizing concepts, will help to clarify these ideas. Each must be correctly used as the dietary manager organizes for effective delivery of products and services.

Steps in the Organizing Process

How exactly does the dietary manager organize for the most effective attainment of dietary goals? How can he or she assure that all activities really help to attain goals? How can the concepts of authority, responsibility, delegation, and accountability discussed above be incorporated into organizing plans? Figure 1.10 outlines the important steps in the organizing process:

Steps 1–3: The need for the dietary manager to be aware of the facility's mission, establish a complementary departmental purpose, and develop goals of the dietary services department compatible with the facility's mission have already been discussed.

Step 4: After dietary services' goals have been established, it is possible to develop the required plans and policies for dietary operations judged best to attain the goals, given the limited resources of the facility. [*Note:* No facility or dietary department has all of the desirable resources (people, food, products and supplies, energy, money, time, etc.). The dietary manager, then, makes decisions about how to best use the limited resources of the institution/department. Many decisions must be made as plans are developed, and each is important in the process of generating action plans to attain dietary department goals.]

Concept	What It Means	Practical Example
1. Authority	Power to command others to do (or not to do) something which is judged to help the facility/department to better attain its mission/goals	A dietary manager has the ability to tell employees what work is to be done—and how it is to be done.
2. Responsibility	Obligation of an employee to do assigned work; having to answer to someone for how one uses authority.	A foodservice worker must do work outlined in an applicable job description to a pre-established quality level when work has been properly assigned.
3. Delegation	The process of giving authority (power) to someone else.	The dietary manager cannot do all work required by the department and may have an assistant schedule staff members.
4. Accountability	Having to answer to someone for how authority which has been delegated has been used	If the person scheduling staff members above does not do it correctly, the dietary manager is still responsible to his/her own supervisor

Figure 1.9 A Close Look at Important Organizing Concepts

Step 5: After required plans and policies are developed, it next becomes necessary to determine activities and procedures required to implement plans. One's knowledge, experience, and common sense, and the activities and procedures currently used in dietary services, can be very helpful in deciding the "best" way to do things.

Steps 6–7: After the dietary manager has determined how work is to be done, it is possible to classify activities into work sections. Perhaps, for example, dietary services will be organized into work sections with clinical (dietetic), production, service, and special-diet responsibilities. Work sections and jobs are illustrated in various organizational charts described later in this chapter.

Much of the discussion about management and supervision in this book will focus on dietary jobs. At this level, the tasks which make up the job should be closely related. For example, a facility would not typically have one position with responsibility for planning the menu, scheduling the workers, preparing the food, delivering and serving meals, and performing miscellaneous required cleanup duties (although, of course, some management and even non-management personnel would be able to perform all of the above and additional tasks).

Steps 8–10: After jobs are developed, the formal authority necessary to require work to be done must be delegated (Step 8). An organization chart showing all relationships among all positions should be developed (Step 9). Also, as illustrated in Figure 1.10, the organization task will need revision as the facility itself evolves (Step 10). [*Note:* Many dietary departments utilize outdated organizational charts which show relationships that no longer exist. When this occurs, the organizational

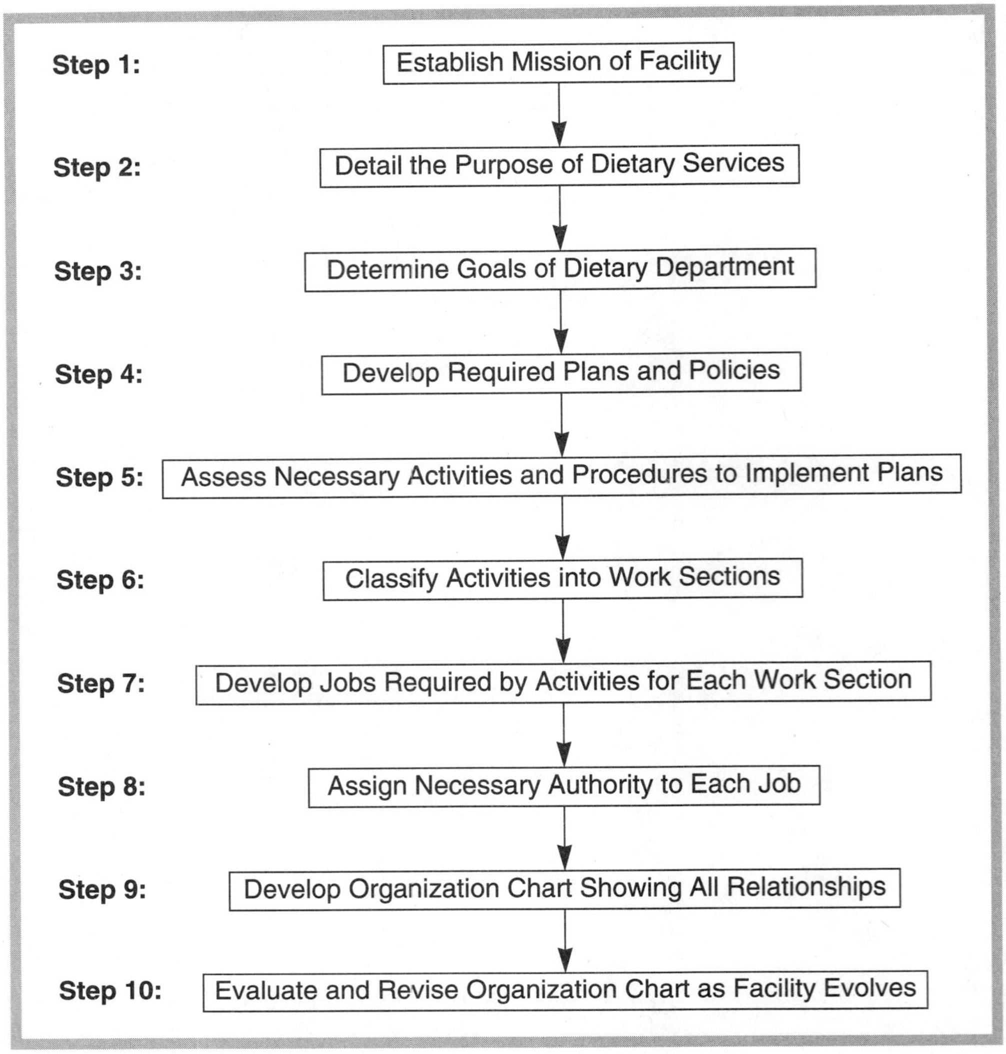

FIGURE 1.10 STEPS IN ORGANIZING PROCESS

chart is not an effective management tool to help in the coordination and communication process.]

A simple example of each element in the organizing process may clarify the role of the dietary manager in the process. Let's assume, first, that the dietary manager is aware of the mission of the facility. (This knowledge has been gained by study of written material and by conversations with top-level administrators.) Likewise, let's assume that the purpose and specific goals are established for the dietary department to illustrate its role in the facility's mission. Let's assume also that one goal relates to economic concerns that budget resources not be exceeded. How, then, can the dietary manager organize to assure that this goal will be met? Plans for and policies regarding the purchasing, receiving, storing, issuing, producing, and serving of required meals can be developed. Ethical concerns at time of purchase; the need to complete various receiving, storing, and issuing documents; the use of portion control tools; the use of leftovers during production, and so on—all these policies must be developed. Standard operating procedures must be developed to specify exactly how, all activities required to implement plans are to be undertaken. Next, the dietary manager can help define which purchasing activities are to be undertaken by the dietary department and which should be the responsibility of the purchasing staff. Work activities relating to product receiving, storing, and issuing can be separated from those relating to food production, service, and other duties. Then the dietary manager can develop all jobs necessary to do required work. For example, perhaps a position, "storeroom manager," will be developed to take care of all tasks involving receiving, storing, and issuing of food products for the facility.

The necessary authority must be given to each job. Who should determine when additional products should be purchased—the storeroom manager or the purchasing official? Who should be responsible for monitoring and making decisions about how and when products should be issued—the storeroom manager or the food production manager, or both concurrently?

The dietary manager must then develop an organizational chart showing the relationship among all positions in the dietary department. He or she should work with other professionals to determine exactly how dietary services will "fit into" the organizational structure for the entire facility. Then relationships can be illustrated for positions external to dietary services.

Finally, as noted in Figure 1.10, the dietary manager must continually evaluate and revise how work is being done and how the relationships among various positions are evolving. For example, the consulting dietitian may provide advice about clinical matters to the dietary manager and about economic concerns to the facility administrator. It would be helpful to show this dual consulting relationship on an organization chart, to specify the nature of the consulting assistance being provided to each position and help avoid possible duplication of effort and different views of "who is supposed to be doing what."

One can see how the above system—formally organizing the dietary department to attain specific objectives compatible with the facility's mission—is much better than an informal approach. For example, a common practice is to hire the dietary manager when the facility opens or when replacing an existing manager. At some point he or she recognizes an inability to do all the work alone. At that time, an additional supervisor is hired. Employees may then be grouped into work sections; the dietary manager may be responsible for one section, and the new supervisor may assume responsibility for the other. There are now three organizational levels (the manager, the supervisor, and other employees). At some future point additional subordinate managers may be hired, the organization will gain additional depth, and departments may be formed. In effect, then, the organization grows from the "top down." However, without constant attention to the facility's mission, purpose, and goals, there is an increased chance that organizations will evolve for the convenience of the managers—rather than for the good of the organization.

It takes much time and analysis to determine exactly how work should be organized. The effort, however, can be very worthwhile and cost-effective if it helps assure that the facility's resources will be most effectively used. A dietary manager who doesn't have time is always busy "putting out fires" (managing crises), and will probably be the victim of administrative problems which could have been resolved by more effective organizing.

Flow of Communication and Organization

An organizational chart does more than show relationships among positions. It also illustrates the flow of communication and authority within the organization. The principles being illustrated are the same regardless of the size or type of organization. As shown in Figure 1.11, the dietary manager has a boss who may be the owner/proprietor in a small proprietary facility, an administrator employed by a board of directors in a voluntary non-profit association, or an administrator whose own boss may be an official in a governmental agency (if the facility is publicly administered). By contrast, in a larger institution where there are specialized top-level positions, the dietary manager's own supervisor may be a business manager, director of auxiliary services, or other official. The dietary manager, in turn, directs the work of two supervisors who, in turn, manage entry-level dietary employees.

Figure 1.11 illustrates one important concept noted earlier. Since top-level administration cannot do all of the work, it must be delegated through several layers

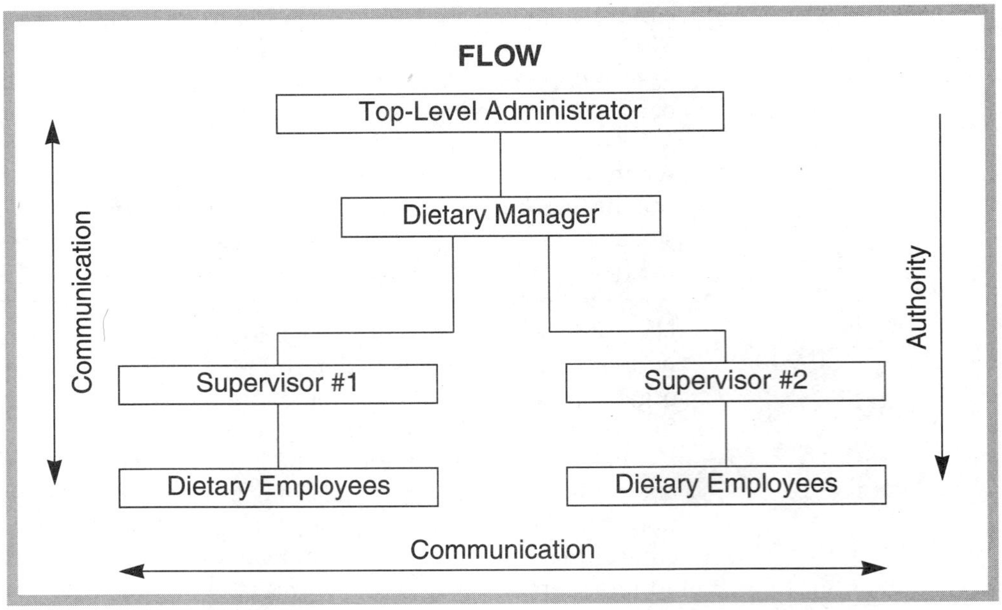

FIGURE 1.11 ILLUSTRATION OF COMMUNICATION AND AUTHORITY

in the dietary department. Said another way, an organizational chart traces the flow of authority from the top level to lower levels of the organization. An organizational chart also shows the flow of communication within the organization.

Unlike authority (which flows downward only), communication flows both down and up the organization. It also flows sideways. For example, top-level administrators may develop policies which must be implemented at the lower levels; information about this policy must flow down through the organization. By contrast, dietary employees may have specialized concerns, and information about these concerns must flow up the organization through supervisors and the dietary managers to, perhaps, top-level administrators if problems cannot be resolved at a lower organizational level. At the same time, dietary supervisors also communicate with other supervisors at the same organizational level.

An organizational chart can help clarify relationships between positions. In Figure 1.11, it is clear that dietary employees, at the base of the dietary services department, are directed by supervisors. It is also helpful to know that (a) dietary employees do not themselves supervise the work of others, and (b) the immediate "boss" of dietary employees is the supervisor. Therefore, if dietary employees have problems, they should address them to their supervisor rather than to the dietary manager.

While Figure 1.11 shows a clear relationship between the supervisor and the dietary manager (the supervisor's boss) and between the supervisor and dietary employees (the latter are managed by the supervisor), what is the relationship between supervisor #1 and supervisor #2? It appears that these two professionals are at the same organizational level; one does not supervise the other. They both have a common boss (the dietary manager) who directs their work. Therefore, if supervisor #1 has a problem, the correct official with whom to discuss it is the dietary manager, not the other supervisor. (In practice, it is common for personnel at the same organizational level to discuss problems, share ideas, and learn from each other's experiences.) The activity of active communication is illustrated in Figure 1.11. However, when there is a difference of opinion, the staff member's supervisor, not peer (a peer is someone who is at the same organizational level), becomes the person to make the decision.

The dietary manager must be concerned about relationships with personnel other than those within the dietary department and in higher levels of administration. For example, there may be a need to interact very routinely and effectively with other department heads. The dietary manager does have concerns about other positions within the organization; an effectively developed organization chart will illustrate these relationships.

Power in Organizations

Power and authority have been shown to mean the same thing: an ability to get others to do or not do something. The formal source of power which is built into one's position has also been discussed. One should also recognize, however, that there are additional sources of power, and that informal power sources can also have a most significant impact upon the dietary department and the entire institutional facility.

Managers in all departments have several possible sources of power available to them as they direct people summarized in Figure 1.12. Several of the sources of power are formalized and are included in one's position. These are legal power, reward power, and punitive power. The remaining two (expert power and referent power) are actually informal sources of power, which supervisors may have (making them more effective) or which non-administrative staff may have (making them informal leaders with whom management staff will have to interact).

Informal power can be thought of as "influence," since people accept it voluntarily. When influence is used, people will react to others without relying on formal policies, rules, or force. Typically, persuasion aimed at consensus and agreement is the tool of influence rather than force, such as may be necessary if one only has formal power. One can see how the dietary manager with both power and influence can be much more effective than the leader with just formal power.

With this distinction as background, power centers within a facility should be considered, and their impact on the work of dietary services. By studying an organizational chart, a very clear and concise trail of authority and responsibility can be traced between positions. In practice, however, an organizational chart (even if current) may not truly specify "how things get done" within a facility. For example, take the case of the director of business services who has had experience as a director of dietary services. He or she may be very knowledgeable about the dietary department, making many decisions and providing input about other decisions which can effectively shape how dietary services is managed. By contrast, he or she may know almost nothing about the engineering/maintenance department. In this instance, then, the chief engineer of the facility is likely to have much more formal

Source of Power	Description of Power Source
1. Legal Power	The power to control others because of one's position.
2. Expert Power	The power to control others because of the expert knowledge, ability, or information that one possesses.
3. Referent Power	The power to control others because of personality, charisma, or respect that others have for the leader.
4. Reward Power	The power to control others by giving or withholding rewards.
5. Punitive Power	The power to control others by punishing them when mistakes are made.

Figure 1.12 Sources of Power

power and influence the director of business services more effectively in an area in which the latter official has no knowledge.

At any given department head meeting, there may be an official without concern for the job (perhaps he or she is about to terminate the position), another with a great deal of interest and enthusiasm but little knowledge, another official with much knowledge and no interest, and a fourth staff member with high levels of both knowledge and interest. Even though all of these professionals hold the same position, who is most likely to influence higher-level decision makers? It all depends upon the situation, but effective administrators are able to "sort out" input from various sources and consider more carefully those from staff members (a) whose interests are compatible with those of the facility and (b) who have creative and carefully considered ideas to suggest.

What should you do if you begin work at a new facility without knowledge about the most influential decision makers? First of all, don't assume that the organization chart will tell who has power and influence within the facility. What can you do? Try the following:

1. Observe what is happening. Who is speaking up at the meetings? What is the reaction, both initially and as plans are implemented, to things being said?
2. Listen to what's being said. Individuals concerned about another's future will often give one clues about others which can help one figure "how they fit into" the informal organizational structure.
3. Ask others for advice, to advance a potential policy or need. Several peers should be asked for their advice. Consider what they say and how they say it. Are their suggestions in concert with others' thoughts? Do they give support or criticism? Do they seem to be concerned about the facility, their department, or others?
4. Initiate some actions. After talking with others and being sure that proposed actions are within given authority and responsibility, initiate an action plan. See what happens! Who gives a reaction? Of what type? Where does support come from? Disagreement? Why?
5. Talk with other supervisors in the department. Ask them about their perceptions of what happens when ideas are advanced outside of dietary services. Who supports and rejects matters affecting dietary services? What past experiences suggest that the "real" power sources may be other than those specified by the organizational chart?

It's true that the strategy to identify centers of power noted above is rather subjective. There are no "hard and fast" rules. However, once one is aware that many personnel at differing levels in the facility can impact the dietary department, he or she will be on the way to understanding his or her organization and how it works.

Organizing Dietary Services

The professional dietary manager tries to avoid common mistakes when organizing the dietary department. One should be alert to these potential problems. When these mistakes occur, it may be because the department is managed ineffectively. The complexity of organizing a dietary services department re-emphasizes the need to apply effective organizing principles.

Some Common Mistakes

Improper Planning: Does the institution and/or dietary service "keep up" with changing mission statements, departmental purposes/goals, and changes in the external environment which create pressure for continual change? For example, as cost control concerns become more important, does the dietary department still use procedures developed and implemented during times when cost emphasis was less important? Does the department organize around existing staff rather than around activities needed to accomplish objectives?

Relationships Not Clearly Defined: When relationships among the employees of dietary services and other departments aren't clearly understood, problems are likely. Mistakes, "personality clashes," and lack of cooperation often arise. Simply stated, each employee in every position must know about the authority and responsibility of that position. They must likewise know the role that others play within the organization, and how their efforts "fit into" the activities of the entire facility. Must an employee follow the commands of someone in another position? Is work done by one staff member being duplicated by another?

Delegation Problems: In some dietary departments, the dietary manager is reluctant to allow subordinates to make decisions. There is a fear that giving others the authority to implement action plans will weaken his or her own position. In reality, of course, the supervisor who doesn't delegate loses the most from this mistake. For example, one cannot be promoted until a qualified replacement has been found. The manager who trains, effectively supervises, and delegates additional work assignments to willing staff members is more likely to have staff that can "fill in" when promotional opportunities arise. Misunderstandings about flow of information will also be minimized.

Failure to Match Responsibility with Authority: Frequently, dietary managers grant authority without corresponding responsibility. Whenever authority is delegated, the employee must be held responsible for what occurs. Conversely, as an employee is made responsible for work activities, the authority necessary to do required work must also be delegated.

Ineffective Use of Staff Specialists: Sometimes there is a conflict between personnel in line and staff positions, for example when staff personnel make decisions that are really the responsibility of line employees. Line personnel may resent the role that staff personnel play in providing information to their departments. Sometimes there is an ongoing conflict between line and staff about "who is responsible for what." These types of problems can be more easily resolved when an effective organizational system is in use and when current organization charts accurately indicate relationships between these personnel.

Too Much Organization: In some dietary departments there is little or no discretion about how objectives are to be attained. For example, detailed standard operating procedures may specify exact details about most activities. Productivity studies have been used to account for seemingly every minute of one's time. The policy manual is thick with policies that dictate action for almost every situation that can arise. While failure to organize properly is, no doubt, a more frequent problem, when there is no decision-making ability left in carrying out a job, a wide range of supervisory, motivational, and other employee-related problems can arise. Over-organization can also create more positions than necessary, and complicate the structure more than is necessary.

A common example arises when an assistant manager must handle fairly routine and/or specialized tasks. Adding unnecessary layers to the organization is never warranted. By contrast, when the dietary manager desires to undertake new responsibilities when he or she must be away from the facility for long periods of time, or when a new staff member is being trained for a management position, the creation of an assistant manager position becomes warranted. In other words, the need for assistant managers varies according to the specific situation. Adding an additional management layer may create a problem rather than solve one.

Basic Principles

Basic principles of organizing work can be recognized and practiced by dietary managers. Most importantly, each part of the facility, including dietary services, must contribute to the objectives of the facility. While there is a wide range of objectives for dietary services, each must be considered carefully and defended for its specific application to the facility. Then the dietary manager should be involved in a process of determining how the objectives will be met. This process must involve analysis and decision making, not an assumption that "we can continue to do things as we have done in the past" without carefully confirming that past procedures are the most effective.

A dietary manager must confirm that his or her department is organized to promote its most efficient operation. While cost concerns have always been important, in these days of cost containment and diagnostic related groups (DRGs), this issue becomes even more important. An emphasis on minimizing expenses while maximizing the attainment of dietary goals is an important force affecting the operation of today's dietary services.

Dietary managers must recognize that there is a limit to the number of employees that a manager can supervise. Factors influencing this number include the supervisor's ability to train, motivate, and direct the work of other employees, and the type of work being done. (A supervisor can typically manage a greater number of employees if each is performing routine and similar work than if the work is highly complicated and unique.)

Authority (power) should flow in an unbroken line from the top to the bottom of the organization. Someone, somewhere in the facility, must have the power to make a decision about any matter that arises. Typically, the authority should be delegated "down the organization" to where the work is being done.

Each staff member should have only one supervisor. While this staff member can be different for varying work shifts or work days, a problem arises when an employee is being supervised by more than one person at the same time. What should he or she do, for example, when one supervisor says that the floor should be swept and another individual wants dishes to be washed? Many of the problems arising in the dietary department are caused, at least in part, by a violation of this important organizing principle.

You should understand the difference between line and staff relationships as the organizational structure is planned. A staff position is one of a highly technical and specialized nature which provides information to decision makers in the "chain of command." Many institutions have personnel, purchasing, and/or accounting departments; typically, personnel in these departments provide help to decision makers "in the line." For example, the personnel department may recommend that a specific applicant be hired, the purchasing department can suggest/develop a purchase specification relating to a specific product, and the accounting department can generate operating statements that suggest specific problems and required action plans. But, in each case, these staff specialists do not typically make decisions binding on other managers.

The organizational charts shown are for information purposes only. There may be few or no facilities with these exact organizational frameworks. Basic organizational structures need to be modified to meet the needs of the specific property.

Organizational charts for various facilities are shown in Figures 1.13–1.16. While the facilities (hospital, nursing home, university/college, military club, correctional institution, or hospitality operation) at first seem vastly different, the organizational charts for each type of operation contain many similarities. First of all, regardless of the facility's size, the same basic tasks are involved in purchasing products, getting them ready for service, and providing them to the consumer. Procedures might be undertaken by more or fewer people in many or relatively few

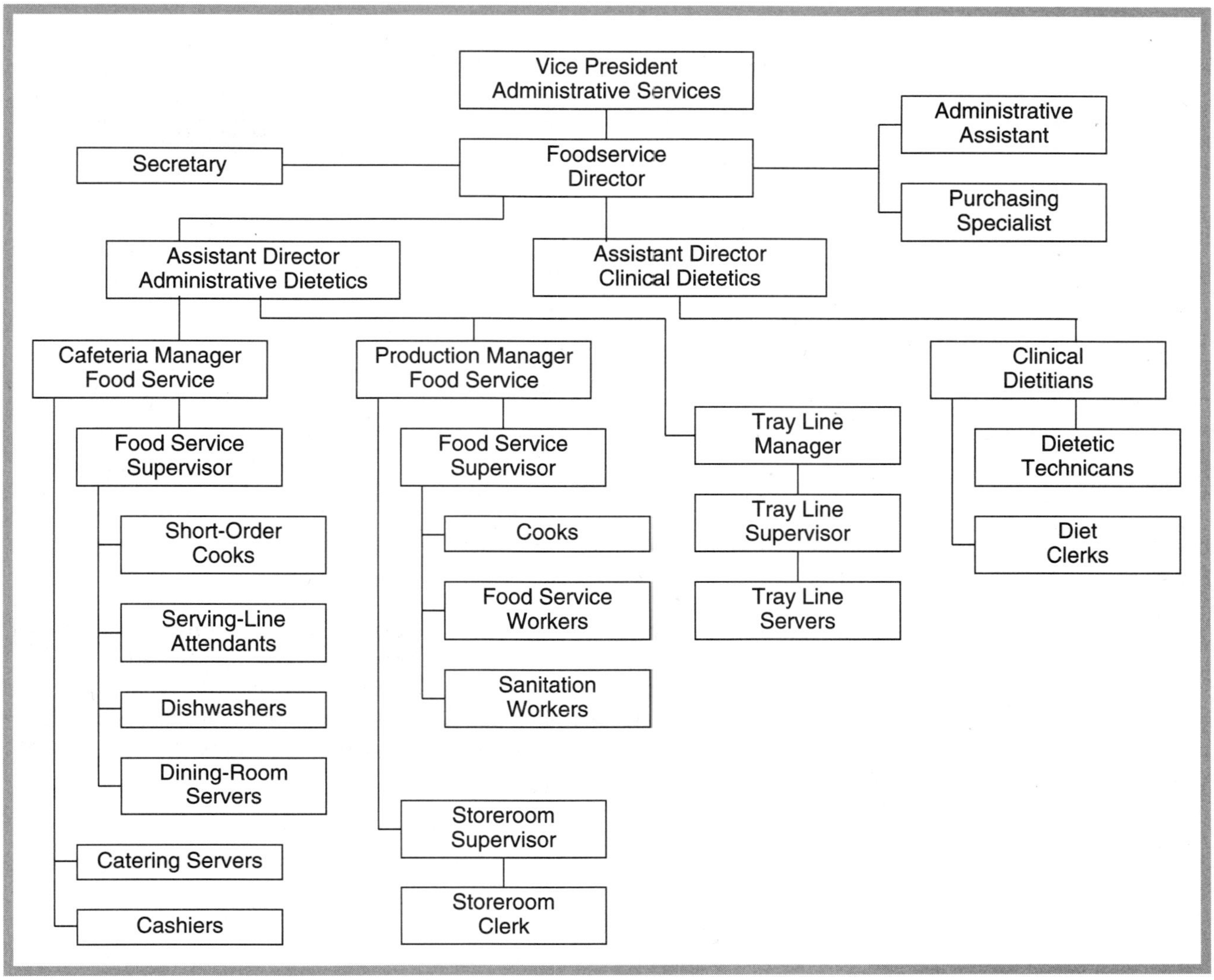

FIGURE 1.13 SAMPLE ORGANIZATIONAL CHART FOR MEDICAL CENTER DIETARY DEPARTMENT

positions, but basic similarities remain. While the missions (and certainly the objectives) of each institutional facility are different, the basic goals of dietary services, which involve nutrition, economics, and concern for the consumer, employees and others, are still basically the same. There may be many employees in each illustrated position in a large facility; there will be only one employee in each illustrated position in a small facility. The need to define the work required of persons within the position, and the need for output to be the same regardless of who does the work, provide additional similarities.

It is generally more difficult to organize and deliver foodservices for a large facility than for its smaller counterpart. However, the structure of personnel and the use of staff advisory specialists help to make the task more manageable.

Figure 1.13 shows a sample organizational chart for dietary services in a large medical center. The foodservice director (whose own boss is the vice president for administrative services) directly supervises the work of five persons (assistant directors for administrative and clinical dietetics, staff purchasing specialist, administrative assistant, and secretary). Each of the assistant directors supervises a range of positions dealing with food production, service, and nutrition. An operation of this size may have 125 or more persons employed in dietary services, many of whom are likely to be part-time staff members. Figure 1.14 illustrates an organizational

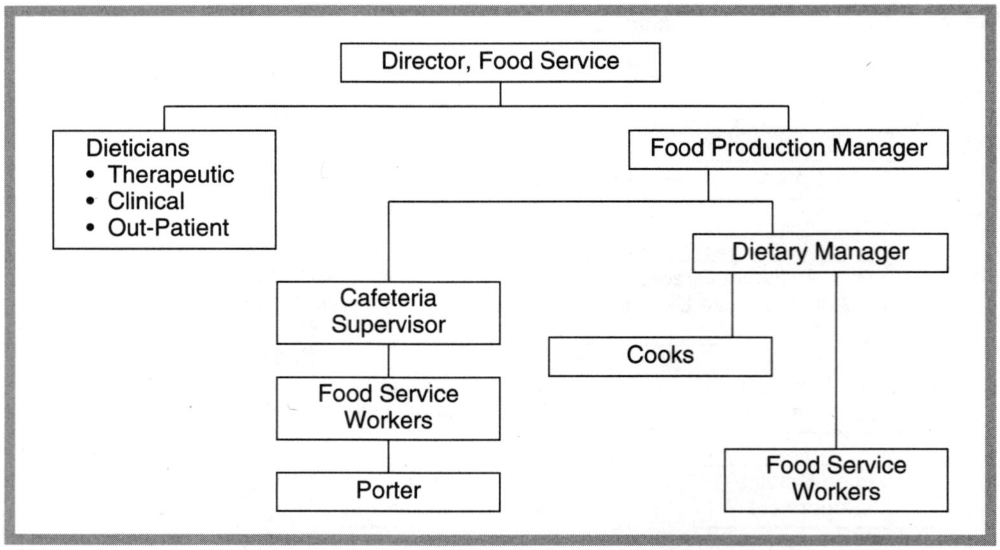

Figure 1.14 Sample Organizational Chart for Small Hospital Dietary Services (200 Beds)

chart for dietary services in a hospital with approximately 200 beds. Notice that, while the number of positions (and personnel) has decreased significantly, the separation of food production, service, and clinical nutrition activities is still evident. Likewise, there are no staff specialists providing advice to the dietary services director. Instead, he or she may assume these responsibilities or share the services with specialists who serve the entire hospital facility.

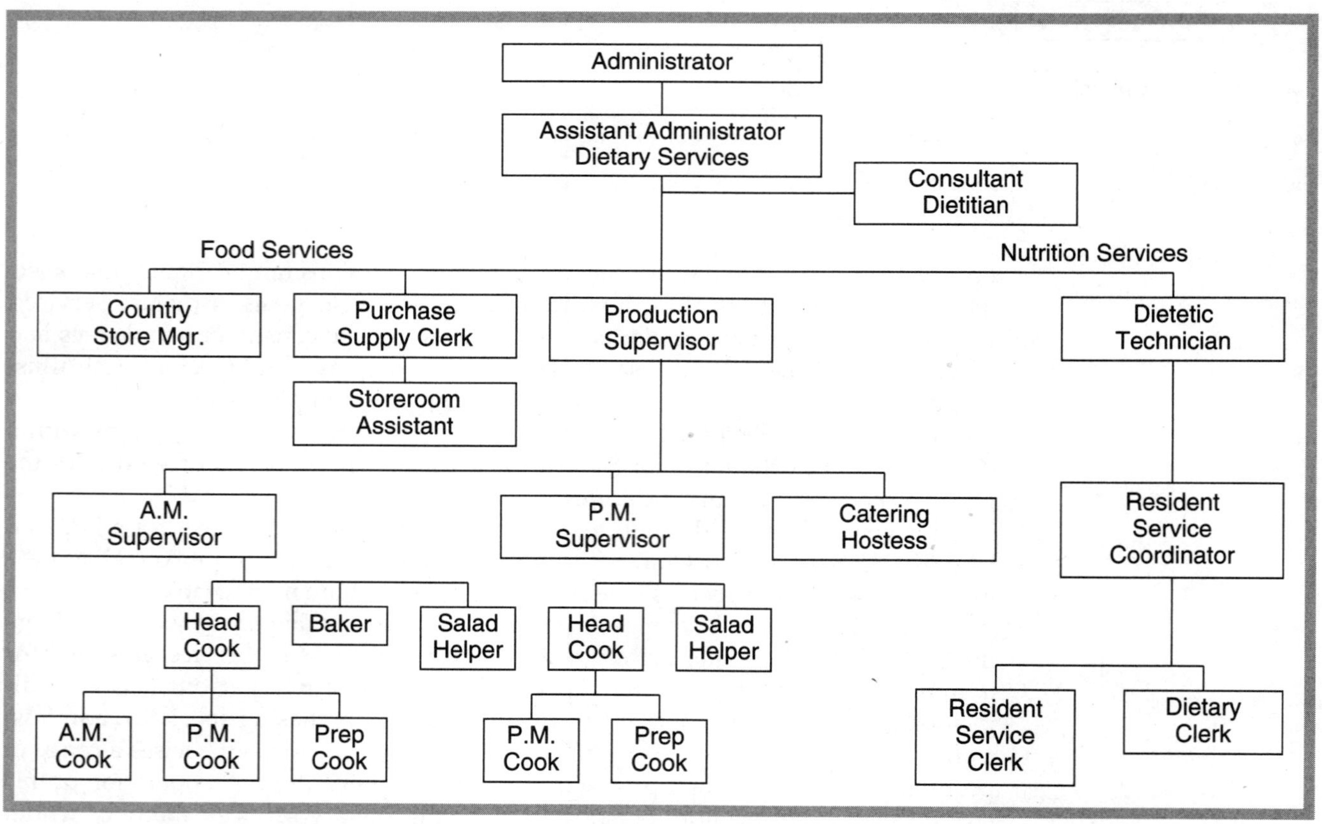

Figure 1.15 Sample Organizational Chart for Retirement Community Dietary Services (365 Beds)

Figures 1.15 illustrates dietary services in a large retirement community. The assistant administrator for dietary services reports directly to the administrator in this large facility. Note that several dietary personnel are on the staff; again, the number of positions and personnel within each position is greatest in a large facility.

The final organizational chart is from a large university (Figures 1.16). Again there are differences in terminology (names of positions), but in each case the organization is developed to attain specific objectives compatible with the mission of the institution it serves.

Systems Approach

To this point the organization of the dietary services department has been the focus. However, dietary services is but one of many departments in an institution. It is an important and integral part of the entire facility, but, at the same time, it must define its role as one element in a total organizational system. Figure 1.17 (Organizational Chart for a Hospital) indicates some of the many different departments found in a hospital. While this book will focus on one—dietary services—it is important to recall that there are many administrative units with specialized concerns making specific demands upon the entire facility; dietary services is only one of them.

Today it is common to discuss a systems approach to organization, which views the total environment of the organization, not just a specific department within it. As such, the organization is in constant change, both because of internal pressures directed by many departments competing for limited resources, and because of differing views of what the facility's mission should be and how it should be attained. External pressures from governing agencies, accrediting commissions, the community, society, also impact upon the evolving nature of institutions.

A systems approach to organization recognizes that an impact in one area is likely to have spin-off effects on another. For example, given limited revenues and

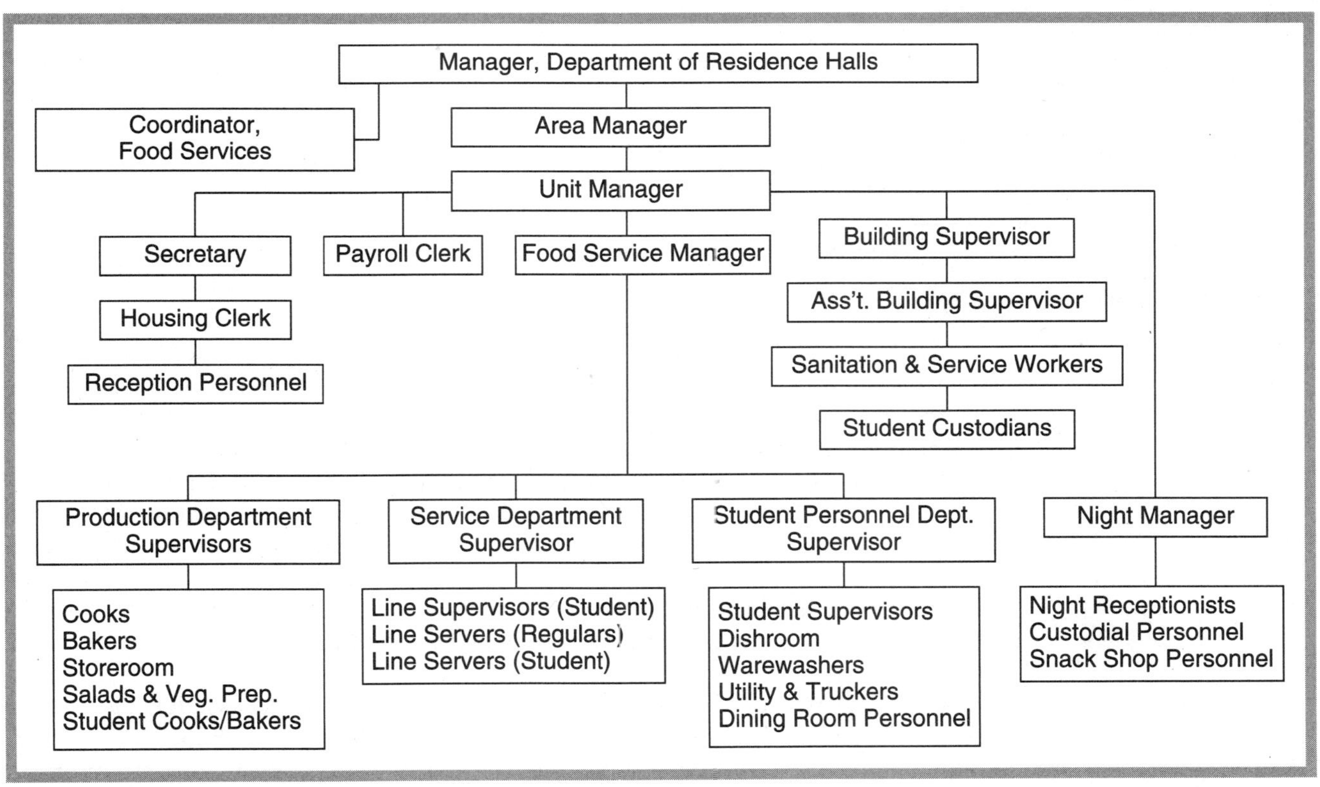

Figure 1.16 Sample Organizational Chart for Large University Food Service*
Adapted from an organizational chart utilized by the Department of Residence Halls, Michigan State University
*Approximately 40,000 students enrolled

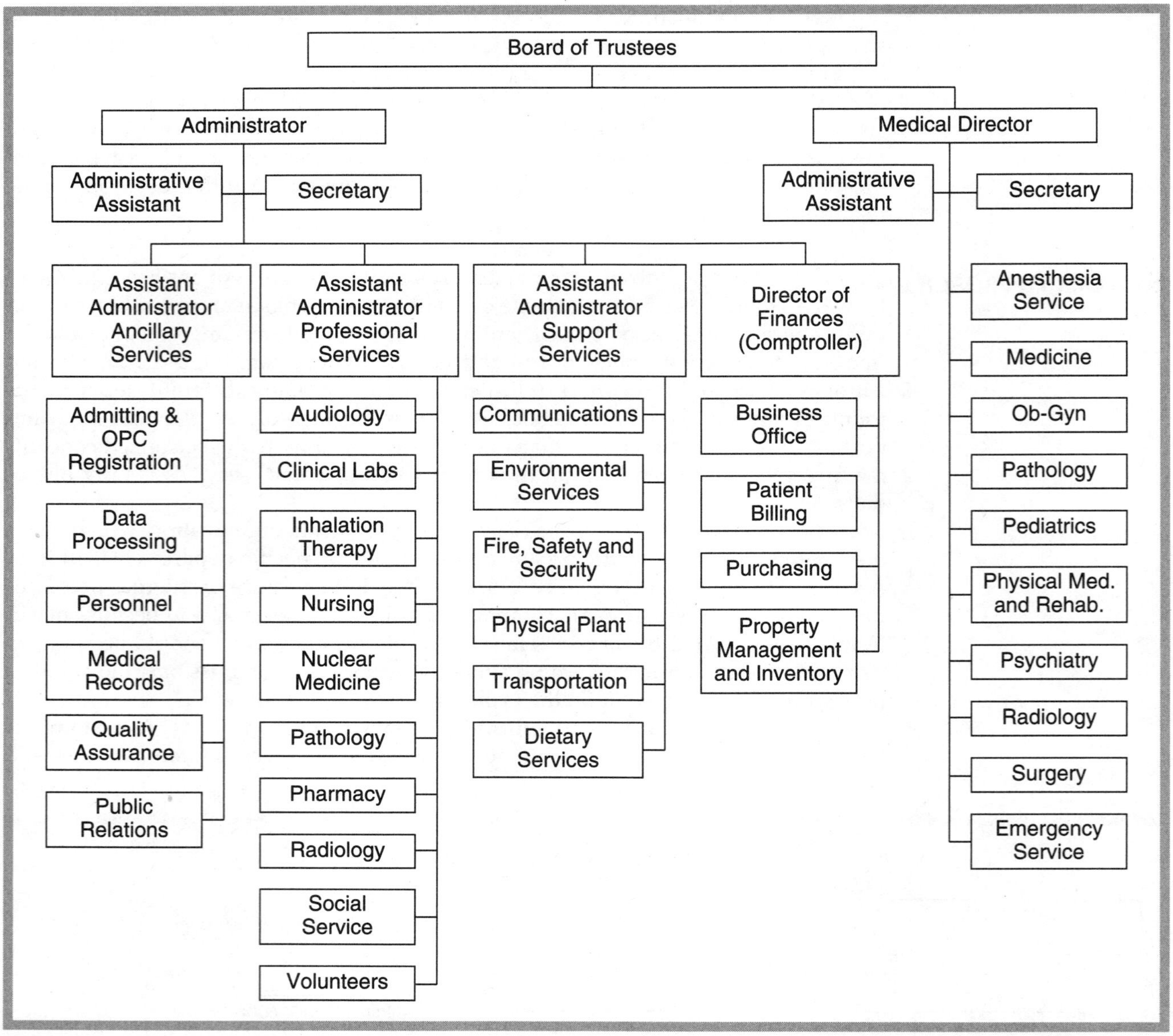

FIGURE 1.17 ORGANIZATIONAL CHART FOR A HOSPITAL

other resources, if more funds are spent in one department, other departments are likely to have fewer resources to use in attaining objectives. While this fact is fairly well understood in concept, frequently department heads, including dietary managers, tend to concentrate their management efforts on their own departments.

While this is good in many respects, it fails to recognize the overall view of the organization and what must be done to maximize the attainment of the institution's overall mission. It is always best to have specific departments working for the mutual benefit of the facility. All too often, however, the attention of administrative personnel within a department may focus on that department rather than on the facility as a whole.

Each department head is like a technical specialist, very knowledgeable about a relatively specific discipline. However, there is frequent need for meetings of personnel representing various departments to focus more generalized attention on matters which concern all departments. It is at this level that dietary service staff sometimes have difficulty. They are experts in dietary services but may frequently lack an ability to see where dietary services "fit into" the organization, how the facility can best attain its mission and, as importantly, how factors affecting the facility as a whole may affect dietary services.

Should an outpatient clinic be established? (What impact does this have on cash cafeteria operations?) Should charges be levied for nutrition education services? (What is the impact on the operating budget?) Should the facility provide foodservices for other sponsors in remote locations? (If so, what is the most cost-effective alternate food production/delivery method?) While the list of examples can go on, the point is that an effective dietary manager is able to contribute to general discussions about the facility's mission and its future. Concentrated attention on dietary services alone is frequently not in the best interest of that department, nor of the facility.

As you have learned, other department heads are colleagues (peers) of the dietary manager. They are on the same organizational level and are charged with the responsibility for operating their own departments as effectively as possible. As such, they are likely to have many concerns in common, such as personnel, recruitment and selection policies; compliance with general operating procedures; and the need to follow the same programs for evaluating personnel and for making decisions about salary/wage increases. Typically, these staff members meet and work together to discuss and resolve problems pertaining to the many areas of mutual concern.

Dietary managers must be aware of the concept of *functional authority:* one department head may be able to make decisions binding on a staff member in an entirely different department. For example, the purchasing department director may specify when food and supply orders must be placed, the laundry department official may require table linens for special events to be picked up or returned by a specified time, and the dietary manager may have the authority to schedule reasonable dining-room hours that will impact upon the scheduling of personnel in many other departments.

There is an obvious need for all department heads to realize the need for functional authority. It is not reasonable for external departments, as part of their standard operating procedures, to create difficulty for other operating departments. There is, likewise, a need for department heads to communicate about the many issues that affect their departments, and to assist in decisions about functional authority. Frequently the administrative official with line responsibility for both affected department heads may solicit input from these personnel and then make a decision binding for both departments.

THE DIETARY MANAGER AS PART OF THE HEALTHCARE TEAM

The dietary manager's work with other professionals in the facility begins at the time the resident is admitted and diet history and/or nutritional assessment information and records are developed. Professional input by a registered dietician must continue as the dietary manager addresses potential nutrition-related problems and conveys these concerns to nursing and medical staff (both informally and through written medical records).

Effective communication is a key to proper medical service. The registered dietitian, dietary manager, and/or other member of the dietary department may be present at client-care planning meetings. A case study, which provides information about the physical and mental condition of the client, is frequently developed; input from dietary personnel is important in the development of all information about the client.

The need for the dietary manager to be a professional and contributing member of the healthcare team is obvious, as important decisions affecting the health and well-being of the client are made. The dietary manager who represents himself or herself, the dietary department, and the facility efficiently and professionally in these meetings is doing a service to all parties, including the client, and represents the type of professional of whom the healthcare profession can be proud.

The dietary manager must be able to interact effectively with personnel at all organizational levels, both within and outside of dietary services. Coordination is a management technique that provides harmony in the individual efforts necessary to help the facility attain its mission.

There will likely be many differences of opinion about how goals can be met as personnel at different levels throughout the organization consider the matter from their perspectives. Frequently, personnel may have the good of the facility in mind but still have honest differences of opinion about what is best for it. The task of coordination, then, begins with ensuring that all personnel understand the facility's mission and exactly how their efforts will contribute toward it. Everyone, not just top-level administrators, must have a basic understanding of the purpose of the institution and the department within which they are employed.

In many ways, coordination means the same thing as communication. It is critical that the relationships established between people, positions, and departments within the facility provide for direct personal communication, since this is the most effective communication method. Face-to-face conversations, group meetings, committee sessions, "open-door" policies of top-level administrators, are among the devices that improve communication. Unfortunately, no one can issue an "order" to communicate and coordinate; procedures that permit this interaction are necessary.

Coordination is not only required when problems arise. Rather, efforts to communicate effectively throughout the facility must be ongoing, and are especially important as plans and strategies to attain them are initially considered.

Each department within the facility is dependent upon the others to provide the variety, type, and quality of products and services necessary. Therefore, when something good or bad happens in one department, it is likely to affect many or all others. Therefore, competition, hostility, or adversarial strategies between departments should not be tolerated.

Frequently the best techniques for coordination involve communication between peers in an organization (such as department heads) rather than vertical communication (such as from a department head to his or her own boss and "back down" to another department head). Again, routine and frequent meetings bringing people with differing responsibilities together are an important element in building coordination within a facility. There is need for continuous, not infrequent, exchange of information. The communication challenge must remain open and should not be "turned on and off" as problems worsen.

Each administrator has an obligation to his or her own supervisor to ensure that efforts are coordinated within the assigned area of responsibility. Therefore, the dietary manager must ensure effective coordination within that department. The dietary manager's own boss must be able to assure higher administrative levels that there is effective coordination between the department heads that he or she supervises. When addressed effectively, "excuses" such as "personality clashes," communication problems, and so on will be less likely to create problems for the facility.

How exactly do you coordinate? You must give advice, make sure that your own employees know the importance and methods of coordination and, as importantly, you must illustrate how coordination "works" through your own actions. Finally, as problems are analyzed, make sure the cause is not ineffective communication/coordination practices.

Written information such as standard operating procedures, memos, bulletins, help in the coordinating effort, but personal contact is still the most effective means. Administrators must also see that the organizational structure itself enhances coordination. Those organizational and department plans that have received benefit from coordinated input developed by a wide range of staff members with differing responsibilities are more likely to be successful than is a plan developed without this coordinated effort.

As institutional facilities and dietary departments grow, the need for effective communication among larger numbers of personnel will become greater. The professional dietary manager recognizes this, and learns and practices principles of coordination to ensure that, first, he or she is not "part of the problem" and, second, that both the department's goals and facility's mission are likely to be attained by coordinated input from all units within the institution. The end result will be a dietary manager well recognized as a part of the healthcare team.

Types of Nursing Care

Nursing homes are generally licensed by the state and then certified for participation in Medicare and Medicaid programs. The basic levels of nursing care are: (a) skilled nursing facility, (b) intermediate care facility, and (c) residential facility:

Skilled nursing facilities provide nursing services to meet the total nursing needs of clients. Licensed practical or vocational nurses or registered nurses are on duty twenty-four hours daily. Nursing personnel include at least one registered nurse on the day tour of duty, seven days a week. Additionally, the facility may provide a range of specialized services, such as physical, occupational, and speech therapy, social services, and recreational activities.

Intermediate care facilities provide care to clients who have chronic but not critical health conditions. Intermediate supervision of these facilities' health services for all days of each week is by a registered nurse or licensed practical or vocational nurse, employed full time on the day shift. At facilities where a licensed practical or vocational nurse serves as the supervisor of health services, consultations are provided by a registered nurse not less than four hours weekly, although this may not be the case in all states.

Residential care facilities provide sheltered living to individuals capable of functional independence. As such, these types of facilities stress the social needs of the resident, as opposed to the medical needs of the patient. Residents in residential care facilities are provided with dietary and housekeeping services, and also receive monitoring of medical needs and the provision of social, recreational, and spiritual opportunities. These services relieve residents of many anxieties associated with old age or disability, and therefore allow residents to live fuller, more productive lives in their later years.

In addition to the three primary levels of nursing care just discussed, other types of facilities are also available:

Skilled Care

Individuals in need of extended, intensive service require skilled nursing. You are most familiar with skilled care involved with the geriatric long-term care industry, commonly referred to the nursing home. Most geriatric patients only need occasional, episodic medical care, yet require long-term care.

Acute Care

In contrast, acute care settings (hospitals) provide technologically sophisticated services to patients requiring hospital-level diagnostic and therapeutic management. Currently, those individuals residing in long-term facilities are transported to an acute care facility when an acute episode occurs, and transported back again when the crisis has ended.

Subacute Care

A new service in health care is available for a short-term recovery or rehabilitation, after acute care in a hospital, to independent living at home. Due to lower inpatient census, hospitals are even setting aside areas to provide this subacute care.

Mental Health and Rehabilitation Care

De-institutionalization of persons with mental retardation/developmental disabilities is presently in process. Persons who formerly resided in large institutions are now integrated into the community at group homes or half-way homes. Successful integration involves collaboration among the family, healthcare providers, and personnel in community agencies. Nurses possess skills that can be useful to families and clients engaged in locating and utilizing resources to meet their needs. The "team" approach has been compared to a string quartet to describe how each of the professionals, like different musical instruments, has a particular part to play in achieving a harmonious outcome. Assessment of food preparation skills, grocery shopping ability, and/or menu planning may need to be done by trained dietary personnel.

Assisted Living

Assisted living is both a philosophy and a reality in some parts of the country. It involves renting a small apartment, perhaps a studio apartment, and receiving as part of the rent numerous personal, spiritual, and social services, as well as some nursing care. The goal behind the concept is to delay or avoid nursing-home admission by allowing the elderly to "age in place."

Assisted living is becoming an attractive addition to long-term care because of the demographic changes in the country, economic constraints, and preferences of the elderly. The philosophy behind it incorporates the values of dignity, privacy, maximum independence, shared decision making, and choice of care and lifestyle.

The care given in an assisted living facility is often based on a service contract drawn up with the client and/or family. The contract stipulates what the client's needs are, as identified by both the client and the nurse; who will meet those needs in a way that is acceptable to the client; and a plan for updating the contract as the client's needs change. Needs of the clients may be met by facility staff or by outside professionals working under contract with the assisted-living facility. For example, some care may be given by home healthcare agencies, mental health agencies, neighborhood churches, or outside social workers.

Most of the staff of an assisted-living facility are nonprofessionals such as kitchen, housekeeping, maintenance, and clerical staff. The majority of personal care (activities of daily living), is provided by nurse's aides, with nursing care being divided between aides and nurses. State regulations may determine whether care must be given by a licensed practical nurse or registered nurse, and how much time a nurse must be on the premises. One of the ways costs are contained in this type of program, especially in small facilities, is by cross-training of staff. This means that in some cases, clerical workers may give some dietary assistance or nurse's aides may help with light housekeeping. It is also true that aides may take on some routine nursing care, delegated by a registered nurse.

Institutional Living

Residents in a facility for the mentally and physically disabled provide a challenge for the dietary manager. Often adaptive feeding devices, food consistency changes, and/or enteral feeding must be assessed to meet their nutritional needs. Orphanages, another institutional living facility, may require the dietary manager to adapt a menu to be more age-specific. Prisons offer a nonselective menu to their incarcerated residents.

Long-term Care for the Chronically Ill

The emergence of the AIDS (Acquired Immune Deficiency Syndrome) virus has evolved, through improved management, from an acute into a chronic condition for an increasing number of affected individuals. An important issue facing health planners and clinicians is determining the optimal care setting for those in whom chronic recurring symptoms and the inability to function in daily activities have become the primary manifestations of the disease.

If their episodes of acute illness are frequent, chronically ill patients will require care in settings where advanced medical care is continually or easily accessible, such as hospitals. However, if patients need medical care infrequently, their need for long-term care would be better served by a continuum of care in settings more oriented toward the delivery of social services and functional assistance. These settings include long-term care facilities, community-based residential homes, and their own homes where they can receive home-care services. While acute care hospitals are well suited to provide the acute care these patients need, they often fail to provide the important functional assistance, personal care, mental care, and spiritual care these individuals need.

An ideal setting in which to care for chronically ill patients would include several levels of care on the same campus, ranging from minimally supervised apartment dwellings to a medically enhanced skilled-nursing facility. Facilities of this type are also more efficient because they share services. Such vertically integrated long-term care communities already exist in various locations to serve the geriatric long-term care population.

Recent trends have prompted some long-term care facilities to include advanced rehabilitative care services and to increase their "acute care" capability. This trend in the long-term care industry has been prompted by several factors, including the following:

1. The geriatric long-term care population has become increasingly aged and frail;
2. Medicare's new prospective payment system has caused acute care patients to be discharged from hospitals earlier, in some cases while the patient may still be in the midst of recovering from an acute illness;
3. There is a movement toward a system of reimbursement based on the resources a facility has used, which has introduced financial incentives for long-term care facilities to provide advanced rehabilitative care.

These changes have led many facilities to shift from treating primarily custodial, low-intensity patients to treating more debilitated patients who require greater levels of nursing and rehabilitative care. In addition, some have begun to offer more intensive services traditionally provided in acute care facilities.

As a result of these changes, some long-term care facilities provide care that approaches the care provided to geriatric patients in acute care facilities for simple acute illness (for example, pneumonia and urosepsis). Moreover, many physicians (particularly geriatricians) who work in long-term care would prefer to avoid transferring elderly nursing-home residents with uncomplicated acute illnesses to hospitals when appropriate resources, such as intravenous therapy and adequate nursing staff, are available.

Although ideal, integrated care settings are not essential for high-quality long-term care. The important concept is that the chronically ill appear to require a range of care settings, not unlike the settings utilized by the geriatric long-term care population, if one recognizes certain key distinctions. In planning settings to care for the growing population of the chronically ill, one should recognize their need for special medical care, mental-health care, spiritual support, and social services.

Medicare and Medicaid Programs

Depending upon the type of facility, there are a wide variety of state and federal regulations pertaining to the degree of care given by the facility. The dietary manager is an important participant in this quality care; since it impacts upon external governing agencies as well as the client, the practice of good communication techniques is an integral part of his/her position.

Nursing homes and other healthcare facilities are regulated by federal, state, and/or local government agencies. In many states, the licensing agent is the state board of health, which establishes and monitors minimum standards for operation of the facility. The federal government establishes its own minimum requirements for facilities participating in federal healthcare reimbursement programs such as Medicare and Medicaid. Applicable regulations and interpretive guidelines are printed in the *Federal Register.* (These regulations are changing; dietary managers and interested others must obtain current information from their state licensing agency.)

What is Medicare? Medicare is a federal insurance program providing a full range of benefits for specific periods of time through providers and suppliers who voluntarily participate in the program. However, regulations prohibit benefits being provided to skilled nursing facilities (SNF) that provide for the care and treatment of mental disease or tuberculosis. Typically, benefits are payable for qualified beneficiaries (most people over the age of 65) or social security beneficiaries (if under the age of 65) who are entitled to disability benefits, or need renal dialysis or renal transplantation. The payment for services is made by the federal government through designated intermediaries.

The Medicare law, an amendment to the Social Security Act, was initially enacted in 1965. It was implemented in 1966. There are two parts. "Part A" is available to people over the age of 65 entitled to disability benefits, and to individuals needing renal dialysis or renal transplantation. Regulations permit the payment for hospital, nursing, and home health agency services. "Part B" is a supplementary medical insurance program which pays for physician services, drugs, durable medical equipment, some laboratory and X-ray services, and other similar services.

Figure 1.18 reviews basic information about the program and the sources and applications of Medicare funds.

Medicaid is a state-administered program, the purpose of which is to provide medical services to persons receiving public assistance under the Social Security Act and, at the state's option, other needy persons. Unlike Medicare, however, only hospitals and skilled-nursing facility services are mandated under Medicaid. Beyond

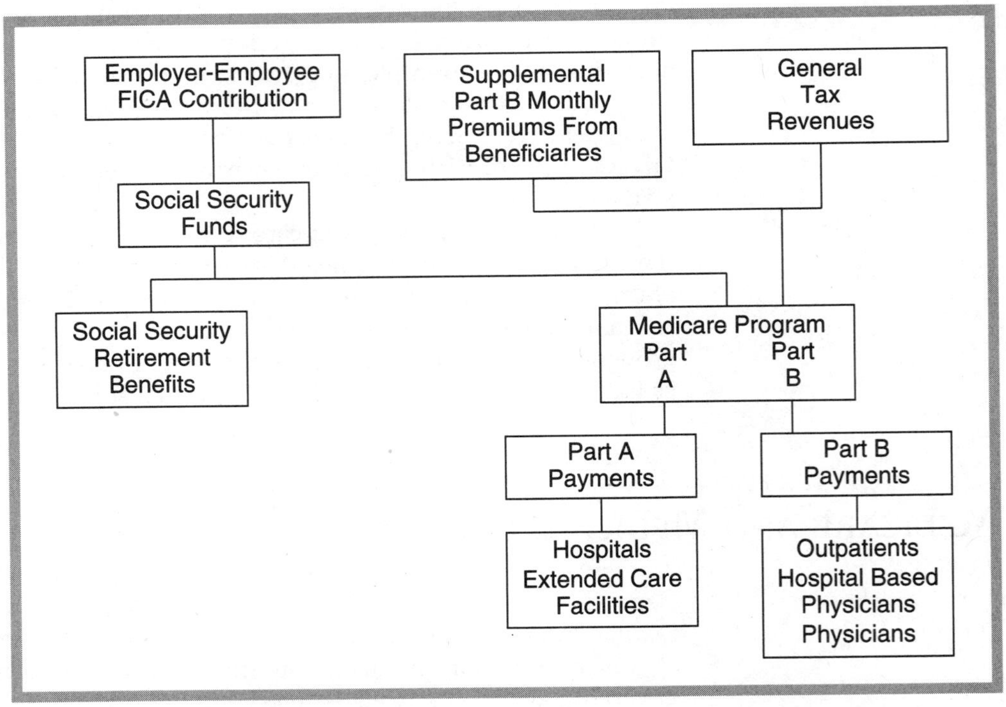

FIGURE 1.18 SOURCES AND APPLICATIONS OF MEDICARE FUNDS

these services, states may decide about the amount, duration, and scope of services, except that care in institutions primarily for the care and treatment of mental diseases may not be included for people over the age of 21 and under the age of 65. Federal regulations prescribe minimum standards for all types of providers and suppliers of Medicare-covered services, and for intermediate-care facilities.

The Social Security Act requires minimum health and safety standards to be met by those participating in Medicare and Medicaid programs. The Secretary of Health and Human Services has designated the Health Care Financing Administration and, within that agency, the Health Standards and Quality Bureau, to administer the standards and certification aspects of the programs.

While Medicare and Medicaid laws constantly change and are, at best, quite complex, the dietary manager must have some basic information about these and related programs. He or she is likely to be asked questions and must give answers within the context of current and applicable federal regulations dealing with reimbursement plans. Since food services are an integral part of the facility's budget, regulations have an impact upon what can and cannot be done within the operation of dietary services.

SUMMARY

Institutions offering dietary services are generally organized into one of three different types of structures: proprietary, philanthropic, and government facilities. Institutional (non-commercial) foodservice programs can be operated by the facility itself (self-operated programs) or by a for-profit management company. While there are potential advantages and disadvantages to each type of operation, each facility must analyze and select the "best" management plan for operation of its dietary services.

Every institutional facility has basic objectives, which may be evaluated regularly using goal statements. Goals may address the following concerns: nutritional, educational, social, economic, community, personal, professional, and societal.

Dietary managers are critical to the success of their department. They need to be familiar with a wide range of technical skills and also possess people skills, as they interact with employees above and below them in the organization. Management can be defined as the process of using resources to accomplish what needs to be done. A supervisor decides how best to use the limited resources to attain desired goals. The management loop identifies each of the components in the management process, including planning, organizing, coordinating, staffing, directing, controlling, evaluating, and revising, and illustrates their relationship.

The task of organizing relates to how work within dietary services will be divided up to better assure that department goals and the facility's mission will be attained. Important organizing concepts include authority, responsibility, delegation, and accountability. There are ten steps that outline the elements important in the organizing process.

An organizational chart does more than show relationships among positions. It also illustrates the flow of communication and authority within the organization. Power and authority have been shown to mean the same thing: an ability to get others to do something. There are six common mistakes a manager should try to avoid when organizing a dietary department.

A systems approach to organization views the total environment of the organization rather than just a specific department within it. This approach recognizes that an impact in one area is likely to have spin-off effects on another. It is required that specific departments work for the mutual benefit of the facility. The dietary manager must be able to effectively interact with personnel at all organizational levels both within and outside of dietary services. Coordination provides harmony in the individual efforts toward fulfilling the facility's mission.

Nursing care in the United States is constantly adapting to the quickly changing needs of society. The basic levels of nursing care are:

- skilled nursing facility,
- intermediate care facility, and
- residential facility. In addition to these three primary levels, other types of facilities are also available.

Skilled care (provided in long-term care facilities), offers twenty-four-hour nursing services and may also offer a range of specialized services such as physical, occupational, and speech therapy. In contrast, acute care is offered in a hospital setting for patients requiring hospital-level diagnostic and therapeutic management. Subacute care is short-term care between hospital and home, providing rehabilitation therapy. Mental health and rehabilitation care serves the needs of people with mental health problems, many of whom were formerly given care in public institutions. Assisted living addresses the demographic changes in America, as well as economic constraints and the preferences of the elderly. The goal behind it is to allow the elderly to "age in place." Institutional living is resident housing.

Although long-term care is not a new concept, recent trends have prompted some long-term care facilities to increase their acute care capabilities, and include advanced rehabilitative care services for those who are chronically ill (AIDS patients, for example). Integrated-care settings would allow a range of care settings for the chronically ill emphasizing their need for special medical care, mental-health care, spiritual support, and social services.

Healthcare facilities are regulated by federal, state, and/or local government agencies. The federal government establishes its own minimum requirements for facilities participating in federal healthcare reimbursement programs such as Medicare and Medicaid. Medicare is a federal insurance program providing a full range of medical benefits for specific periods of time. Medicaid is a state-administered program, the purpose of which is to provide medical services to persons receiving public assistance under the Social Security Act and, at the state's option, other needy persons.

Since foodservices are an integral part of the facility's budget, regulations have an impact upon what can and cannot be done within the operation of dietary services.

KEY TERMS

Accountability
Acute care
Assisted living
Authority
Chronically ill
Continuum of care
Coordination
Delegation
Dietary services
Elderly feeding programs
Feeding programs
Flow of communication
Food management companies
Goal statements
Government facility
Health care market
Institutional foodservice
Institutional living
Integrated-care setting
Long-term care industry
Management loop
Medicaid
Medicare
Mental health and rehabilitation care
Nursing homes
Organization
Philanthropic facility
Principles of management
Proprietary facility
Rehabilitation
Responsibility
Skilled nursing
Sources of power
Student market
Subacute care
Systems approach to organization

QUESTIONS/PROBLEMS/CASES

1. List the three categories of foodservice operations according to the National Restaurant Association. What distinguishes "institutional" foodservice from the others?

2. Identify the major segments in the hospitality industry.

3. What is the difference between commercial and non-commercial/institutional food service?

4. Label each of the following as a proprietary, philanthropic, and/or governmental facility.
   Beaver City Public High School
   Long Brook Nursing Home (owned by Beverly Enterprises)
   Essex County Hospital
   Masonic Home of Lakewood

5. The Spring Valley Retirement Community general manager is looking for a way to reduce the number of hours he spends with the Dietary Mgr. They have decided to hire a food management company to handle their dietary service. During a meeting, he asks you for your opinions on this matter. List three disadvantages to using food management companies. Also provide a suggestion that they might use to monitor the company that is hired.

6. List 5 possible goals of the dietary department of a nursing home.

7. Briefly describe each of the components in the management process.

8. Briefly describe the steps in the organizing process.

9. An experienced dietary manager, finding herself overloaded with responsibility, asked an assistant to schedule staff members for the department. However, the assistant created many problems with his first attempt and the dietary manager was reprimanded by the business administrator. Which organizing concept explains this reprimand? What should the dietary manager have done differently?

10. Describe the difference between formally organizing a dietary department and the informal (top-down) approach.

11. You begin working in a new facility and don't know who the informal power-holders are. What should be your plan for gaining this knowledge?

12. Why is it a good idea to discourage competition, or adversarial strategies, between departments? What management technique speaks directly to this issue?

13. You have a healthy family member who is elderly and in need of help with her "activities of daily living." After doing the appropriate research, you've analyzed the situation and believe you've reached the perfect solution. Which type of facility would you research first and why? What solution have you reached?

14. Why is it necessary for health planners to address the issue of chronically ill patients?

15. Why is an acute care facility not sufficient for those suffering from chronic illnesses?

16. Why should a dietary manager be familiar with programs such as Medicare and Medicaid?

17. Why are long-term care facilities now including advanced rehabilitative care services *AND* increasing their acute care capability?

18. When would a person consider subacute care?

19. What challenges often face a foodservice manager in an institutional living facility?

FOOD PROCUREMENT, PRODUCTION, AND SERVICE

- Menu Planning and Recipes
- Sanitation and Safety
- Purchasing, Receiving and Inventory Management
- Facility Layout, Design and Equipment
- Food Production and Service
- Evaluation of Food and Nutrition Services

2

MENU PLANNING AND RECIPES

CHAPTER OUTLINE

- Planning the Cycle Menu
  - Color
  - Flavor
  - Texture
  - Form and Shape
  - Temperature
  - Consistency
  - Method of Preparation
  - Cost
  - Other Concerns
- Other Menu Types
  - A la Carte Menu
  - Table d'Hôte Menu
  - Du Jour Menu
  - Limited Menu
- Checklist for Menu Planning
- Specific Standards and Procedures in Food Preparation
  - HACCP Principles
  - Hazard Characteristics
  - Using HACCP Format
  - Characteristics of High-Quality Foods
- Standardized Recipes
  - Developing and Evaluating Standardized Recipes
  - Alternate Method to Developing Standardized Recipes
- Menus and the Computer
  - Ingredient Filing
  - Recipe Filing
  - Menu Planning
  - Computer Forecasting
  - Menu Analysis
  - Nutrient Analysis

PLANNING THE CYCLE MENU

A menu is a list indicating food and beverage products available. A small facility may have a basic set of regular and special-diet menus and, perhaps, a separate set of menus for the cash and/or employee cafeterias. Large facilities, like school food-services and correctional institutions, may use a wide variety of menus for different outlets, offsite catering, and special function purposes, along with other menus required for their clients with special dietary needs. Alternative food production-delivery systems may yield a smaller or larger variety of items available, but the need for and procedures to develop the menu (list) of items are similar.

Many institutional facilities use a *cycle menu.* This type of menu changes every day over a specified time period (seven-day, two-week, or four-week, the latter being common in healthcare facilities); the daily menus are then repeated in the same order. Since many facilities have limited resources of time, money, staff, space, or equipment, it is important to plan the meals carefully to help meet the psychological, social, nutritional, and aesthetic needs of the publics being served.

The first step when planning the menu is to provide a block of uninterrupted time and a place away from the busy kitchen. The dietary manager should have records, files, and books, available to help in the development of the menu. First, a decision must be made about the length of the menu cycle. Since the length of stay in an acute care hospital is short, the cycle menu for patients may be correspondingly short. When the average stay is longer (such as in a nursing home) a longer cycle menu, such as four weeks, will be necessary. In both instances, the need to provide variety for the facility's staff will be very important. The U.S. Department of Agriculture has developed and publicized dietary guidelines which can provide helpful assistance for menu planning. Review Figure 2.1 for such assistance.

You typically begin writing a menu by considering the expensive entree items. Write the meat or main-dish items throughout the menu. Popular items may be repeated more than once in a cycle menu. A balance of high- and low-priced items helps keep food costs in line. After selecting the dinner and lunch entrees, move to the vegetable. If the entree has a sauce, select a plain vegetable or a combination of vegetables. The third item to add to the menu is the starch, followed by the salad, the dessert, and breads.

Eat a variety of foods to obtain the nutrients and other substances needed for good health.
Monitor the nutrient content of the food you eat by reading the Nutrition Food Label.

Balance the food you eat with physical activity—maintain or improve your weight.
Evaluate your weight and location of body fat. If you need to lose weight, monitor caloric intake by checking the Nutrition Food Label and increase physical activity.

Choose a diet with plenty of grain products, vegetables, and fruits.
Use the Food Guide Pyramid as a selection guide. Consume at least 3 servings of vegetables, 2 servings of fruit, and 6 servings of grain products a day, with emphasis on whole grains.

Choose a diet low in fat, saturated fat, and cholesterol.
Limit the portion of total calories from fat to 30% with less than 10% from saturated fat.

Choose a diet moderate in sugars.
Avoid excessive snacking, and read the low-calorie food label to check for high sugar content.

Choose a diet moderate in salt and sodium due to association with high blood pressure and loss of calcium.
Limit number of salty snacks or choose those lower in sodium, and monitor sodium content on prepared convenience foods using the Nutrition Food Label.

If you drink alcoholic beverages, do so in moderation.
Children, adolescents, pregnant women, and individuals using medications should not drink.

Source: *Nutrition and Your Health: Dietary Guidelines for Americans.* U.S. Department of Agriculture, U.S. Department of Health and Human Services, Fourth Edition, 1995.

FIGURE 2.1 DIETARY GUIDELINES FOR AMERICANS

The menu pattern will influence the process of writing the menu. A set or non-selective menu offers no choice; everyone receives the same menu. By contrast, a selective menu offers several items from which to choose; greater client satisfaction will occur. Today a variety offering is becoming more commonplace and the increasing emphasis on guest (client) satisfaction almost demands it. The dietary manager first writes a regular or normal diet and then writes modifications of the basic menu for other diets.

There are many factors to consider when writing a menu. Do the clients have preferences in terms of race, religious, or ethnic customs? Consider the season of the year and the availability of foods and holidays to be celebrated. Are nutrition requirements being met? An understanding of pleasing combinations of food based on color, flavor, texture, form, shape, temperature, and consistency is also important. Knowing what to look for when writing the menu can make the menu very pleasing.

Color

Provide a variety of color in each meal. Be aware of meals that become too bland in color. For example, baked fish, mashed potatoes, cauliflower, pear salad, and white cake will not present an attractive offering for the consumer. Use of a reference list of green vegetables or yellow or red products can prompt the dietary manager to use a variety of color. Most food colors combine very nicely (with the exception of some red items, which may not contrast well with some red-orange products).

Flavor

Flavor combinations are concerned with the sensations of sweet, sour, salty, and bitter. Try not to repeat foods with similar taste combinations. Acid or tart foods are frequently served as accompaniments to fatty foods to reduce the fatty taste. Examples are pork and applesauce, lamb and mint sauce, duckling and orange sauce, pork and gooseberries, and roast beef and horseradish sauce.

Texture

Texture refers to the structure of food (whether it feels soft or firm to the mouth). Terms used to describe different textures include grainy, soft, chewy, crisp, hard, and smooth. Provide a variety of textures in the meal. When soup is served, crackers or croutons provide an excellent contrasting texture.

Form and Shape

The shape of food plays a large part in the aesthetic appeal of the menu. When offered potatoes in many forms (mashed, baked, croquettes, fried, au gratin, duchess, hash brown, herb baked, lyonnaise, O'Brien, oven-browned, parmesan, scalloped, stuffed, or cold as in potato salad), clients are less likely to grow tired of them.

Temperature

There are two basic temperatures to remember. Serve hot foods above 140°F and cold foods below 40°F. Temperatures should be checked often during preparation and service. Rather than having a hot meal from soup to dessert, many dietary managers provide some cold foods to give variety.

Consistency

Consistency refers to the degree of firmness, viscosity (resistance to flow), or density of the item. A sauce can be thin, medium, or thick. Try to avoid including menu items with similar consistencies, such as creamed potatoes with a Swiss steak already covered by a heavy gravy.

Method of Preparation

Create variety by using various preparation methods: baking, broiling, braising, boiling, frying, steaming. If the menu items are all plain, the dietary manager may choose to include a sauce or gravy, or to cream, butter, or escallop the vegetables.

Cost

The cost of the menu is an important planning consideration; the topic of pre-costing will be discussed extensively in Chapter Thirteen. The dietary manager should understand the need for a financial limit beyond which, on average, a meal, food cost per client day, or other cost measure should not exceed.

Other Concerns

After taking time to write a menu with a variety of colors, flavors, textures, forms, shapes, temperatures, consistencies, and methods of preparation, it is important to visualize the arrangement of food on the plate. Will the items planned fit on the plate? Is there height? Is the plate and meal balanced and pleasing to the eye? Arrangement of food on the plate is just as important. Foodservice staff can consider the plate to be a picture. Food should be placed in an attractive and pleasing manner. Instruct serving staff to consistently place the meat or main entree in one position. Spills or drips should be removed. This is just as important for meals being served in the cafeteria line as it is for food being pre-plated for service at another site.

What about garnishes? Some plates do not need an added garnish. If the accompanying starch and vegetable provide the color and balance, there may be no need to add an often overused sprig of parsley. In some cases where the accompaniments do not add much contrast, a garnish is appropriate. Some general guidelines for garnishes are that they must be edible, simple, appropriate to the food on the plate, and planned into the plate arrangement.

Classify the garnishes used by color or appropriateness to the item being garnished. For example, the following garnishes are all dark or black in color:

chocolate leaves	spiced prunes
chocolate curls	raisins or currants
chocolate sauce	ripe olives
prunes	blue berries

Another classification divides garnishes into those used for desserts, entrees, and salads. Entree garnishes should complement the meal and not be parsley only. Creative use of peppers, sliced tomato, pimento, spiced apple rings, pineapple, and so on are all excellent, and add variety to the plate.

Other Menu Types

While the majority of dietary managers will use the cycle menu discussed, some will wish to incorporate components of other menu types. Understanding these menus and their characteristics will allow the manager to add diversity for the client accustomed to the typical cycle menu. Figure 2.2 summarizes the characteristics of these different menu types.

A la Carte Menu—Prices each menu item separately

Table d'Hote Menu—Offers a complete meal for one price

Semi a la Carte (Restaurant Style) Menu—Provides the salad, entree, starch and vegetable for one price

Du Jour Menu—Means the "menu of the day" and typically features the special for that day and menu

Limited Menu—Refers to a menu offering 6-12 menu items typically seen in fast food operations

Figure 2.2 Summary of Menu Types

A la Carte Menu

While mostly popular in commercial operations, the a la carte menu allows an individual diner the opportunity to select precisely the items desired, as food items are priced separately. The end result is more revenue for the operator, since selling separate items brings in more revenue than selling items at a group price.

A semi-a la carte, or restaurant-style, menu offers the entree at a single price, but often includes an accompaniment salad, starch, and vegetable with it. Sometimes a beverage is also included, but appetizer, dessert, and other side dishes are typically served for an extra price.

Table d'Hôte Menu

This menu offers a complete meal at a fixed price and is considered the opposite of the a la carte menu. The term table d'hote means table of the host and comes from the "good old days" when room and board were offered to the customer. The room would be the traveler's accommodations, while the board would be the dining table at which the traveler would enjoy his or her food. This table would be, of course, the table of the host and would be included in the price paid for the room and board, thus the all-inclusive pricing when one enjoys a table d'hote menu.

A complete meal might include an appetizer, salad, entree, starch, vegetable, dessert, and beverage. Such grand eating is not as common today; individuals are more concerned about what they eat and how much they eat. Yet, the table d'hote is still popular in some markets and may provide good value for the hearty diner. If entree selections are limited and forecasting precise, the table d'hote menu may be quite appropriate in an institutional setting.

Du Jour Menu

The du jour menu is planned and written daily; it means "menu of the day." It will reflect only the foods produced for that day. The du jour menu makes use of carryover foods, and offers flexibility in production. Often an operation offering a du jour menu is a specialty one serving original and special foods to a limited market.

The du jour menu has been used traditionally in very elegant operations; the menu would be printed special each day and dated accordingly. However, in recent years, with word processing as convenient as it has become with computers in-house, operations are able to print du jour menus readily and successfully at minimal cost.

Limited Menu

The limited menu is a hybrid of the others and offers between six and twelve entree items. Some menus may offer as few as two or three. A representative but small selection of appetizers, salads, desserts, and beverages is also offered.

As a way to improve production control and reduce labor costs, the limited menu has become increasingly popular due to its simplicity. These menus must be written for a relatively specific market since they offer so few items. Fast-food operations have been particularly successful with them.

Checklist for Menu Planning

Since the menu affects every other subsystem in the foodservice operation, its planning must consider a wide variety of issues. Many of these are noted in Figure 2.3 (Checklist for Menu Planning). This form can be used to plan a menu or to evaluate an existing menu.

Specific Standards and Procedures in Food Preparation

Quality (suitability for intended use) is a very elusive term but one that must receive a high priority as recipes are standardized and as food products are produced. Dietary managers sometimes mistakenly believe that all production staff have the same concept about quality and, therefore, there is no need to emphasize it in daily

Personnel

1. The menu communicates the strategy for meeting or exceeding expectations of the patients, residents and staff.
2. The image of the menu is evaluated based on appearance, readability, clarity and pricing strategies.
3. The skill levels of production personnel are evaluated.
4. The skill levels of service personnel are evaluated.
5. Suppliers are asked for preparation and merchandising suggestions.
6. Sanitation, quality and cost control standards are maintained.
7. Counter attendants and servers, if applicable, know the meaning of terms used to describe menu items and their preparation.

Equipment

1. Equipment is selected based on initial costs, capacity, availability of energy sources, operating costs, maintenance costs and skill levels of employees.
2. Equipment is easy to clean and sanitize.
3. Equipment design, layout and installation facilitate both product and people movement in the kitchen and service areas.
4. Special function and catering menus are planned realistically based on the facility's equipment resources.

Inventory

1. The menu achieves the financial objectives of the facility.
2. Records are maintained about the popularity of every menu item.
3. The effect of the menu on the other control points is considered when the menu is planned.
4. Menu item ingredients are cross-utilized as much as possible.
5. High quality convenience foods are evaluated with use of "Make/Buy" analysis and used where appropriate.

Facility

1. Traffic flow in the kitchen service and dining areas is evaluated, and the design and layout of the facility is changed when necessary and possible.
2. The ambiance of the facility is appropriate to the menu and the expectations of those being served.
3. Special function banquets are planned with the limitations of the establishment's facilities in mind.
4. The facility is maintained in a clean and sanitary manner.

Truth-in-Menu

1. Accurate descriptions are used for raw ingredients and finished menu items.
2. Quality or grade statements are factual.
3. Sizes, weights or counts noted in the menu are correct.
4. Frozen or canned items are never called "fresh."
5. Preparation techniques are accurately stated.
6. Additional charges for extras are clearly stated on the menu used for each cafeteria operation.
7. Oral descriptions provided by counter attendants are factual.
8. Dietary or nutritional claims are precise.
9. Points of origin are accurate, not misleading.

FIGURE 2.3 CHECKLIST FOR MENU PLANNING

operations. However, the concern about quality, pervasive throughout the dietary operation, demands constant attention to many details. The dietary manager in charge of the entire operation is responsible for ensuring that quality requirements are met; they are too important to delegate to staff members.

In the context of food production, "quality" refers to a product's taste, texture, appearance, nutritional value, and overall level of excellence. Dietary operations are encouraged to implement ongoing quality-control programs to maintain consistency in the delivery of products of required quality. Consistent quality of food products and service is a goal realized by too few dietary services. Because the quality of food directly relates to the satisfaction of clients, there are likely to be fewer complaints when quality is consistent.

To control quality, dietary managers first develop quality standards. They then train production personnel to incorporate these quality standards into the way that work is done, using proper production techniques to prepare standardized recipes. Some dietary managers like to sample all food products before they are served to help confirm that quality requirements are met on a day-to-day basis.

In these days of cost minimization and cost containment, it becomes relatively easy to sacrifice quality requirements for economic concerns. However, the wise dietary manager attempts to "marry" concerns for cost with concerns for delivery of the proper quality of food products. He or she understands that costs can be minimized in other areas to compensate for added expenses in providing food and service of the necessary quality.

It is difficult to describe the concept of quality, but it is also difficult to operate a dietary operation without constant attention to it. One's experience and understanding about specific menu items and what must be done to best satisfy the client are at the heart of the definition of quality for a dietary operation.

HACCP Principles

The Hazard Analysis and Critical Control Point (HACCP) protocol originated in 1971. In 1989, the National Advisory Committee on Microbiological Criteria for Foods (NACMCF) revised the original protocol, producing the following seven principles:

1. **Conduct Hazard Analysis and Risk Assessment**—A hazard is any biological, chemical, or physical property that may cause an unacceptable consumer health risk. All of the potential hazards in the food chain are analyzed, from growing and harvesting to manufacturing, distribution, retailing, and consumption of the product. A risk assessment of the food is also conducted as discussed below under a more thorough presentation of this first HACCP principle.
2. **Determine Critical Control Points (CCP)**—A CCP is any point in the process where loss of control may result in an unacceptable health risk. A CCP is established for each identified hazard. It is within this principle that the dynamic nature of HACCP is most evident. The emergence of food-borne listeriosis has taught food processors the importance of potential product contamination from the processing environment. Therefore, cleaning and sanitation procedures have recently been included as CCPs in HACCP programs. This is a good example of the expansion of the HACCP approach to meet contemporary needs.
3. **Establish Specifications for Each CCP**—This principle was implicit in the original HACCP protocol, but experience has shown that it is necessary to spell out tolerances at each CCP. Examples of specifications include product pH range, the maximum allowable level of antibiotic residues, and the time and temperature range for reheating food.
4. **Monitor each CCP**—It is necessary to establish a regular schedule for the monitoring of each CCP. The schedule could be, for example, once per shift, hourly or even continuous. Preferably, a printed testing procedure for the monitored parameter should be available. Responsibility for testing must be clearly assigned, and the test results must be recorded.
5. **Establish Corrective Action to Be Taken if a Deviation Occurs at a CCP**—This step has not always been carried out when necessary. Corrective actions

should be clearly defined beforehand, with the responsibility for action assigned to an individual.

6. **Establish a Recordkeeping System**—It has always been important for the food producers to maintain records of ingredients, processes, and product controls so that an effective trace-and-recall system would be available when necessary. Record-keeping will become more and more important.
7. **Establish Verification Procedures**—This principle was also added in anticipation of HACCP-based regulatory programs. Verification can include documentation reviews as well as microbiological, chemical and physical testing.

Hazard Characteristics

The first HACCP principle, hazard analysis and risk assessment, is quite involved. For the sake of uniformity, a standardized procedure for its application has been adopted. Besides the analysis of three hazard characteristics identified in the 1970s, the risk assessment process today has been expanded to include the following six hazard characteristics:

- **Food Intended for Consumption by At-Risk Population**—Awareness of populations at risk for hazards has been heightened by the AIDS epidemic and for other reasons, thus making this point increasingly important to foodservice operators, especially in hospitals and nursing homes, and their vendors;
- **Product Contains Sensitive Ingredient**—A sensitive ingredient is any potential carrier of a hazard, usually a microbiological hazard, such as eggs or poultry;
- **No Process Step to Eliminate Hazard**—Examples include lack of a heat treatment to kill bacterial pathogens and lack of physical devices such as magnets and screens to detect foreign material;
- **Recontamination Potential Before Packaging**—This point was added in response to the proliferation of specialty chilled foods, or high-quality convenience foods popular in homes having two working parents, or in single-individual households. A chilled food which could be recontaminated before packaging could be more hazardous than a food in which no potential for recontamination existed, such as a food which was pasteurized inside its final sealed package;
- **Potential of Product Abuse**—The risk assessment must consider the potential for product abuse in distribution, retailing, or consumer handling which could result in an increased hazard. Such a product might be one held at ambient temperatures for more than several hours on a loading dock, in a car, or at a picnic, which would not have built up a hazardous population of bacteria had it been stored at refrigerated temperatures;
- **No Terminal Heat Process**—This hazard characteristic was added to account for ready-to-eat foods in the risk-assessment process. Since many microbiological hazards are eliminated by pasteurization, a food heated by the consumer should have a greater margin of safety than a food not heated before consumption.

To complete the hazard analysis and risk assessment process, each food is assigned to a product hazard category, depending on the number and type of hazard characteristics present. Foods with no hazard characteristics are designated "0," while foods which possess hazard characteristic A are automatically assigned category "6," the highest risk category. Foods possessing one or more of hazard characteristics B–F are assigned to risk categories "1" to "4." The product hazard categories are helpful in identifying CCPs. If a recipe includes one or more hazardous ingredients, an HACCP flowchart is necessary.

Using HACCP Format

Creating a menu that is tasty, attractive, nutritious and, appreciated is a worthy goal. But, even more importantly, safety and sanitation rules and checks must be incorporated to ensure a meal that is safe to eat.

This is accomplished by identifying critical control points as the food flows through the components of the operation. Critical control points are established at any place along the food flow where something could go wrong that could result in food poisoning or illness.

The food industry and government regulatory agencies are placing greater reliance on the Hazard Analysis and Critical Control Point (HACCP) system to provide greater assurance of food safety. HACCP is a preventative system in which safety is designed into the food formulation and the process by which it is produced. It is more effective than conventional quality assurance programs, which tend to rely on finished-product testing to provide evidence of safety.

While all foods can become hazardous, some are more hazardous than others. Dry cereal can become contaminated with bacteria from some other source but ordinarily would not be considered a hazardous food. Due to their susceptibility to spoilage, high-protein foods such as meat, poultry, fish, eggs, and dairy foods are especially hazardous.

Ideally, a manager will construct HACCP flowcharts and tables similar to those in Figures 2.4 to 2.14 for any recipe that contains one or more hazardous ingredient. Critical control points would be checked during the receiving function, and then the flowchart would continue on through each step of the operation, identifying critical control points in storage, prepping, cooking, and serving.

Characteristics of High-Quality Foods

While quality must be defined for a specific dietary operation, there are some generally accepted "definitions" of high-quality foods on which to base evaluation of products produced for the facility. As a background, the characteristics used to describe any food generally refer to one of the following:

- **Color of Food.** Color of food is of significant importance to its appeal. Most people have a definite opinion about the "proper" color of a food item. Typically, the color should be "natural" and should closely compare with naturally occurring colors. Consider a red tomato, green broccoli, white cauliflower, and orange apricot. These and other fruits and vegetables, when not of

Critical Control	Hazard	Standards	Corrective Action if Standard Not Met
Receiving beef	Contamination and spoilage	Accept beef at 45° F (7.2° C) or lower; verify with thermometer	Reject delivery
		Packaging intact	Reject delivery
		No off odor or stickiness, etc.	Reject delivery
Receiving vegetables	Contamination and spoilage	Packaging intact	Reject delivery
		No cross-contamination from other foods on the truck	Reject delivery
		No signs of insect or rodent activity	Reject delivery

Figure 2.4 HACCP Receiving Process[1]

Critical Control	Hazard	Standards	Corrective Action if Standard Not Met
Storing raw beef	Cross-contamination of other foods	Store on lower shelf	Move to lower shelf away from other foods
		Label, date, and use FIFO rotation	Use first; discard if maximum time is exceeded or suspected
	Bacterial growth and spoilage	Beef temperature must remain below 45° F (7.2° C)	Discard if time and temperature abused
Storing vegetables	Cross-contamination from raw potentially hazardous foods	Label, date, and use FIFO rotation	Discard product held past rotation date
		Keep above raw potentially hazardous foods	Discard contaminated, damaged, or spoiled products

FIGURE 2.5 HACCP STORAGE PROCESS[1]

the "natural" color, will not be judged high in quality whether they are in their raw or cooked form. If a product is not at the color level present when it is at optimal maturity, it is not at its peak of freshness and/or it has been handled/prepared improperly;

- **Texture.** Terms such as toughness, stringiness, crispness, and elasticity are used to define texture. As products deviate from their generally accepted characteristic texture, they will be judged unacceptable. Who likes "soft" crackers, "lumpy" cereal, "stringy" vegetables, or "gritty" butter? One can begin to see the importance of texture as a characteristic of quality;
- **Viscosity.** This term refers to the resistance that various foods have to flow. Who likes "watery" jelly, very thick pudding, liquefied butter or margarine for spreading, etc.?

Critical Control	Hazard	Standards	Corrective Action if Standard Not Met
Trimming and cubing beef	Contamination, cross-contamination, and bacteria increase	Wash hands	Wash hands
		Clean and sanitize utensils	Wash, rinse, and sanitize utensils and cutting board
		Pull and cube one roast at a time, then refrigerate	Return excess amount to refrigerator
Washing and cutting vegetables	Contamination and cross-contamination	Wash hands	Wash hands
		Use clean and sanitized cutting board, knives, utensils	Wash, rinse, and sanitize utensils and cutting board
		Wash vegetables in clean and sanitized vegetable sink	Clean and sanitize vegetable sink before washing vegetables

FIGURE 2.6 HACCP PREPARATION PROCESS[1]

Critical Control	Hazard	Standards	Corrective Action if Standard Not Met
Cooking stew	Bacterial survival	Cook **all** ingredients to minimum internal temperature of 165° F (73.9° C)	Continue cooking to 165° F (73.9° C)
		Verify final temperature with a thermometer	Continue cooking to 165° F (73.9° C)
	Physical contamination during cooking	Keep covered; stir often	Cover
	Contamination by herbs and spices	Add spices early in cooking procedure	Continue cooking at least ½ hour after spices are added
		Measure all spices, flavor enhancers, and additives, and read labels carefully	
	Contamination of utensils	Use clean and sanitized utensils	Wash, rinse, and sanitize all utensils before use
	Contamination from cook's hand or mouth	Use proper tasting procedures	Discard product

FIGURE 2.7 HACCP COOKING PROCESS[1]

- **Flavor.** Flavor refers to the total impression that food has on one's senses when it is eaten. Most people believe that it is the single most important factor in food selection, and, as a characteristic of quality, it is obviously of great importance. The sensation of flavor is a combination of taste, smell, and texture. The four basic taste sensations (bitter, sour, salty, sweet) must be available in just the "right" combination—to the perception of an individual—for food to be judged of proper taste. Smell is also a highly individualistic sense. The fundamental odors (sweet, sour, burnt, and "goaty") can be "mixed" to form a seemingly endless variety of odor sensations that affect one's perception of food quality. Touch (also called "mouth feel") provides a special sensation

Critical Control	Hazard	Standards	Corrective Action if Standard Not Met
Hot holding and serving	Contamination, bacterial growth	Use clean and sanitary equipment to transfer and hold product	Wash, rinse, and sanitize equipment before transferring food product to it
		Hold stew above 140° F (60° C) in preheated holding unit; stir to maintain even temperature	Return to stove and reheat to 165° F (73.9° C)
		Keep covered	Cover
		Clean and sanitize serving equipment and utensils	Wash, rinse, and sanitize serving utensils and equipment

FIGURE 2.8 HACCP HOLDING PROCESS[1]

Recipe Chicken Stew **Serves:** 50 **Date:** 9/15/96

Ingredients	**Measure**	**Amount (50)**
Chicken Pieces, 8 cut, frozen	Lbs	20
Carrots, fresh, peeled, cut in ¾ inch pieces	Lbs	5
Onions, chopped	Qts	1
Potatoes, peeled, cut into ¾ inch pieces	Lbs	7½
Green Peas, frozen	Lbs	4
Margarine	Cups	1
Flour	Cups	3
Chicken Stock	Qts	2
Salt	tsp	2
Pepper	tsp	2

Preparation Steps:

1. Place thawed chicken pieces on sheet pans. Cover and bake at 350°F for 30 minutes.
2. Cut carrots, onions and peeled potatoes into pieces as specified.
3. Cook potatoes, carrots, and peas separately until tender.
4. Remove chicken from oven; drain off juices and fat.
5. Sauté onions in margarine until tender. Add flour and stir until smooth. Add chicken drippings. Add chicken broth as needed for gravy-like consistency. Season with salt and pepper.
6. Combine chicken, cooked vegetables and gravy. Place in deep baking pans.
7. Cover and bake for an additional 30 minutes at 350°F

Product Flow

Source

IQF, 8 cut, 20#/cs from *XYZ Chicken Farms*

→ **Storage**

Chix pieces pulled and thawed in refrigerator; original carton, on sheet pan, bottom shelf; 1 day prior

→ **Pre-preparation**

9 am: move thawed chix from refrig (39°F) to sheet pans; place in pre-heated 350°F oven.
9:30 am: vegetables washed, cut; carrots, potatoes, peas, steamed tender.

→ **Preparation**

10 am Chix removed from oven, drained; gravy prep'd.
10:35 am Chix, cooked vegetables, & gravy combined in deep pans, covered, & placed in 350°F oven

→ **Holding**

11:15 am
Chix Stew removed from oven (170°F)

Placed on steam table, covered.

→ **Service**

11:30 am-1:30 pm
Chix Stew hold on line.

11:30 am	168°F
12:30 pm	155°F
1:30 pm	145°F

→ **Cooling**

2:15 pm Leftovers covered in original pans; placed in refrigerator.

4 pm	100°F
6 pm	80°F
8 pm	60°F
10 pm	40°F

→ **Storage**

In refrigerator, top shelf, 3 days

→ **Reheating**

Reheat in 350°F oven, covered, for 45 minutes.

Final temp: 170°F

FIGURE 2.9 HACCP RECIPE WORKSHEET

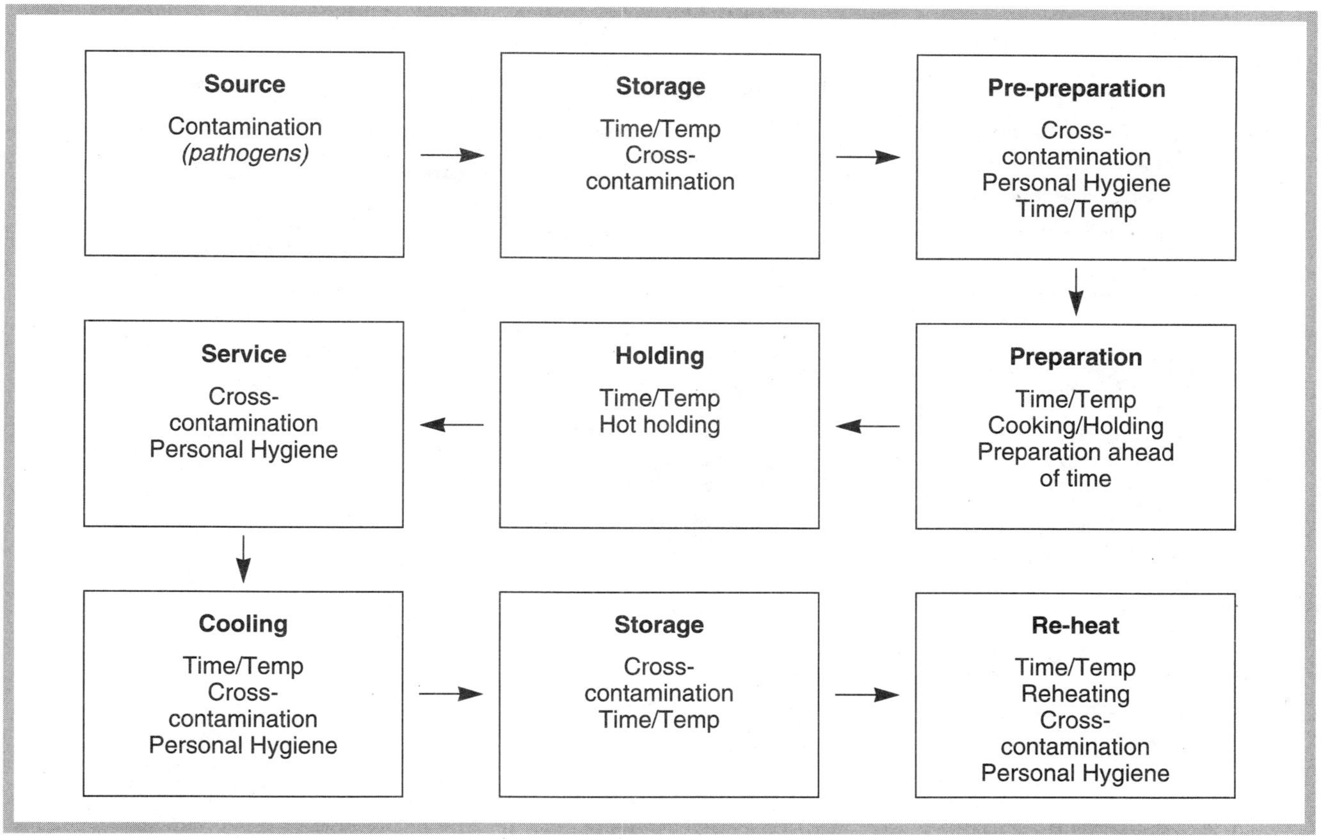

FIGURE 2.10 *CHICKEN STEW* PRODUCT FLOW HAZARDS[1]

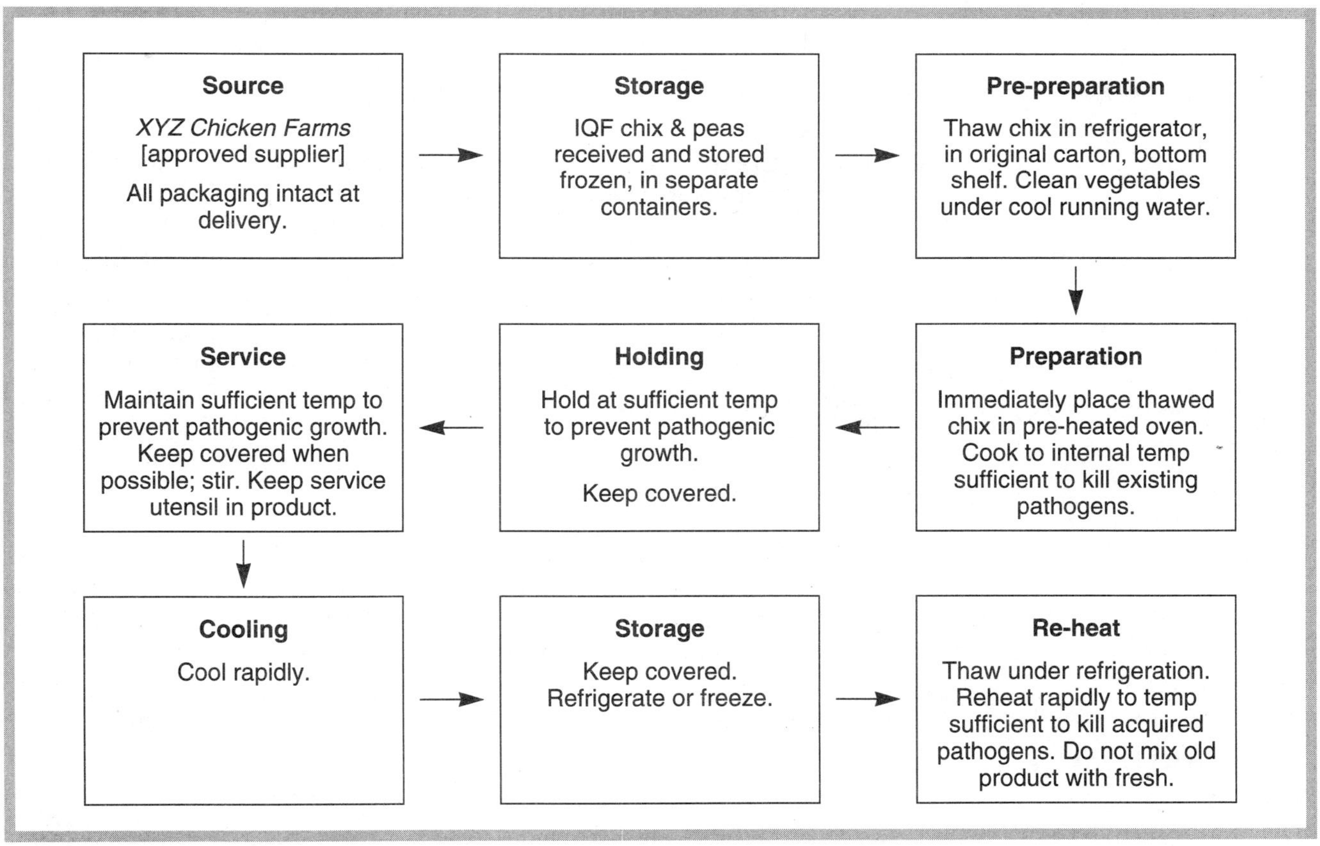

FIGURE 2.11 *CHICKEN STEW* CONTROL POINTS[1]

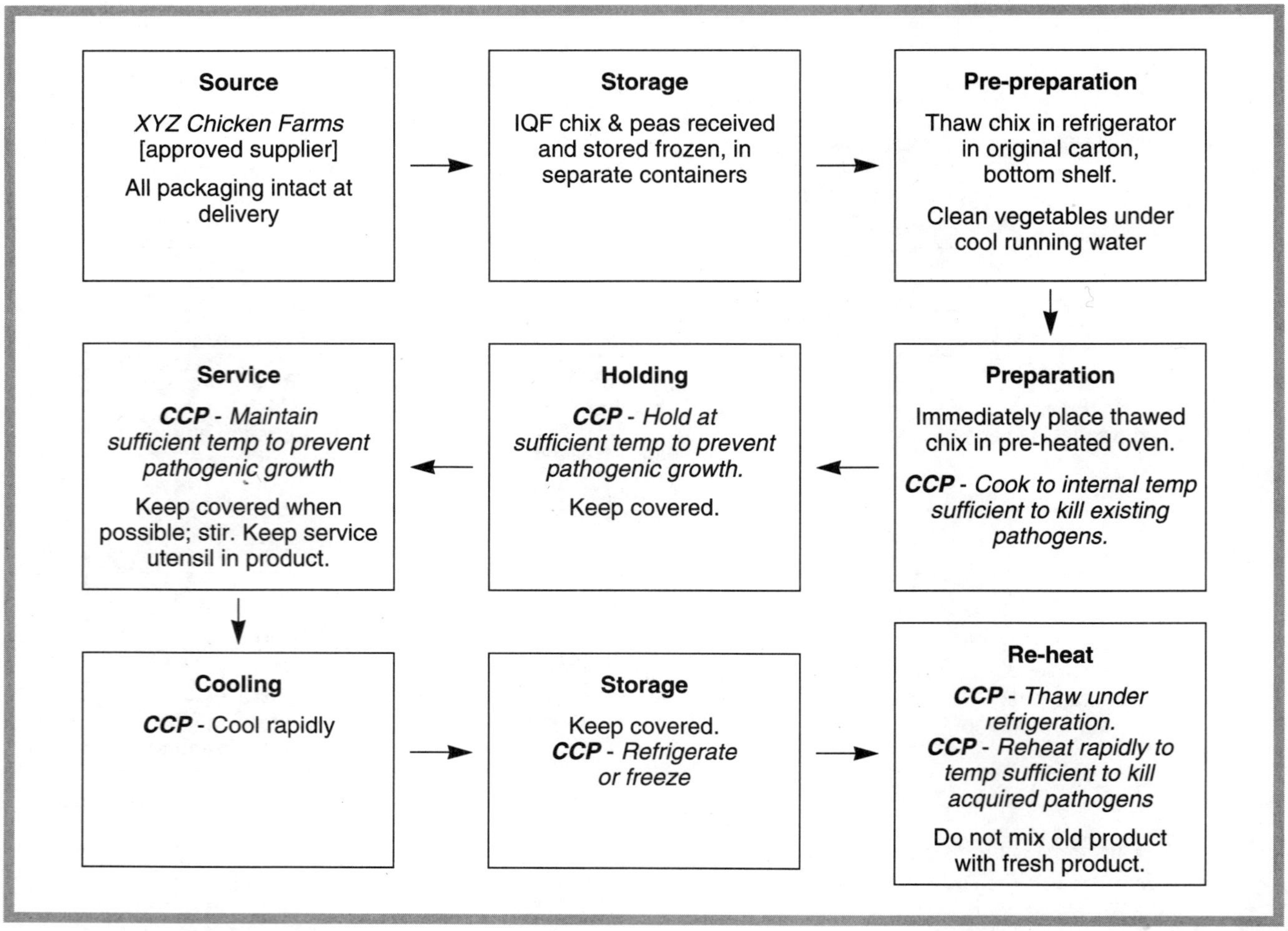

FIGURE 2.12 *CHICKEN STEW* CRITICAL CONTROL POINTS[1]

based upon the texture, consistency, and temperature of products tasted. Finally, food temperature is a characteristic of quality; people have a definite opinion about the temperature of "hot" foods (such as stews, coffee, and spaghetti sauce) and "cold" foods (ice cream, green salads, and watermelon);

- **Other Factors.** For specific food items, a variety of other factors can be important in the definition of "high quality." Consider the "proper" shape of a baked potato, the "height" of a fresh egg yolk, the weight of an "ideal" serving of a meat portion, the length of a "bite-size" cut green bean, etc. Truly, the determination of quality is a highly personal activity; the dietary manager attempting to define quality for products to be produced/served in the facility has a large job.

In the context of food quality, the objectives of food preparation include conserving the food's nutritive value; improving its digestibility; developing and enhancing the flavor and attractiveness of the original color, form, and texture; and freeing it from harmful organisms or substances.

STANDARDIZED RECIPES

There is an old saying in foodservices: "It all starts with the menu." This is true, and dietary managers recognize that menus are implemented by use of standardized

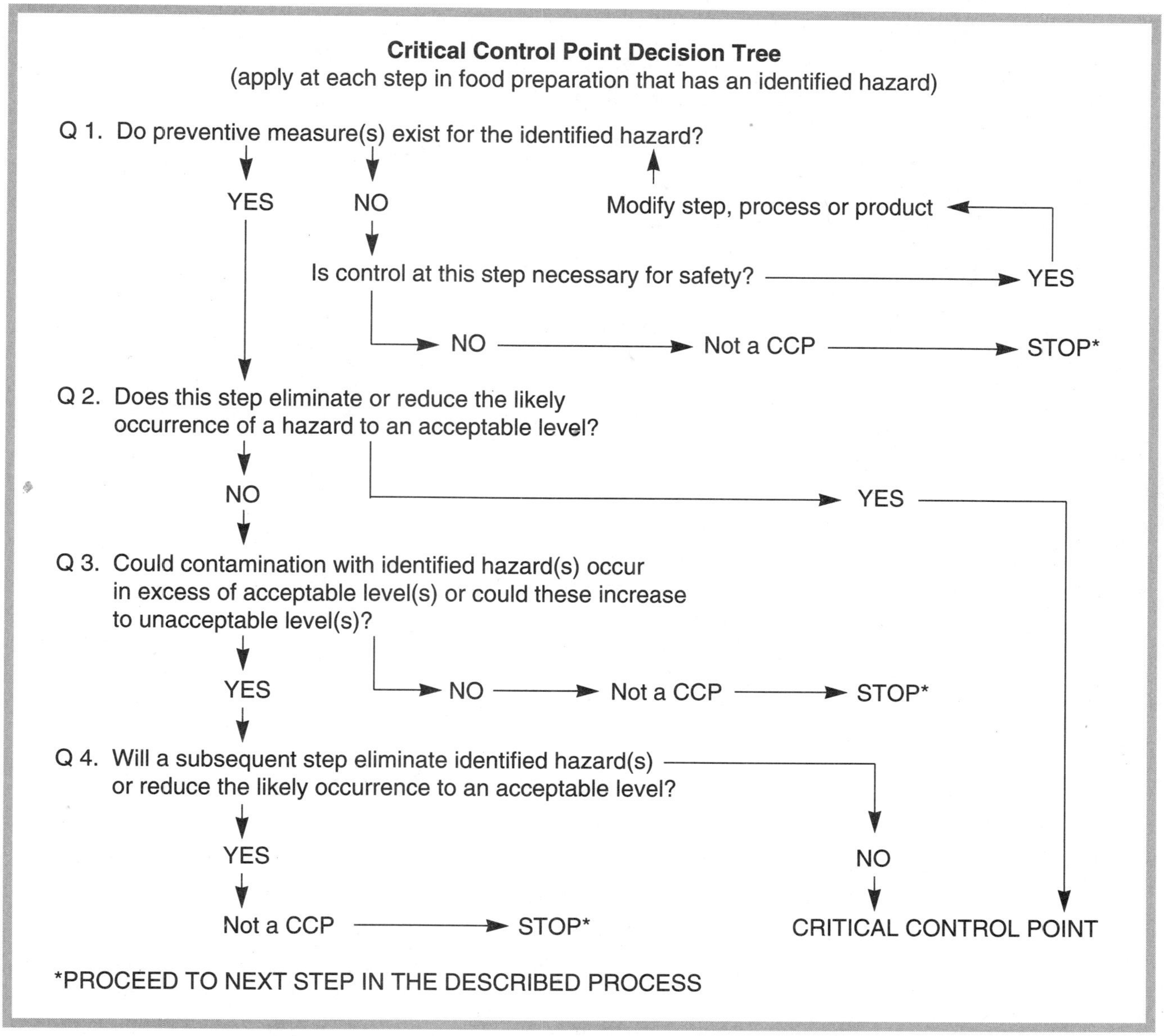

FIGURE 2.13 CRITICAL CONTROL POINT DECISION TREE[1]

recipes. Since standardized recipes dictate the preparation procedures for items to be produced, they affect the quality of food items to be offered by dietary services. The dietary manager must recognize characteristics of high-quality foods and be sure that standardized recipes yield these characteristics.

In addition to developing the "best" recipes, several other procedures are necessary to manage food during its production. For example, pre-production planning is needed to estimate accurately the quantity of food to produce and the number of labor hours required for food production. A wide variety of management practices are necessary to ensure that food products, time, energy, and labor resources are not wasted as the actual food production process evolves.

If you consider the menu to be the "road map" to attaining the goals of the dietary facility, then you can also think of standardized recipes to be the individual "directions" on the road map which help keep the dietary operation on course.

[1]Source: HACCP for Food Service Professionals, Copyright 1996 by Lavella Food Specialists, St. Louis, MO

CCP	Violation	Corrective Action
Receiving	• Product not from approved, inspected source	• Reject order. Do not order from unapproved source
	• Refrigerated (or frozen) product >41°F (or >0°F) at delivery	• Refuse to accept product. Return it.
	• Product packaging not intact or signs of product deterioration	• Refuse to accept product. Return it.
Cold Storage	*Food Temperature:*	
	• 70°F to 120°F more than 2 hours	• Immediately cook food to specified temperature, or discard food.
	• 42°F to 70°F more than 4 hours	• Immediately cook food to specified temperature, or discard food.
Cooking	• Food product below specified final temperature at end of cooking time	• Continue cooking until proper temperature is reached.
Holding/ Handling [*slicing, deboning, mixing, dicing, assembling, serving etc.*]	• Product handled by ill employee	• Discard food.
	• Direct hand contact with ready to eat food	• Discard food
	• Cooked food cross-contaminated with raw food	• Reheat once to 165°F or discard
	• Equipment/utensils contaminated	• Reheat once to 165°F or discard
	• Temperature of cold, ready-to-eat potentially hazardous food:	
	• 42°F–70°F more than 4 hours	• Discard food.
	• above 70°F more than 2 hours	• Discard food
Cooling	*Food Temperature:*	
	• 70°F–139°F more than 2 hours	• Reheat once to 165°F or discard
	• 42°F–70°F more than 4 hours	• Reheat once to 165°F or discard
	• 41°F or less, but cooled too slowly	• Reheat once to 165°F and cool to 41°F within 4 hours, or discard
Reheating	• Food product not at 165°F final temperature	• Continue heating until 165°F is reached
	• Product does not reach 165°F in 2 hours or less	• Discard food
	• Previously held product combined with freshly prepared product	• Reheat once to 165°F or discard

FIGURE 2.14 HACCP CORRECTIVE ACTION TABLE[2]

A standardized recipe is a blueprint for food production, designed and tested so that a consistent product will be produced. Actually, the term *consistent* means almost the same thing as *standard.* If a standardized recipe is used, consistent quality, portion size, and taste will result, and will be appreciated by the client. Standardized recipes will also yield consistent costs and predictable labor hours for food preparation; these are advantages from the perspective of the dietary operation.

[2]Adapted from: Sperber, William H., "The Modern HACCP System," *Food Technology,* June 1991, pp. 116–118.

There are many advantages to using standardized recipes. The consistent quality and costs, which by themselves make use of standardized recipes a "must" for successful dietary services, have already been noted. With standardized recipes will also come predictable ("known") yields. It becomes possible to estimate the number of portions to be prepared. This estimate can be converted into quantities to be produced from a standardized recipe. Without standardized recipes, it is difficult (impossible?) to consistently produce a given volume of food sufficient to serve a specified number of people.

Other advantages to the use of standardized recipes can be cited. For example, less supervision is needed since written procedures for production personnel are readily available. Personnel with fewer or more basic skills can be used. The need for "creative" production staff is lessened, and this can be "translated" into lower labor costs since personnel with less experience can produce the necessary food items.

Standardized recipes also provide useful input to the control system. For example, common menu pricing procedures (in cash cafeteria operations), menu engineering (which relates costs and acceptance to menu planning), pre-cost control and so on all require standardized recipes with associated standardized portion costs.

Dietary managers using standardized recipes become less dependent upon production staff. In the absence of standardized recipes, what happens when a production employee "with the recipes in his or her head" doesn't show up for work? Is someone else available to make the product? Will the product, if made, be acceptable to both the facility and the clients? Marketing concerns are always important.

Standardized recipes provide help in purchasing. If a purchaser knows the number of times an item is to be prepared during the time covered by an order and if he or she knows the quantity of ingredients required by the standardized recipe, it becomes relatively easy to estimate the quantity of food products that must be purchased. (The quantity to be purchased equals the amount needed—from standardized recipe calculations—less the amount of each ingredient on hand.)

Finally, standardized recipes help in evaluation of the dietary operation in at least two ways. First, standardized recipes provide input to the control process, making it possible to evaluate whether economic/financial goals of the facility have been met. Second, food quality requirements are incorporated into standardized recipes. Therefore, the dietary manager and others can evaluate production output to assess whether quality goals are consistently met.

Dietary managers should also be aware of at least two potential disadvantages to the use of standard recipes. First, personnel-related problems may arise. Production staff members who have never used a standardized recipe might allege that they lose the opportunity to be creative. As standardized procedures replace current procedures, some concern about changing the "status quo" may also arise. Participative management approaches that allow input from employees as recipes are standardized can minimize these problems.

A second possible disadvantage in using standardized recipes concerns the amount of time needed to test and implement them. Time will be required to develop the most important production standard control tools (specific procedures are explained below). Since it is not possible to "shut down" the dietary facility until recipes are standardized, the dietary manager may elect to standardize several recipes weekly (or monthly) so that eventually all recipes will be standardized.

Figures 2.15, 2.16, and 2.17 illustrate sample standardized recipe formats. Figure 2.15 shows a recipe which, after standardization, can be used by production staff. In contrast, Figure 2.16 shows a recipe which might be used in an ingredient room operation. Figure 2.17 shows a computerized printout of a standardized recipe with applicable nutrition information. Other recipe formats list diabetic exchanges for each menu item. A supporting nutritional analysis can be developed. (Nutritional analysis information can be developed in-house by the dietary manager or dietitian or can be purchased from external sources. The computer can assist also in gathering

PINEAPPLE UPSIDE-DOWN YAM CAKE					
Yield: 100 servings (2 × 3¾ in.)			Cost per portion ______		
Ingredients	Weights	Measures	For ___ Portions	Cost	Directions
Instant yam flakes* Boiling water	2 lbs.	1qt., 3 cups 2 qt.			1. Add flakes to boiling water. (One quart pineapple juice may be substituted for 1 qt. water.) Let set 5 min. Mix well.
Butter Brown sugar Pineapple slices or crushed pineapple, drained Maraschino cherries (optional)	1 lb. 8 oz. 2 lbs. 6 lbs. 10 oz.	2½ cups 1 qt. 100 slices 1 #10 can 100			2. Melt butter, allowing 6 ounces per pan, in 4 baking pans (12×20×2). 3. Sprinkle brown sugar evenly over butter. Arrange pineapple over brown sugar, and place cherry in center if desired.
CAKE: All-purpose flour Salt Baking soda Cinnamon Nutmeg Oil Sugar Eggs	 3 lbs. 5 oz. 2 oz. 1 lb. 6 oz. 4 lbs. 1 lb. 7 oz.	 3 qts. 3 Tbsp. 2 Tbsp. 2 Tbsp. 2 Tbsp. 3 cups 2½ qts. 13 large			4. Blend flour, salt, baking soda, and spices. 5. Mix oil and sugar. Beat in eggs. 6. Add dry ingredients to oil-sugar-egg mixture. Beat 2 minutes. 7. Pour batter into prepared baking pans over pineapple, allowing about 2¾ qt. batter per pan. 8. Bake at 350° (moderate oven) about 45 minutes or until done.

*Mashed yams may be used in place of flakes and water. Combine 6 lbs. of mashed yams (3 qts.) with 1 cup water.

FIGURE 2.15 SAMPLE QUANTITY RECIPE Used by permission of Joan of Arc Company, Food Service Division, Peoria, Ill.

this data as discussed at the end of this chapter.) An accompanying product flow chart should be developed for each recipe to analyze potential food safety hazards.

DEVELOPING AND EVALUATING STANDARDIZED RECIPES

After the best format for a standardized recipe has been determined, several steps should be used in the actual writing of the recipe:

Step 1: Decide on desirable recipe yield. Typically, standardized recipes for use in quantity operations are based upon 50 portions, 100 portions, or another amount. Some facilities develop a standardized procedure and then illustrate the quantity of ingredients necessary for different yields. For example, a facility may use a ½-cup serving of an entree when served at lunch and a ¾-cup serving when served at dinner (or vice versa). The actual quantity of product needed will then depend upon the meal period for which it is being prepared. Dietary managers recognize this and might show necessary quantities for both yields on the same recipe.

Standardized recipes are usually developed by considering the use of common, modular size pans. For example, a recipe might be sized to yield several 12″ × 20″ × 4″ steam table pans. It is obviously necessary to consider the cooking/baking equipment available as standardized recipes are developed for the facility.

BASIC COFFEE CAKE				
EQUIPMENT:	Mixer bowls, flat paddles Greased counter pans Oven 350°			PORTION SIZE: 0.14 lb. SUGGESTED SERVING UTENSIL: Spatula
NO. PORTIONS		64	384	
PAN SIZE:		12″ × 20″ × 2″	12″ × 20″ × 2″	
NO. PANS		2	12	
INGREDIENTS:		WEIGHTS:		PROCEDURE:
Percent				
27.02	Granulated sugar	2.5 lb.	14.97 lb.	1. Combine in mixer bowl. Cream on #2 speed 10 minutes.
9.19	Shortening	0.85 lb.	5.09 lb.	
8.11	Frozen whole eggs (thawed)	0.75 lb.	4.49 lb.	
33.77	All-purpose flour	3.1 lb.	18.72 lb.	2. Combine dry ingredients in another mixer bowl. Mix on #1 speed for 1 minute.
2.36	Nonfat dry milk	0.22 lb.	1.31 lb.	
1.28	Baking powder	0.12 lb.	0.71 lb.	
0.54	Salt	0.05 lb.	0.30 lb.	
17.73	Water	1.6 lb.	9.83 lb.	3. Add dry ingredients and water alternately to creamed mixture. 4. Mix on #1 speed 3 minutes. Scrape down bowl. 5. Mix on #2 speed 15 seconds. 6. Scale 4.5 lb. batter per pan. Spread batter out evenly. 7. Bake at 350°F. 35–40 minutes.
100%	Handling Loss	3%	3%	8. Cut 4″ × 8″.
TOTAL YIELD	VOL.			
	WT.	9.24 lb.	55.42 lb.	NOTE: May be mixed and panned the day before using. Refrigerate till morning, then bake.
WT. OR AMOUNT PER PAN		4.5 lb.	4.5 lb.	

FIGURE 2.16 STANDARDIZED RECIPE FORM (FOR INGREDIENT ROOM)

Step 2: Decide whether to use weights or measures or both. Accuracy is increased when products are weighed rather than measured. For example, it is common in commercial bakeries to weigh everything, including water.

Step 3: Express all necessary quantities in usable figures. It is always best to avoid fractions. Each measure should be converted into the largest possible unit. For example, you would not indicate that "four cups" of milk are needed; the measurement "one quart" should be used. It is not practical to suggest "¾ of a pound" unless available scales easily express this measure; it is more accurate to specify "12 ounces." As a final example, do production staff understand how to measure "1⅓ tablespoons?" It may be best to specify "1 tablespoon + 1 teaspoon." Dietary managers recognize it is much easier and more accurate for recipe adjustments and extensions to be made in the quiet of the manager's office with a calculator in hand than to trust the arithmetic of busy production staff doing "fast mental calculations."

Step 4: Decide upon the abbreviations to be used and use them consistently. They should be easy to read. Abbreviations such as "T" can be confusing. Does it mean

Recipe: FRENCH TOAST (2 SL)
Serving size: 3.5 ounc

Calories	558.74 Kcal	20.7%
Protein	11.67 gr	20.8%
Fat	13.90 gr	15.4%
Carbohydrate	98.53 gr	26.5%
Calcium	179.71 mg	22.5%
Iron	3.66 mg	36.6%
Sodium	702.11 mg	26.0%
Potassium	257.63 mg	5.6%
Vitamin A	0.00 RE	0.0%
Ascorbic Acid	0.17 mg	0.3%
Folic Acid	47.67 mcg	11.9%
Cholesterol	57.50 mg	19.2%
Nutrient 13	0.00 mg	0.0%
Nutrient 14	0.00 mg	0.0%
Nutrient 15	0.00 mg	0.0%

Do you want a bar chart for this data (1=Yes, 2=No, 99=End)? 1

Recipe Number: 2002 FRENCH TOAST (2 SL) Number of servings: 574

Code No.	Item Name	Quantity Needed
47	MILK NON-FAT DRY	2 Pounds + 2.44 Ounces (weight)
179	WATER,COLD	2 Quarts + 1.74 Pints
96	EGGS FRESH EX LG	14 Pounds + 5.60 Ounces (weight)
68	SPICES NUTMEG	1.952 Ounces (weight)
48	SUGAR,CANE-GRAN DOMINO	5 Pounds + 11.84 Ounces (weight)
174	BK-FS BREAD, WHITE	140 Pounds + 10.08 Ounces (weight)
57	SYRUP PANCAKE MAPLE	8 Gallons + 2.44 Quarts
104	MARGARINE ONE LB SPEC PRNT	14 Pounds + 5.60 Ounces (weight)

DISSOLVE DRY MILK IN WATER
BEAT EGGS, ADD TO MILK
MIX SUGAR AND NUTMEG, ADD TO MIXTURE
DIP BREAD IN MIXTURE
FRY ON 375 F GRILL COVERED WITH MARGARINE
COOK TIL GOLDEN BROWN
SERVE WITH 2 OZ SYRUP

Nutritional Analysis

Name: SAMPLE
Date: 09-14-1984
Prescribed Diet: RDA, Safe & Adequate
Recipe: FRENCH TOAST (2 SL)

Age: 23-50
Weight: 154 pounds
Height: 70 inches
Sex: Male

Activity Level: Light
Lactating: No
Pregnant: No

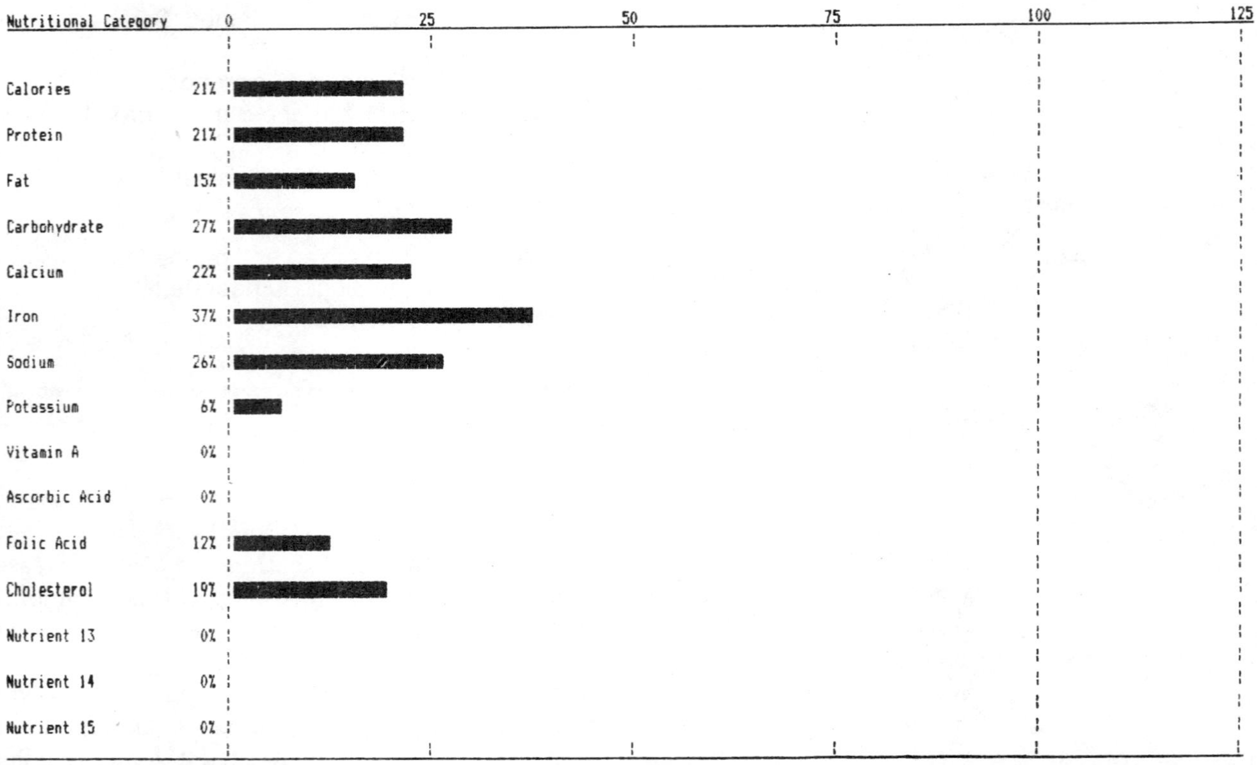

FIGURE 2.17 COMPUTER PRINTOUT OF STANDARD RECIPE
Birchfield Foodsystems, Inc., Annapolis, Md. From their computer assisted precost system.

"tablespoon" or "teaspoon" or another unit? It is better to use the abbreviations or Tbsp. and tsp. to minimize confusion.

Step 5: List ingredients in the order used and with correct terminology. Consider any necessary qualifying statements. For example, what does the following mean:

"One quart whipping cream?" Does it mean "one quart of cream, whipped" or does it mean "one quart of whipped cream"?

Step 6: Give concise directions. Should the product be mixed by hand or by machine? For what length of time? What size and kind of small and large equipment should be used? What is the exact cooking/baking temperature and time? internal temperature?

Step 7: Identify critical control points in the production process, add hazard information to the recipe.

Step 8: Give directions for serving. For example, specify the serving dish to be used, the portion control tool to be used for serving, the number and yield of servings which are expected, and the required garnish and/or sauce.

Frequently, dietary operations utilize a recipe format which allows for pre-costing. Therefore, the per-portion and total ingredient costs of a recipe are also frequently given. Unless a computerized pre-costing system is used, however, recipe costing information quickly becomes outdated.

A coding system is frequently helpful; the busy dietary manager or food production employee can retrieve a recipe more easily when it is coded into, for example, sections (such as entrees or desserts) and number based upon the item being produced.

Generally, standardized recipes for a facility are developed by securing copies of favorite recipes currently used by personnel and other facilities and then modifying them to meet the needs of the specific dietary operation. This approach is much easier than "starting from scratch" and developing recipes in a "test kitchen" approach. When testing a quantity recipe, several steps are important:

1. The recipe should be selected from a reliable source. It should be evaluated as to proportions, methods, yield and costs to ensure that the recipe is practical, suitable, sound and that it will yield the quality of standards desired by the facility;
2. Modifications, if necessary, should be made. Input from dietary production and management staff, administration officials and clients can be helpful at this point;
3. The recipe should first be prepared in a small quantity (perhaps 25 portions) and should then be evaluated. It can then be modified and converted to the desired yield;
4. After testing, the recipe should be converted to the usual yield for the facility.

At this point, it is necessary to check that all "arithmetic" and other procedures are correct. Wise dietary managers realize that it is frequently not possible, for example, to select a recipe for 50 and "multiply it by 10" to yield 500 portions. Adjustments in some ingredients (seasonings, spice, yeast mixtures, etc.) are often necessary.

The "arithmetic" of increasing and decreasing a recipe is not difficult. Figure 2.18 illustrates the basic procedures.

Frequently, the most important step in developing and using a standardized recipe is the actual evaluation of the recipe itself. For all recipes to be tested, a testing committee or panel should be set up. It is important that members of the panel check the following points:

- Is the recipe clear, concise, accurate, and understandable? Is there confusion about the amounts (in weights or measures), the ingredients, methods of instruction, and/or serving directions?

1. Compute adjustment factor.
   a. When reducing, adjustment factor will be les than 1.0.
   b. When increasing, adjustment factor will be more than 1.0.
2. To compute adjustment factor:
   a. Divide new yield by original yield.
   b. Example 1: Recipe yields 100 portions; want yield of 225 portions.

225	÷	100	=	2.25
New Yield		Original Yield		Adjustment Factor

Then use adjustment factor to revise recipe.

Multiply adjustment factor by amount of ingredients in original recipe to determine revised quantity.

Example—Original recipe requires 3 ounces of sugar and adjustment factor is 2.25 (see 2b above).

2.25	×	3 ounces	=	6.75 ounces
Adjustment Factor	×	Original Quantity	=	Quantity for revised recipe

   c. Example 2: Recipe yields 75 portions; want yield of 35 portions; 3 ounces of sugar is required in original recipe.

35	÷	75	=	.47 ounces
New Yield		Original Yield		Adjustment Factor

.47	×	3 ounces	=	1.41 ounces*
Adjustment Factor	×	Original Quantity	=	Quantity for revised recipe

**The dietary manager may consider rounding to 1.50 ounces to ease the measuring task for production personnel.*

3. To change portion sizes:

   Original recipe yields 75 servings of 3/4 cup each; want 125 servings of 1/2 cup each.

   a. 75 × ¾ cup = 56.25 cups (old yield)
   b. 125 × ½ cup = 62.50 cups (new yield)
   c.

62.50	÷	56.25	=	1.11
New Yield		Original Yield		Adjustment Factor

If 3 ounces of sugar were required in the original recipe, the calculation would be:

1.11	×	3 ounces	=	3.3 ounces*
Adjustment Factor	×	Original Quantity	=	Quantity for revised recipe

**This may be changed to Tablespoon/teaspoon measurements if the facility does not have an ingredient scale measuring in 1/3 ounce graduations.*

FIGURE 2.18 PROCEDURES TO INCREASE/DECREASE A RECIPE

- Does the recipe yield a quality product acceptable to the facility?
- Is the menu item nutritious?
- Does the menu item consider and maximize use of time, energy, and the food products themselves?
- Does the recipe help to minimize problems traceable to "human error"?

- Is the recipe suitable for the clients?
- Is equipment (large and small) available to correctly prepare the product?
- Are production staff capable of preparing the menu item within the time frame permitted?
- Is the menu item cost in line with the per-client day or other food cost parameters? If the item is to be sold on the cash cafeteria line, is the per-item cost in line with the proposed selling price?

Figure 2.19 illustrates a format which can be used by individual members of a taste panel to evaluate characteristics of products produced by a standardized recipe.

Date: ______________________ Menu Item: ______________________

Recipe Number: ______________________ Evaluator: ______________________

Instructions: Check (✓) your reaction to each of the following factors used to describe the menu item.

Evaluation Factor	Exceptional	Like Very Much	Acceptable	Like Slightly	Unacceptable

Comments:

FIGURE 2.19 STANDARD RECIPE SCORE CARD

Alternate Method to Developing Standardized Recipes

What do you do when you are aware of the need for and benefits from standardized recipes but already have "recipes" in use which are accepted by production staff? Clearly, the answer to this question is not to discard the recipe and start over. Basic procedures which can be followed include:

- Explain, defend and/or justify the need for standardized recipes. Production staff who have never used standardized recipes will question why "after all this time" changes in recipe formats must be used;
- Closely supervise an experienced production employee as the menu item is prepared. Note the ingredients and quantities which are used, the procedures followed, the type of small and large equipment necessary, etc. Later, organize these into a standardized recipe format;
- Go over the written recipe with the production employee who prepared the item during the closely supervised period. Ask him or her to comment on any inaccuracies;
- Share the tentative recipe with other production employees who might also be called upon to prepare the item. Incorporate any changes which evolve from these meetings;
- Ask an experienced production employee to make the item closely following the standardized recipe which has been "developed." Make any minor changes necessary as a result of this observation period;
- Evaluate the menu item itself to confirm that the recipe yields a product of acceptable quality which meets all other requirements imposed by the facility;
- Duplicate the now-standardized recipe and require its use in the future;
- Supervise production staff on a random but routine basis to confirm that they are consistently adhering to the recipe which has been standardized.

Menus and the Computer

The job of managing has been made easier by the computer by giving management more accurate and more reliable information in a shorter time. This permits better decision making and faster action in response to changing conditions or unexpected developments. The end result of the computer revolution has been better planning, improved organizational control and more up-to-date and complete information for management.

While major computer application came slowly at first to foodservice operations, today it is extended throughout the industry. The key has been the development of integrated systems, with both service and management applications, designed to minimize data handling and streamline data throughput. Software options involving menu planning and beyond include server-cashier and outlet accountability, revenue analysis, sales reporting, prechecking, check tracking, menu-mix analysis, recipe explosion (a recipe can be exploded or increased from 25 to 100, 150, 250 or 1,000 just by giving the computer the right instructions), inventory control, and time and attendance recording.

Office applications can include general-ledger accounting (payables and receivables), cash management, sales and revenue analyses, fixed-asset accounting, inventory control, payroll, budgeting, and financial reporting. Point-of-sales terminals, replacing the old cash registers, can keep track of inventory, sales per hour and per store, menu item sales, and time period. Sales by table are tracked by these POS systems today.

Common computers tasks are discussed here, yet the revolution continues at such a rapid pace that you need to stay abreast of current literature, the press, and information provided by trade associations to fully understand the impact computers are making in the industry today. In other words, software programs available for foodservice operations number in the dozens, and it takes some research to find a system having the right capabilities (too many can be as aggravating as too few) that is cost-effective for any particular operation.

Ingredient Filing

An ingredient file consists of all ingredients listed for recipes. Ingredients are identified in the computer either by their code numbers or their code names. The ingredient code number should be either the same as that used in purchasing or closely related to it.

Changes in recipe or ingredient costs must be input as they occur so that the recipes can be updated and so that the information compiled by the computer reflects what is actually the case. Often a change in the purchase price of one ingredient automatically changes prices in other files. Recipes specify the condition (sifted, beaten, blanched, melted, diced, or strained) in which an ingredient is to be added to others during the preparation of the item, and computers are able to process this information successfully in the cost calculations, thus increasing accuracy of costing.

Recipe Filing

Many menu items in the menu file require special preparation before service, and so must be backed up by one or more recipes. The recipes listed in this manner are kept on what is called a recipe file. An item called Baked Cod Mornay may have two recipes: one for baking the cod in a mornay sauce, and one for making the mornay sauce. Thus, the mornay sauce in the recipe actually becomes an ingredient in the baked cod recipe. These other recipes for sauces and other items supporting the main recipe are sometimes called subrecipes.

As previously discussed, recipes should be standardized to give a known quantity and a known quality at a known cost. Recipes should specify the code number or code name, the total amount of food produced, the number of portions, the portion size, the ingredients, the amount of each ingredient used, and the method of handling ingredients to produce the recipe. Cooking times, cooking temperatures, panning instructions, and other relevant information should also be given. Variations and substitutions can be listed at the bottom of the recipe. Total cost of the recipe and cost per portion are usually listed, and sometimes menu selling price, too. In some cases it may be desirable to identify other items served with the item produced by that recipe, or to include plating or serving instructions along with nutritional information. A picture of how the item should appear is sometimes added (now that computers possess the necessary graphic capabilities).

Menu Planning*

Early use of the computer in foodservice operations came in the areas of payroll, inventory, accounting, and point-of-sales transactions as they were applied from other industries. Computer planning of menus first came in the 1950s and 1960s, with the goal being the production of menus planned to meet nutritional standards within certain cost constraints. These applications were largely for health-related foodservices.

Today, menu-planning programs are used to produce menus that meet specific patron and operational needs within certain cost limitations. Menu programming can include instructions to avoid too much repetition of ingredients or flavors, such as having tomatoes appear a limited number of times in dishes on the menu.

Different forms of preparation can also be specified to ensure that different cooking methods are found in the new items offered, such as a braised meat item, a roast, a broiled meat, and/or a deep-fried meat item. The computer may also be

---

*Adapted from Knight, John B. and Lendal H. Kotschevar, QUANTITY FOOD PRODUCTION, PLANNING AND MANAGEMENT, Van Nostrand Reinhold, 1989, pp. 9–11.

programmed to present a balance in meat, fish, and poultry offerings. If a retirement home wants chicken to appear on the menu for every Sunday dinner, the computer can be instructed to make this happen. Nutritional values for meals can be easily calculated so that management can monitor them to ensure that the proper nutrients are being served.

Constraints or needs can be input to the computer and it will comply with them in generating its menus. Quite flexible programs are possible; often management can override the computer by adding, deleting, or otherwise changing what it does. The list of menu items entered into the computer to use in menu planning is called the menu file.

Computer Forecasting

To obtain an estimate of costs and/or profitability of a specific menu mix (group of menu items), management must develop a projection of the number of menu items that will be sold. This projection is called a forecast.

Forecasting is made so much easier with a computer. Historical data is considered. A popularity index can be kept to record how many portions were sold each time the item appeared on the menu. Another technique is to evaluate the other items competing against a particular menu item and estimate how much they add or detract from its sales.

The effect of weather, conventions in town, athletic contests in the community, and other independent factors may all be input to ensure proper forecasting. Once the forecast is generated, the computer is able to continue its projections regarding costs, profits, and other financial data. The computer is able to read the menu item, select its proper recipes, calculate from the recipes the costs of ingredients and the portion food costs and multiply the latter costs by the number of portions given in the sales forecast, to establish a projected material cost for the menu item. Repeating this process for each item on the menu yields a total food cost figure for the period covered in the projection.

If a selling price for each menu item is input into the computer, the forecast number of sales times the selling price gives the expected income from the item. Again, when this is done for all menu items, the sum of the income figures will equal the total sales. These computations enable management to estimate how well the menu is going to do. If other cost projections are programmed, the computer can generate a net profit estimate and make other projections of great help to management.

Menu Analysis

The computer is useful in performing various menu analyses of special benefit to management for decision making and planning. Many of these have been previously introduced but include calculating quantities to purchase, totaling inventory, keeping track of inventory issues and direct use, setting up receiving reports, maintaining payroll, and making many POS calculations.

Menus can be analyzed in various ways, ranging from highly qualitative methods to complex mathematical ones. Subjective menu evaluation, menu counts (popularity indexes), menu scoring, menu factor analysis, matrix analysis, goal analysis, and break-even analysis are just a few approaches. A detailed discussion of menu analysis is beyond the scope of this text but, as mentioned earlier, the rapid advancement of the computer as a management tool within foodservice operations should encourage you to research the software available today to analyze your menu successfully.

Nutrient Analysis

Nutrient analysis is of great importance to healthcare facilities, school foodservices, and other institutional operations. Analysis by computer is more efficient than ever, yet outside services providing analysis are forever being offered by consulting firms. The key for the dietary professional is to work with someone who is accurate and reliable. As the population ages, and diets become more important, clients seeking and needing appropriate nutrient information will increase due to a need to know the nutritional content of each food. Younger, healthier individuals also seek such information to know what they are eating and to maintain their health through proper diet. Being aware of the fat content or amount of sodium in a food can help in menu planning or dining out. There are six major nutrients for review, including carbohydrates, proteins, fats, vitamins, minerals, and water or fluids. Nutrient analysis must be given careful consideration by all dietary professionals.

SUMMARY

Many institutional facilities use the cycle menu to best utilize the limited resources of time, money, staff, space, and equipment. It changes every day over a specified time period; after this, the daily menus repeat in the same order.

There are many factors to consider when writing a menu, including:

1. color
2. flavor
3. texture
4. form and shape
5. temperature
6. consistency
7. method of preparation
8. cost
9. arrangement of food on the plate
10. garnishes

Different menu types offer variety and serve a different need. While a la carte menus have separately priced menu items, table d'hote menus are just the opposite, offering a complete meal at a fixed price. The du jour menu is the menu of the day, and a limited menu offers no more than six to twelve main items. The planning of a menu is a complex activity involving diverse issues important to the dietary manager.

The Hazard Analysis and Critical Control Point (HACCP) principles provide a greater assurance for the safety of meat and poultry products. There are seven principles set up by the National Advisory Committee on Microbiological Criteria for Foods (NACMCF):

1. Conduct hazard analysis and risk assessment;
2. Determine CCPs;
3. Establish specifications for each CCP;
4. Monitor each CCP;
5. Establish corrective action to be taken if a deviation occurs at a CCP;
6. Establish a recordkeeping system;
7. Establish verification procedures.

The 'Risk Assessment' process has been expanded to the following six characteristics:

A. Food intended for consumption by at-risk population;
B. Product contains sensitive ingredient;
C. No process step to eliminate hazard;
D. Recontamination potential before packaging;
E. Potential for product abuse;
F. No terminal heat process.

HACCP system ensures a greater measure of food safety than finished-product testing. Critical control points (CCPs) are identified and then established at any place along the food flow where something could go wrong that could result in food poisoning or illness.

Standardized recipes ensure consistent quality, portion size, and taste as well as yielding consistent costs and predictable labor hours for food preparation. The advantages of using them include predictable yields, consistent quality and costs, less supervision needed, and help in purchasing. The dietary manager can evaluate production output to assess whether quality goals are consistently met. The disadvantages include the fact that personnel-related problems may arise because there is less opportunity for creativity and the fact that the amount of time needed to test and implement standardized recipes is greater.

Several steps should be used in writing standardized recipes, including:

1. Use common, modular size pans;
2. Decide to use weights, measures or both;
3. Express quantities in usable figures;
4. Decide upon abbreviations to be used;
5. Use correct terminology;
6. Give concise directions;
7. Give directions for serving;
8. Test the recipe.

The most important step in developing and using a standardized recipe is the actual evaluation of the recipe.

The job of managing has been made easier by the computer, by giving management more accurate and more reliable information in a shorter time. Ingredient filing by the computer ensures proper recipe costing as prices fluctuate. Recipe standardization is simplified with computers to give a known quantity and a known quality at a known cost. Menu-planning computer programs are used to produce menus that meet specific patron and operational needs within certain cost limitations. Computer forecasting allows management to obtain an estimate of costs and/or profitability of a specific menu mix. This is accomplished as management develops a projection of the number of menu items that will be sold. The computer greatly assists in making this projection. Finally, computers can be used to analyze menus in various ways, ranging from highly qualitative methods to complex mathematical ones. The rapid advancement of the computer as a management tool within foodservice operations should encourage you to research the software available today to analyze your menu successfully, including its nutritive value.

KEY TERMS

- Cycle menu
- A la carte menu
- Table d'hôte menu
- Du jour menu
- Limited menu
- HACCP (Hazard Analysis and Critical Control Point)
- HACCP principles
- Quality characteristics of food
- Standardized recipes
- Ingredient file
- Recipe file
- Menu file
- Forecast

QUESTIONS/PROBLEMS/CASES

1. There are many factors to consider when writing a menu. Taking these factors into consideration, create a sample menu.

2. What are the advantages and disadvantages of using standardized recipes?

3. Compute the following adjustment factors in order to increase/decrease a recipe:
   a. Recipe yields 120 portions; 180 portions are needed.
   b. Original recipe yields 95 portions; 50 portions are required.
      5 ounces of vinegar is required for the original recipe; compute for the new.
   c. Recipe yields 100 4 oz. portions; 150 6 oz. portions are needed.

4. In determining CCPs, what procedures could be specified control points to prevent product contamination from the processing environment?

5. What should a recipe specify once it is standardized?

6. To obtain an estimate of costs and/or profitability of a specific menu mix (group of menu items), management must develop a projection of the number of menu items that will be sold. This projection is called what, and how does the computer assist in doing it?

7. Describe why it is necessary to use HACCP flowcharting.

8. Complete the following HACCP worksheet for the given baked custard recipe and develop an expanded HACCP flow chart from the worksheet.

BAKED CUSTARD

Yield: 50 custards *Portion:* 4 oz
Oven: 325°F *Bake:* 40-45 minutes

Ingredient	Amount	Procedure
Eggs Sugar, granulated Salt Milk, cold Vanilla	20 (2 lb 3 oz) 1 lb 4 oz 1/2 tsp 1 qt 2 Tbsp	Beat eggs slightly, using wire whip attachment. Add sugar, salt, cold milk, and vanilla. Mix on low speed only until blended
Milk	1 gal	Scald milk by bringing to point just below boiling. Add to egg mixture and blend.
Nutmeg	2 tsp	Pour mixture into custard cups that have been arranged in baking pans. Sprinkle nutmeg over tops. Pour hot water around cups. Bake at 325°F for 40-45 minutes or until a knife inserted in custard comes out clean.

Hazard Analysis Critical Control Point Worksheet

Date: mo. ___ day ___ yr. ___ TIME: Start ___ : ___ A.M./P.M. End ___ : ___ A.M./P.M.

Product ______________________________

Ingredients ______________________________

____

Sources ______________________________

____

TIME	TEMP.	PROCEDURE/OBSERVATION	COMMENT/INTERPRETATION

TIME/TEMPERATURE (°F) CHART

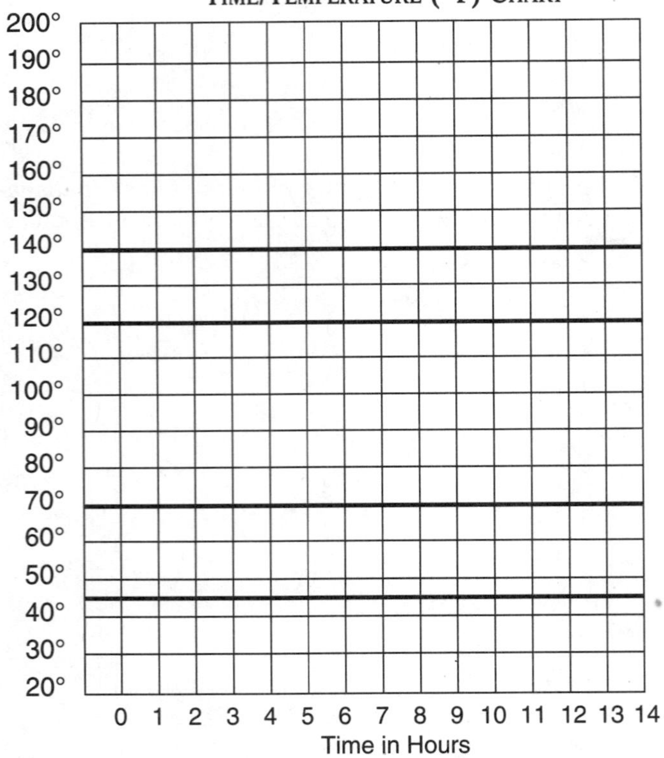

PRODUCT FLOW CHART

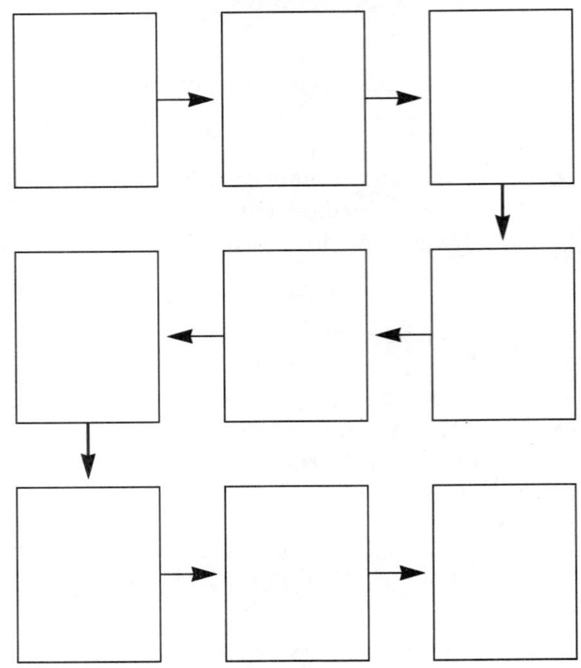

Name of Inspector/Manager ______________________________

9. What needs to be considered when planning an appetizing menu for a summer picnic?

10. Which six groups of nutrients can be analyzed using a nutrient analysis program?

11. What is the easiest way to get a nutrient analysis done?

12. How can a computer be helpful in foodservice?

3

SANITATION AND SAFETY

CHAPTER OUTLINE

- Sanitation
  - Microorganisms and Their Classifications
  - Food-borne Illnesses
  - Prevention of Food-borne Illnesses
  - Personal Cleanliness and Sanitation
  - Guidelines for Safe Food-Handling and Holding
  - Hazard Analysis and Critical Control Point (HACCP)
- Safety
  - Safety Management in Work Areas
  - Causes and Prevention of Foodservice Accidents
  - Safety Inspection Programs
  - Accident Investigation Programs
  - OSHA and Safety Programs
  - Fire Safety and Related Training
  - Hazard Communication Standard (HazComm)

SANITATION

A primary goal of any dietary service is to provide nutritious and safe food. The dietary manager has a very active role in seeing that all food served is clean and wholesome. Food must be purchased, received, stored, distributed, produced, and served with a high-priority concern about sanitation and food safety. Irreparable harm can come to the client—and to the reputation of the dietary department and the facility itself—if basic sanitation practices are not incorporated into the way products are handled and the ongoing supervisory practices of the dietary manager and staff.

There are two basic causes of unsafe food. The first, chemicals, comes from poisons used for cleaning, and from other compounds, pesticides, and residues which get on or into food. The dietary manager can minimize these problems by buying food from reputable suppliers, being sure that employees use care as they work with food, and washing all fruits and vegetables before using. Safe storage practices that keep all chemicals away from food products are of utmost importance.

Microorganisms and Their Classifications

The dietary manager must also have some background information about microorganisms (germs) and other small living things, which are the second and more common source of unsafe food. They are all around and are too small to be seen without a microscope. Some are beneficial to humans; others are not, and may cause illness if they are consumed in food or by other means. In many ways, microorganisms are just like people: They can grow, reproduce, and be healthy if they have the right food and right environment—or unhealthy if they have access to the wrong food and environment. Also like people, they give off waste products, react to temperature and chemicals, live together in groups, and eventually die.

Unfortunately, microorganisms like many of the same types of food that humans do. Products of animal origin, and those containing food products of animal origin, are potentially the most hazardous. These include protein-rich products such as meat, fish, poultry, eggs, and milk. Creamed foods containing milk and eggs, non-acid foods, and products made from combinations of the above foods are the most susceptible.

Microorganisms need moisture to grow and multiply. Two food-preservation methods—drying and freezing—actually stop their growth by denying them access to the moisture they need. However, freezing and drying do not kill most microorganisms; these preservation methods only stop them from growing until they gain access to moisture—which occurs as ice changes to water, when frozen foods thaw, and when moisture is added to dry foods.

Bacteria, one type of microorganism, is about 1/25,000 inch in diameter and has optimal temperature, food acidity, and oxygen requirements. Many bacteria grow best at about body temperature (95°F). They will grow most rapidly if they are in foods held at this temperature. Many bacteria also like foods which do not contain large amounts of acids (unfortunately, animal-origin foods are in the "neutral" acid range). One bacteria, *E. coli* 0157:H7, has been identified to cause illness in thousands, resulting in death on occasion in extreme cases. This bacteria has recently been associated with eating uncooked contaminated ground beef. Person-to-person contact in families and child care centers is also an important mode of transmission Infection can also occur after drinking raw milk. *E.coli* infection can be prevented by thoroughly cooking ground beef, avoiding unpasteurized milk, and washing hands carefully with hot soapy water.

Another recently identified bacteria, Campylobacteria, is commonly found in the intestinal tracts of animals; it is passed through feces through the environment and found in untreated water. Campylobacter jejuni, the strain associated with most reported human infections, may be present in the body without causing illness. Figure 3.1 identifies the sources, symptoms, and control measures for a number of important bacteria.

Some bacteria need oxygen (aerobic) to grow and to live; others (anaerobic) do not. Many of the basic rules of sanitation can be summarized by adhering to one basic principle: keep potentially hazardous foods (those of animal origin and those containing large amounts of products of animal origin) out of the danger zone—40°F to 140°F. If this basic rule is incorporated into the handling of food products, many potentials for food-borne illness will be reduced or eliminated. Although the danger zone is often set at 40°F, the FDA Food Code sets the temperature at 41°F. The best resource for the foodservice manager is to check with local sanitation department to see which temperature they use.

Viruses, the tiniest known living organism, are usually transferred through food or water. Hepatitis, polio, and ornithosis are three virus-caused illnesses, the latter coming from microorganisms carried by birds. For this reason it is very important that birds and other animals are kept out of foodservices. A more recent virus to be identified is the Norwalk Virus, caused by poor personal hygiene and found in the feces of infected persons. Humans are the only known reservoir of the virus. This illness is caused by a viral agent named for the city in Ohio where it was first implicated. Because Norwalk is a virus, it does not reproduce in food but

Campylobacter jejuni

Overview	Sources	Symptoms/Complications	Control Measures
Campylobacter jejuni, though less well known than some other forms of food-borne illness, has recently been recognized as one of the leading causes of diarrhea in the United States. In fact, in most areas of the U.S., cases of food-borne illness caused by *Campylobacter jejuni* equal or exceed those due to *Salmonella* and *Shigella* combined. The illness caused by *Campylobacter jejuni* is called campylobacteriosis.	Poultry, shellfish, livestock and even pets carry the *Campylobacter jejuni* organism. Cases of campylobacteriosis have been attributed to undercooked poultry and meats, raw (unpasteurized) milk and untreated water.	Symptoms of campylobacteriosis include muscle pain, headache, and fever followed by diarrhea, abdominal pain, and nausea that begin one to ten days (usually between two and five days) following ingestion. Convulsions my occur in some young children in association with high fever. The illness most closely mimics that caused by *Shigella* or *Salmonella.*	Wash hands and/or utensils that have come into contact with raw meats in hot, soapy water prior to contact with cooked foods. Cook ground meats (beef, pork, veal, lamb) to a uniform internal temperature of at least 160°F, ground poultry to 165°F, non-ground meat cuts such as roasts (beef, veal, lamb) to an internal temperature of at least 145°F, non-ground pork to 160°F and poultry to 170°F. Once cooked, keep hot foods at or above 140°F. Cold foods should be kept at or below 40°F. Reheat leftovers to 165°F or until steaming hot. Individuals with compromised immune systems should consult a physician regarding special food and food safety recommendations. Never drink unpasteurized milk or other dairy products or untreated water, and never eat raw or undercooked foods of animal origin. Carefully follow "keep refrigerated," "sell by," and "use by" dates. Dogs and other pets should not be allowed in restaurants or other food preparation environments. Always wash hands in hot, soapy water after going to the bathroom and before preparing or eating food.

Figure 3.1 Overview of Specific Bacteria ***Source:*** U.S.D.A.

Clostridium perfringens			
Overview	**Sources**	**Symptoms/Complications**	**Control Measures**
Clostridium perfringens bacteria are everywhere around us—in the intestines of humans and animals, in soil, dust, insects, and sewage. These bacteria are anaerobic—they only grow where there is little or no oxygen. Once ingested, if growth conditions are appropriate, the organism produces a chemical toxin in the gastrointestinal tract, which causes the illness. The illness caused by this type of bacteria is called *Clostridium perfringens* enteritis.	Sometimes referred to as the "cafeteria germ," *Clostridium perfringens* outbreaks frequently occur when large quantities of food are served at room temperature or from a steam table. Foods not cooled properly after serving also contribute to outbreaks of *Clostridium perfringens* enteritis. Meat, poultry, cooked dried beans ("refried" beans), and gravies are the most common carriers of *Clostridium perfringens*. The organism lives in soil, so contamination from unwashed vegetables also is possible.	Symptoms are usually relatively mild and include diarrhea and gas pains which begin between six and twenty-four hours after ingestion and last approximately twenty-four hours. The illness is most serious for the elderly.	When serving foods buffet-style at home, keep hot foods hot (at or above 140°F) and cold foods cold (at or below 40°F). Large leftover portions of cooked foods such as roasts, turkey, stuffing, soups, stews, and casseroles should be divided up for storage (use shallow pans; food should be no more than two inches deep) and cooling in the refrigerator. Leftovers should be heated to at least 165°F (or until steaming hot) before serving. Individuals with compromised immune systems should consult a physician regarding special food and food safety recommendations. Also, be sure to wash away all soil from vegetables, using clean, drinkable water. Carefully follow "keep refrigerated," "sell by," and "use by" dates. Be sure to wash all food preparation utensils and surfaces with hot, soapy water after each use. Always wash hands with hot, soapy water after going to the bathroom and before preparing or eating food.

Figure 3.1 Overview of Specific Bacteria *Continued*

E. coli/E. coli 0157:H7

Overview

Escherichia coli or *E. coli* are a group of bacteria normally found in the intestines of warm-blooded animals including some food animals and humans, and in water contaminated by animal or human feces. When they cause illness due to contaminated food or water, *E. coli* are normally associated with intestinal complaints or diarrhea.

E. coli 0157:H7 is a virulent strain of *E. coli,* a pathogen that can cause serious and potentially fatal diseases. There are currently several rapid methods being used to screen for *E. coli* 0157:H7 in foods. The problem in screening for this and other food-borne pathogens is not a lack of technology; it's problems in sampling. A test to determine whether contamination has occurred may be negative on one surface of a food and positive on another. The industry is currently researching better sampling methods.

Sources

Like other strains of *E. coli, E. coli* 0157:H7 can be transmitted through inadvertent contact with fecal matter during processing of animal foods or because of improper food handling. Improper handling may include contamination by infected food handlers who have not effectively washed their hands before touching the food or utensils that come into contact with the food. *E. coli* 0157:H7 has been identified in ground beef products, unpasteurized milk, and plant foods. Plant foods can become contaminated from fertilization with raw manure, irrigation with contaminated water, or contamination by human contact. Some outbreaks have been attributed to contaminated municipal and recreational water. Person-to-person transmission can occur as well.

Symptoms/Complications

General symptoms of *E. coli* 0157:H7 include severe abdominal cramps and watery diarrhea. *E. coli* 0157:H7 has some potentially serious complications. Hemorrhagic colitis can occur in persons infected with *E. coli* 0157:H7, producing symptoms that include severe abdominal cramps, bloody diarrhea, vomiting, and nausea. In rare cases, symptoms may include a low-grade fever. Symptoms of illness caused by *E. coli* 0157:H7 generally begin three to nine days following infection and may last two to nine days, though complications will prolong illness. A possible complication of hemorrhagic colitis is hemolytic uremic syndrome (HUS), characterized by severe anemia and renal (kidney) failure. HUS develops in approximately 2 to 7 percent of the cases where *E. coli* 0157:H7 is confirmed. HUS is a leading cause of acute kidney failure in children and also poses serious kidney risk for the elderly. Adults may develop HUS or thrombocytopenic purpura (TTP), an illness similar to HUS but with involvement of the central nervous system, which can include strokes and seizures.

Control Measures

While *E. coli* 0157:H7 is a contaminant capable of causing severe disease, it can be effectively controlled by thorough cooking. Cook ground meats (beef, pork, veal, lamb) to a uniform internal temperature of at least 160°F, ground poultry to 165°F, non-ground meat cuts such as roasts (beef, veal, lamb) to an internal temperature of at least 145°F, non-ground pork to 160°F, and poultry to 170°F. Reheat foods to 165°F or until steaming hot. Keep hot foods at or above 140°F and cold foods at or below 40°F. Individuals with compromised immune systems should consult a physician regarding special food and food safety recommendations. It's also important to avoid unprocessed fruit and vegetable juices, and unpasteurized milk and milk products. Wash fruits and vegetables thoroughly, using only clean, drinkable water. Carefully follow "keep refrigerated," "sell by," and "use by" dates. Always wash hands thoroughly with hot, soapy water after going to the bathroom and before preparing or eating food.

Figure 3.1 Overview of Specific Bacteria *Continued*

Listeria monocytogenes

Overview	Sources	Symptoms/Complications	Control Measures
Listeria monocytogenes are food-borne bacteria that enter the intestines of warm-blooded animals including some food animals, and humans, following the ingestion of contaminated food. Once the bacteria are in the body, they begin to multiply, eventually producing numbers sufficient to cause illness. The illness caused by *Listeria monocytogenes* is called listeriosis.	*Listeria monocytogenes* bacteria are commonly found in the intestines of humans and animals, in milk, soil, leafy vegetables, and food-processing environments. The bacteria have been isolated in a variety of foods including raw and cooked poultry, meat, seafood, salads, and sandwiches. Frequent food carriers include unpasteurized dairy products (especially soft cheeses), meat patés, and processed meats. These bacteria can grow slowly at refrigerated temperatures.	Symptoms of listeriosis vary in adults and newborns. In adults, symptoms include the sudden onset of fever, chills, headache, backache, and occasional abdominal pain and diarrhea. Newborns can contract listeriosis from an infected mother during birth. Newborn symptoms include respiratory distress, refusal to drink, and vomiting. Though listeriosis is rare, it's also potentially fatal, because it is capable of producing complications including septicemia (blood poisoning), meningitis, and meningo-encephalitis, which affects tissues around the brain or spine. Listeriosis can also cause spontaneous abortions and stillbirths. Symptoms may begin from one day to several weeks following infection.	Because *Listeria monocytogenes* appear to be a common environmental contaminant, the critical issues are controlling their growth and preventing their survival. Avoid unpasteurized milk and dairy products. Cook ground meats (beef, pork, veal, lamb) to a uniform internal temperature of at least 160°F, ground poultry to 165°F, non-ground meat cuts such as roasts (beef, veal, lamb) to an internal temperature of at least 145°F, non-ground pork to 160°F, and poultry to 170°F. Once cooked, keep hot foods at or above 140°F. Cold foods should be kept at or below 40°F. Individuals concerned about compromised immune systems should consult their physician regarding special food and food safety recommendations. Wash produce thoroughly before preparing, using only clean, drinkable water. Wash all surfaces and utensils that come into contact with raw and cooked foods with hot, soapy water. Since *Listeria monocytogenes* grow at refrigerator temperatures, carefully follow "keep refrigerated," "sell by," and "use by" dates on processed foods. Thoroughly reheat leftovers or ready-to-eat foods such as hot dogs to 165°F or until steaming hot. Always wash hands thoroughly with hot, soapy water after going to the bathroom and before preparing or eating food.

Figure 3.1 Overview of Specific Bacteria *Continued*

Salmonella			
Overview	**Sources**	**Symptoms/Complications**	**Control Measures**
Salmonella bacteria, the most commonly reported cause of food-borne illness, cycle continuously through the environment via the intestinal tracts of animals and humans.	*Salmonella* bacteria are most commonly found in raw or undercooked foods such as poultry, eggs, unpasteurized milk, or other dairy products and meats. As with many other agents of food-borne illness, *Salmonella* also can be present in foods because of cross-contamination. Cross-contamination occurs when a raw (contaminated) food touches a cooked food or surface used to prepare or serve cooked foods. For example, cross-contamination could occur if serving tongs are used to put raw foods on a barbecue grill and are again used to remove foods when finished cooking, without washing between uses. Fruits, vegetables, yeast, and chocolate have also been implicated in *Salmonella* outbreaks.	Salmonellosis, the food-borne illness caused by *Salmonella* bacteria, has symptoms including headache, abdominal pain, diarrhea, fever, and nausea, which generally begin eight to forty-eight hours after eating contaminated food. The symptoms can last anywhere from one to eight days. However, not all infected individuals develop illness. It can be particularly difficult for the average person to determine if he or she has salmonellosis, because the abdominal stress which results is not often associated with food-borne illness. Though abdominal stress in general is likely to be caused by food-borne illness, consumers do not typically make the connection between the symptoms and food.	Thaw susceptible foods such as poultry and meat in the refrigerator or microwave oven and cook immediately after thawing. Avoid cross-contamination of raw and cooked foods and the utensils and surfaces which have contact with foods. Never consume unpasteurized, raw, or undercooked foods of animal origin. Cook ground meats (beef, pork, veal, lamb) to a uniform internal temperature of at least 160°F, ground poultry to 165°F, non-ground meat cuts such as roasts (beef, veal, lamb) to an internal temperature of at least 145°F, non-ground pork to 160°F, and poultry to 170°F. Once cooked, keep hot foods at or above 140°F. Cold foods should be kept at or below 40°F. Reheat leftovers to 165°F or until steaming hot. Individuals with compromised immune systems should consult a physician regarding special food and food safety recommendations. Eggs should be purchased from refrigerated cases, kept in the refrigerator until used, and cooked thoroughly. Carefully follow "keep refrigerated," "sell by," and "use by" dates. Always wash hands in hot, soapy water after going to the bathroom and before preparing or eating food.

Figure 3.1 Overview of Specific Bacteria *Continued*

SHIGELLA			
OVERVIEW	SOURCES	SYMPTOMS/COMPLICATIONS	CONTROL MEASURES
Shigella bacteria are generally found where unsanitary conditions prevail, and can be transmitted through improper food handling. Though the seriousness of shigellosis, the illness caused by *Shigella* bacteria, depends on the strain of the bacterium, the infectious dose is typically very low.	*Shigella* bacteria are carried in the fecal matter of infected humans. No animal reservoir is known. The principal source of this pathogen is contamination of food by a *Shigella*-infected food handler. Because *Shigella* bacteria are effectively eliminated by cooking, the primary food carriers are cold salads (e.g., tuna, chicken, potato) which contain ingredients contaminated by the food handler. Foods of plant origin fertilized with raw manure, irrigated with contaminated water, or contaminated by humans also may carry the bacteria.	Shigellosis can be characterized by a range of symptoms including severe diarrhea (sometimes bloody), nausea, headaches, chills, and dehydration. Some infected individuals may have no symptoms, yet are carriers of bacteria. Symptoms typically begin one to seven days after ingestion of contaminated food. Infections are most common in children ages one to four.	Because outbreaks of illness caused by *Shigella* bacteria have been linked to poor hygiene of food handlers, good hygiene and sanitary food preparation are imperative in the prevention of shigellosis. Care-givers of children in diapers must wash hands with hot, soapy water after every diaper check and change, and teach children to wash hands after going to the bathroom. Carefully follow "keep refrigerated," "sell by," and "use by" dates. Cook ground meats (beef, pork, veal, lamb) to a uniform internal temperature of at least 160°F, ground poultry to 165°F, non-ground meat cuts such as roasts (beef, veal, lamb) to an internal temperature of at least 145°F, non-ground pork to 160°F, and poultry to 170°F. Once cooked, keep hot foods at or above 140°F. Cold foods should be kept at or below 40°F. Reheat leftovers to 165°F or until steaming hot. Individuals with compromised immune systems should consult a physician regarding special food and food safety recommendations. Always wash hands in hot, soapy water after going to the bathroom and before preparing or eating food.

FIGURE 3.1 OVERVIEW OF SPECIFIC BACTERIA *Continued*

Yersinia enterocolitica			
Overview	**Sources**	**Symptoms/Complications**	**Control Measures**
Yersinia enterocolitica are bacteria which are occasionally associated with intestinal disorders. Yersiniosis, the disease caused by *Yersinia enterocolitica,* is not a commonly reported food-borne disease. It has been associated with septicemia, reactive arthritis, tender skin nodules, and other illnesses which occur outside the intestines.	*Yersinia enterocolitica* bacteria are found in the fecal matter of livestock, domesticated, and wild animals. Consequently, *Yersinia enterocolitica* can be found in meats, poultry, unpasteurized milk, dairy products, seafood from sewage-contaminated water, and produce fertilized with raw manure. Foods also can be contaminated by food handlers who have not effectively washed their hands before handling food, or utensils used to prepare food. *Yersinia enterocolitica* bacteria can grow slowly at refrigerated temperatures.	Symptoms of yersiniosis include abdominal pain sometimes mimicking appendicitis, fever, diarrhea and/or bloody diarrhea, and sometimes vomiting. Symptoms typically occur within one to seven days after ingestion and often last for more than a week. Young children are at greatest risk of becoming ill from yersiniosis. Though complications from yersiniosis are rare, the elderly and those with compromised immune systems who have yersiniosis may be at risk of reactive arthritic or anemic conditions, heart problems, and, in rare cases, meningitis.	One of the most important measures for the prevention of yersiniosis is thorough cooking and heating. Cook ground meats (beef, pork, veal, lamb) to a uniform internal temperature of at least 160°F, ground poultry to 165°F, non-ground meat cuts such as roasts (beef, veal, lamb) to an internal temperature of at least 145°F, non-ground pork to 160°F, and poultry to 170°F. Once cooked, keep hot foods at or above 140°F. Cold foods should be kept at or below 40°F. Individuals with compromised immune systems should consult a physician regarding special food and food safety recommendations. Also important are thorough washing of fruits and vegetables, with clean, drinkable water, avoidance of unpasteurized milk and dairy products, good personal hygiene, and safe food handling procedures. Carefully follow "keep refrigerated," "sell by," and "use by" dates. Be sure to wash all food preparation utensils and surfaces with hot, soapy water after use. Always wash hands with hot, soapy water after going to the bathroom and before preparing or eating food.

Figure 3.1 Overview of Specific Bacteria *Continued*

remains viable for an extended amount of time until the food is eaten. Raw vegetables fertilized by manure, cole slaw and other salads, raw shellfish, eggs, and even icing on baked goods have been implicated. Manufactured ice cubes and frozen foods have been vehicles for transmission as well. Since Norwalk virus can survive freezing temperatures and chlorine-sanitizing solutions, it makes control difficult. Emphasis should be placed on good personal hygiene; a potable water supply for drinking and ice-making; reliable, certified seafood suppliers; avoiding cross-contamination; and thoroughly cooking foods. Norwalk virus is susceptible to high heat and cooking temperatures. The symptoms are characterized by nausea, vomiting, diarrhea, abdominal pain, headache, and low-grade fever. The incubation period ranges from 24 to 48 hours, with the symptoms then persisting for an additional 24 to 48 hours. In total, viruses can be extremely dangerous and can cause death in infected human beings.

Parasites are commonly carried in the intestinal tracts of people and animals. They are protozoa-like organisms that live in the soil, on fruits or vegetables, or in other foods, and can be transferred by food handlers on their hands. Tapeworms are an example of parasites. Trichinae, parasites causing trichinosis, are usually found in pork but also can be in rabbit, bear, or other meat. The trichinae larvae grow in the consumer's body and lay their eggs in the muscle of that person, resulting in the disease characterized by nausea, cramps, diarrhea, aching muscles, fever, and chest pain. For this reason pork is always cooked well-done at temperatures above 170°F or higher to ensure that all trichinae present are destroyed.

Another parasite, cryptosporidium, is found in the intestinal tracts of warm-blooded animals. Cryptosporidiosis, the illness caused by cryptosporidium, was first linked with human disease in 1976. While it is a common cause of diarrhea in travelers to developing nations, until recently it has been rare in the United States. It is now recognized as a common cause of community illness and day-care-center illness outbreaks. Many food scientists consider cryptosporidium to be "an emerging parasite/pathogen." The illness causes profuse, watery diarrhea, abdominal cramps, and fever. Careful hand-washing with hot soapy water and safe food handling practices are important measures in controlling the spread of cryptosporidiosis.

Molds are a type of fungus causing food spoilage and sometimes illness in the consumer. They grow on foods which other microorganisms usually do not invade. For example, they may thrive on jellies, smoked meats, and other preserved food items. Molds do not usually grow on highly acidic foods, and are generally destroyed at temperatures above 125°F. An example of a good use for mold would be its injection into cheese, resulting in blue cheese.

Yeasts, like molds, do not cause illness, but they may cause the spoilage of food. Yeasts have many fine uses in food production and are readily seen in bread-making. They are also seen in the production of alcoholic beverages such as beer. Yeasts, single-celled organisms of the fungus kingdom, are present everywhere.

Food-borne Illnesses

The term "food-borne illness" means sickness caused when people eat food containing harmful microorganisms. Every year about 4,000 Americans die from eating contaminated meat and poultry, according to the Centers for Disease Control and Prevention. An estimated five million cases of food-borne illness are attributed to contaminated meat and poultry. There are really three types of food-borne illness: commonly called food poisoning; food-borne infection, foodborne intoxication, and foodborne toxin-medicated infection. A food-borne infection results from eating food containing harmful microorganisms that are alive. A food-borne intoxication occurs from eating food in which microorganisms have grown and produced toxins or poisons. A food-borne toxin-mediated infection results from eating a food containing harmful microorganisms that then produce toxins inside the body.

There are two common food-borne illnesses caused by poisons:

1. Staphylococcal poisoning (staph) is very common. Staph organisms are found on the skin and in the nose and throat of most people. Persons with colds and sinus infections are especially likely to carry these germs. When staph get into warm food and multiply, they produce toxins which cannot be detected by taste, odor, or color. Cooling or reheating food does not destroy poison after it has developed. Correctly cooling cooked foods, covering them for storage, cooking them until hot, and washing hands prior to any food preparation are all important. Excluding employees with respiratory infections, pimples, boils, and infected cuts and burns from food handling duties is important. Using proper hand-washing procedures and the use of rubber gloves should also be a standard precaution. Illness occurs within several hours after eating food, and symptoms include nausea, vomiting, abdominal pain, and diarrhea.
2. Botulism is a rare but sometimes fatal type of food poisoning. It results from eating improperly processed canned food. Therefore, only commercially processed canned goods should be used in dietary operations. The illness occurs within twelve to thirty-six hours after eating food. Symptoms include dizziness, double vision, difficulty in swallowing, speaking, and breathing, and general weakness in muscles.

Another less common food illness comes from clostridium perfringens, microorganisms which produce toxins and are found almost everywhere and can grow without air. They are also very resistant to heat. This toxin-mediated illness occurs within eight to twenty-four hours after eating the food, and symptoms include abdominal pains and diarrhea.

There are several common types of food infections (which occur when microorganisms enter food, grow and multiply into large numbers). Persons get sick when they consume food containing large quantities of these microorganisms. These are three common food illnesses caused by infections:

1. Salmonellosis illness results from the consumption of these organisms, which live in the intestinal tracts of animals and humans. Illness usually occurs within twelve to twenty-four hours; symptoms include abdominal pains, diarrhea, fever, vomiting, and chills;
2. Listeriosis bacteria live in wild and domestic mammals, and are frequently found in soil, water, or plants. Raw vegetables, unpasteurized milk or cheeses, raw meats, and poultry have been connected with this illness. Symptoms include nausea, headaches, and vomiting. This infection has severe results for a pregnant woman or an immuno-compromised individual.
3. Shigellosis (bacillary dysentery), another illness of bacterial origin, occurs in moist prepared foods due to inadequate personal hygiene of foodservice worker. Symptoms of illness include diarrhea, cramps, chills, and possibly fever.

Prevention of Food-borne Illnesses

Each of the above types of food-borne illness can be best controlled by properly handling foods. Be especially careful with the potentially hazardous foods and minimize the amount of time that these products are within the danger zone. Using the sanitary food-handling practices noted in Figure 3.2 will also help to minimize the potential for outbreaks of food-borne illness. Dietary managers should know how to be equipped for food safety as noted in Figure 3.3. Finally, knowing the sanitation terminology as presented in Figure 3.4 will assist dietary managers in the prevention of food-borne illness.

Category of Food-handling	Recommended Practice	Reason for Recommendations
Product (Food) Storage	1. Count inventory immediately and store in proper area. 2. Store food on shelves in freezer, refrigerator, or dry storage. 3. Keep stored food 6″ from wall. 4. Store food in closed containers. 5. Keep stored food away from garbage area. 6. Obtain product directly from storage.	1. Leaving inventory on loading dock promotes spoilage. 2. Food is easily contaminated by dirt on floors. 3. Lets air circulate around food. 4. Airborne particles can contaminate food. 5. Reduces chance of bacterial growth in food. 6. Placing containers on work area soils it and increases possibility of contamination.
Food Preparation	1. Wash fruits and vegetables thoroughly. 2. Use gloves when handling ground meat. Wash gloves thoroughly after use. 3. Prepare foods just prior to serving or cooking. 4. Heat food without interruption. 5. Cook pork until thoroughly done.	1. Removes surface dirt and bacteria. 2. Meat will remain under fingernails and contaminate other foods or surfaces. 3. Prepared foods left at room temperature invite bacterial growth. 4. Incompletely cooked foods invite bacterial growth. 5. Kills Trichinosis organism.
Handling Prepared Food	1. When food is cooked, use it completely or store immediately. 2. Keep food above 160°F or below 30°F. 3. Throw suspicious-looking food out. 4. Refrigerate leftovers at once. 5. Throw returned food away.	1. Refreezing food decreases quality and increases bacterial count. 2. Bacteria thrive in temperatures of 40–140°F. 3. Tasting doubtful food endangers everyone's health. 4. Avoids bacterial contamination. 5. Handling of food by patron can spread disease.
Equipment Use	1. Use different knives and cutting boards for meats and vegetables (may wash, sanitize, and reuse). 2. Clean equipment after use. 3. Dispose of cracked or chipped glassware. 4. Inspect glasses, dishes, and flatware before serving. 5. Use bus help or separate trays to clear soiled dishes. 6. Touch dishes only by the edge, cups by handles, glasses near the base, and utensils by the handles. 7. Let dishware, glasses, utensils, and cooking equipment air-dry or dry in dishwasher. 8. Store glassware inverted.	1. Equipment can spread Salmonella and other microorganisms. 2. (As above.) 3. Bacteria can lodge in cracks. 4. Stuck-on food particles can spread disease. 5. Soiled trays can contaminate food to be served. 6. Can transfer bacteria from hands to eating surfaces. 7. Towels can contaminate surfaces. 8. Airborne bacteria can collect in bowl area.
Personal Habits of Food-Handling	1. Keep person, hair, and hands scrupulously clean at all times. 2. If sick, stay home and call in for a replacement. 3. Practice good public manners. 4. Use proper serving tools. 5. Keep health card valid. 6. Wash hands whenever changing activity and after touching unclean objects or surfaces.	1. Keeps hair, dirt, and germs from contaminating foods and surfaces. 2. Keep from spreading illness. 3. Spitting, nose- or pimple-picking, wiping perspiration with hands, etc. may spread disease (besides being impolite). Sitting or leaning on serving or work areas can transfer contaminants. 4. Avoids contact with food by server's hands. 5. Prevents spread of TB, venereal, and other communicable diseases. 6. Avoids transfer of dirt and bacteria.

Figure 3.2 Sanitary Food-handling Practices
Adapted from material developed by Jeanne Picard while a student at the University of New Orleans

Here's a roundup of some of the products available to help staff prepare food safely.

- Color-coded cutting boards, knives, and scoops that come with posters that indicate, with pictures, which colors should be used with which foods;
- A block of solidified sanitizer that can be sliced on the slicer;
- A water-filled paddle that can be frozen and then used to cool batch-cooked soups, sauces, casseroles, and other kettle ingredients;
- Sanitizing towels to wipe down work areas;
- Nonabsorbent, washable mats to place under color-coded cutting boards. (regular towels, used to anchor boards or wipe up counters, absorb dripping juices);
- No-touch hand-washing stations with infrared sensors and air dryers;
- Recording thermometers allowing temperature information to be automatically downloaded into computers.

FIGURE 3.3 EQUIPPED FOR FOOD SAFETY

Biological hazards	Harmful, disease-causing bacteria, viruses, or parasites that can be supported by, or transmitted in, food.
Chemical hazards	Contamination of food with toxic substances, such as cleaning and sanitizing chemicals and substances.
Clean	Free from visible soil.
Contamination	The unintended presence of harmful substances or microorganisms in food or beverages.
Cross-contamination	Allowing harmful substances from one food product to come in contact with other food products.
Food-borne illness	A disease that is carried or passed to human beings by food.
Food-borne illness outbreak	A reported incident when two or more people report that they have become ill from a common food, which is confirmed through laboratory analysis as the source of the illness.
Environmental hazards	Contamination of food with nonfood items, such as pieces of glass, staples from cartons, or metal shavings from can openers.
Sanitary	Having had many or most disease-causing bacteria removed. Wholesome food handled and prepared in such a way that the food is not contaminated with disease-causing bacteria or chemicals.
Sanitation	The creation and maintenance of healthful conditions.
Spoilage	Damage to the edible quality of food.

FIGURE 3.4 SANITATION TERMINOLOGY

Personal Cleanliness and Sanitation

Dietary service employees must develop and consistently use good sanitary habits. These include personal cleanliness habits as well as techniques for handling food products. Dietary service personnel should have regular physical examinations. Staff members who are ill should not come to work, and employees who have been exposed to infectious diseases should consult a doctor before returning to work.

One should understand that some people can appear healthy but still carry bacteria that can contaminate food. These people, called "carriers," should not handle food—just as a person with a known common visible illness should not. Physical examinations can help assess whether dietary employees are carriers of communicable diseases or those which might be passed along to another human being. Figure 3.5 reviews procedures for personal cleanliness habits which should be practiced by all the dietary employees.

Guidelines for Safe Food-Handling and Holding

Dietary staff members must always observe a wide range of basic principles when working with food. Products should always be purchased from reliable and approved sources. All meat and poultry products should be inspected for wholesomeness. Commercially processed canned goods should be used, rather than "home-processed" products. Receiving practices should confirm that all products are potentially safe (frozen foods have not thawed, refrigerated foods are not warm, there are no dented rims or side seams on canned goods, etc.).

Food in storage areas should be kept off the floor and away from the wall, both to allow for air circulation and proper cleaning, and to eliminate places for rodent and insect nesting or infestation. Storage areas should be kept clean, including shelving and other storage equipment within the area. All foods in storage should be kept covered and maintained at the correct storage temperatures. Foods should be used on a first-in, first-out basis (oldest foods should be used first). Foods which have been thawed should not be re-frozen (since this decreases quality).

When preparing food, raw, packaged, and canned items should be examined before they are used. Hands should be cleaned as often as necessary as foods are be-

Dietary service employees should observe the following behavioral guidelines:

1. Bathe daily.
2. Use a deodorant.
3. Wear clean clothes and underwear.
4. Brush your teeth several times daily.
5. Shampoo hair as often as necessary to keep it clean and healthy.
6. Keep fingernails clean, well trimmed, and free of polish.
7. Don't use excessive makeup and perfume.
8. Wear a hairnet which completely covers the hairline; do not use hairspray.
9. Don't wear jewelry other than wedding bands.
10. Don't smoke or chew gum in food-contact areas.
11. Don't cough or sneeze near food.
12. Don't file nails or comb hair in foodservice areas.
13. Wash hands with soap and warm water as often as necessary.
14. Use disposable towels for drying hands.
15. Don't sample food products with cooking utensils.

Figure 3.5 Personal Cleanliness Habits

ing handled. All food preparation equipment, including small utensils, must be properly cleaned. Special care must be taken when handling potentially hazardous foods (those of animal origin or high in content of animal-origin food). Proper chilling procedures include:

- Divide large quantities to be chilled into smaller shallow pans and place on upper shelves above raw food;
- Do not stack hot pans;
- Stir cooked foods to accelerate the cooling process;
- Leave food uncovered on or near the top shelf until it is completely cooled, then cover;
- Use an ice-water bath;
- Drop food temperature of hot foods in two hours or less.

In other words, foods should be allowed to cool quickly (as stated, use a shallow pan, refrigerate hot foods immediately after cooking, stir hot foods quickly when cooling, and consider setting items in large containers of cold running water). A good rule of thumb is to cool leftovers in no greater volume than two-gallon containers, stirring continuously, while the product is surrounded by cold running water. Place the leftovers in a container, set it in a sink, raised, if possible, to allow cold water to flow underneath the container and stir to cool. Rapid chilling equipment is another method for rapidly-chilling food.

Avoid the use of leftovers whenever possible but, when they must be used, practice sanitation principles to again reduce the time that these products are within the danger zone.

After food is cooked, it must be chilled rapidly or else held above 140° F for service. As always, the objective is to minimize the amount of time food is within the temperature danger zone as illustrated in Figure 3.8. Frequently, cooked foods are placed in steam tables or other holding equipment. Items must be covered to prevent contamination and to retain the proper serving temperatures. The inside temperature of a food product should be monitored with a probe thermometer.

The correct use and calibration of a food thermometer is to maintain accuracy. If used properly, the thermometer should not be a contaminant itself. Take the temperature in the center or thickest part of the food; wait for the needle to be still for 15 seconds, then record the reading. A digital thermometer may need the batteries changed periodically. To calibrate, use either the ice-point method (for cold foods) or the boiling-point method (for hot foods). To use the ice-point method, insert the sensing area of the thermometer into a 50/50 ice-and-water slush until the indicator stabilizes. Then adjust the calibration nut so that the indicator reads 32°F. To use the boiling-point method, insert the sensing area into boiling water until the indicator stabilizes. Then adjust the calibration nut so that the indicator reads 212°F. The boiling point differs daily with atmospheric pressure changes and with the altitude, so adjustments must be made to suit individual altitude levels. The hanging thermometers in refrigeration units sometimes may not be calibrated. In this case, use an approved thermometer to verify the accuracy of each hanging one by placing them side-by-side and taking a comparison reading. Replace an inaccurate thermometer with a new one if calibration is not possible.

Food-holding times must be kept to a minimum if the nutritional value and culinary quality of the product is to be maintained. Proper serving utensils and procedures are necessary. All pre-cooked food must be reheated to an internal temperature of at least 165° F before being placed in warm holding equipment. If reheating will negatively affect the product's quality it should be discarded. Preferably, cooking-to-order is the "best" approach when practical. The need for good sanitary work practices does not end when food is prepared. Food must also be properly handled and served.

A basic rule—"Keep hot foods hot and cold foods cold, or don't keep foods at all"—has serious and useful implications for handling food products during service. Batch cooking of small quantities can help recognize this principle. Use of proper serving counters and other equipment can help maintain foods at their proper temperatures. Provide proper serving utensils so that guests in public and other cafeteria operations cannot handle the eating surfaces of flatware. Food should be kept covered until immediately before serving. State and/or local sanitation and health guidelines typically require sneeze guards or other partitions to reduce the possibility of guests coming in direct contact with food served on the serving counter. When serving foods, use proper utensils such as tongs, spatulas, and spoons; you should not handle foods with your hands. Plastic gloves are used in many dietary operations. While these have great potential for helping to keep foods safe, they can also provide a false sense of security. It is very important to use proper food handling procedures consistently even when plastic gloves are utilized.

Sanitary practices must be followed when cleanup duties are performed. For example, the proper cleaning and sanitizing of dish and flatware, pots and pans, and so on is one of the most important jobs. Organisms can be killed by either heat or chemicals. Some facilities use hot-water dish machines and pot-and-pan sinks that require that surfaces of items being sanitized be exposed to water at least 180° F in temperature for times required by local ordinances. Other facilities use cold-water dish machines and chemical sanitizing agents in pot-and-pan areas to destroy microorganisms by chemical means. Again, the need to comply with all applicable sanitation codes—and to properly instruct and supervise employees to consistently use these procedures—is of utmost importance.

When a dish machine is not available, preparation utensils, service items, and so on should be washed, rinsed, and sanitized in a three-compartment sink using a chemical sanitizer. The items can be pre-soaked and washed in the first sink, and thoroughly rinsed in the second sink. Chemical sanitizing can then be done in the third sink using the correct chemical balance at a temperature between 75 and 120°F. Tableware and cooking equipment should always be air-dried, and should not be handled until ready for use. Unsanitary towels and hands can directly contaminate clean and sanitary dishes and utensils.

Many facilities keep sample plates of all foods produced for twenty-four hours to use for analysis purposes should an outbreak of food-borne illness occur. Of course, if a suspected case or outbreak of food-borne illness occurs, the dietary manager must carefully comply with all requirements and policies issued by the facility. Figure 3.6 illustrates procedures for investigation of food-borne illness at one healthcare facility. Figure 3.7 presents a discussion on AIDS and food handling. Finally, the temperature chart in Figure 3.8 should be made readily available to all employees to ensure proper food safety within operations.

The federal Department of Agriculture 1995 Food Code defines the temperature danger zone as 41—140°F. Since state health departments vary in defining the danger zone, check with local and federal authorities before determining your operational procedures.

Hazard Analysis and Critical Control Point System

The Hazard Analysis and Critical Control Point System (HACCP) emphasizes sanitation concerns and identifies stages where loss of control could present a food safety risk. A careful analysis determines where control is especially necessary to assure that the end product is safe and sanitary.

HACCP identifies sensitive ingredients, critical process points, and relevant human factors as they affect product safety. Critical control points, when not controlled, would result in an unacceptable sanitation risk. Analysis can begin with the development of a process flow diagram that includes all relevant processing factors and details and is specific for the food, process, equipment, and facility involved. Once each step in the processing, packaging, and service or distribution of the product is analyzed, critical control points can be established. The type of potential

STANDARD PRACTICE MANUAL

DIETARY MANUAL Page ____ of ____

DATE ______________________ TIME ________________

NAME OF PERSON ________________________________ AGE _____

ADDRESS __________________________ TELEPHONE ___________

_________ Patient _________ Visitor _________ Employee

If employee; state department and work area ________________________

Did individual partake of the suspected meal? ____Yes ____ No

If yes, date and hour food eaten: ________________________________

Did individual become ill? ____Yes ____No

If yes, date and hour of onset: ________________________________

Below is a list of foods and beverages served at the suspect meal. (Check only those which were eaten)

Food Item Food Item Food Item

____

____

____

Which of the following symptoms did individual have, and how long (in hours) did they last?

Nausea or vomiting ________ Diarrhea __________ Fever __________

Prostration ______________ Paralysis __________ Other __________

Was a physician consulted? ____ Yes ____ No

Diagnosis______________________ Tests ____________________

Name of hospital, if hospitalized ________________________________

Name of other persons who partook of the suspected meal:

____

____

Date ____________________ Investigator __________________________

DATE EFFECTIVE 12-27-81	SUBJECT Case History Questionnaire (suspected food-borne disease)	SUBJECT NO.

Revised 4/82	Revised	Revised	Revised	Revised

STANDARD PRACTICE MANUAL

DIETARY MANUAL Page ____ of ____

A. Report to administrative person in charge.
B. Investigate and establish validity of report.
C. Notify nursing home administrator or designee.
D. If established, administrator will notify: Director of Nursing, Medical Director, Dietitian, laboratory liaison, infection control coordinator, local and state health departments.
E. Conduct thorough investigation.
F. Any leftover food from meals should be sent to lab for cultures.
G. Report findings appropriately.
H. Case history questionnaire follows.

DATE EFFECTIVE 12-27-81	SUBJECT In Case of Suspected Food-borne Outbreaks	SUBJECT NO.

Revised 4/82	Revised	Revised	Revised	Revised

FIGURE 3.6 PROCEDURES FOR INVESTIGATION OF FOOD-BORNE ILLNESS
Used by permission of Heritage Manor Convalescent Center, Flint, Mich.; courtesy of Maurice Latimer

A frequently voiced, but misplaced, fear is that foodhandlers can transmit AIDS (Acquired Immune Deficiency Syndrome). Can the AIDS virus be transmitted through food? Let's review the conditions affecting a foodhandler that may be transmitted to consumers via food and what routes of transmission are of concern.

As stated earlier in this chapter, foodhandlers shedding pathogenic bacteria, viruses and parasites may introduce those organisms into food and if the organism persists in a viable state, the susceptible consumer may become infected.

Foods which are not cooked or require handling in preparation, such as salads and sandwiches, are vehicles for disease transmission. Good foodservice operations policy requires foodhandlers to adhere to stringent handwashing practices on the job and refrain from work when they are infected.

Food has been a vehicle of transmission of agents spread by the respiratory route, such as strep pneumonia. However, transmission of agents from the respiratory tract is a rare occurrence.

Hepatitis A is a viral infection transmitted by the fecal-oral route. Consistent good foodhandling technique is essential for prevention of hepatitis A transmission, because excretion of the agent precedes onset of symptoms by two weeks and continues for two weeks after onset of a clinical illness. Foodhandlers with acute Hepatitis A should be removed from work during the infectious period.

Agents which are present in blood and body fluids and not in feces are not transmitted by the fecal-oral route. Hepatitis B and Human Immunodeficiency Virus (HIV) are in this category. Both agents are transmitted by exchange of blood or sexual secretions. HIV and Hepatitis B are not transmitted through casual contact.

Persons residing with infected people and co-workers who do not exchange blood or have sexual interaction with infected individuals are not a threat to safe food.

When accidents occur in the workplace, injuries resulting in blood or other body fluids on a work surface or equipment should be handled with appropriate precautions in all situations. Surfaces should be treated with disinfectants such as 1:10 solution of household bleach (1/4 cup bleach per gallon of water made fresh daily). Gloves should be worn to protect hands from exposure to the bleach solution to protect them from irritation. And all foods contaminated with human blood or other body fluids should be discarded.

Recommendations to test foodhandlers for HIV antibody or to exclude persons infected with HIV from foodhandling are not necessary to protect the public health. In fact, The American Disabilities Act protects an individual with AIDS and bans discrimination in the workplace, such as transfers or firing. Education of foodhandlers, managers of food services and the general public, concerning agents transmissible by food and appropriate precautions to reduce transmission; would reduce misconceptions about the disease. There is no need however, to be concerned about food-borne HIV.

FIGURE 3.7 WHAT ABOUT AIDS?

Fahrenheit Temperature Scale		Centigrade Temperature Scale
212°	(Boiling point of water)	100°
200°		
180°	Sanitize dishes by rinsing in water at this temperature	82°
160°		
150°	Range of wash water temperature in mechanical dish washing	66°
140°		60°
120°	Hand washing temperature	49°
100°	Range of temperature in which bacteria grow best	38°
90°		32°
80°		
70°	Range of temperature for storage of dry foods	21°
60°		16°
50°		10°
40°	Range of temperature for refrigerated storage (water at sea level freezes at 32°F or 0°C)	4°
32°		0°
20°		-7°
0°	Range of temperature for storage of frozen foods	-18°
-10°		-24°

Danger Zone is 40° to 140° (Fahrenheit)

Danger Zone is 4° to 60° (Centigrade)

FIGURE 3.8 BE CONCERNED ABOUT TEMPERATURES
Source: U.S. Department of Agriculture, *Principles and Practices of Sanitation and Safety in Child Nutrition Program.* U.S. Government Printing Office, Washington, DC, undated

hazard and its critical control point differ with each product, ingredient, package, processing, storage, and handling procedure.

The chief value of HACCP is its ability to predict and monitor problem areas and situations in foodservice operations. The feedback component of HACCP permits management to use this concept as a preventive approach in its quality assurance efforts. The HACCP system can help bring the potential dangers associated with the production of a food product to management's attention. As such, it is a communication tool designed to minimize the errors that can eventually become costly to a foodservice facility and those it serves—both in terms of dollars and health. HACCP is a food safety program that allows every employee to know how to keep food safe. Every manager is responsible for keeping food safe and for using the HACCP standards.

Seven principles involved in operating a HACCP program are summarized here from a more complete discussion in Chapter Two under HACCP Principles:

1. Assess hazards associated with each operational step of growing and harvesting raw materials and ingredients, processing, manufacturing, distribution, marketing, preparation, and consumption of the food; and identify the prevention measures that can be taken at each step to reduce the risk to acceptable levels (although a foodservice operator is not required to assess hazards of growing, etc. only "from dock to dish" in his or her own facility);
2. Determine critical control points (CCPs) required to control the identified hazards;
3. Establish the requirements that must be met at each identified CCP;
4. Establish procedures to monitor each CCP;
5. Establish corrective action to be taken when there is a deviation identified by monitoring of a CCP;
6. Establish effective record-keeping systems that document the HACCP plan;
7. Establish procedures for verification that the HACCP system is working correctly (verification measures may include biological, physical, chemical, and sensory methods); and when needed, establishment of necessary criteria.

While the "philosophy" of HACCP—utilize a system to help assure food safety—certainly applies to all facilities, the use of detailed, written procedures to implement a program is generally applicable only to large operations. For example, a large operation utilizing a commissary production system and/or a facility using a cook/chill or other alternative production/distribution method would likely be advised to implement continuous monitoring, flow-charting, verification tests, and so on which are part of a formalized HACCP system. All dietary managers should, however, be aware of and use applicable procedures at all control points to help assure that food safety standards are consistently maintained. Also, state health department surveyors are incorporating HACCP principles into the survey process.

Safety

In today's foodservices, hazards confront both management and employees. There are few places where one can work that are more potentially dangerous than in the kitchen. There are open flames, high-pressure steam, sharp knives, hot liquids, cutting and grinding equipment, and wet/slippery floors. Heavy objects and trays must be lifted and unsafe conditions could confront the worker at any time. Proper rules of conduct regarding safety are a must, and the dietary manager must enforce any procedures to protect both employees and clients.

Safety Management in Work Areas

Most accidents are unforeseen but are caused by someone's carelessness. Most accidents can be prevented, and the dietary manager must be committed to ongoing employee safety training programs and routine safety inspection activities.

Examples of commitments that dietary managers must make to safety programs include the following*:

1. Take an active role to help reduce the possibility and occurrence of accidents;
2. Assure that safety concerns take priority over convenience; safe practices must be incorporated into all operating procedures;
3. Urge the active participation of all staff members in ongoing safety programs.

In many facilities, the dietary manager has an active role to play in developing and implementing safety programs. He or she

- helps develop work procedures which recognize safety concerns;
- trains employees in work procedures which incorporate safety concerns;
- conducts inspections within the dietary department to ensure that the equipment and facilities lend themselves to safe working practices;
- completes accident reports, assists in accident investigation, and does whatever is necessary to help correct problems which cause accidents;
- whenever necessary, assists in treatment and seeks medical assistance for injured employees or others;
- reports needed repairs or maintenance, changes in work procedures, or other conditions which are potential causes of accidents; and
- conducts ongoing safety meetings and other safety activities.

Dietary employees also have responsibilities in ongoing safety programs. They should observe and closely follow all required work procedures. These includes

- using personal protective equipment and following all requirements for the safe operation of equipment at all times;
- keeping work areas in approved condition;
- reporting any problems requiring repair and/or maintenance as soon as they are observed;
- promptly notifying their supervisor of any accidents, regardless of how minor they might appear.

It should be obvious that all members of the dietary staff—dietary managers, supervisors, employees—are members of the organization's "safety team."

Causes and Prevention of Foodservice Accidents

Some consideration must be given the most common types of accidents which occur in a dietary operation. As you study these possible problems, pay special attention to the rules employees must follow to help protect themselves and others from common accidents.

Many accidents in foodservice operations are caused by burns. Rules to prevent burns include the following[3]:

1. Use dry pot holders when handling hot pots and pans; wet or damp pot holders can cause a steam burn. Never use an apron, towel, or dish cloth;
2. Always open pots on ranges or lids of steam kettles by raising the backside of the lids so that steam will escape away from one's face and body;
3. Always turn on hot water faucets cautiously;
4. Keep handles of pots and pans which are on cooking equipment (such as ranges) out of traffic aisles;
5. Always follow the manufacturer's instructions when using all cooking equipment;
6. Avoid filling pots, pans, kettles, etc. too full;
7. Avoid spattering, splashing, or allowing food to boil over;
8. Stir food with long-handled spoons or paddles;
9. Have a place prepared for hot pans before removing them from a range or oven;
10. Don't use pans with loose handles (which can break off) or rounded bottoms (which can tip);

[3]The remainder of this section is adapted from: *Safety Operations Manual.* National Restaurant Association, Chicago, IL.

11. Use a puller or other proper tool to bring pans to the front of the oven; do not reach into hot ovens;
12. Allow equipment to cool before trying to clean it;
13. If food catches on fire, spread salt or baking soda on the flame; do not use water;
14. Put used matches in a tin container;
15. Always follow the manufacturer's instructions when lighting gas equipment;
16. Always be careful when filtering or changing shortening in deep-fat fryers; use of gloves is recommended;
17. Prohibit horseplay or running in the dietary facility;
18. Food servers should be trained to pour coffee and other hot liquids properly;
19. Counter surfaces below heat lamps can get very hot; alert employees with proper caution signs;
20. Prevent the buildup of grease on stove tops and in ventilation hoods. Do not be afraid to ask for assistance when handling hot and heavy containers;
21. Keep the oven door closed when an oven is not being used;
22. Know how to use fire extinguishers and other safety equipment.

Muscle strains are another frequent cause of accidents in dietary preparation and storage areas. Always have a firm footing before attempting to lift a heavy object. Remember to keep the back straight; do not bend forward or sideways. Bend the knees to pick up low objects; the weight of the lifted object should be on the leg muscles, not on the back muscles. Dietary workers should not try to carry too many or too heavy items at any one time. When carrying a heavy load, ask for help or, better yet, use a cart.

There are some "common sense" rules which can be used to help prevent falls. Next to traffic accidents, falls kill more people than any other kind of accident. You may be interested to learn that most falls are from slips or trips on floor level—not from high places. Some special rules to help prevent falls include the following:

1. Floors should be kept clean and dry at all times. Spills should be wiped up immediately;
2. Floors should be kept free from all hazardous objects such as boxes, mops, brooms, etc.;
3. A sturdy stepladder should be used to remove items from high places;
4. Always walk—never run; always use caution when going through swinging doors;
5. Dietary personnel should wear low-heeled and properly fitting shoes that have non-skid soles. Thin-soled or broken-down shoes or house-slippers should never be worn. The heel and toe should be completely enclosed. Never wear high heels or sandals. Shoestrings should be kept tied to prevent slipping;
6. Always remove snow and ice from entrances and walkways;
7. Areas such as side entrances should be cleaned frequently; floor mats or other protective devices should be kept in good and clean condition;
8. Utilize "slip-resistant" floor waxes;
9. "Caution" or "Wet Floor" signs should be used when appropriate;
10. Mats should be placed in dishroom and by pot sink;
11. Stair treads that are cracked or worn should be replaced;
12. Adequate lighting should be provided in stairwells or other places not frequently traveled;
13. Loose or upturned floor tiles should be replaced as soon as they are noticed.

Cuts are constant hazards for food preparation personnel. Rules to prevent cuts include the following:

1. Knives, cleavers, saws, and other sharp tools should be kept in racks or special drawers when not in use;
2. Always cut away from the body when slicing. Food should be placed on a table or cutting board, firmly grasped, and sliced by cutting downward;
3. Always use cutting tools of correct size and with the proper blade when working;
4. Knives should always be sharp; because dull knives require dietary workers to exert more pressure, slippage problems are more likely to result;
5. Discard or repair knives with loose handles;
6. Collect all sharp tools on a special tray; wash them separately. Never throw knives or other sharp tools into sinks filled with water;
7. Never play with knives or sharp equipment; don't try to catch a falling knife;
8. Always be alert and concentrate when using a knife, slicer, or similar equipment;
9. Don't leave knives on the edge of the counter. Push them back so they can't fall onto the floor or onto a worker's foot;
10. Store knives properly;
11. Clean up broken glass immediately. Minimize the amount of glass permitted in the kitchen. Use a broom and dustpan to sweep up broken china or glass; never use your fingers. If glass breaks in a dishwasher, drain it first and pick up bits of glass with a damp cloth. Always place broken glass or china in a separate refuse container;
12. Use safety guards and any other safety items provided on equipment;
13. Use the feeder/tamper in the hopper of a meat grinder;
14. Clean blades on slicers with a folded heavy cloth, first making sure the slicer is unplugged. Then work slowly and carefully from the center of the blade to the outside cutting edge. Be sure that the blade is in the position recommended for cleaning;
15. Always unplug any foodservice equipment before cleaning it;
16. When chopping food with a knife, bend the fingers and hold the item with your hand. Keep the point of the chopping (French) knife on the block. Never use knives as substitutes for screwdrivers or can openers; always use the proper tools;
17. When using sharpening steels, be sure that there is a finger guard between the handle and the steel. Don't use knives to open cardboard cartons; use the proper tool.

Electrical equipment accidents are common causes of problems in any dietary operation. Special rules which can help prevent electrical equipment accidents include the following:

1. Employees should be instructed in the proper way to disassemble, reassemble, and use all electrical equipment items;
2. A qualified electrician should inspect all electrical equipment, wiring, switches, etc. on a regularly scheduled basis as part of an ongoing preventive maintenance program (see below);
3. All electrical equipment must be properly grounded;
4. The manufacturer's instructions must be carefully followed when operating electrical equipment;
5. Personnel should never touch metal sockets and electrical equipment when their hands are wet or while standing on a wet floor;

6. An electrical cord worn through to the wire should never be used;
7. Before cleaning any piece of electrical equipment, personnel should remove its plug from the outlet;
8. Unauthorized extension cords should never be used; circuits should never be overloaded;
9. Oil- and water-resistant cords should always be used.

The use of proper safety equipment for operation of the many pieces of potentially dangerous food production-related equipment is always of critical concern. Always follow—and train dietary employees about—the manufacturer's instructions. Examples of safety precautions for selected equipment items include:

1. **Ranges**
   a. All new electric ranges should bear the seal of approval of the Underwriters' Laboratories and National Sanitation Foundation International. All new gas ranges should bear the seal of approval of the American Gas Association and the National Sanitation Foundation International.
   b. All electrical connections should conform with the National Electrical Code requirements and all state and local requirements. All gas connections should conform with national, state, and local regulations.
   c. Carbon dioxide or non-toxic chemical fire extinguishers approved by state and local fire regulations should be available near the range. Employees should know their locations and how to use them.
   d. Good lighting in all working areas is essential for safe operation of the range.
   e. Adequate ventilation (hoods and filters) is important;
2. **Deck Ovens**
   a. All electric deck ovens should bear the seal of approval of the Underwriters' Laboratories and the National Sanitation Foundation International. All new gas ovens should bear the seal of approval of the American Gas Association and the National Sanitation Foundation International.
   b. All electrical connections should conform with the National Electrical Code requirements and all state and local requirements. All gas connections should conform with national, state, and local regulations.
   c. Carbon dioxide or non-toxic chemical fire extinguishers approved by state and local fire regulations should be available near the oven. Employees should know their location.
   d. Good lighting is essential for safe operation of any oven.
   e. Adequate ventilation (hoods and filters) is important.
   f. Let ovens cool before cleaning.
   g. Never allow grease to accumulate in cracks of oven; this is a fire hazard. (grease also causes bad odors and attracts roaches and mice.)
   h. Have regular inspections made of all ovens by reliable service persons to ensure safe and efficient operation; the inspections should include a check of the thermostat with the actual oven temperature to make any necessary corrections in the thermostat setting.
   i. To prevent burns, use dry pot holders or oven mitts to remove food from oven. Make certain space is available to place the hot pans which are removed.

j. When you remove heavy containers, ask for help and know where the container may safely be placed. Always be sure that the work area is clear of other employees before moving hot containers.
k. Always keep oven doors closed when not in use.
l. Do not close door on gas models until gas is ignited.
m. Ventilate gas ovens before lighting;

3. **Tilting Braising Pans**
a. Guard against possible steam burns when raising the kettle's lid.
b. To prevent burns, use long-handled paddles, dippers, spatulas, and turners.
c. Use dry mitts or pot holders when holding hot utensils.
d. Wipe up any grease that may spatter on the floor when emptying the tilting braising pan;

4. **Steam Jacketed Kettles**
a. Guard against possible steam burns when raising kettle's lid.
b. See that proper water level is maintained in water jacket.
c. If the water jacket has gone dry, do not add water to the jacket without first allowing it to cool.
d. Be sure that the safety valve is in good working order.
e. If steam pressure rises above safety level, turn off and call service person.
f. To prevent burns, use long-handled paddles for stirring and long-handled dippers for removing food.
g. Wipe up any grease that may spatter on floor when using the kettle;

5. **Compartment Steamers**
a. Guard against possible steam burns when opening door.
b. Be certain that the safety valve is in good working order.
c. If steam pressure rises above safety level, shut off steam and call service person.
d. Prevent burns in removing food from steamer. Use dry pot holders or mitts and make certain that space is available to place hot baskets or pans when they are removed.
e. Clean up spilled foods at once.
f. See that proper water level is maintained in self-contained steamers.
g. Check water level at intervals during operations. Never use without water.
h. If steam leaks around the door after tightening, have steamer checked by service person;

6. **Deep Fryers**
a. Be sure that the unit is operated under adequate ventilation hoods.
b. Have the proper type of fire-extinguishing equipment available for ready use.
c. Insert and remove baskets from deep fryers carefully to reduce splashing of fat.
d. Allow excess fat to drain from food before moving baskets across work aisles. Floors and other spaces can become very slippery if fat is dripped onto them.
e. Carefully follow all manufacturer's requirements regarding cleaning of the unit.
f. Do not place wet/damp food into the deep fryer. This will cause fat to splatter.

g. When practical, wear a long-sleeved shirt/uniform when working with the deep-fat fryer.

h. Use proper equipment and techniques for straining/draining/cleaning the deep fry unit;

7. **Mixers**

a. All electrical connections should conform with the National Electrical Code requirements and other state and local requirements.

b. Be sure to have correct electrical connections according to identification plate on mixer.

c. When cleaning mixer, do not let water come in contact with the motor or electrical wiring.

d. Select the correct bowl for the type of mixture and then select correct beater or whip.

e. Be sure to fasten bowl, beater, and whip securely before starting the motor.

f. Do not put hand or spoons into bowl while the mixer is in operation.

g. Stop machine before scraping down sides of bowl or loosening materials on the bottom during mixing process.

h. Always use a rubber scraper, flexible spatula, or long-handled spoon to scrape down sides of bowl and to remove food from beater or whip.

i. Use mixing bowls for mixing only; do not put them on the range or in the oven.

j. If mixer is used on a continuous basis, always allow time for motor to cool;

8. **Food Slicers**

a. All electrical connections should conform with the National Electrical Code requirements and other state and local requirements.

b. When cleaning a slicer, do not let water come in contact with the motor or electrical wiring.

c. Never use slicer when blade guard is off.

d. Always keep hands away from blade when machine is in operation; never catch food with hands.

e. Keep plug out of socket when machine is not in use. Be certain guard is on slicer before putting plug in socket.

f. Always make certain the switch is off and the plug is pulled out of socket before cleaning.

g. When disconnecting slicer pull the *plug; not* the cord.

h. Never use a metal tool to scrape off food particles from slicer blade.

i. Make sure your hands are dry before operating the slicer.

j. Be sure cord is dry and free from grease.

k. Do not use very hot water or steam when cleaning slicer.

l. Keep blades sharpened according to manufacturer's instructions;

9. **Food Choppers**

a. Never put hands in bowl when chopper is in use.

b. Wait until knives have stopped revolving before removing food or cleaning.

c. Do not overload the bowl; fill no more than two-thirds full.

d. Use large spatula rather than your hand to guide food into cutters; move in direction opposite to bowl rotation.

e. Do not use for cutting meat with bones and gristle.

f. After cleaning, make sure knives are replaced in the proper position.

Safety Inspection Programs

The safety program for the dietary department must begin with an awareness of the importance of protecting the safety of employees and residents/patients. It must be followed by a training program designed to teach employees about safe work practices. A routine safety inspection program is also important, to confirm that the facility is safe and that employees are utilizing safe working practices.

While the dietary manager may wish to design a safety inspection checklist unique to the property, one should be aware that several are currently available and one (Figure 3.9) is included in this chapter. Representatives of insurance companies, municipal fire department staff members, and representatives of the local safety council are among experts who can provide specialized assistance as necessary.

How often should safety inspections be made? It depends in part upon the findings of the initial safety inspection. In many facilities, a routine safety inspection is made monthly. However, the supervisor can make daily, and more frequent, inspections as part of ongoing supervisory responsibilities.

Safety hazards noted at the time of safety inspections must be corrected promptly. If employees are observed to be using unsafe practices, they must be coached, retrained, and/or more closely supervised to be sure these problems do not recur.

Employees should be trained about safety concerns as an integral part of their initial training. Concerns noted during safety inspections can be reviewed as part of ongoing staff meetings.

Safety inspection reports should be kept to help the dietary manager review the effectiveness of ongoing safety programs and to provide useful information if any external agency questions the safety and work practices of the facility.

To Locate Hazards

The following checklist covers both physical factors in the property and work practices of your personnel. During your inspection be as aware of unsafe acts as much as you are of unsafe conditions.

Area	Yes	No	Comments
Receiving Area:			
Are floors in safe condition? (Are they free from broken and defective floor boards? Are they covered with nonskid material?)			
Are employees instructed in correct handling methods for various containers, etc., that are received?			
Are garbage cans washed daily in hot water?			
Are garbage cans always covered?			
Are trash cans leak-proof and adequate in number and size?			
If garbage disposal area is adjacent to a part of the general receiving area, is there a program that keeps floors and/or dock areas clear of refuse?			
Is there a proper rack for holding garbage containers? Are garbage containers on dollies or other wheel units to eliminate lifting by employees?			
Are adequate tools available for opening crates, barrels, cartons, etc. (hammer, cutter, cardboard carton opener, and pliers?)			
Is crate-, carton-, and barrel-opening done away from open containers of food?			

Figure 3.9 Foodservice Safety Checklist (Continued on next page)
Revised from materials originally developed by the National Safety Council, *Safety Check List to Locate Hazards.* Chicago, Ill., no date

Area	Yes	No	Comments
Storage Area:			
Are shelves adequate to bear weight of items stored? Are employees instructed to store heavy items on lower shelves and lighter materials above?			
Is a safe ladder provided for reaching high storage?			
Are cartons or other flammable materials stored at least two feet from light bulbs?			
Are light bulbs provided with a screen guard?			
Is a fire extinguisher located at the door?			
Are employees carefully instructed in the use of detergents to prevent irritation of dermatitis, etc.?			
Do you have a program for disposition of broken glass or china?			
Where controls are in a passageway, are they recessed or guarded to prevent breakage or accidental starting?			
Are dish racks in safe condition (if wooden, free from broken slats and smoothly finished to eliminate splintering; if metal, free of sharp corners that could cause cuts)? Are these racks kept off the floor to prevent tripping?			
Serving Area:			
Are steam tables cleaned daily and maintained regularly (are gas or electric units checked regularly by a competent serviceperson)?			
Is safety valve equipment operative?			
Are serving counters and tables free of broken parts and wooden or metal silvers and burrs?			
Do you have regular inspections of:			
Glassware?			
China?			
Silverware?			
Plastic equipment?			
If anything breaks near the food service area, do you remove all food from service adjacent to breakage?			
Are tray rails adequate to prevent trays from slipping or falling off at the end or corners?			
Are floors and/or ramps in good condition (covered with nonskid material, free from broken tile and defective floor boards)?			
Are these areas mopped at least daily and waxed with nonskid wax when necessary?			
Is there effective traffic flow so that customers do not collide while carrying trays or obtaining foods?			

FIGURE 3.9 Continued

Area	Yes	No	Comments
Dining Areas:			
Are floors free from broken tile and defective floor boards? Are they covered with nonskid wax?			
Are pictures securely fastened to walls?			
Are drapes, blinds, or curtains securely fastened?			
Are chairs free from splinters, metal burrs, broken or loose parts?			
Are floors "policed" for cleaning up spillage and other materials?			
Is special attention given to the floor adjacent to water, ice cream, or milk stations?			
Are vending machines properly grounded?			
If customers clear their own trays prior to return to dishwashing area, are the floors kept clean of garbage, dropped silver, and/or broken glass and china?			
If trays with soiled dishes are placed on conveyor units, are the edges guarded to keep customers from catching fingers or clothing?			
If dishes are removed from dining areas on portable racks or bus trucks, are these units in safe operating condition (for example, are all casters working, all shelves firm)?			
Soiled Dish Process Area:			
Are floors reasonably free of excessive water and spillage?			
Are floor boards properly maintained and in safe condition (free from broken slats and worn areas that cause tripping)?			
Are all electrical units properly grounded?			
Are switches located to permit rapid shutdown in the event of emergency?			
Can employees easily reach switches?			
Pots and Pans Room or Area:			
Are duckboards or floor boards in safe condition (free from broken slats and worn areas which could cause tripping)?			
Are employees properly instructed in use of correct amounts of detergent and/or other cleaning agents?			
Are adequate rubber gloves provided?			
Is there an adequate drainboard or other drying area so that employees do not have to pile pots and pans on the floor before and after washing them?			
Do drain plugs permit draining without the employee placing hands in hot water?			

FIGURE 3.9 Continued on next page

Area	Yes	No	Comments
Walk-in Coolers and Freezers (Refrigerators):			
Are floors in the units in good condition and covered with slip-proof material? Are they mopped at least once a week (and whenever spills occur)?			
If floor boards are used, are they in safe condition (free of broken slats and worn boards which could cause tripping)?			
Are portable and stationary storage racks in safe condition (free from broken or bent shelves and set on solid legs)?			
Are blower fans properly guarded?			
Is there a by-pass device on the door to permit exit if an employee is locked in (or, is there an alarm bell)?			
Is adequate aisle space provided?			
Are employees properly instructed in placement of hands for movement of portable items to avoid hand injuries?			
Are heavy items stored on lower shelves and lighter items on higher shelves?			
Are shelves adequately spaced to prevent pinched hands?			
Is the refrigerant inthe refrigerator nontoxic? (Check with your refrigerator service manual.)			
Food Preparation Area:			
Is electrical equipment properly grounded?			
Is electrical equipment inspected reguarly by an electrician?			
Are electrical switches located so that they can be reached easily in the event of an emergency?			
Are the switches located so that employees do not have to lean on or against metal equipment when reaching for them?			
Are floors reguarly and adequately maintained (mopped at least daily and waxed with nonskid wax when necessary; are defective floor boards and tiles replaced when necessary)?			
Are employees instructed to immediately pick up or clean up all dropped items and spoilage?			
Are employees properly instructed in the operation of all machines?			
Are employees forbidden to use equipment unless specifically trained in its use?			
Are machines properly grounded?			
Don't Overlook:			
Lighting—is it adequate in the:			
Receiving area?			
Storage area?			
Pots and pans area?			
Walk-in coolers and freezers?			

FIGURE 3.9 Continued

Area	Yes	No	Comments
Food preparation area?			
Cooking area?			
Serving area?			
Dining area?			
Soiled dish processing area?			
Doors—do they open into passageways where they could cause an accident? (List any such locations.)			
Are fire exits clearly marked and passages kept clear of equipment and materials? (List any violations.)			
Stairways and ramps—			
Are they adequately lighted?			
Are the angles of ramps set to provide maximum safety?			
Is stairs are metal, wood, composition, or marble, have abrasive materials been used to provide protection against slips and falls?			
Are pieces broken out of the casing or front edge off the steps?			
Are clean and securely fastened handrails available?			
If stairs are wide, has a center rail been provided?			
Ventilation—is it adequate in the:			
Receiving area?			
Storage area?			
Pots and pans area?			
Walk-in coolers and freezers?			
Food preparation area?			
Cooking area?			
Serving area?			
Dining area?			
Soiled dish processing area?			
Other Safety Concerns:			
Do employees wear good shoes to protect their feet against injury from articles that are dropped or pushed against their feet?			
Is employee clothing free of parts that could get caught in mixers, cutters, grinders, or other equipment?			
Are fire extinguishers guarded so they will not be knocked from the wall?			
If doors are provided with a lock, is there an emergency bell or a by-pass device that will permit exit from the room should the door be accidentally locked while an employee is in the room?			
Is there a pusher or tamper provided for use with the grinders?			
Are mixers in safe operating condition?			
Are the mixer beaters properly maintained to avoid injury from broken metal parts and foreign particles in food?			

FIGURE 3.9 Continued

Accident Investigation Programs

Unfortunately, even when the facility uses effective training programs and ongoing safety inspection tools to combat safety problems, accidents may still occur. It is important that all dietary staff be trained in procedures to be followed immediately after an accident occurs. It is also important that dietary staff learn from accidents to help keep them from happening again. Figure 3.10 shows the type of information asked for on the Employer's Basic Report of Injury, which is typically required for Workmen's Compensation purposes. A typical procedure requires that copies of the form be sent to the insurance company, the employee, and the state regulatory agency. Of course, a copy should be retained for the facility's records.

OSHA and Safety Programs

The Occupational Safety and Health Administration (OSHA), part of the U.S. Department of Labor, was created to help make working conditions in businesses of all types and sizes safer for employees. It developed programs, procedures, and requirements designed to help encourage both employers and employees to reduce work hazards. OSHA regulations affect essentially every employer. Dietary operations in institutions are generally covered.

OSHA sometimes receives unfavorable publicity because of requirements based on standards thought to be impractical. However, the "spirit and intent" of the act is commendable since it urges constant attention to the availability of safe and healthful working conditions.

There are several elements in OSHA laws which affect the dietary manager. First, federal and/or state and local inspectors can visit the facility and search for potential safety hazards. If any are found, a closed meeting will be held to discuss and review probable violations. Recommendations for remedial action, and time frames for their completion, will probably be parts of this process. Follow-up inspections will also be held.

If a facility is in violation of basic OSHA requirements and does not take required remedial action, violations can be cited. There are important procedures for penalties, appeals, and posting of job safety and health protection information.

Record-keeping requirements are also part of OSHA laws. Some records are required for reporting occupational injuries or illnesses, and additional information may be necessary. Since the requirements of OSHA change and may be affected by the state or local jurisdictions within which a facility is found, dietary managers should check with local Department of Labor officials for current and relevant information.

Fire Safety and Related Training

Another common cause of accidents in dietary operations is fires. The benefits of an effective fire prevention program are:

- protection of life and property;
- lessened chance of costly shutdowns;
- reduced possibility of a serious fire;
- promotion of good sanitation and housekeeping practices.

Compliance with a fire protection program means the training of the employees in adopting fire prevention habits, in the use of fire protection equipment, and in assisting the client at the time of fire. The dietary manager's obligation is to protect both the client and the employee from injury by fire, and to preserve the facility from interruption, loss, or destruction due to fire.

Fire can be prevented by the following:

A. *Portable fire extinguishers* should be

1. properly located and in working order;
2. of proper type for a fire which may occur;

Form 100
Rev. 1-82

OSHA
Case or File No. ________

DEPARTMENT OF LABOR
Bureau of Worker's Disability Compensation
LANSING, MICHIGAN

COPIES TO BE DISTRIBUTED
Yellow and Green – Bureau of Workers's Disability Compensation, Lansing, Mich.
Blue – Insurance Company
Pink – Employer File
White – Employee

EMPLOYER'S BASIC REPORT OF INJURY

Employers must report to the Bureau on Form 100 all injuries, including diseases, which arise out of an in the course of the employment and cause: 1. Seven (7) or more days of disability not including Sundays or the day of injury. 2. Death. 3. Specific Losses. In case of DEATH also file immediately an additional report on Form 106.

1. **INJURED EMPLOYEE** ________ Soc. Sec. No. ____/____/____
2. Address ________ Telephone No. ________
3. Birthdate - Month ____ Day ____ Year ____ If under 18, date working permit issued ________ ☐
4. Sex: ☐ Male ☐ Female Number of injured employee's children under age 16 living with injured ________
5. Marital status: ☐ Married ☐ Single If married male, is wife living with him? ☐ Yes ☐ No
6. Number of other family members or relatives at least 50% supported by injured ________
7. **DATE OF INJURY** ________ Last day worked ________ Did employee die? ☐ Yes ☐ No If yes, date ________
8. Location of Injury City ________ State ________ County ________
9. Was place of accident or exposure on employer's premises? ☐ Yes ☐ No ☐
10. Name and address of physician ________
11. If hospitalized, name and address of hospital ________

12. DESCRIPTION OF ALLEGED INJURY (Complete and specific information needed for each category) ☐

A. Describe the injury or illness
Examples: Amputation, Burn, Cut, Fracture, Sprain, etc. ☐

B. Part of body - The part of body directly affected by the injury or illness.
Examples: Head, Arm, Leg, Circulatory system, etc. ☐

C. Describe the events that caused the injury. Examples: Fell, Operating machinery, Exposure to chemicals, etc. ☐

D. Name the object or substance which directly injured the employee.
Examples: Knife, Band Saw, Acid, Floor, Oil, Punch Press, etc. ☐

13. Occupation of injured employee (be specific) ________ ☐
14. Department ________ Foreman or supervisor ________
15. Total Gross Wages - Highest 39 of 52 weeks preceding date of injury
Total Gross Weekly Wages $ ________ No. of weeks used in calculation ________
Average weekly wage $ ________
16. Complete the following only if the injured employee received wages from a second employer.
Name of second employer ________
Mailing address ________
17. Date returned to work ________ or estimated lost time from work ________ ☐

18. IS EMPLOYEE CERTIFIED AS VOCATIONALLY HANDICAPPED? ☐ Yes ☐ No ☐
19. IS EMPLOYEE RECEIVING UNEMPLOYMENT INSURANCE BENEFITS? ☐ Yes ☐ No

20. **EMPLOYER** MESC. No. ________
A. ________ Federal ID No. ________
B. ________
21. Location (if different from mail address) ________
22. **TYPE OF BUSINESS** ________ ☐
23. **INSURANCE COMPANY (Not agent)** ________ Carrier ID No. ________
24. **HAS WHITE COPY OF THIS REPORT BEEN GIVEN TO EMPLOYEE?** ☐ Yes ☐ No ☐

Questions or errors should be immediately reported to the employer representative indicated below

Date of Report ________ Prepared by ________
Signature (in ink) **Employer** or Representative Tele. #

FIGURE 3.10 EMPLOYER'S BASIC REPORT OF INJURY

3. used if the fire is discovered while still small enough;
4. used if the fire is discovered by a person ready, willing, and able to use it. (A fire extinguisher should be used only when there is no clear danger to the user. Fire officials warn against employees fighting fires unless it is absolutely clear that it can be immediately contained).

The extinguisher to be used is dependent upon the type of fire that could occur in the area to be protected. Four classes of fires are defined:

1. Class A fires are fires in ordinary combustible materials, such as paper or plastic;
2. Class B fires are fires in flammable liquids, gases, and greases (grease fires, however, require agents suitable for this special hazard);
3. Class C fires involve live electrical equipment, and a non-conducting extinguishing agent is required;
4. Class D fires are fires in combustible metals such as magnesium and titanium.

B. *Detection systems* can perform the multiple functions of summarizing assistance from the local fire department as well as notifying occupants for evacuation:

1. Smoke detectors can be either ionization or photoelectric. Ionization detectors detect visible and invisible products of combustion. Photoelectric detectors detect only visible (smoke, flame) products of combustion;
2. Heat detectors are either thermostats, which are widely used, or fusible links, which are used in certain applications, wherein the link separates when its rated temperature is reached, actuating an alarm;
3. Rate of Rise Detectors operate on a principle of a temperature increase exceeding a predetermined rate in number of degrees per minute;
4. Flame detectors sense radiant energy.

Any detection system should be carefully and properly engineered to provide the protection necessary. A professional consultant is of obvious significant assistance in the design of an effective system.

C. *Sprinkler systems* are the most effective means of automatically controlling fires in buildings. In addition to the savings in direct fire losses due to sprinkler protection, there is a saving represented in the reduced interruption of business, as well as the savings in insurance premiums. There are three major types:

1. Wet-pipe system is filled with water under pressure. When a fire occurs, the fusible link on a sprinkler head melts, opening the water supply;
2. Dry-pipe system contains compressed air. When a sprinkler head is opened, the compressed air is released, causing water to flow through the system. This is effectively used in areas where water might freeze;
3. Pre-action system is a variation of the dry-pipe system. The water is held out of the system by a valve operated by a detecting device. The water flows into the system when the detecting device is actuated. With the sound of the alarm, it is sometimes possible to extinguish a fire with portable units prior to the opening of the sprinkler heads.

Unsatisfactory sprinkler performance is in most cases due to the system being closed. The other major cause of poor performance is partial protection. A system must be properly installed and then maintained in operable condition.

To summarize, fires can be controlled by the following:

1. Adequate fire extinguishing equipment should be available; personnel should know where it is located and how to use it. Local fire authorities can be consulted about the purchase, use, and inspection of correct fire-extinguishing equipment;
2. Authorized and frequently tested fire-detection devices should be available. These may be specialized equipment items which can detect smoke, flame and/or heat;
3. Automatic sprinkler systems are a very effective means of controlling fires. They may be required by local fire ordinances, but even if they are not, they may be a very wise investment. Special fire-extinguishing equipment under ventilation filters is usually required by local ordinance. Regardless of the type (dry-chemical, carbon dioxide, or chemicals in special solutions), they can only be effective if they are professionally designed, installed, and maintained.

It is obviously important that all local, municipal, and other ordinances be followed. Dietary employees should know the location of all emergency exits, and fire drills should be conducted on a regular and routine basis. Dietary managers should check to see that all exit doors open to the outside. They should be sure that all fire exits are kept clear of furniture, food products, and so on at all times.

It is wise to keep the phone number of the local fire department handy. Local fire officials can also be contacted for help in designing training programs for dietary staff.

Dietary staff should be familiar with the location of all portable fire extinguishers. These items, of the proper type, should be located close to the most probable source of fires. Naturally, they must be regularly inspected and maintained.

Dietary operations suffer from three types of fires: Class A fires, which involve combustible materials such as paper, plastics, etc.; Class B fires, which are caused by flames in gases and greases; and Class C fires, which involve electrical equipment. While there are many types of specialized fire extinguishers, a multi-purpose dry-chemical extinguisher is useful in fighting fires of all three types noted above.

Obviously, personnel must be trained in the proper use of extinguishers. Typically, a locking pin must be pulled out before the unit can be operated. When a multi-purpose unit is used, the operator should attempt to cover all burning areas with the chemical in order to minimize sources of re-ignition. If the fire is too large, personnel safety becomes of primary importance. The facility's designated fire-fighting official should be notified, and the local fire department should be called. Even if the fire is small and can be extinguished with equipment available in the facility, it is always best to contact the facility fire official and/or local fire department for necessary follow-up activities.

Hazard Communication Standard (HazComm)

The U.S. Occupational Safety and Health Administration (OSHA) has issued a regulation requiring employers, including healthcare facilities, to inform workers about the possible dangers of chemicals they may use to do their jobs, and to train them to use these chemicals safely. This regulation is referred to as the Hazard Communication Standard (often called HazComm).

Five steps are needed to comply with the HazComm Standard:

- Read the standard;
- List the hazardous chemicals at the facility;
- Obtain a Material Safety Data Sheet (MSDS) from each supplier for applicable chemicals used at the facility and make the sheets available to employees;
- Properly label all chemical containers;
- Develop and implement a program which explains MSDS information and labeling procedures to employees, and informs them about hazards and protective measures.

The MSDS will indicate whether a chemical is hazardous: look for words such as "caution," "warning," "combustible," "flammable," or "corrosive" on the label. The list of hazardous chemicals must be available to employees whenever they wish to see it, and a procedure for keeping the list up-to-date must be in place.

Some chemicals are exempt from the HazComm Standard. For example, rubbing alcohol in a first-aid station would be exempt from the standard because it is intended for personal use by employees.

The facility must assure that an MSDS is on file for all hazardous materials. If there is none, the facility must contact the chemical manufacturer.

MSDSs can be filed by hazardous ingredients, or location—whatever way will make it easy for employees to find an MSDS in cases of emergency. They must be available during all workshifts and should not be stored in areas that will be locked during some shifts.

A sample MSDS is shown in Figure 3.11. An MSDS should include the following information:

- Chemical identity;
- Hazardous ingredients;
- Physical and chemical characteristics;
- Fire and explosion hazard data;
- Health hazards;
- Precautions for safe handling and use;
- Control measures.

Chemical manufacturers must provide proper labeling for chemicals. Employers should double-check these labels for completeness and accuracy. The label must contain the name of the chemical, hazard warnings, and the manufacturer's name and address. If no label is provided, the facility must prepare a label from the MSDS or ask the manufacturer to provide one.

To make the label quick to read and easy to understand, a labeling system with color, letter, and number codes may be used. For example, a red label might indicate that the chemical poses a physical hazard; the letter "F" might indicate that the chemical is flammable; and the number "four" (on a scale of one to four, with four being high) could indicate that the hazard is very dangerous.

Caution should be exercised in transferring chemicals to other containers unless full labeling is used on the new container. There are many rules of safe storage for hazardous materials, and the use of protective gear, including goggles, gloves, and so on, during use is a must. It is the manager's responsibility to provide such gear and monitor all chemicals found within the operation.

SUMMARY

The dietary manager has an active role in seeing that all food served is clean and wholesome. There are two basic causes of unsafe food: chemicals and microorganisms. Chemicals come from poisons used for cleaning, and other compounds, pesticides, and residues which get on or into food. Microorganisms are all around us and are too small to be seen without a microscope.

Microorganisms are classified in many ways, are all around, and are too small to be seen without a microscope. Bacteria, one type of microorganism, is about 1/25,000 inch in diameter and has optimal temperature, food acidity, and oxygen requirements. Viruses are the tiniest known living organism and are usually transferred through food or water. Parasites are commonly carried in the intestinal tracts of people and animals. They are protozoa-like organisms that live in the soil, on fruits or vegetables, or in other foods, and can be transferred by food handlers on their hands. Molds are a type of fungus causing food spoilage and sometimes illness in the consumer. Yeasts are single-celled organisms of the fungus kingdom that are present everywhere.

CLOROX

The Clorox Company
7200 Johnson Drive
Pleasanton, California 94566
Tel. (415) 847-6100

Material Safety Data Sheet

Clorox—HMIS	
HEALTH	2*
FLAMMABILITY	0
REACTIVITY	1
Personal Protection	8

I Chemical Identification

NAME: REGULAR CLOROX BLEACH — **CAS no.** 7681-52-9

DESCRIPTION: CLEAR, LIGHT YELLOW LIQUID WITH CHLORINE ODOR — **RTECS no.** NH 3486300

Other Designations	Manufacturer	Emergency Procedure
EPA Reg. No. 5813-1 Sodium Hypochloride Solution Liquid chlorine bleach	The Clorox Company 1221 Broadway Oakland, CA. 94612	Notify your Supervisor Call your local poison control center or Rocky Mountain Poison Center (303) 573-1014

II Health Hazard Data

*Causes severe but temporary eye injury. May irritate skin. May cause nausea and vomiting if ingested. Exposure to vapor or mist may irritate nose, throat and lungs. The following medical conditions may be aggravated by exposure to high concentrations of vapor or mist: heart conditions or chronic respiratory problems such as asthma, chronic bronchitis or obstructive lung disease. Under normal consumer use conditions the likelihood of any adverse health effects are low. FIRST AID: EYE CONTACT: Immediately flush eyes with plenty of water. Remove contact lenses first. If irritation persists, see a doctor. SKIN CONTACT: Remove contaminated clothing. Wash area with water. INGESTION: Drink a glassful of water and call a physician. INHALATION: If breathing problems develop remove to fresh air.

III Hazardous Ingredients

Ingredients	Concentration	Worker Exposure Limit
Sodium hypochlorite CAS# 7681-52-9	5.25%	not established

None of the ingredients in this product are on the IARC, NIP or OSHA carcinogen list.

IV Fire and Explosion Data

Not flammable or explosive. In a fire, cool containers to prevent rupture and release of sodium chlorate.

V Special Protection Information

Hygienic Practices: Wear safety glasses. With repeated or prolonged use, wear gloves.

Engineering Controls: Use general ventilation to minimize exposure to vapor or mist.

Work Practices: Avoid eye and skin contact and inhalation of vapor or mist.

VI Spill or Leak Procedures

Small quantities of less than 5 gallons may be flushed down drain. For larger quantities wipe up with an absorbent material or mop and dispose of in accordance with local, state and federal regulations. Dilute with water to minimize oxidizing effect on spilled surface.

VII Reactivity Data

Stable under normal use and storage conditions. Strong oxidizing agent. Reacts with other household chemicals such as toilet bowl cleaners, rust removers, vinegar, acids or ammonia containing products to produce hazardous gases, such as chlorine and other chlorinated species. Prolonged contact with metal may cause pitting or discoloration.

VIII Special Precautions

Keep out of reach of children. Do not get in eyes or on skin. Wash thoroughly with soap and water after handling. Do not mix with other household chemicals such as toilet bowl cleaners, rust removers, vinegar, acid or ammonia containing products. Store in a cool, dry place. Do not reuse empty container; rinse container and put in trash container.

IX Physical Data

Boiling point	212°F/100°C (decomposes)
Specific Gravity (H_2O=1)	1.085
Solubility in Water	complete
pH	11.4

0174m 7/86

FIGURE 3.11 MATERIAL SAFETY DATA SHEET

There are three types of food-borne illness: food-borne intoxication, toxin-mediated infection, and food-borne infection. Food-borne illness occurs when people eat food in which microorganisms have grown and produced toxin (poison). Two common food-borne illnesses caused by poison are staphylococcal poisoning (staph) and botulism. There are several common types of food-borne infections including Salmonellosis, Listeriosis, and Shigellosis.

Safeguards which must be established to prevent food-borne illnesses include personal hygiene, food protection, facility and equipment sanitation, and rodent and insect control. Personal cleanliness habits, as well as techniques for handling food products, are essential in foodservice. It is possible to appear healthy but still carry microorganisms that can contaminate food.

Dietary staff members must always observe a wide range of basic principles when working with food. Food-holding times must be kept to a minimum if the nutritional value and culinary quality of the product is to be maintained. The need for good sanitary work practices does not end when food is prepared. Recognizing the potentially hazardous foods and the temperature danger zone are critical to food safety. Food must also be properly handled and served. The need to comply with all applicable sanitation codes and to properly instruct and supervise employees to consistently use these procedures is of utmost importance.

HACCP emphasizes sanitation concerns and identifies stages where loss of control could present a food safety risk. The type of potential hazard and its critical control point differ with each product, ingredient, package, processing, storage, and handling procedure (refer to Chapter 2). For the manager, training staff to monitor and take corrective action at critical control points is mandated for food safety.

The dietary manager must be concerned about safety to prevent accidents which can cause harm to employees and clients. Dietary managers' commitment to safety include

1. taking an active role to help reduce the possibility and occurrence of accidents;
2. assuring that safety concerns take priority over convenience and that safe practices are incorporated into all operating procedures; and
3. urging the active participation of all staff members in ongoing safety programs. Dietary employees also have responsibilities in ongoing safety programs. They, along with dietary managers and supervisors, are members of the organization's "safety team."

Some of the most common types of accidents in a dietary operation are burns, muscle strains, falls, cuts, and electrical equipment accidents. The use of proper safety equipment for operation of the many pieces of potentially dangerous food production-related equipment is always of critical concern. Dietary employees should be trained about manufacturer's instructions on safety precautions.

Safety inspection programs for dietary departments begin with an awareness of the importance of protecting the safety of employees and clients, followed by a training program, and then a routine safety inspection program which confirms that the facility is safe and the employees are utilizing safe working practices.

Furthermore, safety inspection reports should be kept to help the dietary manager review the effectiveness of ongoing safety programs and to provide useful information if any external agency questions the safety and work practices of the facility. It is also important that all dietary staff be trained in procedures to be followed immediately after an accident occurs. A facility may have effective training programs and ongoing safety inspection tools, yet accidents may still occur.

The Occupational Safety and Health Administration (OSHA) is part of the U.S. Department of Labor. It was created to help make working conditions in businesses of all types and sizes safer for employees. It developed programs, procedures, and requirements designed to help encourage both employers and employees to reduce work hazards.

Another common cause of accidents in dietary operations is fire. Again, training is important in adopting fire prevention habits, in the use of fire protection equipment, and in assisting clients at the time of fire. Fires can be controlled by portable fire extinguishers, detection systems, and sprinkler systems.

Dietary employees should know the location of all emergency exits, and fire drills should be conducted on a regular and routine basis. All local, municipal, and other ordinances must be complied with also. Additionally, local fire officials can be contacted for help in designing training programs.

An OSHA issued regulation requiring employers, including healthcare facilities, to inform workers about the possible dangers of chemicals they may use to do their jobs, and to train them to use them safely is referred to as the Hazard Communication Standard (HazComm). Five steps are needed to comply with the HazComm Standard:

- Read the standard;
- List the hazardous chemicals at the facility;
- Obtain a Material Safety Data Sheet (MSDS) from each supplier for applicable chemicals used at the facility and make the sheets available to employees;
- Properly label all chemical containers;
- Develop and implement a program which explains MSDS information and labeling procedures to employees and informs them about hazards and protective measures.

KEY TERMS

- Microorganisms
- Food poisoning
- Bacteria
- Viruses
- Parasites
- Molds
- Yeasts
- Food-borne illness
- Food-borne infection
- Food-borne intoxication
- Food-borne toxin-mediated infection
- HACCP (Hazard Analysis and Critical Control Point)
- Safety inspection programs
- OSHA
- Fire prevention programs
- Hazard Communication Standard (HazComm)

QUESTIONS/PROBLEMS/CASES

1. On Sunday evening, Joanne prepared chicken breasts for dinner. She also prepared a cooked pudding, a favorite dessert among the residents of the nursing home where she was currently employed. Because several residents were away from the home and Joanne had not been told, she prepared more chicken breasts and pudding than were necessary.

   Joanne thought that she would just use the leftover chicken to make chicken salad later in the week, and serve the pudding then as well. She refrigerated the leftover chicken and pudding in five-gallon containers in an air temperature of 40 degrees F. until she was ready to prepare lunch later that week.

   Friday morning, Marie, the dietary manager, saw Joanne preparing the chicken salad, fresh fruit, cole slaw, and pudding for lunch. Marie asked Joanne if the chicken and pudding were leftovers from earlier in the week, and when Joanne confirmed to her that they were, Marie asked Joanne to stop preparing the lunch.

   Why did Marie do this?

   What should Joanne have done in a better manner?

2. What is meant by the "danger zone" concerning sanitation?

3. Describe the distinction between food-borne intoxication and food-borne infection?

4. List the four safeguards that must be established to prevent food-borne illnesses.

5. What is meant by the basic rule, "keep hot foods hot and cold foods cold, or don't keep foods at all"?

6. You are the dietary manager of a large facility. How would you implement a safety program?

7. Describe the process taken after receiving a bad OSHA review.

8. What are the benefits of an effective fire prevention program?

9. How are fires best controlled?

10. The employees in a small cafeteria had scraped every dish and utensil and placed them in the racks that automatically fed into the high-temperature dishwashing machine. When the wash and rinse cycles were complete, one of the employees noticed that the dishes were spotted. The thermometer that registered the final rinse temperature for the sanitizing cycle had a reading of 140°F. instead of the required 180°F. The employee told the manager and the manager immediately called the manufacturer's representative to come and examine the dishwashing machine. In the meantime, what could be done to clean and sanitize the dishes and utensils?

11. A chef begins the day by making her award-winning recipe of chili. She first cuts up the onions and tomatoes, shreds the beef, and mixes all with the appropriate seasonings and kidney beans. After simmering for hours, the chili is allowed to cool uncovered on a side table. Mid-afternoon, the janitor decides to sweep the floor and passes by the chili with his broom, scattering particles of dust into the air as he cleans the floor. He sneezes as he goes by the chili. Bacteria settles onto the chili, although the contamination was not noticed because foods contaminated with staph bacteria have no particular odor or taste.

    The chef then decides to top the chili with cheese prior to service. Using her unwashed hands, she grates the cheese, places it on the chili, and allows the pan to remain on the table, figuring that her night chef will bake her chili for service. Unfortunately, he neglects to bake it and, in a hurry upon receiving an order for it, dashes a bowl of it into the microwave, thinking that zapping it will bring the chili to correct temperature. The bacteria have produced their toxins into the food, thus contaminating the chili.

    The customer has no idea that the chili had been unrefrigerated all day and does not complain when receiving the bowl of chili which is only warm, not hot. About six hours later signs of nausea, vomiting, diarrhea, dehydration, and cramps appear as the customer retires for the evening at home.

    1. What caused the customer to become sick?

    2. Name two of the control measures in the prevention of staphylococcal intoxication that could have been used in this case.

3. What was the food or foods involved in this food-borne intoxication?

4. What could be done if the customer should come back to complain?

12. What steps are needed to comply with the Hazard Communication Standard?

4

PURCHASING, RECEIVING, AND INVENTORY MANAGEMENT

CHAPTER OUTLINE

- Definitions Are Important
  - Purchasing
  - Buying/Ordering
  - Selection
  - Procurement
- Purchasing/Procurement Process
  - Primary Procurement Objectives
  - Importance of Procurement
  - Line and Staff Functions
- Use of Purchase Specifications
  - Responsibility for Developing Specifications
  - Minimum Requirements for Specifications
  - Advantages and Disadvantages of Purchase Specifications
- Determining Quantity of Food to Purchase
  - EP and AP Conversions
  - Assessing Quantity Needs
  - Purchase for Immediate Use
  - Purchase for Inventory: Minimum/Maximum Systems
  - Calculating Order Quantity and Forecasting
- Overview of Accounting Records in the Purchasing Process
  - Small Dietary Operations
  - Large Dietary Operations
  - Price Reduction Procedures
  - Payment Policies
  - Supplier Selection Process
- Ethics in Purchasing
  - Security Concerns in Purchasing
  - Proper Payment Method Reduces Theft
  - Competitive Bidding Procedures
  - Prime Vendor
- Make/Buy Analysis—Overview
  - Making the Decision
  - Factors of Critical Importance
  - Possible Advantages of On-Site Production
  - Possible Disadvantages of On-Site Production
  - Possible Advantages to Use of Convenience Food Products
  - Possible Disadvantages of Convenience Food Products
  - Conclusions
- Make/Buy Analysis—Procedures
  - Introduction
  - Make/Buy Analysis Process
- The Receiving Process
- Effective Food Storage Practices
  - Record-Keeping During Storage
  - Perpetual-Inventory System
  - Assigning Values to Inventory
  - Ways to Reduce Inventory Costs
  - Security Concerns in Storage
  - Computerized Inventory Systems
  - Food Distribution (Issuing) Practices

DEFINITIONS ARE IMPORTANT

Purchased goods and services represent a large percentage of total operating expenses in institutional dietary operations.* An emphasis on product quality must begin before food products are issued to the kitchen and processed as part of the food production task. It is important to design and implement an effective system to assure that costs are reduced without sacrificing quality requirements. This emphasis begins as purchasing procedures are planned. The definition of "purchasing" includes a variety of activities.

PURCHASING

The term "purchasing" technically refers to three components of the procurement process:

- Negotiation for price;
- Physical aspects of the purchase decision;
- Payment for products received.

In foodservices, however, the term refers to every step in the process by which goods and services are "bought" and brought into the dietary operation. This expanded definition of purchasing will be used interchangeably throughout this chapter with the term "procurement."

BUYING/ORDERING

These terms refer to steps in the procurement/purchasing process.

Buying relates to the exchange of money (or other commodity) for a product or service. *Ordering* refers to the communication between buyer and seller at the time an agreement to exchange money (or another commodity) for goods and services is made. Examples are communication with a distributor sales representative (DSR) in a meeting or on the telephone, or communication via computer or facsimile machine (fax).

SELECTION

This term technically means to "choose between alternatives." It is obvious that the purchaser must select between alternative products as the purchasing decisions are made.

PROCUREMENT

This term refers to an entire system of decision making and implementation of plans that involves:

- requisitioning necessary products/services by kitchen personnel;
- determining necessary quality requirements;
- assessing quantity needs;
- selecting suppliers;
- arranging for delivery;
- negotiating price(s);
- making the actual purchase decision;
- arranging for payment;
- following-up (expediting) on "orders;"
- receiving;

*Sections of this chapter discussing definitions, a review of procurement and make/buy decisions are from: Dietary Managers Association. *Professional Procurement Practices: A Guide for Dietary Managers.* Lombard, Ill. 1991 (pp 3–8; 89–96).

- maintaining necessary records;
- maintaining proper vendor relations;
- dispensing of surplus equipment and other items if necessary (frying fat, beverage containers, etc.);
- inspecting;
- storing;
- controlling inventory;
- researching and studying needs of the dietary operation; and
- obtaining information to make the purchasing decision.

PURCHASING/PROCUREMENT PROCESS

The tasks involved in "purchasing" include many duties and responsibilities undertaken both before and after the time an order is actually placed with a supplier.

"Purchasing" is much more than calling in an order. The dietary manager must consider the job of purchasing to include *all* of the various components in a *system* of purchasing/procurement. Regardless of whether the facility is "big" or "small," the tasks outlined above must be completed by someone. Larger facilities may have a specialized buyer or purchaser; small operations may incorporate the tasks into the job of a manager or another official. However, the primary tasks must be completed by someone as products and services are purchased.

The purchasing task is ongoing. Through experience with suppliers, products, and services, the dietary manager can develop a very effective system to help control costs and to assure that quality requirements are met. A purchasing system is not generally developed "overnight"; procedures are incorporated and systems are modified as conditions warrant action and as changes prove necessary. Procurement is a "living," never-ending process which must keep up with changes in the industry, the facility, and the dietary operation.

The purchasing system must be designed to attain stated objectives which are much more than "buying the products we need at the best cost and getting them here when we need them." While this should be obvious, in practice very little thought is often given to what the purchasing system must accomplish.

PRIMARY PROCUREMENT OBJECTIVES

The objectives of a purchasing system must involve, at least, "assuring that the *right* product, of the *right* quality, is received at the *right* time. It must be obtained at the *right* price from the *right* supplier." While these objectives are easily stated, they are not easily accomplished. Much time and effort are necessary to design a purchasing system to accomplish these things.

Quality Goals. The dietary purchaser must obtain the *right* quality products and services. This is not always the *highest* quality available. It is not possible to consider the quality aspects of a product without considering its price at the same time. The relationship between the two is referred to as "value."

Quantity Goals. Products must be purchased in the *right* quantity. If an insufficient quantity of product is purchased, stockouts (running out of items with increased possibility of client dissatisfaction as well as increased operating problems) can result. When an *excessive* quantity of products is purchased, inventory and cash-flow problems often occur.

Price Goals. The *right* price for the *right* quality must be assessed; it can often be negotiated. The dietary buyer has a responsibility to obtain required quality products at the "best" price; this price is a function of related services which the supplier provides.

Supplier Selection Goals. It is important that products be obtained from the *right* source. It is not reasonable either to "buy from anybody" or, conversely, to deal with one source of supply because "we've always purchased from him or her."

Delivery Schedule Goals. Products must be received at the *right* time. Delivery should not be beyond the control of the dietary operation. While occasional problems must be anticipated, supplier selection should be based in part on reliable delivery schedules.

Importance of Procurement

The foundation for a successful control-of-costs program begins with the purchasing process. Wise dietary managers know that "good" product quality cannot be derived from "bad" quality products that are purchased. Increasingly, facilities are utilizing "quality assurance," "quality control," or related programs that emphasize the relationship between cost and quality within the operation.

In healthcare dietary services, a quality assurance program focuses upon both the clients (what's "best" for them) and upon the facility. How can costs be controlled? (The objective of quality assurance, then, involves combining an emphasis on the client with the facility's cost goals.) The challenge is to provide what the client needs in the most cost-effective manner. Effective procurement is at the heart of a quality assurance program.

Effect on Cash Flow. Even large, high-volume healthcare facilities can have cash-flow problems. Cash must be available to pay bills when they become due. The quantity of items purchased, their price, and the timing of their delivery ultimately affect the amount of money (cash) required to satisfy payment obligations.

A qualified manager should make decisions about decreasing purchases (which increase possibilities of stockouts) and about increasing the quantity of purchases (which can yield discounts). However, input from purchasing staff can be helpful as these decisions are made. Purchasers can (and should) arrange for deliveries in required quantities at required times. These tactics can help assure that cash-flow problems do not result from ineffective purchasing practices.

Line and Staff Functions

If the facility utilizes a full-time purchaser, this staff member serves in a staff function within the property. That is, as a technical specialist in a very specific area (procurement) the purchaser provides assistance to ine decision makers (administrators with decision-making authority). This distinction is very critical. Decision makers plan menus (which dictate items to be purchased). Line managers also should be responsible for making product-quality decisions, for forecasting volumes of products to be produced, and for determining whether products should be made on-site or be purchased in a ready-service format. In other words, purchasers help line managers obtain the products that are needed, but do not make these decisions for those with this responsibility.

Why the emphasis on line and staff relationships? In some properties, roles are reversed. Production personnel prepare items with those products available to them. Often, little if any input from management/production personnel has been obtained, and technical specialists (purchasers) make decisions with little knowledge about quality, client preferences, and/or equipment or production personnel capabilities. In small facilities where managers assume purchasing duties, there is less of a problem. Still, dietary managers/purchasers must interact with their own supervisors; line-staff relationships become important as financial, labor, and other decisions are made.

Supply of Purchasing Information. The purchasing task includes soliciting information and researching new products. It is important in the fast-changing foodservice industry for managers to keep up with new technology. Purchasing personnel must be in constant contact with many suppliers who, in turn, are in contact with manufacturers, other suppliers, and other facilities. They can be a valuable source of information about "what's new," as they collect new ideas and pass them on to those who can utilize them.

Continuity of Supply. Purchasers must help assure that products are available at the right time. The concept of continuous supply is critical to client satisfaction. From the perspective of production personnel, it is the "fault" of purchasing personnel if required products are not available when needed. Purchasing staff must expand their responsibilities to include *expediting* (following up on orders to help assure that suppliers meet contractual requirements regarding quality, quantity, delivery dates, etc.).

Purchasing Success Affects Profits. Many institutional facilities operate cash operations (cafeteria lines, banquet functions, etc.) which are planned to yield a profit. Reduced costs brought about by more effective purchasing increase profits. An example illustrates the significant impact which purchasing has on profits. Assume two identical facilities: through effective purchasing, one is able to reduce its food costs by 5 percent.

	FACILITY A		FACILITY B
Sales	$100,000		$100,000
Less Food Purchased (40%)	40,000	Less 95% of $40,000	38,000
	$ 60,000		$ 62,000
Less Other Costs	5,000		5,000
"Profit"	$ 10,000		$ 12,000

Note that a 5-percent decrease in purchased food costs ($38,000 rather than $40,000) results in a 20-percent increase in profit level ($12,000 instead of $10,000). Isn't it interesting! All of the $2,000 in decreased food costs "fell" to the profit line—which increased by $2,000. Want to save costs? If so, increase purchasing effectiveness!

USE OF PURCHASE SPECIFICATIONS

A purchase specification describes the quality requirements for products purchased by the dietary operation. Specifications must be developed and given to suppliers before orders are placed, so that price quotations consider the desired quality of the products needed. The dietary department will benefit greatly from developing purchasing specifications for the most expensive and frequently used items.

The term "quality" refers to the suitability of a product for its intended use. The closer a product comes to being "suitable," the greater is its quality. Quality does not always refer to the highest possible quality. For example, large olives—which are perfectly shaped and of uniform size (and also expensive)—are not necessary if the product is to be chopped for a salad. A "broken pieces" product is acceptable; it is the proper quality of olive. The term "quality" means that the product serves the purpose *for which it is intended* better than any other product.

The concept of quality can be related to price. This relationship is defined as "value"; in fact, price and quality cannot really be separated. A product becomes a better value when quality remains constant and the price decreases, or when quality increases and the price stays the same. Conversely, a product represents a lower value when the price stays the same and the quality decreases, or when the quality stays the same and the price increases.

The purchase specification is a quality statement that indicates what requirements must be met in order for a product to be "suitable" for its intended purpose. After the dietary manager decides what is needed, he or she must describe the quality characteristics acceptable for products used in the operation. There may be more than one specification written for each product. For example, preportioned hamburger patties of several sizes may be necessary for different entrees. If olives are used for garnishes in a catered event as well as for the salad bar, two different products are needed.

Responsibility for Developing Specifications

The dietary manager must accept primary responsibility for developing food-purchase specifications; however, there are several sources of information:

Suppliers. Suppliers generally have very detailed information about the products they sell. They can be asked for comments about purchase specifications as they are developed.

Dietary Staff. In large facilities with specialized purchasing departments, production personnel must ultimately decide what quality is necessary. Their role in developing a quality purchase specification includes (a) accurately defining product need, (b) providing expertise in developing the purchase specifications, (c) making suggestions about which suppliers should be contacted, and (d) evaluating and testing samples and trial order products.

Purchasing Staff. Personnel with primary purchasing responsibilities can also provide much helpful input as purchase specifications are developed. They can learn about products by reading trade magazines, attending trade shows, visiting suppliers and competitors' properties, and reading material published by the U.S. Department of Agriculture, trade associations, and various other sources.

Minimum Requirements for Specifications

Certain requirements are generally necessary for all specifications:

1. Specifications must accurately describe quality aspects;
2. They must be realistic; quality definitions cannot be so strict that few or no products will be acceptable;
3. Specifications must be stated in clear and simple terms;
4. Specifications should enable suppliers to provide readily available products;
5. Specifications must be written so as to make it possible for several suppliers to quote prices and supply products;
6. Specifications must provide some flexibility for both the supplier and the buyer.

Figure 4.1 shows a format for general information that can be incorporated into purchase specifications.

Advantages and Disadvantages of Purchase Specifications

There are several basic advantages to the use of purchase specifications. Specifications provide a clear understanding of required products. There are likely to be fewer "communication" problems between the facility and supplier, since both parties will clearly understand the quality of products required. There are likely to be reduced purchasing costs, because the dietary manager and others think carefully about the required quality of product. They are less likely to purchase products of

____

(name of dietary operation)

1. Product name: ______________________________

2. Product used for:

   Clearly indicate product use (such as olive for garnish, hamburger patty for grill-frying for sandwich, etc.).

3. Product general description:

   Provide general quality information about desired product. For example, "iceberg lettuce; heads to be green, firm without spoilage, excessive dirt or damage. No more than 10 outer leaves; packed 24 heads per case."

4. Detailed description:

   Purchaser should state other factors that clearly identify the desired product. Examples of specific factors, which vary by product being described, include:

   - Geographic origin
   - Variety
   - Type
   - Style
   - Grade
   - Size
   - Portion size
   - Brand name
   - Density
   - Medium of pack
   - Specific gravity
   - Container size
   - Edible yield, trim

5. Product test procedures:

   Test procedures occur when the product is received and as or after the product is prepared/used. Thus, for example, products to be at a refrigerated temperature upon delivery can be tested with a thermometer. Portion-cut meat patties can be randomly weighed. Lettuce packed 24 heads per case can be counted.

6. Special instructions and requirements:

   Any additional information needed to clearly indicate quality expectations can be included here. Examples include bidding procedures, if applicable, labeling and/or packaging requirements, and delivery and service requirements.

FIGURE 4.1 PURCHASE SPECIFICATION FORMAT

higher quality than necessary. Increased competition can also result, as several suppliers quote prices on the same product.

Specifications help in the receiving process; the staff member receiving products will have an understanding consistent with that of the purchaser about required quality.

There are some potential disadvantages to using purchase specifications. Time, effort, and expertise are required, and there will be an occasional need for updating; the development of purchase specifications requires increased work for someone on the staff. Another potential problem is that the minimum quality desired may become the maximum quality delivered.

In addition to purchase specifications, some general information is needed for all orders placed by the dietary manager. The following information should *not* be included in specifications for each product, but should instead be provided to the eligible suppliers as general information:

- Delivery instructions
- Names / positions of personnel authorized to purchase / receive products
- General bidding / ordering procedures
- Qualifications of eligible suppliers
- Quantity needed
- Agreed-upon price
- Purchase unit size

MEATS

Specification factors can include:

- Inspection (mandatory)
- Grading (if desired)
- IMPS/MBG descriptions
- Weight/thickness limitations
- Fat limitations
- State of refrigeration
- Miscellaneous (tying, boning, packaging, etc.)

SEAFOODS

Specification factors can include:

- Type (fin fish or shellfish)
- Market form (whole, eviscerated, etc.—fin fish; alive, whole, shucked, etc.—shellfish)
- Quality requirements (describe flesh, eyes, skin, gills, etc.
- Grade (if desired)
- Inspection (voluntary)
- Processing requirements

POULTRY

Specification factors can include:

- Kind (chicken, turkey, duck, goose)
- Class (typed by age)
- Grading
- Inspection (mandatory)
- Style (whole, breasts, breasts w/ribs, etc.)
- Size (weight limitations)
- State of refrigeration
- Grade (if desired)

FRESH FRUITS AND VEGETABLES

Specification factors can include:

- Grade (if desired)
- Variety
- Size
- Type of pack
- Count per container
- Growing area

PROCESSED FRUITS AND VEGETABLES

Specification factors can include:

- Grade (if desired)
- Drained weight
- Packing medium
- Can (container) size

FIGURE 4.2 PURCHASE SPECIFICATION FACTORS

In addition to the general information, some specific information must be provided for each product purchased. Figure 4.2 includes purchase specification factors applicable to some categories of food products purchased by dietary managers.

DETERMINING QUANTITY OF FOOD TO PURCHASE

It is very important that the proper quantity of food products be purchased to minimize the following problems:

1. Excessive money tied up in inventory. Cash flow and other problems arise when available cash must be used to pay suppliers rather than for another purpose;
2. Need to pay increased insurance, interest, and storage costs because of improper inventory management;
3. Possibility of quality deterioration and product damage with longer storage times;
4. Risks of theft and pilferage.

There are also problems when insufficient quantities of products are purchased:

1. Stockouts may result. There can be problems with client dissatisfaction, last-minute changes in production scheduling, and "small batch" cooking (with inefficient use of labor) when necessary products are unavailable;
2. Emergency and rush orders may need to be placed. These take time, cost money, and create anxiety;
3. Discounts from volume purchases (which can reduce product cost) are lost.

EP and AP Conversions

Three abbreviations are often used in dietary management:

- EP refers to edible portion (EP) and means the raw, uncooked quantity after all trimming is done; it is the quantity that one actually cooks.
- AP, on the other hand, means "as purchased" (AP), and refers to the untrimmed quantity in the same form in which it was purchased; it is the amount for which one pays.
- EY refers to edible yield (EY), and is determined by calculating the percentage difference between what is bought and what becomes the useable product.

Using these three abbreviations correctly can be tricky at times, but if you are purchasing precut, portion-control steaks of fish fillets, and cooking and presenting them just that way, the EP and AP costs are the same. In the case of fruits and vegetables, EP costs can be far different from AP, as skins, cores, seeds, and so on are discarded and the end product is presented in its final form. The same is true for a cut of beef, which must have excess fat and bone removed prior to cooking and service.

The formula to determine (EP) edible portion is:

$$\text{EP cost} = \text{AP} / \text{EY}$$

This can be determined by weighing or measuring what amount of product remains after it is processed into the form needed to be served. An example would be the following:

Filet Tenderloin Price:	\$6.75 per pound
Weight untrimmed:	5.0 pounds
Weight trimmed into useable product:	4.0 pounds

The edible yield (EY) is 4.0/5.0 or 80%

Knowing that the EY is 80% and the (AP) price is \$6.75 per pound, the EP cost is calculated as follows:

$$\text{EP} = \$6.75/80\%$$
$$\text{EP} = \$8.44$$

Therefore, the actual price for the usable filet tenderloin is \$8.44 per pound. Particularly with beef products, the EP cost could vary significantly, depending upon how much fat trimming and bone needs to be discarded in order to reach the usable portion for the client.

Assessing Quantity Needs

Products can be purchased for immediate use or inventory:

Immediate use. Perishable products (such as fresh produce, bakery, and dairy items) must be purchased in a quantity which can be used within a very short time period;

Inventory use. Non perishable products (such as frozen meats and canned grocery items) can be purchased in quantities which permit longer storage times if this is desirable.

In either instance, the quantity to be purchased is an important consideration. Basic procedures involve the following calculations:

For perishable products:

Quantity needed (–) Quantity available = Quantity to purchase

(If five cases of lettuce are needed and two cases are available in the walk-in refrigerator, three cases should be purchased.)

For inventory products:

Quantity desired in inventory (–) Quantity available = Quantity to Purchase

(If eight cases of 6 #10 cans of corn are desired for inventory and five cases are available, three cases should be purchased [8 cases needed – 5 cases available = 3 cases to purchase].)

Procedures must be developed to assess the quantity of items needed for immediate use and for inventory.

Purchase for Immediate Use

Normally a standard procedure is utilized to determine the quantity of perishable products needed for immediate use:

1. The dietary manager and purchasing staff must "know" the general usage rates of these products. For example, in an average three-day buying cycle, a specific number of cases of various products, pounds of fresh meat, and number of chicken fryers are used;
2. Purchasers then determine the quantity of each product available and subtract it from the quantity deemed necessary to determine the amount to purchase;
3. Routine quantities needed must be adjusted if the volume of meals to be produced fluctuates;
4. The need to revise forecasting procedures becomes obvious when spoilage or waste occurs (suggesting that excessive quantities are being purchased) and/or as stockouts and "emergency" orders consistently occur (suggesting that inadequate quantities are being ordered).

Generally, through a trial-and-error process, purchasers can establish a useful, reasonably accurate process to determine necessary quantities of perishable products.

Dietary managers can use a quotation call system to purchase perishable products. Using the Perishable Product Quotation Call Sheet form in Figure 4.3, the quantity to order can be calculated (columns 1–4) and suppliers eligible for selling to the facility can be asked to quote current prices. (Since all sellers have copies of required specifications, prices should be quoted for products of similar quality.)

Orders can be awarded to the supplier quoting the lowest price on a by-order or by-item basis. (Minimum delivery weights and/or dollar minimums are of concern with the latter alternative.)

Purchase for Inventory: Minimum/Maximum Systems

Determining purchase quantities of nonperishable products presents a different set of circumstances to the dietary manager; he or she can buy either for short-term use or long-term (inventory) storage. When buying for inventory, he or she needs an accurate and efficient method of calculating the amounts of nonperishable products to purchase. A minimum/maximum system of inventory management may prove useful. It is based on two reference points for each product included:

1. ***The minimum allowable*** quantity of the product (inventory levels should not fall below this figure);

Item (1)	AMOUNT Needed (2)	On Hand (3)	Order (4)	SUPPLIER NAME A & B Co. (5)	Green Prod. (6)	XYZ Co. (7)
Spinach	6 cs	2½ cs	4 cs	22/cs = 88	19.88=79.40	21.70=86.80
Ice Lett.	8 cs	1 cs	7 cs	17/cs = 114	16.75=117.25	18.10=126.70
Carrots	3 20#	20 #	2 20#	14.70=29.40	13.90=27.80	13.86=27.50
Cabbage	2 sacks	½ sack	2 sacks	18.60=37.20	18.00=36.00	18.10=36.20
				$861.40	$799.25	$842.15

FIGURE 4.3 PERISHABLE PRODUCT QUOTATION CALL SHEET
Source: Jack D. Ninemeier, *Planning and Control for Food and Beverage Operations.* Third Edition. Educational Institute of American Hotel and Motel Association, East Lansing, Mich., 1990.

2. ***The maximum allowable*** quantity of the product (inventory levels should not rise above this figure).

By calculating how much of the product is needed to bring the inventory level to maximum at the time of delivery, the dietary manager can determine the quantity to order.

Definitions of terms used in the minimum/maximum system follow:

Purchase unit—the package, container or amount in which a product is usually purchased, that is, a *case* (containing, for example, six cans), a *pound* (of fresh meat), or a *drum* (of fat for deep-fat frying);

Usage rate—number of purchase units normally used between deliveries. If a facility generally uses four cases of canned pears between any two monthly deliveries, the usage rate of canned pears is four cases. Naturally, the usage rate will vary over a short period, so the dietary manager will have to use trial-and-error methods for an extended period to arrive at an accurate estimate of amounts used;

Lead time—the number of purchase units used from the time the product is ordered until it is delivered. If two cases of canned pears are used between order and delivery, the lead time is two cases. There are two ways that lead time can be determined: (1) The time required for an "average" order, or (2) The time required for the longest order.

If usage and safety (minimum) levels have a "cushion" for unanticipated problems, a small variance in lead time isn't critical. If these two numbers are tightly calculated, a longer lead time is warranted.

Other situations where a dietary manager should consider allowing long lead times are when (1) suppliers aren't dependable; (2) there is only one supplier;

(3) the dietary operation is in a remote location; or (4) there are erratic conditions in markets, distribution channels, and so on.

Safety level (minimum level)—the lowest allowable number of purchase units in inventory. This safety factor helps prevent stockouts by allowing for unexpected increased use, for late deliveries, and so on. Setting the safety level requires consideration of other factors:

1. ***Lead time.*** If delivery becomes less frequent, the number of lead units increases. If delivery times and frequency aren't predictable, the safety level should be increased;
2. ***Usage rate.*** If product usage rises, safety levels may need to be increased to reduce the possibility of a stockout. Clients will be especially dissatisfied if the dietary department runs out of a popular item.

Order point—the number of purchase units in stock indicating that an order should be placed. In other words, when a product is ordered at the order point, the quantity in stock will drop to the safety (minimum) level by the time the order is received. In numerical terms, the number of purchase units at the order point equals the sum of lead time units and safety level units.

EXAMPLE: Given that: lead time = 6 cases; safety level = 7 cases
lead time units + safety level units = order point units

$$6 + 7 = 13$$

The purchaser should order additional units when there are 13 cases on hand (order point). By the time the order is delivered, only 7 cases (safety/minimum level) will remain:

order point units – lead time units = safety level units

$$13 - 6 = 7$$

Maximum level—maximum number of purchase units allowed in inventory. The maximum level is equal to the usage rate (units used during order period) plus the safety level (minimum units allowed in inventory).

Examples of the process which incorporates the components of the minimum/maximum system are presented in Figure 4.4.

The minimum/maximum system can best be used:

1. for food products that are standardized, i.e., when quality characteristics do not change between orders and products are readily available from more than one supply source;
2. when prices are relatively stable;
3. when products are used in essentially consistent quantities;
4. for products that are costly;
5. for products purchased in large quantities;
6. when products will continue to be used in the future;
7. when products do not have a limited shelf life;
8. when desired maximum quantities do not present storage space problems.

Stated another way, there is little practical need to use the minimum/maximum system for inexpensive, low-volume, nonperishable items that have a long storage life. As these products are withdrawn from inventory, they can be reordered; there is less concern for lead time.

Assume:

Purchase unit = case
Usage rate = 3 case per day
Order period = monthly (30 days)
Monthly usage rate = 3 cases/day × 30 days = 90 cases
Lead time = 4 days
4 days @ 3 cases per day = 12 cases
Safety level = 12 cases
Order point

Lead time	+	Safety level	=	Order point
12 cases	+	12 cases	=	24 cases

Maximum level

Usage rate	+	Safety level	=	Maximum level
90 cases	+	12 cases	=	102 cases

Quantity to buy at order point:

If an order for a product is to be placed when the order point is reached, the following process is used:

Units at order point	24 cases
Order monthly usage rate	90 cases
Total cases will equal	114 cases

However, during time from order to delivery (lead time), daily usage rate has continued; deduct lead time (12); 114 cases – 12 cases = 102 cases (maximum level from above)
Maximum stock level will then be maintained.

Quantity to buy before order point:

If any order is to be placed *before* the order point is reached (as would occur when an order of many products is being put together for price quotations from suppliers) the following process is used:

Assume 30 cases in storage

Excess over	=	Amount in storage	–	Order point
6 cases	=	30 cases	–	24 cases

Amount to order	=	Usage rate	–	Excess over order point
84 cases	=	90 cases	–	6 cases

The decision to order 84 cases can be proved:

Order 84 cases	84 cases
Amount available	+ 30 cases
Total	114 cases
Less lead time	– 12 cases
Maximum Inventory level	102 cases

Figure 4.4 Minimum/Maximum Purchasing System: Examples

Calculating Order Quantity and Forecasting

Calculating order quantity requires certain factors to be kept in mind. First, the number of people to be served in a given period must be known. Historical client/sales data will be helpful in providing this information. Portion sizes must also be known, as well as the weights and sizes of the various products to be purchased.

Purchasers must know production results to be able to predict accurately how many portions a given amount of purchased goods will yield. The dietary manager must work with the chef and/or the kitchen staff to accurately determine order quantity.

Forecasting is defined as a technique for utilizing past information in a systematic way to estimate future needs. It is a planning function or tool for production used by the manager in estimating the amount of food to prepare, scheduling equipment and planning labor for the preparation and service of food for the customer.

In the past, the good forecaster was a person who could be the most accurate in determining customer menu item selections. This individual bore the responsibility for forecasting amounts of menu items that allowed cooks to feel secure in preparing these amounts. Some forecasters felt the pressure of "not running out" so strongly that they over-forecast. Over-forecasting led to leftover or wasted food and under-forecasting led to food that ran out before customer demand was satisfied.

The emphasis on forecasting in a foodservice organization depends upon the philosophy of the management. The most rewarding results of an accurate forecast are customer satisfaction, personnel pride, job satisfaction, manager confidence, operational controls, and profit or break-even financial status.

Customer satisfaction is one of the most important results of an accurate forecast method and a well-managed production operation.

Personnel pride and job satisfaction occur in the food production area if menu items meet quality standards and are available when the customer wants to eat a meal. The personnel tension or stress within the work areas is likely to be reduced when the quantities of food items to produce are at an accuracy level that results in opportunities to have a well-run production area.

Manager confidence is attained when the manager is provided with information for managing scarce resources, thus improving the bottom line and accountability.

Operational accuracy is attained when forecast records are used as an operational tool in a well-structured production unit.

Profitable financial status is enhanced or improved with forecasting control. With control, over- and under-production costs are minimized with reduced chances of preparing too much or too little of the menu items.

Actions needed by the foodservice manager to forecast menu items are summarized below:

1. Select a forecasting team consisting of a foodservice manager, forecaster, head cook, and data recorder, and identify a team leader;
2. Discuss the concept of updating the forecasting method and review anticipated results;
3. Review the current forecasting method and evaluate the data accuracy;
4. Study and revise, if necessary, the menu, recipes, production scheduling, and customer choices of menu items. Each of the documents must be current and must contain accurate information including dates, days of week, menu item forecast, and the amount actually sold (or customer demand);
5. Revise food production documents, if needed, or establish some draft documents, such as menu, recipes, production schedules, and customer choices or sales information, to enhance the forecasting method.

Overview of Accounting Records in Purchasing Process

Personnel with accounting or bookkeeping responsibilities generally pay the bills. To do this effectively, they must work within a system that assures them at the time of payment that the items to be paid for were, in fact, ordered and received.

The role of the accounting department deserves special attention in this discussion about purchasing, since all products received must be paid for. Designing a system that makes the accounting function an integral part of the purchasing task is very important. In small dietary operations, the owner or manager may be both the purchaser and the bill-payer. As operations become larger, these tasks are split between operations and accounting or bookkeeping and "office" personnel. As dietary operations grow bigger still, the purchasing responsibilities for receiving and/or storage may be assumed by the accounting department in an increased effort to separate duties. This result is desirable to reduce the possibilities of theft and fraud, which are otherwise more possible when one official is responsible for everything.

Typically, a flow of "paperwork" is used to help the dietary manager, facility accountant-bookkeeper, and supplier communicate with each other. The term "source document" refers to the source of original entry for financial information into the accounting system. For example, a time card may be a source document for payroll. Several source documents will be discussed in the purchasing system below. As accounting systems are designed, there is always a trade-off between accuracy and practicality. While some paperwork is necessary, it is obvious that more-than-necessary accounting forms can be burdensome and less than cost-effective; the output (information) is not worth the input (time and effort) required. Let's look at the flow of source documents in small and large dietary operations.

Small Dietary Operations

In a small dietary operation, several procedures might be used to process bills for payment. Figure 4.5 reviews the source documents and flow of accounting information in a small facility, from the time that an order is placed until the supplier is paid.

Quantities of products to be ordered are determined through a visual observation of what's available in storage, a production forecast, and/or study of physical and perpetual inventory records. Quantities, prices, and so on, are entered on a purchase record form (see Figure 4.6) when the order is placed with the distributor sales representative. A copy is also sent to the employee(s) with receiving duties. When the products are received, incoming items are accepted only if they have been noted on the purchase record form. Incoming products are also compared against the accompanying supplier's delivery invoice, which is signed only if it agrees with the purchase record (and if product quality meets requirements of the purchase specifications).

At the end of the day or shift, the purchase record forms and delivery invoices are forwarded to the manager or bookkeeper. The bookkeeper has several tasks to perform. He or she must:

- assure that there are no differences in quantity and/or price between items ordered (purchase record) and received (delivery invoice);
- assure that arithmetic extensions on the delivery invoice are correct;
- file the invoice with the purchase record attached for payment; pull the invoice or statement at the appropriate time and ready it for payment.

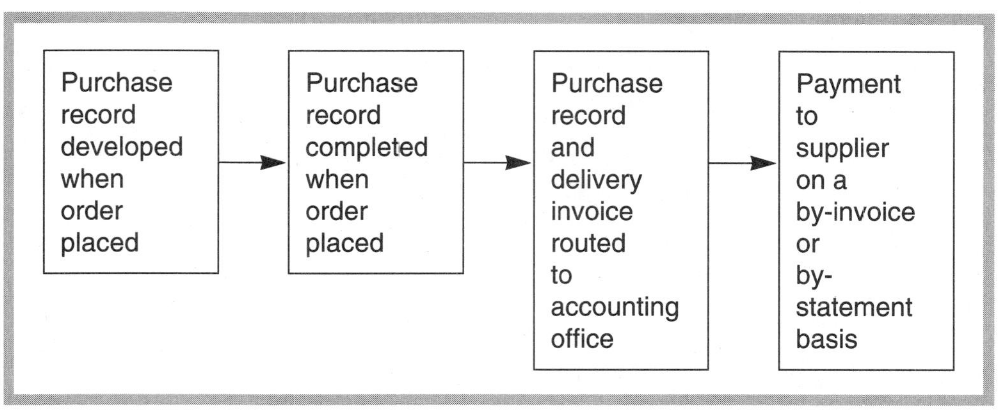

Figure 4.5 Source Document Flow in Small Facility

(supplier)

Date Ordered	Item Description	Unit	Price	Number Units Purchased	Total Purchase Cost	Invoice #	Comments

FIGURE 4.6 PURCHASE RECORD

LARGE DIETARY OPERATIONS

Procedures may be modified by larger dietary facilities as outlined in Figure 4.7. A purchase requisition (Figure 4.8) may be used by storeroom personnel to inform purchasing personnel about additional products which must be purchased. Request for price quotations (Figure 4.9) and purchase orders (Figure 4.10) are then com-

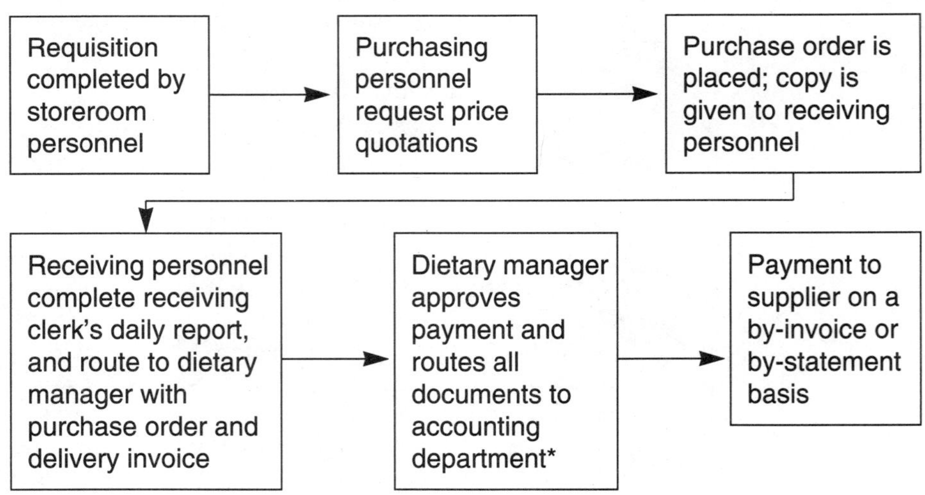

*In some facilities, forms may be routed to the purchasing department which matches its copy of the purchase order before forms are forwarded to the accounting department.

FIGURE 4.7 SOURCE DOCUMENT FLOW IN LARGE FACILITY

Purchase Requisition

Needed by ______________________ Requisition Number ______________________
(Department)

Date needed ______________________ Date ______________________

Item	Purchase Unit	Number of Units	Specification Number

____
(signature of authorizing staff member)

FIGURE 4.8 PURCHASE REQUISITION
Source: Dietary Managers Association. *Professional Procurement Practices: A Guide for Dietary Managers.* 1991. (pg. 183.)

Request for Price Quotation

Date ___________ Request Number ___________

To

(supplier/address)

Please quote your price and delivery on the following products. Return to this office by ________

____

Product Description	Quantity			Price	
	Unit	Total		Per Unit	Total

Date of Delivery ____________________ Request by

Price valid for ____________________ (number of days)

____________________ (company)

Signed ____________________ (supplier)

____

____

____________________ (address)

____________________ (authorized signature)

____

____

____________________ (address)

____________________ (authorized signature)

FIGURE 4.9 REQUEST FOR PRICE QUOTATION

Source: Dietary Managers Association. *Professional Procurement Practices: A Guide for Dietary Managers.* 1991. (pg. 186.)

Purchase Order

Purchase Order Number ____________ Order Date ____________________

Payment Terms ______________

To ______________________________ From/Ship to ______________

(supplier) (name of foodservice)

______________________________ ______________________________

(address)

______________________________ Delivery Date ______________

(address)

Please Ship

Quantity Ordered	Description	✓	Units Shipped	Unit Cost	Total Cost

Total Cost ____________________

IMPORTANT: This Purchase Order expressly limits acceptance to the terms and conditions stated above, noted on the reverse side hereof, and any additional terms and conditions affixed hereto or otherwise referenced. Any additional terms and conditions proposed by seller are objected to and rejected.

____

(authorized signature)

FIGURE 4.10 PURCHASE ORDER

Source: Dietary Managers Association. *Professional Procurement Practices: A Guide for Dietary Managers.* 1991. (pg. 189.)

pleted by purchasing staff to formally order products. A copy of the purchase order is sent to the receiving and accounting departments. When products are accepted, the receiving clerk must compare the purchase order and delivery invoice, and must assure that purchase specifications are complied with. Additionally, a receiving clerk's daily report is completed. Each of these forms, when completed for each order received, can be forwarded to the accounting personnel.

Accounting-bookkeeping staff must perform the same basic functions used by personnel in small facilities to process bills for payment. These will be reviewed later in this chapter. One additional duty is the need to match up the documents with the receiving clerk's daily report.

Price Reduction Procedures

Both the dietary manager and suppliers are concerned about the price of products to be purchased. There is frequently a range of prices within which compromise is possible. Dietary managers want to spend at the lower end of that price range; paying less is to their benefit. Suppliers want to sell at the high end of that price range; collecting more is to their advantage. Dietary managers are not doing their job when they simply ask for a price for necessary products and then pay it.

What Is the "Right" Price? What is the right price? It depends on whether the question is answered by the dietary manager or the supplier. Holding quality constant, the dietary manager wants to pay as little as possible, and sets an upper limit to what he or she will pay. It is affected by:

1. How badly the product is desired. The range of prices which will be paid increases for necessities and decreases for optional purchases;
2. How much other suppliers charge. Competition is a great equalizer of prices. Over a long time period, a buyer will not pay more for a product than he or she must pay elsewhere.

The seller obviously wants to receive as much as possible for the products being sold and sets a minimum limit to the amount he or she will accept. It is affected by:

1. What prices other suppliers are charging for a similar quality product;
2. Whether the buyer is price-conscious. (Some purchasers emphasize price concerns above quality, service, and other aspects of purchasing decisions.);
3. Supplier's cost. A supplier must generally at least cover the cash cost for the product being sold;
4. Supplier's overhead and profit requirements. His or her definition of a "fair" price would obviously be one that contributes a reasonable amount to associated overhead and profit requirements;
5. His or her control of the market. When a supplier has few competitors, prices will be set at a rate that is favorable ("fair") to the supplier. As competition increases, prices will be adjusted downward.

Procedures to Reduce Purchase Price. Dietary managers can use several procedures to reduce the purchase price of products:

Negotiate with the seller. The "art" of negotiation can be a most effective procedure to reduce purchase price;

Purchase in larger quantities. Suppliers may provide discounts for volume purchases. Careful study may indicate that these discounts benefit the dietary operation;

Re-evaluate the need for high-cost items. As the prices of optional items (such as garnish ingredients and menu items which do not need to be offered) increase, creative judgment may suggest that lower-cost products can be substituted for these high-price items;

Pay cash. When possible, pay cash, to provide an incentive for a supplier to reduce prices. He or she may have cash-flow problems, and this alternative can frequently benefit both the buyer and the supplier;

Speculate about purchase price trends. If the dietary manager anticipates rising or falling prices, he or she may take advantage of probable price changes by increasing or decreasing the quantities of products purchased;

Change the purchase unit size. Price per pound, quart, and so on may decrease as larger packaging units are purchased. For example, one pound of flour may cost less when purchased in a 100-pound sack than when bought in a 10-pound unit;

Use a new kind of buying. For example, cooperative (pool) purchasing may be helpful. This plan, which involves combining needs from several facilities in order to increase purchase quantities, may yield cost savings because of volume purchase discounts;

Use competitive bidding procedures—either formally or informally. These can be very effective price-reduction techniques. Too many dietary purchasers get comfortable with a supplier and fail to get competitive prices for needed products (this strategy will be discussed later in this chapter);

Enter into creative price agreements with suppliers. For example, some suppliers, when assured of the business, will agree to a price markdown based on changing wholesale market prices. Another possibility is long-term commitments at lower prices for purchases in a predetermined quantity;

Take advantage of promotional discounts (for new or slow-moving products) and "opportunity buys" (for discontinued or damaged products which are usable);

Bypass the supplier and purchase directly from a distributor / manufacturer / grower if you are a large-volume purchaser. Cost savings from eliminating the middleman can be significant.

The Art of Negotiation. Dietary managers can influence the prices paid for required products. The practice of negotiating prices must be on the list of potentially useful tactics to obtain low prices. Negotiation is simply a process used to reach agreement on all matters important to a purchase. Examples of concerns include product specifications, delivery times, and price.

Both buyer and seller must "give and take" in the process of reaching agreement. The objective is to show that the best interests of both parties are served when they move closer to meeting each other's objectives.

Basic principles of negotiation can help the dietary manager become an effective "persuader." These include:

1. The dietary manager must know about limitations. Can he or she obligate the dietary operation? Are there price or total cost limits beyond which top administrative input is required?
2. *Almost all* purchases should involve some price negotiation. Major purchases involving significant costs certainly deserve the effort. Small cost items routinely purchased over a long time period also represent large dollar values;
3. The dietary manager must know that he or she is negotiating with the proper official. While salespersons might be authorized to make minor price adjustments, major price negotiations may need to be conducted with the sales manager or another officer of the company;
4. A formal meeting should be held for discussing major price items. Rarely can a "hallway chat" or telephone conversation be adequate for large-dollar concessions;
5. Purchasers should know in advance what they will initially offer and the highest price they can pay. They should also attempt to consider what concessions

the supplier is likely to make. Other aspects of the purchase agreement should be thought out. For example, will the purchaser provide reduced services for a lower price?

6. The conversation should not become emotional; it should remain calm, professional and friendly;
7. Areas of agreement should be highlighted. Also, when the supplier has conceded a point, the next one brought up by the purchaser should be one that he or she doesn't mind losing;
8. The agreement, once made, should be summarized in writing;
9. Purchasers should not lie or make threats they can't live with. For example, to lie about "the other guy's prices" or to suggest that "I can take my business elsewhere" (if this can't be done) are not statements made by an effective negotiator;
10. Suppliers must be able to predict the effect of their negotiations; they should understand that they will get the order if their price is low and, conversely, they will not get the order if their price is high;
11. The purchaser should be concerned about major points of the negotiation; he or she shouldn't get wrapped up in details unless or until it is necessary;
12. A buyer should negotiate for the long term. Be alert to the need to make short-term concessions that might lead to an increased advantage over the long run. For example, to pay a bit more for a product when it is plentiful may prompt the supplier to give the buyer first priority when the supply is limited;
13. The purchaser should be sure that all information and facts used in the negotiation are correct.

Payment Policies

Prices paid for products purchased can be affected by the method of payment. Payment procedures must be of concern to the dietary manager even if these decisions are made by top-level administrators. Basic principles can guide the design of an effective payment policy:

1. Bills should be paid when due; it is not to the advantage of the dietary operation to pay bills before they are due, unless a discount is offered;
2. Suppliers do not like to deal with "slow payers." Any bargaining or negotiating advantage is lost if the facility has the reputation of paying bills late;
3. If there is a discount for prompt payment, the operation should take it if cash flow permits (if there is not a discount offered, bills should be paid when due);
4. Payment terms should be negotiated after the price is agreed on (so discounts aren't added to the price before it is quoted);
5. If there is a problem paying a bill, the dietary manager should discuss it with the supplier. Don't try to hide it or make excuses. Most suppliers are willing to work out payment terms with facilities that are honest and professional in their dealings with suppliers;
6. Generally, bills should be paid by check. This helps provide an "audit trail" of purchases from the time the order is placed until it is paid. Internal security (theft) problems are also minimized when cash is not routinely used for payment of purchases. There may, however, be times when cash payments are in order.

Supplier Selection Process

It will do little good for the dietary manager to develop detailed purchase specifications, calculate the quantity of foods to be purchased, and otherwise design and implement an effective purchasing system if competent suppliers cannot be found. Experienced dietary managers realize that not every supplier who "carries the product" should be permitted to do business with the facility. They realize that quality, price, service, and dependability are other concerns that require careful thought before selecting eligible suppliers.

Reasons for selecting the best supplier include:

1. the facility's desire to purchase products at a fair price;
2. the need to consistently obtain the quality and quantity of desired products;
3. the need for products to be received on a timely basis;
4. the amount of information and other assistance a good supplier can provide the dietary operation;
5. the provision of supplier services such as delivery schedules, payment policies, etc., of interest to the operation.

Definition of a "Good" Supplier. The dietary manager will want to deal with "good" suppliers. Therefore, the selection decision will identify the perception of what a "good" supplier is. Figure 4.11 lists characteristics that might be included in the description of a good supplier.

Both dietary managers and suppliers should realize that their own interests are best served as they work together to develop a cooperative relationship. Even price-conscious dietary managers must understand that it takes more than offering the "cheapest" price to make a supplier "good." The product purchased at a low price which does not arrive when it is needed, or the supplier in a "shaky" financial position with his or her own suppliers, cannot be helpful to the dietary operation.

Sources of Information About Suppliers. In order to select a supplier, it is necessary to identify those who can provide the needed products and services. The need to identify as many sources of supply as possible is important. Dietary managers who currently purchase obviously know some suppliers who can provide necessary products and services. However, they may not be aware of all, or even the best, sources of supply. Some techniques to identify possible sources of supply are:

Past experience. The experiences that the dietary manager has had with suppliers who are currently used (or not used) are among the most available and popular methods used to identify eligible suppliers. If a supplier has been acceptable in the past, it is likely that the relationship will continue. The reverse may also be

THE "GOOD" SUPPLIER MUST:

- be honest and fair as he/she does business with the dietary operation.
- know the product, the market, and the needs of the dietary operation.
- consistently be able to meet quality and quantity needs for products on a timely basis.
- operate with and be able to maintain a sound financial position.
- offer fair, reasonable prices.
- desire to improve products and services.
- offer services which the foodservice operation believes to be important.
- be accessible. It should be easy to contact him/her about problems, to negotiate any concerns, etc.
- be careful. The supplier will take care in delivery of products and in after-delivery followup.

FIGURE 4.11 CHARACTERISTICS OF A "GOOD" SUPPLIER
Adapted from Jack D. Ninemeier, *Purchasing, Receiving, and Storage: A Systems Manual for Restaurant, Hotels and Clubs.* CBI Publishing Co., Inc., Boston, Mass., 1983.

true; unless significant changes have occurred within a supplier's operation (such as new management), there is little reason for a dietary manager to believe that past unsatisfactory relationships will be changed;

Salespeople. Good salespersons know who their competition is. Many also have at least some familiarity with other suppliers with whom they do not directly compete;

Supplier catalogs. Catalogs are frequently provided by foodservice equipment dealers, paper and disposable goods companies, grocery (especially "one-stop") shopping outlets, and others. These printed materials will indicate what types of products are available from the supplier, and may also provide important general information about the supplier;

Trade journals and papers. Advertisements in hospitality trade publications can be good sources of information about "who carries what." The printed material received in response to the ads can provide additional useful information about suppliers;

Yellow pages. The local telephone directory should not be overlooked as a very handy, helpful source of supplier information;

Mailing brochures. If the dietary manager has maintained a file of mail advertisements on a by-product basis, this can also help to identify possible suppliers of selected products;

Trade shows. Exhibits manned by representatives attending various local, state, and national shows are additional sources of supplier information. Dietary managers who attend these shows and talk with exhibitors about their product needs can frequently determine whether a supplier and his or her products can be useful;

Other facilities. Dietary managers can talk with staff members in other facilities about their experiences with suppliers, and for ideas about new sources of supplies;

Other sources. Employees of the dietary operation itself, buyer's guides, professional industry associations, directories furnished by Chambers of Commerce, and sales literature distributed by suppliers all provide information.

Factors to Consider When Selecting Suppliers. After possible suppliers have been identified, the dietary manager must evaluate them according to specific selection factors. Generally the process of supplier evaluation must involve an analysis of each supplier's ability to consistently provide necessary products and services at the desired quality, price, and quantity.

Factors which should be considered include:

Location of supplier. A close location shortens delivery times and transportation costs and reduces the possibility of accidents and other problems that cause delay;

Visit to supplier's facility. This trip can help a dietary manager assess sanitation levels (important when food and beverage products are being purchased), procedures used to process orders, variety and quantity of items in current stock, morale levels and expertise of employees, and so on;

Financial stability. A "good" supplier does not go out of business, nor does he or she have difficulty obtaining products from his or her own suppliers because of poor credit management. The Dun and Bradstreet credit service provides, at little cost, valuable information about the financial soundness of potential suppliers;

Technical ability of supplier's staff. Good salespersons are more than just people who take orders. They *know* their products and are able to tell foodservice officials whether products will or will not meet their needs.

Compatible attitudes. The working relationship between the dietary manager and the supplier is enhanced if their business attitudes are compatible;

Honesty and fairness. It is easy and obvious to say that a "good" supplier will be honest and fair. It is much more difficult to determine that a supplier does in fact have these traits. These characteristics cannot be assumed; they must be *seen* in the business practices of the supplier;

Local purchasing. Some institutional administrators desire to purchase from local sources when possible to promote good community relations (although other officials believe the "best" price is a more important concern);

Other purchasing issues. There are several other purchasing issues that must be addressed by the dietary manager. These include security concerns, competitive bidding procedures, make/buy analysis, and capital equipment purchases.

ETHICS IN PURCHASING

While Chapter 15 presents Professional Ethics, the issue of ethics in purchasing must be well understood by all dietary managers. Inappropriate purchasing activity is not only detrimental to operations, but management may find itself in serious trouble neglecting the "common sense" rule of proper purchasing ethics.

A wide variety of theft practices can be used by "creative" purchasers. Examples include purchasing for one's own benefit, purchase of products "wholesale" for selected employees, and so on. Each can be controlled by using an effective purchasing system.

Personnel with purchasing duties may be offered gifts, free meals, attendance at holiday parties, and so on. All of these activities are designed to increase the supplier's business. Basic purchasing ethics suggest that buyers must put the facility first and make decisions on the basis of what is best for it, rather than on the basis of what is best for the buyer.

SECURITY CONCERNS IN PURCHASING

Several security concerns are important at time of purchase. In small facilities where the dietary manager purchases the products, there is less concern about theft at time of purchase. In these operations, concerns might focus on developing an assurance that value (price relative to quality) is received; theft can occur when low-quality products are substituted for high-quality products (even though "high-quality prices" are charged). Even when dietary managers purchase products, other staff members may be involved in receiving and storage activities; security control procedures are still necessary.

As a dietary operation gets larger, more personnel become involved in more purchasing-related tasks; dollar amounts "at stake" also grow larger. More detailed control procedures are important to reduce the possibility of losses due to dishonest suppliers or employees.

Types of Theft at Time of Purchase. There are several common methods of theft at time of product purchase:

Kickbacks. Kickbacks involve the purchaser working in collusion with someone from the supplier's company. In one type of kickback scheme, products are purchased at higher than necessary prices; the two thieves split the difference between the real and inflated price. The "payment" can be in money or gifts; either way, the dietary operation is the loser. This type of theft is best controlled by the facility owner or business office manager routinely reviewing the invoices. (For example, why are so many products purchased from the same supplier?) and soliciting price quotations on a random basis to assure that the prices being paid are the "best" for the required quality product;

Padding the invoice (adding items that were not received and/or increasing the invoice by adding unreasonable "handling" or other charges). Since this scheme works well when the employee who purchases also does the receiving, the dietary manager should design a system which separates the purchasing and receiving tasks;

Fictitious companies. Personnel who purchase can steal by setting up a "dummy" company to submit invoices for products that were never received. A dietary manager should periodically review payees' names on company checks. Unless he/she is specifically familiar with a supplier, checks should *never* be sent to companies with a Post Office box address (unless another address is provided on invoices);

Processing thefts. Suppliers may "send an invoice through" twice if the facility does not have an internal system to verify which invoices have not been paid and cancel invoices that have been paid;

Credit memo problems. Theft can occur when products are not delivered or rejected and when no credit memo is issued to reduce the original delivery invoice by the value of the non-delivered items. Dietary managers should always require that a credit memo be issued and attached to the delivery invoice whenever shortages or related problems occur;

Delivery invoice errors. Intentional arithmetic errors, short weight/counts, quality problems, and similar "mistakes" can cost dietary services money. It is important for both the dietary manager and business-office personnel to check the arithmetic on invoices and for proper receiving practices to be undertaken to catch these "mistakes." Regardless of whether these are innocent errors or intentional frauds, the "bottom line" is the same: the facility is going to lose money;

Quality substitutions. Downgrading a product with the hope that it won't be noticed is another type of theft. Paying more for a lower-quality product can be prevented by proper receiving practices. Brand label substitutions can also become frequent problems if receiving personnel are not familiar with products the facility orders;

Security in Receiving. Security concerns become important at time of receiving since there are many opportunities for employee and supplier theft. Consider the following examples:

- Receiving the wrong items (such as 30-percent fat-content ground beef instead of 20-percent fat-content beef) and paying a higher price for lower-quality products;
- Short weight or count. The dietary operation pays for more product than was received;
- Receiving thawed meat or seafood products which are represented as fresh and for which a higher price is charged;
- Grinding ice into ground meat products, adding fillers such as soy products or non-fat dry milk extenders in applicable products, selling meat with excess trim, etc.;
- Including the weight of ice and/or packaging in the amount of product for which a price is charged.

The list of possible ways that suppliers or their employees can steal from the dietary facility appears endless. Problems can occur with almost any product ordered. To help guard against theft at the time products are received, basic principles should be followed. Receiving tasks should normally not be done by the same person who purchases; someone must be trained to receive. To the extent possible, product deliveries should be made at non-busy times so that receiving staff will have time to correctly receive the product. Receiving staff verify goods against order. A delivery may be rejected, or shortage recognized at that time. Delivery should be made to a specified area of the facility. After receipt, products should be moved to storage immediately, and the salesperson, delivery/route persons, and so on should not be permitted in the storage area. As a final example of security procedures, the receiving door should be locked. An audio signal can be installed to permit delivery staff to signal when they have arrived. With this plan, delivery persons will be under visual supervision of receiving staff during the entire time they are in the facility.

Proper Payment Method Reduces Theft

There are generally two methods used to pay suppliers for purchased products. With the "by-invoice" plan, processed invoices (those approved for payment) are filed by due date and paid when due. For example, if an approved bill is due on August 10, it may be "pulled" on August 6 and processed for payment. It might be signed and mailed on August 7 to allow adequate time for delivery.

Bills can also be paid on a "by-statement" basis. With this plan, processed invoices which have been approved for payment are filed on a "by-supplier" basis awaiting receipt of the statement of account. When the statement is received, applicable invoices are pulled and processed for payment. All invoices covered by the statement (less adjustments, if any, required by credit memos) are paid at one time.

Regardless of whether bills are paid "by-invoice" or "by-statement," similar procedures are necessary to prepare the documents for payment:

1. Invoices must be matched with applicable purchasing documents and with the delivery invoices. All such forms must be compared; the *same* items that were ordered must be received;
2. Any credit memo problems requiring changes to the delivery invoice must be noted and adjustments made;
3. All arithmetic extensions must be verified;
4. Delivery invoices which have been properly processed are noted "approved to pay" by the business office;
5. Invoices are then filed until time for payment.

When invoices are to be paid (either singularly or with others covered by a statement), order and delivery forms should again be checked in a manner similar to that above. Business-office personnel should total all invoices to be paid with one check and should then prepare the check for signing. Each invoice paid should be marked to indicate the date and amount of payment, and the check number. Marking should be done in a way that it is possible to verify payment has been made. (It is important to minimize the possibility of an invoice being paid twice.)

Competitive Bidding Procedures

Competitive bidding incorporates the basic principle that price differences will occur when more than one supplier quotes a price on a similar product. The dietary manager can then accept the lowest quoted price resulting in cost savings to the dietary operation.

Competitive bidding will help assure the dietary manager of getting the lowest price when:

- the order is large enough to justify the time and expense involved,
- specifications are clearly known by all suppliers, and
- there are several suppliers desiring to quote prices on the order.

Competitive bidding can be done through an informal or formal process.

Informal Process. This method is used when one "calls around" for prices. Some informal negotiation might also be possible. For example, before prices are obtained from suppliers, the buyer may attempt to secure a lowered price quotation.

Basic principles of an informal bid purchasing system include:

1. The quoted price and other terms of the agreement must be clearly understood; a purchase decision will be made on the basis of the understanding between the buyer and seller at the time of the price quotation;
2. The price quoted by the supplier must remain "firm" for the length of time needed by the purchaser to make a decision;
3. All suppliers must quote a price on the same level of quality of the product and otherwise agree to comply with the same terms of the order;
4. All eligible suppliers should be allowed to quote on the order;
5. Purchases should be distributed among suppliers whenever possible in order to keep several supply sources interested in dealing with the dietary operation;
6. A purchase order, return telephone call, or other procedure is necessary to confirm the agreed-upon price and other terms under which the order will be placed.

Formal Process. A formal process of competitive bidding is rarely, if ever, used by small facilities. It is more likely to be used by large facilities. In this process, suppliers are invited to submit sealed bids on a detailed, written prospective order. Bid bonds may be required. Most dietary operations will improve their purchasing success by utilizing an informal rather than a formal competitive bidding process.

Prime Vendor

In contrast to competitive bidding, the prime vendor concept is based upon an agreement to purchase the majority of a specified supply category from one vendor. The prime vendor may supply from 60 percent to 80 percent of the items. The remaining percentage is supplied through other vendors. A prime vendor agreement is usually for a specified quantity of items in the category.

Prime vendor purchasing improves the consistency and quality of food purchased because the products do not change with minor price fluctuations, as is common with competitive bidding. Cash flow increases with a known and constant supplier, as lower inventory levels may be established. The receiving process also is more efficient with a reduced number of vendors. Vendor performance has been noted to improve with a prime-vendor agreement because of the value of the contract and the commitment of the customer. Value added services, such as computer software for menu analysis, or order entry, may also be viewed as an advantage resulting from the prime vendor/customer relationship.

Prime vendor purchasing can have several disadvantages, including the loss of a reliable backup vendor, a limited inventory, and an increase in prices due to lower competition. Two methods a buyer can use to help ensure optimal results with a prime vendor system are to choose an efficient and credible vendor, and to establish a periodic bidding process. This process is essential to maintain low cost, and may serve to retain interest and reliability in the backup supplier.

Make/Buy Analysis—Overview

The question of whether to "make or buy" in dietary operations generally relates to the use of **convenience foods:** products that have all or some of the labor necessary to prepare them built into the product at the time of purchase. The subject sometimes creates a subjective debate between those who favor or oppose their use.

Making the Decision

Decisions regarding the usage of convenience foods are important and hard to make. Except for a few "traditional" items (such as frozen French fries, fresh-baked bread products, and some canned grocery items) a great deal of emotion sometimes clouds the convenience-foods issue, and, in the minds of many dietary managers, the definition of convenience foods is not clear. In actuality, since few facilities have their own farms and sources to grow needed fresh-food items, all of the meats, produce, processed fruits and vegetables, seafood, and so on, are purchased in some convenience-foods form; the labor necessary to raise the products is not provided on-site. Canned, dried, and frozen (processed) fruits and vegetables, portioned meats and seafoods, bakery and dairy products, and so on, are all really convenience foods; in these "convenient" forms, they are used by almost every dietary operation.

Make/buy decisions are time-consuming to make if all of the factors which affect the decisions are considered. Some elements—such as the energy costs to bake desserts—aren't known and are difficult to calculate. Others—such as quality and perceived client reactions—are subjective and hard to measure. Ideally, both economic and non-economic factors which affect the make/buy decision must be considered.

A make/buy analysis can be done for almost every product produced by the dietary operation. This is obviously not practical. Some facilities with equipment and space limitations and other "challenges" have, in effect, no decision to make regarding convenience-food usage as an alternative for some products. They must either buy those products ready-prepared or exclude them from the menu.

Decisions Are Not "All or Nothing." Decisions about the use of convenience foods are not of the "all-or-nothing" type. Few facilities use either "all or no" convenience food items. The many types of convenience-food products permit dietary operations to add a little or extensive amounts of on-site labor. Consider one item: loaf bread. It is available in several forms:

- sliced, ready-to-serve;
- unsliced, ready-to-serve;
- frozen, proofed, ready-to-bake;
- frozen, unproofed, ready-to-proof;
- in the form of raw ingredients such as flour, salt, yeast, shortening, etc. (the product can be totally prepared on-site).

According to the needs of the individual dietary operation, more or less labor can be added to loaf bread on-site. The decision to "make or buy" loaf bread is not that simple; it must be modified to consider "how many preparation tasks should be done on-site, or should we purchase it completely made?"

Is a Make-or-Buy Study Necessary? The make-or-buy decision-making process is affected by many factors which must be analyzed, including:

- New product usage. As menus are redesigned and new items are added, dietary managers will need to consider "make or buy" implications of new products;
- Extensive revision of menus;
- Problems with supplier performance. If, for example, suppliers cannot consistently deliver convenience-food products or raw ingredients of the required quality, this may suggest a need to reexamine the form in which the product is being purchased;
- Quality problems. If, for any reason, there is a problem with the existing quality of prepared or purchased products, a make/buy study may be in order;
- Increasing or decreasing client demand for specific products;

- When items must be purchased in very large or very small volumes;
- When the facility has limited space and/or inadequate funds for capital purchases deemed necessary for new (expanded) item production;
- When there is a change in the quality of work or level of experience of current or prospective employees;
- When there is concern about retaining a continuous source of supply.

Factors of Critical Importance

The concerns basic to the purchase of any product apply to the purchase of convenience-food products. Several factors are of critical importance:

- **Quality is important.** If the required quality cannot be purchased in a convenience-food product, no analysis is necessary; the product must be prepared on-site if it is to be available to clients. If an acceptable quality product is available, analysis of other factors becomes necessary. It may be that two producers make an acceptable quality item; analysis then must be among both products *and* the alternative of preparing the item on-site. It is likewise important to assure that the proper quality product can be made by the dietary operation. There may be no alternative but to purchase the required items ready-made because specialized equipment or skill is not available;
- **Quantity is important.** Perhaps so much or so little of a product is needed that the only practical possibility (assuming acceptable quality) is to purchase the item ready-made. On the other hand, perhaps such a small quantity is needed that no source is interested in supplying the item; then it must be made on-site;
- **Cost is important.** When quality is comparable for two options, cost considerations are frequently the primary basis on which a make/buy decision is made. Unfortunately, reality is not so clear-cut. The cost to buy an item is known; the seller sets a price which must be paid. However, when a product is to be prepared on-site, costs must usually be estimated. This is time-consuming and risky; the estimate might be wrong. Therefore a known higher supply cost might be better than a slightly lower, estimated on-site production cost;
- **Service is important.** All of the technical and followup assistance suppliers can provide is important, whether service applies to providing ready-to-serve products or ingredients for on-site production. There may, however, be a larger problem with convenience-food products than for raw ingredients. Continuity of suppliers is of potentially greater concern when convenience foods are purchased;
- **Timing is important.** If the convenience-food product is to be utilized, it must be at the property when needed. If the item is to be prepared on-site, it must be ready at the correct time.

Possible Advantages of On-Site Production

Several possible advantages to on-site production should be considered. Here are some examples:

- If only small quantities of the product are needed, the amounts might be integrated with existing personnel schedules and equipment;
- Quality needs might be better assured through on-site production, supervision, and quality control;
- There may be more assurance of continued supply;
- If no suppliers for the needed product exist, it must be made on-site;
- It may be less expensive;

- On-site preparation may serve to better utilize available personnel and/or equipment;
- There may be "emotional" reasons favoring on-site production for example, less employee resistance and resentment;
- House "specialty" items may need to be produced on-site for marketing reasons.

Possible Disadvantages of On-Site Production

Disadvantages are really the opposite of the benefits cited above. On-site items may be more expensive or of lower quality; equipment and personnel expertise may not be available, and so on. Other possible disadvantages to on-site production include:

- There is less of a purchasing/receiving/storage control problem when, for example, one item (such as a ready-serve entree) must be purchased as opposed to the individual purchase of all the ingredients needed to produce the item "from scratch" at the facility;
- Reliance on skilled cooks to show up daily for work may be more of a problem than reliance on manufacturers to make (and suppliers to deliver) required products. Some of this pressure is relieved when standard recipes are used. Still, someone must prepare the required items;
- More and greater levels of on-site supervision are required when items are produced on-site. Locating and paying these personnel are, then, possible disadvantages to on-site production;
- When facilities are designed and equipment is purchased for convenience-food operations, it is frequently awkward or impossible to utilize on-site production methods.

Possible Advantages to Use of Convenience-Food Products

There are selected advantages to use of convenience foods. Benefits to be evaluated as a make/buy analysis is undertaken include:

- Limited space and equipment may require use of convenience foods; lower capital investments often result;
- Lack of skilled personnel favors convenience-foods use;
- Productivity of production personnel may increase (if labor hours are reduced as convenience foods are used);
- Menu variety can often be increased without the offsetting operating and management control-related problems;
- The quality of convenience-food products might be consistently better than the comparable quality of on-site produced items;
- When all costs are considered, convenience foods might be less expensive than on-site prepared products;
- Product waste might be reduced if portion control items are prepared as they are needed.
- Nationally recognized "brand" convenience foods, such as pizza or tacos may add marketing value.

Possible Disadvantages of Convenience-Food Products

Specific factors in an individual dietary operation may point to disadvantages in the use of convenience foods:

- Quality and cost considerations may be negative factors;
- As costs increase, profits decrease. These two factors must be considered simultaneously;
- Reliance on out-of-facility personnel (for product and supply) may be viewed as a disadvantage;

- Public acceptance might be reduced. Consider, for example, the facility that prides itself on "homemade" menu items and assertively uses this facility "advantage" in marketing efforts to the community. Consider also the facility which believes that the quality of dietary services helps distinguish it from other competitors. If this facility believes that "fresh is best," its fear of decreasing public acceptance would probably establish a policy (or at least a philosophy!) excluding conversion to convenience-food products;
- Increased freezer storage space may be necessary for holding many convenience-food products;
- Employee resentment (perhaps even fear of job loss) may result from the use of convenience foods;
- Reduced employee needs may not be taken advantage of when personnel must be available for production of other on-site prepared items;
- If only one supplier is available, there may be concern that price increases will need to be accepted; there will be no alternative source of supply.

Conclusions

Dietary managers should generally be aware that:

- The dietary operation can best be improved when administrative officials have an open, "neutral" attitude toward convenience foods;
- Convenience-food products may or may not be best for the facility. It depends upon, first, the specific product and, second, the specific operation;
- Dietary managers must recognize the importance of careful analysis to determine whether products should be prepared on-site or purchased in a ready-to serve form;
- While it is time-consuming to consider details of analysis and comparison of products, the time and effort spent to quantify these details are well spent;
- Specific procedures should be followed as an analysis of make/buy alternatives is undertaken. These are reviewed below.

Make/Buy Analysis—Procedures

Specific activities to be performed by purchasing personnel in large facilities include many services necessary to accurately consider the alternative of purchasing convenience foods. These are:

Introduction

- identifying suppliers, along with information about their dependability, expertise, and service;
- identifying available products;
- assembling samples and general information materials;
- discovering accurate cost estimates for the purchase alternative;
- providing other supportive information.

Personnel in production units are required to meet the financial and quality expectations of top-level administrators. Working in close cooperation with them, dietary managers must make the decision, which essentially involves:

- gathering information about the "make" option in the analysis;
- assessing quality differences between purchased and on-site prepared items;
- making the final decision or, at least, a recommendation to their own supervisors.

Make/Buy Analysis Process

Several procedures provide general guidelines to be followed in make/buy analysis.

Step One: Define the problem.
Purchasing and production personnel must know:

- What is prompting the analysis to be undertaken? Perhaps one or more of the factors emphasizing the need for analysis (need for new product, alleged quality issues, convenience, supplier performance problems, etc.) have become a critical concern;
- What will determine the "best" solution? Are quality, cost, service, client acceptance or other factors most important? How will analyses applicable to these and other factors be undertaken?
- What else must be known "up-front?" (Examples include opinions or attitudes of key personnel, definite limitations imposed by space, existing equipment, available funds and corporate-level policies for multi-unit facilities, etc.).

Step Two: Consider quality first.
The need to determine the desired level of quality is obvious. If desired quality cannot be made, it must be purchased; if desired quality cannot be purchased, it must be made.

- If more than one purchased product is available, the analysis will need to assess whether the product should be produced on-site or whether one (and which) of the alternative products is "best."
- Quality is much more than an assurance that samples submitted during the analysis period attain minimal quality expectations. There is a need to assure that all products will have a consistent quality over the life of any resulting purchase decision.

Step Three: Consider costs of all alternatives.
Costs incurred in the purchase of convenience-food alternatives are generally easier to assess than costs of their on-site produced counterparts.

- The direct costs of buying must be converted to an edible portion (EP) per-meal or per-serving cost. Purchase costs often include warehousing and delivery costs incurred by the supplier. If not, these must be added to the product costs.
- There is a wide array of other overhead, direct, and indirect costs associated with provision of convenience foods.

How to Calculate Cost Comparison. An example would be to consider two different meat suppliers, one offers to sell an 8oz New York strip prepared to one's specifications for $7.25 per pound. The other supplier can offer the same specifications, but will not cut or trim the steaks. The price is $5.15 per pound for this untrimmed product. It would appear that the supplier that offers the lower price would gain the business. To accurately determine this, a cost comparison using the (EP) and (AP) conversions would apply. Consider the following:

Supplier A	Supplier B
Precut 8oz New York strips $7.25 per pound cost per steak $3.63	Whole New York strips, 18 pound average, $5.15 per pound Edible Yield 60% EP = 5.15 / 60% EP = $8.58 cost per steak (8oz) $4.29

This example clearly shows that supplier A, although having the higher (AP) price, offers a steak with a cost, in the end, considerably less. This same comparison may be used in determining the purchase of several convenience foods, such as soups, lasagna, stews, and a variety of desserts.

Production of items on-site involves assessment of several categories of other costs:

- Purchase cost of raw ingredients. The cost (converted to edible portion per serving or per meal) must be established. When standard recipes are used, this task is somewhat easier since a definite quantity of raw ingredients is utilized each time a quantity of the product is prepared;
- Indirect costs must be estimated. The categories of costs are the same for both convenience foods and on-site prepared items, including those for purchasing, receiving, and inspection. These may be lower for convenience-food products since a reduced number of ingredients, otherwise handled separately, can be processed together;
- Direct labor costs. Costs of actual product preparation and service should be lower for convenience-food products; this is, after all, one of the major reasons why they are used. However, labor costs are only reduced if total labor hours are cut back with the result that lower total salaries and wages are paid and benefit costs are reduced. If labor hours are not reduced, product costs will be higher, labor costs will be identical, and the "bottom line" will be increased operating costs when convenience foods are utilized;
- Allocated inventory and storage costs. A "fair share" of these costs might be assessed against alternative products being considered. It is possible that storage costs might be higher for convenience foods when frozen storage space is required;
- Direct energy costs. Utility costs incurred in the preparation of on-site items will often be higher than costs incurred in reconstituting convenience foods;
- Capital costs. If new equipment is needed to produce or reconstitute on-site or convenience-food products, these costs must be assessed. Likewise, there must be enough space for the equipment and space costs (for heating, insurance, interest payments, and similar costs) must be prorated.

Step Four: Consider other factors.

In addition to quality and costs, other factors are sometimes important:

- Acceptance of product(s) by employees;
- Suitability of convenience food packaging;
- Expertise of suppliers in providing technical help;
- Consistency of portion sizes;
- Compatibility of product, (either convenience food or on-site prepared) with the market, facility, and equipment.

Step Five: Make comparisons.

After cost and other factors associated with products of acceptable quality have been developed, comparisons of alternatives can be made. Important points include:

- Purchasing-staff input is advisory only; they should not make the final decision;
- Production personnel working with top administrative personnel should be responsible for arriving at the decision;
- Ideas and suggestions should be solicited from affected production department employees;

- It is generally a wise idea, when practical, to ask selected clients about their taste preferences for alternative products.

Step Six: Implement the decision.
After the decision is made, it must be implemented. This involves:

- Developing purchase specifications; in the case of convenience foods this is most effectively done by specifying a brand designation (perhaps with an "or equal" statement if similar products are available);
- Purchasing the required products;
- Purchasing, locating, and installing any necessary equipment;
- Training affected staff in all required procedures;
- Closely monitoring employee and product performance during periods of initial use.

Step Seven: Evaluate the decision.
Even with careful analysis and implementation, it is necessary to evaluate acceptability of the decision and to assure that no problems with product handling have arisen since the implementation of the decision. Careful review of the current operation may suggest additional areas of study, factors which may affect the convenience food/on-site preparation decision, and so on.

THE RECEIVING PROCESS

A typical receiving practice in some institutional foodservice operations permits "whoever is closest to the back door" when a delivery is made to "sign the sheet" and place items in storage. While oversimplified, it is unfortunately an all-too-accurate review of receiving practices which are totally unacceptable.

Forty percent or more of all dollars spent by most dietary services are used to purchase food and supplies. It is essential that the right products in the right quantity at the right price and from the right supplier be received at the right time. It is not possible to be sure that the incoming products are "right" for the facility without paying attention to the receiving process. Dietary managers must implement receiving systems which incorporate basic management principles.

EFFECTIVE RECEIVING SYSTEM COMPONENTS

There are several components in an effective receiving system. Trained staff must be available to perform required tasks. Employees with receiving duties must:

- know quality specifications for each product;
- recognize required quality;
- understand how products are received by the facility;
- know how to handle problems;
- have the time to perform required receiving tasks;
- know how to complete receiving records.

Specialized skills and knowledge learned through training are necessary to do each of the above activities, but it is generally not practical to train all employees. In small facilities, the dietary manager (who may also be responsible for purchasing) and, perhaps, the head cook and/or other responsible person can perform the receiving tasks.

Another requirement for effective receiving is adequate space. In small facilities, a "wide spot in the hallway" may be sufficient. However, as the volume of deliveries increases, additional space becomes important. Generally, the receiving area should be located near the delivery door. (Many union contracts for delivery personnel permit "inside back door" delivery only.) Security concerns arise when non-employees are allowed access to back-of-house areas. Some space is also necessary for receiving equipment. The most space-consuming item may be the receiving scale, but carts, dollies, and other items may also be necessary. If so, space must be allowed for them.

A calculator is necessary if arithmetic extensions are to be verified by the receiving employee. He or she may also need a desk, chair, file cabinet, or other office-style equipment.

A thermometer and other small items are necessary to confirm the internal temperature of products delivered. Clipboard, pencils, and marking and tagging equipment may also be necessary. Plastic or other bins provide a place to put top levels of produce as interior layers are checked. Containers to hold ice removed from fresh poultry and fish help with weighing. Tools to open wooden, cardboard, plastic, and other containers are also helpful.

Receiving Procedures

Several procedures are important to assure that incoming products are properly received:

Step 1: Check against purchase records.

It is helpful to have an in-house record to describe products which have been ordered. A copy of the purchase record can then be sent to receiving personnel so they will know what supplier is to deliver what products, the amount (weight/count) to be delivered, size of purchase unit, agreed-upon price, basic specification information, and approximate delivery date.

Large facilities may use a formal purchase order (see Figure 4.10) to solicit prices, make purchase decisions, and formally commit funds for specified products to a recognized supplier. In these facilities, incoming products should be checked against the purchase order to confirm that products being received are, in fact, those which were ordered.

Without exception, the quantity of all items received must be verified. Said another way, each item must be weighed, counted, and/or measured. Normally, if items are purchased by the count (a case of six #10 cans, a fifty-pound bag of flour, etc.), counting is sufficient. If items are purchased by weight (50 pounds of ground beef, 10 pounds of five-ounce hamburger patties, etc.), items should be weighed. It is also important to randomly weigh portion-control items. If, for example, a six-ounce patty is purchased, the facility may not accept items weighing more than ¼ of an ounce more or less than the agreed-upon weight.

Items should be weighed separately. For example, 15 pounds of pork chops and 15 pounds of ground beef will weigh 30 pounds when received in a shipping carton. However, if 20 pounds of ground beef and 10 pounds of pork chops were ordered, the dietary operation will be paying a higher price than necessary for the ground beef. Ice, packaging material, cardboard casing, and so on should be removed when weighing items. Items purchased by count (such as 96 count lemons or 24 count lettuce) should be counted on a spot-check basis to be sure that the proper size is received;

Step 2: Inspect against specifications.

After the receiver knows that the correct products have been delivered, quality assurance becomes important. Products should be compared with the written purchase specification. Staff with specialized training know and recognize the proper quality. They must take care that all products meet specifications (for example, by detecting chickens that have thawed on the surface, a case of five-ounce rather than six-ounce meat patties, or ground beef which is 30 percent fat instead of 20 percent fat).

Receiving staff should not be rushed by delivery persons. If suppliers are dissatisfied with the time it takes for proper receiving, agreements can sometimes be made to have the products delivered at the supplier's risk with the invoice signed and mailed after thorough inspection;

Step 3: Inspect against delivery invoice.

Products must be compared with the delivery invoice (which the supplier will use as the basis for calculating the bill). It is obviously important that items be included on the delivery invoice in the correct quantity and at the correct price. If there are no corrections to the invoice, the receiving employee will be asked to sign it. One copy should be retained by the dietary operation.

If there are corrections to the invoice (for example, recorded products may not be received or only a partial delivery may have been made), these corrections must be recorded on the invoice before it is signed. Depending upon the supplier's system, a credit memorandum may be used to show the amount which is owed. Signed delivery invoices and other receiving documents should be given at least daily to the dietary manager, accounting department, or other responsible person;

Step 4: Accept (reject) products.

After the receiving person is sure that there are no problems, he or she signs the delivery invoice, indicating that products were received in acceptable order. Products then become the property of the dietary operation.

Receiving staff must be aware of procedures to reject products. It is generally much easier to reject items before they are accepted than it is to return them after they have been accepted. Reasons for refusing products include: they were not ordered, they were not of required quality, the price was not that quoted, and / or they were not delivered on time.

If the receiving employee notes errors during the receiving process, he or she should alert the purchaser, dietary manager, head cook or other personnel. If, for example, a quality problem is noted but the product can still be used, a price reduction might be negotiated. Typically, the receiving employee can neither make this decision nor negotiate a price; the dietary manager must be contacted.

If only a partial quantity is delivered or the required item is not available, the dietary manager should be notified. In these and related instances, a credit memorandum is usually issued by a supplier. Figure 4.12 illustrates a sample credit memorandum;

CREDIT MEMO

No.______________

To: ____

Address: ____

City, State ______________________ Date: ______________

Please send credit for the following:

Invoice	Item	Quantity	Unit of Sale	Unit Price	Extension

Reason:

Delivery Person ______________________ Authorizing Signature ______________________

FIGURE 4.12 CREDIT MEMO

Step 5: Complete receiving report.
Large operations have several uses for a receiving report:

- It provides a record of products received which can be a check on status of and payment for delivery invoices;
- It provides a record of product transfer to storage in facilities where receiving and storage tasks are performed by different personnel;
- It can be used as a partial basis for calculating food costs.

The report with attached invoices can be used as the authorizing source of entry of information about received products in a perpetual inventory system.

A sample of a receiving clerk's daily report is illustrated in Figure 4.13;

Date ______________

Name of Receiving Employee ______________________ Page No. _____ of _____

Supplier	Item	Amount	Purchase Unit	Unit Price	Total Value	Classification		Storage (✓)*
						Direct	Storage	

Totals _____ _____

Receiving Employee ______________________
(signature)

*The final column (Storage ✓) is used to confirm that the receiving employee has placed each delivered item in storage. If there are separate receiving and storage employees, the latter (storeroom clerk) should initial this column to confirm that he or she accepts responsibility for the items.

FIGURE 4.13 RECEIVING CLERK'S DAILY REPORT: FOOD

Step 6: Remove to storage.

After products are received, they must be immediately removed to the proper secure storage area, to prevent deterioration in quality and potential theft.

In some dietary facilities, items are marked or tagged at time of receipt. The delivery date and price can be written directly on the can, case, bottle or other packaging unit before it is placed in storage. This helps with inventory and food cost calculations; the price can easily be recorded without having to "look it up." It also becomes easier to confirm that stock rotation plans are in use; products on the shelves longer will be used first, and fewer items will deteriorate in quality and/or spoil;

Step 7: Monitor Hazard Analysis and Critical Control Point (HACCP) throughout the receiving process.

Three critical control points (CCPs) may be identified in receiving which should not go uncorrected.

1. If product packaging is not intact or signs of product deterioration has occurred, refuse to accept the product and return it.
2. If the refrigerated or frozen product is above 40 degrees or 0 degrees, respectively, refuse to accept the product and return it.
3. If the product is not from an approved, inspected source, reject the order, as one should never order from an unapproved source.

Finally, after these steps have been completed, it is important to confirm that extensions (the number of purchase units times the price per purchase unit) are verified before bills are paid. In some facilities, a dietary employee initially verifies the calculations, which are then checked by an accounting department staff member as bills are processed.

Effective Food Storage Practices

There are three basic concerns to be addressed by the dietary manager as products are stored. Effective storage plans are required to:

- ensure that product quality is retained during storage,
- develop inventory records needed for accounting purposes, and
- prevent theft of items in storage.

If products are effectively purchased and received, it is more likely that items of the proper quality will be available within the dietary operation. However, quality can deteriorate if items are not properly stored. Food must be rotated so that items in storage the longest will be used first. Dating products at time of receiving and a policy that new products are placed under and/or behind those already in storage will help.

Items must be stored at the proper temperature and humidity. Dietary managers should use accurate thermometers to check that temperatures for refrigerated items are kept below 40°F, that dry-storage area temperatures range from no less than 50°F to no more than 70°F and that frozen foods are kept between 0°F and –10°F. Storage records need to include temperature of storage units taken at regular intervals. Food safety during storage is a regulatory requirement; the dietary manager cannot be too careful in keeping the appropriate records.

Foods must be stored in clean storage areas. Routine cleaning for all frozen, refrigerated, and dry-storage areas is important. Effective storage practices also require proper ventilation and air circulation. Ongoing programs to control rodent and insect infestation are necessary. Typically, items should be stored in their original packing containers, and items which absorb odors (such as flour) should be stored away from items that give off odors (such as onions). Most food should be stored in airtight containers, and all products should be stored in covered containers.

Record-Keeping During Storage

Dietary managers must know the quantity of products in inventory and the amount which is used. This practice can help reduce theft, assess food costs, and determine the quantities of products which must be purchased. Generally, it is not sufficient to "place products in storage, take them out when needed, and order more when necessary." Rather, there must be a planned and systematic process to control items in storage. Both a physical inventory system and a perpetual inventory system (for selected food products) can help.

A physical inventory system involves counting products in inventory. This should be done routinely at least once each fiscal period to assess the quantity of items on hand and to determine the actual cost of food used. (This information is needed to develop financial statements when accrual accounting systems are used.)

Many small facilities use only a physical inventory system to track items in storage. With this plan, a once-a-month tally indicates the quantity of items in inventory. Generally, an assumption is made that the value of low-cost items and those in process and in workstation storage areas "average out;" that is, the value of these items remains approximately the same from month to month. Thus, the value of items in storage is represented only by those products which are counted. The "constant value" of low-cost and other items not counted may be added to the total assessed cost of products to determine the inventory value for the period.

It is important that the employee responsible for control of items in storage not be the individual who conducts the physical inventory count. Typically, someone from the accounting department, the dietary manager, and/or another official is responsible for this task. A sample copy of a physical inventory form is illustrated in Figure 4.14. Information from the physical inventory form can be used to calculate monthly food costs.

There are several advantages to use of a physical inventory system. It is easy, and consumes a minimal amount of time. It also enables small dietary facilities to make periodic calculations of product inventory values.

There are, however, several disadvantages to use of only a physical inventory system. For example, a physical inventory only tells the quantity of products in storage; it does not indicate how much product *should* be in storage. It may also be necessary to physically count items in storage each time an order is placed to assess the quantity of items to be purchased.

Small dietary operations should consider using a physical inventory system to assess the quantity of most products in inventory. However, expensive items (meats, seafoods, etc.) might be better controlled through use of a simplified perpetual inventory system.

Perpetual-Inventory System

A perpetual-inventory system keeps track of storage items on a continuous basis. A "running balance" of the quantity in inventory is kept. As items are received and placed in storage, the balance is increased; as items are withdrawn (issued), the balance is decreased.

All dietary operations can probably benefit from using a perpetual-inventory system, at least for expensive and/or theft-prone items. In addition to limiting access and keeping storage areas secure, this procedure helps to provide tight control over high-cost items.

It is easier to use a perpetual-inventory system when a record is kept only of the quantity rather than the value of products in inventory. Since a physical count must still be used to compare perpetual-inventory records with the quantity of items actually available in storage, there is no need to keep a continual balance of inventory value.

Type of Product ____________________

Month ____________________ Month ____________________

Product	Unit	Amount in Storage	Purchase Price	Total Price	Amount in Storage	Purchase Price	Total Price

FIGURE 4.14 PHYSICAL INVENTORY FORM

A perpetual-inventory system enables the user to maintain one food control standard not possible when only a physical inventory system is used. It indicates the quantity of product which *should* be available. This amount can be confirmed by a physical count. Any discrepancy between what should be and what is available becomes a measure of the effectiveness of the inventory storage system. A sample Perpetual Inventory Form is shown in Figure 4.15.

Perpetual inventories must be verified; it is necessary to confirm the accuracy of this count with a monthly physical count (see above). The quantity determined from physical count should equal the amount noted in the perpetual-inventory record.

Personnel who maintain perpetual-inventory records should not be involved in taking the physical count. This would defeat the purpose of the physical inventory. Therefore, the dietary manager and, perhaps, someone from the accounting department (in a large facility) or an employee involved with food production (in a small facility) can perform the counts together.

The first step in the process is to arrange perpetual-inventory sheets in the same sequence as the items are located in storage. One employee then counts the prod-

Product Name ____________________ Purchase Unit Size ____________

Date	In	Out	Balance Carried Forward ____	Date	In	Out	Balance Carried Forward ____

FIGURE 4.15 PERPETUAL INVENTORY FORM

ucts while the second staff member compares this quantity with the amount noted on the perpetual-inventory record. Any difference, of course, must be explained.

There is a need to continually update the balance (number of items available) of the perpetual-inventory system. The source of information about additional items added to inventory is the signed delivery invoice and/or the receiving report. The document used to reduce the quantity of products under perpetual inventory is the Food Requisition Form (see Figure 4.16). These forms are collected when issues are made. The storage area is otherwise kept locked so that removal of items is limited to only a few times daily. Note that this form includes pricing on it such that the one receiving the product from storage knows its value.

Small dietary operations may not find it practical to use a formal food requisition system. These facilities might, however, require that a dietary manager be physically present at the time withdrawals are made from inventory. Small facilities

REQUISITION FORM

Date: ______________

Location: ______________________________

Number	Unit	Description	Unit Price	Extension

Authorized ______________________ Received by ______________________

FIGURE 4.16 FOOD REQUISITION FORM

can also use a form (similar to Figure 4.16) taped to the wall or door of the storage area. Staff members authorized to withdraw products from storage can then enter information onto the form as they do so. Dietary managers using this system are cautioned that close supervision is necessary to assure that personnel adhere to this procedure.

Most dietary managers recognize that much of their inventory investment is represented by a relatively small number of items. If, for example, a facility purchases 400 products, perhaps only 100 or fewer of these items represent the largest cost (for example, meats and seafoods are much more expensive than cereal products, baked items, etc.). The concept of "ABC analysis" suggests that dietary managers should:

- Study purchases to determine which products are most costly ("A" items), next costly ("B" items), and least costly ("C" items). This refers to the price of an individual item and not the total cost of that item per week or per month. In other words, while breads, cereals, and dairy items may represent a significant cost because of the quantity used, it is the use of costly "A" items that are of interest in "ABC analysis";
- Categorize items in this manner to set priorities in purchasing, receiving and storing. For example, costly "A" items must be carefully controlled; less expensive "C" items need less control or, certainly, should not demand attention until control of all "A" and most "B" products has become systematized.

Advantages to thinking about purchased items in terms of their cost and, therefore, relative importance include:

- The dietary manager's time and efforts will be better spent in controlling the most costly items;
- Inventory investments can be minimized (since the dietary manager can carefully consider the minimum and maximum quantities of "A" products to carry in inventory);
- Specific policies and procedures will be developed to purchase, receive, and store top-priority items.

How can the concept of "ABC analysis" be used in storage? For example, small facilities might designate one section of a reach-in refrigerator or freezer for storage of most expensive items. These units can be kept locked and a perpetual-inventory system can be used to monitor the quantity of "A" items in these areas. Perhaps a lockable shelving unit can be installed in the walk-in refrigerator to house the most expensive fresh items—which would also be kept under perpetual inventory. The "precious room" concept—locked storage within a locked storage area—might be useful to safely store the most expensive dry items, including chafing dishes, buffet utensils, and other expensive supplies and materials.

Assigning Values to Inventory

Procedures to assign values to products in inventory must be developed. There are at least three common methods:

Method 1: First-in, First-out (FIFO). The value of products in inventory is represented by the price paid for the product which has been placed in inventory most recently (since the first products placed in storage are used first). For example, if a case of applesauce in storage was purchased three weeks ago for $22.50 and applesauce in a more recent delivery is valued at $23.25, cases in inventory are priced at the rate of $23.25.

Method 2: Last-in, First-out (LIFO). The value of products is represented by the price paid for the products in the inventory the longest (since LIFO attempts to match current income with current expenses). In the example above, cases of applesauce would be valued at $22.50.

Method 3: Weighted Average. This method considers the actual cost of products in storage. If there are three cases of applesauce at the earlier price and five cases of the product at the most recent price, the value of a case of applesauce is $22.97 (three cases @ $22.50 + five cases @ $23.25 ÷ eight cases = $22.97).

Ways to Reduce Inventory Costs

Cash-flow problems or, at the least, minimized investment return occurs when inventory levels are too high. Procedures for reducing inventory costs include the following:

- Reduce the quantities of products purchased; if stocks are too large, the facility may be able to "live on inventory" for some time period;
- Reduce requirements for delivery time and stockout safety levels. Inventory levels can be adjusted downward if there is less concern about late deliveries and/or stockouts;
- Attempt to obtain more frequent deliveries of smaller quantities by negotiation with suppliers;
- Be sure that the "par" levels of inventory are of the correct size;
- Standardize the type of products carried. For example, perhaps only two or three rather than four or five different sizes of hamburger patties need to be utilized and, therefore, carried in inventory;
- Refuse early deliveries (which must be paid for sooner than products delivered on an appropriate, timely delivery schedule).

Security Concerns in Storage

A third basic concern at time of storage is security. As already noted, it is best if the dietary manager knows not only how much product is available but also the amount of product which should be available. Even a small property can use a perpetual-inventory system for the most expensive "A" items, as has already been discussed.

Basic security principles are required to reduce theft of products in inventory.

Security Principle 1. There should be limited access. It is generally unwise to let everyone into storage areas. Only authorized personnel should be allowed to enter storage spaces.

Security Principle 2. Storage areas should be lockable. It should be possible to lock the freezer and the dry storage areas. A lockable walk-in refrigerator might also be useful, at least in large facilities.

Security Principle 3. Inventory control practices must be consistently used, and items judged expensive and "theft prone" should be controlled by a perpetual-inventory system.

Security Principle 4. Items in workstations should be placed under central inventory control at the end of each shift.

Computerized Inventory Systems

Today's increasing use of the computer helps ease the task of storeroom record-keeping. A wide variety of systems are available depending upon the needs and available funds of the specific operation. Some systems link storage (inventory) files with ingredient files. As this is done, it is possible to monitor stock levels, assess re-order points, and calculate actual product usage and variances between actual usage and expected usage based upon production/serving records. These systems also calculate the value of inventory, which is useful for several accounting purposes.

Efficient systems can track products through purchase, storage, issuing, and usage (production) control points. Systems can convert purchase units (such as case of #10 cans) to production units (such as cups or ounces). After production an automated system should be able to update inventory records by entering production units used (from standard recipe information) for comparison with quantities of products issued and subsequent reductions in inventory levels.

As is true with the purchase of any computerized system, it is first necessary for the dietary manager to determine exactly what the system must do. Unless there are unique circumstances, it is likely that a system is available for purchase in today's marketplace. The purchase of stand-alone systems should be evaluated for compatibility with existing facility computer hardware and software.

Food Distribution (Issuing) Practices

An effective food distribution (issuing) system has three objectives:

1. To utilize security procedures;
2. To "match up" items removed from storage with those used in actual food production;
3. To determine the quantities of items issued for record keeping and food costing procedures.

The process of food distribution basically involves completion of food requisition forms (see Figure 4.16). Each facility must establish policies; for example, who is to complete the form and authorize inventory withdrawal? When should products be issued? Who is to complete the daily food cost records? A basic plan may be that the cook, after noting the item and quantity to be prepared, completes the food withdrawal record for those menu items to be prepared for the next meal period. A standardized recipe will indicate the types and quantities of necessary ingredients. After the food requisition form is completed, it should be reviewed by the cook's supervisor and then taken to the storeroom for issuing.

There are many variations to the process just described, but the process remains the same in every case. The process of food distribution or issuing is the movement of ingredients to production and service areas. For example, perhaps food requisition forms are made out the night before for the following morning. As the person responsible for issuing comes to work, supply carts can be stocked with those items required by the food requisition form. As a second example, some weighing, measuring, and so on might be done in the storage area or in a separate ingredient room, the latter designed to provide the kitchen with exactly what is needed ingredient-wise to complete the recipe. With this plan, the actual quantity of each item needed for a specific recipe may be issued.

Large facilities with full-time storeroom clerks, and smaller facilities with specific personnel assigned to issue at specified times, are able to control access to storage areas. This is a prime concern in security at time of food distribution. After items are issued and transferred to food production areas, the issuing process is complete. The food withdrawal record should be retained by the storeroom clerk or other person with issuing duties. These forms have several purposes:

- They can be used by the dietary manager, storeroom clerk, or other staff members with responsibilities for maintaining perpetual-inventory records;
- They can be used to calculate the value of food issues—a component in the process to calculate daily food costs;
- They can be used by the head cook, dietary manager, or other staff member in an attempt to "match up" the quantity of items withdrawn from inventory with that used in actual food production.

The objective in issuing is to distribute needed items for production efficiently, safely, and economically. Related to this first objective is to keep food stocks secure from theft and pilferage, and record-keeping is an adjunct, supportive service, but not an objective unto itself. The end result is effective food distribution throughout the operation.

Other Issuing Concerns. Some dietary facilities may utilize food distribution systems which maintain par inventory levels. Consider, for example, quantities of items on nourishment carts in nursing stations, or supplies of all sorts in ward or "rethermalization" kitchens. As items in these areas are reduced to a predetermined minimum level, a specified quantity of additional products is issued to build the inventory levels to a predetermined maximum level. A modification of this system is the exchange cart process; a cart may be properly stocked with required supplies and wheeled to a ward kitchen in exchange for the cart with a reduced supply of items, which is then taken to a storage area for restocking.

Some dietary facilities today (and many more in the future) utilize computerized issuing systems. With this plan, perpetual-inventory records are easily kept. The quantity of products leaving storage areas is calculated; a constant value of products in inventory is maintained. Some facilities use optical reading devices which "automatically" read information from universal product codes (bar codes) and enter it into computerized information systems.

Some facilities utilize "stockless" inventory systems. For example, a satellite food-receiving unit may have no or little inventory on hand. Products to be prepared/served are brought to the facility daily; any remaining products are taken back to the central preparation area at the end of the serving period. While not practical in many operations, some facilities have very little food storage areas; very frequent deliveries of necessary products are made so that very little product inventory is kept at the facility.

Even small facilities can utilize basic principles of issuing control. Perhaps expensive and/or theft-prone items can remain in locked storage. Management staff can be present for issuing of these relatively few items at specific times preceding production. Other items would be available in storage areas on an as-needed basis by production personnel. Consistently enforced policies regarding storage areas being "off limits" to unauthorized personnel can also be utilized to reduce the number of employees who "issue" products to themselves. Use of a perpetual-inventory system to manage selected items and the matching of production records with changes in inventory volumes can also help the small facility monitor the effectiveness of issuing procedures.

As one can see from this discussion, there are a large number of basic management and control principles which should be incorporated into plans for the management of products and materials under control of the dietary manager. Regardless of the size of the dietary operation, these principles must be known and practiced to ensure a proper quality of products, constantly available, without excessive costs.

SUMMARY

In foodservices the term "purchasing" (used interchangeably with the term "procurement") refers to every step in the process by which goods and services are "bought" and brought into the dietary operation. Purchasing includes a variety of activities:

- Buying/Ordering refers to steps in the purchasing process;
- Selection refers to choosing between alternatives;
- Procurement refers to decision making and implementation of plans.

The objectives of a purchasing system must involve, at least, "assuring that the *right* product, of the *right* quality, is received at the *right* time. It must be obtained at the *right* price from the *right* supplier." Procurement is a "living," never-ending process which must keep up with changes in the industry, the facility, and the dietary operation.

The challenge in the healthcare dietary services is to provide what the client needs in the most cost-effective manner. Effective procurement is at the heart of a quality assurance program. A qualified manager should make decisions about decreasing purchases (which increase possibilities of stockouts) and about increasing the quantity of purchases (which can yield discounts).

The purchase specification is a quality statement that indicates what requirements must be met in order for a product to be "suitable" for its intended purpose. Specifications must be developed and given to suppliers before orders are placed, so that price quotations consider the desired quality of the products needed.

Specifications provide clear understanding between the facility and supplier, so there are likely to be fewer "communication" problems. Time, effort, and expertise are required, however, and there will be an occasional need for updating, so developing purchase specifications require increased work for someone on the staff.

It is important that the proper quantity of food products be purchased for various reasons. EP and AP conversions are important in this process.

Also, procedures must be developed to assess the quantity of items needed for immediate use and for inventory. To purchase perishable products for immediate use, a quotation call system may be used. The quantity to order can be calculated, then suppliers eligible for selling to the facility can be asked to quote current prices.

When buying for inventory, a minimum/maximum system may prove useful. It is based on two reference points for each product:

1. *The minimum allowable quantity* of the product (inventory levels should not fall below this figure);
2. *The maximum allowable quantity* of the product (inventory levels should not rise above this figure).

By calculating how much of the product is needed to bring the inventory level to maximum at the time of delivery, the dietary manager can determine the quantity to order.

Calculating order quantity must be reviewed. A flow of paperwork ("source documents") is used to help the dietary manager, facility accountant-bookkeeper, and supplier communicate with each other. There will be a flow of accounting information from the time an order is placed until the supplier is paid. A smooth flow of paperwork expedites the bill-paying process. Forecasting is defined as a technique for utilizing past information in a systematic way to estimate future needs.

Since dietary managers want to reduce the purchase price of products, and suppliers want to receive as much as possible for their products, compromise must be negotiated. Negotiation is a process used to reach agreement on all matters important to a purchase. Examples of concerns include product specifications, delivery times, and price. The objective is to show that the best interests of both parties are served when they move closer to meeting each other's objectives.

Prices paid for products purchased can be affected by the method of payment. Payment procedures must be of concern to the dietary manager even if these decisions are made by top-level administrators. An effective payment policy can be designed by using basic principles.

The issue of ethics in purchasing must be well understood by all dietary managers. Inappropriate purchasing activity is not only detrimental to operations, but management may find itself in serious trouble neglecting the "common sense" rule of proper purchasing ethics.

Several security concerns are important at time of product purchase. More detailed control procedures are important to reduce the possibility of losses due to dishonest suppliers or employees as an operation becomes larger. There are several common methods of theft at time of product purchase: kickbacks, padding the invoice, fictitious companies, processing thefts, credit memo problems, delivery invoice errors, quality substitutions, and other "creative" methods. Each can be controlled by using an effective purchasing system.

Decisions regarding the usage of convenience foods are important and hard to make. Ideally, both economic and non-economic factors which affect the make/buy decision must be considered. Quality is a primary issue in make/buy analysis, as well as quantity and cost.

On-site production ("make") has advantages and disadvantages, and since each facility has unique issues to address, advantages and disadvantages must be assessed for each specific facility. Likewise, there are advantages and disadvantages in the use of convenience foods ("buy"). It depends upon, first, the specific product and, second, the specific operation. While it is time-consuming to consider details of analysis to determine whether products should be prepared on-site or purchased in a ready-to-serve form, the time and effort spent to quantify these details are well spent.

Since 40 percent or more of all dollars spent by most dietary services are used to purchase food and supplies, it is essential that the right products in the right quantity at the right price and from the right supplier be received at the right time. There are several procedures in an effective receiving system:

- Check against purchase records;
- Inspect against specifications;
- Inspect against delivery invoice;
- Accept/reject products;
- Complete receiving report;
- Remove to storage;
- Monitor CCP's.

Receiving staff must be trained in procedures to reject products. Each item must be verified by counting, weighing, and/or measuring. To help guard against theft at the time products are received, basic principles should be followed.

There are three basic concerns to be addressed by the dietary manager as products are stored. Effective storage plans are required to (a) ensure that product quality is retained during storage, (b) develop inventory records needed for accounting purposes, and (c) prevent theft of items in storage.

There must be a planned and systematic process to control items in storage. A physical inventory system involves counting products in inventory routinely to assess the quantity of items on hand and to determine the actual cost of food used. A perpetual-inventory system keeps track of storage items on a continuous basis. A running balance of the quantity in inventory is kept. Perpetual inventories must be verified; it is necessary to confirm the accuracy of this count with a monthly physical count. The quantity determined from physical count should equal the amount noted in the perpetual-inventory record.

There are three common methods to assigning values to products in inventory:

1. First-in, First-out (FIFO);
2. Last-in, First-out (LIFO);
3. Weighted Average.

Procedures exist to reduce inventory costs - the goal is to keep inventory levels low.

Basic security principles are required to reduce theft of products in inventory.

- There should be limited access.
- Storage areas should be lockable.
- Inventory control practices must be consistently used, and items judged expensive and "theft-prone" should be controlled by a perpetual inventory system.
- Items in work stations should be placed under central inventory control at the end of each shift.

Computers help ease the task of storeroom record-keeping. Some systems are available depending upon the needs and available funds of the specific operation. Some systems link storage (inventory) files with ingredient files. It is then possible to monitor stock levels, assess reorder points, and calculate actual product usage and variances between actual usage and expected usage based upon production/serving records. These systems also calculate the value of inventory, which is very useful.

An effective food distribution (issuing) system has three objectives:

1. To utilize security procedures;
2. To "match up" items removed from storage with those used in actual food production;
3. To determine the quantities of items issued for record keeping and food costing procedures.

The need for security is important at the time of food distribution. Issuing practices should recognize the possibilities for theft, and should counter them with control procedures that properly document items being issued.

Regardless of the size of the dietary operation, basic management and control principles should be incorporated into plans for the management of products and materials under control of the dietary manager.

KEY TERMS

- Purchasing
- Buying
- Ordering
- Selection
- Procurement
- Continuous supply
- Purchase specification
- ABC analysis
- Quotation call system
- Minimum/maximum system
- Forecasting
- Source document flow
- Purchase requisition
- Negotiation
- Security concerns
- Purchase record system
- Competitive bidding
- Prime vendor
- Make/buy analysis
- Ethics
- Receiving system
- Physical inventory system
- Perpetual inventory system
- FIFO
- LIFO
- Weighted average
- Computerized inventory system
- Food requisition form

QUESTIONS/PROBLEMS/CASES

1. The objectives of a purchasing system involve assuring that the right product, of the right quality, is received at the right time, at the right price, from the right supplier. What does this mean for the dietary manager?

2. You are the dietary manager of a large facility and one of your responsibilities is to develop food-purchase specifications. Who are your available sources of information and what might they offer you? What should be included in purchase specifications?

3. In purchasing products for inventory, the quantity to be purchased is an important consideration. What is the procedure to determine quantity if the "quantity needed" is eleven cases and the "quantity available" in the walk-in refrigerator is four cases?

4. Dietary managers are not doing their job when they simply ask for a price for necessary products and then pay it. Why is this?

5. List two ways to control theft in creating an effective purchasing system.

6. Why would a dietary manager consider using a prime vendor in purchasing? What are possible disadvantages of having a prime vendor?

7. The make or buy decision-making process is affected by many factors which must be analyzed. Several procedures provide general guidelines to be followed in make/buy analysis. What are the seven process steps involved in this analysis?

8. List steps in receiving products, define, and include reason for each step's importance.

9. How does a computer help ease the task of storeroom record keeping?

10. Describe hazards to food safety described in this chapter.

11. What are the main objectives of an effective food distribution system?

12. What is one use of a food requisition form?

13. List and describe three inventory valuing methods used in inventory management.

14. What is an ABC analysis and how is it useful to the dietary manager?

15. List security concerns identified in purchasing, receiving, and storage.

5

FACILITY LAYOUT, DESIGN, AND EQUIPMENT

CHAPTER OUTLINE

- Facility Design and Work flow
  - Design Principles
  - Design of Receiving and Storage Areas
  - Design of Food Preparation and Service Areas
  - Design of Other Dietary Areas
- Types of Kitchens
  - Cook-Serve
  - No-Cook
  - Cook-Chill
- Capital Equipment Purchases
  - Selecting the Supplier of Major Equipment
  - Important Factors in Equipment Selection
  - Financing Capital Equipment Purchases
  - Purchasing Used Equipment
- Selecting and Using Foodservice Equipment
  - Receiving Equipment
  - Refrigeration and Chilling Equipment
  - Preparation Equipment
  - Cooking Equipment
  - Holding and Serving Equipment
  - Other Equipment for Cleanup Purposes
- Equipment Maintenance
- Managing the Cost of Supplies

FACILITY DESIGN AND WORK FLOW

The way that the facility is designed has a dramatic impact on the efficiency of personnel within the dietary operation. If the facility is improperly designed, there may be too much space, requiring unproductive efforts to move between workstations and additional time will be required for cleaning the space. If space is too small, it may be inadequate to house the equipment and provide working space for necessary personnel. The quality (and frequently the quantity) of food products produced will suffer. Since a large capital cost is incurred for building space, there is a need for careful thought as decisions about space and equipment are made.

Several factors affect the layout of the dietary facility. Among these are:

- **The menu.** As meals must be prepared for three or more meal periods and as an extensive variety of items must be offered, there is an obvious need for additional storage and preparation space. Since the menu dictates the types of food products to be prepared, it also indicates food items which must be purchased, stored, and produced. Again, implications for facility layout are obvious;

- **Amount of convenience foods used.** As the number and quantity of items which have some labor "built into them" increases, there will be lessened needs for food production space and equipment. Conversely, if a large number of items are to be made from "scratch," on-site needs for space and equipment will increase;
- **Quantity of food to prepare.** The dietary facility preparing meals for large numbers of clients will need more space and equipment than will its counterpart producing fewer meals;
- **Necessary equipment.** As the amount of necessary food production equipment increases, the space and utilities necessary to provide for this equipment must also increase. Today there is a wide range of highly specialized production equipment which will frequently consume more space than will multi-purpose equipment items. One should also recognize, however, that space-efficient items, such as convection and microwave ovens and high-capacity pressure steamers, and so on, consume less floor space than do their older counterparts;
- **Funds.** The amount of money to be spent on dietary space and equipment has an obvious implication on the project. It is likely that dietary services will need to "compete" with other departments in the facility for the limited amount of resources available for remodeling and/or new building activities;
- **Space.** The number of square feet allocated for dietary services will affect both the facility layout and the amount and type of equipment which can be used. Since space can be equated with capital cost, the dietary services will probably compete with other departments for available space (dollars). The facility may not (will likely not!) make available the ideal amount of space (dietary operation's perspective), and compromises in design are almost always the rule—not the exception;
- **Production Systems.** Facilities using commissary-type systems (such as cook-chill or bulk food transport) must adjust space needs accordingly. If the former system (cook-chill) is used, production space may be lessened (meals can be produced at off-peak times) and refrigerated space will need to be increased (to hold products until rethermalization and service). If the latter system (bulk food transport) is used, no production and little storage space will be needed for the "satellite" serving centers.

Design Principles

Preparation facilities must be designed to help insure an efficient flow of products and personnel through each sequence in the food production/service cycle. Figure 5.1 illustrates the concept of work flow in dietary services. Note that products must be received and then stored in the appropriate area. Products must be issued for baking, meat, and/or vegetable preparation. Products must be cooked, prepared, and served. Supportive activities, including pot-washing and dishwashing, are also required. There is a relationship between the serving and dining activities. In many institutional operations, intermediate steps of preportioning products on tray assembly lines make the work flow process even more complex. It is necessary to consider each of the functions which must occur in the facility, to allocate space for the function, and to design the facility so that there is an obvious and helpful relationship among the spaces allocated for each function.

Many factors must be considered as food preparation areas are designed. Among the most important is the menu, since space, employees, equipment and ingredients must be available to prepare each item required by the menu and the production/delivery system in use. Typically, facilities are designed by considering work load requirements. Then work centers are developed.

For example, consider the activities, space, and equipment necessary to prepare bread dough in a bake shop. While recipes differ, it is obvious that activities must

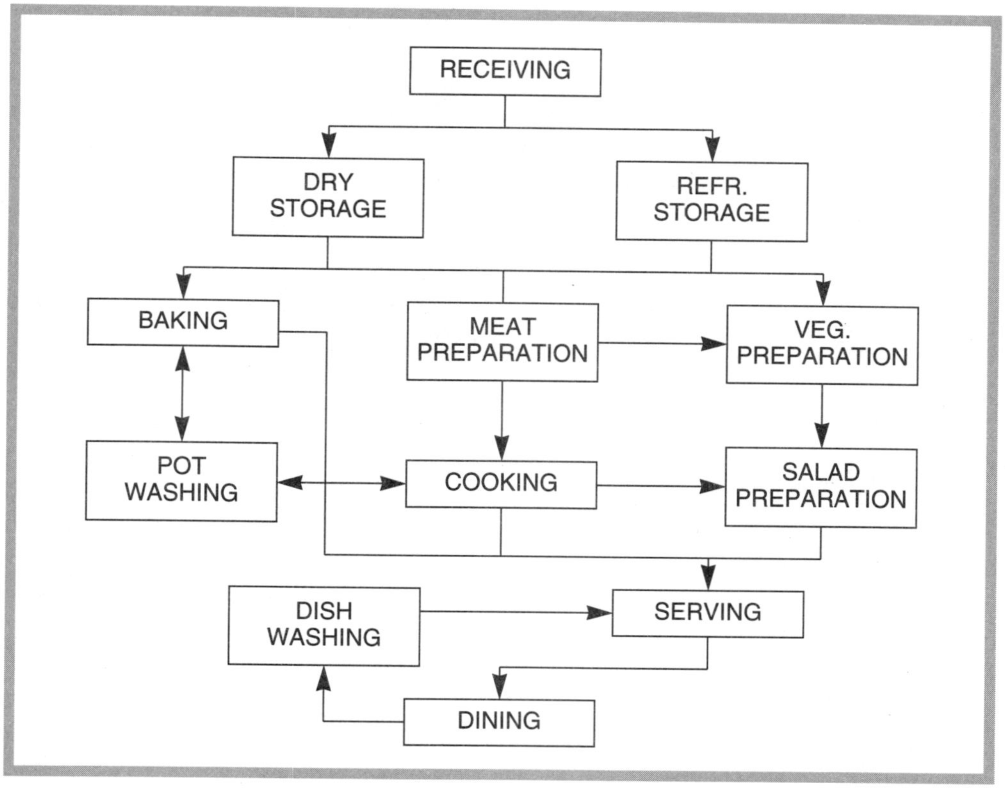

FIGURE 5.1 WORK FLOW IN DIETARY SERVICES
Source: E. Kazarian, *Food Service Facilities Planning* (3rd ed.). Van Nostrand Reinhold. New York, N.Y., 1989, pg. 92

include weighing of dry ingredients, combining dry and liquid ingredients in a mixer, proofing prepared bread dough, dividing and rounding bread and roll portions, panning, proofing, and baking. Each of these tasks must be considered as the work center for bread and roll preparation is designed. Then, each of these work centers is combined into a workstation (the bakery area, for example, is a workstation). Along with bread baking, the production of dessert sauces, baked desserts, and a wide range of other products might also be within the responsibility of the bakery work section.

Note: Unfortunately, the design process is more complicated than this "simple" example suggests. Bread (rolls) can be purchased as bulk or preportioned dough or already baked (sliced or unsliced). The market form of the product to be purchased must, then, be considered. Problems arise when, for example, changes in desired market form are made after the facility is constructed.

The task of designing foodservice departments is complex. The dietary manager and his or her staff should be part of the design team. Their input, along with that of other facility representatives, the project architect, perhaps a specialized foodservice design consultant, and others, will also be useful as the design project evolves.

There is a wide range of other special concerns which must be considered as the department is designed. For example, much physical work will be performed in kitchen areas. Therefore, concern for the reduction of physical fatigue becomes important. These concerns are recognized as designers reduce distances employees must travel, adjust heights of work areas to fit the needs of employees, and develop comfortable locker room, restroom, employee dining, and related areas.

There is typically much noise in food preparation areas. This can distract clients as well as employees. Use of soundproofing materials and the selection of less noisy equipment can help reduce these problems.

Much detail work is done in foodservice departments; therefore, lighting concerns become important. Work in food preparation areas can also be very hot. Concerns about temperature are appropriate as air conditioning needs are considered, and as cooking and cleaning equipment selection decisions are made.

Safety and sanitation concerns are important. Security concerns are always of top priority in the design. For example, should storage areas be located close to the back door (which makes food theft more of a potential problem)? Should receiving and preparation areas be under the view of the dietary manager, and, therefore, should glass partitions be used rather than solid walls in the dietary manager's office? While the list of questions can continue, the point is that the control of food and materials during production and service is influenced by the amount of security "built into" the facility at time of construction.

Design of Receiving and Storage Areas

Foodservice designers must pay attention to areas used for receiving and storage of food products. Receiving areas should typically be as close as practical to the storage areas. They should also be large enough to place all items being received, so that effective receiving practices can be used. There must be room available for proper receiving equipment. Storage areas must include space sufficient to house the required quantity of dry, refrigerated, and frozen products, as well as a wide variety of disposable, cleaning, linen, and other supplies necessary for conduct of dietary services. To limit access by unauthorized persons, storerooms should be designed with walls that extend from the floor to the ceiling and with ceilings that cannot be entered from an adjoining room.

Design of Food Preparation and Service Areas

Ingredient preparation areas might be planned as part of or adjacent to dry-storage areas. The need for storage space, aisleways to house supply carts, space for counters, measuring and weighing equipment, and so on becomes important.

If food is to be preportioned onto tray assembly lines, the design of service and dining areas must include space for the necessary equipment. Additional space will be needed for mobile carts, transport equipment, and personnel necessary to staff the tray assembly line.

If cafeteria serving lines are to be used in the foodservice area, space for the equipment needed must be allocated. Sometimes, cafeteria lines are stationary, in straight-line, L-shaped, U-shaped, or other formats. In other systems, "scrambled" designs are used so that clients using the facility can go directly to service areas where desired food items are located. If food items are to be prepared on an as-ordered basis, utility hookups, ventilation systems, and space to house necessary equipment in service areas must be considered. Equipment to hold hot and cold food items near the point of service will be needed. Sometimes cafeteria operations utilize hot and/or cold food "pass-throughs" so that production staff can make items readily available for service without having to go into public foodservice areas.

If cafeteria operations are to collect cash, space for cashiers, register equipment, and other necessary items must be included.

Dining area planners must consider not only the number of persons to be served at one time, but also the flow of soiled dishes back to washing areas. In some facilities, table service is provided, necessitating serving stations with a wide range of service equipment and supplies.

Dining areas greatly influence the clients' impressions of foodservice. The atmosphere of the facility itself, the cleanliness and condition of dining room furniture, fixtures and equipment, lighting, and a wide range of other concerns are important to these impressions.

How many clients must be fed at one time? How much space should be allocated for each diner? What other activities besides dining services will occur in dining areas (in many facilities, dining areas become multi-purpose rooms at non-feeding times of the day)? Many questions must be carefully answered and many people consulted as dietary areas are planned.

Design of Other Dietary Areas

In addition to food storage, production, assembly, serving, and dining areas, other spaces must be considered for dietary services. Consider the need for an office for dietary management officials. What about space for dish and pot washing, holding of refuse until pickup, space for washing mobile transport, and shelving equipment, and so on? Where will cleaning and other chemicals be stored? What about space for refrigeration equipment for walk-in units? Where will mobile transport equipment be stored?

In some facilities, de-centralized "ward kitchen" or "rethermalization center" space must be allocated. Preportioned hot and cold food items are sent in frozen or chilled condition to decentralized (satellite) kitchen areas at time of service. These items must be rethermalized, placed on appropriate serving trays, and moved from these centers to the clients. How much space should be provided for this activity? What equipment will be needed?

Space must also be allocated on client units for nourishment centers in many facilities. These incurred costs may be borne by nursing services. However, the dietary manager, as an "expert" in foodservice within the facility, is likely to have ideas about how nourishments can be protected from theft and other misuse, and can offer this advice as a service to the proper officials.

If the proper design of foodservice areas sounds like a difficult and complex job, it is! However, it is a very important task which will dramatically affect the long-term effectiveness of dietary services. While the dietary manager may not be knowledgeable about every activity involved in proper facility design, he or she will still have many excellent ideas. This creative input should be solicited and utilized as facility planners make decisions which impact upon dietary services.

Types of Kitchens

Many terms are used to describe different types of kitchens. Traditional kitchens (cook-serve) prepare foods from ingredients and cook food according to client preference. No-Cook and Cook-Chill kitchens are so named for the specific techniques of preparing food in them and serving it to the customer. Each of these types are considered further in the following sections.

Cook-Serve

A traditional foodservice has six subsystems, each with its own space requirements and each equipped for specific functions including receiving, storage, preparation, cooking, serving, and clean-up. The equipment required by each is discussed further in another section of this chapter. Figure 5.2 indicates the breakdown of space allocations for the traditional 6,000-square-foot kitchen.

No-Cook

The no-cook, decentralized, or satellite kitchen is where preportioned hot and cold food items are sent to a rethermalization center where the food must be rethermalized, placed on appropriate serving trays, and moved from these centers to the clients. The backup to a no-cook system, of course, is the traditional kitchen, or central commissary, where most of the pre-preparation and cooking occurs.

Cook-Chill

This is a technology that has been around for several decades but is now finding new applications. Its use has been expanding into organizations where foodservice needs to prepare food for large numbers of people in multiple locations in the safest, most efficient manner possible.

Traditional Cook-Serve Kitchen		
Subsystem	**Space Allocation**	
Receiving	120 sq. ft.	3.00%
Storage	1,120 sq. ft.	28.00%
Preparation	1,100 sq. ft.	27.50%
Cooking	470 sq. ft.	11.75%
Serving	800 sq. ft.	20.00%
Clean-up	390 sq. ft.	9.75%
Subtotal	4,000 sq. ft.	100.00%
Fixed Space*	2,000 sq. ft.	*includes janitorial storage, restrooms, lounge area, etc.
TOTAL	6,000 sq. ft.	

Figure 5.2 Space Allocations for the Traditional Kitchen

Cook-chill is a production process whereby just-cooked foods are rapidly chilled (generally within one to two hours) to an internal temperature of 38°F or below). The rapid chilling leaves little or no opportunity for harmful microbial growth. There are three basic types of cook-chill "chilling" technology:

Tumble Chillers. Imagine a huge washing machine full of ice water. Next, picture a large kettle full of spaghetti sauce that is being pumped into heavy plastic bags, which are mechanically sealed, given an identification tag and placed into the ice water bath. When cooked, the sauce had a temperature of 180°F. After being placed in the tumble chiller, the internal temperature is quickly reduced to 38°F. Once this process is complete, the bag of sauce is removed and placed in a refrigerator at no more than 32°F. until it is needed. Under normal operating conditions, the bag, the sealing process, and the quick chilling technique will permit the spaghetti sauce to be held for up to six weeks.

Blast Chill. If foodservice staff were to take that same spaghetti sauce and place it in a 2.5-inch deep steam table pan, they could then place it in a blast chill refrigerator. A blast chill refrigerator looks like the commercial refrigerator found in most kitchens. The difference is that blast chill equipment has a high horsepower motor that permits cooked food to be chilled to a temperature of 38°F. in two hours or less. Since the food has not been bagged, its effective shelf-life will be approximately five days. Heavy-duty plastic bags can be placed in pans or on trays and into the blast chiller to get similar cooling results.

Sous Vide. This is a French term that literally means "cooked under vacuum." With sous vide preparation, foods are prepared and placed in heavy-duty plastic pouches and slow-cooked at lower than normal temperatures in a vacuum chamber. At that point, products are either blast chilled or frozen. If chilled, they will have a shelf-life of approximately twenty days. If frozen, most items will retain full quality for up to a year. While certainly more expensive in terms of cost, sous vide products eliminate the need to employ a highly paid chef or cook if only a few people are to be served or there is a need to serve a large number of persons in a very short period of time. This type of food would be purchased from approved commercial sources.

CAPITAL EQUIPMENT PURCHASES

The dietary manager will occasionally need to purchase capital dietary equipment (expensive, long-lived) carried on the balance sheet of the facility. Purchase of capital equipment generally requires the use of procedures different from those used to purchase dietary products and supplies. Because capital equipment items are purchased infrequently, the facility probably does not have routine procedures which can be used. Since the purchases will have a long life, the dietary operation will have to "live with" the purchase decision for many years. Capital equipment purchases affect the way the dietary facility operates; labor productivity, sanitation, and safety may all be affected by the purchase decision.

In many facilities, a requisition for purchase of a capital equipment item must be preceded by a specific budget appropriation. Also, there is a need for a greater lead time for purchase, more extensive negotiations with suppliers, and more detailed records about the equipment for accounting, security, and maintenance/repair purposes. There also may be less frequent price fluctuations with capital equipment than with less expensive items.

Several basic procedures must be used to purchase capital equipment items:

Step 1: There must be a need. Typically, the dietary manager and other staff members in the dietary department recognize the need for equipment purchases. There may be recurring problems; existing equipment may break down and may not be "worth" repair costs; manufacturers may introduce new items of great interest or benefit to the facility;

Step 2: Consider the budget. Since the purchase of large equipment items will involve significant expense, these items generally must be included and approved in a capital budget separate from the department's operating budget;

Step 3: Facility staff play a role in the equipment purchase. In large facilities with a purchasing department, personnel with this responsibility may obtain general information from equipment suppliers about potentially useful items, provide help with cost benefit studies, and develop final purchase specifications. Purchasing staff may also be involved in requesting price quotations from suppliers, comparing quotations, undertaking supplier negotiations, and advising the dietary manager about decisions to be made.

In smaller facilities without a purchasing department, these tasks will probably be done by the dietary manager and/or representative from the business office.

In facilities of any size, the dietary manager must be involved in:

- determining the exact equipment needed;
- explaining cost effectiveness and defending equipment needs to administrators;
- working with suppliers to determine specific equipment needs, such as wiring;
- analyzing information about alternative equipment items;
- developing economic analyses to determine which equipment should be purchased;
- determining compatibility with other equipment and impact on workflow;
- evaluating equipment safety and ease of use;
- equipment placement in the food preparation area;
- helping to develop purchase specifications;
- working with the supplier awarded the order to coordinate installation, training, and/or other activities;

- promptly notifying top-level administrators about any problems which might require their attention.

Important Factors in Equipment Selection

It is obvious that capital equipment must be suitable for its intended use. The purchase must also be cost-effective. Special elements in the definition of these concerns must be evaluated. The dietary manager must first select equipment that meets the needs of the menu planned.

The equipment needs to arrive in a timely fashion, be compatible with existing equipment, and be properly ordered for wiring considerations. How well does the new equipment enhance work and traffic flow? The dietary manager must be concerned with its placement for maximum efficiency within the operation.

Other important factors in equipment selection include sanitation and safety, equipment flexibility, warranty coverage, maintenance and service issues, reliability, and ease of use. These are discussed further in the section of this chapter, titled "Selecting and Using Foodservice Equipment."

Selecting the Supplier of Major Equipment

Many dietary managers determine the specific brand of desired equipment and then select suppliers from those carrying the desired brand. In some areas of the country there may be only one supplier carrying a specific brand; the supplier selection decision will be made "automatically" when the brand of equipment is selected. However, with many brands of equipment, alternative suppliers are available.

Among the factors the dietary manager should consider when selecting a supplier for large equipment items are the following:

1. The supplier's reputation, which could affect warranty and service;
2. The amount of pre-purchase assistance which is given (many suppliers provide helpful ideas, make creative suggestions, and genuinely try to help the facility as a decision is made);
3. Differences in payment terms, price, credit arrangements, etc.;
4. The amount of assistance given after purchase. Some suppliers may include in their price quotation costs for delivery, installation, on-site testing, demonstration, training, and even initial maintenance. In contrast, other suppliers may exclude all or many of these services. It is important for the dietary manager to clearly understand what is and is not included in the price quotation.

Financing Capital Equipment Purchases

A significant number of dollars are necessary to purchase capital equipment. Financing may be a special concern—especially when adequate funds are not available, when cash flow problems may arise if equipment is purchased without assistance, and/or if the alternative of leasing is not feasible.

There are several methods for financing large equipment. For example, the supplier may finance the purchase (and, in fact, his or her willingness to do so may be a factor in the supplier selection decision). When this financing arrangement is used, some "up-front" money will probably be necessary at the time equipment is ordered, to protect the supplier against costs incurred if the order is canceled. Another payment may be required at the time of delivery, and the remaining balance may be financed by the supplier, often with interest rates lower than the going rate. It is necessary for the dietary manager to work closely with the business office to consider these and other arrangements for financing of equipment purchases.

Purchasing Used Equipment

Used equipment presents another alternative for dietary managers. Potential reasons for purchasing used foodservice equipment include lower price, immediate availability, and limited need (indicating that new and expensive equipment cannot be justified). Used equipment may also be more compatible with existing, older equipment, and institutional facilities may not need equipment with long life. For the facility desiring to "experiment" with a satellite delivery program, loaned or leased equipment may be helpful in this short-term "trial study."

Dietary managers must be familiar with potential disadvantages in purchasing used equipment. For example, there typically is not a warranty, the equipment may be sold on a "cash only" basis, and responsibilities for moving and installing the equipment may rest with the buyer. The life expectancy of used equipment is typically shorter than that of new equipment, and used equipment may not have newer, preferred design qualities. There may be a need for increased maintenance, and it is unlikely that competitive bids are possible (or, at least, can be evaluated). Dietary managers will also find it difficult to match required specifications with used equipment items that are available. It will be difficult to determine the severity of previous use, and the dietary manager may need to deal with unfamiliar "supplier" sources and find difficulty in securing required service or parts.

The dietary manager must have a clear understanding of the specific need for an equipment item and must carefully consider all sources. If used equipment is to be considered, the dietary manager should recognize that equipment suppliers may have some used "trade-ins." There may also be sales or auctions of discontinued businesses. Government agencies may have surplus items for sale; other commercial and/or institutional facilities may have unused items for sale; there are even used-equipment dealers in some larger municipalities. Also, leasing companies may have equipment items that remain from expired leases and/or from leasing contracts which have been terminated.

Selecting and Using Foodservice Equipment

Dietary managers must have some knowledge about procedures to select and use foodservice equipment. Equipment selected will have an overt impact upon the efficiency of the operation and the quality of the products produced. A greater lead time is necessary for purchasing equipment than for food and other items. There will be more extensive negotiation with suppliers. The cost of capital equipment is less likely to be affected by frequent price fluctuations than are food and other products.

Basic selection factors become important when dietary managers consider new equipment. These include:

- **Suitability for intended use.** Since a wide range of equipment products is available for almost any purpose, it is important that the dietary manager carefully consider the suitability of each product. In large facilities with staff purchasing departments, some of this responsibility might be shared with the staff purchasing office;
- **Durability.** It is necessary to confirm that the product will "stand up" under the use to which it will be put. Obviously, warranty information is important and must be studied;
- **Cost.** It is necessary to confirm that the equipment is worth more to the facility than what it costs. Payback analyses, cost-effectiveness studies and other tools should be used to confirm that the purchase will be cost-beneficial;
- **Ease of operation.** The dietary manager must confirm that the equipment will be easy to use. The availability of easy-to-read instruction and training manuals and on-site visits from the supplier and/or equipment manufacturer representatives may help personnel to use the equipment properly;
- **Construction concerns.** Closely aligned with durability is the integrity of the equipment's construction. Seals of approval from the National Sanitation

Foundation International, Underwriters Laboratories (for electrical equipment), and/or American Gas Association (for gas-operated equipment) are important considerations which impact upon the value of a proposed equipment item;

- **Sanitation/safety concerns.** Equipment being considered must be safe to operate and must lend itself to sanitary food production. Therefore, equipment must be easy to clean and safe to operate, and these concerns must be high on the list of selection factors;
- **Compatibility with existing equipment.** It is important that equipment "works" with other items currently available. For example, trays being purchased must fit into existing carts, and attachments for electric mixers must usually be of the same brand. Be sure equipment being purchased will fit into available space and can be moved through existing doorways.

The dietary manager is responsible for developing procedures for maintaining, operating, and cleaning foodservice equipment. Once developed, these procedures must be incorporated into training and supervision activities for all affected employees.

The basis for applicable procedures will be found in the manufacturer's instructions accompanying the equipment. While many dietary operations review information accompanying foodservice equipment, a common practice is to discard it or "file it" in an inconvenient location. In contrast, the wise dietary manager carefully studies this information and incorporates it into standard operating procedures for cleaning, maintenance, and operation. The manufacturer's recommendations about equipment maintenance can be transferred to a preventive maintenance form and repair log as seen in Figure 5.3. Instructions about cleaning can be used as the basis for developing cleaning procedures to be taught to all employees. Information about proper operation must also be taught to employees and can also be the basis for written procedures posted on or near each equipment item.

In addition to information from manufacturers that accompanies the equipment, many dietary managers utilize their past experience with similar equipment items to help modify procedures for maintenance, cleaning, and operation. Suppliers can often provide additional information as well.

Once developed, this information can be summarized in an equipment operations manual. For each equipment item, procedures for cleaning and operation should be recorded. This manual can then become a training tool to show new staff members how to use each equipment item properly. The manual can also become a basis for supervision, for safety inspections, and for development of "refresher information" for ongoing staff training programs. Figure 5.4 shows a sample policy and procedure statement for cleaning an equipment item in a nursing home.

Receiving Equipment*

The typical receiving equipment found in foodservice operations includes scales, moving equipment, and miscellaneous items such as calculators, desks, chairs, and file cabinets.

Scales must give accurate weights down to ounces. Large receiving scales usually are able to weigh items in the range from 50 to 1,000 pounds. Figure 5.5 shows the typical scales found in the receiving area of operations. The dietary manager will know what scales are needed in the operation by considering the weight of the items usually ordered, whether in portion or case lots for most facilities.

Dollies, trucks, and other mobile equipment may be needed to move purchases from the receiving dock to storage. The shelving used for storage should be suited to the receiving equipment used.

*The following discussion is loosely based upon: Knight, John B. and Lendal H. Kotschevar, *Quantity Food Production, Planning and Management*, Van Nostrand Reinhold, 1989, pp. 80–106.

Service	Type Machine	Equipment No.
Location	Serial No.	Model No.
Make	Date Purchased	Purchase Cost

PREVENTIVE MAINTENANCE PROCEDURE

Function	Interval

SPECIAL INSTRUCTIONS

SPECIFICATIONS

Voltage	Drive
Amperage	Belts
Phase	Fuse
Pressure	Lubrication
Horsepower	Filter
RPM	Fluids

SPARE PARTS REQUIRED

Part	Mfr. Part No.	Hotel Stock No.	Quant.

Date	By	Work Performed	Hours	Mat'l	Labor	Cost To Date

FIGURE 5.3 EQUIPMENT MAINTENANCE AND REPAIR LOG

DATE: 0/00/00

NAME OF FACILITY:	DEPARTMENT:
ABC Nursing Home	Dietary
APPROVAL BY: Joe Jones, Dietary Mgr. Sally Smith, Administrator	SUBJECT OR TITLE: Cleaning Electric Mixers

POLICY (STATEMENT)

It is the policy of ______________________ (name of facility) that electric mixers be properly cleaned after each use according to the following procedures.

EXPLANATION (IF NECESSARY):

PROCEDURE:
(1) Immediately after use, take bowls, beaters, and all removable parts to pot-sink for washing and sanitizing according to manual pot-washing instructions.
(2) Fill both compartments of pail with warm water. To the wash compartment, add Cream Suds in the ratio of 2–4 oz. per gallon of water; to the rinse side, add Mikroklene in the ratio of 1 oz. per gallon of water. Use separate sponges for wash and rinse compartments.
(3) Use sponge and detergent solution to thoroughly scrub all stationary parts of mixer. Pay particular attention to underside of head, corners, handles, and underneath rolled rims.
(4) Rinse thoroughly with sponge dipped in sanitizing rinse solution and squeezed nearly dry. Dip and wring sponge frequently so all parts are sanitized.
(5) Dry with clean cloth.
(6) Replace removable parts.
(7) Return cleaning equipment to proper storage.

FIGURE 5.4 SAMPLE POLICY AND PROCEDURE: EQUIPMENT CLEANING

REFRIGERATION AND CHILLING EQUIPMENT

Refrigeration and chilling equipment exist to minimize the deterioration of stored foods and to reduce the likelihood of contamination. Adequate storage capacity is necessary to protect food, ensure proper sanitation, and maintain high food standards. The storage area provided should be designed to receive and hold the specific food stored in it.

Equipment in this area keeps food cool or frozen to preserve flavor, color, texture, and nutritional elements. Refrigeration temperatures range from 28°F to 40°F, while chilling equipment range from –10°F to 10°F. Units offering these temperatures come in a variety of types: walk-in, reach-in, and roll-in models. Figure 5.6 shows how flexible and convenient such roll-in refrigeration equipment can be.

PREPARATION EQUIPMENT

The list of preparation equipment is ever expanding as manufacturers attempt to ease the tasks of fruit and vegetable cleaning and cutting, salad preparation, and meat cutting and trimming. Depending upon how many menu items are prepared from scratch within the operation, many preparation equipment items can be called for.

Scales can again be an important equipment item as portion sizes of menu items are made to be uniform each time they are prepared. Food mixers vary in size from 5 to 140 quarts, and may be counter, bench, or floor models, as seen in Figure 5.7.

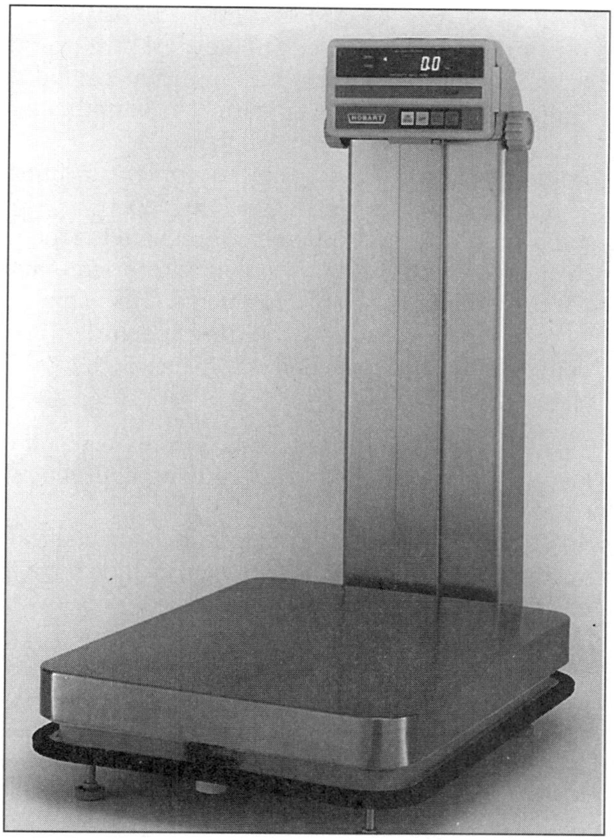

FIGURE 5.6 ROLL-IN REFRIGERATION EQUIPMENT
Source: Photo courtesy of Hobart Corporation.

FIGURE 5.5 RECEIVING SCALES
Source: Photo courtesy of Hobart Corporation.

counter model | bench model | floor model

FIGURE 5.7 FOOD MIXERS: (A) COUNTER MODEL (5-QT CAPACITY); (B) BENCH MODEL (20-QT. CAPACITY); (C) FLOOR MODEL (140-QT. CAPACITY) ***Source:*** Photo courtesy of Hobart Corporation.

Food cutters, known traditionally as Buffalo Choppers, consist of a rotating bowl that moves food into the path of a spinning blade. The vertical cutter and mixer (VCM) chops, cuts, mixes, blends, emulsifies, purees, and homogenizes foods in a matter of seconds, working similar to a home blender with two knife blades whirling at the bottom of a deep bowl. A smaller version of the VCM is a food processor which has become a common piece of preparation equipment in most kitchens today. Figure 5.8 shows the Buffalo Chopper, and VCM.

Food slicers, vegetable peelers, and meat-processing equipment round out the number of major preparation equipment items found in many foodservice operations. Figure 5.9 provides a picture of each of these important equipment items. Other smaller pieces of preparation equipment may include blenders, breading machines, can openers, coffee grinders, knife sharpeners and waste collection and disposal systems.

Cooking Equipment

The cooking and baking of foods is a focal point of most kitchens. While ovens play an important role here, broilers, fryers, griddles, ranges, steam-cooking equipment, and tilting pans all are found in the cooking subsystem.

There are five oven types seen in operations including conventional, mechanical, convection, microwave, and rethermalizing. While conventional ovens include the all-purpose, reel, draw-plate, and deck ovens, they are each characterized by a lower heat source, and possibly an overhead source as well, in an enclosed chamber. The mechanical oven is similar but has a mechanically moving interior that shifts the foods around to different parts of the oven, whether by revolving-tray, traveling-tray, or rotary mechanism. Convection ovens have a fan in them which causes the heat to move within the enclosed chamber, resulting in faster cooking with less heat. In fact, temperatures are set at 50°F less than the recipe suggests and the time is reduced by 30 percent in a convection oven. Microwave ovens use a form of electromagnetic energy intermediate in frequency and wavelength between radio and infrared waves. When microwaves penetrate food, molecular activity or movement takes place within the food, creating friction that heats the food internally. When appropriately used, the microwave oven offers flexibility and speed for bringing small quantities of frozen and chilled food to a hot state in minutes. Rethermalizing

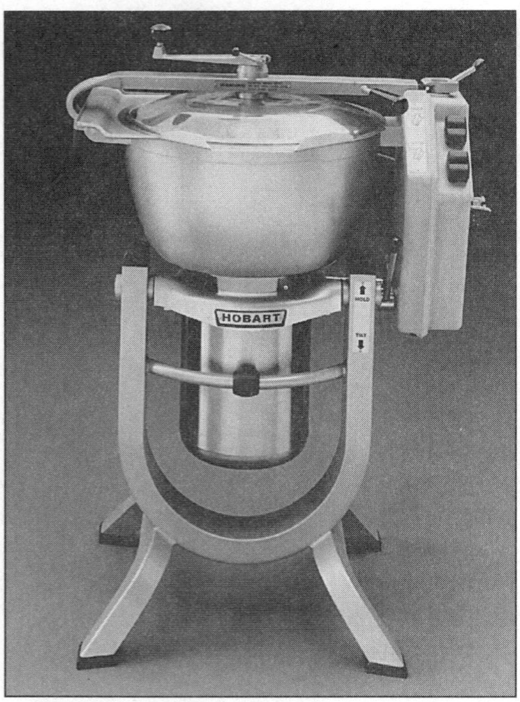

verticle cutter and mixer

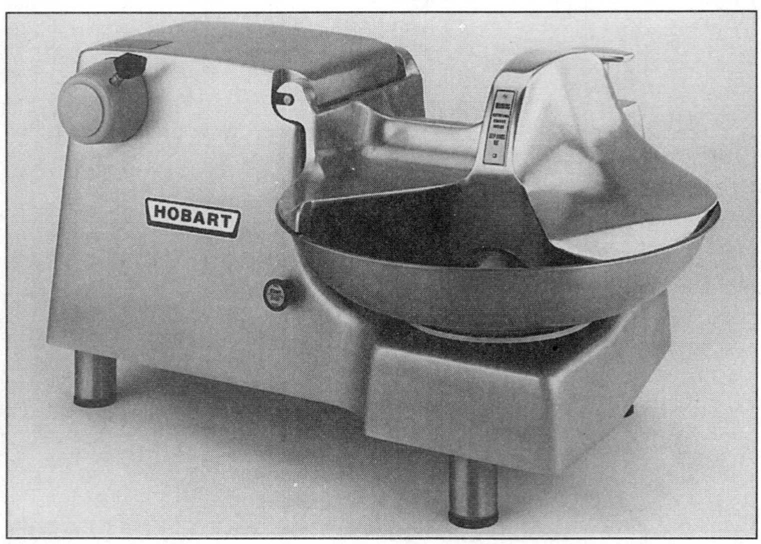

food cutter (Buffalo chopper)

Figure 5.8 Food cutters: (a) verticle cutter and mixer (food processor); (b) food cutter (Buffalo chopper)
Source: Photo courtesy of Hobart Corporation.

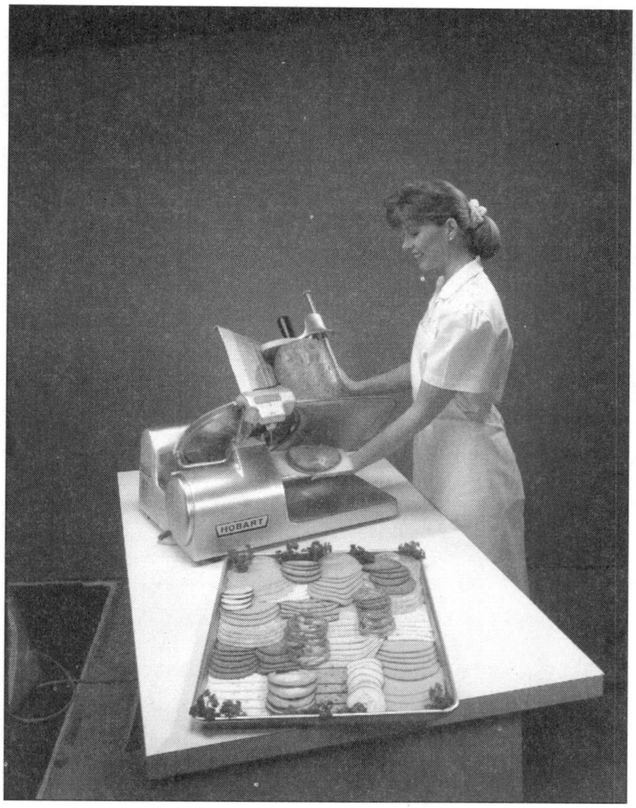

food slicer

chopper

vegetable peeler

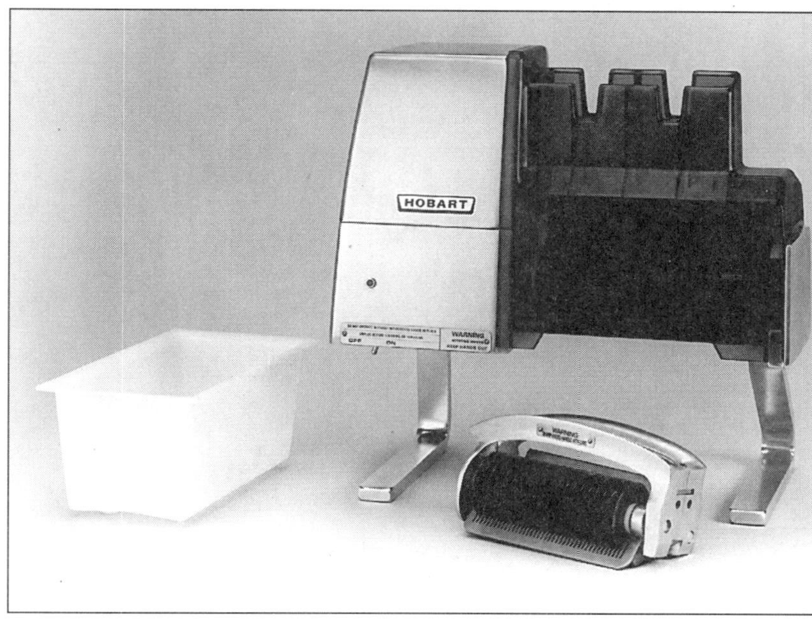

tenderizer

FIGURE 5.9 FOOD PREPARATION EQUIPMENT: (A) FOOD SLICER; (B) VEGETABLE PEELER; (C) CHOPPER; (D) TENDERIZER
Source: Photo courtesy of Hobart Corporation.

ovens use radiation to bring foods from thawing to serving temperatures quickly. Heat is transferred by infrared waves in these units, reaching temperatures as high as 850°F. Figure 5.10 shows different foodservice oven types in use within operations.

Broilers use radiated heat energy to cook food similar to how the sun tans an individual lying in the sun. Most broilers heat from above the product, although some

all-purpose

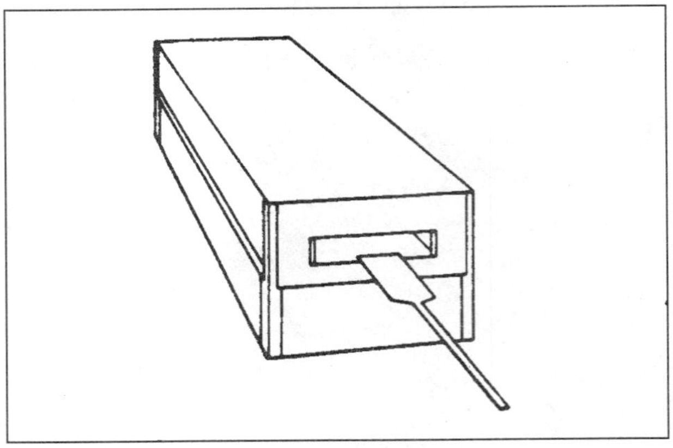

reel oven

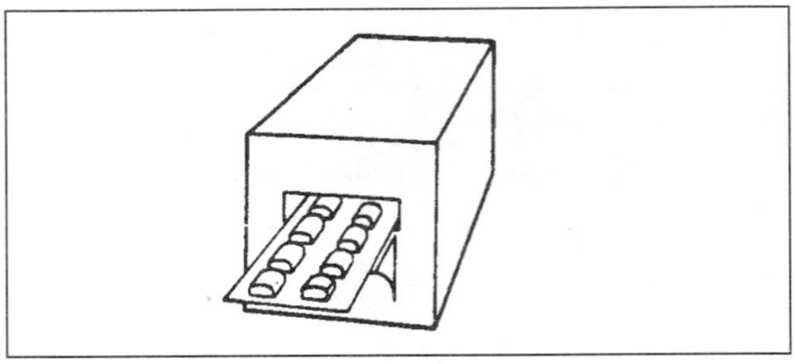

draw-plate oven

deck oven

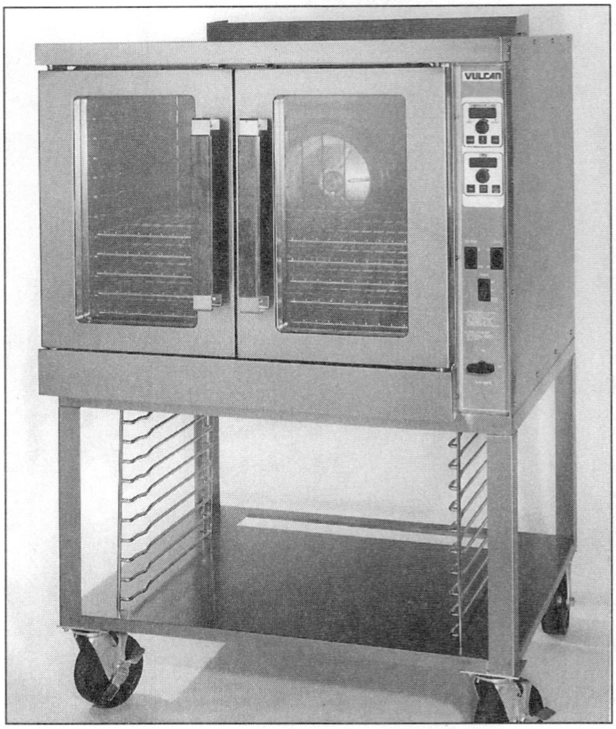

convection

cook from the side or even the bottom of the unit. Fryers cook food in a bath of hot fat, producing a browned, crisp outer coating with a nutty flavor and completely cooked, moist interior. The range includes a combination of an oven and cooking top within one unit. Griddles are found on top of a range or as a stand-alone unit. Food is cooked on the griddle surface in a small amount of fat, much as it would be

double ovens with rectangular and high-speed French hot plates on top

griddle on top of range

gas burners with griddle on double ovens

backshelf broiler attachable to back of range

FIGURE 5.10 FOODSERVICE OVENS: CONVENTIONAL (A) ALL-PURPOSE; (B) REEL OVEN; (C) DRAW-PLATE OVEN; (D) DECK OVEN. RANGES (E) CONVECTION (F) DOUBLE OVENS WITH RECTANGULAR AND HIGH-SPEED FRENCH HOT PLATES ON TOP; (G) GRIDDLE ON TOP OF RANGE; (H) GAS BURNERS WITH GRIDDLE ON DOUBLE OVENS; (I) BACKSHELF BROILER ATTACHABLE TO BACK OF RANGE.
Source: Photo courtesy of Vulcan-Hart Corporation.

cooked in a fry or sauté pan. Steam-cooking units include steam cookers and steam-jacketed kettles, the former bringing steam into a chamber where it comes directly into contact with the food, and the latter working much as a double boiler would, with steam surrounding the food contained in a separate compartment. Tilting pans or skillets are highly versatile and can do the job of a range top, griddle, small steam kettle, stock pot, or fry pan. They tilt up to 90 degrees on a horizontal axis. Figure 5.11 presents various pieces of cooking equipment. Figure 5.12 includes utensils, pots, pans, and other small tools and equipment needed in the cooking subsystem.

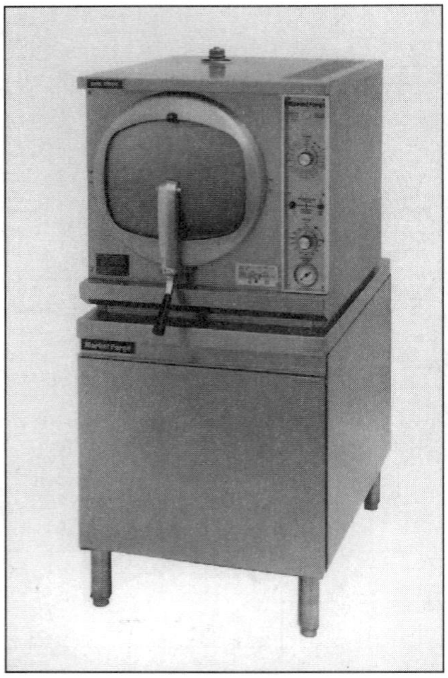

high-compression compartment steam unit

low-compression compartment steam unit

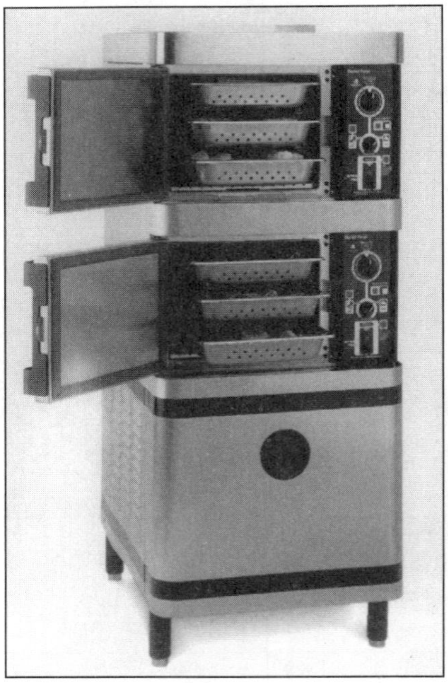

convection steamer

steam-jacketed kettle

FIGURE 5.11 VARIOUS PIECES OF COOKING EQUIPMENT: (A) HIGH-COMPRESSION COMPARTMENT STEAM UNIT; (B) LOW-COMPRESSION COMPARTMENT STEAM UNIT; (C) CONVECTION STEAMER; (D) STEAM-JACKETED KETTLE

Source: Photo courtesy of Market Forge

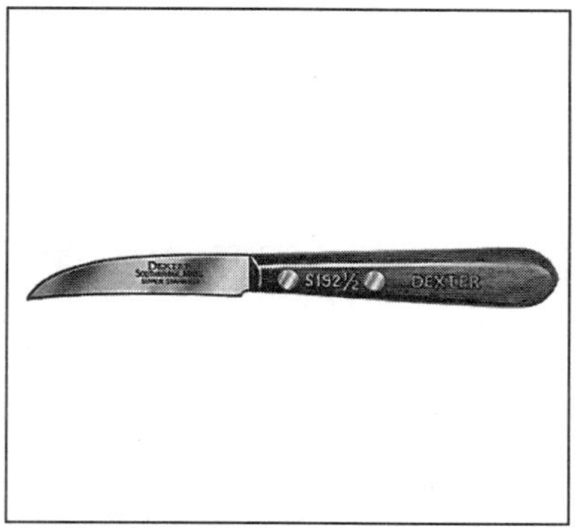

paring—curved

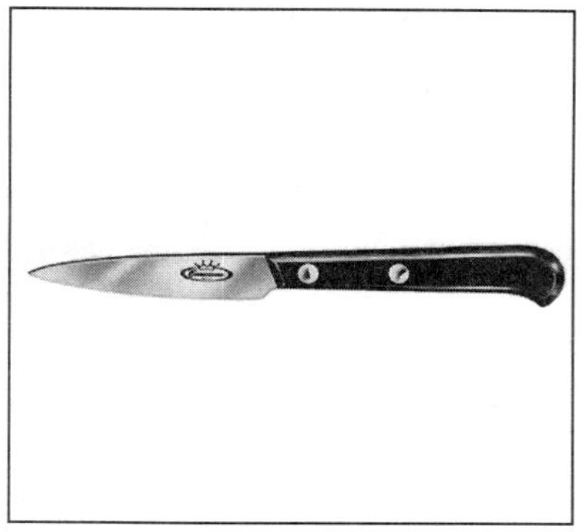

paring—spear

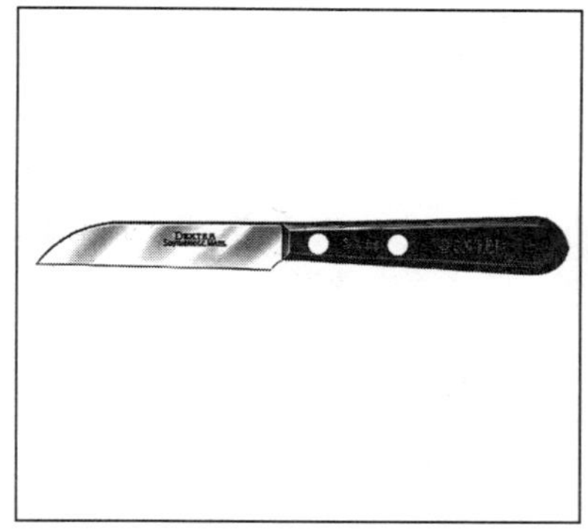

paring—sharp

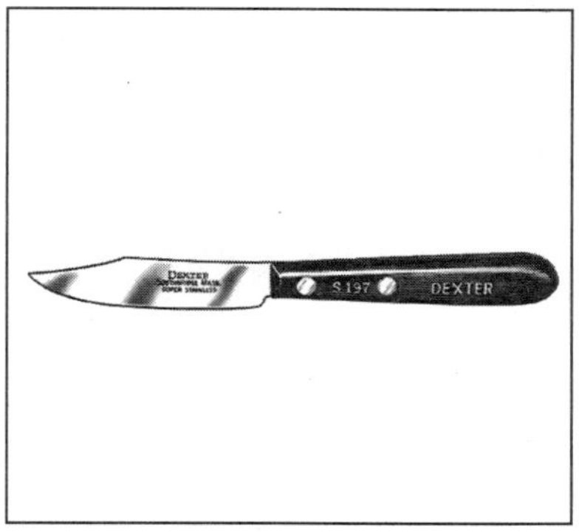

paring—clip point

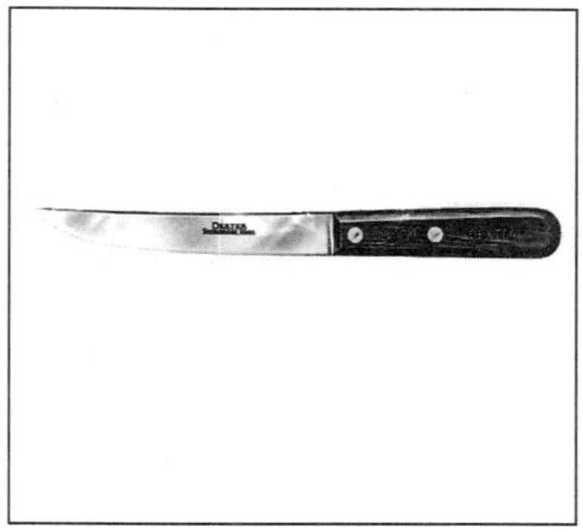

boning—wide

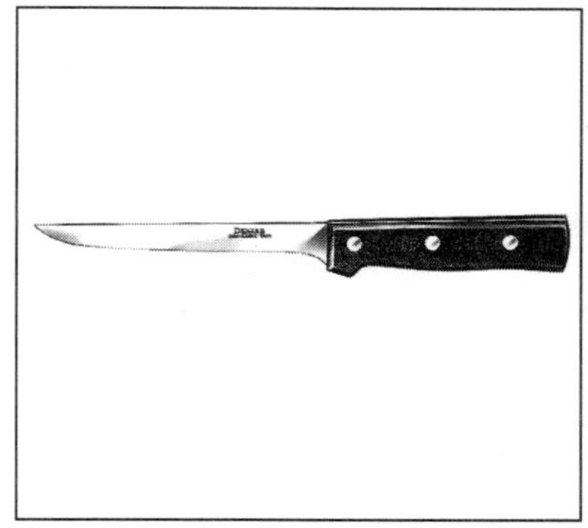

boning—narrow stiff and flexible

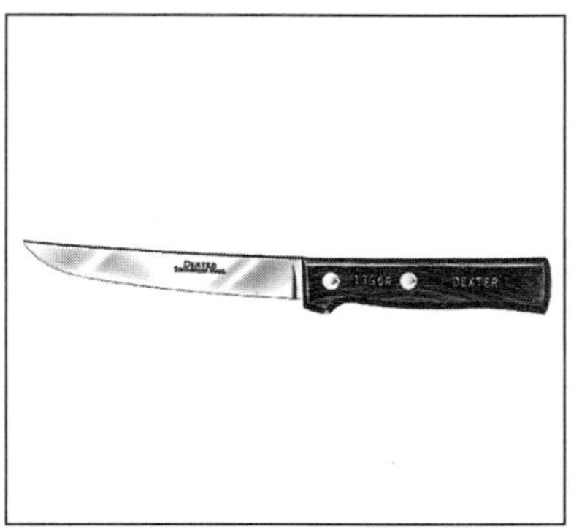

boning—wide stiff

curved cimeter

butcher

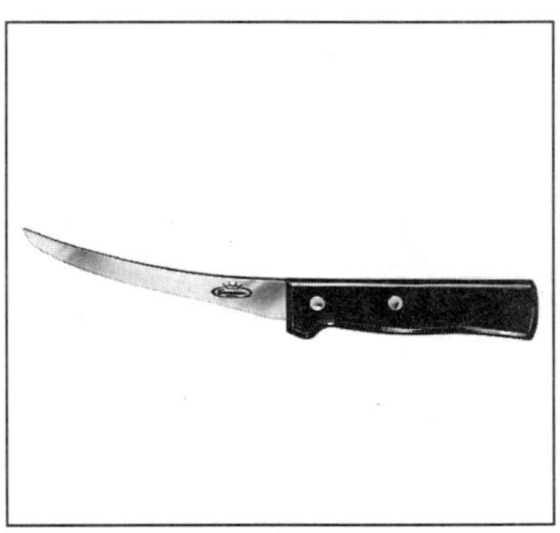

boning—curved

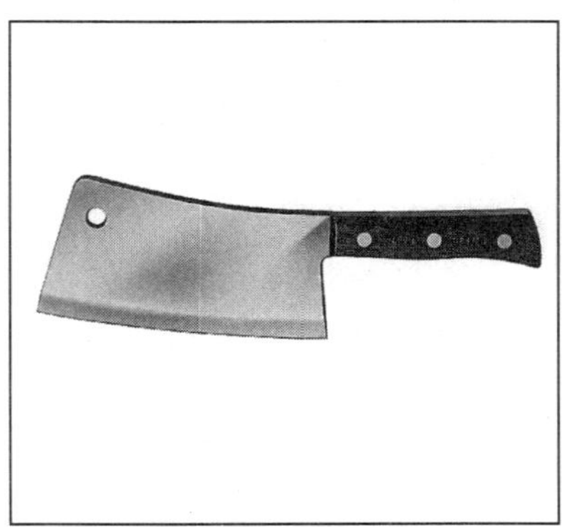

cleaver

forged

Figure 5.12 Various Small Tools for Cooking Areas: (a) knives; (b) utensils; (c) pots and pans
Source: Photo courtesy of Russell Harrington Cutlery, Inc. (photos 1–28) and Crestware (photos 29–49)

regular chef

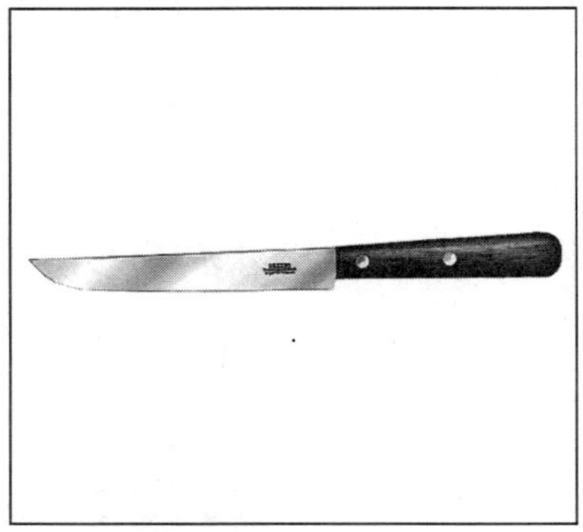
cold meat slicer

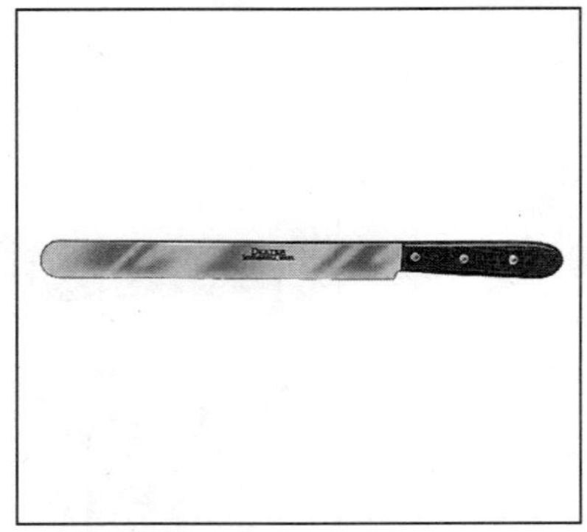
roast beef slicer

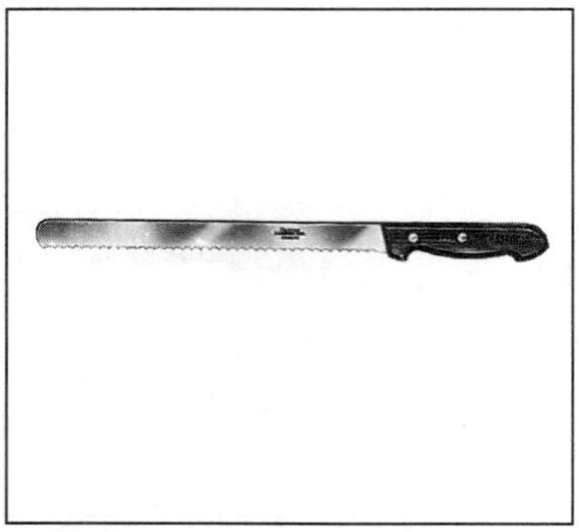
"dur-edge" roast slicer

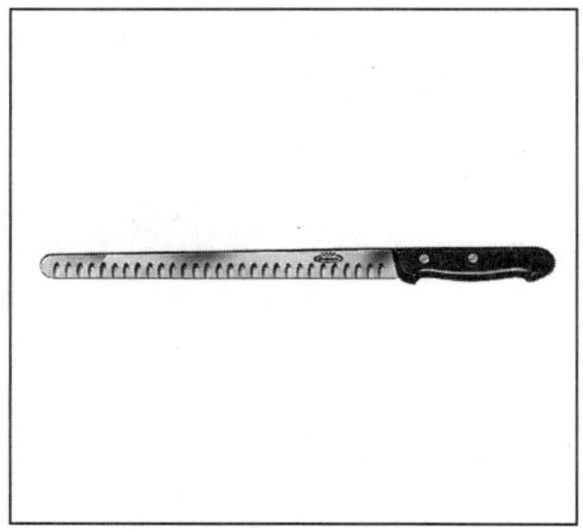
ripple edge slicer

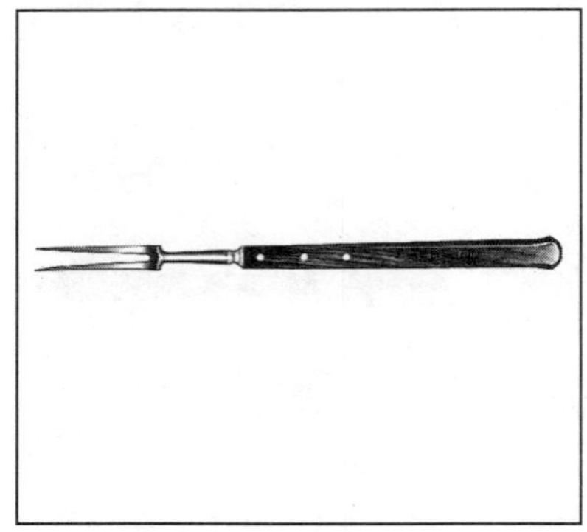
cook's fork

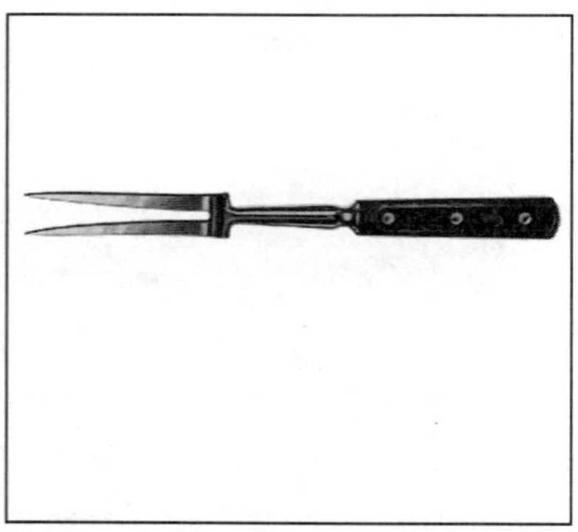
broiler fork

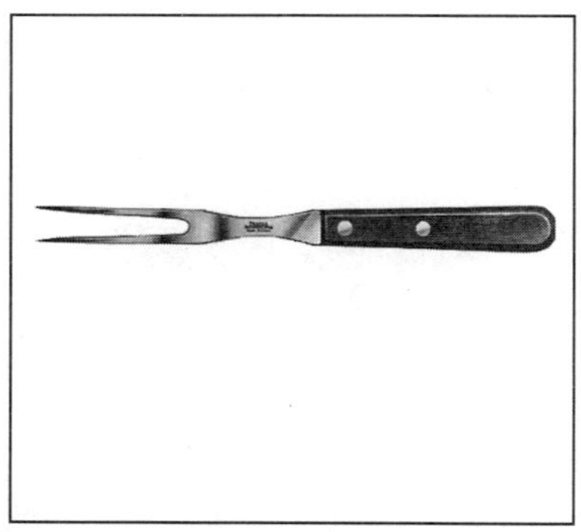
carver fork

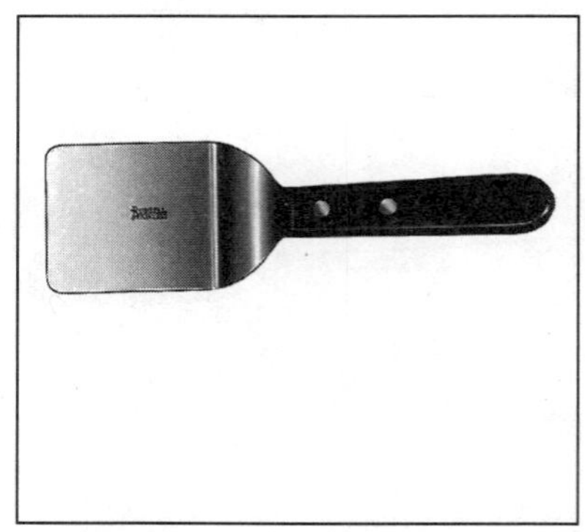
hamburger or cake turner

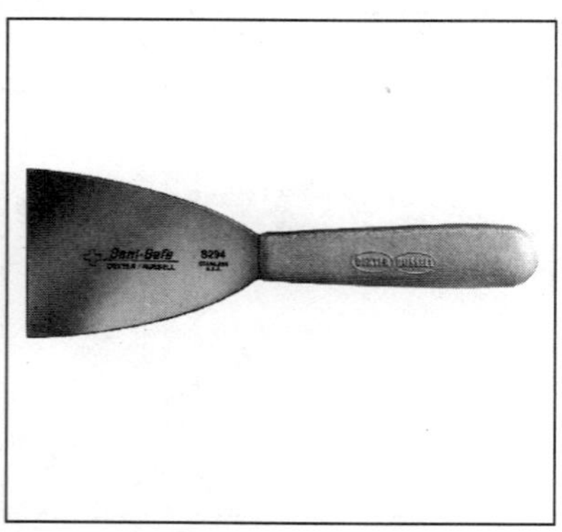
cookie spatula

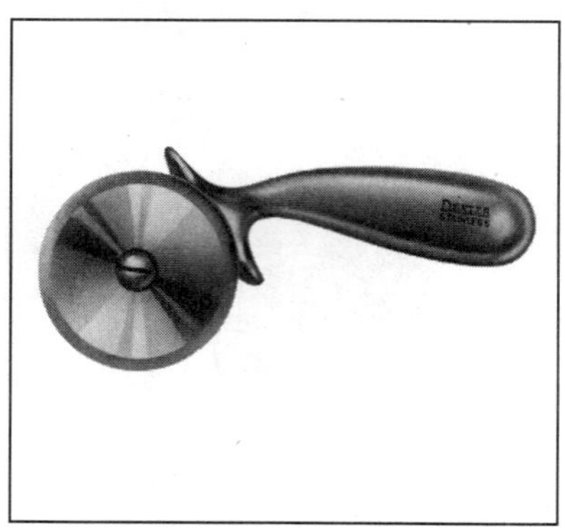
pizza cutter

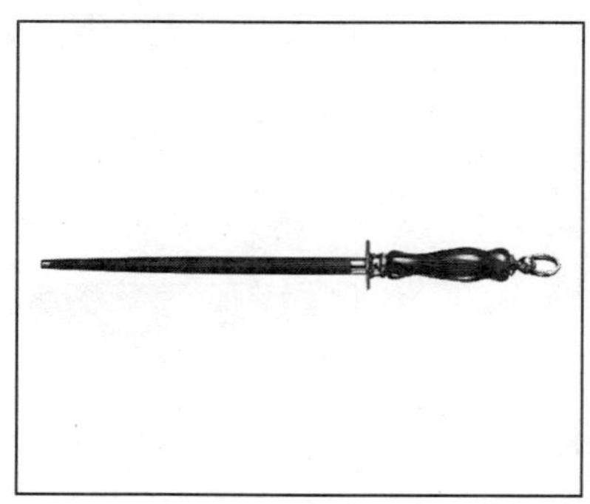
chef's steel—used to sharpen cutting edge

FIGURE 5.12 CONTINUED

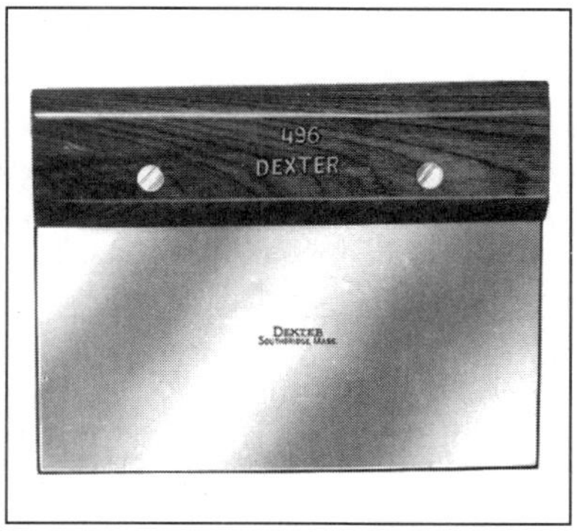

dough cutter—scrapes dough from baker's table

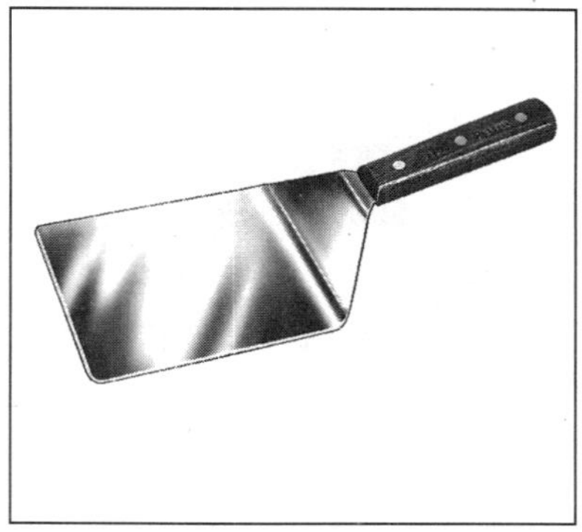

pan scraper—used on griddle tops to remove waste materials

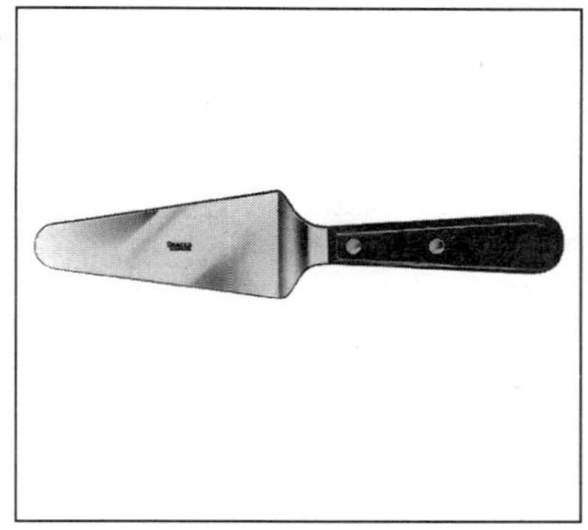

pie knife—removes pie pieces from tin

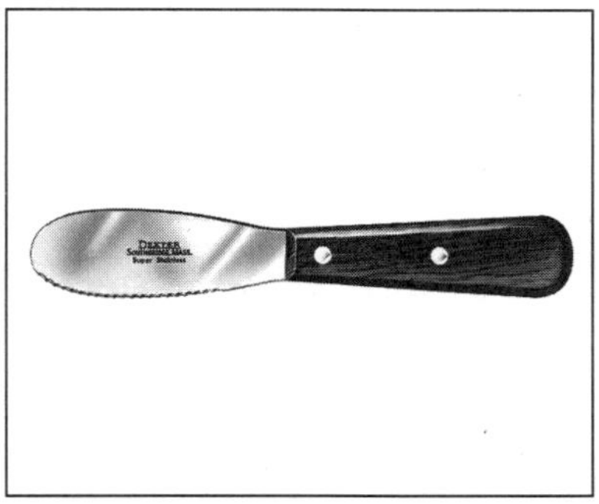

sandwich spreader

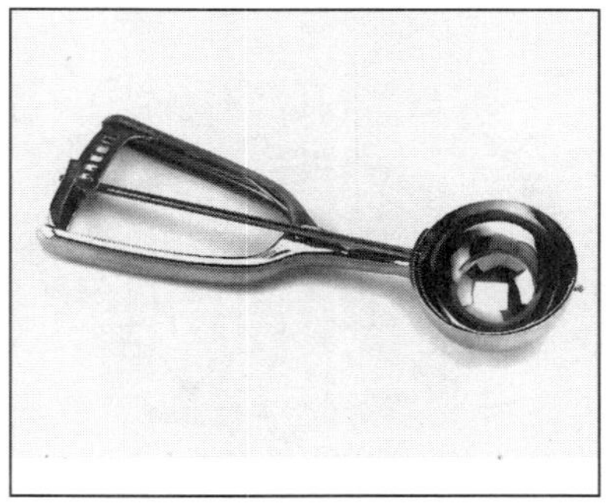

all-purpose disher

scoop

collander

measure

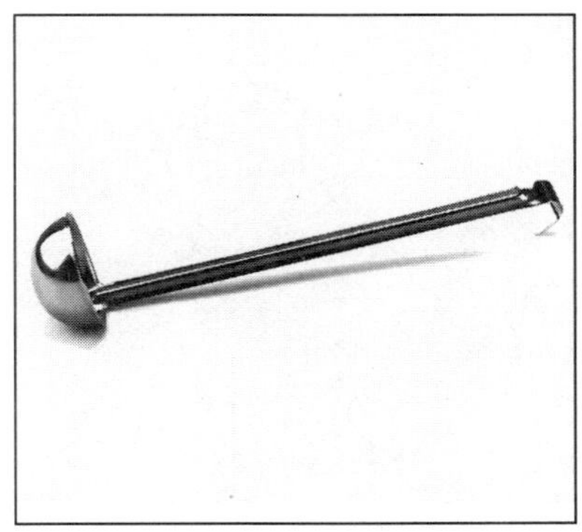

ladle

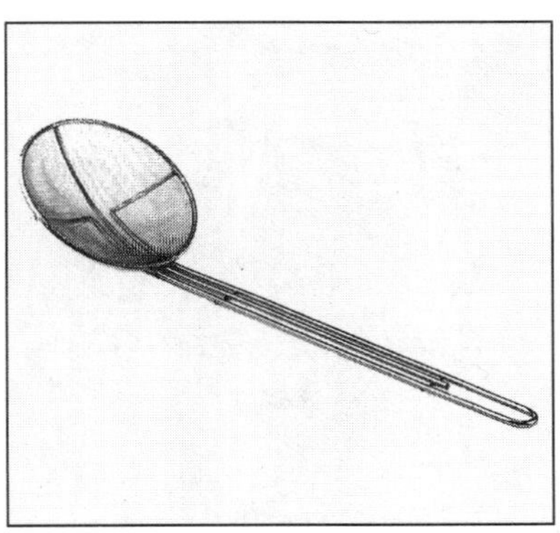

wire skimmer

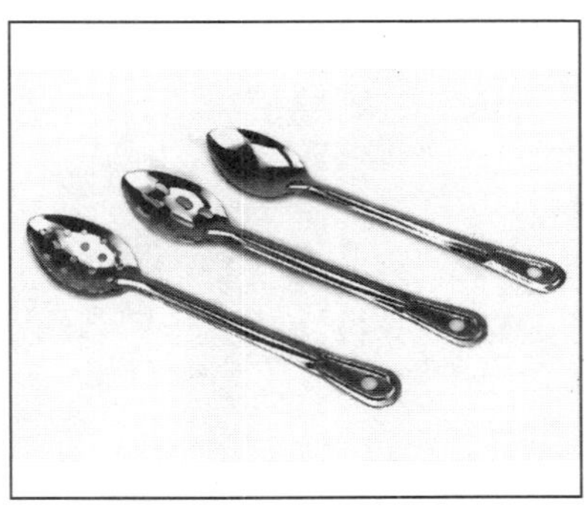

perforated, slotted, and solid spoon

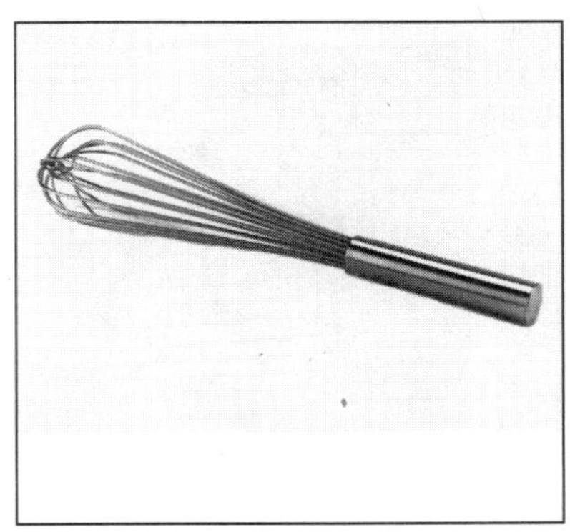

wire whisk

FIGURE 5.12 CONTINUED

steam table pans

sauce pans

fry pan

sautée pan

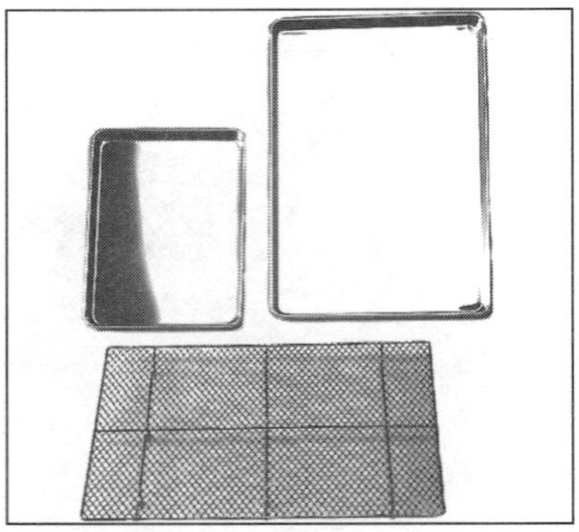

sheet pan

pie tin

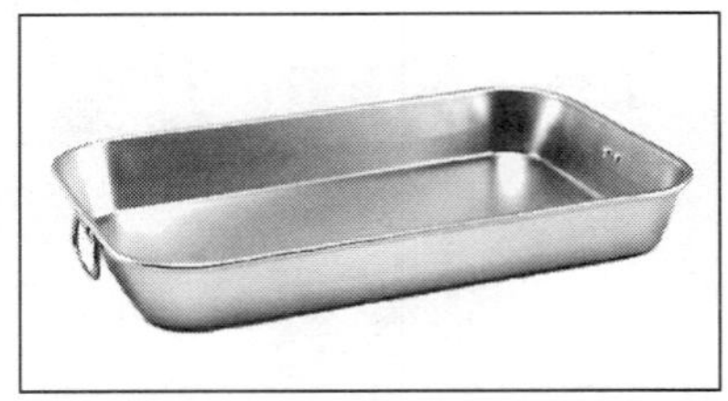

straight-sided bake pan

layer cake pan

muffin pan

bain marie pot

steam table inset

stock pot

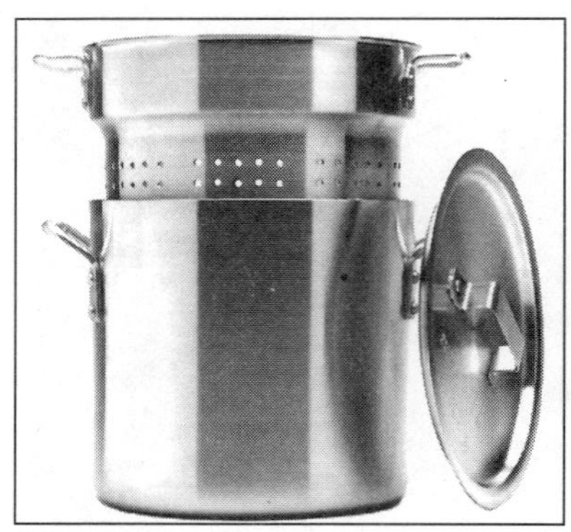

pasta cooker

FIGURE 5.12 CONTINUED

Holding and Serving Equipment

Holding equipment is important in the serving subsystem as the assembly of food occurs and the arrangement of food takes place prior to service. Holding equipment for hot food must keep product hot from 140 degrees F. to 190 degrees F. Holding equipment for cold food should never allow temperatures to rise above 41 degrees F.

Serving equipment includes chafing dishes, mobile carts and display cases. Coffee machines, ice machines and beverage dispensers may also be found in this subsystem.

Other Equipment for Cleanup Purposes

Cleaning up is an ongoing process that begins before each meal and continues throughout preparation, cooking and service. Waste-removal equipment including disposers, compactors and pulpers are important. Dishwashing equipment (see Figure 5.13), including counter and undercounter models, free-standing models,

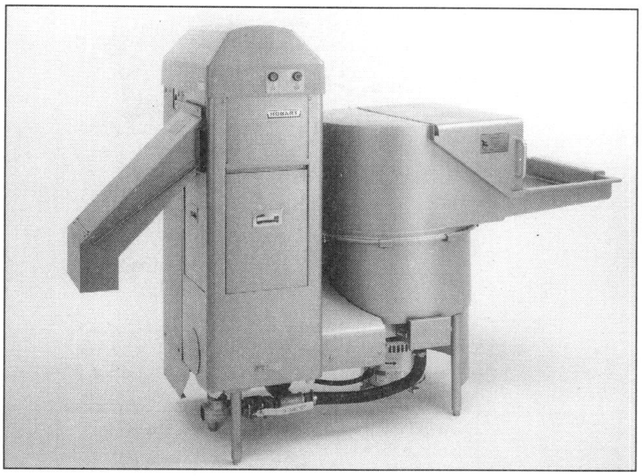

pulper

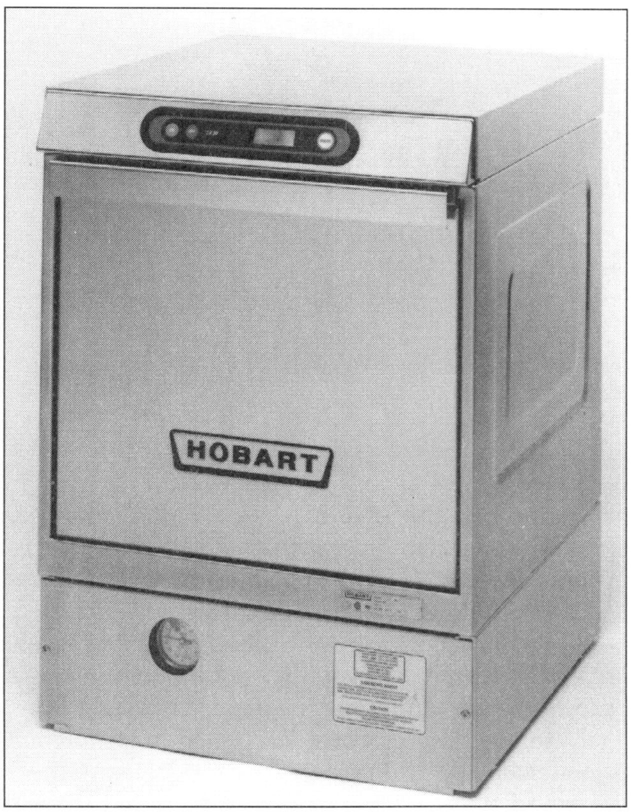

undercounter model

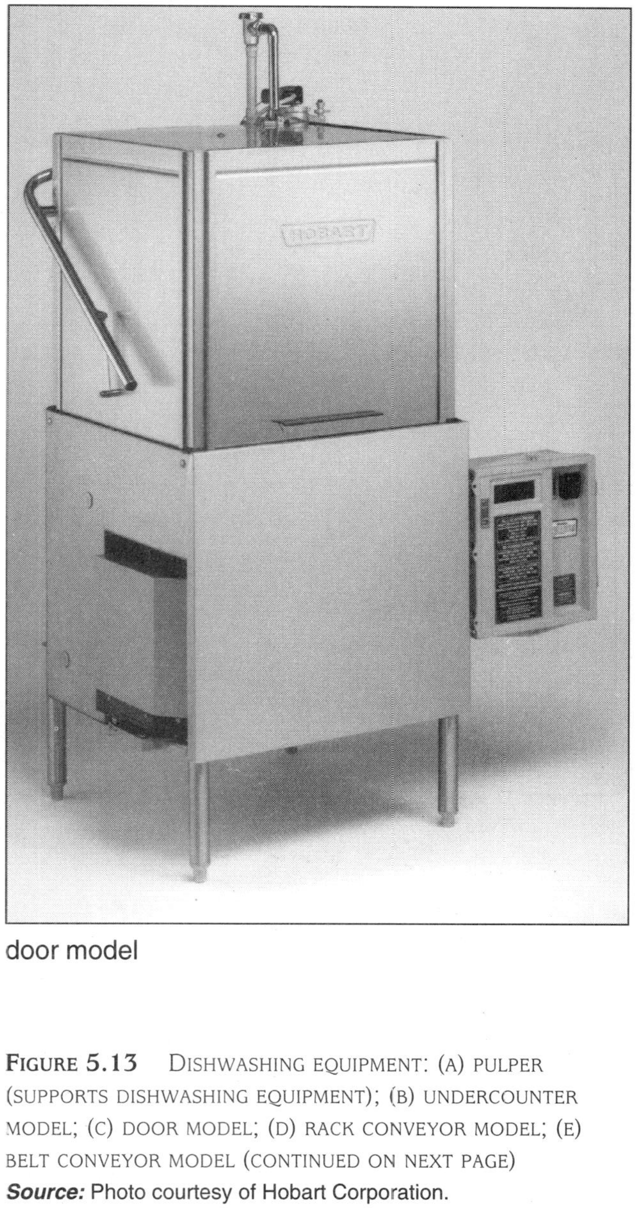

door model

FIGURE 5.13 DISHWASHING EQUIPMENT: (A) PULPER (SUPPORTS DISHWASHING EQUIPMENT); (B) UNDERCOUNTER MODEL; (C) DOOR MODEL; (D) RACK CONVEYOR MODEL; (E) BELT CONVEYOR MODEL (CONTINUED ON NEXT PAGE)
Source: Photo courtesy of Hobart Corporation.

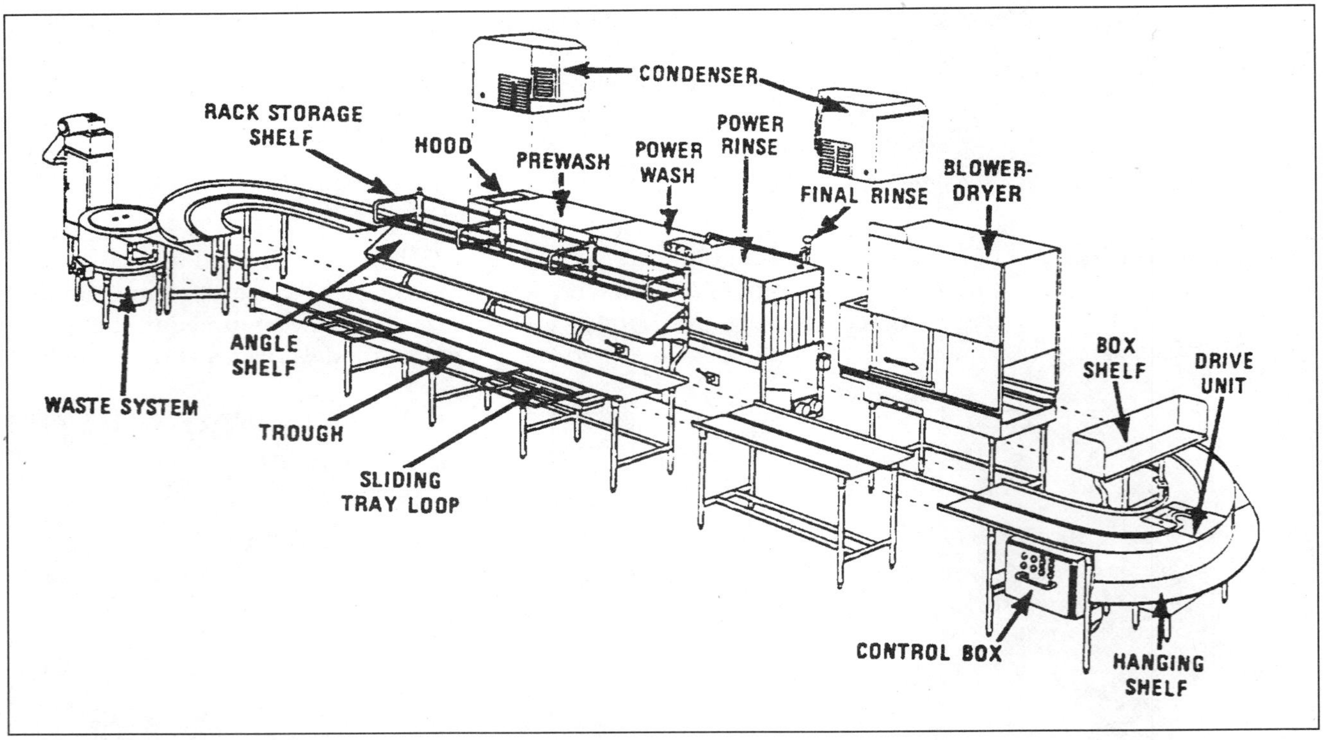

rack conveyor model

belt conveyor model

FIGURE 15.13 CONTINUED

door models, rack conveyor models, and belt conveyor models, are all available to do the job correctly for specific types of foodservice operations.

The key to successful selection and use of foodservice equipment is to know what that equipment will be used for and how to operate it correctly. Computers are continuing to assist in all phases of equipment selection and use. Whether a new software package is used to purchase equipment wisely or a computer controls a piece of equipment to ensure its more efficient operation, the dietary manager is being assisted by the revolution of technology that improves equipment selection and use yearly. A discussion with a manufacturer or dealer of foodservice equipment will keep the dietary manager informed as to what is new and improved in each subsystem.

Equipment Maintenance

There are two basic types of maintenance: crisis maintenance, in which repairs are made as breakdowns occur; and preventive maintenance, a system of pre-scheduling adjustment, cleaning, calibration, lubrication, component replacement, repairs, or other needed services on a regular and routine basis. Preventive maintenance keeps equipment working, and is less costly than crisis maintenance.

The dietary manager must be concerned about the development and implementation of an effective preventive-maintenance program. As this is done, several objectives will be realized:

- Equipment will operate at maximum efficiency; energy and other savings can result;
- Equipment will work correctly;
- Operating costs will be reduced;
- Equipment will attain its maximum life expectancy;
- Unscheduled down-time will be minimized;
- Inventory levels for spare parts will be reduced.

Several basic steps can be used to develop preventive-maintenance programs. First, all equipment in the dietary facility which needs periodic checking/maintenance should be identified, not only preparation and cleanup equipment in the kitchen area itself but also equipment in serving, unit kitchen, and other areas.

The second step is to assess maintenance requirements. Typically, this information is developed by the manufacturer and supplied with the equipment which is sold. This data should be available in the facility. If it is not, the supplier and/or manufacturer should be contacted for an additional copy. This information can be summarized on a maintenance record. One form should be completed for each piece of equipment under the preventive-maintenance program. (Figure 5.3 illustrates a form which might be used.)

The next step in developing the preventive-maintenance program is to set up a schedule of routine inspections. Depending upon the equipment item, maintenance work may be necessary on a weekly, semi-annual, or other basis. Figure 5.14 illustrates a preventive-maintenance schedule form used for this purpose. Note that the form recaps required preventive-maintenance activities for a six-month period. The form is completed by indicating with a check-mark the week during which necessary work is to be performed on each equipment item. Computerized systems to track and identify this information are in increasing use.

Wise dietary managers know that noting required maintenance activities on a preventive-maintenance schedule does not mean that required work will be done on schedule. It is very difficult to give priority to preventive-maintenance work when maintenance/engineering staff are facing building system or major equipment breakdown problems. It is, however, part of the dietary manager's job to check consistently that required work is done by maintenance/engineering staff, if applicable, or by another individual.

Some facilities make use of maintenance or service contracts with suppliers. Under this plan, eligible suppliers bid on the facility's maintenance needs. Quotations may be based upon actual time spent at the facility, a monthly fee, or another alternative. Some companies include discounts on necessary parts in their quotations for the maintenance contract.

The dietary manager should make effective use of equipment suppliers; input is of value as equipment selection decisions are made. Frequently supplier representatives have information about how other facilities have solved operating problems, and suggestions about equipment items which might be useful.

Equipment	Work	MONTH	JANUARY				FEBRUARY				MARCH				APRIL				MAY				JUNE			
Item	Necessary	WEEK	1	2	3	4	1	2	3	4	1	2	3	4	1	2	3	4	1	2	3	4	1	2	3	4

FIGURE 5.14 PREVENTIVE MAINTENANCE SCHEDULE

The services of the supplier do not end when an equipment selection decision has been made. Many suppliers make suggestions about the most effective placement of equipment and about the best type of utility service to be used. After the equipment is installed, suppliers may conduct training programs to instruct staff members in proper use of the equipment. As the dietary manager develops the operations manual or preventive-maintenance procedures for each piece of equipment, the supplier representative should provide useful input. Suppliers can also help with ideas about how best to integrate new equipment with other equipment, procedures, and systems used by the facility.

Some suppliers offer preventive-maintenance contracts to facilities; equipment covered by a maintenance contract will be routinely serviced by the supplier. This plan is frequently useful when personnel skilled in servicing sophisticated equipment are not available within the institution. Many operators, however, do not put new equipment items under preventive-maintenance contracts for the first year (since items are likely to be covered by the manufacturer's guarantee for this or a similar time period).

MANAGING THE COST OF SUPPLIES

A hospital serving 1,000 clients and employees a day can easily spend $1,000 or more per month for chemicals needed to clean dishes, pots and pans, and work areas pertaining to dietary services. Many dietary managers are unaware of the significant cost implications for cleaning and related supplies. Most are aware, however, of the need to use the "right" chemicals in the "right" quantities to assure that cleanliness and sanitation goals are met.

Today, modern technology has made a wide range of chemicals available for use in dietary services. Check with your supplier for ideas about available items and recommended uses, and use your supplier representative as a "partner" to help resolve cleaning and sanitation problems in the facility.

As is true with all resources available to dietary services, cleaning supplies must be properly controlled. While employee theft may be of less concern, it is still necessary to deal with the "best" supplier. When considering a supplier of cleaning agents, consider his or her location, financial stability, technical ability (the extent to which he or she can provide help to you as you encounter problems related to effective cleaning), price, attitude, and the extent to which your past experiences with the supplier have proven beneficial.

A cost-benefit study is usually necessary to confirm which product is the most potentially useful. To undertake this study, first define what the product is to do; ask suppliers for suggestions about and/or samples of products that they believe will be useful. Using the instructions provided by the supplier and/or those on the container itself, use each product properly. Then objectively determine which meet the facility's quality requirements. All further analysis should only consider those products which provide the proper quality of cleaning services to the facility.

The next concern is cost. For example, one gallon of a cleaning agent may cost $50 but clean twice as many square feet to your quality requirements as another gallon costing less than this price. Study is necessary to define the cost per square foot, rack of dishes, load of laundry, and so on, to make a fair comparison.

To effectively control supplies cost, first consider the usage cost—not purchase cost. Since the amount required per use may vary between products, the cost of amount used per month should be compared. Second, dietary staff must be trained in proper use of products. The quantity of items to be purchased should be considered. Frequently, suppliers will assist the facility in making this decision. The supplier's representative may keep track of the number of purchase units bought and used, and will make recommendations on a monthly or other basis about the quantity to purchase. (While there is some merit to this system, this plan does not relieve the dietary manager of the ultimate responsibility for determining purchase quantities.)

Ongoing supervision assures that the correct amount of all cleaning supplies is used. Sometimes an employee has the mistaken notion that "if three ounces is good, then six ounces will be better." In addition to providing training and on-site supervision, the dietary manager should provide, where applicable, the correct measuring or portioning devices to help eliminate guesswork by the employees.

Cleaning supplies should be kept in non-food-storage areas. Since these products are expensive, a formal issuing system similar to that used to control expensive food products may be in order. Dietary managers also recognize the need to track usage of products. With a stable participation level, why would an increasing—or decreasing—amount of cleaning supplies be needed? These questions must be routinely asked—and answered!

When cleaning supplies are used with equipment such as dish and ware washers, laundry equipment, and so on, proper maintenance and service of the equipment is necessary to minimize the amount of cleaning supplies needed. Some cleaning supply services offer maintenance and service work on affected equipment (with service costs being charged back to the facility as part of the product cost).

Automatic mixers are available which "automatically" dispense proper quantities of cleaning supplies. High-pressure cleaning systems with applicable chemicals are also used for cleaning many items of dietary service equipment.

The need for utilizing a good supplier is just as important for the purchase of chemicals as it is for the purchase of food products, capital equipment items, and other purchases. The "good" supplier must be honest, fair, and knowledgeable about the product needs of dietary services. He or she must consistently meet the quality and quantity requirements of the facility and deliver the needed supplies on time. He or she should also charge reasonable prices, and have a desire to continue to improve the product and services being provided. As is true with any supplier, the supplier of cleaning agents must be accessible to the dietary manager and facility, careful in planning and making product delivery, and able to provide necessary followup service.

SUMMARY

The design of a facility impacts the efficiency of personnel within the dietary operation. Several factors affect the layout of the dietary facility:

- The menu;
- Type of production used;
- Quantity of food to prepare;
- Necessary equipment;
- Funds;
- Space;
- Production systems.

The most important factor to consider as food preparation areas are designed is the menu, since space, employees, equipment, and ingredients must be available to prepare each item required by the menu and the production/delivery system in use.

Special concerns include designing a facility that would reduce physical fatigue among employees, reducing the noise level by using soundproofing materials and selecting less noisy equipment, installing proper lights, considering temperature concerns around specific cooking and cleaning equipment, and safety and sanitation concerns.

Receiving areas should typically be as close as practical to the storage areas and large enough to place all items being received, so that effective receiving practices can be used.

Dining-room planners must consider not only the number of persons to be served at one time but also the flow of soiled dishes back to washing areas. The atmosphere of the facility, the cleanliness and condition of dining room furniture, fixtures and equipment, lighting, and a wide range of other concerns are important to the clients' impressions of foodservice.

Additionally, other spaces must be considered for dietary services: an office for dietary management, space for dish and pot washing, holding of refuse until pickup, space for washing mobile equipment, space for storing cleaning and other chemicals, and space for refrigeration equipment for walk-in units.

The proper design of foodservice areas, a difficult and complex job, is very important, and will dramatically affect the long-term effectiveness of dietary services. Cook-Serve kitchens have six subsystems, each with its own space requirements and each equipped for specific functions. No-Cook and Cook-Chill kitchens are so named for the specific techniques of preparing food in them and serving it to the customer.

Capital equipment purchases affect the way the dietary facility operates. There are many factors to be considered in order to determine equipment selection. Capital equipment must be suitable for its intended use. The purchase must also be cost-effective and the special elements of concern must be evaluated.

When selecting a supplier, consider supplier's reputation pre-purchase assistance, difference in price and terms, and post sale assistance.

Financing may be a special concern, especially when adequate funds are not available. There are several methods for financing large equipment. The purchasing of used equipment is an alternative for dietary managers.

Procedures for maintaining, operating, and cleaning foodservice equipment will also need to be developed; once developed, these procedures must be incorporated into training and supervision activities for all affected employees.

There are two basic types of maintenance: crisis maintenance, in which repairs are made as breakdowns occur; and preventive maintenance, a system of pre-scheduling adjustment, cleaning, calibration, lubrication, component replacement, repairs, or other needed services on a regular and routine basis. In fact, some suppliers offer preventive-maintenance contracts to facilities so that equipment covered by a maintenance contract will be routinely serviced by the supplier.

As is true with all resources available to dietary services, cleaning supplies must be properly controlled. After choosing the best supplier, the dietary manager will want to undertake a cost-benefit study to determine which products will meet the facility's quality requirements. Finally, ongoing supervision is necessary to assure that the correct amount of all cleaning supplies is used, and a formal issuing system may be in order.

KEY TERMS

- Work flow
- Cook-Serve kitchen
- No-Cook kitchen
- Cook-Chill
- Capital equipment
- Receiving equipment
- Refrigeration and chilling equipment
- Preparation equipment
- Cooking equipment
- Holding and serving equipment
- Waste-removal equipment
- Preventive maintenance
- Crisis maintenance
- Cost-benefit study

QUESTIONS/PROBLEMS/CASES

1. You are a dietary manager who appreciates the input of your staff, so you've called them to a meeting to provide input to the design team for the foodservice department in a new addition to the foodservice area. They inform you that the employee turnover has been high in the past because of the physical strain that they are under, as well as the heat and noise factors in the facility. You realize that it is in the best interest of the facility to meet the needs of the employees. What are some things that you might consider as selection decisions are made for the new facility?

2. You've been asked to serve a large number of people at multiple sites with flexible schedules. What method of cooking might you consider for such a production?

3. What factors should a dietary manager consider when selecting a supplier for large equipment items?

4. After considering several sources, your facility has decided to purchase used foodservice equipment. Where would you begin looking for good used equipment?

5. Since purchasing large equipment represents a long-term investment, and since the equipment selected will have an overt impact upon the efficiency of the operation and the quality of the products produced, what factors become important when considering new equipment?

6. Plan a subsystem of a foodservice operation, such as receiving and describe what might typically be included in this subsystem.

7. In making equipment selection decisions, how might an equipment supplier representative be of help?

8. Describe the steps involved in the undertaking of a cost-benefit study for purchasing supplies.

9. What factors affect the layout of the dietary facility?

10. Identify which type of kitchen each of the following descriptions fit.

    Elmwood City School District operates the following kitchens.

    The Central Commissary uses a new technology called sous-vide to prepare entrees that are shipped to most school kitchens.

    Most schools rethermalize the sous-vide foods, add appropriate cold foods, and serve school lunches.

    One small kitchen at North Elmwood is located the furthest from the Central Commissary and prepares its own meals for the small population it feeds.

11. Describe the steps involved in developing and implementing an effective preventive maintenance program.

6

FOOD PRODUCTION AND SERVICE

CHAPTER OUTLINE

- Pre-production Planning
- Food Production Control
- Food Production Principles
  - Meat Preparation Principles
  - Poultry Preparation Principles
  - Thawing Meats and Poultry
  - Fish, Egg, and Cheese Preparation Principles
  - Vegetable and Fruit Cookery Principles
  - Salad Preparation Principles
  - Stock and Soup Preparation Principles
  - Sauce Preparation Principles
  - Principles of Bread and Cereal Preparation
  - Sandwich Production Principles
  - Dessert Preparation Principles
- Monitoring Food Waste and Managing Solid Waste
- Identifying the Type of Service Needed
- A Close Look at Food Transport Equipment and Systems
- Tray Line Systems
  - Metal Pellet System
  - Use of Insulated Trays
  - Thermostatically Controlled Dishes
  - Infrared Radiation System

PRE-PRODUCTION PLANNING

Experienced dietary managers recognize that things don't "automatically" happen as products are being prepared. A wide range of pre-production activities involved with purchasing, receiving, storing, and issuing must first be undertaken. Once products are "in the house" and ready to use, pre-production planning becomes important. In many, especially small, institutions, pre-production planning may be done "in the head" of the dietary manager and/or head cook. In larger facilities, it may be a very formalized process with weekly or other scheduled production meetings of various personnel to coordinate planning necessary for upcoming routine and special production needs.

There are several advantages to production planning:

1. Plans must be developed so that food products, personnel, and equipment are available in necessary quantities;
2. Coordination between production and service staff must take place to prevent resources available to dietary services from being over- or under-utilized;
3 Effective planning decreases the likelihood that problems will arise.

Procedures for pre-production planning must be developed for each specific facility. Several basic principles are important:

Portions. Regularly scheduled pre-production planning meetings should be held to plan the number of portions of each menu item to prepare. The dietary manager and head cook in a small facility may meet weekly to review plans for the following week. Sales-history records can be reviewed and used as a guide to estimate production forecasts for the upcoming week. Season of the year, weather, special events within the facility, and similar factors are also considered in an attempt to estimate production needs. In some facilities with a constant client count, these elements may not be relevant; however, in hospitals, schools, and other facilities with a varying number of meals to be served, estimates of the quantity of food to be produced become very important.

How does one determine the quantity of food produced and served during a previous time period? Some ways include analysis of sales journal tapes from cash registers (in cash cafeteria operations) and review of production/leftover records (in non-cash operations). Figure 6.1 shows a form which can be used for a food production planning and leftover worksheet. Each item to be prepared is noted (column 1). The portion size and number of portions to be prepared are also stated

Date: ______________________

Meal: ______________________

Item	Portion Size	Number of Portions to Prepare	Employee Assigned	Comments	Number of Portions Left Over	Actual Number Served
1	2	3	4	5	6	7

FIGURE 6.1 FOOD PRODUCTION PLANNING AND LEFTOVER REPORT

(columns 2 and 3). The employee assigned the production task and any special comments are also noted (columns 4 and 5). At the end of the meal period, the number of portions left over is reported (column 6). The actual number served (column 7) can be computed (column 3 minus column 6).

Information about leftovers and number of portions served (from the food production planning and leftover worksheet) can be used to complete the worksheet for future meal periods. The food production planning and leftover worksheet therefore serves a third purpose: providing a sales history useful to assess the number of meals to prepare for subsequent meal periods;

Labor. In addition to planning the number of portions of each menu item to prepare, pre-production planning meetings can also be used to schedule required labor hours. The actual number of labor hours required will be dependent upon the number of clients to be served. The maximum number of hours scheduled for each "routine" shift cannot, of course, exceed the maximum allowed in the staffing guide. The dietary manager must be creative in scheduling staff members for exceptionally busy or slow shifts, and for special functions or other non-routine dietary events;

Equipment. It may also be necessary to schedule equipment for specific time periods. For example, equipment scheduling may become necessary when a special catered function requires production of items in quantities not normally needed.

After the pre-production planning sessions are completed, the required number of portions of each menu item is known. It then becomes possible to prepare purchase orders for perishable products and to confirm that dry and frozen inventory levels for these products are sufficient.

When special catered functions require greatly increased quantities of food products, or a special event requires products not normally carried in inventory, it becomes very important to assure that these products will be available. Pre-production planning maximizes communication and coordination among the dietary manager, the purchasing official, and other interested parties.

Food Production Control

Food production involves preparing and assembling required food products. Procedures to maintain quality and to comply with planned cost concerns must be implemented. Quality control—especially defining quality and adhering to required standards—is of prime concern. It does little good, for example, to purchase proper quality food products, to use procedures designed to maximize quality during storage, and to be sure standardized recipes (which dictate procedures to maintain quality during production) are available in the work station if you do not supervise closely to ensure adherence to standards.

The dietary manager and his or her assistants must constantly supervise work being done. They must see that products in sufficient quantity for production needs—no more or less—are withdrawn from inventory. They must make sure that all required food production procedures relating to quality, cost control, safety and so on are being followed. Food waste during production must be minimized by designing efficient production techniques.

Employee eating/drinking policies must be followed. Productivity decreases, sanitation problems increase, and food costs rise if reasonable policies are not developed and enforced.

Spoiled food resulting from either improper storage and/or incorrect production must be discarded. The dietary manager must recognize the impact of these wasteful practices on food costs. As this occurs, the dietary manager becomes more acutely aware that basic management principles have been violated and that corrective action and closer supervision are necessary.

The need for production-planning records cannot be over emphasized. Supervision is required to ensure that the quantities of food items produced, the number of labor hours scheduled, the times for specific equipment items to be used, and so on match those specified during pre-production planning.

Production "bottlenecks" during busy periods should be detected and problems resolved. Often, affected personnel themselves will have ideas about how procedures can be improved and how costs can be reduced in the process.

Weighing and measuring tools and equipment should always be used in preparation of food items. Portion control tools (scoops, ladles, etc.) should always be used as food items are being portioned. Communication and coordination among work sections within the dietary department, and between the dietary department, and other work units within the facility are very important as plans are "put together" and implemented.

Records kept during production can guide the future planning of the operation and provide input to accounting systems. There are definite control implications to:

- the design of record-keeping systems,
- the accuracy of information (and subsequent decisions) from the record-keeping system, and
- the timeliness of information and generated reports.

Said another way, accounting information (such as actual food and labor costs from operating statements) will be affected by the actual production process, and should be used as a foundation against which to measure how well plans have been carried out.

Use of labor-saving food (convenience foods) and equipment must do just that: Labor must be reduced at least to the level where savings will pay for the increased food or equipment costs. If not, food or equipment costs will increase, labor costs will stay the same, and total costs will be higher than before the use of the "labor-saving" food and/or equipment item.

Consider the following example: The dietary manager may determine that labor costs can be reduced if a specified piece of labor-saving equipment (such as a patty-making machine or a bread/roll slicing machine) is purchased. The equipment is purchased, but labor is not reduced. The "paper savings" from the preliminary analysis does not in itself yield reduced operating costs.

The Food Production Planning and Leftover Report (see Figure 6.1) must be accurately completed and used as a future reference to "fine-tune" the process of assessing the quantity of items to be prepared. Leftovers should be creatively used in future production. The need to control food costs by using leftovers, however, must always be balanced by the need to constantly maintain established food quality levels.

Food Production Principles

Entire books have been written to detail principles of quantity food production. It is therefore impossible to review details important to help assure *quality* quantity food production. The information which follows provides examples of important food preparation techniques.

Meat Preparation Principles

A. Cook at low temperatures.
   1. This will soften connective tissues.
   2. This produces tender, juicy meats with minimum shrinkage.

B. Use appropriate cooking methods indicated by tenderness of meat.
   1. Dry heat (for tender cuts such as steaks, roasts, tenderized portions): roasting, baking, broiling, pan broiling.
      a) Tender cuts of beef
      b) Most cuts of lamb and pork since they are young in age. (See Figure 6.2)
   2. Moist heat (for less tender cuts such a stewing meat, shanks, and those having a lot of connective tissue): braising and stewing.
      a) Less tender cuts of beef.
      b) Pork and lamb shanks.
      c) Methods of moist heat cookery.
         1) Braising: to braise meat, a skillet or grill is used to brown the product. A high temperature of 475°F is used to carmelize the meat to add flavor. The meat is then placed in a pan with a tight-fitting lid with a small amount of fluid, and cooked at medium heat until the internal temperature is 185°F. Continue cooking for 30 minutes. The internal temperature, cooking time, and water all combine to tenderize the meat.
         2) Stewing: to stew, meat is first browned to caramelize the meat for deeper color and richer flavor. The meat is then covered with water and simmered at 185°F until the connective tissue is softened.

C. Use a meat (or instant-read) thermometer. (The internal temperature of the meat is the only accurate way to determine when the meat is done).

D. Use meat timetables as a general guide for cooking meat. (Timetables are useful in determining when to start cooking meat in order for it to be done when needed).

E. Thawing procedures for meat are similar to those for poultry. (See the next section.)

Poultry Preparation Principles

A. Cook at low temperature 325°–350°F (to produce a tender juicy product).

B. Use appropriate cooking methods indicated by the tenderness of bird.
   1. Dry heat (for young poultry) such as sautéing, roasting or ovenfrying

FIGURE 6.2 SPICE RUBBED PORK TENDERLOIN
Source: Photo courtesy of National Pork Producers Council

a) Roasting of poultry.
   1) Whole turkeys, turkey roasts, and portioned products such as bone-in or boneless breasts can be roasted. Follow processor's preparation instructions when preparing these items.
   2) To reduce cooking time of whole turkeys, debone flesh from the carcass.
   3) Never stuff a turkey with dressing before roasting.
b) Ovenfrying of poultry.
   1) Is a popular method of preparing chicken in quantity.
   2) Brush cooking oil or margarine over the poultry, place on a greased sheet pan, and bake at 350°F until done (use a thermometer).

2. Moist heat (less tender birds) such as braising, steaming or stewing.
   a) Braising of poultry (for technique refer to braising meat above).
      1) Few poultry items are prepared by the braising method.
      2) Braising temperatures should not exceed 185°F.
   b) Steaming of poultry.
      1) In the preparation of à la kings, curries, and creamed poultry dishes, the steaming of poultry under pressure in the compartment steamer will greatly reduce the cooking time.
      2) Do not oversteam, as poultry overly done is tough and rubbery.
   c) Stewing of poultry (for technique refer to stewing meat above).
      1) Steam-jacketed kettles can be used to stew poultry.
      2) Poultry that has been prepared in this fashion can be used in stews, à la kings, and curries.
      3) Stewing temperatures should not exceed 185°F.

C. Use a meat (or instant read) thermometer when roasting turkey. (The internal temperature of the meat is the only accurate way to determine when the meat is done). Turkey is done when the thermometer reads 180°–185°F in inner thighs of whole turkey or 170°F in turkey roast.
D. Use timetables as a general guide for cooking poultry. (Timetables are useful in determining when to start cooking poultry in order for it to be done when needed).
E. Stuffing for poultry should be baked separately.

Thawing Meats and Poultry

A. Schedule thawing so that the meat or poultry will be cooked soon after it is thawed.
B. DO NOT THAW AT ROOM TEMPERATURE.
C. Remove from freezer storage only the amount of meat or poultry needed for one day's use.
D. Remove from the carton and thaw in original wrappings in the refrigerator at 35° to 40°F.
E. Space packages of meat or poultry on refrigerator shelves so that air can circulate around them. Put packages into a shallow pan to catch any moisture leakage.
F. Allow 1½ hours per pound of meat for thawing in the refrigerator.
G. Allow the following thawing time for poultry.
   1. Chicken, whole or cut-up—overnight.
   2. Turkey, whole:
      a) 18 pounds and over—two to three days.
      b) Under 18 pounds—one to two days.
      c) Turkey parts—about one day.
      d) Turkey breasts—overnight.
H. Do not start cooking meat or poultry one day and finish it the next.
I. Alternative methods for thawing:
   1. The use of the microwave oven for thawing is recommended only when the manufacturer's instructions are available for consultation. Consult these in-

structions whenever considering the thawing of any product in a microwave oven.

2. Thawing under running *cold* water (never warm or hot water) is appropriate if the thawing process may be completed in two hours or less. Thus, only small items, not large ones like whole turkeys, may be thawed in this manner.

Fish, Egg, and Cheese Preparation Principles

Cooked Fish Preparation

A. Cooked fish should be juicy, flavorful, tender and well done (145°F for 15 seconds) as indicated when it flakes easily.

B. Fish should generally be cooked at a moderate temperature. Fish should be cooked rapidly enough to retain juices and moisture, but slowly enough to insure thorough cooking.

Egg Preparation

A. Cooked eggs should be tender and evenly cooked.
   1. Directions for using fresh eggs:
      a) Cooked in compartment steamer.
         1) Steam eggs in the shell in a perforated pan 15 minutes at 5 pounds per square inch (psi).
         2) Remove from heat and cool under cold running water.
         3) Crack shells by stirring lightly. Peel from large end of egg.
         4) Use immediately or refrigerate for future use.
            Note: Convection steamer equipment is in use in many institutional kitchens. Follow the manufacturer's instructions for preparation of food products using this equipment.
      b) Cooked in a steam-jacketed kettle.
         1) Cover eggs in shell with cold water; heat to boiling point at 212°F and then simmer (180°–211°F) for 20 minutes.
         2) Follow procedures for cooking eggs in a compartment steamer (above).
      c) Cooked in oven.
         1) Remove shells from eggs.
         2) Place about 25 eggs onto a greased baking pan (12″ × 20″ × 2″). Add ½ cup of water to each pan.
         3) Set pan of eggs in a pan of hot water; cover and bake at 350°F for 30 minutes or until eggs are firm.
         4) Use immediately or chill in refrigerator.
   2. Directions for using frozen eggs.
      a) Thaw amount of frozen eggs needed.
      b) Follow directions for cooking fresh eggs in the oven.
      c) Caution must be exercised in using frozen eggs.
         1) Storage and thawing:
            a. Store frozen eggs at 0°F or below in the freezer.
            b. Thaw only the amount needed at one time.
            c. Thaw in a tight container in refrigerator or under cold running water.
            d. Since frozen eggs are highly perishable, use thawed eggs within 24 hours.
         2) Special caution: Do not use frozen eggs in uncooked or slightly heated foods such as egg-milk drinks, ice cream, uncooked salad dressings, cream puddings, soft custards, omelets, or scrambled eggs cooked on top of the range.
   3. Directions for using dried whole eggs:
      a) Sprinkle dried whole eggs over water and beat to blend.

b) Pour into greased baking pan (12″ × 20″ × 2″) to depth of ½ inch (two quarts per pan). Bake at 325°F for 15 minutes until egg mixture is firm.
c) Use immediately or chill in refrigerator. Do not hold hard-cooked eggs prepared from dried whole eggs overnight.
d) Special caution: Use dried eggs in only those products which will be thoroughly cooked, such as baked breads, cakes, long-cooked casseroles, and baked custards.

B. Eggs should be cooked at low or moderate temperatures to avoid toughening of egg white, discoloration and toughening of the yolk, and an unpleasant flavor (see Figure 6.3).

C. New food safety recommendations include the use of pasteurized eggs when cooking for healthcare clients. The problem with salmonella contamination through egg preparation is ever-present. Caution in egg preparation must be exercised at all times.

D. Food safety recommendations for the characteristics of all cooked eggs, as well as their serving termperatures, have also been made. They include that eggs and egg dishes should be cooked until the yolk and white are firm or 160°F.

Cheese Preparation

A. Cooked cheese should be smooth and flavorful.

B. Cheese should be cooked at low temperatures to avoid curdling, toughness, and stringiness.
   1. Ripened cheese has better cooking qualities than medium-cured or unaged cheese.
   2. Ripened cheese also blends better with other mixtures.

C. Common cheeses used in non-commercial foodservices include:
   1. Muenster;
   2. Romano;
   3. Parmesan;
   4. Mozzarella;
   5. Provolone;

FIGURE 6.3 HARVEST FRITTATA IS A TEST OF EGG COOKERY SINCE IT MUST NOT BE OVERCOOKED YET FOLLOW SAFE FOOD GUIDELINES.
Source: Photo courtesy of American Egg Board.

6. Cheddar;
7. Swiss;
8. Brick;
9. Cream.

Vegetable and Fruit Cookery Principles

A. General Principles of cooking in water or by steam.
   1. Cook vegetables *only* until they are done, with the degree of doneness depending upon the client to whom you are serving them. (An older client may prefer a more well-done product for ease of chew or palatability.)
      a) Use a small amount of water, bring to boil, add product, return to boil, and cook in simmering water (185°–205°F).
      b) Cook until tender but firm.
      c) DO NOT OVERCOOK; overcooking destroys many valuable nutrients and harms their color, flavor, texture, and shape.
      d) Schedule vegetable preparation as close to serving time as possible.
   2. Cook in as large pieces as possible and cook vegetables (such as potatoes and carrots) in their skin whenever possible to save nutrients. (see figure 6.4)
      a) Care must be taken in removing any vegetable skin.
      b) Excessive loss of edible material should be kept to a minimum.
   3. When cooking mild-flavored vegetables on top of the range, cook them in a covered pan (strong-flavored vegetables such as cabbage and brussel sprouts should be cooked in an uncovered container).
   4. Cook vegetables in a steamer whenever possible.
      a) Use a perforated pan for fresh and frozen vegetables.
      b) Vegetables cooked in a perforated pan should be salted and seasoned *after* they are cooked.
      c) Cabbage cooks better in a steam-jacketed kettle.
      d) Batch cooking is preferred, as vegetables will always be freshly cooked.

FIGURE 6.4 FRESH BABY CARROTS, TENDER COOKED VEGETABLES WITH PARSLEY GARNISH.
Source: Photo courtesy of California Fresh Carrot Advisory Board.

Note: Cooking information (charts) are typically provided by equipment manufacturers. This data should be used as a guide when establishing cooking times/temperatures for the facility's standardized recipes.

5. The color of green vegetables is affected by long cooking, and by minerals and acids (such as vinegar) in the presence of heat. To avoid discoloration, boil vegetables without a cover on the cooking vessel.
   a) Intense heat, acids, and minerals turn green vegetables a brownish color.
   b) Alkali (such as baking soda) deepens green color (but it may also cause a loss of Vitamin C); NEVER add baking soda to green vegetables that are a major source of Vitamin C.
6. Oven cooking may cause yellow vegetables to become pale in color.
7. Red vegetables (such as beets) may lose color in water; alkali in hard water cause the vegetables to turn bluish color; acid makes the color brighter.
8. White vegetables (such as cauliflower) become dissolved in vegetable juices; they turn yellow in alkaline or hard water. To maintain the color of white vegetables, cover the cooking vessel.

B. Cooking fresh vegetables
   1. To prepare fresh vegetables for cooking, procedures such as washing, paring, trimming, cutting, and soaking may be required.
   2. Clean vegetables deteriorate less; therefore, fresh produce should be cleaned and stored as soon as possible after delivery.
   3. Some vegetables (such as potatoes and carrots) may require scrubbing; others (such as greens) may require soaking.
      a) Dirt may be removed from greens by soaking for no more than six minutes in salted water (adding one teaspoon of salt per gallon of water will assist in loosening soil).
      b) Some vegetables (such as cauliflower, broccoli and cabbage) may contain tiny mites, which may be removed by soaking in cold, salted water for 30 minutes.
   4. Do not use the wash water from the vegetables after they are cleaned.

C. Canned vegetables
   1. Since canned vegetables are fully cooked, only a very short heating time is needed.
   2. Schedule the heating of canned vegetables so they will be served soon after they are heated.
      a) Always heat the vegetables before placing them on the serving counter.
      b) To heat, strain liquid; bring liquid to a boil and add the vegetables. Remove them as soon as the liquid returns to a boil.
      c) The serving counter should be used to keep the vegetables warm, not to heat them initially. The temperature of the serving counter is not hot enough to bring the vegetables to proper temperature in a short period of time.
   3. Season canned vegetables well.

D. Frozen vegetables
   1. Most frozen vegetables can be cooked without thawing.
   2. Vegetables such as spinach and broccoli spears, however, do cook better if they are partially thawed. Partial thawing under running *cold* water (never warm or hot water) is appropriate and should be completed with the product in its original packaging.
   3. Follow the manufacturer's instructions to properly use your equipment to cook frozen vegetables.

E. Fruits
   1. Fresh fruits.
      a) Fresh fruits may be served whole, halved, or in pieces (see Figure 6.5).

FIGURE 6.5 FRESH FRUIT MAY BE SERVED (A) WHOLE, (B) HALVED OR (C) IN PIECES IN A SALAD.
Source: Fruit salad photo courtesy of USA Rice Council

   b) Fresh fruits should be washed thoroughly before using and some (such as peaches and bananas) should be dipped in ascorbic acid or lemon juice after peeling or cutting to prevent them from turning a dark color.
2. Canned fruits may be purchased in various concentrations of syrups.
3. Dried fruits may be served as stewed fruit or in pies, cobblers, crisps, whips, and salads.
4. Frozen fruit should be served as soon as it has thawed (preferably before all the ice crystals have melted).

Salad Preparation Principles

Salad Ingredients

A. Salads may be made from vegetables, meat, poultry, seafood, cheese, fruits, nuts, and eggs.
B. Almost any vegetable can be used in a salad. Use your imagination, since there are many possible salad combinations.
   1. Examples of raw vegetable combinations:
      a) Beets on romaine lettuce;
      b) Celery, carrot, and zucchini sticks;
      c) Corn, green pepper, onion, pickle relish, pimento;
      d) Kidney beans, wax beans, and green beans.
   2. To prepare raw vegetables for use in salads, they must be properly cleaned.
      a) Vegetables such as cauliflower, broccoli, and cabbage may contain tiny mites (which can be removed by soaking in cold, salted water for six minutes).
      b) When vegetables have finished soaking, lift them out of the water within six minutes. Do not leave them in the water; water-soluble vita-

mins may be lost and leafy vegetables like lettuce may rust if in contact with water too long.

c) After cleaning vegetables, drain them thoroughly.

1) If the vegetables must be stored until serving time, place them in a tightly covered container in the refrigerator at 40°F.

2) The vegetables may be covered with plastic film wrap or aluminum foil if covered containers are not available.

3. Examples of leafy vegetables:
   a) Romaine lettuce;
   b) Bibb lettuce;
   c) Spinach;
   d) Chinese cabbage;
   e) Curly endive;
   f) Escarole;
   g) Mustard greens;
   h) Kale.
4. Leafy vegetables should be washed gently but thoroughly in cool water.
   a) Remove any damaged leaves.
   b) To loosen soil, soak raw vegetables in cold, salted water.
   c) To clean lettuce, remove the core and wash the head under cold running water; be sure to drain thoroughly.
   d) Wash cabbage under cold running water and drain.
   e) Store leafy vegetables in a refrigerator at 40°F.

C. Fruit salads are also popular.
   1. Canned, dried, fresh, and frozen fruits may be served.
   2. Fruits must be properly prepared for use in salads.
      a) *Canned fruits* should be chilled and drained thoroughly before used. (The drained juice can be used in salad dressings, gelatin desserts, dessert and meat sauces, fruit beverages, and punches).
      b) *Dried fruits* should be soaked and then drained thoroughly for use in salads.
      c) *Fresh fruits* should be washed and chilled for use in salads.
         1) To avoid ascorbic acid loss, cut fruit just prior to service.
         2) To avoid browning or discoloration, wash cut fruit in an acid or salt water, or cook sufficiently to deactivate the enzymes.

Preparing Salads

A. Plan salads carefully (see Figure 6.6).
   1. Color can be pleasing when it exists as several shades of one hue, as contrasting colors, or as different colors that blend well together. Some examples are:
      a) Avocado and unpeeled apple—contrasting colors;
      b) Celery, carrot, and zucchini sticks—different colors that blend well;
      c) Bibb lettuce, romaine, and spinach—several shades of one hue.
   2. Flavors should be combined imaginatively but carefully. Combine mild and strong flavors, salty with bland, or tart with sweet. Some examples are:
      a) Beet, carrot and turnip sticks—mild and strong flavor;
      b) Chopped raw cranberries, diced apples and banana—tart with sweet;
      c) Olives with hard-cooked eggs and celery—salty with bland.
   3. Texture combinations may include soft with crisp foods, fibrous with smooth foods, tender with chewy foods, and juicy with crunchy foods. Some examples are:
      a) Avocado, apple and grapefruit—soft with crisp;
      b) Celery sticks stuffed with peanut butter—fibrous with smooth;
      c) Green pepper in cottage cheese—tender with chewy;
      d) Peach slices in Waldorf salad—juicy with crunchy.

FIGURE 6.6 SALAD BARS OFFER THE CLIENT A CHOICE OF GARDEN FRESH INGREDIENTS INCLUDING CROUTONS AND DRESSINGS.
Source: Photo by Chef Jeremy Corson

4. Shape should be varied such as:
    a) Bite-size pieces of spinach;
    b) Fruit sections;
    c) Shredded vegetables.

B. The parts of a salad.
1. The salad base or under-garnish is often a lettuce leaf. Head lettuce such as iceberg, Boston, and bibb offer the best cups. The base helps to shape or confine salads. They give height and provide a frame for the salad. The rim of the plate may also be used as the frame, in which case the salad should never flow beyond or over the frame in which it should be found. Other base materials are:
    a) Leaf lettuce;
    b) Romaine;
    c) Spinach;
    d) Endive.
2. The salad body.
    a) It can be made up of:
        1) Fruits;
        2) Vegetables;
        3) Meat;
        4) Fish;
        5) Poultry;
        6) Cheese;
        7) Eggs;
        8) Pasta products.
    b) The topography of a salad has psychological value. Appropriate height lends importance.
        1) Ingredients should be in bite-size pieces.
        2) DO NOT OVERCHOP SALAD INGREDIENTS
3. The salad dressing.
    a) Various salad dressings are:
        1) Oil and seasonings;

2) French;
3) Mayonnaise;
4) Sour cream;
5) Honey.

b) ADD DRESSING JUST BEFORE SERVING TIME so the salad greens do not become wilted. The oil in the dressings wilt salad greens.
c) Dressings act as complements to salads by adding flavor and sometimes color.
d) There are three basic types of salad dressings: cooked, French, and mayonnaise.
   1) All of these can be made in most kitchens.
   2) Many kinds of salad dressings can be made from the three basic dressing recipes.
   3) Salad dressings are most appetizing when served chilled, except for a basic oil and vinegar, which is usually served best at room temperature.
e) Prepared salads need to maintain their chilled condition; place salad materials on prechilled plates and maintain completed salad in a refrigerator at 40°F.

3. The salad garnish is the fourth part of the salad and contributes much to the acceptability of a salad if used to accent or complement colors, flavors, shapes, and textures of the ingredients.
   a) Some examples of garnishes are:
      1) Bacon bits;
      2) Frosted grapes;
      3) Gelatin cubes;
      4) Plumped prunes or raisins;
      5) Watercress;
      6) Fresh croutons.
   b) All garnishes must be edible.

Relishes

A. Relishes must be clean, fresh, and crisp.
B. Cut celery and carrots into sticks.
C. Tomatoes should be sliced or cut into wedges.
D. Cucumbers, pared or unpared, may be sliced, quartered or cut into chunks.
E. Small radishes may be served whole.
F. Other relish possibilities are:
   1. Pepper rings and turnip sticks;
   2. Celery, carrot and zucchini sticks;
   3. Celery, cucumber, green onion, radish, and green pepper tray;
   4. Celery sticks stuffed with peanut butter, whole cherry tomatoes, pickle sticks, and cauliflower buds.

Stock and Soup Preparation Principles

Stock Preparation

A. Most soups start with a richly flavored stock.
   1. The usual flavors for stock come from beef, veal, chicken, and fish.
   2. Commercially prepared soup bases (which contain large concentrations of salt) are available for use.
   3. Commercially prepared stock (food) bases are available which often yield a very high-quality product when prepared according to the manufacturer's instructions.
B. Stock classification.
   1. Brown, from browned cracked bones of beef with vegetables and seasonings.

2. White, from rinsed beef and veal bones, not browned, with vegetables and seasonings.
3. Chicken, from following the procedures for a white stock but using chicken bones.
4. Fish, from following the procedures for a white stock but using fish bones.

C. Procedure.
1. Ingredients used are shank, neck, knuckle, fowl carcass, or fish bones cut into 3″–4″ pieces so the water can draw out the nutritive and flavor-giving substances.
2. If meat is included with the bones, the stock becomes a broth or bouillon, both meaning a rich, flavorful stock.
3. Six pounds of bones are needed for each gallon of stock.
4. One pound of mixed vegetables, known as mirepoix (50% onion, 25% celery, 25% carrots) to five quarts of fresh unsalted cold water are used to make one gallon. A bouquet garni (also known as a sachet bag) of bay leaf, marjoram, crushed peppercorns, thyme, and parsley can be added for flavor.
5. To get the best flavor, start the bones in the cold water, and slowly bring to a simmer (185°F), cooking six to eight hours for brown, four to six hours for white, three to four hours for chicken and forty-five minutes for fish. Add the vegetables and seasoning halfway through the simmering process. In the case of the white, chicken, and fish stocks, restart with fresh cold water if the initial water is cloudy upon the stock coming to a simmer; the end product will be much clearer.
6. After cooking, remove bones through a colander and strain the stock for later use.
7. Cool the stock quickly in a water bath by stirring. Refrigerate at 35°–40°F.
8. Remove the congealed fat from the surface of the chilled stock and use to make soup or sauces.

Kinds of Soup

A. Appetizer soups are those that precede a full meal.
1. They should be stimulating and light.
2. Appetizer soups include thin, clear soups such as consommés, bouillons, and broths, and the light, delicate creams and purées.

B. Main dish soup should be more nutritious in substance and generous in portion size.
1. It may take the place of an entree.
2. It may complement a salad or sandwich.
3. Examples of main dish soups.
   a) Bisques.
   b) Chowders.
   c) Cream soup.
   d) Gumbos.

Sauce Preparation Principles

There are several basic sauces.

A. Simple sauces;
B. Butter sauces;
C. Bread sauces;
D. Sauces thickened with egg;
E. Tart or savory sauces;
F. Starch-thickened sauces.

Preparation Techniques and Principles For Preparing Sauces

A. Simple sauces.
  1. Au jus is made from the drippings of roasted meat.
     a) The caramelized drippings are dissolved in water by stirring over heat.
     b) No thickening is added.
  2. Concentrated canned soups may be used without diluting .
     a) They are heated and served hot.
     b) If desired, a small amount of water may be added to thin the sauce.

B. Butter sauces.
  1. Butter will add richness and flavor as a sauce.
  2. Butter is a good carrier of additional seasonings.
     a) Seasonings may be beaten into the butter.
     b) When added to hot food, the butter melts and carries the added seasonings to the food.

C. Bread sauces.
  1. Vary in consistency from dry to moist, and do not result in a smooth sauce.
  2. Browned and buttered dry bread sauce is prepared by stirring and browning bread crumbs in a hot skillet with melted butter.
  3. A moist sauce is prepared by using two ounces of dry bread crumbs to thicken one quart of stock.

D. Sauces thickened with eggs.
  1. Sauces thickened with eggs include mayonnaise and cooked sauces such as Hollandaise.
  2. The principles involved in the preparation of these sauces include the absorption of fat into the egg yolk and the ability of the egg yolk to act as an emulsifying agent and hold oil in suspension, as is the case in mayonnaise.
  3. Eggs must be handled carefully and cooked fully since they can cause foodborne illness; the potential of salmonella poisoning with eggs is always present.

E. Tart or savory sauces.
  1. Tomato-flavored barbecue sauce and ketchup are the most popular.
  2. These sauces are often used on baked, broiled, and grilled meat, poultry, and fish.
  3. Marinades are used to flavor and tenderize meats. The acid ingredients break down the connective tissue of the meat.
  4. The main principle involved with the preparation of these sauces is the amount of time permitted for the ingredients to blend and develop a unique flavoring.

F. Starch-thickened sauces.
  1. Sauce success calls for an understanding of the characteristics of starches.
  2. There are two types of starches used.
     a) Cereal starch from wheat, corn, and rice.
     b) Root starch from potatoes, tapioca, and arrowroot.
  3. The two types of starch react differently.
     a) Cereal starch requires a boiling temperature to complete gelatinization, or the swelling of the starch granules which causes thickening to take place. Boiling must continue for five minutes to insure complete swelling.
     b) Root starch begins to gelatinize when heated at 150°–160°F, and complete swelling is accomplished before boiling. If boiling continues the starch granules will break down; the sauce will lose its thick appearance and become sticky.
  4. The thickening power of starches differ; to thicken one gallon of sauce the following quantities of starch could be used:
     a) Pastry flour—8 ounces;
     b) Cornstarch—5½ ounces;
     c) Tapioca—7 ounces.

5. Avoid lumping of starch granules by using these techniques and by stirring continuously.
   a) Separate the starch granules with a fat.
      1) This is called a roux. Blend equal volumes of melted fat and flour, and cook them together three to five minutes for a white roux, five to seven minutes for a blond roux, and ten minutes for a brown roux. Depending upon the color needed in the end product, whether soup or sauce, you would use the light to dark colored roux.
      2) Add to hot liquid off the burner, whipping with a wire whip.
   b) Separate the starch granules with other dry ingredients. Cornstarch can be separated with sugar.
   c) Separate the starch granules with a cold liquid such as cold water. This is known as a slurry and does not provide the same quality as a roux in the end product, since the starch has not had the advantage of being cooked first. By being cooked, the starchy flavor is more likely to be removed and not tasted in the end product.
6. Sauces are identified by their color.
   a) Blond or white sauce.
      1) Sauces made from flour which has not been browned.
      2) Liquid may be milk, milk and cream, light cream, and/or white stock.
   b) Other names given to blond or white sauce.
      1) White sauce: sauce made with milk.
      2) Cream sauce: sauce made with cream.
      3) Béchamel: sauce made with part milk or cream and white stock.
      4) Veloute: sauce made with white stock only.
   c) Brown sauce (Espagnole): The chief differences between a brown and blond sauce are the following:
      1) A browned roux is used. The color is achieved by cooking the flour and fat until the flour browns as noted above;
      2) Mixed vegetables of carrots, celery, leeks, onions, turnips, and cabbage are used;
      3) Seasonings of bay leaf, parsley, thyme, and marjoram tied up in a cheese cloth are used.
7. With the basic blond and brown sauces, many different sauces may be made.

Principles of Bread and Cereal Preparation

Bread Preparation

A. Breads may be yeast breads (which are leavened with yeast). See figure 6.7
   1. Lean dough: A dough made with little or no sugar and shortening.
      a) Bread—white, wheat, French.
      b) Rolls—white, brown-and-serve, hamburger.
   2. Sweet dough: A dough made with sugar, shortening, and eggs.
      a) Bread—raisin.
      b) Rolls—maple, caramel, peanut butter, pecan
   3. For best results in bread baking:
      a) Proper equipment is needed;
      b) Be sure temperature controls on ovens are accurate;
      c) Use standardized recipes;
      d) Use good-quality ingredients;
      e) Weigh or measure ingredients accurately;
      f) Know and use the specific techniques recommended in the recipes.
         1) Punching involves folding the dough over from the sides into the middle until most of the gas is expelled. This relaxes the gluten and remixes the ingredients so yeast obtains new food.

FIGURE 6.7 (A) PANETTONE BREAD & PRETZELS; (B) BREAD MONTAGE: A VARIETY OF YEAST BREADS AND ROLLS.
Source: Photos courtesy of the Wheat Foods Council

2) Proofing: The fermentation of the sugar in the dough. The yeast multiply producing CO_2 which leavens the dough. A temperature of 80°–85°F and humidity of 75 percent is desirable. When dough has doubled, proofing is complete. Proofing usually requires from 15 to 45 minutes.
3) Kneading: The mixing of the dough to develop the gluten.

g) Scale or measure the prepared product into baking pans.

h) Keep the oven temperature constant for the specified baking time.
1) Well-proofed bread—425°F for 15 minutes, then 375°F for 45 minutes.
2) Under-proofed bread—375°F for 60 minutes.
3) Rolls—425°F for 15 to 30 minutes.

i) Know how to judge quality yeast bread. When evaluating appearance consider:
1) Volume: 125–155 cubic inches per pound loaf;
2) Shape: pleasing to the eye;
3) Color: pleasing brown.

B. Breads may be quick breads (which are usually leavened with baking powder and/or soda, an acid).
1. Biscuits.
a) Rolled and cut—cheese.
b) Dropped.
2. Muffins—portioned into muffin tins (such as blueberry, raisin, date).
3. Loaf breads—portioned into loaf pans (such as Boston brown, banana, date).

C. To save time when making yeast and quick breads:
1. Rolling and cutting yeast breads is quick and gives a uniform product (this includes hamburger and hotdog buns).
2. To make biscuits:
a) Cut biscuits in squares rather than using a biscuit cutter and rerolling the dough; several biscuits may be transferred to the baking pan at one time using a long, wide spatula.
b) A second method is to roll out biscuit dough in pan and cut in squares or diamond shapes with dough cutter.

Cereal Products

A. These include items such as rice, macaroni, noodles, and spaghetti.
B. Cereal products are cooked to increase digestibility and to develop flavor.
C. Cereal products should be cooked according to directions.

D. General cooking principles are to:
   1. Cook quickly in boiling saltwater until tender;
   2. A small amount of salad oil added to the water while cooking keeps pastas and rice from sticking together and foaming. At serving time there will be no need for additional fat;
   3. Drain quickly and stir in fat, if desired;
   4. Avoid overcooking;
   5. Pasta products should have resistance to the bite. The term used to describe this texture in the cooked product is "al dente"
   6. Rice should be tender, but not excessively soft (see Figure 6.8).
E. Enriched rice SHOULD NOT be washed before it is cooked; this procedure washes away valuable nutrients.

Sandwich Production Principles

A. The variation in bread and rolls can provide variety in flavor, texture, size, and shape.
   1. Enriched white bread.
   2. Rye bread.
   3. Pumpernickel bread.
   4. French bread.
   5. Raisin bread.
   6. Italian bread.
   7. Boston brown bread.
   8. Cheese bread.
   9. Whole-wheat bread.
   10. Hamburger, frankfurter rolls.
   11. Hard and soft rolls.
B. The variation in fillings can provide variety in flavor and texture.
   1. Sliced cold or hot meats.

FIGURE 6.8 RICE MILANO—RICE AND VEGETABLES COOKED CORRECTLY AND PLATED ATTRACTIVELY.
Source: Photo courtesy of US Rice Council.

2. Sliced cold or hot cheeses.
3. Combined ingredient fillings.
4. Cold or hot fish.
5. Cold or hot eggs.

C. To prepare sandwiches.
1. Have all ingredients ready to use.
   a) Soften butter by letting it stand at room temperature. Allow 8½ ounces of butter for 100 sandwiches (one-half teaspoon each).
   b) Wash lettuce thoroughly; core, separate leaves, drain, and crisp. Allow five medium heads of lettuce for 100 sandwiches.
   c) Evenly slice foods such as tomatoes, cheese, and meats. Cross-stack sliced ingredients such as cheese and meat for quick and easy pickup.
2. Allow plenty of space to work. One slice of bread or a bun takes up at least four square inches.
3. Assemble all equipment and ingredients in advance and place within easy reach toward back of the table. Arrange ingredients in the order to be used.

D. To Assemble Sandwiches
1. Using both hands (gloved), grasp bread and drop off slices in four rows of five each.
2. With narrow spatula in right hand, spread butter to edges of bread with one sweeping motion. With left hand, scoop a portion of sandwich filling into center of each slice.
3. With right hand, use a stroke of the spatula away from you and a stroke toward you to spread filling evenly to edge of bread. With left hand, place lettuce on filling.
4. With both hands, grasp bread and drop off two slices over each filled slice, matching edges of bread.
5. Repeat steps 2 through 4 two more times until there are 60 sandwiches in stacks of three. Stacks must be kept low so cold air in the refrigerator can penetrate the filling.
6. Hold sandwiches together with thumb and first finger of left hand. Cut through several stacks at one time with a sawing motion.
7. Place in sandwich bags or waxed paper or in pans with covers, and refrigerate. Do not cover sandwiches directly with a damp towel, as the moisture in the towel may promote bacterial growth. Serve sandwiches the same day they are made.

E. Precautions for Sandwich Production.
1. Make sandwiches the day they are to be served.
2. Make prepared fillings only in such quantities as will be used during one serving period.
   a) Avoid leftovers.
   b) Never hold over any perishable protein foods or fillings that have been at room temperature for four hours or more.
3. Handle bread and fillings as little as possible during preparation.
   a) Avoid the use of hands in direct contact with foods if tools can do the job efficiently.
   b) Consider plastic gloves, tongs, scoops, forks.
4. Avoid stacking sandwiches for refrigeration more than three high; overstacking will insulate the filling and prevent proper storage temperature.

Dessert Preparation Principles

Gelatins

A. Varieties
1. A mold—a dissolved gelatin base that is flavored and (with or without added foods) poured into a container and allowed to congeal (set or become firm).

2. A whip—a gelatin base which (when partially congealed) is beaten until much air has been whipped in and then chilled to recongeal as a foamy dessert.
3. A snow—a gelatin-based mixture to which egg whites are added and beaten until the mixture resembles snow (either white or pastel colored) and then chilled to recongeal.
4. A chiffon-type pudding or pie filling—a gelatin based mixture with fruit juice, sugar, and egg yolks, cooked in a double boiler to a custard consistency; when chilled and partially congealed, the mixture is folded into stiffly beaten egg white.
5. A banana cream or mousse—similar to chiffon mixtures but the product is further enriched by adding whipped cream.

B. Gelatins require liquid and heat to dissolve, and a cool place, usually a refrigerator, to congeal.
C. Whenever possible, use fruit juice for the liquid in the gelatin to add nutrients and flavor.
D. Never use fresh or fresh-frozen pineapple juice in gelatin (this fruit contains an enzyme which prevents the gelatin from congealing).
E. Gelatin will be gummy or have a rubbery bottom layer if the gelatin is not completely dissolved; the liquid must be hot and the gelatin must be stirred sufficiently.
F. To prevent fruits from sinking to the bottom, the gelatin must be allowed to congeal until it is like thick syrup before the fruit is folded in.
G. Gelatins may be flaked, cubed, whipped, or layered for variety.

Cakes and Cookies

A. Use only standardized recipes to make cakes and cookies.
B. Use highest-quality ingredients and weigh or measure them carefully.
   1. Butter or fat used should be at room temperature to give the batter a better texture and volume. Eggs, because they are potentially hazardous, should be kept at refrigerated temperature until needed for batter preparation.
   2. Egg whites, if to be foamed, are an exception and should be at room temperature for greater volume, realizing the foam will be well cooked prior to service.
C. Preheat oven to desired temperature.
D. Blend ingredients thoroughly but do not overmix; use one of the combining methods.
   1. Conventional method (cakes)—produces best quality of cakes.
      a) Cream sugar and shortening to incorporate air into the cake batter.
      b) Add eggs and blend to aid in producing fine grain to the cake.
      c) Add one-third sifted dry ingredients to creamed mixture.
      d) Add one-half liquid and mix.
      e) Repeat with one-third sifted dry ingredients and one-half liquid and mix.
      f) Add last one-third of sifted dry ingredients and mix.
   2. Muffin method—a quick method.
      a) Dry ingredients are placed in one bowl.
      b) Liquid ingredients are placed in another container. Oil or melted fat is used, since creaming of sugar is omitted.
      c) The liquid ingredients are poured into the dry ingredients and blended together.
E. Measure or weigh batter to go into pans. Only the bottoms need to be greased. Leave the pan sides ungreased for a larger volume cake.
F. Place pans in preheated oven so that they do not touch one another; always allow for free circulation of heat.
G. Bake only until done and remove from oven immediately.
H. Cool in pans for 15 minutes.

Pastries and Pies

A. In making pastries it is very important that proper ingredients in correct amounts be used. The ingredients are flour, salt, fat, and water. The proper ingredient ratio is six parts flour, two parts fat, and one part water.
   1. All-purpose or pastry flour should be used.
   2. Shortening should be chilled to achieve extra flakiness in the pie pastry.
   3. Too little shortening will cause the crusts to shrink or be tough.
   4. Too much water will cause the dough to be sticky and hard to roll; this will also make the crust tough.
   5. Too little water will cause the dough to be crumbly and hard to roll.

B. The dough should be mixed and handled lightly; too much mixing and handling will cause the crust to be tough. The correct mixing technique is:
   1. First mix the flour and salt.
   2. The fat is then cut into the flour using a pastry knife if a mixer is available, or a pastry blender if done by hand. Cut the fat to the size of rice kernels.
   3. Iced or cold water is added drop by drop as the flour mixture is mixed.
   4. As the flour becomes moistened, remove from mixing bowl.
   5. Divide pastry and roll out for cobblers, pies, and deep dish pies.

C. Single pie crusts are usually baked from 425° to 450°F for 15 minutes.

D. Bake double crust pies at 425° to 450°F for 10 minutes, then drop the temperature to 350°F for approximately 45 minutes. Pie crusts should be lightly and evenly browned in appearance with a rich, flaky texture; if a crust is cooked in too slow an oven, the crust may shrink or be soggy. Deep-dish pies and cobblers can also be made from this pastry.

E. Some popular pie fillings are cream puddings, chiffons, custards, and fruits.

F. Meringue or other toppings should be added just before serving.
   1. Meringue is egg white with bubbles of a gas trapped by layers of the egg white.
   2. Technique for making a meringue.
      a) While egg whites are at room temperature to increase meringue volume, food safety cautions that proper cooking of meringues be observed to decrease the potential of any food poisoning.
      b) Whip with hand rotary beater, electric mixer, wire whip, or mechanical mixer.
      c) Stages of meringue formation:
         1) Foamy stage:
            a. White is beaten briefly;
            b. Bubbles form on the surface but liquid remains in the bowl;
            c. At this point add cream of tartar and some of the sugar;
            d. Continue to add sugar as whites are beaten.
         2) Soft-peak stage:
            a. The white will peak and just bend over as the beater is slowly pulled out of the meringue.
            b. This is appropriate for soft meringue.
         3) Stiff-peak stage:
            a. The white will peak and remain straight up when the beater is slowly pulled out of the meringue;
            b. This is appropriate for hard meringues.

G. Most fruit pies are improved if they are slightly warm when served.

H. Fruit pie fillings should be moist but the fruit should hold its shape.

I. Cream pie fillings should be stiff enough to stand up, but the filling should bend slightly when served with a topping.

MONITORING FOOD WASTE AND MANAGING SOLID WASTE

Food waste occurs when food is purchased and then discarded before it is served. However, food products not used for the intended purpose, and/or products which are prepared and cannot then be used as leftovers, are also wasted. Purchasing in excessive quantities, improperly storing and handling foods, poor sanitation practices, overproduction, oversupply, improper cooking, theft, and pilferage are also causes of food waste.

In today's dietary operation with an ongoing emphasis on cost containment, every dollar spent for food must be effectively "managed." The dietary manager cannot afford to devote "one or two percent to inventory shrinkage" (a term referring to unexplained inventory losses) or to "buy more than we need so we're sure to have enough."

Basic procedures should be used to monitor food waste. First of all, procedures to purchase food in the right quantity and of the right quality are necessary. Proper receiving practices must be used to confirm that all products are received for which suppliers will be requesting payment. Proper storage practices following basic sanitation principles are necessary to be sure that quality deterioration problems do not arise. Rotation of products and use of the "first in-first out" system of food issuing is also necessary.

A very important rule which must be followed consistently at time of food storage is: No food can be discarded without prior approval of the dietary manager. This rule is not meant to question the ability of subordinate staff to identify products that have spoiled and must be discarded, but is designed to make the dietary manager aware of storage problems. It is obvious that these problems cannot be corrected unless the dietary manager knows about them. Figure 6.9 can be used as an integral part of the food waste monitoring activity. The dietary manager can record the value of food products discarded during the month and can use this system on an ongoing basis to evaluate effectiveness of supervisory practices.

It is very important that employees who receive products observe the quality of raw products received. This concern refers not only to products of inferior quality (which may have to be discarded) but also to products that will yield a smaller than required quantity (which will increase food cost).

Production personnel should clean and prepare foods carefully in order to not waste excessive amounts. The relationship between as-purchased (AP) weight and edible-portion (EP) weight should be monitored. The vegetable cook who trims excessive amounts of "peelings" from potatoes, discards an excessive number of outer leaves of lettuce or cabbage, discards parsley stems, celery trimmings, and so on, is not concerned about food costs. (Many trimmings can be used for soups, stock, and other items.)

All foods should be prepared properly. Standard recipes should be used. The proper quantity of products needed should be prepared. Each of these and related practices can be useful in reducing waste and in decreasing food costs.

Concern about employee theft and pilferage also relates to food waste. If products are purchased but stolen before preparation, food costs will increase. The cook who constantly "nibbles," staff members who receive free meals, and other staff members who remove products from the premises, are all contributing to higher-than-necessary food costs.

Today we are all familiar with concerns about the "garbage" crisis. It is true that foodservice operations—including non-commercial facilities—generate only a rather small amount of the total waste product in this country; but it is also true that dietary managers must do their part to manage product waste:

- There are increasing legislative concerns—if facilities do not do something on their own, the "government" will;

Month: ______________________ Storage Area: ______________________

Date	Item	Amount	Purchase Cost	Cost per Purchase Unit	Total Cost	Comments

Total Cost of Food Waste:

FIGURE 6.9 REPORT OF FOOD WASTE

- There are social concerns—as community citizens dietary managers want to make a contribution to the reduction of this problem;
- There are client concerns—they want something to be done.

Environmental concerns are certainly in the news today—both the news we hear and read about as citizens and in the trade press, which focuses these issues specifically on the foodservice industry.

The U.S. Environmental Protection Agency has noted a four-edged approach to managing food wastes. Stated in order of preference, they are:

1. *Source reduction*—As we use less there is less to discard. Reusable containers, along with other packaging alternatives, come to mind. In many ways source reduction—procedures to consume less—is similar to the strategy dietary managers have been practicing since the early 1970s about energy management: How can we alter our foodservice operation without sacrificing quality while, at the same time, reducing energy consumption? Warewashing or use of disposables pro-

vides an example of source reduction: should we wash dishes or use single-serve items? Today environmental concerns, along with cost comparisons, become important as these decisions are made.

2. *Recycling*—This alternative is receiving lots of attention today. Dietary managers can recycle containers along with much of the paper, cardboard, plastic, and other materials they utilize.

3. *Incineration*—Modern technology has developed clean-burning systems which can even provide usable power from the heat generated. Incineration can reduce the volume of municipal solid waste significantly; there is much less volume of waste which must be removed to landfills.

4. *Landfills*—While all landfill sites have an ultimate capacity (finite life span) there are suitable land sites available in many areas. However, it is becoming difficult to build landfills on a site, because of legislative and social concerns. Therefore, the above alternatives, which reduce the amount of product needing to be sent to landfills, should receive a priority in the facility's food waste disposal strategies.

What can the dietary manager do about food waste? First, be well informed about the problem and potential solutions; have an attitude about concern that "every little bit helps" and that the facility has a role to play in the resolution of the problem. Second, do what is possible to reduce the volume of food waste. Lastly, tell clients, other staff within the facility, and citizens of the community in general about the efforts being made by the dietary operation to contribute to the resolution—not creation—of this significant problem.

Identifying the Type of Service Needed

One of the main purposes of the dietary manager's job is to ensure that tasty food of high quality is served to clients according to their prescribed diets. There are many types of service patterns which can be used, but the judgment must be based on the physical design of the kitchen and location of the dining room, along with the requests and needs of the customers. Customers (anyone provided service: client, family, visitor, staff, vendors, etc.), the preferences of the administrator, dollars available to make changes, and the total time available for service are all important factors. A few types of service will be presented in this chapter.

There are several ways that facilities can serve meals to clients. Obviously, the method(s) chosen must be in compliance with laws established by state and/or other regulatory bodies. A common method involves *tray service* in a cafeteria setting. In one basic plan, diners pick up flat or compartment-style trays and pass through a serving line. Either they or foodservice attendants may portion hot and/or cold foods onto the serving trays. When flat trays are used, food items are placed onto service ware (plates, bowls, etc.) and are then placed on the serving trays. Tray service is obviously self-service for the customer and can save in labor costs for the manager. On the other hand, customers who are unable to help themselves or carry their trays will be in need of assistance, which can add to labor costs substantially.

An increasingly popular tray service method uses a *scramble system* for serving line arrangement. With this plan, clients may go to different service areas to select food items; for example, separate serving areas may be set up for salads, entrees, and desserts. This system eliminates waiting lines, as areas with less traffic tend to attract the customer anxious to be served quickly. The end result is savings in time and energy for both customer and management.

When all clients come to one central dining area, there is the possibility of using *family-style service.* With this plan, a group of four to eight people may sit at a table.

Each person has a complete place setting of necessary china, silverware, and glassware. The food is passed in bowls or platters around the table; each person serves himself or herself. Customers unable to physically pass the food may need some assistance. People on modified diets prescribed by the physician may receive preplated portions of food, but may still sit at the table and enjoy the companionship of the group. Obviously, labor costs are limited in this setting, but customers must be willing to pass the food among themselves, and that takes skill without assistance in some facilities.

The *waiter/waitress service* style of dining may take many forms. The presentation style may be French, Russian, American, English or modified American service. Most of these styles are not used, due to high costs of labor or equipment necessary to execute the presentation. The dietary manager should know about them, however, because they may be useful in the conduct of special catered events.

A simplified version of *French service* occurs when food is brought to the dining room fully or partially cooked. The waiter/waitress finishes the cooking process on a cart. The food is plated by the waiter/waitress and placed in front of the client or guest. This is more formal and increases labor costs considerably. On the other hand, some customers will pay for this upgrade and actually attract other customers to dine with them because of their pride in the ambiance created.

Russian service is characterized by the waiter/waitress bringing platters of food, which have been carefully arranged and garnished in the kitchen, to the dining room. He or she transfers the food from the platter in the left hand to the customer's plate with a spoon and fork in the right hand and serves the customer on the left side. This is economically feasible when large crowds are dining together and are having the same menu items, as would be the case in a banquet.

English service incorporates the cooking of food in the kitchen except for portioning the meat or main item. The meat is carved in the dining room by a host or hostess, who then plates the meat and passes it to the customer or guest. Other food items are in bowls and platters, and are passed family-style.

In *American service,* all food is fully cooked and plated in the kitchen. The waiter/waitress picks up the plated food and carries it to the guest in the dining room. The guest is served on the left side by the waiter's left hand. Removal of empty plates and beverage service take place with the right hand on the right side of the guest. The *modified American service* consists of food fully cooked and plated in the kitchen. The waiter/waitress brings several servings to the dining room at once on a cart. The waiter/waitress serves one table before moving to the next.

A *buffet* is a display of food from which people select what they desire. Figure 6.10 A buffet can be attractive because of the careful arrangement, quantity, and variety of foods offered. The buffet line should be kept filled with products throughout service. Garnishes of many types can enhance the food items on the buffet line. Serving sequence and arrangement of food are also important. Many dietary managers prefer to set up the line in the order of a menu: appetizers, main course, and desserts. In other operations, the cold items are placed first on the line with hot foods following these items; the hot food will be warmer if it is picked up last. Still other dietary managers place the most expensive items first on the line and then follow with the least expensive items. In all cases, sauces and gravies should be placed next to the item with which they are to be served. Buffet service may be refined by separating the desserts from the other foods. It is a good idea to start each line with plates or other appropriate service ware.

A *box lunch* or *box dinner* is another form of meal service. The Food Pyramid can be used to make selections for the box meal. This type of service may be used for groups going on excursions away from the facility; it may also be appropriate when meals are distributed to people in their homes. Service to people who are unable to get their own groceries or have special dietary needs is often called a "Meals-On-Wheels" program.

FIGURE 6.10 ELEGANT BUFFET SET FOR SERVICE

A Close Look at Food Transport Equipment and Systems

There are basically two ways to transport food, regardless of whether the food is to be transported within the facility and/or to a remote site. Food can be transported in bulk or in preportioned form.

When food is to be transported in bulk, it is prepared (unless convenience foods are used) and placed in large transport containers. Figure 6.11 illustrates one type of bulk food transport chest commonly used. The unit can be insulated, and it can be heated. The heat source can be either electric or canned liquid/paste fuels. One disadvantage of electric heat is that it generally cannot be applied to the contents while the transport equipment is enroute. Disadvantages of canned fuel are its higher cost, and safety problems if the fuel remains lighted as equipment is transported.

Some facilities use electrically heated, insulated transport chests which are preheated before use. The hot food is placed into the chest, which, immediately upon arrival at the ward or satellite kitchen, is again connected to a heat source.

For sanitation purposes, hot foods should be kept above 140°F or below 40°F. If the internal temperature of a hot food transport chest is set too high, the food can continue to cook; this reduces food quality unless plans are developed for the food to cook while being transported. (Undercooking is difficult to plan for and carry out!) On the other hand, if the food is not kept above 140°F, other problems arise.

Transport equipment for moving food in bulk is generally sized to fit modular steam table pans. For example, hot foods can be placed in 12″ × 20″ × 4″ pans, which are then covered. If items being transported contain liquids, as would casserole dishes, aluminum foil can be placed on the pans before putting on the lid. Tight-fitting pan lids with gasket seals are also available.

After a transport chest is filled, the door should be closed. Units can be stacked on top of one another; when dollies are available for transportation, this is a common practice.

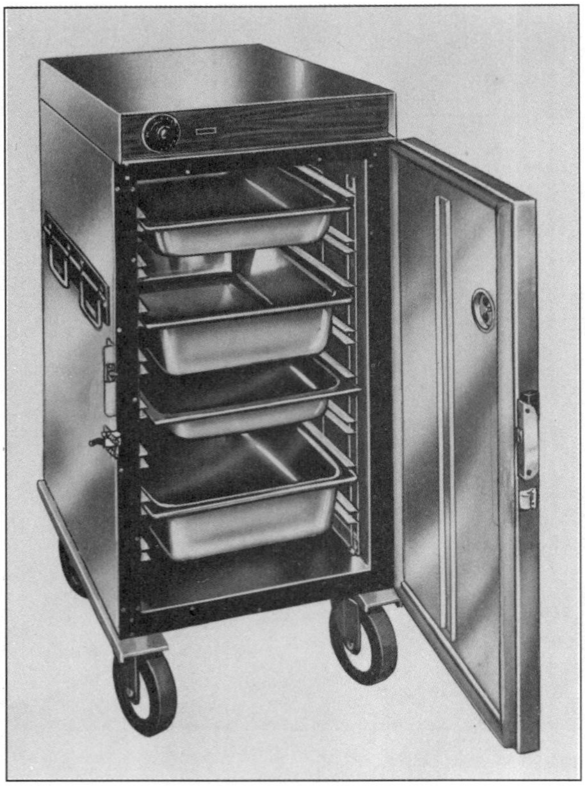

FIGURE 6.11 BULK FOOD TRANSPORT CHEST

FIGURE 6.12 BULK FOOD TRANSPORT CANISTER

Figure 6.12 shows a bulk food transport canister which can be used to transport liquid such as coffee, soup, and sauces. The canister is insulated and can be fitted with a draw-off valve, or the top lid can be removed and food products ladled out of the canister. As a third alternative, circular inserts can be used to pack several different types of food products into the canister.

Items to be served at room temperature (such as baked desserts, sandwiches, etc.) and chilled foods must also be transported. How is this done in a bulk food delivery system? It is possible to utilize various types of insulated or uninsulated mobile transport equipment. Insulated transport chests similar to those illustrated in Figure 6.13 can also be used.

Whenever food is to be transported even for short distances through non-public service corridors within the building, food must be covered. Pans with aluminum foil or other lids are necessary, as a minimum. As the quantity of products to be transported becomes greater, the dietary manager should investigate mobile or other equipment specifically designed for food transport.

In addition to transporting bulk food in hot, ready-to-serve condition, alternate food production/delivery methods provide for bulk foods to be transported in chilled or even frozen condition. Convenience foods can also be purchased in bulk for reheating as necessary in ward or satellite serving kitchens.

As noted, foods can be preportioned for delivery to other areas of the facility. Again, preportioned items can be transported in hot, ready-to-eat, chilled, or frozen states. Specialized food transport equipment is available to safeguard food quality and meet safety and sanitation requirements during transport.

Institutional facilities producing a large volume of preportioned meals frequently use automated tray assembly lines to assist with the preportioning task. If preportioned items are to be transported in a hot state, trays are quickly preportioned and placed in heated, insulated transport equipment for moving to the remote site. Frequently, however, preportioned meals are chilled after preportioning for later transport and reheating. With this plan, preportioned meals may be

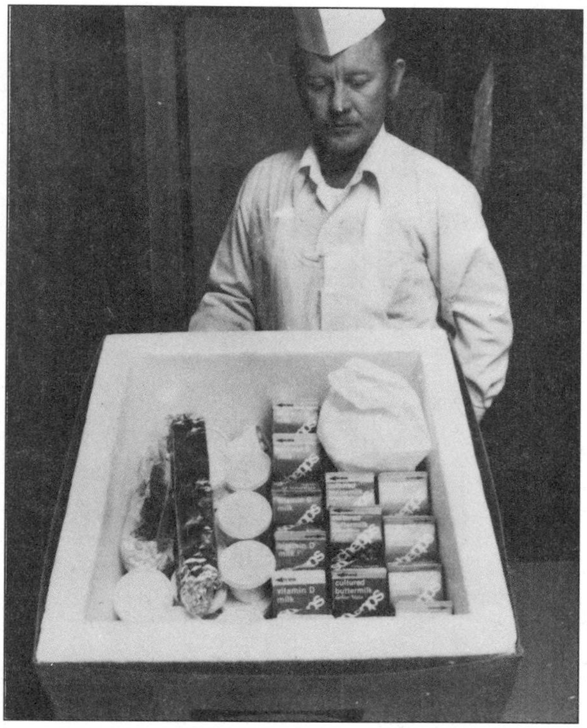

FIGURE 6.13 INSULATED TRANSPORT CHESTS

"racked" and placed on mobile transport dollies. Frequently, insulated "blankets" are placed over the equipment, and meals are then stored in a walk-in or other refrigerated unit until delivery to the remote site. (See Figure 6.14 for an example of preportioned items in transport racks.)

Some facilities utilize blast freezers to quickly freeze preportioned meals for later transport and rethermalization at a remote site. This equipment is similar to a normal freezer except that colder temperatures may be used and a fan is used to circulate the cold air. Blast chill refrigerators may be used to chill 45 lbs of food in 90 min. (Figure 6.15).

Some institutional facilities, in effect, operate "convenience-food factories." For example, convenience foods are purchased, some food may be produced on site, and both types of food items are then preportioned and frozen. With this plan, the amount to produce is that needed to build frozen food inventories up to pre-established par levels. There is less relationship between daily quantities of items requested and actual production needs.

This plan enables institutions to use a "restaurant-style menu" (an example is shown in Figure 6.16). Clients may order from a wide variety of menu items. As orders are transferred to the kitchen personnel, menu items are "pulled" out of frozen inventory (frequently the day before service); items are then stored overnight in a refrigerated unit. Prior to the time of service, these preportioned items are placed on service trays as required and are transported to ward kitchens (also called "rethermalization" galleys) and may be stored in an on-site roll-in refrigerator in the galley. At time of service, hot foods are "rethermalized" in a convection or other oven, and completed food trays are then served (by either dietary or nursing staff) to residents or clients in the area.

FIGURE 6.14 PREPORTIONED FOODS IN TRANSPORT RACKS

Used by permission of St. Lawrence Hospital, Lansing, Mich.

FIGURE 6.15 BLAST CHILL REFRIGERATOR
Source: Photo courtesy of Traulsen & Co., Inc., Ft. Worth, TX

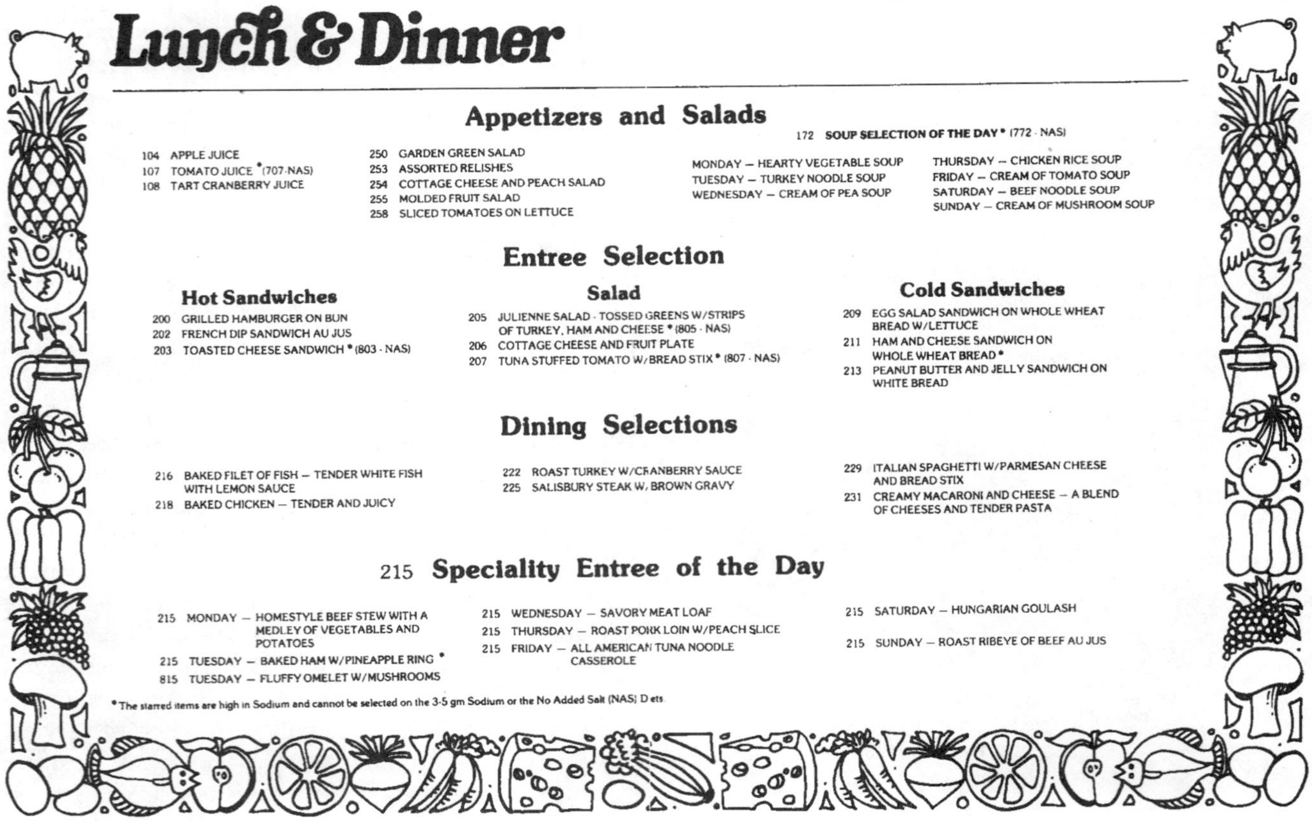

Lunch & Dinner

Appetizers and Salads

104 APPLE JUICE
107 TOMATO JUICE *(707-NAS)
108 TART CRANBERRY JUICE

250 GARDEN GREEN SALAD
253 ASSORTED RELISHES
254 COTTAGE CHEESE AND PEACH SALAD
255 MOLDED FRUIT SALAD
258 SLICED TOMATOES ON LETTUCE

172 **SOUP SELECTION OF THE DAY** * (772 - NAS)

MONDAY – HEARTY VEGETABLE SOUP
TUESDAY – TURKEY NOODLE SOUP
WEDNESDAY – CREAM OF PEA SOUP
THURSDAY – CHICKEN RICE SOUP
FRIDAY – CREAM OF TOMATO SOUP
SATURDAY – BEEF NOODLE SOUP
SUNDAY – CREAM OF MUSHROOM SOUP

Entree Selection

Hot Sandwiches

200 GRILLED HAMBURGER ON BUN
202 FRENCH DIP SANDWICH AU JUS
203 TOASTED CHEESE SANDWICH * (803 - NAS)

Salad

205 JULIENNE SALAD - TOSSED GREENS W/STRIPS OF TURKEY, HAM AND CHEESE * (805 - NAS)
206 COTTAGE CHEESE AND FRUIT PLATE
207 TUNA STUFFED TOMATO W/BREAD STIX * (807 - NAS)

Cold Sandwiches

209 EGG SALAD SANDWICH ON WHOLE WHEAT BREAD W/LETTUCE
211 HAM AND CHEESE SANDWICH ON WHOLE WHEAT BREAD *
213 PEANUT BUTTER AND JELLY SANDWICH ON WHITE BREAD

Dining Selections

216 BAKED FILET OF FISH – TENDER WHITE FISH WITH LEMON SAUCE
218 BAKED CHICKEN – TENDER AND JUICY

222 ROAST TURKEY W/CRANBERRY SAUCE
225 SALISBURY STEAK W/BROWN GRAVY

229 ITALIAN SPAGHETTI W/PARMESAN CHEESE AND BREAD STIX
231 CREAMY MACARONI AND CHEESE – A BLEND OF CHEESES AND TENDER PASTA

215 Speciality Entree of the Day

215 MONDAY – HOMESTYLE BEEF STEW WITH A MEDLEY OF VEGETABLES AND POTATOES
215 TUESDAY – BAKED HAM W/PINEAPPLE RING *
815 TUESDAY – FLUFFY OMELET W/MUSHROOMS
215 WEDNESDAY – SAVORY MEAT LOAF
215 THURSDAY – ROAST PORK LOIN W/PEACH SLICE
215 FRIDAY – ALL AMERICAN TUNA NOODLE CASSEROLE
215 SATURDAY – HUNGARIAN GOULASH
215 SUNDAY – ROAST RIBEYE OF BEEF AU JUS

* The starred items are high in Sodium and cannot be selected on the 3-5 gm Sodium or the No Added Salt (NAS) Diets

FIGURE 6.16 RESTAURANT-STYLE MENU
Courtesy of St. Lawrence Hospital, Lansing, Mich.

Tray Line Systems

There are several different tray line systems used in facilities. The simplest system involves a worker pushing a tray in front of him or her. The food is placed on the tray according to the diet. Another tray system involves a tray moving on rollers. The tray moves with the help of gravity and passes in front of the workers for the addition of food items. A third style uses an electric motor to power a conveyor belt. The speed of the conveyor can be regulated.

Computer controls have entered the realm of tray service. In one system, the employees wear headphones to assist in placing the correct food on the tray as it passes in front of them.

Some tray lines use straight-line configurations, with hot and cold food wheeled into place next to the tray line. Other tray lines operate in a circle.

As you have learned, there are many different delivery systems available to dietary managers today. Some of the systems start with hot food; others begin with food in the chilled or frozen state. Systems reviewed in this chapter make use of plate pellets, insulated trays, dishes with metal contacts, and rethermalization of food from infrared heat or convection and microwave ovens.

Metal Pellet System

The metal pellet system requires heating of a base in a hot oven before use. Some manufacturers have designed a special oven to hold and heat the pellets, while other systems use a conventional oven to heat the pellets. Some pellets are shaped like a donut and others are shaped to surround a dinner plate. In addition to the heated pellet, a cover is used to hold in the heat. The cover may be constructed of stainless steel or structural foam. Select a cover which has ample height for your entree and can be easily stacked on top of another. (See Figure 6.17 for illustrations of pellet system equipment items.)

Figure 6.17 Illustration of Pellet System Equipment

Use of Insulated Trays

The insulated tray is generally a rectangular tray with indentations for food. The idea behind this tray is to hold hot foods hot and cold foods cold. Some of the trays are patented to use special china or disposable dinnerware. A lid or cover helps to keep the food hot, and separates the hot food from the cold food (see Figure 6.18 for a picture of an insulated tray and cover).

There are some partially insulated and contoured trays that fit on a standard tray to hold cold food. Once again, the dinnerware must fit this section of the tray. The hot food is separate, so regular china or other insulated dinnerware is used.

Thermostatically Controlled Dishes

Thermostatically controlled dishes and heating units are a third style of delivering hot food. The plates and bowls used for hot food have metal buttons on the bottom of the dish. This button helps provide the contact between the electric conductor rails in the oven and the plate. The plates or bowls have matching lids. The process for thermalizing the food has the following steps: The food is produced and refrigerated until it is needed. Food to be served hot is placed into the special oven and heated to 165°F. Once this temperature is reached, it is held or maintained until the food is removed from the oven. While the food is in the oven, hot beverages or frozen/chilled foods are added to a tray of refrigerated food.

Infrared Radiation System

A system using infrared radiation to reheat the refrigerated, cooked food uses a special porcelain plate and a bell-shaped stainless-steel cover. Two horizontal tubes emit infrared rays that heat the food. The tube above heats the cover, and the tube below heats the plate. During the regeneration process, the cover is always at a higher temperature than the plate, so no condensation will occur. The porcelain plate, having heat-producing capacity but little thermal conductivity, serves as an accumulator of heat. The stainless steel cover, with little heat-producing capacity but good conductivity, serves as the emitter of dark infrared rays acting directly on the food. The plates are removed with special tongs from the shelves of the oven and placed on the service tray with other refrigerated items.

Figure 6.18 Illustration of Insulated Tray and Cover

Convection ovens are the source of heat for another system. One cart holds the cold foods in a refrigerated section and the food to be heated in another. When the cart is wheeled into position in a pantry kitchen, a convection oven is used to heat the food. (The cold food cart is held under refrigeration.) A convection oven has forced air circulating throughout the cavity. Regular china can be used with this system. Food can be plated chilled or hot in the kitchen. The hot food item is then matched with the cold food tray and delivered to the client.

A microwave oven can also be used to boost the temperature of food. Generally, one plate is placed in the microwave at a time. If several plates will be needed simultaneously, a bank of microwave ovens could be purchased. A manual indicating how long to cook each item provides a more consistent product to the client, and can reduce anxiety of the employee heating the food. Following the heating process, the food is added to the tray of refrigerated or frozen items.

Carts are generally used to transport food from the preparation area to the service area. There are many styles of carts available. Some are automated and run on a monorail, and others are pushed to their destination. Some styles use open shelving and others are enclosed. Whenever food is transported, it must be covered to be kept sanitary. Dietary managers can purchase carts to hold hot food only, cold food only, or both hot and cold foods.

The central concern behind all food production/delivery systems is to deliver and serve food at proper temperatures to the client. Facilities of different size will warrant different systems. If the dietary manager is trying to optimize cooking and serving times to avoid a rush or to even out the slow periods during the day, he or she may want to consider the cook/chill or cook/freeze preparation methods. Both the cook/chill and cook/freeze methods require more refrigeration space than a normal kitchen has, so preparations to change from cook/hold to another system will require design changes in a kitchen.

A decision to change to a new delivery system offers the opportunity to write to several companies to seek information about their systems. Ask the company representatives where their system is in use in the local area. Visit the facility, ask questions, and eat a meal. Find out whether the silverware is too cold to handle or the packages difficult to open.

There are both advantages and disadvantages to any method of food production/delivery system being considered. Quality, acceptance by clients, capital and operating costs, labor (especially union), and other concerns must all be addressed and quantified for the specific facility. The dietary manager should not be prejudiced for or against any system. Instead, he or she should be aware of all the many alternatives available, and should know the procedures necessary to conduct a cost-benefit analysis for the specific facility. Frequently, visits to nearby facilities utilizing the alternative methods can provide a great deal of insight and suggestions about the "practicality" of the alternate for use in the specific facility.

SUMMARY

As products are being prepared, a wide range of pre-production activities involved with purchasing, receiving, storing, and issuing ought to be carried out. There are several advantages to pre-production planning:

- Effective planning assures that food products, personnel, and equipment are available in necessary quantities;
- Coordination between production and service staff prevents available resources from being over- or under-utilized;
- Effective planning decreases the likelihood that problems will arise.

There are several sales analysis procedures. Some ways include analysis of sales journal tapes from cash registers (in cash cafeteria operations) and review of production/leftover records (in non-cash operations).

Sales history records can be reviewed and used as a guide to estimate production forecasts for the upcoming week, as well as the season of the year, weather, special events within the facility, and similar other factors considered in an attempt to estimate production needs.

In addition to planning the number of portions of each menu item to prepare, pre-production planning and meetings can also be used to schedule required labor hours, as well as for scheduling equipment for specific time periods.

Food production involves preparing and assembling required food products. Quality control is of prime concern. The dietary manager should make sure that all required food production procedures relating to quality, cost control, safety, and so on are being followed. Food waste during production must be minimized by designing efficient production techniques.

The Food Production Planning and Leftover Report must be accurately completed and used as a future reference to "fine-tune" the process of assessing the quantity of items to be prepared.

Food production principles include many important food preparation techniques. Among them are meat and poultry preparation principles; fish, egg and cheese preparation principles; vegetable and fruit cookery principles; salad preparation principles; sauce preparation principles; bread and cereal preparation principles; sandwich production principles; soup preparation principles; and dessert preparation principles.

Learning to manage every dollar spent for food will minimize food waste. Purchasing in excessive quantities, improperly storing and handling foods, poor sanitation practices, overproduction, oversupply, improper cooking, theft, and pilferage are all causes of food waste.

Basic procedures should be used to monitor food waste:

1. Procedures to purchase food in the proper quantities are necessary;
2. Proper receiving practices must be used to confirm products requested;
3. Proper storage practices following basic sanitation principles are necessary;
4. Rotation of products and use of the "first-in, first-out" system of food issuing is also necessary.

A very important rule of food storage is: No food can be discarded without prior approval of the dietary manager. A report of food waste can be used as an integral part of the food waste monitoring activity and then can be used to evaluate effectiveness of supervisory practices.

Production personnel should clean and prepare foods carefully in order to not waste excessive amounts. Using standardized recipes and preparing proper quantity of products are useful practices in reducing waste and decreasing food costs.

Dietary managers need to do their part to manage product waste. There are not only legislative concerns but, there are also social, client, and environmental concerns as well.

The U.S. Environmental Protection Agency has noted a four-edged approach to managing food wastes:

1. Source reduction;
2. Recycling;
3. Incineration;
4. Landfills.

A dietary manager should be well informed about the problem of food waste and potential solutions, and have an attitude about concern that "every little bit helps" and that the facility has a role to play in the resolution of the problem.

There are several ways that facilities can serve meals to clients. A common method involves tray service in a cafeteria setting. Other types of service include:

1. Family-style service;
2. Waiter/waitress service;
3. French service;
4. Russian service;
5. English service;
6. American service (and modified American service);
7. Buffet service;
8. Box meal service.

There are basically two ways to transport food, in bulk or in preportioned form. When food is transported in bulk, it is prepared and placed in large transport containers. The unit can be heated by either electricity or canned liquid/paste fuels. Some facilities use electrically heated, insulated transport chests which are preheated before use.

For sanitation purposes, hot foods should be kept above 140°F or below 40°F. Food quality is reduced if the internal temperature of a hot food transport chest is set too high, because the food will continue to cook.

Transport equipment for moving food in bulk is generally sized to fit modular steam table pans. After sealing them, the units can be stacked on top of one another for transportation, when dollies are available.

Other equipment items used for transporting food are canisters (for liquids), and various types of insulated or uninsulated mobile transport chests. In addition to transporting bulk food in hot, ready-to-serve condition, alternate food production/delivery methods provide for bulk foods to be transported in chilled or even frozen condition.

Preportioned items can be transported in hot, ready-to-eat, chilled, or frozen states, and there is specialized food transport equipment available to safely transport those items as well.

There are several different tray line systems used in facilities. While some tray systems involve pushing one's own tray as food is placed on the tray according to diet, other tray lines may operate in a circle, or may be operated by a conveyor belt where the speed is regulated.

There are many different delivery systems available to dietary managers today. Some of the systems start with hot food: others begin with food in the chilled or frozen state. Modern delivery systems include:

1. Metal pellet system, which requires heating of a base in a hot oven before use;
2. Insulated trays are generally rectangular with indentations for food;
3. Thermostatically controlled dishes and heating units are another way of delivering hot food;
4. Infrared radiation systems use infrared radiation to reheat the refrigerated, cooked food.

Carts are generally used to transport food from the preparation area to the service area. Carts can be used to hold hot or cold food only, or both hot and cold foods.

When evaluating food systems, quality, acceptance by climate, capital and operating costs, labor, and other concerns must all be addressed and quantified for the specific facility.

KEY TERMS

- Pre-production planning
- Food production planning and leftover report
- Food production principles
- Food waste
- Source reduction
- Recycling
- Incineration
- Landfills
- Tray service
- Family style service
- Waiter/waitress style service
- Buffet service
- Box meal service
- Bulk food transport method
- Preportioned food transport method
- Metal pellet system
- Insulated trays
- Thermostatically controlled dishes
- Infrared radiation system

QUESTIONS/PROBLEMS/CASES

1. As dietary manager of a retirement home, you have been asked to plan for an annual Christmas holiday buffet for the residents and their invited guests. What might you consider in the pre-production stage of planning?

2. Answer the following question concerning food preparation techniques:

   a. Moist heat is suggested for what cut of beef? and why?

   b. Why is it necessary to cook poultry at low temperatures?

   c. Why is it necessary to use thawed eggs (after freezing) within 24 hours?

   d. Why should cheese be cooked at low temperatures?

   e. What happens to vegetables when they are overcooked?

   f. What process stops fresh fruit from turning a dark color?

   g. Which vegetables may contain tiny mites, which can be removed by soaking in cold, salted water for six minutes?

   h. Give an example of each "part" of a salad.

   i. What are the principles involved in the preparation of sauces thickened with eggs?

j. Which type of starch begins to gelatinize when heated at 150°–160°F and complete swelling is accomplished before boiling?

k. Which kind of soup precedes a full meal?

l. What is meringue?

m. To insure complete swelling, how long does flour have to boil?

n. What is a white sauce made from?

o. Describe the steps in the muffin method of mixing ingredients.

3. Why has product waste become such an issue in this country?

4. What does source reduction and recycling have to do with management of solid waste?

5. List the different delivery systems and their distinctions.

6. List the types of service that Mercy Hospital provides.

Most Mercy Hospital patients receive meal trays in their room. In one unit of the hospital, patients go to a dining room and are served plated food from a waitress who brings several servings to the dining room on a cart.

Mercy Hospital employees can get most meals in one of three ways: select foods from various stations in a cafeteria, eat from a buffet line, or order a box meal.

7

EVALUATION OF FOOD AND NUTRITION SERVICES

CHAPTER OUTLINE

- Internal Quality Control
  - Defining and Establishing Food Standards
  - Training Employees to Produce a Standard Product
  - Testing Product Quality
  - Implementing Quality Control Checks and Necessary Changes
  - Evaluating Food Acceptance
  - Evaluating Food Quality
  - Observing and Recording Food Intake
  - Preparing and Serving Special Nourishments and Supplemental Feedings
  - Developing Foodservice Quality Control Procedures
  - Evaluating Operating Procedures
  - Evaluating Strategies
  - Evaluating Dietary Goals
  - Procedures for Self-review
  - Procedures for Improving Dietary Services
- External Quality Control
  - Joint Commission on Accreditation of Healthcare Organization (JCAHO)
  - Governmental Agencies and Evaluation
  - Omnibus Budget Reconciliation Act (OBRA)
  - Details of Licensure
  - Preparing for Surveys and Challenging Them

INTERNAL QUALITY CONTROL

DEFINING AND ESTABLISHING FOOD STANDARDS

Each dietary operation must establish its own standards. A good quality standard should cover the essential characteristics that indicate a quality product. These standards may be shown on a recipe card in the form of a color picture with a descriptive verbal explanation. The card can then be laminated or placed in an enclosed plastic covering to keep it from getting wet or covered with food.

TRAINING EMPLOYEES TO PRODUCE A STANDARD PRODUCT

Both training programs and use of standardized recipes will help to attain quality objectives of products to be served. Involve employees in the production and evaluation process. The employee should first receive quality products or ingredients. The product must then be processed in a minimum amount of time to enhance the final product. Before being served, the final product must be tested for flavor and correct temperature. Work with employees if the product does not meet the standard so that they produce the standard product the next time it is on the menu.

Client reactions to the final product should be shared with employees. When the product receives praise, do not hesitate to pass this recognition on to the staff members who produced the food item. Information about a product that has been overcooked or overseasoned should also be shared. Discuss whether the equipment is at fault, the recipe is a problem, or human error played a part in the unacceptable product.

Testing Product Quality

A testing instrument and taste panel can help determine whether a product meets the given standard. The people on the panel should have knowledge about food standards and the ability to distinguish flavors, and generally should be nonsmokers. (If a desirable judge stops smoking for two to three hours before a test, he or she may regain the ability to identify differences in the samples.) Inform the judges that being well rested and free from colds also helps in the decision process. The best time of day to judge food is an hour before lunch or dinner. The testing instrument considers taste, odor, flavor, color, texture, and appearance of the sample product.

People can distinguish among four tastes: sweet, salty, bitter, and sour. One can also smell the odor associated with the food. Taste and the odor yield the flavor of a product. Taste sensitivity decreases with age, increasing the need for seasoning for elderly clients.

Color is also important. Many foods have characteristic colors closely identified with certain highly acceptable qualities. For example, the desired color of an apple is the color present when the fruit is at its peak of maturity. If the color is darkened or faded, the fruit is not of the "best" color. Color sometimes does not reflect quality, as in the example of oranges. They may be mature in flavor and nutritive value but still be green in color.

Texture is judged by the food item's characteristic texture, which may be stringy, velvety smooth, crisp, mushy, tough, tender, or hard. Appearance refers to the exterior, interior, and portion size in a bowl or on a plate. Factors to consider include a characteristic and/or regular shape, unbroken pieces, correct portion size, proper moistness level, and good color. Is the interior appealing in terms of texture and color? Does the portion look attractive? Does it fit the container in which it is to be served? All of the factors of taste, odor, flavor, color, texture and overall appearance are generally subjective, based on personal preference or bias. The information or feedback received, however, is valuable, and changes can be made to achieve a more acceptable and standard product. A sample of a product score sheet is illustrated in Figure 7.1.

Implementing Quality Control Checks and Necessary Changes

Some quality control checks have already been discussed. Employees must be trained to be responsive to quality control standards before service. It is a good practice to use the first tray at the beginning of service as a test tray. Give this tray of food the same treatment as the other food. Deliver it to the eating area and, after all the food has been placed in front of each person, check the food items on the test tray. Compare the food to these standards:

- Are hot foods served above 140°F[1]?
- Are cold foods served below 40°F?
- Are colors bright and fresh looking?
- Are items on the tray in the correct location?
- Are a variety of textures and flavors present?

---

[1] Poultry and stuffed meats should be cooked to a minimum temperature of 165°F. Potentially hazardous food must also be reheated to a minimum of 165°F to minimize the possibility of food-borne illness.

Name N.S. (Person on Taste Panel) Date 8/16/84

Name of Product Chicken broccoli casserole

	Extremely Poor	Very Poor	Poor	Between Poor & Fair	Fair	Between Fair & Good	Good	Very Good	Extremely Good
Taste Sweet—#1 Salty—#2 Bitter—#3 Sour—#4							✓		
Odor							✓		
Flavor								✓	
Color									✓
Texture							✓		
Appearance								✓	

FIGURE 7.1 PRODUCT SCORE SHEET

If "yes" is answered to these questions, a fine job is being done. If "no" was the answer to any one of the questions, time should be spent researching and making corrections. Use this test tray idea every day for every meal until favorable results are consistently obtained.

The feedback provided to staff is important. The dietary manager may decide to work with one employee at a time to make corrections, or he or she may use group meetings for a team approach. The group meetings could be for the hot-food preparation staff only or for the entire dietary staff. Staff should be told how clients and managament feel about the job being done. Pass words of praise on to them.

Changes may be necessary after receiving feedback from the clients served. Look at the changes in terms of food category, equipment, or scheduling. For example, if the vegetables receive constant complaints about being cold, mushy, and/or unappetizing, try steaming them instead of boiling them. Prepare smaller batches and keep replacing these small pans of product on the tray line throughout the service. Other ideas include plating the food cold in the kitchen and raising the temperature at the location where it will be served.

Next, look at equipment changes in the kitchen. If the chopped sirloin steak is not desirable when cooked in an oven, try grilling the meat. When meat is grilled, you can control the time it is on the heated surface; the flavor will be different and it will be a nicer brown color. Serve this product as soon as possible after taking it off the grill.

A third area for change may come in the scheduling of products. Work first with the product that takes the longest to prepare or cook. Then schedule the second, third, and fourth products. For example, the order of production with the following menu for 100 servings may be as follows:

1. Apple Waldorf salad with bibb lettuce underliner (start 2 hours 45 minutes before service; hold under refrigeration);
2. Cranberry crunch dessert (begin 1 hour 45 minutes before service);
3. Chicken broccoli casserole (start 1 hour before service);
4. Oven-browned potatoes (45 minutes are needed);
5. Warm whole-wheat dinner rolls (10 minutes are required);
6. Beverage (portion when served or plated).

It is a good idea to look at the service of food for changes in procedure if the food is not being served hot. Look for answers to the following questions and establish standards for the dietary operation so that hot food is served hot and cold food is served cold:

- Does staff start with warm dinnerware for hot food and chilled dinnerware for cold food?
- Is the food hot when it gets to the steam table?
- Is there a draft coming from above the steam table?
- How many employees help set up the trays?
- How long does it take to serve the first tray plated?
- When is the cover removed from the tray or plate?

Evaluating Food Acceptance

Identifying food preferences should be a continual process. Interview the client to find out the client's food likes and dislikes. The list of food items is recorded on a card and placed into a file. Another method of verifying preferences involves use of the three-day food intake study. This study provides information about exactly what the client consumes, which can be compared with preference record. Both of these sources provide an opportunity to ask and see first-hand what the client is willing to accept and what food he or she rejects. When a food product is rejected on the three-day study, the dietary manager can follow up and ask whether it was the preparation method or non-interest in the food product that day.

The dietary goal must be to serve quality food and watch each step of preparation and service to ensure that the best quality food is being delivered and served. Another approach to identify client food preferences or food problems can be to use survey cards or personal visits to ask a sampling of persons for comments on the food. The survey card can be placed on the dining-room table in a card holder or on a tray. The card seeks information on overall quality of the meal and then asks specific questions about each food item. The person making the comment has the opportunity to sign his or her name and give the date so the dietary manager can respond to the client personally. One may want to offer pencils with the cards on the table or tray. Figure 7.2 illustrates a sample of a meal survey.

	EXCELLENT	GOOD	FAIR	POOR
Overall, my meal was:		X		
Specifically, my				
Appetizer was:	X			
Salad was:		X		
Entree was:		X		
Vegetable was:		X		
Dessert was:	X			

Additional Comments: ______

Signature: *John Good* Date: *7/18/85*

Figure 72. Meal Survey

Visiting with clients in the dining room is another effective approach for gathering comments on the food. People are either going to provide their opinion or indicate that everything is satisfactory. The dietary manager can build rapport with clients by changing a product if enough people indicate that a change is preferred, but will not build rapport if he or she asks for comments and then does not accept responses or does not change a product after several complaints are received. Figure 7.3 is a food and nutrition patient questionnaire to be completed by the client to provide appropriate feedback to staff.

Food & Nutrition Service Patient Questionnaire

1. What is your diet order?
   Regular ________ Modified ________ Don't know ________

2. Which meal do you enjoy most?
   Breakfast ________ Lunch ________ Dinner ________

3. Do you receive the meal items you requested?
   Always ________ Frequently ________ Seldom ________

4. Have your meals been served at about the same time every day?
   Yes ________ No ________

5. Please rate the Food and Nutrition personnel who served you your meals:

	Always	Frequently	Seldom	Never
Knock on door before entering	________	________	________	________
Greeted you upon entering?	________	________	________	________

6. Please rate the following areas:

	Excellent	Good	Fair	Poor
Quality of food	________	________	________	________
Hot foods hot?	________	________	________	________
Cold foods cold?	________	________	________	________
Appearance of tray	________	________	________	________
Variety of foods	________	________	________	________
Correct items on tray	________	________	________	________

7. Additional Comments/Suggestions?

____

____

THANK YOU FOR YOUR HELP! Optional.

Name ____

Room Number Date

FIGURE 7.3 FOOD AND NUTRITION PATIENT QUESTIONNAIRE
Used by permission of Food and Nutrition Services, Shands Hospital at the University of Florida.

When people are hesitant to indicate that a product is not what they are used to eating, the dietary manager may decide to conduct a plate-waste study in the dishroom. This study provides an overview about which products were consumed or rejected. To conduct a plate-waste study with more specific information, use a card on the tray to identify the person and look at the food left on the tray at the end of the meal. (This study is not always considered accurate because someone may move an empty glass or cup from one tray to another tray.) The benefit from conducting a plate-waste study is the overall information received about a specific food product. One format for a plate-waste study is shown in Figure 7.4.

A sampling of at least twenty trays can be helpful. This information will also be helpful when the menu is planned. If a product is repeatedly refused, you may decide to take it off the menu.

After gathering data about food preferences, the dietary manager must summarize and analyze the information obtained. What is being done correctly? Should you consider changes in procedures for delivering food to the client, serving the food, preparation methods, food temperatures, menu, quality of food being purchased, quantity of food prepared, employee skill, or equipment capabilities? Look at one area at a time as changes are made.

Evaluating Food Quality

The temperature and quality of food served to the client affects whether he or she accepts or rejects the food. Dietary managers should always prepare foods under sanitary conditions, hold hot foods for as short a period of time as possible, and keep cold foods under refrigeration. Vegetables, fruits, starch items, desserts, and products made with milk deteriorate and lose quality as they are kept under holding temperatures of 160°–200°F. Ideally, french fries are deep-fat fried, drained for 30 seconds, then served directly to the consumer. Since many facilities are unable to attain this goal, the next best alternative is to make small batches of french fries, drain them, place them under a heat light on the serving line and serve them as quickly as possible. If soggy, semi-warm french fries still result, perhaps other forms of potato or starch items should be used on the menu.

Time and temperature have a direct relationship to good quality. Frozen sweet peas placed in boiling water or steamed to an internal temperature of 200°F for 1½ minutes will be hot and tasty. They will have a dark green color and be slightly crunchy. Frozen sweet peas held on a 212°F steam table for 30 minutes will look pale green and be mushy in texture. Figure 7.5 shows what happens in 45 minutes to the temperature of food transported from a kitchen to the client, using three different insulation methods.

Always check the temperature of the food during preparation. Do not transfer hot food to the tray line if the product is below 140°F. Also check the temperature of food just before serving. Take the temperature again midway through service and,

Indicate with a slash the number of people who refused the product; use the second column to show how many plates came back with ½ the product, and the third column for emply plates.

Cycle Menu Week 1, Day 3, Meal 3	Plate full of Product	½ the food consumed	Empty plate
Soup	III	IIIII	IIIII IIIII II
Juice			
Salad	I	II	IIIII IIIII IIIII II
Entree	II	IIIII I	IIIII IIIII II
Vegetable	IIIII II	IIIII IIII	III
Dessert	I	II	IIIII IIIII IIIII II

Figure 7.4 Plate-Waste Information

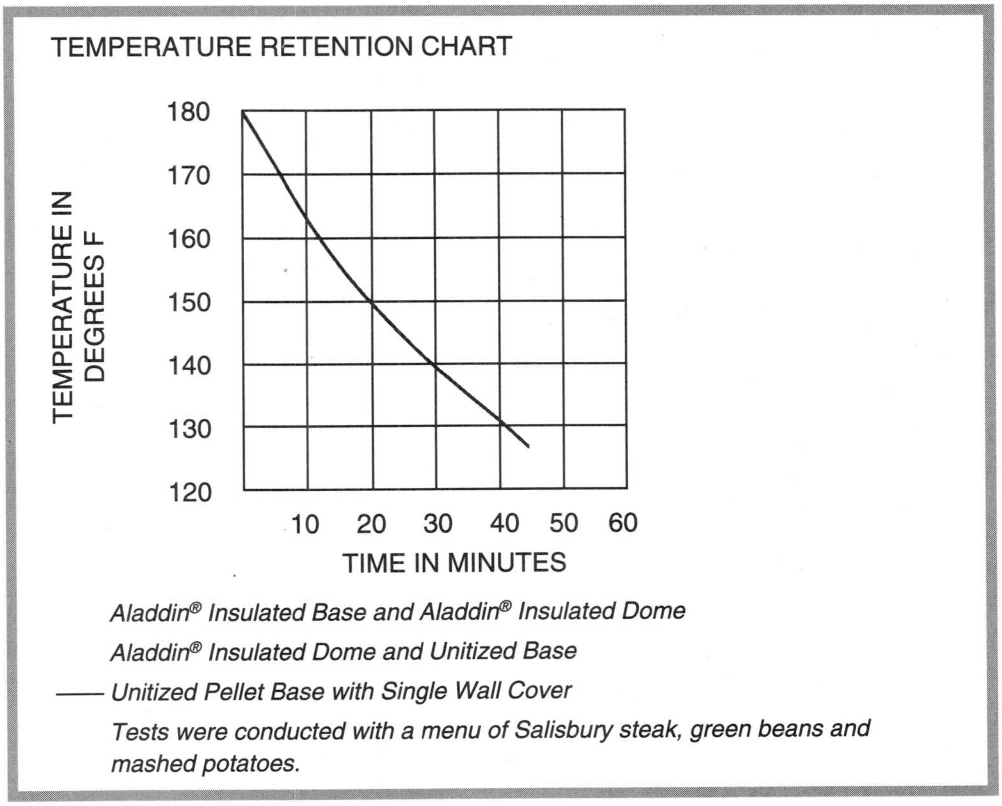

FIGURE 7.5 TIME/TEMPERATURE RELATIONSHIPS
Source: Aladdin Company, Synergetics Inc., 1 Vantage Way, P.O. Box 100888, Nashville, Tenn. 1981.

finally, at the point of service. Some facilities plate food for a tray not to be consumed and record the hot and cold food temperatures at the beginning and end of service. Chart the food temperatures in your facility to find out how long it takes to serve, and how temperatures change over this time period.

Observing and Recording Food Intake

It is a good idea to visit the clients while they are eating to discover their feelings about the food being consumed. It is important to know whether a client is refusing any type of food on a continual basis. The nurses may be of some assistance if they record food consumed. However, wise dietary managers do not rely on them for all observations. You may use a three-day food intake form, used normally for calorie counts, to study the eating habits of each client.

Preparing and Serving Special Nourishments and Supplemental Feedings

The physician generally prescribes nourishment or supplemental feeding programs for clients. After the dietary manager has gathered data about a client and found that the client needs extra nourishments, he or she may write in the medical record that the client could benefit from a nourishment program. The individual who has ultimate responsibility to determine need and to document should be carefully considered; in some states and/or facilities this choice may be dictated by licensure laws and/or policies of the facility.

Some healthcare facilities have found between-meal feedings have greater acceptance if they are not given to the client too close to another meal period. Therefore, mid-morning, mid-afternoon, and early to mid-evening (before bedtime) periods are generally accepted as times when the client is most willing to eat. Some nourishment programs highlight high-calorie milkshakes for weight gain; others individualize the program to meet the modified diet and likes or dislikes of the client.

The purpose of supplying a nourishment is lost if the client does not consume the product. Therefore, a variety of nourishments may increase the client's acceptance of the product. Figure 7.6 shows an example of a nourishment sheet listing the names of the clients, the day of the week, time when the nourishment is given, and the product consumed. Figure 7.7 is used by the nursing staff to record how much of the product was consumed.

Once the dietary manager has determined who is to receive a nourishment and what it will be, dietary employees can help with preparation. The preparation time will vary depending on the number and variety of products. In Figure 7.6, notice that on Wednesday several clients are receiving half a banana. The employee could slice the bananas, place the slices in a small amount of orange juice, cover them with clear wrap, and then mark the name on each serving and refrigerate. The dietary manager can time approximately how long this process will take; it can then become a standard procedure. It is a good practice to have the employee make a checkmark on the nourishment form and write his/her initials at the bottom of a column to be sure that each nourishment has been prepared and delivered to the nurses' station or to the client. This system makes the employee accountable for his or her actions.

Allow enough time for the nourishments to be passed to each client, but not so much time that the product becomes a health hazard from sitting at room temperature. The arrangements for picking up soiled dishes should be made in writing if the nursing staff distributes and picks up the dishes from the clients. It is a good practice to have dietary employees travel only once to pick up the dishes in a central location.

NOTE: Dietary Staff—Please place a check mark in the box after you have made the nourishment, written the name on the nourishment, and delivered it to the nurses' station. Place your initial at the base of the column to identify the person making the nourishments.

Room Name	Date 12/1 Mon	12/2 Tues	12/3 Wed	12/4 Thurs	12/5 Fri	12/6 Sat	12/7 Sun
9:00 AM							
101 Johnson	½C cranberry jc.	½C pineapple jc.	½C apple juice	½C cranberry jc.	½C prune juice	½C grapefruit jc.	½C tomato juice
2:00 PM							
202 Olson	medium apple cubed	1C van. milkshake	½ banana	1C choc. milkshake	½C pear slice	1C strawberry milkshake	½C peach slices
101 Johnson	medium apple cubed	1C van. milkshake	½ banana	1C choc. milkshake	½C pear slice	1C strawberry milkshake	½C peach slices
H/S Feeding							
202 Olson	½C choc. pudding	½C custard	½C lemon pudding	½C yogurt	½C tapioca pudding	½C van. ice cream	½C lime sherbet
101 Johnson	½C choc. pudding	½C custard	½C lemon pudding	½C yogurt	½C tapioca pudding	½C van. ice cream	½C lime sherbet
303 Flower	½C skim milk + 5 van. wafers	½C skim milk + 2 graham crackers	½C skim milk + 2 pkgs. soda crackers	½C skim milk + 5 van. wafers	½C custard	½C skim milk + 2 graham crackers	½C skim milk + 2 pkgs. soda crackers

FIGURE 7.6 NOURISHMENT INTAKE RECORD

NOTE: All Nursing Staff—Please record the acceptance or refusal of the following nourishments daily, using the recommended codes:

(O) = Did not receive from dietary
(R) = Refused nourishment
(S) = Sleeping
(1) = Accepted all of the nourishment
(¾) = Accepted 50–75% of the nourishment
(½) = Accepted 25–50% of the nourishment
(¼) = Accepted 10–25% of the nourishment

Room Name	Date 12/1 Mon	12/2 Tues	12/3 Wed	12/4 Thurs	12/5 Fri	12/6 Sat	12/7 Sun
9:00 AM							
101 Johnson	1	½	S	¾	R	¼	1
2:00 PM							
202 Olson	¾	S	1	R	½	1	¾
101 Johnson	R	S	R	S	½	S	R
H/S Feeding							
202 Olson	1	½	¾	1	¾	½	1
101 Johnson	1	1	1	1	1	1	1
303 Flower	½	½	½	½	¾	¼	½

FIGURE 7.7 NOURISHMENT INTAKE RECORD (NURSING STAFF)

DEVELOPING FOODSERVICE QUALITY CONTROL PROCEDURES

Every dietary service should have an ongoing quality control program. Food quality means that food is at the peak of freshness. When handled properly, this freshness can be passed on to the client. The quality of food served at one's facility can be measured against a standard. However, a standard in one area of the United States may not be the same as that in another area. An example is chili. The southwestern states may desire a more spicy product than other areas of the country. Dietary managers should establish standards for products which they produce and/or serve. These standards would develop as standardized recipes are created.

Once standards are established, employees must be trained to achieve the standard as the food product is prepared. Dietary managers can use a panel of judges to taste the products and provide feedback. Clients can also score or react to food products served. When a selective menu is used, watch the products circled or checked most often for food preference, and also note which products come back to the dish machine uneaten.

EVALUATING OPERATING PROCEDURES

The dietary manager cannot resolve short-range operating problems or develop strategies for long-term goal attainment unless he or she evaluates. Figure 7.8 illustrates the steps in evaluation.

In step 1, dietary department goals are established. Goals must be in harmony with the broad purposes of the institution and must help the facility to better achieve those purposes. In step 2, strategies to attain dietary goals must be planned and, in step 3, specific operating procedures must be developed. The dietary manager must utilize a basic decision-making process to develop procedures judged most useful in attaining the dietary goals identified in step 1.

After specific operating procedures are developed, they must be implemented (step 4). Many dietary managers feel most comfortable with steps 3 and 4; they are

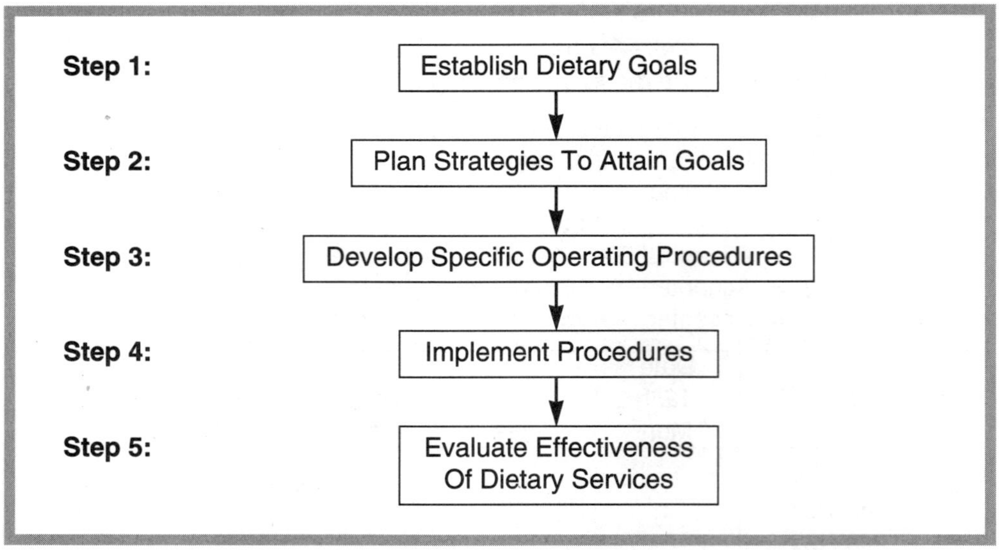

FIGURE 7.8 EVALUATION PROCESS: OVERVIEW

actively and continuously developing and implementing operating procedures. One can begin to see that, if adequate time has not been spent on the establishment of goals and in the planning of strategies to attain them, time spent in developing and implementing procedures may be less than effective.

In step 5 of Figure 7.8, the dietary manager begins to evaluate the effectiveness of dietary services. For example, as a result of implementing procedures (step 4), information will become available to the dietary manager. The monthly departmental operating statement illustrates economic aspects of dietary services. Input from clients, nursing staff, administrators, and others provides information about the delivery of dietary services. Input from clients tells the dietary manager about food quality, variety, and so on. It becomes the dietary manager's job to consider all of this information and to make evaluation decisions.

For example, the specific operating procedures which have been developed (step 3) should be evaluated. Do they utilize most effectively the limited resources available? Do they create operating or other problems not considered at the time they were planned? Are there "spin-off" effects on other aspects of dietary services or on other departments within the facility? As a result of this analysis, the dietary manager may be able to modify specific operating procedures.

EVALUATING STRATEGIES

The dietary manager can also evaluate the broad strategies which have been implemented. Is the type of food production/delivery system really the "best"? Are the facility's quality concerns addressed as foods are purchased, received, stored, and processed? Are the very best strategies in effect to recruit qualified personnel? Again, without specific attention given to this concern, the dietary manager is likely to be caught up with operating problems and neglect these broader concerns.

EVALUATING DIETARY DEPARTMENT GOALS

As a final example of evaluation, the dietary manager should consider the extent to which dietary department goals are being met. Recall the need to state goals in a measurable way so that evaluation will be easier. For example, the dietary manager who knows that dietary costs cannot exceed $500,000 will be in a much better position to evaluate economic goals than will his or her counterpart who must only "minimize expenses." Are meals provided to clients really nutritious? Are goals about personal and professional development for dietary employees really being met? Are sanitary practices being followed? Again, the dietary manager will not know unless a focused analysis is undertaken.

In summary, then, the dietary manager must assume the responsibility for a program of ongoing evaluation of dietary services. This evaluation must focus on dietary goals and the extent to which they are attained. The dietary manager who does not assume this responsibility not only violates the basic management principle that requires the need for evaluation, but also risks the possibility that the facility's limited resources will not be used optimally.

Procedures for Self-review

A formalized process for evaluation is necessary; it is not possible to "informally" evaluate dietary services with the degree of accuracy possible with a more focused procedure. How, then, should self-evaluation be done? Many facilities make use of checklists to aid in the evaluation process. With this plan, areas of specific concern are identified, listed on an evaluation form, and routinely assessed.

How is a checklist developed? Perhaps a brainstorming session can be conducted at a dietary meeting. At this time, all attendees could be asked to suggest points of concern that should be included on a checklist for a specific topic. The dietary manager could then add additional points, based upon his or her experience and knowledge of the specific operation.

Many reference books, including this text, include checklists; frequently they can be used, perhaps with modification, as the basis for developing a checklist for a specific facility. The facility's own policies and procedures manual also presents a source of information which can be abstracted into a checklist.

How is a checklist used? Perhaps the dietary manager can set aside one period monthly to review the checklist and compare it with practices and procedures actually followed; perhaps one or more checklists can be completed by a supervisor who then discusses results with the dietary manager.

What purposes are served by a checklist? The need to evaluate the current operation has already been emphasized. A checklist can help the dietary manager recall what practices are of concern and how they should be done. A checklist can also be a very effective training tool to teach new employees, and to review required procedures with experienced staff members.

When possible, changes stemming from self-evaluation analysis should be implemented gradually. For example, perhaps several staff members on one work shift could try revised procedures, or perhaps the dietary manager himself or herself could perform some work in question to get a personal feel for changes being made. It is also necessary to consider exactly how improvements being implemented will be evaluated. For example, to what extent will they bring the dietary services closer to attaining required goals? How will the impact of change on the clients, administrators, employees, and so on be evaluated?

Wise dietary managers allow some time after program improvements are made before undertaking the evaluation process. It takes time, for example, for employees to become experienced with new procedures and for clients and others to understand exactly how the changes will affect them. Time is also needed to generate operating statistics which will help define the extent to which measurable goals are better attained.

After procedures are finalized, they should be written down. Some facilities have standard operating procedures and/or policy manuals. Affected portions of these documents should be revised, dated, signed, and issued to all employees. All personnel affected by the revisions should be notified. Again, facilities with formal documents may also have formal routing procedures to ensure updating of all manuals.

Many basic management principles important in using self-evaluation tools to improve dietary services have been discussed. Let's consider a specific example to see how these principles really work. Assume that the dietary manager has an operating budget which specifies that only $350,000 can be spent for food, and that specified nutritional and other quality requirements have been established. Assume also that the dietary manager has reviewed the actual food cost information (from the monthly operating statement) and the allowable food costs (from the monthly operating budget). This comparison may indicate that actual food costs are higher than permitted. What should the dietary manager do? He or she has developed a good cost-control checklist and may be reasonably sure that all of the policies/practices required by this checklist are in use, but has he or she really confirmed that these concerns are addressed in the way people work?

How can the food costs be higher than allowable if all practices are followed and the budgeted food costs were reasonable? It is possible, of course, that food purchase costs have increased beyond the amounts estimated by the operating budget, that more meals were served than were anticipated, that errors were made in calculating actual costs in the departmental operating statement, and so on. These and related potential problems do need investigation; however, it is also possible that some of the management principles incorporated into policies and procedures and addressed in the control checklist are not being followed. The dietary manager should review each of the points addressed in the checklist and then spend some time actively supervising to confirm that all practices are being followed. As a result of this supervision, the dietary manager may note that a recently hired employee with food-receiving duties is not following all required procedures. While he or she can "blame" the new employee's supervisor for not providing proper orientation/training, it is important to recall that the responsibility for meeting food-cost goals cannot be delegated; the dietary manager is responsible. What should he or she do?

A meeting with the supervisor of the new employee can be scheduled to discuss the problem and to confirm that the supervisor does, in fact, know required procedures. The supervisor may then quickly schedule necessary training activities and closely supervise the new employee to confirm that the required receiving practices are being followed. The dietary manager can also supervise this activity more closely to confirm that the supervisor and employee are not experiencing further difficulties needing corrective action by the dietary manager. Similar problems can develop with long-term employees as well.

Let's also look at this situation from the supervisor's perspective. He or she should first review required procedures with the new employee. At this time, he or she can explain, defend, and justify the need for the practices. Perhaps on-the-job training will be done. If so, the supervisor may receive several incoming shipments with the new employee watching. At that time, the supervisor can explain what he or she is doing, how it is to be done, and why required procedures are followed. The employee can then be permitted to receive incoming shipments with the supervisor watching closely, making comments as necessary, and coaching the employee about the "right" way to receive. After this step, the supervisor may closely supervise the employee until he or she is confident that the employee knows the required procedures. From that point, routine supervision can resume.

From this above example, one can see how the dietary manager must be an "expert" in each management function and must undertake evaluation as a routine part of his or her job. Note also that employees at several organizational levels may need to be involved in necessary corrective actions and, as importantly, that operating problems cannot be resolved unless the supervisor is aware that they are occurring. Self-evaluation is the management tool necessary to provide this information.

Procedures for Improving Dietary Services

The effective dietary manager will conduct self-evaluation on a routine basis. Preceded by careful study of those factors judged most important, the review will then focus on the extent to which those factors are addressed in work undertaken by dietary services staff. What procedures should then be used to improve dietary services?

The dietary manager must first give priority to resolving problems. While this seems obvious, it is sometimes overlooked. For example, the dietary manager may feel "comfortable" working on routine, recurring activities, and may rationalize that time is not available for program improvement efforts. Other dietary managers are "fire fighters"—resolving crises which could have been avoided if proper planning, evaluation, and program improvement efforts had been undertaken earlier.

What should a dietary manager do if self-evaluation indicates that more than one problem needs correcting? Perhaps some activities can be delegated to others. If not, the dietary manager may have to decide which concern most dramatically affects the attainment of dietary services goals, and address this concern first.

Frequently, observed problems can be resolved without external assistance. Sometimes, if requested, other administrators within the facility are able to help. It is important to note that the dietary manager is the foodservice expert in the facility and that his or her advice will be required regardless of the alternative chosen for problem resolution.

It is generally best to modify existing procedures, if possible, rather than to discard the entire procedure and begin over. In effect, then, the dietary manager serves as an internal consultant about dietary operations for the facility. A wise consultant typically tries to utilize existing procedures as much as possible and to then modify them only as necessary to resolve the problems identified. Since employees may resist change, you need to minimize changes as new procedures are implemented. As the dietary manager considers alternatives to resolve problems noted at the time of self-evaluation, there is a need to involve employees, consider alternative methods, do limited testing (if practical), and so on. One should recall that the dietary manager is judged either good or bad according to his or her ability to manage these non-routine problem-solving activities. While the job of the dietary manager is difficult, the greatest challenge often comes in addressing specialized, non-recurring concerns identified by internal performance evaluation.

Once the dietary manager determines and implements improvements necessary to resolve problems, the changes must be evaluated. Several management principles become important at this point. First, affected employees must be involved in required changes. The dietary manager should explain, defend, and/or justify the need for changes. Employees should also be involved to the extent practical in the decision-making process leading to changes being proposed. They must be trained in revised procedures and provided with the necessary tools/equipment.

External Quality Control

Both governmental and private associations may be involved in the evaluation of dietary services. The dietary manager who has developed enlightened dietary goals and effective operating procedures to attain them and who can conduct ongoing self-evaluation is likely to have little, if any, problem in meeting requirements of external evaluators. Let's consider some of the applicable concerns of external evaluators.

Joint Commission on Accreditation of Healthcare Organizations (JCAHO)*

The JCAHO is a private not-for-profit organization dedicated to improving the quality of patient care in organized healthcare settings. This is accomplished through standards setting, survey evaluation, accreditation, and education. Healthcare organizations voluntarily seek JCAHO accreditation because it raises community confidence and provides an educational tool to improve care, service, and programs.

Consistent with JCAHO's standards development process, a task force was organized to identify the important aspects and processes of nutrition care. The identified processes included ordering the diet, communicating the diet order, preparing the diet, distributing the diet, and monitoring nutrition care.

The focus of nutrition care in healthcare organizations consists of providing appropriate nutrition care in a timely and effective manner, using all appropriate resources to provide this care efficiently. As a function of patient care, the nutrition care process as overviewed in Figure 7.9 consists of the following processes that

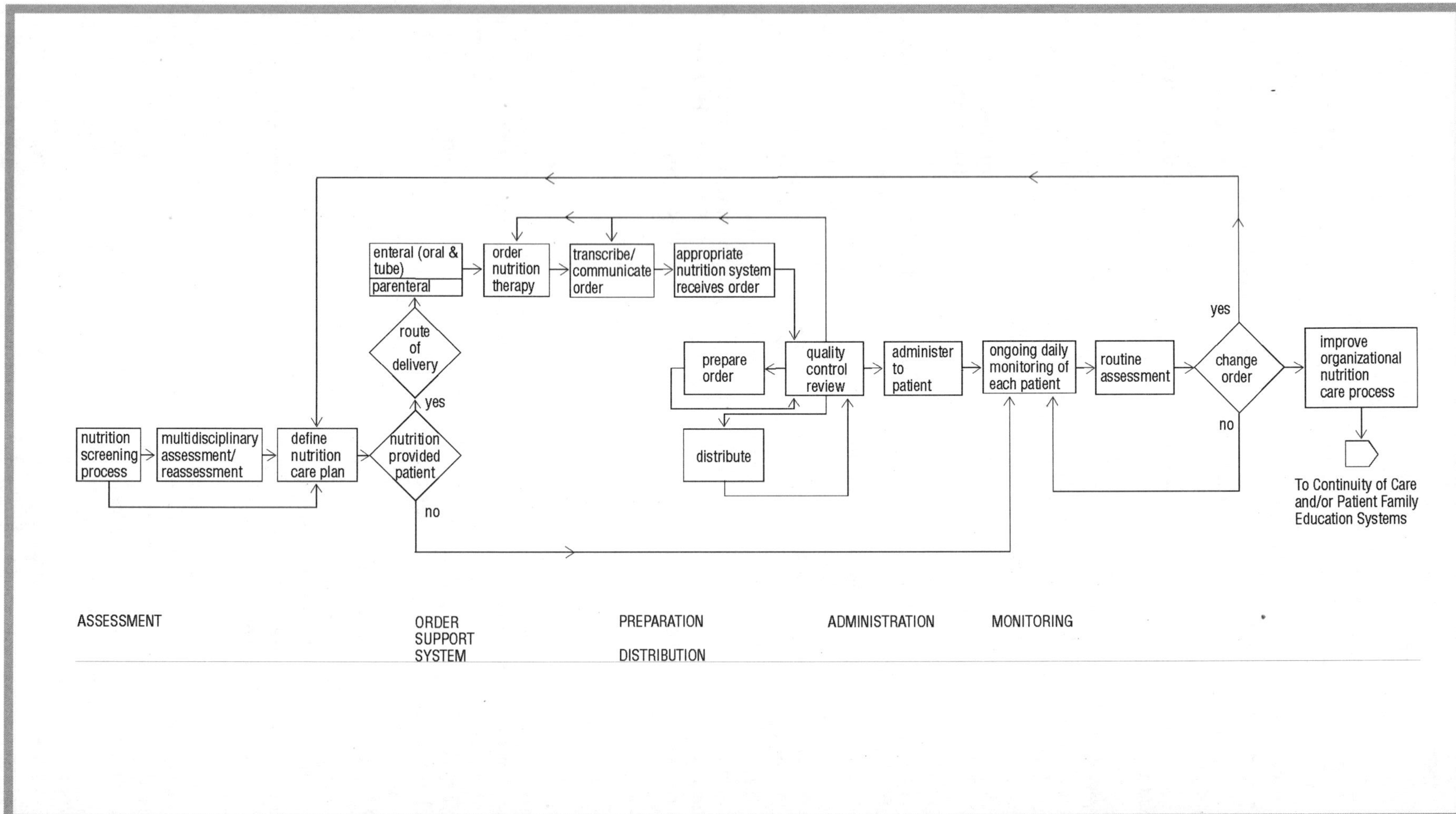

FIGURE 7.9 NUTRITION CARE PROCESS

Adapted from "National Coordinating Committee Clinical Indicators of Nutrition Care," Journal of the American Dietetic Association; Oct. 1994; p. 1168.

must be performed well: patient screening; assessment and reassessment of needs, as appropriate; development of a nutrition care plan through an interdisciplinary approach; ordering of nutrition therapy; communication of the order to nutrition and/or pharmaceutical service; preparation of the order; distribution/administration of nutrition therapy; monitoring of the process and provision of continuous reassessment; and improvement of the nutrition care process.

Information management is the focus of JCAHO. The quality and accessibility of patient information in the patient record for the purpose of monitoring quality are the main concerns. The goal, effective organization-wide information management, is seen as you review the three major sections of JCAHO standards as seen in Figure 7.10. For the purposes of the dietary manager, an understanding of JCAHO standards in nutrition care is most important; these standards, as referenced in Figure 7.11 (Medical Records Analysis Worksheet), can be summarized as follows:[1]

- For an organization to score well on this standard (TX.4), it must show that it has defined criteria under which a plan for nutrition therapy is developed and that developed plans are consistently implemented. A plan may be as simple as a prescription for a regular diet or may involve multiple prescriptions and interdisciplinary team involvement for an at-risk patient who has several complications;
- For patients determined to be at nutritional risk, the nutrition care plan includes measurable goals and a plan to achieve them;
- People who prescribe/order food and nutrition products are authorized legally and through the granting of clinical privilege to do so; food and nutrition product prescriptions/orders are recorded in the patient's medical record by an authorized person before the food or nutrition product is provided to the patient;
- Food and nutrition therapies are to be prepared and stored under proper conditions of sanitation, temperature, light, moisture, ventilation, safety, and security;
- This standard (TX.4.4) addresses the need for food and nutrition therapies to be distributed and administered in a safe, accurate, and timely manner to the patient for whom they have been ordered;

[1] Krasker, Glenn and Lucy Balogun, "(1995) JCAHO Standards: Development and Relevance to Dietetics Practice," *Journal of the American Dietetic Association*, Feb. 1995.

Section One

RI Patient Rights and Organizational Ethics (RI.1 - RI.3)
PE Assessment of Patients (PE.1.1 - PE.7.4)
TX Care of Patients (TX.1 - TX.7.4)
PF Education (PF.2 -PF.4.2)
CC Continuum of Care (CC.2 - CC.7)

Section Two

PI Improving Organizational Performance (PI.3.4.2.4 - PI.4.1.3.7)
LD Leadership (LD.1.6 - LD.1.7.1)
IM Management of Information (IM.7.2.1 - IM.7.10)

Section Three

MS Medical Staff (MMS.2.16.1 - MS.3.6)

Figure 7.10 JCAHO Standards—Three Major Sections
Adapted from *Information Management: A Guide to the JCAHO Standards;* pp. 84–106.

JCAHO STANDARDS	% required to score a 1	% required to score a 2	% of records with the documentation	Place a score of 1, 2, or N (non-compliance), or NA (not applicable)	Who is responsible for documenting the information?	Comments
TX.2.3—Records include measurement and assessment of physiological status during surgery.	100	95–99				
TX.2.4.1—Records show that patients are discharged from the postanesthesia care unit by an LIP or by using discharge criteria.	not stated	not stated				
TX.3.4.1—Records describe the effects of medications, including the patient's perceptions.	91–100	76–90				
TX.4—Records show that plans for nutrition therapy are consistently implemented.	not stated	not stated				
TX.4.1—For patients at nutritional risk, records include an interdisciplinary plan that is revised as needed.	91–100	76–90				
TX.4.2—Records show that authorized individuals prescribe or order nutrition.	91–100	76–90				
TX.4.3—Records document that the organization has defined and assigned responsibility for handling food.	not stated	not stated				
TX.4.4—Records show that nutrition is distributed and administered safely, accurately, and timely.	not stated	not stated				
TX.4.5—Records show that each patient is monitored for the nutrition's effectiveness and appropriateness.	91–100	76–90				
TX.4.6—Records show the organization has a functioning process for providing nutrition when diets are altered.	not stated	not stated				
TX.4.7—Records show that the organization has a standard mechanism to communicate nutrition care processes throughout the organization.	not stated	not stated				
TX.5—Records show the medical staff has defined and approved the content for operative assessments.	not stated	not stated				
TX.5.1.1–5.1.5—Records of patients undergoing operative and/or invasive procedures include:						
.1 a review of the patient's history,	91–100	76–90				
.2 a review of the patient's physical status,	91–100	76–90				
.3 a review of diagnostic data,	91–100	76–90				
.4 an assessment of the risks and benefits, and	91–100	76–90				
.5 an assessment of the need to administer blood or components.	91–100	76–90				
TX.5.2.1–5.2.2—Records show that operative patients have been told about alternative options and the need for and risk of blood transfusions.	91–100	76–90				

FIGURE 7.11 MEDICAL RECORDS ANALYSIS WORKSHEET

- The ongoing nutrition care monitoring of each patient for effectiveness and appropriateness of nutrition is addressed here. Results of any patient nutrition care monitoring are documented in the medical record and used in the assessment and, as appropriate, in the revision of the patient's nutrition care plan;
- As a general patient-rights issue, this standard (TX.4.6) pertains to an organization's need to satisfy a patient's unique diet needs. Such unique needs may relate to religious and/or cultural beliefs;
- Once the organization has identified standard practices and commonly recognized processes, the goal of this standard (TX.4.7) is to formalize these practices into policies and procedures and, perhaps, to develop a diet manual (*not* required; but a system to communicate standardized nutrition care activities is required).

Figure 7.12, a sample nutrition assessment form for documenting malnutrition diagnoses, may be of assistance to the dietary manager.

The JCAHO has established a goal of eliminating and combining standards that do not have a direct impact on the quality of care. The JCAHO also is moving forward in implementing a Continuous Quality Improvement (CQI) process to replace the existing Quality Assurance (QA) program. The move to CQI is to meet the needs, wants, and perceptions for quality as demanded by the customers. A customer is a client, employee, family, staff, visitor, vendor, regulator, and any "end-user" of the system.

CQI is a process (system) for continuous improvement of processes through design and redesign. Its purpose is to eliminate variances and defects, and to build service and quality into the product the first time. At all steps of the process it is assumed that the quality can be improved. CQI is proactive and is focused on correction of the process. It is the responsibility of all and is designed for cross-functional teams to problem-solve by employees at all levels. It is a shared value, a strategy, and a management process. The JCAHO role in implementing CQI[1] is as follows:

- Develop standards to replace current QA standards with provisions that foster CQI;
- Refocus standards on functions and processes that have a significant impact on quality, and eliminate those that are outdated or irrelevant;
- Collect indicator data that have proven valuable in focusing organizational attention to key quality related activities;
- Improve the survey process so that it more directly aids organizations in implementing and operating effective CQI programs;

JCAHO requirements for dietary services include:

- Have a written organizational plan;
- Have well-established working relationships with other departments within the facility;
- Have qualified personnel, including top-level administration, available;
- Be staffed by an adequate number of dietitians;
- Be staffed with an adequate number of hours of professional service, including those directed to nutritional aspects of patient care;
- Have adequate space, equipment, and supplies to undertake dietary services;
- Take precautions to avoid contamination;
- Follow safety precaution policies;

[1]Quoted from Quality Letter (QL) Perspectives, May 1990 *From QA to QI: The Views and Role of the Joint Commission.* James S. Roberts, MD, FACP and Paul M. Schyre, MD, FAPA.

DATE	TIME	☐ **Consultation** ☐ **Nutritional Screening** ☐ **Patient/Family Request**
S Usual Weight	Weight Change?	

Previous Diet Instructions/Home Diet

Other Comments

O Age	Sex ☐ M ☐ F	Ht.	Current Wt.	IBW	Diet History Obtained? ☐ Y ☐ N
Admit. Wt.	% Usual Wt.	% Ideal Wt.	% Wt. Change	Adjusted Body Weight for Obesity	

DIAGNOSES

PAST MEDICAL HISTORY

CURRENT DIET | PRESENT INTAKE

Nutritionally Pertinent Medications

LABORATORY			
DATE			
ALB			
GLU			
CHOL			
HGB			
HCT			
TLC			

Other:

A Nutritional Diagnostic Statement

☐	Protein Depletion Malnutrition (Kwashiorkor)
☐	Severe Calorie Malnutrition (Marasmus)
☐	Severe Protein Calorie Malnutrition
☐	Moderate Malnutrition
☐	Mild Malnutrition

Above per approved criteria

Estimated Nutritional needs for ☐ GAIN ☐ LOSS	☐ MAINTENANCE		TPN ONLY
Kcal: (BEE kcal × stress factor)	Gms Pro: (gm/kg IBW)	Ml Fluid: (1ml/kcal)	Max. CHO Load:

Estimation of Nutritional Support
Current ☐ TF ☐ TPN as ordered ( ) will provide:

kcal	gms pro	ml water

To meet estimated needs, will need GOAL of for ☐ TF ☐ TPN

Instructions Given? Written/Verbal information included
☐ Y ☐ N

Pt. &/or S.O. Comprehend instructions? ☐ Yes ☐ No Evidenced by:

Expected Compliance ☐ GOOD ☐ FAIR ☐ POOR

Other

P **GOAL of Nutritional Therapy**

Recommendations/Suggestions:

- ☐ Supplemental feedings: ____________
- ☐ Alterations in diet: ____________
- ☐ Lab tests/other: ____________
- ☐ Referral to: ____________

Actions Taken:

- ☐ Initiate 3-day calorie count to assess intake
- ☐ Calorie count in progress
- ☐ Weekend calorie counts will be calculated on Monday
- ☐ Providing high kcal, high pro supplement
- ☐ Offer 6 small feedings
- ☐ Monitor for potential nutritional problems
- ☐ Follow-up: ____________
- ☐ Other: ____________
- ☐ RD name and phone number provided

Dietitian ____________

FIGURE 7.12 SAMPLE NUTRITION ASSESSMENT FORM FOR DOCUMENTING MALNUTRITION DIAGNOSES.
Adapted from *Journal of the American Dietetic Assoc.* April 1995. p 473.

- Have written policies and procedures regarding all dietary activities;
- Have an up-to-date diet manual and procedure for documenting physicians' orders in medical records; and
- Have evaluation assistance from the dietitians.

The emphasis placed by JCAHO on evaluation is apparent. Its design of a self-assessment form to assist in the evaluation of dietary services is a helpful way to implement this concern. The above points are very basic; they are required for all dietary services.

Governmental Agencies and Evaluation

The National Social Security Act mandates that facilities participating in Medicare and Medicaid programs meet minimum health and safety standards. Medicare is a federal insurance program with payment for services made by the federal government through intermediaries. Medicaid is a state program which provides medical services to people receiving public assistance under the Social Security program (and to other needy persons as well). The requirements pertain to hospitals, skilled nursing facilities, and a wide range of other providers and suppliers of health services. The Medicare program is administered by the U.S. Department of Health and Human Services, which issues minimum requirements to be met by participating institutions. States may also establish additional requirements under the Medicaid program. Typically, the federal government sets minimum standards; states may develop more specific standards, and those that provide the greatest degree of control will apply.

A state agency is designated in each state to carry out the requirements of the Social Security Act. Among other requirements are the need to visit facilities to assure that minimum standards are met, to complete various records, and to comply with other requirements.

While state-level officials are generally responsible for conducting on-site surveys for Medicare and Medicaid requirements, the federal government will have several responsibilities:

- It reviews survey and certification reports submitted by state agencies;
- It evaluates fiscal, administrative, and procedural aspects of its agreements with the states;
- It conducts some on-site surveys of Medicare and Medicaid facilities;
- It reviews and approves state budgets and expense reports dealing with survey / certification activities.

Each state agency designated to administer the Medicare and Medicaid programs has several duties, which, taken together, are referred to as the certification process: Since the standards used will change, they are not included in this text. Dietary managers must monitor how the dietetic services have changed and their role in CQI. The Journal of the American Dietetics Association, Journal of Clinical Nutrition, publications from the JCAHO, and other professional journals provide information on current requirements. It is one's own responsibility to be knowledgeable.

These basic standards will still be applicable but may be combined into an overall facility requirement. While the dietetic services department will need to have job descriptions, orientation, on-the-job training, and continuing education available through cooperation with all departments within the facility, the state agency will be responsible for the following:

- It must identify as many qualified providers and suppliers of health services as possible; there must be eligible facilities on a statewide basis;

- It conducts investigations and fact-finding surveys to determine how well participating facilities comply with requirements. Often this investigation is done in conjunction with the state's own licensure and other regulatory programs;
- It completes certification, re-certification, and periodic follow-up reports dealing with whether facilities are qualified to participate in programs. The states can take final action only on facilities participating in the Medicaid program but must make recommendations to the federal government about facilities participating in Medicare programs;
- It provides consultive services to providers and suppliers and to those seeking eligibility for the program in order to help them, respectively, maintain required standards and qualify for participation.

It is the dietary manager's responsibility to be very familiar with the rules and regulations established in the state for the type of facility where he or she works. In general terms, the dietary manager must provide a nutritionally adequate diet. The diet should supply the nutrients for the age group being served.

The modified diets ordered by the doctor should be followed using the guidelines set forth in the diet manual approved at the facility. Do not change a diet without permission. The dietary manager may make suggestions in the medical record, but the individual who has ultimate responsibility to determine need and to document should be carefully considered; in some states and/or facilities this choice may be dictated by licensure laws and/or policies of the facility. Always follow the guidelines of the State Board of Health. In addition, the minimum time allowed between the last meal in the evening to the first meal in the morning may be specified in requirements or protocol. A facility that participates in Medicare must also meet the conditions established by the federal government. Discuss these conditions with the administrator in order to understand the role that dietary services play in meeting the requirements.

Dietary managers should be concerned about professional liability and should ask the administrator about the type of insurance the facility carries. The dietary manager should be included in this insurance coverage while working. Ask questions to be sure that there is adequate coverage and under what situations the insurance will be applicable.

There is a close relationship between the certification process, state license requirements, programs for professional accreditation (such as JCAHO) discussed above, and medical assistance standards. Typically, the relationships among these standards require close coordination and information exchange. For example, healthcare facilities cannot qualify for Medicare assistance unless they have first been licensed by the state. Standards used by JCAHO generally meet many of the standards issued by the federal government. Said another way, then, the facility is not faced with sets of conflicting standards which make compliance with each very difficult (or impossible). The guidelines, recommendations, standards, and interpretations of each regulatory agency and professional association interface to provide guidelines for managing healthcare facilities.

The dietary manager aware of applicable standards, interpretive guidelines, and survey procedures will have both an insight into preparing for the survey and excellent guidelines for self-evaluation. Figure 7.13 gives guidelines for survey procedures and reviews detailed information applicable to surveys for dietary services. The standards noted are rules of law which must be followed. The interpretive guidelines are used to educate surveyors and facility administrators about the standards; they are not, however, rules of law themselves. The figure should be studied to ensure that each standard is implemented in the dietary facility. Questions to ask about each standard include:

- Is this standard currently being met?
- Who is responsible for training employees in the applicable standard?

Guidance to Surveyors—Long-Term Care Facilities

Tag Number	Regulation	Guidance to Surveyors
F360-A	**§483.35 Dietary Services.** The facility must provide each resident with a nourishing, palatable, well-balanced diet that meets the daily nutritional and special dietary needs of each resident.	
F361	(a) **Staffing.** The facility must employ a qualified dietitian either full-time, part-time, or on a consultant basis. (1) If a qualified dietitian is not employed full-time, the facility must designate a person to serve as the director of food service who receives frequently scheduled consultation from a qualified dietitian. (2) A qualified dietitian is one who is qualified based upon either registration by the Commission on Dietetic Registration of the American Dietetic Association, or on the basis of education, training, experience in identification of dietary needs, planning, and implementation of dietary programs.	**Interpretive Guidelines: §483.35(a)** A dietitian qualified on the basis of education, training, or experience in identification of dietary needs, planning and implementation of dietary programs has experience or training which includes: • Assessing nutritional needs of geriatric and physically impaired persons; • Developing therapeutic diets; • Developing "regular diets" to meet the specialized needs of geriatric and physically impaired persons; • Developing and implementing continuing education programs for dietary services and nursing personnel; • Participating in interdisciplinary care planning; • Budgeting and purchasing food and supplies; and • Supervising institutional food preparation and service. **Survey Procedures and Probes: §483.35(a)** If you find problems in resident nutritional status: • What practices of the dietitian or food services director contributed to the identified problems in residents' nutritional status? • What are the educational, training, and experience qualifications of the facility's dietitian?
F362	(b) **Sufficient staff.** The facility must employ sufficient support personnel competent to carry out the functions of the dietary service.	**Interpretive Guidelines: §483.35(b)** "Sufficient support personnel" means enough staff to prepare and serve palatable, attractive, nutritionally adequate meals at proper temperatures and appropriate times. **Survey Procedures and Probes: §483.35(b)** Observe kitchen and food preparation: [Sufficient staff preparation] Y = Food is prepared in scheduled time frames in accordance with established professional practices. N = Food is not prepared in scheduled time frames in accordance with established professional practices. Observe food service: [Sufficient staff services] Y = Food leaves kitchen and is served to residents in scheduled time frames. N = Food does not leave kitchen and is not served to residents in scheduled time frames.

Figure 7.13 Guidelines for Survey Procedures *(continued on next page)*

Source: Healthcare Financing Administration 1992. Standards change; check with your surveying agency for the latest update.

GUIDANCE TO SURVEYORS—LONG-TERM CARE FACILITIES

Tag Number	Regulation	Guidance to Surveyors
	(c) **Menus and nutritional adequacy.** Menus must—	
F363	(1) Meet the nutritional needs of residents in accordance with the recommended dietary allowances of the Food and Nutritional Board of the National Research Council, National Academy of Sciences;	**Survey Procedures and Probes: §483.35(c)(1)** • Are residents receiving food in the amount, type, consistency and frequency to maintain usual weight and acceptable nutritional values? • If food intake appears inadequate based on meal observations, or resident's nutritional status is poor based on Quality of Care review, are menus adjusted to meet the caloric and nutrient-intake needs of each resident? • If a food group is missing from the resident's daily diet, does the facility have an alternative means of satisfying the resident's nutrient needs? [Menu adequately provides the daily basic food groups] Y = Menu provides for meeting basic nutritional needs (e.g., 2 or more serv @ 3 oz/serv of edible meat or a meat substitute, 2 cups fruit/vegetable, 4 servings bread/cereal, 2 cups milk). N = Menu does not supply the basic nutritional needs. NOTE: This guidance is used primarily for menu planning and food purchasing. It is not intended to meet the nutritional needs of all residents. In order to be functional, this guide must be adjusted to consider individual differences. Some residents will need more due to age, size, gender, physical activity, and state of health. There are many meal planning guides from reputable sources such as: Food and Drug Administration, American Diabetes Association, American Dietetic Association, American Medical Association, or U.S. Department of Agriculture that are available and appropriate for use when adjusted to meet each resident's needs.
F364	(2) Be prepared in advance; and	**Survey Procedures and Probes: §483.35(c)(2)** [Menu prepared in advance] Y = Dated cycle menus for both regular and modified diets. N = No dated cycle menus for both regular and modified diets.
F365	(3) Be followed.	**Survey Procedures and Probes: §483.35(c)(3)** [Menu followed] Y = Food is served as planned. N = Food is not served as planned. Obtain appropriate documentation from diet card, record review, and interviews with food service manager or dietitian to support reason(s) for deviation from the written menu.
	(d) **Food.** Each resident receives and the facility provides—	
F366	(1) Food prepared by methods that conserve nutritive value, flavor, and appearance;	**Interpretive Guidelines: §483.35(d)(1)** Food preparation that conserves nutritive value does not destroy vitamins because of prolonged food storage, light exposure, prolonged cooking of foods in a large volume of water, addition of baking soda, and overcooking for soft texture. **Survey Procedures and Probes: §483.35(d)(1)** Review nutritional adequacy in §483.25(i)(1). [Food—appearance] A = Food has distinctly appetizing aroma *and* appearance, such as attractive use of garnishes and variety in color as plated. B = Food has unappetizing aroma *or* appearance. Little use of color or garnishes. C = Food has unappetizing aroma *and* appearance, such as foods run together and no variety in color as plated.

FIGURE 7.13 continued

Guidance to Surveyors—Long-Term Care Facilities

Tag Number	Regulation	Guidance to Surveyors
F366 Cont.		[Food—flavor] A = Food is generally well seasoned (for example, is not too bland or spicy) *and* acceptable to residents. B = Some food item(s) are poorly seasoned *or* flavor unacceptable to residents. Seasoning will likely reduce consumption. C = Food is generally poorly seasoned (for example, too bland or too spicy) *and* flavor unacceptable to residents. Seasoning likely to significantly reduce consumption. [Conserves nutritive value] Y = Food preparation does not destroy vitamins. No food adulteration because of prolonged food storage, light exposure, prolonged cooking in large amounts of water, addition of baking soda, or overcooking for soft texture. N = Food preparation destroys vitamins, resulting in adulteration of nutritive value.
F367	(2) Food that is palatable, attractive, and at the proper temperature;	**Survey Procedures and Probes: §483.35(d)(2)** [Food—temperature] Y = Food served at appropriate temperature (hot foods are served hot and cold foods are served cold). N = Food served at inappropriate temperature (hot foods are served tepid or cold; or cold foods served warm). Refer to §483.35(h)(2).
F368	(3) Food prepared in a form designed to meet individual needs; and	**Survey Procedures and Probes: §483.35(d)(3)** [Food—form] Y = Food cut, chopped, or ground for individual resident's needs. N = Food not cut, chopped, or ground to meet individual resident's needs.
F369	(4) Substitutes offered of similar nutritive value to residents who refuse food served.	**Interpretive Guidelines: §483.35(d)(4)** A food substitute should be consistent with the usual and ordinary food items provided by the facility. For example, if a facility never serves Alaskan crab legs, they would not be required to serve this as a food substitute; or the facility may, instead of grapefruit juice, substitute another citrus juice or vitamin C rich juice that the resident likes. **Survey Procedures and Probes: §483.35(d)(4)** [Substitutes available] Y = Residents who refuse food offered substitute of similar nutritive value. N = Residents who refuse food not offered substitute of similar nutritive value. • [Individual] If you refuse to eat what is being served at a meal, are you offered a substitute? (If yes) What is the substitute?
F370	(e) **Therapeutic diets.** Therapeutic diets must be prescribed by the attending physician.	**Survey Procedures and Probes: §483.35(e)** • Is the therapeutic diet that the resident receives prescribed by the physician? Also, see §483.25(i), *Nutritional Status.*
	(f) Frequency of meals.	
F371	(1) Each resident receives and the facility provides at least three meals daily, at regular times comparable to normal mealtimes in the community.	
F372	(2) There must be no more than 14 hours between a substantial evening meal and breakfast the following day, except as provided in (4) below.	**Interpretive Guidelines: §483.35(f)(2)** A "substantial evening meal" is defined to mean an offering of three or more menu items at one time, one of which includes a high-quality protein such as meat, fish, eggs, or cheese. The meal should represent no less than 20 percent of the day's total nutritional requirements.

Figure 7.13 *(continued on next page)*

Guidance to Surveyors—Long-Term Care Facilities

Tag Number	Regulation	Guidance to Surveyors
F373	(3) The facility must offer snacks at bedtime daily.	**Interpretive Guidelines: §483.35(f)(3) and (4)** "Nourishing snack" is an offering of items, single or in combination, from the basic food groups. Adequacy of the "nourishing snack" will be determined both by resident interviews (e.g., is the offered snack usually satisfying?) and by evaluation of the overall nutritional status of residents in the facility. **Survey Procedures and Probes: §483.35(f)(3) and (4)** • [Individual] Do you eat bedtime snacks? Is the snack usually satisfying?
F374	(4) When a nourishing snack is provided at bedtime, up to 16 hours may elapse between a substantial evening meal and breakfast the following day if a resident group agrees to this meal span, and a nourishing snack is served.	
F375	(g) **Assistive devices.** The facility must provide special eating equipment and utensils for residents who need them.	**Interpretive Guidelines: §483.35(g)** Assistive devices maintain or improve residents' ability to eat independently, for example, improving poor grasp by enlarging silverware handles with foam padding, aiding residents with impaired coordination or tremor by plate guards, or providing postural supports for head, trunk, and arms. **Survey Procedures and Probes: §483.35(g)** Review sampled residents comprehensive assessment for eating ability. Observe these residents during *Dietary Service System Assessment.* [Assistive devices] Y = Effective adaptive utensils used to promote maximum resident independence in dining. N = Adaptive utensils to promote maximum resident independence in dining are needed, but are not used.
	(h) **Sanitary conditions.** The facility must—	
F376	(1) Procure food from sources approved or considered satisfactory by Federal, State or local authorities;	**Survey Procedures and Probes: §483.35(h)(1)** [Food source] Observe fluid milk and milk products, dry milk and milk products, fresh and frozen shellfish, fresh and pasteurized eggs, canned foods, fresh produce, meat, poultry, and fish. Y = Foods are obtained from sources approved or considered satisfactory by Federal, State, or local authorities. N = One or more foods are not obtained from approved sources.
F377	(2) Store, prepare, distribute, and serve food under sanitary conditions; and	**Interpretive Guidelines: §483.35(h)(2)** "Sanitary conditions" means storing, preparing, distributing, and serving food properly to prevent food borne illness. Prevention of food borne illness focuses on potentially hazardous food; foods subject to continuous time/temperature controls in order to prevent either the rapid and progressive growth of infectious or toxigenic microorganisms. Potentially hazardous food tends to focus on animal products including, but not limited to, milk, eggs, poultry, fish, meat, and synthetic food ingredients. Some fruits and vegetables (e.g., cantaloupe and baked potatoes) as well as specialty foods (e.g., garlic and oil) are also potentially hazardous foods. Hot foods should leave the kitchen (or steam table) above 140° F and cold foods below 45° F. Refrigerator temperatures should be maintained at 45°F or below. **Survey Procedures and Probes: §483.35(h)(2)** [Sanitary food storage] Observe food storage rooms and food storage in the kitchen. Y = Containers of food stored off the floor and on clean surfaces in a manner protecting it from contamination. N = Food stored in an unsanitary manner, making it subject to contamination.

Figure 7.13 continued

Guidance to Surveyors—Long-Term Care Facilities

Tag Number	Regulation	Guidance to Surveyors
F377 Cont.		[Refrigerated storage] Check all refrigerators and freezers for readily visible thermometers. Use your thermometer to evaluate the internal temperatures of questionable units. Y = Potentially hazardous foods stored at 45° F or below and frozen foods kept at 0° F or below. N = Potentially hazardous foods stored above acceptable temperatures. [Food preparation] Use a sanitized thermometer to evaluate food temperatures. In addition, how do kitchen staff treat leftovers? What do kitchen staff do to thaw frozen foods? Y = Staff handle and cook potentially hazardous foods properly. No risk of food-borne illness. N = Staff mishandle or fail to cook potentially hazardous foods properly, increasing resident risk of food-borne illness. [Food service] Using thermometer, properly sanitized, check the temperatures of food under refrigeration and held hot. Y = Potentially hazardous foods are kept at an internal temperature of 45°F or below in cold food storage unit, or at an internal temperature of 140° F or above in a hot food storage unit during display and service. N = Potentially hazardous foods are not kept at proper temperatures and safe time periods during display and service. [Food distribution] Observe food as it is transported to the dining rooms and residents' rooms. Y = Food is transported in a way that protects against contamination (covered containers, wrapped, or packaged). N = Food is transported in a way that may result in contamination. [Pest free] Is the area pest free? (See §483.70(h)(4).) Y = There is no sign of rodent or insect infestation. N = There is evidence of rodent or insect infestation. [Water source] Y = The water source is safe; sufficient hot and cold water under pressure. N = Water source unsafe or insufficient water pressure to support sanitary food preparation practices. [Dishwashing] The current Food Service Sanitation Manual, DHHS, FDA, PHS recommends the following water temperatures and manual washing instructions: **MACHINE:** • Hot Water: —140° F Wash (or according to the manufacturer's specifications or instructions). —180° F Rinse • Low Temp: —120° F + 50 ppm (parts per million) Hypochlorite (household bleach) on dish Surface **MANUAL:** • 3 Compartment Sink: —75° F—50 ppm Hypochlorite (household bleach) or equivalent, or 12.5 ppm of Iodine. —Hot Water Immersion at 170° F for at least 30 seconds. [Dishwashing] Y = Food preparation equipment, dishes, and utensils effectively sanitized to destroy potential disease carrying organisms. N = Food preparation equipment, dishes, and utensils not effectively sanitized. For example, wash/rinse temperatures too low, wash/rinse cycles too short, manual sanitation methods inadequate (chlorine or iodine solutions to weak).

FIGURE 7.13 *(continued on next page)*

GUIDANCE TO SURVEYORS—LONG-TERM CARE FACILITIES

Tag Number	Regulation	Guidance to Surveyors
F377 Cont.		[Sewage] Y = All sewage, including liquid waste, is properly disposed of by a public sewerage system or by a sewage disposal system constructed and operated in accordance with State or local law. N = Sewage improperly disposed of. [Plumbing] Y = Potable and nonpotable water systems are in accordance with State or local law. N = Potable and nonpotable water systems are not in accordance with State or local law. [Preventing Contamination] Y = Handwashing facilities are convenient and properly equipped for dietary services staff use. Staff uses hygienic practices and staff with communicable diseases or infected skin lesions do not have contact with food if that contact will transmit the disease. N = Handwashing facilities are not convenient or are not properly equipped (for example, no towels or soap). Staff does not wash hands as needed to prevent contamination of food or food utensils. Staff with communicable diseases or infected skin lesions have contact with food when that contact may transmit disease. [Hazard Free] Y = Toxic items (such as insecticides, detergent, polishes) are properly stored, labeled, and used. N = Toxic items are not properly stored, labeled, or used.
F378	(3) Dispose of garbage and refuse properly.	**Survey Procedures and Probes: §483.35(h)(3)** [Garbage/refuse] Observe garbage and refuse container construction, and outside storage receptacles. Y = Garbage and refuse containers are in good condition (no leaks) and waste is properly contained in dumpsters or compactors with lids or otherwise covered. N = Garbage and refuse containers are not in good repair, or waste is not properly contained (inadequate number of containers, garbage containers are malodorous and/or uncovered).

FIGURE 7.13 continued

- Who is responsible for supervising staff members to make sure that standards are being followed?
- How will the surveyor be able to determine whether this facility is in compliance with the standard?
- Does the standard suggest typical operating procedures which should be, but are not currently, used?
- Does this facility have adequate documentation to confirm that it is in compliance with the standard?

Study of the information will confirm the usefulness of the standards and procedures necessary to implement them. As stated above, they present useful guidelines regardless of whether the facility is a hospital or a skilled-nursing facility receiving Medicare and/or Medicaid funds.

The Dietary Services System Worksheets are very important. See Figure 7.14 (Dietary Services System Worksheets). The most important aspect of standards is *assessment* guidelines used by the facility.

DEPARTMENT OF HEALTH AND HUMAN SERVICES
HEALTH CARE FINANCING ADMINISTRATION

DIETARY SERVICES SYSTEM WORKSHEET-SANITATION, PREPARATION AND DISTRIBUTION

Provider Number	Surveyor Name

Instructions: Observe food service sanitation and food preparation for a meal. Record and document all "B", "C" or "No" ratings.

Meal: ☐ Breakfast ☐ Lunch ☐ Dinner Date: ________ / ________ / ________
MO DAY YEAR

A. Food Service Sanitation		RATING	TAG NUMBER(S)	DOCUMENTATION
Food Source	(Y/N)		F376	
Sanitary Food Storage	(Y/N)		F377	
Refrigerated Storage	(Y/N)		F377	
Food Preparation	(Y/N)		F377	
Food Distribution	(Y/N)		F377	
Food Service	(Y/N)		F377	
Garbage/Refuse	(Y/N)		F378	
Pest Free	(Y/N)		F377/F483	
Preventing Contamination	(Y/N)		F377	
Hazard Free	(Y/N)		F377	
Water Source	(Y/N)		F377	
Dishwashing	(Y/N)		F377	
Sewage	(Y/N)		F377	
Plumbing	(Y/N)		F377	
B. Food Preparation				
Menu Provides RDAs	(Y/N)		F363	
Menu Prepared in Advance	(Y/N)		F364	
Menu Followed	(Y/N)		F365	
Conserves Nutritive Values	(Y/N)		F366	
Sufficient Staff-Preparation	(Y/N)		F362	
Sufficient Staff-Service	(Y/N)		F362	

C. Food Distribution *(Complete if you detect problems that warrant sampling test trays.)*

Time left kitchen: ______ Time arrived floor: ______

Time last tray served: ______ Time last resident begins eating: ______

		REGULAR	PURÉED	MECHANICALLY ALTERED	TAG NUMBER(S)	
Food-Flavor	(A,B,C)				F366	
Food-Appearance	(A,B,C)				F366	
Food-Temperature	(Y/N)				F367	

Additional Documentation

FORM HCFA-679A (4-92)

FIGURE 7.14 DIETARY SERVICES SYSTEM WORKSHEETS *(continued on next page)*
Source: Healthcare Financing Administration 1992

DEPARTMENT OF HEALTH AND HUMAN SERVICES
HEALTH CARE FINANCING ADMINISTRATION

DIETARY SERVICES SYSTEM WORKSHEET-DINING AREA OBSERVATION

Provider Number	Surveyor Name

DINING ROOM

Instructions: Observe dining area(s). Record and document all "B", "C" or "No" ratings. See Interpretive Guidelines and Survey Procedures and Probes for the individual regulatory citations for a detailed explanation of requirements.

Location ________________		RATING	TAG NUMBER	DOCUMENTATION
Odors	(A,B,C)		F260	
Cleanliness	(A,B,C)		F260	
Orderly	(A,B,C)		F261	
Lighting	(A,B,C)		F475	
Ventilation	(A,B,C)		F476	
Adequately Furnished	(A,B,C)		F477	
Sound	(A,B,C)		F265	
Accommodate Needs	(A,B,C)		F253	
Sufficent Space	(A,B,C)		F478	
Hazard Free	(Y/N)		F329	
Temperature	(Y/N)		F264	
Pest Free	(Y/N)		F483	

Additional Documentation

FORM HCFA-679B (4-92)

FIGURE 7.14 continued

DEPARTMENT OF HEALTH AND HUMAN SERVICES
HEALTH CARE FINANCING ADMINISTRATION

DIETARY SERVICES SYSTEM WORKSHEET-RESIDENT DINING OBSERVATION

Provider Number	Surveyor Name

Name	Site of Observation	Date	Meal

Instructions: Observe resident's quality of dining during two different meals, if any of the following apply. Record and document all "B", "C" or "No" ratings. See Interpretive Guidelines and Survey Procedures and Probes for the individual regulatory citations for a detailed explanation of requirements.

Basis of Observation *(check all that apply)*

- ☐ Dining Complaint during Interview
- ☐ Nutritional Deficiency (protein-calorie malnutrition)
- ☐ Weight Change of more than 5% in one month or 10% in 6 months.
- ☐ Therapeutic/Mechanically Altered Diet
- ☐ Complaint of Hunger, and/or not being fed
- ☐ Presence of a Pressure Sore
- ☐ Dysphagia
- ☐ Other *(please specify)*

Diet Served

		RATING	TAG NUMBER	DOCUMENTATION
Clothing	(Y/N)		F241	
Grooming	(Y/N)		F241	
Assistive devices	(Y/N)		F375	
Assistance with eating *(if dependent)*	(A,B,C)		F317/314	
Assistance with eating *(if independent)*	(A,B,C)		F314	
Food-form	(Y/N)		F368	
Food-appearance	(A,B,C)		F366	
Substitutes available	(Y/N)		F369	
Amount eaten	(Y/N)		F332	
Conforms to diet order	(Y/N)		F332	
Proper Positioning	(Y/N)		F316	

Additional Documentation

FORM HCFA-679C (4-92)

FIGURE 7.14 continued

Omnibus Budget Reconciliation Act (OBRA)*

On October 16, 1987, a proposed federal rule was published that would establish consistent requirements for skilled Medicare nursing facilities and for intermediate and skilled Medicaid nursing facilities. This federal rule, called the Omnibus Budget Reconciliation Act of 1987 (commonly known as OBRA '87), was established to enforce requirements that improved quality of care and life for each long-term resident. Note that, with revisions and amendments, enforcement of OBRA was delayed until October 1, 1991.

The Health Care Financing Administration (HCFA) contracted with the Institute of Medicine to study and prepare a regulatory system to ensure satisfactory resident care. HCFA rulings provide clarification and interpretation of complex or ambiguous provisions of the law or regulations relating to Medicare, Medicaid, and related matters, and are decisions that serve as precedent, final opinions, orders, and statements of policy.

The following areas of OBRA are most representative of the long-term care industry's acceptance of the challenge before it:

- The admission process—requirements may be met by developing orientation programs and organizing family support groups;
- Resident rights—requirements may be met by preparing handbooks and scheduling regular resident council meetings;
- Restraint reduction—requirements may be to establish restraint policies and programs with ongoing monitoring by a restraint reduction committee;
- Restorative care—requirements may be met by promoting a strong interdisciplinary approach to each individual resident's needs to reach the optimal level of care. This interdisciplinary approach might involve such disciplines as occupational therapy, physical therapy, recreational therapy, nursing, and/or social services among others. Dietary services would evaluate appropriate nutritional matters.

Within the OBRA regulations and interpretive guidelines exist the themes of quality of care and quality of life. Organizations are expected to guarantee that the resident's condition will improve or be maintained unless a medical cause prevents that goal.

The minimum data set is a mandatory resident assessment instrument used as a part of client data collection. Departments or disciplines, as noted above, such as rehabilitation, dietary, and social services, provide information to formulate a complete picture of the resident. The time allowed for completion of these assessments is defined under both state and federal guidelines.

Identifying a resident's needs and problems may trigger an additional assessment specific to that need (a nutritional assessment, for example). Then, a plan can be developed specific to the resident's need.

Communication between departments in developing a restorative plan of care occurs on an ongoing basis. Each discipline offers its knowledge and expertise to the others for consideration. Ideas are listened to and reflected on among departments. Working together to implement the OBRA regulations has challenged and strengthened the team. As long-term care providers, staff members pool their knowledge and expertise with other disciplines and develop a give-and-take relationship when prioritizing goals in the treatment approach.

Unlike past approaches to the development of care plans, whereby each department isolated goals and treatment intervention, OBRA '87 has encouraged interaction among all departments. The resources of individual disciplines and the sharing of these resources has increased ten-fold.

---

*This section adapted from Hensel, Terry, "OBRA Regulations," *Topics in Geriatric Rehabilitation*, Sept. 1995.

Details of Licensure

Specific procedures used for a licensure/certification survey vary among states and sometimes among different consultants within a state. The sequence of activities, however, typically includes the following:

1. The consultant arrives at the facility (generally unannounced) early in the morning. An entrance interview is held with the facility administrator, the official responsible for dietary services, and/or the dietary manager. The consultant will review the facility's plan of correction developed as a result of the previous on-site survey. He or she will confirm that all deficiencies noted during the last survey were, in fact, corrected. Purposes of and procedures for the survey are discussed; the consultant may inquire about any problems the facility is experiencing so that he/she may be alert for potential resolution suggestions.

   The surveyor will select at least a 25-percent sample of clients in each of eleven special care categories. The samples may include tube-fed clients, colostomy/ileostomy care clients, and individuals with pressure sores;
2. A tour of the dietary operation—from the back door through storage, production, serving, and reconstitution/dining areas—is undertaken, frequently with any or all of the personnel who were present for the entrance interview. The consultant uses the tour as an opportunity to become familiar with the facility and to observe available equipment, personnel practices, and sanitation problems. In some states/areas, the consultant undertakes the only sanitation inspection done by governmental representatives. In that case, there may be detailed sanitation code forms which must be completed;
3. Typically, a great deal of paperwork must be completed. The consultant will have prepared for the survey by studying reports of previous visits and by discussing the facility with his or her supervisor and/or other consultants to assess any special concerns which should be reviewed. Matters identified by this process will be given special attention as the survey is undertaken and as survey forms are completed. Figure 7.15 illustrates a survey form similar to one used by a foodservice consultant in one state. It is typical of the concerns addressed by consultants during their reviews of dietary operations. Note the wide variety of records and documents which will need to be available and studied as the survey evolves;
4. A great deal of the surveyor's time will be spent in observation. Food production, tray service, and food transportation practices will all be observed carefully. The consultant will be concerned about temperatures, special diets, and all special matters which affect the duties of the dietary manager;
5. The consultant will watch clients being fed and eating. He or she will probably also consume a meal and may use this time for discussion with the dietary manager and/or other facility officials, or may prefer to eat alone to observe, study, write, or plan later review activities.

   Surveyors will probably spend ten to twenty minutes with each client. They must address the following items when interviewing and observing:

   - clients' rights;
   - dietary needs;
   - grooming/hygiene;
   - skin;
   - social services needs;
   - activity needs.

   The surveyor will also review the medical record to determine if:

   - an assessment has been completed;
   - a care plan is developed;

Name of facility____________________ Date____________________
Name of administrator ____________________ Reviewer____________________
Name of dietary manager____________________ Census ____________________
Capacity ____________________

Part I: Review of Dietary Department Materials

1. Copies of reports from previous dietary inspections.
   Deficiencies corrected Yes _____ No ______
   Comments:

2. Copies of contracts, job descriptions, and report of dietary consultant (if applicable).
   Name of dietary consultant ____________________
   ADA registration number ____________________
   Comments:

3. Name of certified dietary manager (or foodservice supervisor):
   ____
   Proof of required education ____________________
   Comments:

4. Dietary department operating manual (to include departmental policies, work procedures, job descriptions and policies) including such areas as:
   - nutritional assessment
   - food acceptance records
   - patient care plans/progress reports
   - replacements/substitutions
   - nourishments

   Comments:

5. Daily work assignments:
   - for current week
   - for past three months
   - reflecting call-ins and terminations

   Comments:

6. Written records of in-service education programs, including, at least, but not limited to:
   - infection control
   - accident prevention
   - fire and disaster planning
   - patient rights and preservation of confidentiality

   Comments:

7. Written records of departmental orientation in employee personnel file.
   Comments:

8. Records of T.B. skin tests or X-rays and other pre-employment physical information (where applicable) in employee personnel file.

Part II: Nutrition and Food

9. Copy of Facility Diet Manual (revised by R.D. Consultant if necessary to reflect facility routines):
   - in kitchen
   - in each nurses' station

   Comments:

10. Number of patients:
    a. regular diets ______
    b. modified diets ______
    c. with Decubitis ulcers ______
    d. insulin dependent ______
    e. renal dialysis ______
    f. on weight gain diets ______
    g. number on supplemental feedings ______

Comments:

Figure 7.15 Sample Dietary Survey Form *(continued on next page)*

11. Review of menus (30 days for intermediate care facility, or 90 days for skilled nursing facility):
    a. regular—preplanned in writing and served as planned
    b. therapeutic—preplanned in writing and served as planned
    Are menus posted? Regular _________ Therapeutic _________

12. Review of food acceptance records:

	After admission	After diet change	At nutrition risk
a. Breakfast			
b. Lunch			
c. Dinner			
d. Nourishments			

    Study of patient charts (problems) ____________________

13. Review of patient care plans:
    a. goals
    b. implemented approach
    c. evaluation efforts
    d. revision according to patient response
    Comments:

14. Nutritional assessment for every patient upon admission
    Comments:

15. Written meal census records
    Comments:

16. Food invoices (three months)
    Comments:

17. Review of tested recipes with appropriate yields
    Comments:

18. Nutritional information for combination entrees/diabetic exchange equivalents
    Comments:

Part III: Sanitation and Special Concerns

19. Food storage practices:

20. Food handling practices:

21. Food serving practices:

22. Dishwashing procedures:

23. Pot/pan washing procedures:

24. Other sanitation concerns:

Part IV: Specific Recommendations (cite statutes where applicable)

Signed: ______________________________ Date: ______________
(Name of Consultant)

FIGURE 7.15 CONTINUED

- realistic outcome goals are defined and accepted;
- intervention is carried out;
- evaluation and follow-up are completed;

6. The surveyor will review personnel files of dietary employees. What problems are observed? How are personnel evaluations done? What are evaluations of orientation and in-service training? What training has been received by staff members? Are employee health records maintained? These and a wide variety of other concerns are addressed by a study of personnel records;
7. The surveyor will conduct an exit interview (probably with the same officials involved in the entrance interview). Findings will be discussed and recommendations will be made. This conversation is likely to focus on resolution of past problems, if any, and suggestions/recommendations for further improvements. Challenges to the surveyor can be made. The exit interview provides an excellent opportunity to mutually agree upon any necessary corrective action plans and also to get ideas about non-required program improvement efforts;
8. A written statement of deficiencies will be sent to the facility after consultation with the facility administrator. The dietary manager must develop and implement a plan of correction (POC) to resolve deficiencies. This POC must address the *causes* of the problem and details to ensure that, after correction, problems do not recur. The POC must include reasonable timelines for implementation of corrective action procedures. A followup letter may be requested by the surveyor. Usually, the facility administrator writes the letter after consultation with the dietary manager. Information from the consultant should be routed to the dietary manager, followup actions should be taken, and all written correspondence should be filed for future reference.

Preparing for Surveys and Challenging Them

Surveys done by government and/or private associations should be considered necessary and helpful because they help ensure that facilities will provide quality care. This monitoring is good not only for the facility but also for the clients. Some dietary managers, however, are intimidated by the prospect of a survey. They see them as "necessary evils" which are required in order to obtain "federal and state money."

However, the professional surveyor is a specialist and a consultant who can help dietary managers resolve many of the operating problems which they face. Information can be given as it applies to the standards being reviewed; since surveyors visit many different facilities, they are sources of information about how other institutions have resolved a wide range of operating problems.

A survey is in the best interest of both the facility and the clients. The dietary manager operating a facility according to standards which are both required and useful can be assured that the dietary department is providing clients with products and services of consistently high quality.

How does a dietary manager prepare for a survey? Surveys are conducted with little, if any, advance notice; however, facility administrators can request informal consultation at a specified time. It is also probable that checking times of past survey visits may give some indication about when future surveys will be conducted. (For example, surveys must be conducted prior to relicensing; if this is an annual requirement, surveys will be made several months prior to the specified date.)

An important first step in preparing for the survey is to be familiar with all applicable regulations. Dietary managers can contact the applicable state regulatory agency and request a current copy of regulations, interpretations, and suggested procedures. Some states utilize a standardized surveyor review form. In these states, copies of the forms can be made available to the facility; dietary managers will have a better idea of exactly what the surveyor will be reviewing. (Even in states without standardized forms, copies of forms from several reviewers can be requested and studied; survey documents utilized by different surveyors will probably be very similar.)

The dietary manager who studies the standards, understands their interpretation and knows the types of concerns likely to be addressed by the surveyors will be prepared for this survey. If he or she continually implements/evaluates standards within the dietary department, the manager will be sure that the dietary operation is in harmony with requirements.

Figure 7.16 recaps some preliminary tasks for gathering materials/records which should be readily available when the consultant visits the facility for a dietary survey.

During the visit, the dietary manager should be as helpful as possible in providing records, answering questions, helping the surveyor become familiar with the fa-

Approximately six months before survey

- Secure copies of the survey forms, regulations (JCAHO, state survey, etc.) and review
- Meet with the registered dietitian or accreditation manager to discuss requirements
- Meet with the staff. Assign responsibilities
- Survey, audit department using the surveyors guidelines
- Review all policies and procedures. Check for signatures, date, applicability

Approximately three months before survey

- Re-survey department using surveyors form
- Meet with staff, go over deficiencies/results, assign responsibilities

Approximately one month before survey

- Begin the collection of documents
- Contact peers to discuss their survey results
- Discuss at staff meeting.
- Inspect department for sanitation/safety problems; correct

One week before survey

- Finalize the gathering of all information
- Check all bulletin boards for posting of organizational chart
- Review disaster call-list
- Check all fire routes

Day of survey, check for

- Copies of previous dietary inspections indicating corrections (certifying agencies, health inspections, JCAHO, etc.)
- Policy manuals
  —Hospital
  —Department
  —Personnel
- Job descriptions—signed and dated
- Organizational charts: current, signed, and dated
  —Hospital
  —Department
- Orientation
  —Infection control: hospital and department
  —Patients' rights and responsibilities
  —Hazardous material management
  —Fire emergency procedures
  —Disaster
  —Department safety policies
  —Accident
- Education
  —Inservices
  —Continuing education
- Professional licenses/registration/ certifications
  —Registered dietitians
  —Certified dietary managers
- Schedules: Daily work schedules by hours of work
- Copy of approved diet manual
- Copy of menu and analysis
  —Substitution list
  —Special events
  —Regular and modified
- Written meal census report
- Written quality improvement process
  —Approved QIP reports
  —Annual report

Other

Any other materials that your facility may request be available

- Make a final round before the surveyors arrive; check for sanitation (area, equipment, personnel) and safety

FIGURE 7.16 DIETARY SURVEYS: PRELIMINARY TASKS

cility, and so on. (Regulations generally require that the dietary manager provide the surveyor with requested materials; however, the courtesy and cooperation is obviously appreciated.) He or she should also feel free to ask questions and to learn from the surveyor.

What should the dietary manager do when the surveyor questions a policy, procedure, record, and so on? It depends upon whether the surveyor is correct in both the observation/finding and/or in the interpretation of the applicable regulation. If the surveyor is correct, action should be taken immediately to resolve the problem and to bring the dietary operation into compliance with the regulations. As noted above, a plan of correction, addressing the resolution of procedure, policy, and other deficiencies leading to the observed problem(s), must also be developed. However, since surveyors are people, they do make mistakes. They may reach conclusions and suggest corrective measures with which the dietary manager does not agree.

It is possible to challenge surveyors on their interpretations, conclusions, and directives. The challenge should not be done negatively and should not be hostile. A reasonable and acceptable process of questioning the surveyor is in order. The following procedures can be helpful:

- First, know the regulations;
- Ask the following question: "Is this facility deficient according to your interpretation of the regulation or according to a statute?"
- If the surveyor believes the facility to be in violation of a statute, the dietary manager should ask for a specific citation of the statute and, if possible, a copy of the statute itself. After studying this document, the facility administrator and/or dietary manager may become aware that there is, in fact, a problem. If, however, there is a concern that the statute is not violated, the dietary manager should seek an interpretation from the facility administrator; perhaps legal counsel may also be in order;
- If the violation stems from the surveyor's interpretation, the dietary manager should ask for the basis of the interpretation. Again, the surveyor may be correct, but the dietary manager may wish to discuss differences of opinion about the interpretation with the surveyor. The controversy can be brought to the attention of the administrator whose views may support or be in disagreement with those of the dietary manager;
- If corrective action is required, ask the surveyor for recommendations. Be sure to find out whether the surveyor is saying "it must be done this way" or is only making suggestions;
- If the dietary manager wishes to challenge the surveyor, he or she should do so with permission from the facility administrator. Then, the challenge should begin with the surveyor. Offer an interpretation of the regulation or ideas about corrective action. Many times this will reduce the surveyor's concerns about problems within the facility. If this approach does not lead to satisfaction, it becomes necessary to appeal to a higher level of authority;
- The next step in the challenge process should involve contacting the surveyor's supervisor, usually termed the "licensing officer" for the facility. In many facilities, this will be undertaken by the facility administrator, not by the dietary manager. Since policy is established by the facility, the requirements of each institution will determine who should make this contact. When contacting the surveyor's supervisor, it is important to "tell one's own side of the story" and to ask his or her consideration of those ideas. The initial conversation can take place by phone. A followup letter is always a good idea, especially if the licensing officer does not accept your position;
- If the problem has not been resolved, it may be necessary to contact someone at a higher level in the state agency. This contact should normally be made by

the facility administrator. The dietary manager should seek his or her assistance before this step is taken.

The surveyor can make errors in judgment, and so can the dietary manager. Because both parties are especially concerned about the clients and are aware of the need for the highest quality of health care possible, the need for a partnership rather than an adversarial relationship is obvious. While the dietary manager is on the firing line every day, he or she can and should consider the external evaluator to be a source of additional information which can help a dietary operation better attain its goals.

The dietary manager has a responsibility to use the tools available to implement needed changes and improvements. The dietary manager can do at least the following to provide quality care to the client.

- Be knowledgeable of duties and responsibilities of the job.
- Constantly read, study and question changes, policies and technology.
- Seek a mentor, role model.
- Network within the profession, and learn from others.
- Be ethical; maintain confidentiality.
- Prioritize tasks; use time management techniques.
- Keep materials up to date by reviewing and revising policies, procedures, and inservices.
- Motivate yourself and help employees to meet their needs.
- Develop leadership skills.
- Delegate, delegate, delegate, and train an understudy.
- Market yourself, the department, and your facility.
- Practice good personal hygiene; good nutrition, and dress appropriately.
- Share your ideas with others; help them to grow.

Good personal attributes will help you be a better dietary manager, serve your fellow man and, hopefully, reduce malnutrition in society.

SUMMARY

Each dietary operation must establish its own standards. Both training programs and use of standardized recipes will help to attain quality objectives of products to be served. The dietary manager should work with employees if the product does not meet the standard so that they produce the standard product the next time it is on the menu.

A testing instrument and taste panel can help determine whether a product is at the given standard. The testing instrument considers taste, odor, flavor, color, texture, and appearance of the sample product. The feedback received is valuable, and changes can be made to achieve a more acceptable and standard product.

Quality control checks compare the food to the following standards:

Are hot foods served above 140°F?
Are cold foods served below 40°F?
Are colors bright and fresh looking?
Are items on the tray in the correct location?
Are a variety of textures and flavors present?

Testing a tray of food every week is good practice. If the standards aren't met, spend time researching and implementing necessary changes. After receiving feedback, look at the changes in terms of food category, equipment, or scheduling.

Identifying food preferences should be a continual process. When a food item is rejected, the dietary manager can then follow up and ask whether it was the preparation method or non-interest in the food product that day. The dietary goal is to serve quality food and watch each step of preparation and service to ensure that the best quality food is being delivered and served.

Approaches to identifying client food preferences or food problems include:

1. Using survey cards;
2. Visiting with clients in the dining room to gather comments;
3. Conducting a plate-waste study.

The temperature and quality of food served to the client affect whether he or she accepts or rejects the food. Dietary managers should always prepare foods under sanitary conditions, hold hot foods for as short a period of time as possible, and keep cold foods under refrigeration. Charting food temperatures, starting with warm dinnerware to hold the heat, and using chilled dishes for frozen or cold items are good strategies in retaining proper temperatures.

It is important to know whether a client is refusing any type of food on a continual basis. A three-day food intake form may be used to study the eating habits of each client.

If a dietary manager finds that a client needs extra nourishments, he or she may write in the medical record that the client could benefit from a nourishment program. Some nourishment programs highlight high-calorie milkshakes for weight gain, while others individualize the program to meet the modified diet and likes or dislikes of the client.

Every dietary service should have an ongoing quality control program; once standards are established, employees must be trained to achieve the standard as the product is prepared. The dietary manager cannot resolve short-range operating problems or develop strategies for long-term goal attainment unless he or she evaluates. The steps in evaluation are:

1. Establish dietary department goals;
2. Plan strategies to attain goals;
3. Develop specific operating procedures;
4. Implement procedures;
5. Evaluate effectiveness of dietary services.

A formalized process for evaluation is necessary, so many facilities make use of checklists to aid in the evaluation process. A checklist can help the dietary manager recall what practices are of concern and how they should be done. A checklist can also be a very effective training tool, to teach new employees and to review required procedures with experienced staff members.

When possible, changes stemming from self-evaluation analysis should be implemented gradually. Time is needed not only for employees to become experienced with new procedures, but also to generate operating statistics which will help define the extent to which measurable goals are better attained.

Management principles are important in using self-evaluation tools to improve dietary services. The dietary manager should review each of the points addressed in the checklist and then spend some time actively supervising to confirm that all practices are being followed. If the dietary manager notices that an employee is not following all required procedures in receiving, for example, he or she would schedule a meeting with the employee's supervisor to discuss the problem and to confirm that the supervisor does, in fact, know required procedures. The supervisor would then watch closely, making comments as necessary, and coaching the employee about the "right" way to receive.

If self-evaluation indicates that more than one problem needs correcting, some problem-solving activities can be delegated to others. It is best to modify existing procedures rather than discard the entire procedure and begin over. A dietary manager is judged either good or bad according to his or her ability to manage these non-routine problem-solving activities. Both governmental and private associations may be involved in the evaluation of dietary services.

The Joint Commission of Accreditation of Healthcare Organizations (JCAHO) is an organization dedicated to improving the quality of patient care in organized healthcare settings. This is accomplished through standards setting, survey evaluation, accreditation, and education. Healthcare organizations voluntarily seek JCAHO accreditation because it raises community confidence and provides an educational tool to improve care, services, and programs. The JCAHO is moving forward in implementing a Continuous Quality Improvement (CQI) process to replace the existing Quality Assurance (QA) program. CQI is proactive and is focused on correction of the process, is the responsibility of all, is designed for cross-functional teams to problem-solve by employees at all levels; it is a shared value, a strategy, and a management process.

The National Social Security Act mandates that facilities participating in Medicare and Medicaid programs meet minimum health and safety standards. Medicare is a federal insurance program and Medicaid is a state program which provides medical services to people receiving public assistance under the Social Security program. The federal government and the state agency have several responsibilities, which, taken together, are referred to as the certification process.

It is the dietary manager's responsibility to be very familiar with the rules and regulations established in the state for the type of facility where he or she works. Dietary managers should be concerned about professional liability and should ask the administrator about the type of insurance the facility carries. The dietary manager should be included in this insurance coverage while working.

There is a close relationship between the certification process, state license requirements, programs for professional accreditation (such as JCAHO), and medical assistance standards. The guidelines, recommendations, standards, and interpretations of each regulatory agency and professional association coordinate to provide guidelines for managing healthcare facilities. These guidelines for survey procedures review detailed information applicable to surveys for dietary services. The interpretive guidelines are used to educate surveyors and facility administrators about the standards.

The Omnibus Budget Reconciliation Act of 1987 (OBRA '87), is a federal rule to establish consistent requirements for skilled Medicare and Medicaid nursing facilities. Under the "restorative care" area of OBRA, guidelines exist that enable a facility to improve or maintain the resident's condition. This includes the dietary department of a facility, and provides assessment time limits for a department to completely develop a restorative plan for a single resident. Of main concern are:

1. Residents' rights;
2. Quality of life;
3. Quality of care;
4. Dietetic services;
5. Administration.

Specific procedures used for a licensure/certification survey vary among states and sometimes among different consultants within a state. The sequence of activities typically include the following:

1. The consultant arrives at the facility and holds an entrance interview;
2. A tour of the dietary operation is undertaken;
3. Paperwork is completed (reports and survey forms);
4. Observation will take place;

5. The consultant will watch clients being fed and eating;
6. Personnel files of dietary employees will be reviewed;
7. An exit interview will be conducted;
8. A written statement of deficiencies will be sent to the facility after consultation with the administrator; the dietary manager must develop and implement a plan of correction (POC) to resolve deficiencies.

A survey is in the best interest of both the facility and the clients, and there are steps to take in preparing for it. The dietary manager who studies the standards, understands their interpretation, and knows the types of concerns likely to be addressed by the surveyors will be prepared for this survey.

It is possible to challenge surveyors on their interpretations, conclusions, and directives. A reasonable and acceptable process of questioning the surveyor is in order and should not be done negatively or hostilely. Because the surveyor and the dietary manager are both concerned about the clients and are aware of the need for the highest quality of health care possible, there is a need for a partnership rather than an adversarial relationship.

KEY TERMS

Quality standards
Testing instrument
Plate-waste study
Survey cards
Three-day food intake form
Nourishment program
Steps in evaluation
Self-evaluation
Checklists
JCAHO (Joint Commission on Accreditation of Healthcare Organization)
OBRA (Omnibus Budget Reconciliation Act)
Continuous Quality Improvement (CQI)
National Social Security Act
Licensure/certification survey
Entrance interview
Exit interview
Plan of Correction (POC)

QUESTIONS/PROBLEMS/CASES

1. When checking the food items on a test tray, by what standards should one compare the food?
2. Why would a dietary manager be interested in identifying food preferences?
3. If the dietary goal of your facility is to analyze which foods are *not* being consumed and why they're rejected, describe each step in the evaluation process.
4. What are the advantages of using checklists in a facility?
5. Why might a *wise* dietary manager "modify" rather than discard existing procedures if a problem arises internally?

6. What does the CQI process involve? What is its purpose and how does it relate to healthcare?
7. Why might a healthcare organization seek JCAHO accreditation?
8. You are part of an assessment team, as a dietitian, and the patient complains of unsteadiness and weakness. Which disciplines might offer their expertise? How might you contribute to the development of a restorative plan based on OBRA guidelines?
9. Summarize the roles of federal government and state agencies, and the responsibilities of dietetic services, where evaluation is concerned.
10. Summarize what a dietary manager might expect from a licensure survey.
11. What is the best way to prepare for a survey?
12. What are three procedures that would be helpful when challenging surveyors on their interpretations, conclusions, and directives?

ADMINISTRATIVE AND HUMAN RESOURCE MANAGEMENT

- Staffing and Scheduling
- Human Resource Development
- Supervisor as Manager of Change
- Leadership
- Communication: Internal and External Relations
- Financial Management
- Marketing Management
- Professional Development

8

STAFFING AND SCHEDULING

Chapter Outline

- Procedures for Human Resource Planning
- Tools of Human Resource Management
- Job Breakdown Procedures
  - Job Descriptions
  - Job Specifications
- Role of Dietary Manager in Employee Recruitment and Selection
  - Employee Recruitment Procedures
  - Sources of Employees
  - Obtaining Information About Applicants
  - The Interview Process
  - The Selection Decision
- Employee Labor Control
  - Performance Standards
  - Writing Work Performance Objectives
  - Scheduling Employee Hours
  - Techniques for Schedule Writing
  - Informing Employees About Their Schedules
  - Scheduling Salaried Personnel
  - Controlling Overtime
  - Managing Employee Turnover
  - Determining Actual Labor Hours
  - Payroll Information Systems
  - Comparison of Standard and Actual Labor Hours
- On-the-Job Concerns
  - Equal Employment Opportunity Commission (EEOC)
  - Americans with Disabilities Act (ADA)
  - Sexual Harassment

Procedures for Human Resource Planning

Today's dietary manager has many "full-time" jobs. One of the most important involves determining human resource needs and recruiting and selecting the best employees. Once brought "on board," these staff members must be properly oriented, trained, and supervised to ensure that they make a maximum contribution to the attainment of the department's goals.

Sometimes, dietary managers use the "warm-body syndrome" as their basic human resource strategy. This term implies that there is little, if any, attention given to the need for staff until there is a vacancy. Then, because of the pressure of ongoing work, the first "warm body" making application for a job is retained.

By contrast, professional dietary managers use basic principles of human resource planning and management to guide them as they develop and implement strategies to hire the applicants most likely to be effective and contributing members of the department.

Many, especially larger, institutions may utilize staff planning programs at all organizational levels and for all departments—including dietary services. There are many institutions, however, that do not have organization-wide human resource planning programs. It is for them that this section is written.

Human resource planning involves all procedures in the process by which a dietary manager anticipates the future—and what it will require in personnel. By taking an inventory of currently employed staff, one can determine the need for more or less personnel with the same or differing knowledge, skill and experience levels. For example, if computerized aspects of dietary services will expand (and this is likely!), the dietary manager knows that, at some point, a person with knowledge in computer applications for dietary services will be necessary. Is that person available on staff now? Is there a person currently employed who can be trained? Must a new person be retained? If so, when?

There are several important objectives of a human resource planning program:

1. To reduce personnel problems and costs by managing human resources so that awkward and expensive personnel-related issues do not arise;
2. To allow for human resource planning on a timely—not crisis—basis;
3. To consider ways that societal concerns for minority employment and advancement can be met by the facility;
4. To ensure that personnel are always available to do required work;
5. To promote an awareness of the need for human resource planning;
6. To provide tools useful in evaluating the effectiveness of human resource management plans and policies.

The dietary manager must make sure that all policies dealing with human resources are developed within the framework of concerns established by the institution. The organization, then, lays the foundation for concern about people—and how they are managed. An effectively operated department will have goals and developmental programs for staff members who are new, in training, or in career advancement modes, and even for those who are leaving the facility.

Dietary managers should be flexible as human resource planning systems evolve. Today's fast-changing dietary services may foster personnel concerns we are not even aware of now that will be of dramatic importance to the facility's success tomorrow.

When human resource planning programs are used, the facility recognizes that people—employees—are an investment, not an operating cost, and that it is to the facility's and the employees' mutual benefit to maximize their effective use.

All too often we think of the need for training and educating relatively new staff members and forget about the need to provide attention to the growth and development of long-tenured staff members. Employees of all ages and at all stages in their employment with the facility should be active in a carefully designed career development program. A properly developed human resource planning program, providing opportunities for employees to improve their knowledge and understanding of job requirements, will be compatible with an individual's career development program. This is even more true when the dietary manager is truly concerned about the personal and professional growth and development of staff members.

The term "managerial obsolescence" means that current employees can be victims of rapid change affecting foodservices and the institution for whom they are employed. How do currently employed staff "keep up" with new job demands and responsibilities required by change? What is the responsibility of management staff to provide employees with opportunities, information, and activities to remain effective in changing times?

Recall the concern that employees be treated as investments, not as expenses. The facility that recognizes this and develops plans for staff members to improve themselves is more likely to meet goals and remain stable during increasingly difficult economic and externally regulated times.

Dietary managers in facilities with human resource departments can generally obtain a great deal of assistance in their staff-planning efforts. Typically, a working team comprised of human resource department representatives, top dietary department officials and other management staff within the department are used.

The basic steps in human resource planning are illustrated in Figure 8.1. Human resource planning begins with a forecast of future personnel needs. Will more or fewer staff be needed? Will the same or different types of skills be needed in each position? Will growth in services and products provided require more staff or fewer staff (if productivity can be increased)? Assess the views of top-level administrators about the institution's plans for both the present and the future so that the forecasting of future human resource needs can be in harmony with the growth patterns and plans of the institution itself.

The second step in the human resource planning process is to conduct an inventory of current staff. What are the current jobs in the dietary department? How, if at all, will these need to change in the near and long-range future? What are the skills, abilities, interests, and needs of currently employed staff members? An updated job analysis can be very helpful in this inventory. At this step one must also consider planned vacancies. How many staff members will be retiring within the next several years? Is one aware of other employees whose education will be completed, whose changes in family life impact upon their jobs, and/or of other facts to help assess which staff members will be able to assist the facility in the future?

The third step (assessing human resource planning needs) becomes possible by comparing information gained from steps one and two above. The dietary manager must consider the department's needs for additional personnel and the types of knowledge and skills necessary in these additional staff members.

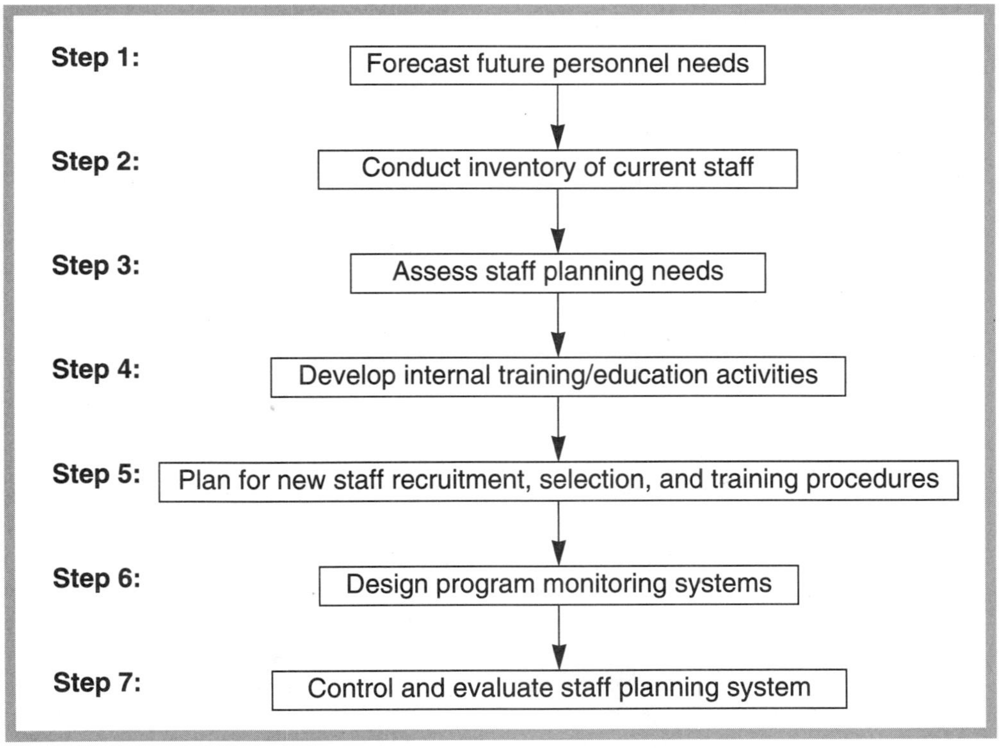

FIGURE 8.1 ELEMENTS IN THE HUMAN RESOURCE PLANNING PROCESS

At this point two separate strategies can be developed. The first is suggested by step four, development of internal training/education activities to upgrade the abilities of those existing staff members who will need to perform activities different from their present job. The second strategy is suggested by step five. It is necessary to plan for new human resource recruitment/selection and training procedures. Of course, if personnel are not needed for several years, it is probably too early to begin this step. However, the dietary manager can be alert for chances to fill positions with current staff members whose potential is evident. One can also carefully evaluate all existing staff; potential candidates for a future position may have been overlooked because of work or personal problems which may have only short-term consequences. If so, these employees present additional options to the manager concerned about planning for the future.

How well is the human resource planning process working? With step six, a careful plan to monitor the effectiveness of the human resource planning process becomes important. How many new positions do we expect to fill at a specific point in time? How many were filled? How many employees have been trained—and in what topics? Program monitoring makes it possible to control and evaluate the human resource planning system (step seven in Figure 8.1).

If planning for future human resource needs sounds complicated, it really isn't. It involves an awareness that planning for the future is the only effective way to ensure that the number of "surprises" will be minimal. No one can predict what will happen in the future. However, the dietary manager who rationalizes that human resource planning is impossible is also failing to fulfill a very important part of the job.

Tools of Human Resource Management

The dietary manager must be aware of and use three human resource management tools. One of these—organizational charts—was discussed in Chapter One. Review this information if desired to glean a clearer understanding of how organizational charts (which show the relationships among each position in a facility) can help with human resource planning. Job descriptions and job specifications are discussed here.

Job Breakdown Procedures

A job breakdown is a very useful tool to develop standard operating procedures which specify how work should be done. Once completed, its results can become the basis for training programs, performance appraisal, and the development of standard operating procedure manuals. The correct way to do required work must be determined before quality requirements of a job can be defined and productivity standards developed. Figure 8.2 shows a sample job breakdown for washing service-ware. Notice that it divides the task of washing service-ware into individual elements, and indicates specifically how each sub-task is to be done.

Developing task analysis information for all work activities undertaken by dietary services personnel will take some time. Perhaps a schedule can be developed so that task analysis for one or more activities noted in a job description can be done weekly as part of ongoing staff meetings; or perhaps the dietary manager can develop a job list, indicating specific activities which are part of the job. Then, individual supervisors can each be assigned one task and develop a tentative analysis for it. Meetings can be held to "fine-tune" efforts undertaken by individual supervisors. With this plan, within a year or less a dietary department might develop task analysis information for all of the more important activities. When one considers that this information will be useful for programmed planning, controlling, and monitoring purposes, as well as for training, the results of the effort certainly will make it cost-effective in many operations.

JOB BREAKDOWN

Job Breakdown #84: The ability to wash service-ware
Equipment needed: Dish, glass, and silver racks; dish machine; silverware soak tub; garbage can w/liner

What to Do	How to Do It	Additional Information
1. Scrape and sort.	1. a) Use a "decoy system" by setting up one piece of each type of service-ware as a lure for service personnel to help sort according to the "decoys." b) Deposit all linen napkins and tablecloths in a linen bag. c) Scrape all food into garbage cans using heel of hand. d) Place all silver in soak tub and soak before washing.	1. a) Cooperation with service personnel will make your job and their job easier. Organizing the dishwashing function will speed the process and increase efficiency. b) Protect linens—they are expensive. c) A special rubber scraper may be used to scrape food if preferred. d) Soak tub should have one tablespoon of detarnish powder and be two-thirds full of water. Presoaking makes washing easier, and detarnish solution reduces spots.
2. Rack and prewash.	2. a) Rack each type of china separately to avoid breakage. b) Rack glasses in glass racks. c) Miscellaneous items should be racked in open racks. d) Spray service-ware with warm water from the prewash spray. Push racks into the machine. e) Sort silverware from the soak tub. Place silverware in plastic cones with the handles down.	2. a) Heavy china will bump against delicate service-ware, causing breakage if racked together. b) There are special glass racks for each size of glasses. Do not mix glasses. c) Do not overcrowd or overload the racks because the wash and rinse water must reach all surfaces to clean the items. d) Prewashing removes some of the food particles that otherwise would enter the dish machine. It also reduces the number of times that wash water will need changing. e) Presorting reduces handling of clean silverware.
3. Feed the machine and wash dishes.	3. a) Turn on conveyor and pump. b) Push the rack of soiled items into the machine far enough for the conveyor to engage the rack; the conveyor will move it through the machine. c) Rack more items and feed into machine as fast as it will take them.	3. a) Push black buttons on control panel to start; Push red buttons to stop. b) The rack should engage at one-third to one-half of the way in. Check wash temperature to be sure it is at least 140°F. Rinse temperature should be at least 180°F. If temperatures are low, stop machine and contact your supervisor. c) Do not allow soiled dishes to pile up and hinder the service personnel. Help them unload trays and bus tubs. Work to maintain good relationships with other employees.
4. Remove clean racks.	4. Machine will push racks out of rinse end. Pull them completely free. Shake rack to remove excess water. Allow items to air dry before removing.	4. If rinse water is 180°F, items will air-dry quickly. Service-ware should never be wiped dry.
5. Stack and store service-ware.	5. Store glasses in the wash racks. Stack china and store in clean dish area.	5. Plates and bowls are placed on dish carts. Glassware is left in racks and placed on glass carts. Silverware is placed in flatware racks for transport to service stations.
6. Check for service-ware not properly cleaned.	6. Look for food, waterspots, chips, cracks, or other problems which indicate items cannot be used.	6. You are the quality control inspector of clean service-ware. Check carefully and rewash all soiled items. Remove all chipped and cracked items and discard. Guests judge the cleanliness of the kitchen by the condition of the service-ware.

FIGURE 8.2 SAMPLE JOB BREAKDOWN

Source: L. Forrest, *Training for the Hospitality Industry.* Second Edition. Educational Institute of American Hotel and Motel Association. East Lansing, Mich., 1990, pp. 34–35.

Job Descriptions

As a result of effective job analysis, job descriptions can be prepared. A job description lists all of the various tasks and related information which, when taken together, make up the job or work position. For example, the job of a tray line worker may involve tasks including transporting food and supplies to the tray line, portioning food, cleaning the tray assembly line and area after work is completed, and even transporting food to wards or other areas. Each facility is different, and job descriptions should be written to indicate "who must do what" in a specific facility.

A job description can be the basis for organizing work, and is very useful in training personnel. Since tasks are spelled out in the job description, it can also be the basis for employee evaluation.

A job description must be task-oriented; it is written for a position, not for a person. In other words, when the dietary manager develops job descriptions, don't think "I have a cook named Sally; what does she or should she do?" Rather, the manager should consider "What are the tasks I can reasonably expect any cook to do?" Currently employed staff may not be employed in the future; rotation of shifts, promotion, and continued changes within jobs are other reasons why it is not wise to plan or define job tasks on a by-person basis.

A job description should be written for all positions in the dietary operation. The task of writing a job description does not have to be time-consuming or difficult. Brief statements can be sufficient. Sample job descriptions for selected dietary positions are included later in this section. They provide illustrations of how to write descriptions, which generally explain "what the job is all about." However, since each facility is unique, these job descriptions cannot be used "as is." The job description for each position in an ongoing operation must be designed to fit the exact needs of the specific property.

Job descriptions for a specific department are complete when all tasks necessary to carry out all aspects of that department's operation are included in the job description of some position. Planning tools begin with the facility's mission statement, continue to the development of dietary purposes and specific goals, consider the most effective ways to utilize the resources allocated to the department, and then yield an organization chart and specific job descriptions.

Many factors can be addressed in a job description. These include:

- Job title;
- Section or department in which position is located;
- Supervisor name and title;
- Description of basic responsibilities;
- Summary of job tasks (duties);
- Equipment used to perform the job;
- Details regarding working conditions (which can identify potential job hazards); and
- Listing of positions supervised by the employee in the job.

Job descriptions are very important. They answer several questions for each position within dietary services: What, exactly, are all the tasks a worker in this position must perform? What position supervises a worker in this position? What are any other factors which will make clear what this position involves and how it relates to other positions within the department and facility?

There are several important uses served by a job description. They tell managers and employees what tasks are the responsibility of each position (who receives food deliveries—the foodservice supervisor or the cook?) Knowledge of this information can resolve many disagreements regarding "who should do what."

Job descriptions also indicate how each position relates to all other positions in the dietary department. As such, they lay the foundation for the flow of communication, authority, and responsibility throughout the organization.

Job descriptions help organize positions into work sections so that effective labor control systems can be developed and implemented. They also help with hiring tasks; an employee considering a job wants to know what it involves. Task requirements of the job are listed in the job description, and applicants can then quickly and concisely learn "what the job is all about."

Job descriptions provide managers with an overview of tasks involved in all the positions supervised, and they also help implement the organizational chart.

Once developed, job descriptions should be combined into a job description handbook or human resource manual. As jobs change, job descriptions will need to be updated as necessary to provide a current view of all tasks involved in each job.

What work is likely to be performed by the dietary manager? Many of the tasks have been identified by the Dietary Managers Association (Figure 8.3).

Let's look at some job descriptions for positions which impact on and are part of the dietary department. The figures which follow are:

Figure 8.4—Job Description for an Assistant Administrator, Dietary Services. This official coordinates activities of the dietary department;

Figure 8.5—Job Description for an Assistant Administrator, Financial Services. This official is responsible for economic aspects of the facility, including dietary services;

Figure 8.6—Job Description for a Foodservice Director;

Figure 8.7—Job Description for a Food Production Manager;

Figure 8.8—Job Description for a Chief Clinical Dietitian;

Figure 8.9—Job Description for a Clinical Dietitian;

Figure 8.10—Job Description for a Dietary Manager;

Figure 8.11—Job Description for a Hospital Cook;

Figure 8.12—Job Description for a Hospital Foodservice Worker;

Figure 8.13—Job Description for a Nursing Home Cook;

Figure 8.14—Job Description for a Nursing Home Foodservice Worker.

Supervise employees in approved sanitary/safety procedures
Implement physician's diet order
Monitor food quality, portion size, and accuracy of diet order
Comply with requirements and standards established by regulatory agencies
Supervise dietary employees in day-to-day operations
Attend continuing education programs
Establish sanitation procedures
Monitor safety procedures
Purchase food and supplies
Develop/maintain employee work/time schedules
Supervise employees in equipment use/maintenance
Supervise employees in food production
Establish department infection control practices
Interview and select employees
Confirm physician's diet order
Document nutrition information in medical records
Maintain department records, i.e., fiscal, schedules, etc.
Identify nutrition problems and develop appropriate care plans
Orient new employees to facility and department

FIGURE 8.3 TASKS WITH HIGHEST IMPORTANCE RATINGS

Theresa Strand. *A National Survey of the Job Tasks and Knowledge/Skills of Dietary Managers.* Evanston, Ill. Educational Testing Service. 1990. (pp 24–25).

FUNCTION

Plans, organizes, directs, and coordinates the activities of the Dietary Department to provide services for residents, staff, and guests. Responsible and accountable to the Administrator of Otterbein Home.

DUTIES

Establishes departmental regulations and procedures, in conformance with Federal, State, local regulations, as well as administrative policies, and develops standards for organization and supervision of dietetic service. Determines quality and quantity of food required, plans menus, and controls food costs. Reviews regular diet menus as to cost and suitability to facility and standardized recipes for menu requirements. Makes frequent inspections of all work, storage, and serving areas to determine that the regulations and directions governing dietetic activities are followed. Recommends or institutes changes in techniques or procedures for more efficient operation. Develops and prepares policies and procedures governing handling and storage of supplies and equipment, sanitation, keeping records, and compiling reports. Prepares job descriptions, organizational charts, manuals, and guidebooks covering all phases of departmental operations for use by employees. Makes final determination of kinds and amounts of supplies and equipment needed.

Interviews and makes final selection of applicants for employment. Reviews work schedules for personnel and job performance ratings. Administers and monitors payroll, benefits, and staffing.

Selects, upon supervisory recommendation, personnel for transfer, promotion, and special training to insure most effective utilization of individual skills and employee development.

Reviews records and reports covering number and kinds of regular and therapeutic diets prepared, costs of raw food, and labor and inventory of equipment and supplies. Develops and directs control system. Prepares and evaluates annual department budget.

Confers with other Department Heads regarding technical and administrative aspects of dietetic service. Establishes effective relationships with medical staff, nursing, and other resident care services. Serves on facility-wide committees as assigned.

Attends administrative staff meetings as executive staff member and transmits information to Department Staff regarding new developments and trends. Attends and contributes to all Board meetings. Delegates authority to Supervisory Staff for task details to facilitate smooth flow of materials.

Responsible for activities in the Country Store.

Assists Administrator as assigned and to substitute in his or her absence. Assist in public relations and interpretation of the Home to the public as requested by the Administrator.

FIGURE 8.4 JOB DESCRIPTION FOR AN ASSISTANT ADMINISTRATOR, DIETARY SERVICES
Used by permission of Otterbein Home, Lebanon, Ohio; courtesy of Jerrold Blackmore

OVERALL FUNCTION

This position is the Chief Financial Officer (C.F.O.) of the Hospital. The C.F.O. is responsible for the financial management of the Hospital, which includes the departments of Admitting, Data Processing, Finance, and Patient Billing. The incumbent summarizes, analyzes, interprets, and communicates financial and budget reports to Management and Board of Trustees, and makes recommendations to Administrative Staff on Financial Issues. Responsible for Capital Financing and administers the Hospital Insurance Program.

DISTINGUISHING FEATURES

The incumbent supervises others at the supervisory, professional, and clerical level, and operates under the general direction of the Administrator and in coordination with the Associate Administrator. Decision-making authority affects the entire Hospital. Effective performance requires regular contact with Administrative Staff at the Hospital and frequent contact with ranking representatives of outside organizations.

EXAMPLES OF DUTIES

- Provides assistance to the departments of Finance, Admitting, Patient Accounting and Data Processing in planning, organizing, problem-solving, goal setting, budgeting, and performance evaluations. Approves departmental policies.
- Formalizes and directs financial budgeting program.
- Controls and coordinates Hospital insurance policies with Hospital broker.
- Reviews and evaluates (and may implement) other administrative projects. Also provides financial input into many other areas and projects.
- Acts as a consultant to Administrative Staff.

DATE PREPARED: ____________________ APPROVED BY: ____________________

Assistant Administrator

FIGURE 8.5 JOB DESCRIPTION FOR AN ASSISTANT ADMINISTRATOR, FINANCIAL SERVICES [ALSO COMMONLY CALLED CONTROLLER, BUSINESS MANAGER, VICE PRESIDENT OF FINANCIAL AFFAIRS]

Used by permission of North Charles General Hospital, Baltimore, Md; courtesy of Pat Parker

OVERALL FUNCTION

This position is responsible for planning, organizing, coordinating, and directing the operation of the Hospital's food service in compliance with Hospital rules, local, State, and Federal laws and accrediting agency regulations.

DISTINGUISHING FEATURES

The incumbent supervises others at the supervisory and professional level, and operates under the general direction of the Assistant Administrator, General Services. Decision-making authority affects the Dietary Department. Effective performance requires occasional contact with department managers at the Hospital and regular contact with vendors. Contact with State and local health regulation agencies is occasional.

EXAMPLES OF DUTIES

- Oversees the purchase, preparation, and service of all food products for patients and cafeteria.
- Makes frequent inspections of all work, storage, and serving areas to determine that regulations and direction governing dietetic activities are followed.
- Formulates departmental policies in conformance with administrative policies, and develops standards for organizing and supervising dietetic service.
- Prepares departmental objectives, budgets, and inservice programs to comply with Hospital objectives.
- Recommends or institutes changes in techniques or procedures for more efficient operation or to comply with Hospital, local, state, federal, and accrediting agency standards and regulations.

FIGURE 8.6 JOB DESCRIPTION FOR A FOODSERVICE DIRECTOR
Used by permission of North Charles General Hospital, Baltimore, Md; courtesy of Pat Parker

POSITION TITLE: Food Production Manager

SUPERVISOR: Director of Dietary Services

DEPARTMENT: Dietary Services

DATE: April 17, 0000

APPROVAL: ______________________________

CHARACTER OF THE POSITION

Under the direction of the Director of Dietary, incumbent is responsible in the assigned areas of food production management. Procures and receives supplies and equipment following established procedures. Estimates food consumption and requirements to determine type and quantity of all food items. Assists in the implementation of established cost-control procedures. Compiles data for use in evaluating the food service system. Assists in the preparation of the operating budget. Assigns, supervises, and coordinates food production personnel. Supervises food production and service. Plans master schedule for food production personnel. Plans cafeteria menu in the absence of the Director. Supervises, directs, and schedules Food Service Supervisors. Prepares weekly payroll records. Participates in staffing needs and on-the-job training. Maintains records of work assignments, hours of operation, and inventory control. Attends meetings as assigned. Performs additional duties as assigned.

KNOW HOW

1. Comprehensive knowledge of food production.
2. General knowledge of budgets.
3. General knowledge of personnel and hospital policies and procedures.
4. Requires an associate degree with a major in Dietetic Technology. In lieu of degree, 15 years previous experience and enrollment in an approved Dietetic Technology program may be substituted. Minimum of five years experience in a supervisory capacity is required. Membership in either Dietary Managers Association or the American Dietetic Association is required.

PROBLEM SOLVING

1. Has latitude to cope with most production problems.
2. Refers unusual problems to Food Service Director.

FIGURE 8.7 JOB DESCRIPTION FOR A FOOD PRODUCTION MANAGER
Modified from job description from North Charles General Hospital, Baltimore, Md; courtesy of Pat Parker

A. GENERAL SUMMARY

Responsible for nutritional care and follow-up of patients and communicating information appropriately to other health professionals. Assists in quality assurance audits, inservice, and community education programs.

B. DUTIES AND RESPONSIBILITIES

1. Coordinates and integrates the administrative and clinical aspects of Nutrition Services.
2. Organizes, directs, and supervises work of Clinical Dietitians, Food Service Supervisors assigned to patient care, Galley Technicians and Line Aides in patient related activities. Assists Director in hiring and disciplinary decisions; evaluates performance.
3. Functions as relief dietitian to maintain continuity in the nutritional care of patients.
4. Functions as the Clinical Nutrition Representative in developing healthcare protocol with physicians, nursing staff, and other health professionals.
5. Writes and revises policies and procedures relating to clinical nutrition, and implements and maintains these procedures to provide optimal nutrition care.
6. Coordinates departmental quality assurance program by developing, implementing, and overseeing the maintenance of Quality Assurance standards, in accordance with JCAH, Board of Health, and departmental guidelines.
7. Schedules and plans department inservice education and community service nutrition programs by assessing department needs, researching and developing programs, obtaining speakers, lecturing, etc.
8. Responsible for writing and printing of patient menus, diet manuals, and patient nutritional materials.
9. Coordinates out-patient data counseling program by scheduling appointments and counseling outpatients.

C. SUPERVISION GIVEN AND/OR RECEIVED

Reports to:	Director, Food and Nutrition Services
Supervises:	Food Service Supervisors, Patient Care, Clinical Dietitians, Galley Technicians, Line Aides

D. WORKING CONDITIONS

Hazards typical of institutional kitchen facilities (contact with infectious diseases, electrical equipment, hazardous floor surfaces, contact with patients with physical impairments.

E. PHYSICAL DEMANDS

Moderate amount of walking.

FIGURE 8.8 JOB DESCRIPTION FOR A CHIEF CLINICAL DIETITIAN
Modified from job description from North Charles General Hospital, Baltimore, Md; courtesy of Pat Parker

A. GENERAL SUMMARY

Under general supervision, responsible for nutritional care and follow-up of patients and communicating information appropriately to other health professionals. Assists in quality assurance audits, inservice, and community education programs.

B. DUTIES AND RESPONSIBILITIES

1. Screens patients designated "at risk" according to established priorities. Assesses nutritional status; develops and charts nutritional care plan by analysis of charted and observed data.
2. Instructs patient and/or significant other on diet as ordered by physician using written materials; evaluates and charts patient comprehension of diet information according to behavioral objectives.
3. Evaluates appropriateness of diet orders.
4. Communicates with other health care professionals (i.e., staff nurse, physician) of information pertinent to care of patient.
5. Responsible for nutritional adequacy and adherence of menus to prescribed diets. Calculates patients' nutrient needs and records actual food intakes.
6. Develops and revises diet instructional materials to provide patients with written guidelines.
7. Teaches and/or participates in hospital or community group meetings as assigned.
8. Participates in evaluating quality assurance audits and developing criteria for area of nutrition services.

C. SUPERVISION GIVEN AND/OR RECEIVED

Reports to: Chief Clinical Dietitian

Provides functional supervision to: Galley Technicians

D. WORKING CONDITIONS

Hazards associated with patient contact (i.e., exposure to infectious diseases).

E. PHYSICAL DEMANDS

Moderate amount of walking.

FIGURE 8.9 JOB DESCRIPTION FOR A CLINICAL DIETITIAN
Modified from job description from North Charles General Hospital, Baltimore, Md; courtesy of Pat Parker

1. Establishment Job Title(s)

Dietary Manager

2. List Overall Purpose or Summary of this Job

Manages food operations in institutions, such as hospitals, nursing homes, and other educational and community feeding centers. Responsibilities include management of food service personnel, food supplies, kitchen equipment, food production, and routine nutritional aspects of food services. Utilizes services of Dietititan (Consultant) as required for development of special diets and menus.

3. List Important or Regularly Performed Tasks

1. Collaborates in gathering nutritional data from patients/clients and identifying dietary needs.
2. Manages implementation of dietitian's nutritional plans or dietary orders from physicians.
3. Develops and manages appropriate food services for patients/clients.
4. Collaborates in nutritional education programs for patients.
5. Manages food facility personnel, including hiring, supervision, and evaluation.
6. Develops plans/procedures for food facility and its personnel.
7. Collaborates in developing external relations of facility with outside groups.
8. Manages kitchen supplies and equipment using safety, sanitation, and efficiency principles.
9. Manages food production and distribution services.
10. Collaborates in management of facility business operations, e.g., purchases, meal costs, wages.

4. (a) List Employer's Hiring Requirements: (education, vocational training, experience, other)

Generally must have 3 to 5 years experience in food service jobs plus high school education. Must complete a formal vocational training (minimum 90 hours of classroom, plus 150 hours of field experience) program approved by Dietary Managers Association. As of 1984, the title "Dietary Manager" will be based on a credential awarded by the Dietary Managers Association Credentialing Board.

4. (b) List Machines, Tools, Equipment, or Work Aids the Worker Uses to Perform Duties

Food production equipment, such as bulk blender, mixer, cooking range/stove, oven, tray conveyor belts. Must also work with patient charts and medical records.

Figure 8.10 Job Description for a Dietary Manager

Modified from job description from North Charles General Hospital, Baltimore, Md; courtesy of Pat Parker

A. GENERAL SUMMARY

Under limited supervision, prepares all hot food and desserts requiring on-premises cooking/baking for patients, cafeteria, and special events.

B. DUTIES AND RESPONSIBILITIES

1. Prepares and cooks hot food, bakery products, and garnishes for patients, cafeteria, and special events as assigned, according to standardized recipes and safe food-handling practices. Utilizes kitchen equipment such as broiler, deep fat fryer, electric slicers, ovens, and steam kettles.
2. Utilizes and properly rotates any overproduction of food items.
3. Cleans and sanitizes assigned work area.
4. Portions out food for blast freezing according to portion control standards.
5. Completes production sheets with amounts of food utilized.
6. Fills out meat yield chart according to specifications.
7. Assists in production planning by providing input at daily production team meetings (i.e., forecasting needs, assisting in standardized recipe development).

C. SUPERVISION GIVEN AND/OR RECEIVED

Reports to: Supervisor, Food Service

D. WORKING CONDITIONS

Hazards typical of institutional kitchen such as hot cooking surfaces, sharp objects, electrical equipment, wet floors. Frequent exposure to temperature extremes (from hot oven area to freezer). Exposure to hot, spattering grease. Handles some potentially hazardous cleaning supplies.

E. PHYSICAL DEMANDS

Moderate to heavy lifting, constantly on feet, carrying hot pans, and pushing medium-size carts.

FIGURE 8.11 JOB DESCRIPTION FOR A HOSPITAL COOK
Modified from job description from North Charles General Hospital, Baltimore, Md; courtesy of Pat Parker

A. GENERAL SUMMARY

Under general supervision, performs a variety of housekeeping duties to maintain order and sanitary conditions in institutional kitchen and eating areas.

B. DUTIES AND RESPONSIBILITIES

Performs variety of duties which may include the following:

1. Sweeps and mops floors; vacuums cafeteria daily.
2. Operates dishmachine following established policy to wash, unload, and put away patient, cafeteria, and special events dishes.
3. Washes, sanitizes, and puts away pots and pans.
4. Collects trash and operates compactor.
5. Cleans and sanitizes work areas (may include ovens, deep fryer, and ceilings).
6. Performs emergency cleaning jobs as necessary.
7. Puts stock away in proper storage areas to keep coolers organized.
8. Reports needed equipment repairs to supervisor.
9. Works patient tray line as needed.

C. SUPERVISION GIVEN AND/OR RECEIVED

Reports to: Supervisor, Food Service

D. WORKING CONDITIONS

Hazards typical of institutional kitchen (i.e., hot cooking surfaces, electrical equipment, wet and/or greasy floors, sharp objects). Exposed to inclement weather while compacting trash, to very cold temperatures in coolers, and to potentially hazardous cleaning chemicals.

E. PHYSICAL DEMANDS

Some heavy lifting, pushing tray carts, constantly on feet, standing on ladder for high cleaning.

FIGURE 8.12 JOB DESCRIPTION FOR A HOSPITAL FOODSERVICE WORKER
Modified from job description from North Charles General Hospital, Baltimore, Md; courtesy of Pat Parker

JOB TITLE: NURSING HOME COOK

RESPONSIBILITIES

Ensures proper preparation, portioning, and serving of foods according to standardized recipes.

Supervises all employees in the absence of the food supervisor.

Performs other related duties as assigned.

WORK STANDARDS

Quality food products prepared according to standardized recipes and menus.

Food ready at the specified time.

Adaptability to a variety of job duties and situations.

Follow departmental procedures including sanitation, safety, and cleaning schedules.

Function as a team member, often requiring leadership abilities.

PHYSICAL DEMANDS

Stands and walks for short distances most of working day. Stoops and reaches, lifts and carries food and kitchen equipment. Tastes and smells food to determine quality and palatability. Hand dexterity to prepare food.

SPECIAL DEMANDS

Must have a genuine interest in geriatric work. Willingness to work for best interests of institution. Ability to supervise and work cooperatively with others. Considerable initiative and judgment involved in setting up meals, seasoning food, estimating food requirements, utilizing leftovers, and presenting food in an attractive and palatable manner. Works under general supervision. Follows standard recipes and menus but makes frequent independent decisions relative to type of meal to be served and method of preparation.

WORKING ENVIRONMENT

Works in clean, well-lighted, and ventilated kitchen. Atmosphere is warm and humid from cooking foods and dishwashing. Is exposed to sudden temperature changes when entering refrigerator, and is subject to burns from hot foods and utensils, and cuts from knives. Possibility of injury from falls on slippery floors.

FIGURE 8.13 JOB DESCRIPTION FOR A NURSING HOME COOK

Used by permission of Willowbrook Manor Nursing Home, Flint, Mich.; courtesy of Maurice Latimer

JOB TITLE: GENERAL FOOD SERVICE WORKER

IMMEDIATE SUPERVISOR: Dietary Service Supervisor or Cook in the absence of the food supervisor

RESPONSIBILITIES

Properly wash and sanitize all dishes, utensils, and cooking equipment. Put away.

Assist in tray assembly and deliver carts to Units.

Properly dispose of refuse.

Assemble and deliver floor supplies.

General cleaning as scheduled.

Properly put away all deliveries of food and supplies.

Performs other related duties as assigned.

WORK STANDARDS

Accurate tray assembly.

Efficient use of time to complete assigned work.

Follow departmental procedures including sanitation, safety, and cleaning schedules.

Function as a team member.

FIGURE 8.14 JOB DESCRIPTION FOR A NURSING HOME FOODSERVICE WORKER
Used by permission of Willowbrook Manor Nursing Home, Flint, Mich.; courtesy of Maurice Latimer

It is unlikely that all of the job descriptions noted in Figures 8.4 to 8.14 will be specifically applicable to your facility. However, review of this information will give you an idea about (a) what work tasks are included in various positions, and (b) how job descriptions can be written.

Job Specifications

Job specifications indicate the personal qualifications judged necessary to successfully perform in a position, and which are then outlined in a job description. Job specifications should be kept simple and should accurately represent needs for the position. If, for example, experience and other requirements are higher than necessary, it will decrease the pool of candidates applicable for the position; unless you offer a higher wage/salary rate to compensate fairly. Dietary managers will then "pay more" for personnel who may get bored and frustrated with the lack of challenging work to do. By contrast, if job specifications understate personal qualities, staff members hired may become frustrated and discontented, and will be less able to do the work required of them. Work quality is likely to suffer, length of time required for training is likely to increase, and the institution, the employee, and the client being served will probably suffer, in part because of an inadequate job specification.

In some areas, facilities may be unable to hire appropriate trained and/or experienced staff members. Then, training becomes extremely important. Dietary operations which utilize effective human resource policies and procedures will be more able to attract and retain qualified staff than will other facilities.

Job specifications should be written around tasks required by applicable job descriptions. They should not be developed around personnel currently employed by the dietary services. Don't ask "What is Mary's background?" Instead, consider what qualifications are needed to perform tasks to a minimal level of acceptance.

Factors included in a job specification (other than required education, experience, knowledge, and training) can include necessary physical skills, communication abilities, ability to use and maintain equipment, and so on.

A job specification can be used to help identify which applicants for vacant positions are eligible and should be considered for positions. Job specifications set acceptable standards for initial employment in a position. Only individuals who possess the personal qualifications outlined by the job specification will be considered for employment in the position.

Job specifications can also help identify existing staff who should be considered for advancement. (If only qualified personnel are eligible, concerns about employee favoritism are lessened.) In the context of human resource planning noted earlier, the staff member being considered for a new position can be evaluated against the job specification required for that new position. Areas where additional training, experience, and/or education are necessary will be identified. The staff member can then be guided into continuing education/training activities which will be useful when the job change is made. Figure 8.15 illustrates a more detailed job specification for a cook position.

Role of Dietary Manager in Employee Recruitment and Selection

The human resource tools already discussed (organization chart, and job descriptions, and specifications) can help the dietary manager in recruiting and selecting the best employees. The dietary manager will understand (a) the positions needed for effective operation, (b) the tasks which must be performed by employees in each position, (c) personal qualifications necessary for employees to be successful in each position and (d) how, at least formally, each position relates to each other. These tools are at the heart of the human resource management system.

Large institutions will likely have human resource departments, to assist with recruiting and selecting. In small facilities, top-level administrators may be involved

Work Schedule
Must be able to work approximately 40 hours weekly; varied daily schedules but hours for the position range from 6:00 AM to 11:30 PM.

Experience
At least two years' experience in quantity food production; four years of total foodservice experience in progressively more responsible positions. Experience must include entree, salad, and soup preparation, and some meat cutting.

Special Skills/Abilities
Perform basic arithmetic calculations (must pass test on recipe extensions); *speak and write effectively;* supervise and motivate foodservice workers. Use and know how to maintain all foodservice production equipment in the kitchen. Develop and maintain three-month *on-the-job training* program for newly hired foodservice workers which corresponds to requirements in the facility's training manual.

Personality Requirements
Even disposition. Dependability. Concern for detail in work.

Physical Requirements
Able to lift 50 lbs., with good eyesight (correctable with glasses or contact lenses if necessary). Able to work, standing up, long hours in facility with hot cooking equipment.

Education
High school, General Educational Development (GED), or equivalent.

Other Concerns
References must be contacted. Should be able to make the following standard recipes: brown sauce, scalloped potatoes, and/or other items as part of employment test. Must also pass written test on recipe extension and be able to review/outline procedures to be used for on-the-job training for newly employed cooking personnel.

NOTE: This sample job specification is shown for illustrative purposes only. The actual specifications for a facility will need to be developed to fit the needs of the specific institution.

Figure 8.15 Sample Job Specification: Cook

in the process. However, dietary managers working in facilities of every size must have a thorough understanding of how the recruitment and selection process works, and they should have an opportunity to provide input as the process evolves.

Employee Recruitment Procedures

Employee recruitment is the process by which applicants are sought out and screened for suitability for positions within the dietary operation. The process essentially involves announcing job vacancies through useful sources and then evaluating applicants to determine who may be suitable. The selection process begins with recruiting and ends with hiring. Both the dietary manager and the immediate supervisor of the position to be filled should be involved in the task of recruiting and selecting staff. Both of these staff members can assist by:

1. Reviewing and updating (if necessary) the job description and specifications before the position vacancy is announced;
2. Routine screening to determine the most qualified applicants;
3. Interviewing eligible applicants;

4. Reviewing application forms and other information supplied by the applicants;
5. Checking education and references;
6. Helping make the hiring decision.

Sources of Employees

There are several sources which can be used to recruit employees for dietary services, including both internal and external as explained below:

1. *Friends and relatives of current employees.* There are advantages and disadvantages to employing friends and relatives of existing staff members. Advantages include: (a) employees' knowledge of the requirements of the job and what it is like to work for the facility (if they have favorable impressions they might be "good salespersons" to recruit others), and (b) current employees' relationships with many of the same types of people who would be good candidates for vacant positions.

One disadvantage is that, if several friends or family members work for the same facility, all may be affected by a single event. For example, if one of the group is disciplined, the entire group may react negatively;

2. *Promotion of current employees.* In a "career ladder" program a good employee can be trained for advancement. Good employees should be encouraged to stay with the operation. An example of a "career ladder" might be a foodservice worker becomes an assistant cook and then, after training and experience, a cook. When a manager position opens, he indicates that he has taken training to become a dietary manager, and applies for the position. Lateral transfers from one section to another section or department are also possible.

Advantages of internal promotion/transfer may include building morale, encouraging existing employees to perform better, and encouraging employees to remain with the facility. However, dietary managers should know that employees who are successful in one position may not be effective in the job to which they are promoted. Continuous human resource development efforts are helpful in screening employees for promotions;

3. *External sources.* Applicants for vacant positions may be recruited from newspaper advertisements. Public and private employment agencies can be helpful in locating applicants. Government and other groups which work with and train handicapped and disadvantaged persons may be helpful. Some facilities have had success when hiring trainees from these sources—especially for entrance level positions. Professional organizations, colleges, universities, vocational and secondary schools with distributive education, and similar programs are also sources for new staff members.

Obtaining Information About Applicants

Information must be gathered about personnel making application for vacant positions. Sources of information include:

1. *Job application form.* The job application form provides basic information to help tell whether the applicant meets minimum job qualifications.

The application form should be simple and require only information important for consideration of job suitability. A sample job application form is illustrated in Figure 8.16.

General types of information included in job application forms are:

- name;
- address;
- education;
- references;
- experience.

NORTH CHARLES GENERAL HOSPITAL
NORTH CHARLES AT 26TH ST. • BALTIMORE, MD. 21218

Employment Application

Date ______________

PLEASE COMPLETE ALL QUESTIONS—PRINT CLEARLY OR TYPE

Name: Last / First / Middle	Social Security Number
Address: Number / Street / City / State / Zip Code	Home Phone: ______ Business Phone: ______

Notify in Case of Emergency: Name / Residence / Relationship / Phone

How referred to NCGH?	Have you worked for NCGH before?	If yes, when:	What capacity?:

Position(s) Applying For:	Type of Employment: Permanent ______ Full Time ______ Temporary ______ Part Time ______

Date Available:	Salary Expected:	Hours Preferred:	If Temporary, How Long?

PLEASE LIST ALL EMPLOYMENT FOR PAST YEARS—BEGIN WITH YOUR LAST EMPLOYER FIRST—ACCOUNT FOR ALL PERIODS OF UNEMPLOYMENT.

EMPLOYER	TITLE AND DUTIES	DATE EMPLOYED	SALARY
Name: Address: Phone: Supervisor's Name & Title:		From To May We Contact Your Employer? Reason for Leaving	Start Final
Name: Address: Phone: Supervisor's Name & Title:		From To May We Contact Your Employer? Reason for Leaving	Start Final
Name: Address: Phone: Supervisor's Name & Title:		From To May We Contact Your Employer? Reason for Leaving	Start Final
Name: Address: Phone: Supervisor's Name & Title:		From To May We Contact Your Employer? Reason for Leaving	Start Final

AN EQUAL OPPORTUNITY EMPLOYER

FIGURE 8.16 JOB APPLICATION FORM *(continued on next page)*

Used by permission of North Charles General Hospital, Baltimore, Md.; courtesy of Pat Parker

NAME AND ADDRESS OF SCHOOL	DATES ATTENDED	HIGHEST GRADE COMPLETED	MAJOR	DIPL./DEGREE
Grade or High School				
College				
Graduate				
Vocational or Other Training				

Typing WPM ___________

Shorthand WPM _________

Use Dictating Machine

____

Other Skills or Qualifications: (Office Machines, Professional Registration, Certification, or Licensure)

U.S. Military Service:	Date of Entrance:	Date of Discharge:

Describe your duties in the military:

Are you under 18 years of age? Yes _________ No _________	If not a U.S. Citizen, give visa class, number and expiration date

Health Limitations Please describe:	Do you receive a disability pension? Do you now receive Workman's Compensation?

Have you ever been convicted for any reason other than a minor traffic violation?

If yes, explain and give dates: Yes _________ No _________

*Existence of an arrest or criminal record does not constitute a bar to employment

Please read the following:

1. Under the Maryland law an employer may not require or demand any applicant for employment or prospective employment or any employee to submit to or take a polygraph, lie detector or similar test or examination as a condition of employment or continued employment. Any employer who violates this provision is guilty of a misdemeanor and subject to a fine not to exceed $100.
2. I certify that this information, to the best of my knowledge, is true and I understand that any misrepresentation or willful omission of facts may be cause for immediate dismissal. I understand that I'm subject to pass a physical examination as a conditon of employment.

Signature: ____ Date: ____________________

REMARKS: PERSONNEL OFFICE USE ONLY

DOH: ________________ PEP: ________________ DOB: ________________

TITLE: ____________________________________ M/S: ________________

FTE: ________________ R/N: ________________

PG/S: ________________ SALARY: _________/hr NEW: ________________

VAC: ________________ REPL: ________________

ID: ________________ REQ #: ________________

Figure 8.16 Job Application Form *(continued from previous page)*

Care in structuring of questions included in application forms is important because of federal, state, and perhaps local Equal Employment Opportunity Commission (EEOC) and other laws dealing with age, race, and other types of discrimination practices. (A listing of information which can and cannot be solicited from applicants before an employment decision is made is presented in Figure 8.17.) Figure 8.18, selected equal employment opportunity laws, may assist in recruiting and selecting applicants also.

SUBJECT	LAWFUL PRE-EMPLOYMENT INQUIRIES	UNLAWFUL PRE-EMPLOYMENT INQUIRIES
NAME:	Applicant's full name. Have you ever worked for this company under a different name? Is any additional information relative to a different name necessary to check work record? If yes, explain.	Original name of an applicant whose name has been changed by court order or otherwise. Applicant's maiden name.
ADDRESS OR DURATION OF RESIDENCE:	How long a resident of this state or city?	
BIRTHPLACE:		Birthplace of applicant. Birthplace of applicant's parents, spouse, or other close relatives. Requirement that applicant submit birth certificate, naturalization or baptismal record.
AGE:	*Are you 18 years old or older?	How old are you? What is your date of birth?
RELIGION OR CREED:		Inquiry into an applicant's religious denomination, religious affiliations, church, parish, pastor, or religious holidays observed. An applicant may not be told "This is a Catholic (Protestant or Jewish) organization."
RACE OR COLOR:		Complexion or color of skin.
PHOTOGRAPH:		Requirement that an applicant for employment affix a photograph to an employment application form. Request an applicant, at his or her option, to submit a photograph. Requirement for photograph after interview but before hiring.
HEIGHT:		Inquiry regarding applicant's height.
WEIGHT:		Inquiry regarding applicant's weight.
MARITAL STATUS:		Requirement that an applicant provide any information regarding marital status or children. Are you single or married? Do you have any children? Is your spouse employed? What is your spouse's name?
SEX:		Mr., Miss or Mrs., or an inquiry regarding sex. Inquiry as to the ability to reproduce or advocacy of any form of birth control.

**This question may be asked only for the purpose of determining whether applicants are of legal age for employment.*

FIGURE 8.17 PRE-EMPLOYMENT INQUIRY GUIDE *(continued on next page)*
State of Michigan, Michigan Department of Civil Rights, Lansing, Mich.

Subject	Lawful Pre-Employment Inquiries	Unlawful Pre-Employment Inquiries
HEALTH:	Do you have any impairments, physical, mental, or medical which would interfere with your ability to do the job for which you have applied? Inquiry into contagious or communicable diseases which may endanger others. If there are any positions for which you should not be considered or job duties you cannot perform because of a physical or mental handicap, please explain.	Inquiries regarding an individual's physical or mental condition which are not directly related to the requirements of a specific job and which are used as a factor in making employment decisions in a way which is contrary to the provisions or purposes of the Michigan Handicappers' Civil Rights Act. Requirement that women be given pelvic examinations.
CITIZENSHIP:	Are you a citizen of the United States? If not a citizen of the United States, does applicant intend to become a citizen of the United States? If you are not a United States citizen, have you the legal right to remain permanently in the United States? Do you intend to remain permanently in the United States?	Of what country are you a citizen? Whether an applicant is naturalized or a native-born citizen; the date when the applicant acquired citizenship. Requirement that an applicant produce naturalization papers or first papers. Whether applicant's parents or spouse are naturalized or native born citizens of the United States; the date when such parent or spouse acquired citizenship.
NATIONAL ORIGIN:	Inquiry into languages applicant speaks and writes fluently.	Inquiry into applicant's (a) lineage; (b) ancestry; (c) national origin; (d) descent; (e) parentage, or nationality. Nationality of applicant's parents or spouse. What is your mother tongue? Inquiry into how applicant acquired ability to read, write, or speak a foreign language.
EDUCATION:	Inquiry into the academic, vocational, or professional education of an applicant and the public and private schools attended.	
EXPERIENCE:	Inquiry into work experience. Inquiry into countries applicant has visited.	
ARRESTS:	Have you ever been convicted of a crime? If so, when, where, and nature of offense? Are there any felony charges pending against you?	Inquiry regarding arrests.
RELATIVES:	Names of applicant's relatives, other than a spouse, already employed by this company.	Address of any relative of applicant, other than address (within the United States) of applicant's father and mother, husband or wife and minor dependent children.
NOTICE IN CASE OF EMERGENCY:	Name and address of person to be notified in case of accident or emergency.	Name and address of nearest relative to be notified in case of accident or emergency.
MILITARY EXPERIENCE:	Inquiry into an applicant's military experience in the Armed Forces of the United States or in a State Militia. Inquiry into applicant's service in a particular branch of United States Army, Navy, etc.	Inquiry into an applicant's general military experience.
ORGANIZATIONS:	Inquiry into the organizations of which an applicant is a member excluding organizations, the name or character of which indicates the race, color, religion, national origin, or ancestry of its members.	List all clubs, societies and lodges to which you belong.
REFERENCES:	Who suggested that you apply for a position here?	

Figure 8.17 Pre-Employment Inquiry Guide *(continued from previous page)*

Federal Laws and Executive Orders	Type of Employment Discrimination Prohibited	Employers Covered
Equal Pay Act of 1963	Sex differences in pay, benefits and pension for substantially equal work	Private
Title VII, 1964 Civil Rights Act	Discrimination in all human resource activities based on race, color, sex, religion or national origin, established Equal Employment Opportunity Commission to administer the law	Private; federal, state, and local governments; unions; employment agencies
Executive Order 11478 (1969)	Discrimination based on race, color, religion, sex, national origin, political affiliation, marital status or physical handicap	Federal government
Equal Employment Opportunity Act of 1972	Amended Title VII, made EEOC more power to enforce and extended coverage	Educational institutions, other employers
Vocational Rehabilitation Act of 1973, Executive Order 11914 (1974)	Discrimination based on physical or mental handicap	Federal government and federal contractors
Vietnam Era Veterans Readjustment Act of 1974	Discrimination against disabled veterans and Vietnam veterans	Same as above
Pregnancy Discrimination Act of 1978	Prohibits discrimination in hiring, promoting, or terminating because of pregnancy, pregnancy to be treated as medical disability	Same as Title VII
Age Discrimination in Employment Act of 1967 (as amended in 1986)	Age discrimination against those 40 years of age or older	Private, unions, employment agencies
Americans with Disabilities Act (1990)	Bars discrimination of disabled individuals in hiring and employment	Businesses with over 25 employees; as of 7/26/94 also businesses with 15–24 employees

Figure 8.18 Selected Equal Employment Opportunity Laws
Adapted from Supervision in the Hospitality Industry, 2nd Ed. Miller, J., Porter, M., Drummond, K., p. 160.

The application form is used to screen out applicants who do not meet job specification requirements. It is not intended to be the only selection tool.

There are several advantages to the use of formal job application forms:

a. They test the applicant's ability to read and write English;
b. They provide basic information useful in asking questions in a subsequent employment interview;

c. They indicate the past experiences of the applicant and provide a clue as to whether the current vacancy logically seems to fit within a planned career progression for the applicant;

2. *Check of applicant references.* All references (especially business/professional sources) provided by the applicant should be verified; also, education and/or credentials should be verified. The dietary manager or human resource officer should confirm the accuracy of information contained in the application form and can attempt to "draw out" relevant information about work and personal habits.

Telephone conversations with past employers can help provide information during the screening process. It will take a past employer less time to conduct a telephone conversation than to write a letter, so he/she may be more cooperative. This is also the time when the human resource official or dietary manager can inquire about eligibility for rehire.

Employer references may be more helpful than personal references, since the applicant will probably note only friends or others who may give a uniform, biased, positive recommendation. Past employers, on the other hand, may provide more objective observations. If an employer does provide negative information, it may be helpful to discuss the matter with the applicant; it is possible that, from the applicant's perspective, there is information which should be made known. The applicant can then "tell his or her side of the story."

Applicants who will be handling cash can be bonded. In this case the bonding company provides an application form which must be completed. The bonding company, through its independent background check of the applicant, may uncover information which makes the applicant unbondable without higher bond payment rates . If this is the case, there may be a serious question about the suitability of the applicant for the position. An Applicant Reference Check form is shown in Figure 8.19. It can be used to record comments obtained from past employers when reference checks are made;

3. *Selection tests.* Selection tests are a third potential source of information about job applicants. Formal selection tests are not frequently utilized by small facilities; however, it may be wise to consider use of some physical means to determine an applicant's suitability for employment. Note, for example, that an applicant for a cook's position which requires previous experience might be required to prepare one or more food items using a standardized recipe. An experienced food server can be expected to know how to use portion control tools or to help patients/residents needing assistance with foodservice. These procedures involve little expense and may quickly prove worthwhile when they affirm or question the applicant's statements on the application form and in subsequent interview(s);

4. *Medical exams.* Medical exams provide another source of information about job applicants. Obviously, one's physical health is of critical concern for work in institutional dietary services. Since medical exams cost money (even if they are self-administered by the facility), they are typically a final step in the recruitment/selection process and are only given to those applicants who have met all other standards for employment.

State or other laws may address medical exams (how often they must be administered and minimal requirements for them). For example, in at least one state, medical exams are required initially upon employment and at least once every three years thereafter, and the exam must include a check for tuberculosis. While medical exams are no insurance that a dietary employee is healthy (one can become sick with a cold the day after he/she takes an exam and can contaminate food and other products with which he or she comes in contact), they are probably very cost effective;

Part I. General Information
Name of applicant: ______________________________
Previous employer: ______________ Job Title: ______________
Name of reference: ______________ Title: ______________
Dates worked: ________ to ________ Pay: Start ________ End ________

Part II. Job Information
Duties: ______________________________
____
____

Supervisor's evaluation of work: ______________________________
____
____

Applicant's strengths: ______________________________
____

Applicant's weaknesses: ______________________________
____

Comments, if any, about:
(a) Attendance and punctuality: ______________________________
____

(b) Attitude and character: ______________________________
____

(c) Work habits: ______________________________
____

(d) Relationships with co-workers: ______________________________
____

(e) Other factors: ______________________________
____

Would you rehire? Yes ______ No ______
Expressed reason for leaving: ______________________________
____
____

Part III: Interviewer's Comments
____
____
____
____
____

Date of reference check: ___________
Signature of interviewer: ______________________________

Figure 8.19 Applicant Reference Check

5. Drug testing. Drug testing may be a preemployment requirement for selected positions and required periodically thereafter. This information is worthwhile to a facility for safety and financial reasons.

6. Americans with Disabilities Act (ADA) requirements. This landmark civil rights law states, in part, that employers may not discriminate against an individual with a disability in hiring if he or she is otherwise qualified for the job. This law, including implications for selection, is discussed in depth later in this chapter.

The Interview Process

Much information about job applicants can be gained from application forms, reference checks, selection tests, and medical exams. However, one or more pre-employment job interviews are also essential to match the "right" employee with a job vacancy.

A preliminary or screening interview should be conducted by the human resources department or top-level administrator in order to assess the attitudes of the applicant and to inform him or her about the facility, the dietary operation, and the job itself. It is also used to obtain additional information to determine which applicants should be considered further.

If the dietary manager and/or immediate supervisor is not involved in the preliminary interview, he or she should be involved in an interview with the applicant before the final selection decision is made. The purpose should be to assess, from the perspective of the manager who will be directly supervising the applicant, the abilities, attitudes, and compatibility of the applicant for the position. It is very important that the immediate supervisor be involved in the applicant selection process; the interview provides a formalized opportunity for this to occur. Figure 8.20 assists the interviewer with appropriate questions. [*Note:* The basic principles of interviewing applicants for vacant positions are also useful in interviewing employees for problem-solving, disciplining, performance appraisal, and other purposes.)

An interview is really a planned conversation. As such, some planning is required about the direction the interview should take. An interview between an official of the facility and the job applicant is really a specialized kind of information interview. Each party needs to obtain information from the other; an interview provides a format for this information transfer.

Often, there are three separate interviews utilized during the recruitment/screening process. A second selection interview may be used to reduce the number of applicants to two or three of the most eligible applicants. At this point, there may be a third interview by a personnel department or top-level administrative official, the dietary manager, and, if applicable, the immediate supervisor. Figure 8.21 provides additional interviewing tips.

There are two basic types of interviews: directive and non-directive. A directive interview requires the interviewer to ask specific questions formulated in advance and followed in almost checklist fashion. Questions asked should solicit important information. Examples of directive interview questions include: What did you do in your last job? Why did you leave your last position? Why do you want to work in this facility? What do you think are your three most important strengths and weaknesses? Directive interview questions solicit facts and do not seek opinions or subjective responses to questions. All topics of directive questions should directly impact on how the applicant views the job and on matters relevant to the job. Any other questions may be in violation of EEOC or other laws.

Figure 8.22 lists additional questions for directive interviews typically asked in employment interviews. Some questions may be more important than others and can be given additional weight as responses are considered. Frequently, the interviewer can record responses to questions as they are given, and in many directive interviews the interviewer may speak almost as much as the interviewee.

When directive interviews are used, it is important that the job applicant be given time to ask questions and that the interviewer provide basic information about the job.

The second type of interview is non-directive. While questions are also planned and perhaps written down in advance, they are less structured and more open-ended so that the interviewee can provide creative responses. Examples of open-ended questions include: Why do you think you'll like this job? What elements do you consider important when you consider a new position?

In addition to asking the initial question, many interviewers like to use responses given as a springboard for additional questions. With this approach, the interviewer can go in depth to find out "where the applicant is coming from."

1. Why did you choose to interview with our company?
2. Describe your ideal job.
3. What can you offer us?
4. Where do you want to be in five years? ten years?
5. Do you plan to return to school for further education?
6. What skills have you developed?
7. Did you work while going to school? In what positions?
8. What did you enjoy most about your last employment?
9. What did you enjoy least about your last employment?
10. What did you learn from these college work experiences?
11. Have you ever quit a job? Why?
12. Why should we hire you rather than another candidate?
13. Why did you choose your major?
14. What do you consider to be your greatest strengths?
15. Can you name some weaknesses?
16. Do you prefer to work under supervision or on your own?
17. Would you be successful working on a team?
18. Of which three accomplishments are you most proud?
19. In which campus activities did you participate?
20. Have you ever dropped a class? Why?
21. Why did you select your college or university?
22. What do you know about our company (product or service)?
23. Which college classes did you like the best? Why?
24. Which college classes did you like the least? Why?
25. Who are your role models?
26. Do you think you received a good education at ______________________?
27. What is your overall GPA? What is your major GPA?
28. Do your grades accurately reflect your ability?
29. Were you financially responsible for any portion of your college education?
30. Have you worked under deadline pressure? When?
31. Are you able to work on several assignments at once?
32. Do you prefer large or small companies? Why?
33. How do you feel about working in a structured environment?
34. How do you feel about working overtime?
35. How do you feel about travel?
36. How do you feel about the possibility of relocation?
37. Do you have any hobbies?
38. What problems have you solved in your previous positions?
39. Are you willing to work flextime?
40. Have you ever done any volunteer work? What?
41. Define success. Failure.
42. Have you ever had any failures?
43. How does your college education or work experience relate to this job?
44. How did you get along with your former professors (supervisors and co-workers)?
45. How many classes did you miss because of illness or personal business?
46. What are your ideas on salary?
47. Tell me about yourself.
48. Do you have any computer experience?
49. Have you ever spoken to a group of people? How large?
50. Would you be willing to take a drug test?

FIGURE 8.20 FREQUENTLY ASKED INTERVIEW QUESTIONS
Source: CRS Recruitment Publications/Cass Communications, Inc., Evanston, Illinois.

Interviewing Tips

When you interview a prospective employee, you are indirectly setting the tone for the relationship that may follow if that individual is hired by your organization. The interview serves as recruitment tool and public relations opportunity, and can ultimately be construed as a legally binding description of both the job opportunity and your company's own value system (or lack of it).

The following interviewing tips are also adapted from a more extensive section on this subject in St. Francis Hospital's guidebook for employees, *Interviewing Guidelines, Strategies, and Mechanics.*

- Respect a candidate's feelings and self-esteem at all times. Strive to put the candidate at ease.
- Begin with pleasant, professional introduction and appropriate "light" conversation.
- Remember that the interview is a public relations tool, as well as an assessment of past performance and future potential. To the candidate, *you* are the organization.
- Don't give excessive encouragement verbally or non-verbally at any point.
- Examine candidate evidence in areas of:
  - Past performance and achievement
  - Work philosophies and beliefs
  - Interview behavior
- Use verbal rejoinders to trigger additional response in crucial areas, such as "Tell me more . . .", "Give me another example," etc.
- Use nonverbal reminders, such as nodding, facial gestures, etc. to maintain a steady flow of information.
- Take notes as needed and in a natural sequence. Don't make a final appraisal of notes until the interview is concluded.
- If you don't see a desired characteristic, ask for it specifically; if it is still not apparent, score the interview accordingly.
- Make yourself thoroughly knowledgeable about the candidate prior to the interview and use that knowledge throughout it.
- Portray the available position adequately and accurately; question candidate to determine specific qualifications.
- Have a set questioning precess prepared prior to the interview; seek specific data to match against the job description.
- Don't wander into EEOC-sensitive information unless you are seeking BFOQ—Bona Fide Occupational Qualifications. Avoid areas such as age, race, marital status, and any other sensitive areas unless information is volunteered by candidate.
- Let the candidate do the majority of the talking.
- Maintain an overall limited emotional profile and avoid emotive reactions.
- Listen attentively, accurately and actively.
- Postpone all *final* judgments until after the interview.
- Interrupt the candidate only when necessary, and then with tact and brevity.
- Call the candidate by first name, appropriate title, or preferred nickname—whichever enhances comfort and flow.
- Ask candidate for permission to take notes or merely inform candidate you will do so.
- Control excessive applicant rambling by introducing the next question or a rejoinder.
- Ensure the candidate answers a question at hand completely before moving on to another area.

FIGURE 8.21 Interviewing Tips
Source: *Food Management,* April 1996

Frequently, one can discover much about an applicant when a non-directive interview is used. Applicants left to speak on their own will usually provide much more information than is given to "yes" or "no" questions.

Use of situational interview questions is increasing since they have proven to be effective in determining which candidate will be compatible with the department.

1. Interviewer should provide basic information about:
   - A. ○ Working hours and location
   - B. ○ Equipment applicant will use
   - C. ○ General information about the facility
   - D. ○ General information about the dietary department
   - E. ○ Most important policies and procedures which impact on applicant's work
   - F. ○ Nature of the work environment
   - G. ○ Other information considered important
2. Specific questions to ask applicant:
   - A. ○ How does your past experience apply to this position?
   - B. ○ How does this job match your interest in the job?
   - C. ○ What skills do you have which will help in this job?
   - D. ○ How much judgment do you think is necessary to perform this job?
   - E. ○ What are your main strengths for this job?
   - F. ○ What major weaknesses will need to be overcome for you to do this job adequately?
   - G. ○ How do you think your performance in this job should be measured?
   - H. ○ Will you have any problems getting to work?
   - I. ○ What other information can you provide which will help me to understand your capabilities for this work?
   - J. ○ What are your thoughts about this facility?
   - K. ○ What questions do you have about the job?
   - L. ○ When would you be able to begin work?

FIGURE 8.22 SAMPLE FORMAT FOR DIRECTIVE INTERVIEWS
Used by permission of McLaren General Hospital, Flint, Mich.

These questions ask a candidate to describe a type of situation and their decisions and/or actions. Some examples are listed below:

- Tell me about a time when you knew a co-worker was not following work procedures and what you decided to do.
- Describe a personal conflict that you had with a co-worker and tell me how you solved it.
- If you knew someone was dishonest or stealing, what would you do?
- Can you think of a time when you disagreed with a company policy? Tell me what you decided to do.
- If you saw an unsafe situation, what would you do?

This type of interview question is used in second and third interviews to select, from three qualified candidates, the one who will be most compatible (long-term employee) and effective in work teams.

There is much more to an interview than just asking questions. The interviewer must properly prepare for it. A private environment free from interruptions is best. Set a beginning time—and stick to it. Read over the application form and any other information available about the applicant. Provide enough time so that information can be solicited without the need to rush. Review the checklist of questions which you will ask and be sure that all questions are directly relevant to the selection decision.

Some basic principles help develop good interview techniques. The applicant should be put at ease. He or she is likely to be nervous, so a small amount of beginning conversation (about the weather, the local sports team, or current events) can be helpful in developing the relationship necessary for a good interview. A friendly handshake, a hospitable greeting, and perhaps a cup of coffee are always good ways to start.

Once the interview begins, ask simple questions first. If an outline has been developed, stick with it. Be aware of the time and don't allow yourself to get rushed. *Listen* to what is being said. While this seems obvious, an interviewer sometimes listens with a bias or is thinking about other things and the "real" message of the interviewee is lost. When the interviewee is speaking, don't be thinking about the next question you will ask. Also, don't be so busy writing that you miss clues about additional questions or the "real" meaning of the applicant's words.

Remember that the purpose of the interview is to get—and give—information. It is not to "editorialize" about remarks made or to give your own impressions or attitudes. Remain neutral; if an applicant believes you have a positive or negative bias, he or she may pick up on it and give a response that you want to hear.

Don't ask leading questions (such as, "You would like to work here, wouldn't you?"). Questions of this nature are useless and contribute nothing to the process.

Follow-up after the interview is necessary. If you are certain at the conclusion of the interview that the applicant will not be considered further, let him or her know. Perhaps there is another vacant position for which the interviewee will be eligible. Put yourself in the interviewee's place. Wouldn't you like to know about the interview results as soon as possible? If you believe the applicant is qualified but want to interview others, it is fair to tell the interviewee that also. Give a time by which you will let him/her know about your selection decision. Adhere to the schedule—or apprise the interviewee of the revised date for the decision. If you believe the interviewee is qualified and you have no other applicants to consider, you may inform the interviewee that a job will be offered. Regardless of the outcome of the interview, let the interviewee know how you feel.

We have noted basic principles that should be followed during an employment—or any other type of—interview. Now let's look at some problems which should be avoided:

1. Remember the "halo effect" (hiring people like yourself); don't let your personal biases influence decisions about the interviewee;
2. Don't be rushed; if you are not prepared for an interview or feel pressure to make a decision immediately, you are likely to obtain incorrect or incomplete information about the applicant;
3. Don't make unreasonable comparisons; for example, if you compare an applicant with another employee with many years of experience, perhaps no applicant will be judged acceptable. The comparison which *is* necessary involves comparing the job applicant with the job specification and with your understanding of his or her ability to perform required work;
4. Follow principles of effective interviewing; if you fail to follow the principles discussed in this section, your interview may be ineffective;
5. Don't oversell your facility or the job; many of us may feel very strongly about our institution. An unreasonable buildup may initially excite the applicant—who will then discover unforeseen problems when the job begins. Always tell the truth and let the applicant make decisions based upon a fair and reasonable assessment;
6. Don't omit important information; tell the applicant everything he or she should know to make a decision;
7. Leave the applicant with a good impression about your facility; if a job will be offered, this is obviously important. Even if you will not be offering a job, the

applicant is likely to be a member of the community and will have feelings about the facility;

8. Don't ask discriminating questions; be aware that EEOC and other applicable laws have a definite impact upon the type of questions that can and cannot be asked. Be sure that all questions you propose to ask are cleared by officials with current knowledge of applicable laws, and be careful not to violate these laws.

Computer-assisted interviews provide an interesting "high-tech" approach to applicant interviewing. After completing an application form, interviewees respond to a series of questions displayed on the monitor of a personal computer. Questions posed can relate to those asked on the application form itself and/or to matters involving knowledge tests based upon experience, psychological, attitudinal, and other matters. A printout provided to the interviewer indicates:

- Inconsistencies, if any, between information cited on the application and provided during the computerized response process;
- Answers for which additional information may be solicited. For example, if an applicant indicated "trouble on a previous job" follow-up information may be desired;
- Implications about honesty, work habits, and other issues identified by other questions.

Computer-assisted interviews are not likely to replace the human element in the process. Rather, they are designed to provide the interviewer with additional information that can be helpful in posing and analyzing questions/information relevant to an applicant's qualifications.

The Selection Decision

As a result of obtaining applicant information, one or two applicants may remain as prime candidates. Who should be offered the position? Typically, this decision is made by considering the views of the human resource department (in large facilities) and/or top-level administrators (in small facilities) and those of the dietary manager. It is very important that the latter be consulted. If the new employee will be supervised by someone other than the dietary manager, this supervisor's input should also be solicited. These concerned officials can review applicant information, consider the relevance of pre-employment training and education, determine the extent to which previous experience will be helpful and, in general, try to match the applicant with the position being filled.

In many instances the "right" applicant will not be perfect for the job. It then becomes a matter of considering the strengths and weaknesses of each final candidate to determine the one best qualified. While some dietary managers and others believe that they have a "knack" for picking the best applicant, a thorough review of available information and earnest discussions with other affected staff members are always in order.

The selection decision is important. Significant time and money will be spent in properly orienting and training even entry-level staff members. These costs are higher when management positions are filled. Many times, facilities with high turnover rates can trace problems to incorrect procedures and inadequate decisions made at the time of recruitment and selection.

All information developed from the recruitment and selection process should be maintained on file in the new employee's personnel records. Sometimes reasons why other applicants were not selected may also be important. (For example, many facilities earnestly attempt to recruit and hire minority employees, and records to support this search are important.) Documentation of information is very important and must be emphasized as permanent files are developed.

A final step in the recruitment/selection process is to notify promptly those applicants who will not be made an offer. They have a right to know about your decision so that they can make other personal and professional plans. The need to recognize that the public relations image of the facility is important even at time of recruitment and selection of new staff members has already been emphasized.

Employee Labor Control

Dietary managers know that labor costs are one of the two largest categories of operating expenses (food costs are, of course, the other). They must consider minimum quality requirements for work, develop performance standards, incorporate these requirements into a staffing guide, and use this information to schedule personnel.

Performance Standards

Performance standards are specific statements of job tasks and the required skill level for each. A group of related job tasks could be the focus of a training meeting, for example, sanitation.

What can a dietary manager do if performance standards are not met? One alternative may be to schedule more labor hours to perform required work. Labor costs are likely to increase but, at the same time, the quality of work output may improve. It becomes important for dietary managers first to define the minimum quality requirements for work to be done and then to schedule labor as efficiently as possible. As this process is followed, the dietary manager can make great efforts to satisfy both the clients' desires and the facility's concern for costs.

Let's see how quality makes a difference. Suppose that, in one facility, an extensive amount of prepared convenience foods is used and that no choice is given to residents/patients. The amount of production labor required to produce meals in this facility will be less than in a facility where all items are prepared "from scratch," and clients are given a choice of two or three items in each menu category (entree, vegetable, dessert, etc.) in each meal period. Of course, one cannot generalize that the quality of food production and service will be higher in the latter facility, but the quality standards are different and, therefore, separate standards must be assessed for each facility.

Dietary managers should carefully consider minimum quality requirements and closely examine how well these requirements are incorporated into work done. The supervisor may notice problems. His or her employees and, in fact, top-level administrators and others may also be able to identify areas where quality expectations are not consistently met. This type of self-analysis can set the foundation for development of productivity requirements.

Labor costs must be controlled—but not at the expense of quality. Ask the question, "Given a minimum level of quality, how can labor costs be most effectively controlled?" One popular approach is to establish performance standards and procedures to be followed as employees work. These procedures can then be considered when time requirements to undertake work assignments are established.

For example, experience may indicate that 16 hours of assistant cook labor are needed when 75 percent of the beds in the facility are occupied; only 12 labor hours may be necessary when 60 percent of the beds are occupied. These standard labor hours represent the allowable time to do work according to pre-established quality levels. If performance standards can be established for all positions, it is possible to develop staffing guides which incorporate productivity and quality requirements.

[*Note:* Some labor is "fixed"; the number of labor hours will not vary according to the number of meals to be produced and/or the number of clients to be served. For example, if the cash cafeteria line is open for three hours, it is likely that one cashier will be necessary for the entire period. Above some level determined by the property, additional cashier hours may be necessary for "peak periods." Likewise, regardless of whether the facility will serve one meal or many more, one cook will be required for a minimum number of hours. After some point, additional cook hours will be necessary. The staffing and scheduling procedures discussed in this chapter apply to those labor hours required above the fixed minimum number of hours necessary for the facility to operate.]

Three essentials are necessary in producing an effective performance standard system. Employee participation comes first as the worker frequently knows the job to be done better than the dietary manager. In fact, the employee may set a higher performance standard than the manager would have set. As you know, the employee who assists in the particulars, including goal setting, job responsibilities and performance evaluations, is going to work harder, feel recognized and contribute to the well being of the whole, so important to good morale.

Second is positive supervisory leadership and support by management at all levels. The dietary manager, of course, is responsible for the procedures and standards of performance, but how flexible he or she is to the concerns of employees is important. Specifying performance standards must be a result of joint acceptance of the work and responsibility for accomplishing it.

The final essential is the reward system designed and implemented. Employees will be motivated if they sense a fair reward is given based on merit. Hard workers do not wish to see those less motivated being equally rewarded. He or she exceeding the standards set should receive the promotion, raise, better hours, etc. Even if material recognition is not possible, a word of praise, a handshake or similar note of thanks can be as meaningful to the deserving employee.

There is an order of steps to develop a performance standard system as seen in Figure 8.23. A performance standard is to be developed for each unit of the work. The first step is to define the purpose for which the standards are to be used. Once the purpose has been defined, the next step is to analyze the job and break it down into units. The unit is the "what" of the objective. The tasks become the "hows" that make up the standard procedures. When a standard has been added for each unit, a performance standard is complete.

Often it is appropriate to define three levels of performance: an ideal level, a realistic level, and a minimum level. An ideal level describes how a fantastic crew would do the work. A realistic level is an estimate of what constitutes a competent job and the way good steady employees are doing it now. A minimum level is rock bottom—below this level is unacceptable.

It is best to write performance standards for a realistic level. A minimum level sets the standard for trainees or new employees during their first week on the job. An ideal level is appropriate for the high achiever who is not challenged by a goal that is too easy. High level achievement must be rewarded if you want that kind of effort to continue.

The fourth step is to develop standard procedures. The procedures state what a person must do to achieve the results, and tell the employee exactly how things are to be done in the facility.

The next step is developing a training program with a training objective for each standard. Each training objective will have a time limit or other measurable criteria included in each required performance standard. The results of the training will be tested.

The final test is to evaluate employee performance on the job using the performance standards. This first evaluation is a test of both the employees and the system so far. If the employee rates below standard, the dietary manager has to diagnose the trouble. Is the standard too high? Are the procedures confusing, misleading, or impossible to carry out? Or is it the employee? If it is the employee, what corrective action does he or she need? If the employee is far below standard in everything, is there hope for improvement, or should the employee be terminated?

Once a performance standard system is used and adjusted if needed, a permanent set of instruments is in place for describing jobs, defining a fair day's work for

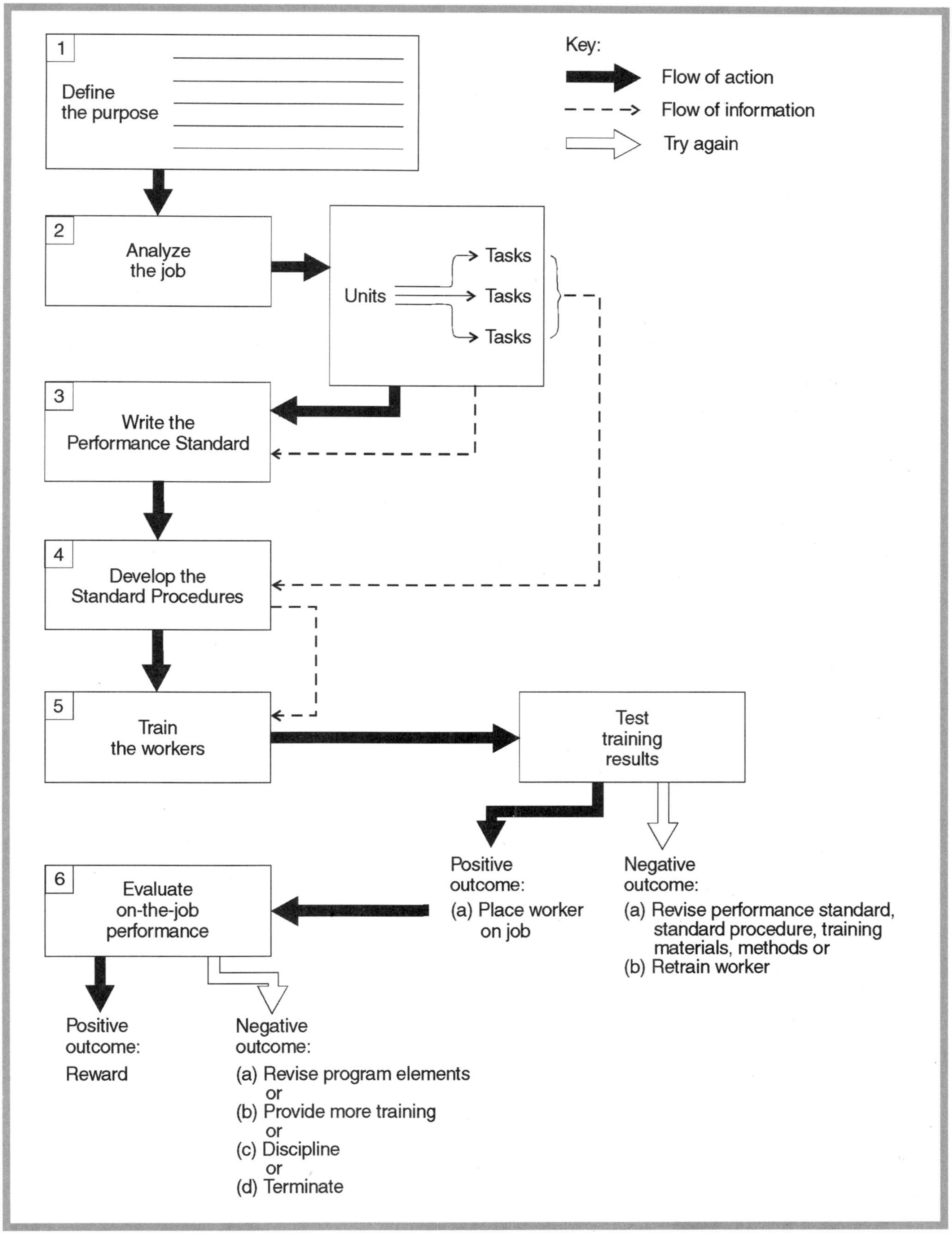

FIGURE 8.23 FLOW CHART FOR DEVELOPING A PERFORMANCE STANDARD SYSTEM

From Miller, Jack, Mary Porter and Karen Eich Drummond. *Supervision in the Hospitality Industry.* John Wiley & Sons, Inc. 1992. p. 131.

each job, training employees to standards, evaluating performance, and rewarding achievement.

After performance standards are developed, they can be incorporated into a staffing guide. In many facilities, the number of meals to be produced daily does not vary significantly. The staffing guide need only list, by position, the number of labor hours needed each day. In other facilities, a different number of meals will be produced. In this instance, the staffing guide will need to be developed over a range of client meals to be produced. Once a staffing guide is developed, it can be utilized to schedule employees.

Writing Work Performance Objectives

A performance standard is a concise statement made up of three elements that together describe the way a unit of work is to be carried out in a given operation. The essential features are:

- Describe the work to be done
- Identify how it is to be done
- Specify the speed, quality, amount or accuracy required

For example, if the first unit on a server list is "stocks serving station," this abbreviated description could become more precise by limiting the scope of the work sequence and specify the quality and time. The resulting performance standard: "The server will stock the serving station for one serving area for one meal as described in the Service Station Procedures. The server will stock the station completely and correctly in 15 minutes or less."

The following criteria must be followed in developing performance standards:

1. The statement must be specific, clear, complete, and accurate. It should tell the employee exactly what you want. There should be nothing that is confusing or could be misunderstood.
2. The standard must be measurable or observable behavior. "Good" and "well" are subjective terms; use "correct" and "accurate" in writing a performance standard. Examples: The tray delivered is correct if it is what the client requested. The cook follows recipes accurately, which is reflected in inventory quantities. The supervisor will use this standard to evaluate the employee's work performance.
3. It must be within the physical and mental capabilities of the employees and job conditions. If expectations are unrealistic, the manager should reexamine the standard.
4. The standard must adhere to company policies, company goals, and applicable legal and moral constraints. It should not require illegal acts of an employee.
5. Standards should have a time period set for achievement.

Writing performance standards can be the most challenging part of developing a performance standard system. The process is valuable since it makes expectations clear. Review figure 8.24 for a further discussion on developing procedures.

Scheduling Employee Hours

The staffing guide discussed above can be used for scheduling labor hours. It answers the question, "How many labor hours will be needed for each position, given the number of meals I anticipate serving?" The variable labor staffing guide indicates the number of labor hours which can be scheduled for each position, given the forecast of meals to be served. If, for example, it is estimated that 200 patients/residents will be served next Tuesday, the schedule planner can refer to the staffing guide, assess the number of allowable labor hours for this number of meals, and then schedule accordingly.

Developing Procedures

Standard procedures state what a person must do to achieve the results—they give the instructions for the action. They tell the worker exactly how things are supposed to be done in the establishment. They are developed by spelling out, step by step, each task of each unit in a given job. There may be many tasks involved to describe precisely how to carry out that unit of the job.

There are various means of presenting the materials that make up each procedure: individual procedure sheets, pages in a procedural manual, diagrams, filmstrips, videotapes, slides, and photographs. It depends on what will be easier to understand and what will best meet the requirements of the individual standard. The important thing is to have them in some form of accessible record so that they can be referred to in cases of doubt or disagreement, and so that the trainers can train workers correctly.

When evaluating a written policy, whether it's a new one or one that's being revised or updated, the following guidelines should be applied:

- The policy should be neither too broad nor too narrow. It should establish standards that can be met.
- Staff members who will be affected by a policy should be involved in writing or revising it.
- Policies should be reviewed periodically, preferably once a year, and outdated ones revised to reflect current practice.
- Inservices on all new or rewritten policies and procedures should always be provided, with attendance mandatory and documented.
- Once staff members receive training in a particular procedure, they should be held responsible for following it.
- Copies of all applicable policies and procedures should be easily accessible, so they can be consulted as needed.

The reward for diligence will be policies that protect rather than imperil.

Figure 8.24 Developing Procedures

When the number of standard labor hours noted on the staffing guide is not exceeded, dietary managers have some assurance that personnel worked efficiently. Specific procedures for using the staffing guide to schedule labor hours include:

1. **Set a time frame for scheduling personnel.** For example, some dietary managers may do their schedules each Monday for the following two weeks (Monday-Sunday). Personnel in other facilities may develop schedules for a longer or shorter time period, but the need for a routine procedure is important;
2. **Estimate the number of patients/residents to be served.** Since the staffing guide has been developed by planning the range of meals normally served for a specific meal period, the estimated number of meals must be known. Meal count information (which is also used to order food, schedule salaried labor, etc.) will be helpful;
3. **Schedule labor hours on the basis of number of meals forecast.** For example, if 250 clients are expected next Thursday and if the standard labor hour staffing guide indicates that 18 hours of dishwasher labor are necessary, then

18 labor hours are scheduled. If fewer than 18 labor hours are scheduled, the quality of cleanup, quantity of cleaning, etc. may decrease because personnel will be rushed. If more than 18 labor hours are scheduled, employees will not work efficiently; labor costs will be higher and efficiency will be lower than permitted by the labor performance standards expressed in the staffing guide. In this example, the 18 hours can be allocated as necessary. (For example, one dishwasher may work six hours, finishing lunch cleanup and covering the early part of the evening shift; another dishwasher might work six hours, coming in when the dinner period begins and staying to close; a third employee might work six hours, being available for the busy period.) Regardless of how the 18 labor hours are "shuffled," labor is controlled if the number of meals actually forecast are served and if the number of standard labor hours is not exceeded.

Techniques for Schedule Writing

Dietary managers should use several principles when scheduling personnel.

1. **Schedule staff to fit work needs.** It is *not* generally useful for all staff to begin and end shifts at the same time. They should be scheduled as the volume of work requires. (This is called "staggered scheduling.") For example, one dishwasher might be scheduled to begin work one hour before the evening meal period begins. This time may be used to clean up any remaining dishes from lunch and get ready for the dinner period. A second service employee might be brought in one-half hour before the time of service to perform other duties. (Both employees will be ready for the evening rush period.) Other personnel would be scheduled through a process which provides the required number of staff for the volume of meals to be served at different hours. The first employee in will be the first employee to leave; staggered ending times are also important to assure maximum worker efficiency.
2. **Use creative schedule plans.** Since work flow may not be constant and there is frequently less "rush" time than "normal" or "slow" time, personnel should be scheduled accordingly. Since "staggered" scheduling frequently reduces necessary labor hours, there is less need for full-time personnel. Priority should normally be given, however, to full-time personnel for key management positions.

   To the extent that there are insufficient management tasks for a full-time position, perhaps a title such as "Head" Dishwasher can be developed: a full-time job is made up of management tasks and the non-management task of dishwashing. Salary or wages can be set on the basis of reasonable pay for all the work performed so that both the dietary operation and the employee can benefit from the arrangement.

   Part-time staff can be hired to work short shifts (3/4/5-hour periods). If some of these staff members want longer hours, perhaps a split shift (two short shifts in one day separated by a nonworking time period) can be arranged. Temporary employees can also be used. Many facilities have names of people who don't want "steady" work but who do like to work occasionally. If there is a special event, employee illness, or other need for temporary assistance, these personnel can be very helpful.
3. **Consider personnel preferences whenever possible.** "Schedule Request" forms may be used by personnel for indicating in advance those days/shifts when they wish to be off duty. Dietary officials should honor these requests when possible.
4. **Review policies, if any, applicable to employee scheduling.** There may be policies relating to a need to rotate arrival times of staff members or kitchen cleanup tasks at closing times, and so on.
5. **Past experience in allocating labor hours to each employee generally provides the best basis for scheduling personnel.**

Informing Employees About Their Schedules

When the schedule worksheets have been developed, the hours to be worked by each employee are known. The hours for each person should be posted onto an Employee Schedule, which is then provided for employee review and use. An employee schedule indicates the days and hours of each shift that each employee in the "cook" position will work for an entire week. An employee can develop personal plans around the posted work schedule.

The total of all labor hours scheduled for all employees in the position should not exceed the hours planned on the schedule worksheet.

Dietary managers and employees know that things do not always go according to plans; persons become ill or "no-show," or volumes of meals to be produced require more or fewer hours to be scheduled. The written, posted schedule is an attempt to provide employees with the best possible advance notice of their work shift requirements. Dietary managers must continually seek employee cooperation in complying with posted schedules. Policies regarding "on-call" staff may be useful to "protect" the property when personal problems reduce the number of employees available.

Scheduling Salaried Personnel

Management tasks such as record-keeping, purchasing, work scheduling, and so on can often be scheduled during non-peak production periods. During busy times, managers must normally be free to perform supervisory and operational duties.

Salaried personnel may perform tasks that waged personnel might otherwise perform if overtime would otherwise need to be paid to a waged employee. Union rules or agreements may impact on this. There may also be a need for hourly-paid managers who are required as production volume increases beyond specified levels.

[*Caution:* Normally, salaried personnel should be scheduled when they are needed to perform work required by their job descriptions; do not consider them as personnel "who can work any time for any length of time because they don't cost any more." Efficiency, attitudes, and abilities are all affected by the length of the work week. Top-level turnover can often be traced to these types of problems.]
Some scheduling concerns for salaried personnel include:

1. Consider salaried personnel's preferences in schedules when possible;
2. Develop responsibilities, tasks, and volume of work which managers are to do first; schedule waged personnel to perform those tasks which managers are not to perform. In other words, schedule waged personnel "around the base" of work initially assigned to salaried personnel;
3. While dietary managers must "know how to do everything," back-up plans (as when a cook doesn't come in) should not necessarily be "have the manager do it";
4. A basic general rule for scheduling salaried personnel should be to determine what they should do (per the job description) and schedule them in a way that permits time to do the required tasks;
5. Tasks of salaried personnel must be considered in analyses of work for development of staffing guides.

Controlling Overtime

What is overtime? Overtime refers to time worked in excess of the allowable amount beyond which laws require payment of one and a half times the hourly rate for every hour worked. If, for example, applicable laws require the payment of time and a half when more than 40 hours are worked within seven consecutive days, a dietary employee paid $8 per hour and working for 44 hours would receive an overtime payment of $16 (four hours overtime at $4 per hour = $16) in addition to the $32 of regular pay for the additional four hours.

Overtime of this type is very expensive and must be minimized. If it occurs frequently, ineffective schedules are being developed, the number of meals and/or amount of work to be undertaken are inaccurately estimated, or perhaps both of these problems are occurring.

Some employees are exempt from overtime pay. Employees who meet the following tests can be exempt from the overtime provisions of the Wage and Hour Law as executives:

1. They must supervise two or more other employees;
2. Their salary must be the minimum amount determined by the Wage and Hour Division (which changes periodically);
3. They must have the power to hire and fire or their recommendations must carry significant weight;
4. Their primary duty must be managing: they can't do non-exempt work more than 40 percent of the time in any given workweek. Generally, they can't do the work of the people they supervise. They must be able to exercise discretionary powers and set policies on the job. Often only the department manager can set policies within that department, and all others follow those policies. If so, only one person in a department is usually considered exempt as an executive. However, the Wage and Hour Division has recently been interpreting this rule to allow an assistant manager who is working on an entirely different shift from the manager to be exempt if the other requirements are met.

In addition, an exempt employee who earns more than $250 a week may perform work not directly related to the exempt executive status as long as it doesn't exceed 50 percent of the working time.

Another commonly used exemption is for "administrator." An administrative employee performs office or non-manual work which must directly assist an executive. It must be done only under general supervision; the bulk of the work must be specialized or technical, requiring special training, experience or knowledge. The worker must be able to make discretionary judgments and must not perform non-exempt work more than 40 percent of the work week.

There is another type of overtime which is also expensive to the facility—and which also must be avoided: time worked by an employee above the hours scheduled. If, for example, a staff member is scheduled to work 36 hours but works additional hours, there is a problem with the labor control system. Unless there are acceptable and explainable reasons, overtime hours, even if not compensated at a higher-than-normal rate, mean that planned labor costs will be exceeded.

The dietary manager should require advance approval for any overtime to be scheduled. Schedule writers use the staffing guide to determine the allowable number of labor hours which can be scheduled. Then the schedule would be developed. If hours in excess of those permitted by the staffing guide are to be scheduled, the schedule writer would have to receive advance approval. This might occur when a new employee is being scheduled for training or work activities not covered by the staffing guide (such as a unique catering event) are being planned. If top-level officials agreed with the schedule, they could certify advance approval. Unless this approval was received, supervisors would be held responsible for all overtime.

Managing Employee Turnover

Employee turnover is all too common in many dietary operations. Some employees leave the job for explainable reasons such as relocation, graduation, and retirement. Other turnover is welcomed, such as occurs when staff members are terminated. Most frequently, however, turnover occurs for unknown reasons and, from the dietary manager's perspective, is undesired.

Turnover is expensive, even for entry-level positions. How much does it cost to recruit, select, orient, and train new employees? What is the cost of lowered productivity caused by the "old" employee, after the termination decision is made and before employment ends, and time required by the "learning curve" for the new employee?

Operations are disrupted as the "rookie" must be taught on the job and as employee teams are affected. Clearly, procedures to control undesired turnover must be a priority for all dietary managers.

Controllable turnover occurs when someone leaves a place of employment to assume another position because the current job does not provide job satisfaction. Much turnover occurs early in employment and happens because of mistakes made during recruitment/selection or early job experiences—or both. Principles of supervision discussed throughout this chapter, then, address the turnover issue.

Frequently, several factors individually or in combination lead to turnover:

- Lack of opportunities for professional growth and development;
- Lack of effective supervision;
- Inadequate levels of trust between the employee and the supervisor;
- Lack of participative opportunities;
- Perceived subjectivity and inequality regarding how employees are treated;
- Improper use of human relations principles;
- Low compensation.

Procedures that address the above problems can significantly reduce turnover within the department. Use of appropriate employment tests can help assure that the "right" employee is hired. Use of basic principles of supervision discussed throughout this book help to reduce job dissatisfaction. Fair compensation and human resource benefit programs are also of help. Use of attitude surveys, team-building sessions and provision of adequate professional development activities are relevant. Exit interviews to discover why employees leave help identify problems which can then be addressed by the dietary manager.

One "no-cost" strategy which can also be helpful is to ask the following question: "How would I like to be treated if I were an employee here?" Often the answer may identify areas where supervision or other problems exist. Once identified, the dietary manager can undertake corrective action to help make the job and the job environment more conducive to higher levels of satisfaction.

How can employees "mesh" their personal concerns with the goals of the facility? Answers to this question, which identify ways that personal goals can be attained at the same time organizational goals addressed, are also part of the "recipe" for managing employee turnover.

Determining Actual Labor Hours

Development and use of the staffing guide will help to control labor hours and costs. The actual number of labor hours incurred must also be known:

1. For administrative and financial purposes. Payroll for waged personnel is based upon the number of actual labor hours worked. Information generated is also necessary for financial statements, operating budgets, and so on;
2. To assess the effectiveness of the labor control system. Actual results are compared with standard plans, and corrective action is taken when there is a variance between the two.

The assessment of actual labor begins with use of a weekly labor hour report. This form is used to collect information about the actual number of labor hours worked by all personnel within the dietary department. The form is completed in the following manner:

1. The supervisor of each section records the number of actual hours worked daily by each employee during the week;

2. If the actual reported hours are to be used as the basis for payroll purposes, they should be verified with time cards or other source documents;
3. The total number of weekly planned (standard) labor hours scheduled for each employee should also be entered on the form. This information can be transferred to the form by the supervisor as employee schedules are written. Reasons for differences, if any, between actual and standard labor hours worked for each position during the week should be written on the form.

The completed form should be reviewed by the appropriate administrator to assess the extent to which standard labor hour goals were met and to plan for corrective action, if necessary.

Payroll Information Systems

It is very important that hours worked by waged employees be accurately reported. Use of a time clock is probably the best method, although a "sign-in log" or "hours worked review form" completed by the dietary manager or supervisor may be acceptable in small operations. Regardless of the method, accuracy is necessary since information is used as the basis for determining (a) wages earned and (b) whether corrective action is necessary to bring labor productivity into line with plans.

Payroll systems can be of two types: manual and automated. A manual payroll system involves processing of payroll information "by hand." The source of the information can be a time clock or "hours worked" reports completed by managers. Information about the hours worked by waged employees can be taken directly from the weekly labor hour report, which tells the actual number of hours worked each week by each employee. While this information can be used alone as input for the payroll system, procedures would be strengthened through use of time cards either punched through a time clock or signed by the supervisor. (Personnel generally are more careful about assessing actual labor hours when they know information will be used for payroll purposes in addition to "control" purposes.)

Manual processing of payroll information generally involves:

1. Assessing/calculating the number of hours worked by each waged employee;
2. Multiplying hours worked by applicable wage rates to calculate gross pay;
3. Determining the amounts of withholding, FICA, and other employee taxes;
4. Determining the pay due to the employees;
5. Writing checks and supplying withholding and other payroll information via check stub reports;
6. Completing required federal and state reports used to submit tax payments to governmental agencies;
7. Monitoring and administering the payroll checking account. (Some facilities choose to set up and utilize a separate checking account for payroll purposes. This account along with the general operations checking account are the only two checking accounts required by many institutions.)

If a time clock is used, definite policies regarding its use are necessary. All employees must know all the policies. Dietary managers must constantly monitor to make sure that policies are consistently followed. As a minimum, consider the following:

1. Employees must "punch out" immediately after finishing work (some facilities establish time limitations to regulate how long employees can be at the institution before and after work);
2. No employee is to use another employee's time card;
3. Any errors should be brought immediately to the attention of the dietary manager (who must sign the time card at any point where a change is to be approved).

Computerized time clocks, which can be programmed to accept specific time cards only at selected times, are now on the market. Very detailed labor reports, providing almost any labor-related information required by the facility, can be developed by these time clock systems. For example, based upon pre-established employee number codes, information about hours worked by and the labor costs for each work section can be easily generated. This equipment can also be programmed to automatically develop payroll reports which must be submitted to governmental agencies.

Even relatively small dietary operations might benefit from a low-cost, automated payroll system offered by banks and bookkeeping/accounting services, or from owning a personal computer system. Some large facilities may have computer capabilities to which smaller institutions may be linked through shared computer access. Systems may be programmed to calculate and print payroll checks, to provide data of any detail for control purposes, and to develop and print payroll reports and other information.

These systems are relatively inexpensive (often costing less than the wages paid to a bookkeeping clerk or secretary for performing the same tasks) and can be tied to systems which coordinate operating budget projections and comparisons. When the processing is done by a bank, it may also be possible to arrange for net total payroll costs to be charged directly to the facility's payroll account and to have such charges transferred from the general operating account to its payroll account (when two accounts are used and both are with the same bank).

Comparison of Standard and Actual Labor Hours

Labor standards stated in staffing guides must be compared with actual hours, to assess whether the labor control program is effective. Generally, a minimal deviation is permitted. If the actual labor hours exceed this variance, analysis/investigation is in order. The amount of variance permitted before corrective action becomes necessary depends upon:

1. Whether the dietary manager permits standards to be exceeded. If he or she believes that standards are reasonable and necessary to meet financial goals, allowable deviations are likely to be small;
2. Whether there are larger control problems in other areas, such as food or energy which require more immediate attention (the value of excessive costs is greater);
3. Whether variances can be explained. It is one thing when labor hours are excessive because a new employee is being trained; it is another matter when allowable hours are consistently exceeded without knowing why.

Comparison can be undertaken on a weekly basis. If comparisons are made too infrequently, time is wasted and labor dollars are lost before there is an indication of a problem. On the other hand, if comparisons are made too frequently, excessive time and costs are necessary to develop the system, assemble the data, and make comparison decisions. Some time is necessary for hours and costs to "average out." Labor hours can be greater than performance standards on some days and less than performance standards on other occasions; it is the "average" costs and efficiency that become important to dietary managers.

Use of a weekly information collection and comparison system satisfies both points noted above; information is obtained before a long lapse of time has occurred, and enough time is allowed for labor "averaging."

The difference between standard and actual labor hours represents potentially lower operating costs for the facility. As variance levels increase, the amount of potential savings becomes larger and the need for corrective action is stronger. The comparison step in the labor control process enables the dietary manager to see the results of the labor control efforts and helps to assess whether corrective action is necessary.

When standard and actual labor hours are compared, several questions may be asked when a difference exceeds the allowable variance:

1. Are the labor standards correct? It is possible that the labor staffing guide is incorrect? If unacceptable variances are a recurring problem, perhaps an updated position productivity performance analysis should be performed;
2. Was the estimated production forecast correct? Additional labor hours may have been necessary if actual meals served were in excess of the planned number of meals to be served. If this happens frequently, the system used to estimate meals to be served should be examined;
3. Are tasks being performed which are not in the job description (and, therefore, were not considered as the initial position performance analysis was developed)?
4. Are different (and more time-consuming) procedures used to perform tasks than were used when standards were developed?
5. Is there an increased number of new employees who aren't able to perform as efficiently as the employees during the initial position performance analysis?
6. Have factors affecting labor efficiency (menu, amount of ready-service foods, etc.) changed? If so, an updated analysis leading to revised labor standards will be necessary;
7. Has equipment become inoperative?
8. Are there personal or professional problems among staff which affect efficiency?
9. Have elements in labor cost changed? For example, salaried labor and/or fringe benefits may have been included in the labor standards but *excluded* at the time of the actual labor cost calculations;
10. Is the difference between standard and actual operating results similar to the differences from other periods? (For example, if the variance has averaged approximately 2 percent for the past six months, a variance of 6 percent this month probably needs investigation.)

As a result of the comparison process, the dietary manager will know (a) if there is a variance between expected and actual labor results, and (b) if the variance is great enough to warrant further attention.

Acceptable Variances—A variance between standard and actual labor hours does not automatically mean that problems exist that deserve immediate corrective action. The comparison and analysis process may indicate some acceptable or at least understandable reasons for the variance. While dietary managers must decide what these might be for the specific operation, examples may include:

1. New employees have been hired; and their training hours are included in the Weekly Labor Report(s);
2. Inoperative equipment created the need for additional labor hours;
3. New menu items and/or new work procedures have been implemented; a training/transitional period requires additional labor In this instance, labor performance standards may need to be changed to reflect the revised necessary procedures;
4. Changes in record-keeping procedures may require adjustments and can account for explainable differences between labor expectations and actual operating results.

These and similar circumstances, once identified, may provide reasons for the variance, and corrective action is not necessary. The dietary manager is aware of the problem, understands what caused it, knows its expected duration, and can estimate costs. "Acceptable" reasons are those, then, which account for variances and are understood by the dietary manager.

Unacceptable Variances—The comparison/analysis of differences between labor performance standards and actual labor results may also indicate unacceptable reasons for variances. These must also be defined specifically for the facility but include:

1. Personnel use unacceptable procedures (any procedure not used when the position performance analysis was done);
2. Employees work inefficiently (slowly, with unnecessary work stoppages; commit errors which require work to be redone, etc.);
3. Supervisors make schedule, communication, and similar errors, yielding more hours of work input.

Comparisons between expected and actual labor results will point out these problems so that they can be resolved. The comparison between standard and actual labor hours may indicate variances which cannot be explained; while it is obvious that a problem exists, reasons for and ways to resolve it are not immediately obvious. If the dietary manager is certain that labor standards are reasonable, it will be necessary for him or her and the supervisor(s) of the affected position to work together to resolve the matter. Perhaps one or both staff members should work in the "problem" position for one or more shifts. Employees themselves can be questioned about the problem. This occurrence, while rare, must receive a high priority to ensure that labor costs are controlled. Once identified, procedures for corrective action must be undertaken.

On-the-Job Concerns

Increasingly today, one more area of expertise must be assumed by dietary managers: knowledge about legal issues. There are a growing number of things managers can and cannot do, which bring their facility into the legal domain. In today's litigious society and with laws reducing the manager's discretion, it becomes increasingly important to know how to supervise employees legally.

There are many laws that affect what one can and cannot do. Some may believe that their facility's attorneys and top-level administrators are the only ones who need to keep up with these laws. Not true! In fact, if you break a law out of ignorance, you and/or the employer (the facility) may still be held responsible and liable.

The following information reviews some of the laws about which you must be knowledgeable. Of course, you should check with the facility's legal counsel whenever possible to be sure of the legal implications of a situation.

Equal Employment Opportunity Commission (EEOC)

Discrimination is the practice of treating someone differently—usually wrongly—based on a factor such as the individual's race or nationality. When one discriminates, he or she does not bother to get to know people as individuals or relate to them according to their merits as an individual. Rather, one puts people in categories based on their color, religion, sex, and so on, and treats everyone in that category the same. Since this treatment is based on ignorance of the individuality of the members of these various categories, they usually are subject to the stereotypes and prejudices held about the category in which these individuals are placed.

Employment discrimination at all organizational levels is prohibited by law in the United States. The amended Civil Rights Act of 1964 contains a section, **Title VII,** that deals with employee selection and guarantees the right of an individual to work in an environment free from discrimination based on race, sex, religion, or national origin. All employees must be treated equally by both managers and co-workers. In fact, a hospital or other healthcare facility may be held liable for the discriminatory acts of its employees even if administrators were unaware of those acts. Discrimination includes practices where the effects may not have been intended, such as using human resource tests that have not been validated as a selection device.

Dress codes and standards for personal appearance also have discrimination implications. Men and women, of course, are allowed to dress differently, but the same general standards must apply to each sex and the standards must be reasonable, appropriate, and consistent. For example, if a facility requires some employees to be clean-shaven (for example, in the Admissions Department) this requirement should probably be imposed on other "service" employees working, for example, in dietary and gift-shop areas. There must be facility-wide consistency in the interpretation of what is appropriate for employees. Individual departments or managers must not be allowed to make contrary decisions or rules.

Religious discrimination must be avoided. Employees must be scheduled so their work requirements will not conflict with religious commitments/beliefs, and it is necessary to make whatever schedule and other adjustments are necessary to meet these special requests. An employee's personal appearance may reflect religious heritage (length of hair, for example) and human resource policies must *accommodate* these special circumstances. ("Accommodate" means allowing reasonable modifications that fit within the criteria for sanitation, appearance, etc.)

Dietary managers must not discriminate on the basis of sex. For example, personnel specifications such as weight or height that discriminate based on gender are unlawful unless they reflect essential attributes required for performing the job. These essential attributes are called **bona fide occupational qualifications** (BFOQ). An example of a legitimate BFOQ might be that storeroom workers must be able to lift or move heavy boxes of canned goods. Since this task can be done by a woman employee, you might have difficulty defending a discrimination charge filed by a woman if all of these positions were filled by men. Discriminating against pregnant women or refusing to hire women (or men) because of uniform, locker space, or other problems are examples of unlawful practices.

The Discrimination in Employment Act of 1967 was enacted to prohibit arbitrary discrimination based upon age. It applies to persons over the age of 40. Offering different fringe benefit packages to older workers, refusing to train or promote them, and mandating their retirement are all examples of illegal acts.

Some laws require organizations doing business with the government to protect the rights of veterans. Generally, organizations must rehire employees who complete military service. Further, time off (without pay) must be provided to those employees with Military Reserve obligations.

Federal and state laws also protect employees against invasion of their privacy. The Federal Right of Privacy Act covers employee records, locker and personal inspections, background investigations, and other matters. Normally, employees are entitled to a reasonable expectation of privacy and, if this is denied, legal liability can result.

Americans with Disabilities Act (ADA)

The Americans With Disabilities Act (ADA), passed in 1990, requires covered organizations (including many healthcare facilities) to take steps to accommodate disabled persons, including employees, and to employ qualified disabled job applicants.

The law's definition of disability is important: "A physical or mental impairment that substantially limits one or more major life activities of such individuals; a record of such an impairment; or being regarded as having such an impairment." This definition includes persons with a wide range of disabling conditions such as blindness, hearing impairments, arthritis, heart conditions, emphysema, shortness of stature, amputees, and others, in addition to the more traditional "definition" involving persons requiring wheelchairs.

Regulations are detailed and yet vague in many respects about defining what organizations must do (that which is "readily achievable") and what needs not be done because it is an "undue burden." Issues such as costs, financial resources of the institution, and its relationship, if any, with a parent corporation are all taken into account as these and related issues are assessed.

Generally, public accommodations must remove architectural barriers in existing facilities if such removal is "readily achievable" (easily accomplishable and able to be carried out without much difficulty or expense). Each public accommodation is to evaluate its facilities and determine what can be done. If a problem exists, the organization typically must provide the goods, services, facilities, and accommodations through alternative methods.

In regard to the facility itself, there are several priorities:

- First is actual access to the public accommodation (doorways, entrance ramps, etc.);
- The second priority is access to goods and services (for example, do all disabled visitors have access to the cash cafeteria operation?);
- The third priority is access to restroom facilities;
- The fourth priority is access to any other services, goods, or facilities offered by the organization.

A wide range of regulations become applicable when there is new construction or alterations to existing facilities. Likewise, enforcement provisions include opportunities for victims of discrimination to go to court.

Most healthcare facilities have been designed to accommodate persons with disabilities and, in fact, *exist* to provide health services for them. However, healthcare facilities may be confronted with the same types of issues as are other organizations relative to the employment of persons with disabilities. Figure 8.25 reviews major concerns which must be addressed in the personal policies and procedures of most employers, while Figure 8.26 (Americans with Disabilities Act Legislation in Review) presents the key points of the ADA.

EMPLOYMENT

✓ Employers may not discriminate against an individual with a disability in hiring or promotion if the person is otherwise qualified for the job.

✓ Employers can ask about one's ability to perform a job, but cannot inquire if someone has a disability or subject a person to tests that tend to screen out people with disabilities.

✓ Employers will need to provide "reasonable accommodation" to individuals with disabilities. This includes steps such as job restructuring and modification equipment.

✓ Employers do not need to provide accommodations that impose an "undue hardship" on business operations.

Who needs to comply:

✓ All employers with 25 or more employees must comply, effective July 26, 1992.

✓ All employers with 15–24 employees must comply, effective July 26, 1994.

FIGURE 8.25 AMERICANS WITH DISABILITIES ACT REQUIREMENTS FACT SHEET: EMPLOYMENT

- Hotels, restaurants, theaters, stores, offices, transit stations, museums, social service agencies, parks, schools, and gyms must not discriminate against individuals with disabilities.
- Barriers in existing facilities must be removed when removal can be accomplished without undue difficulty or expense. If not, alternative methods of making goods and services available must be in place.
- Altered facilities must be accessible. In major structural alterations, a path of travel to the altered area nd restrooms serving the altered area must be accessible.
- New facilities must be accessible, unless structurally impractical.
- Auxiliary aids and services are required, unless the business can demonstrate undue hardship.
- Elevators need not be provided in buildings with fewer than three floors or with less than 3,000 square feet per floor, other than in shopping centers and healthcare buildings.
- Bona fide private clubs and religious groups are not covered by these provisions.

FIGURE 8.26 AMERICANS WITH DISABILITIES ACT REVIEW
Source: The President's Committee on Employment of People with Disabilities

SEXUAL HARASSMENT

Today, sexual harassment in the workplace receives significant attention and is one of the most frequent reasons for employee litigation. In March 1980, the Equal Employment Opportunity Commission (EEOC) issued specific guidelines dealing with sexual harassment. The EEOC has confirmed that sexual harassment is a violation of Title VII and has presented information about conduct that constitutes unlawful sexual harassment. Simply stated, in order for conduct to be considered sexual harassment, the conduct must (1) be sexual in nature, and (2) be unwelcome. Sexual harassment may be physical, verbal, (including suggestive comments) or visual (for example, displaying pornographic photographs).

While the laws and their interpretations may vary, some principles appear established. The manager and/or employer will probably be held liable for sexual harassment if an employee is deprived of a tangible job benefit (e.g., promotion) because of a refusal to provide sexual favors. If an employee's work environment is negatively affected (in the employee's opinion) by the sexual harassment of a supervisor or co-worker, and if the employer knows or should have known of this conduct and does not take immediate action, the employer will probably be held liable. The dietary manager and the facility could also be found liable for the harassment of employees by patients or their guests and vendors if unwanted activities occurred, facility personnel were aware of them, and did not take immediate corrective actions.

The facility must exercise reasonable care to prevent sexual harassment. In the event a manager is informed that an employee is being sexually harassed, the following steps should be taken:

1. Notify your own boss;
2. Investigate the situation according to your facility's policy;
3. Seek legal advice before further action is taken (see steps 4 and 5);

[1]EEOC Guidelines on Discrimination Because of Sex. 29 C.F.R. Section 1604.11. Sexual harassment.

4. Confront the accused party, and get the accused party's side of the story;
5. Take any necessary disciplinary action(s).

There are, of course, a wide range of other supervisory activities affected by laws and legal issues. Effective dietary managers understand the importance of keeping up with the legal aspects of their profession. They consistently utilize practices which recognize the rights of the employees, clients, and others with whom they interact.

The following main points provide some specific action to be taken to deal effectively with the issue of sexual harassment:

1. Management should be familiar with the company's policy. This policy should include disciplinary guidelines for both the individual who is guilty and guidelines for harassers who retaliate against those who report them. Policy should include a formal complaint procedure for employees to use if they think they have been victims of sexual harassment, with provisions for immediate investigations and prompt disciplinary actions when appropriate;
2. Employees should be educated on how to recognize sexual harassment, how to report it when it occurs, and the steps that will be taken if an employee is guilty of sexual harassment. All cases of possible sexual harassment must be investigated according to this policy set by management;
3. Follow-up needs to be provided after all instances of sexual harassment. Victims must be contacted and witnesses need to be asked if the sexual harassment has indeed stopped and no retaliation is taking place.

SUMMARY

Human resource planning involves all procedures in the process by which a dietary manager anticipates the future—and what it will require in personnel. There are several important objectives of a human resource planning program including:

1. To reduce human resource problems and costs;
2. To allow for human resource planning on a timely—not crisis—basis;
3. To consider ways that societal concerns for minority employment and advancement can be met by the facility;
4. To ensure that personnel are always available to do required work;
5. To promote an awareness of the need for human resource planning;
6. To provide tools useful in evaluating the effectiveness of human resource management plans and policies.

Employees of all ages and at all stages in their employment with the facility should be active in a carefully designed career development program. The basic steps in human resource planning are:

1. Forecast future personnel needs;
2. Conduct inventory of current staff;
3. Assess human resource planning needs;
4. Develop internal training/education activities;
5. Plan for new staff recruitment, selection, and training procedures;
6. Design program monitoring systems;
7. Control and evaluate human resource planning system.

A job breakdown is a very useful tool to develop standard operating procedures which specify how work should be done. This information is useful for programmed planning, controlling, and monitoring purposes as well as for training, which will make it cost-effective in many operations.

A job description is prepared after the job breakdown analyzes all tasks. It is written for a position, not for a person, and describes what the job is all about. Job descriptions for a specific department are complete when all tasks necessary to carry out all aspects of that department's operation are included in the job description of some position. Once developed, job descriptions should be combined into a job description handbook or human resource manual.

Job specifications indicate the personal qualifications judged necessary to successfully perform in a position, and which are then outlined in a job description. Factors which might be included in a job specification other than required education, experience, knowledge, and training can include necessary physical skills, communication abilities, ability to use and maintain equipment, and so on. Additionally, job specifications can help identify existing staff who should be considered for advancement.

Employee recruitment is the process by which applicants are sought out and screened for suitability for positions within the dietary operation. Both the dietary manager and the immediate supervisor of the position to be filled should be involved in the task of recruiting and selecting staff.

There are several sources which can be used to recruit employees for dietary services. These include:

1. Friends and relatives of current employees;
2. Promotion of current employees;
3. Other sources including employment agencies, government trainees, colleges, universities, and vocational and secondary schools with distributive education.

Information about personnel making application for vacant positions may be gathered by:

1. The job application form;
2. Verifying applicant references;
3. Selection tests;
4. Medical exams;
5. Americans with Disabilities Act (ADA) requirements.

An interview between an official of the facility and the job applicant is a specialized kind of information interview. Each party needs to obtain information from the other; an interview provides a format for this information transfer. Often, there are three separate interviews utilized during the recruitment/screening process: an initial screening interview; a second screening interview, and a selection interview.

There are two basic types of interviews: directive and non-directive. Directive interview questions solicit facts and do not seek opinions or subjective responses to questions. Non-directive interview questions are less structured and more open-ended so that the interviewee can provide creative responses. Situational interview questions will reveal candidates' on the job decision-making and potential for work-team compatibility.

Some problems that should be avoided during an interview are:

1. Letting personal biases influence decisions about the interviewee;
2. Being rushed;
3. Making unreasonable comparisons;
4. Failing to follow the principles of effective interviewing;
5. Overselling the facility or the job;

6. Omitting important information;
7. Leaving the applicant with a bad impression;
8. Asking discriminating questions.

When the "right" applicant will not be perfect for the job, it becomes a matter of considering the strengths and weaknesses of each final candidate to determine the one "best" qualified. The selection decision is important. Many times, facilities with high turnover rates can trace problems to incorrect procedures and inadequate decisions made at the time of recruitment and selection.

Dietary managers should carefully consider minimum quality requirements and closely examine how well these requirements are incorporated into work which is done. Three essentials must be built into the system from the beginning, if a successful performance standard is to be created:

1. Employee participation;
2. Active supervisory leadership and assistance throughout;
3. A built-in reward system.

There is a definite order of steps to be taken in developing a performance standard system:

1. Define the purpose;
2. Analyze the job (and break it down into units);
3. Write the performance standard;
4. Develop the standard procedures;
5. Train the workers (and test);
6. Evaluate on-th-job performance.

After performance standards are developed, they can be incorporated into a staffing guide. Once a staffing guide is developed, it can be utilized to schedule employees. When the number of standard labor hours noted on the staffing guide is not exceeded, dietary managers have some assurance that personnel worked efficiently.

Performance standards are a specialized and demanding form of communication, and writing them may be the most difficult part of developing a performance standard system. But it is precisely this process that requires you to make things clear. If it forces you to figure out just what is expected from the employees, then a valuable lesson will have been learned.

Specific procedures for using the staffing guide to schedule labor hours include:

1. Set a time frame for scheduling personnel;
2. Estimate the number of patients/residents to be served;
3. Schedule labor hours on the basis of number of meals which are forecast.

Dietary managers should use several principles when scheduling personnel:

1. Schedule staff to fit work needs;
2. Use creative schedule plans;
3. Consider personnel preferences whenever possible;
4. Review policies, if any, applicable to employee scheduling;
5. Consider past experience in allocating labor hours to each employee which generally provides the best basis for scheduling personnel.

The total of all labor hours scheduled for all employees in the position should not exceed the hours planned on the schedule worksheet. Dietary managers must continually seek employee cooperation in complying with posted schedules.

Some scheduling concerns for salaried personnel include:

1. Consider salaried personnel's preferences in schedules;
2. Develop responsibilities, tasks, and volume of work which managers are to do;
3. Back-up plans should not include "working" the manager;
4. Determine what salaried personnel should do, and schedule them in a way which permits time to do the required tasks;
5. Tasks of salaried personnel must be considered in analyses of work for development of staffing guides.

Overtime refers to time worked in excess of the allowable amount beyond which laws require payment of one and a half times the hourly rate for every hour worked. If it occurs frequently, ineffective schedules are being developed, the number of meals and/or amount of work to be undertaken are inaccurately estimated, or perhaps both of these problems are occurring.

Some employees are exempt from overtime pay. Employees who meet the following tests can be exempt from the overtime provisions of the Wage and Hour Law as executives:

1. They must supervise two or more other employees;
2. Their salary must be the minimum amount determined by the Wage and Hour Division;
3. They must have the power to hire and fire or their recommendations must carry significant weight;
4. Their primary duty must be managing: they can't do non-exempt work more than 40 percent of the time in any given workweek.

Another commonly used exemption is for "administrator." An administrative employee performs office or non-manual work which must directly assist an executive. The dietary manager should require advance approval for any overtime to be scheduled. Unless advance approval was received, then, supervisors could be held responsible for all overtime.

The actual number of labor hours incurred must also be known:

1. For administrative and financial purposes;
2. To assess the effectiveness of the labor control system.

The weekly labor hour report is completed in the following manner:

1. The supervisor of each section records the number of actual hours worked daily by each employee during the week;
2. If the actual reported hours are to be used as the basis for payroll purposes, they should be verified with time cards or other source documents;
3. The total number of weekly planned hours scheduled should also be entered on the weekly labor hour report for evaluation.

Payroll systems can be of two types: manual and automated. A manual payroll system involves processing of payroll information "by hand." Automated payroll systems, offered by banks and bookkeeping/accounting services or from a personal computer, can calculate and print payroll checks and print payroll reports and other information.

The difference between standard and actual labor hours represents potential savings for the facility. As a result of the comparison process, the dietary manager will know (a) if there is a variance between expected and actual labor results, and (b) if the variance is great enough to warrant further attention.

Employment discrimination at all organizational levels is prohibited by law in the United States. The amended Civil Rights Act of 1964 contains a section, **Title VII,** that deals with employee selection and guarantees the right of an individual to work in an environment free from discrimination based on race, sex, religion, or national origin. The Discrimination in Employment Act of 1967 was enacted to prohibit arbitrary discrimination based upon age, and the Federal Right of Privacy Act covers employee records, locker and personal inspections, background investigations, and other matters.

The Americans With Disabilities Act (ADA), passed in 1990, requires covered organizations (including many health care facilities) to take steps to accommodate disabled persons, including employees, and to employ qualified disabled job applicants. Each public accommodation is to evaluate its facilities and determine what can be done. If a problem exists the organization typically must provide the goods, services, facilities, and accommodations through alternative methods.

In March 1980, the Equal Employment Opportunity Commission issued specific guidelines dealing with sexual harassment. To be considered sexual harassment, the conduct must (1) be sexual in nature, and (2) be unwelcome. Sexual harassment may be physical, verbal, or visual. The facility must exercise reasonable care to prevent sexual harassment.

KEY TERMS

- Human resource planning
- Managerial obsolescence
- Job description
- Job specifications
- Employee recruitment
- Interview
- Overtime
- "Actual" labor hours
- "Standard" labor hours
- Variance
- Payroll system
- Equal Employment Opportunity Commission (EEOC)
- Sexual harassment
- Americans with Disabilities Act (ADA)

QUESTIONS/PROBLEMS/CASES

1. As dietary manager, what strategy would you employ in gathering information about personnel making application for a position in your facility?

2. Johnson Nursing Homes employed 200 employees in its facilities. George Hanson, the director of human resources, had held this position for the past seventeen years. He prided himself on his ability to conduct interviews effectively. When Sue Platts was hired as a new assistant human resources manager, Hanson took great pleasure in "breaking in" this recent college graduate on the practical aspects of effective interviewing.

   In speaking with his new assistant, Hanson stated, "I can size anyone up in ten minutes or less in an interview. My record shows how good I am at this, and I'll give you a few tips. We don't use written tests anymore because of EEOC hassles with them. It's just as well, because I didn't put much faith in what those tests showed anyway. As for personal interviews, we use several interviewers for important positions to get the effect of a group interview. All of the interviewers ask the questions that they feel are important, and they report to me anything outstanding or particularly negative that turns up. My interview with a prospective employee is the one that usually counts the most, though. I'm looking for 'hard drivers' and people who I think will succeed around here. In just a few minutes, I can tell by the way they look at me, the kind of clothes they wear, and their general confidence in themselves whether or not they're likely to be good employees. For example, you can tell a lot about a man by the kind of shoes he wears and how well they are polished. Also, I put a lot of stock in whether or not the applicants have finished the education they began, whether it's high school, junior college, or university. It shows that they can finish things and can stick to their tasks."

Hanson continued, "The best technique I've found to separate the poor applicants from those with real promise is to ask them how they would handle the following situation. I give them two alternatives to stop employees from arguing constantly with each other. First, the employees could be told either to work it out among themselves or to get a transfer out of the department. Second, the supervisor could sit down with the employees and work out the difficulties together. Whichever approach the applicant picks, I tell them that they are wrong. If they select the first method, I tell them that their job is to develop and help employees to perform better. If they select the second, I tell them they have more important things to do than to work out personal problems between employees. By doing this, I see how applicants handle stress and find out what they're made of. Good potential employees will stick by their guns and give me some good reasons why their approach should be followed. With all this information, I can usually make a good decision in a pretty short time. I've found that I am seldom wrong."

Questions for Discussion

1. Evaluate Hanson's interview techniques. What are the strengths and weaknesses of Hanson's system.

    a. Is it possible to do an adequate job of interviewing in so short a time? Discuss.

    b. How valid is the stress aspect of the interview?

    c. What recommendations, if any, would you make to Hanson in regard to his interviewing?

    d. What recommendations, if any, would you make to the new assistant, Sue Platts, concerning whether or not she should adopt the same interviewing approach as that of her supervisor?

2. Describe five ways to recruit new employees from inside and outside the facility.

3. What are the advantages of promoting from within?

4. Tony is a long-time employee whose performance as a cook has generally been adequate. Recently, however, he has been quite sloppy, and other workers have had to cover for his mistakes. What does this situation call for?

5. As dietary manager, you are responsible for estimating excessive labor costs. You reference the weekly labor hour sheet and notice that the cooks (average hourly rate = $12), "actual" labor hours for the week totals 150 hours, yet the "standard" labor hours total 136 hours. Since the standard, planned hours have been exceeded, calculate how much over budget labor costs will be.

6. Circle any of the following questions that is considered job-related and legal to ask an applicant during an interview:

    a. Where were you born?

    b. Are you a U.S. citizen?

    c. What is your religious affiliation?

    d. Are you 18 years of age or older?

    e. May I have a picture of you to attach to the application form?

    f. How old are you?

7. What is meant by BFOQ?

8. Describe how sexual harassment is taking place, if at all, in each of the following situations and how the situation should be corrected.

    Situation 1. Linda is the dietary manager of a large nursing home where she has worked hard to rise to her present position. She is considering her next move which might place her in a regional position over five care centers. She has been asked out to dinner on a number of occasions by her boss, but has refused since she wishes to maintain her professionalism. One day in the office, he tells her that the regional position may be available soon and that she would be wise to discuss the matter over dinner with him.

    Situation 2. Jake is a newly hired assistant waiter in the dining room having moved from being dishwasher after three years. He reports to Sally the head waitress who refers to her male assistants as "boys". Jake is twenty-four years old and is uncomfortable with being called boy.

    Situation 3. Deb is in the kitchen placing an order with the cook when she overhears the manager and chef telling crude jokes. She is offended by both the content of the jokes and the language being used by these fellow employees.

9. List the major components of a job description.

10. How is a job description different from a job specification?

11. Write a performance standard for an employee who prepared cold foods, including salads and desserts.

12. How can a dietary manager control overtime?

9

HUMAN RESOURCE DEVELOPMENT

Chapter Outline

- Motivation
  - Importance of Motivated Staff
  - Maslow's Human Needs Theory
  - Maintenance-Motivation Theory
  - McClelland's Achievement, Power, Affiliation Theory
- Orientation and Training
- Employee Training Programs
  - Characteristics of Good Trainers
  - Adult Learning Theory
  - Steps in the Training Process
  - On-the-Job Training Procedures
  - Checklist for Effective Training
- Employee Performance Evaluations
  - Types of Performance Reviews
  - The Use of Job Descriptions with Performance Reviews
  - Possible Problems with Performance Review Programs
- Employee Corrective Action
  - Corrective Action Process
  - Specific Corrective Action Procedures
  - Negative Action
  - Causes of Corrective Action Problems
  - Classification of Corrective Action Problems
  - Principles of Employee Corrective Action Procedures

Motivation

Motivation has been defined as an internal force which makes employees do something in order to reach a goal. It is often difficult to effectively practice motivation principles on the job. Notice that one defines motivation to be an internal drive—a force which must develop within the employee. The dietary manager cannot motivate subordinates alone. What he or she can do is to provide job conditions that help employees to attain goals which have been developed internally. It becomes the mission of the dietary manager, then, to match the employees' goals with those of the dietary department.

The task of dietary managers is to hire people capable of doing the jobs that are assigned to them. If they are not capable of doing the jobs, no amount of training will make them effective. Moreover, they must also be willing to do the job. They can have the ability to do the job, but if they don't really want to do it, they probably won't be effective. The third part of this interconnection is this: employees can be willing to do the job and perfectly capable of doing the job, but if they are not shown how to do the job, they still may not be effective.

Once employees are capable, willing, and trained, the ongoing challenge then is to figure out how to get them to do it, and for them to do it graciously. In order to do this, it is important to understand why people do what they do, to know what motivates them.

Motivation comes from within people. One cannot motivate people to do things. They must have a reason for wanting to do what managers want them to do, and that comes from within them. The task as managers is to figure out what motivates the employees. To be able to do that, it is important to know them. The goal is to create a delicate set of conditions wherein they can somehow meet their needs while doing what management wants them to do.

There are numerous theories of motivation that address the question of why people do things. Money is often thought to be a motivator. The lack of adequate or equitable compensation can have a very negative effect on employee productivity and attitude. However, in the long run, money alone will rarely be enough to make up for insufficient support or unsatisfactory job matches.

Another view is that satisfied or happy workers will be motivated. It is true that people who are satisfied with their jobs will be absent less often and will tend to hold their jobs longer. In this view, inadequate compensation and lack of job satisfaction are seen as negative motivators; adequate money and good job satisfaction are seen as positive motivators.

The third view is that most people strive to reach their full potential. How far they have advanced toward reaching their full potential will determine what motivates them. The idea here is that if managers know where on this spectrum of potential they are, they will know what motivates them and can therefore provide the appropriate incentives that will encourage them to do the tasks associated with their jobs. The best-known theory of this third view is Abraham Maslow's hierarchy of needs.

Importance of Motivated Staff

Why does the dietary manager want motivated employees? The goals of the dietary department—and of the facility itself—cannot be attained unless staff at all levels work together.

It is important for the dietary manager to maintain good employee morale. Raising morale can also be an objective of effective motivation strategies, since morale is the combination of all the feelings that one has about all aspects of the job: the work to be done, feelings about staff members with whom one comes in contact, and the facility and work environment itself.

The dietary department and the entire facility will gain from having staff members with high morale levels. It becomes important, then, for the dietary manager to consider the personal goals of employees so that these goals can be meshed with those of the facility. Simply stated, when an employee desires to accomplish the same things as does the dietary department, he or she is likely to judge required work to be interesting and challenging. The work is also likely to be done according to required quality levels, and cooperation among affected staff is likely to improve. The staff member who "feels good" about the job may, in part, feel that way because of the opportunity to attain personal goals through work.

Maslow's Human Needs Theory

Psychologist Abraham Maslow answered the question, "What motivates people to work?" when he developed his motivation theory. He stated basically that individuals would satisfy their needs and wants by the way they behave. Since needs and wants are inexhaustible, he went on to say that as soon as one need is satisfied, another would arise to take its place. His proposed hierarchy of universal human needs represents the order in which these needs become motivators of human behavior (Figure 9.1).

The physiological needs of survival, including food, water, etc., are at the base of the pyramid and are the focus of one's attention should they not be readily available. When these needs are being met, an individual moves from focusing on them

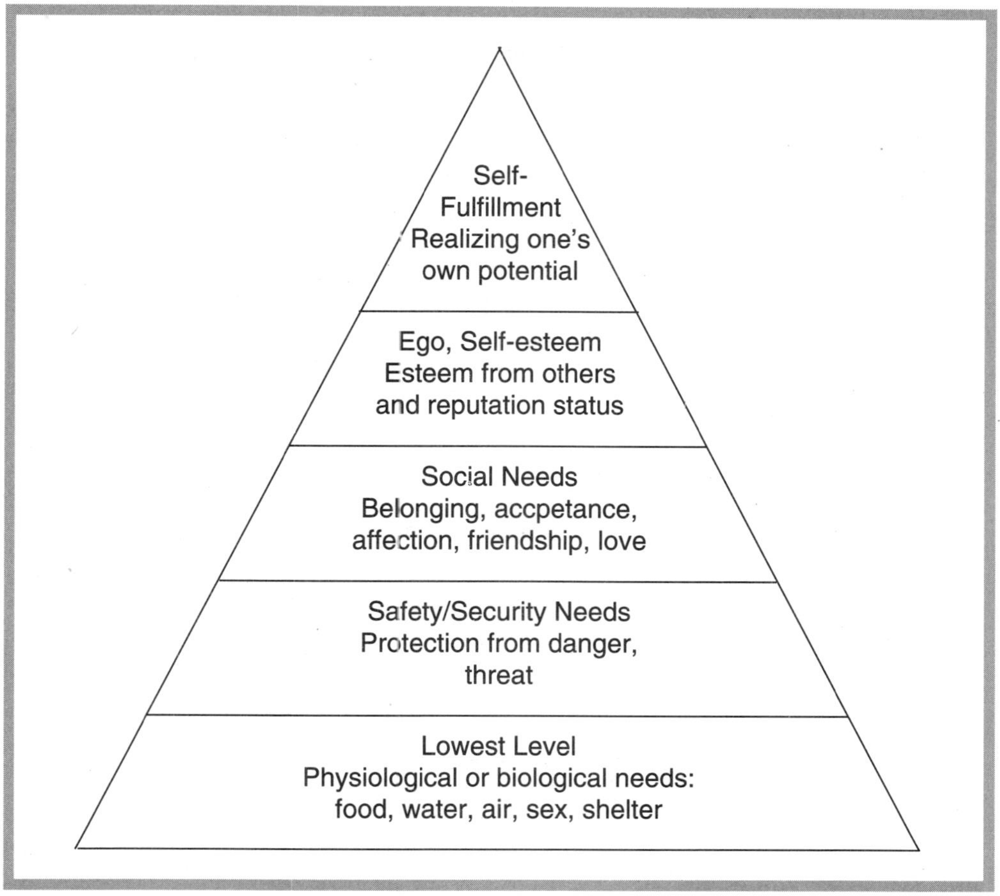

FIGURE 9.1 MASLOW'S HIERARCHY OF NEEDS*
Source: Maslow, 1954

to the next level of needs, involving security and safety, such as stability, protection and freedom from fear and chaos. Social needs motivate behavior next and revolve around friendship, love and the need to belong.

As each of these primary needs are met, the individual moves to a level of ego needs centered on self-esteem. One of them is the desire for self-esteem or self-respect and for the strength, achievement, mastery, competence, confidence, independence, and freedom that provide such self-esteem. Another is the desire for the esteem of others, including status, fame, glory, dominance, recognition, attention, importance, dignity, and appreciation. The need for esteem gives rise in some people to the need for power as a way of commanding the esteem of others. Satisfaction of the need for self-esteem leads to feelings of self-confidence, strength, and worth. When these needs go unsatisfied, they produce feelings of inferiority, weakness, and helplessness.

At the top of the hierarchy is the need for self-fulfillment, or what Maslow called self-actualization. This level includes the need to be doing what one is best fitted for, the desire to fulfill one's own potential.

One or another of all these personal needs or various combinations of needs are what motivate people to do what they do. If a lower need goes unsatisfied, people will spend all their time and energy trying to fill it, and they will not experience the next level of needs until the lower needs are met. When a need is satisfied it is no longer a motivator, and the next level of needs becomes the predominant motivation.

---

*Detailed information about Maslow's Hierarchy of Needs Theory will be found in: Abraham Maslow, *Motivation and Personality.* Harper and Row, New York, N.Y., 1964.

As one is motivated to accomplish what is a need at a lower level, he or she is presented with a new need as the first is met. Since wants and needs are always present, the employee continually is in a cycle attempting to reach the top of the pyramid or, at least, the level which is of interest at that moment.

A dietary manager might use these ideas to help an employee who has personal problems that relate to job security. The dietary manager can emphasize pay rates, promotion opportunities, job security, and related aspects of the work to help the staff member see how his or her concern for physical needs might be met on the job.

What if the dietary manager believes a staff member is concerned about social needs? He or she might emphasize how these needs can be met through work-related activities. Creative supervisors can become aware of specific employee concerns and address these as his or her relationship with the staff member evolves.

Employee needs can be met on the job in a variety of ways:

- Physiological—Rest breaks, pay checks, bonuses;
- Safety / Security—Consistent application of work rules, policies, non-threatening environment, proper working equipment;
- Social Needs—Committee assignments, friendship with fellow employees, sponsoring social activities such as bowling teams, employee picnics, newsletters;
- Ego—Awards (employee of month, year; service pins), attendance at seminars, recognition, personal letters from boss;
- Self-fulfillment—paid tuition; involvement in planning of goals, objectives, and budgets; creative projects.

Maintenance-Motivation Theory

Fredrick Herzberg and others have considered two sets of factors necessary in a work environment to promote motivation. One set is called maintenance factors. These factors include wages, salaries, and other economic concerns, seniority privileges, the ability to interact with one's peers, adequate working conditions, and so on, and they will not cause motivation. If they are not present, however, dissatisfaction will result. These elements, provided on the job in a quantity judged sufficient from the staff member's perspective, can prevent dissatisfaction.

The second basic set of factors, called motivation factors, provide conditions necessary to motivate employees. Examples of motivation factors include work which is challenging, feelings of personal accomplishment, a recognition for work well done, the ability to perform work of increasing responsibility, and so on.

Figure 9.2 reviews elements in the job which commonly prevent dissatisfaction (maintenance factors) and which generate job commitment (motivation factors). It is generally true that:

- The staff member who is interested in his or her work is more likely to have the internal motivation which will benefit the employee, the dietary department, and the facility itself;
- The staff member who can identify with the organization and believe in it will be more willing to help the organization than will one motivated only by punishment and reward;
- Many employees do not consciously know about their personal goals or needs; much motivation may be subconscious. Few people make an effort to objectively analyze themselves about "where they are going." The dietary manager may have a difficult time considering aspects of the staff member which the employee may not even be able to verbalize;
- Money is not a primary and important motivator for a large number of employees. In fact, money is often a maintenance—not a motivation—factor;

MAINTENANCE FACTORS PREVENT DISSATISFACTION

1. Economic—wages, salaries, and fringe benefits
2. Security—procedures for grievances, reasonable work rules, policy and discipline programs, etc.
3. Social—the change to interact with one's peers both on and off the job
4. Working conditions—proper levels of heat, light, ventilation, work hours, etc.
5. Status—job titles, work privileges, and other signs of position and rank

MOTIVATION FACTORS GENERATE COMMITMENT FROM STAFF MEMBERS

1. Challenging work
2. Feelings of personal acocmplishment
3. Recognition for achievement
4. Opportunities to gain increased job responsibilities
5. Feeling important to the organization
6. Having access to information
7. Participating in the decision-making process

FIGURE 9.2 A CLOSE LOOK AT MAINTENANCE/MOTIVATION FACTORS

- Competition among employees or groups of staff members within the same facility does not generally motivate. For example, in some instances, employees who "lose" competitions may become uninterested in the "winning" team. Therefore, many types of competition within a dietary department (such as among service staff on different shifts) can have more negative than positive impact.

McCLELLAND'S ACHIEVEMENT, POWER, AFFILIATION THEORY

David McClelland's work on achievement motivation resulted in the development of a technique with which to measure an individual's achievement motivation, and determine how behavior varies in a number of situations as a function of the level of the "need for achievement."

Drawing on principles of learning obtained from human and animal studies, the findings of attitude-change research, and principles of psychotherapy, McClelland developed formal courses that teach achievement motivation to adult men. From these training sessions, he derived a series of principles or guidelines, the use of which he believes can induce a change in the level of need achievement (or of any other motive).

The first objective of his training is to instill confidence in the participants that the program will work. Training techniques are more likely to be effective if the person believes that he will (and should) develop this new motive. The techniques are also more effective if the person is able to see their relevance to the real world, that is, how the person can use what he is learning.

McClelland also believes that motivational changes are much more likely to occur if a person feels warmly and honestly supported, as well as respected, by both trainers and other employees. These people should reaffirm the person's belief in his or her ability to direct the course of his or her own future behavior.

From his studies, McClelland concluded that people with high achievement needs will, in their everyday activities (and particularly in their work) seek situations that will allow them to satisfy these achievement needs. They will set certain achievement standards for themselves and then work hard to reach those standards.

ORIENTATION AND TRAINING

Appropriate orientation and training is the start to motivating employees and instilling good morale among them. When employees have been employed and before they actually begin work, they should be oriented to the facility and the department. The orientation is a time when the new employee has an opportunity to observe, demonstrate, and practice the job duties that they will be expected to be performed before actually performing them.

Proper orientation of new employees is one of the most important first steps in introducing the new employee to the job. Orientation to the whole facility, usually done on the first day of employment, is organized and conducted by the human resource division. Orientation to the specific department is usually done by the new employee's supervisor.

Proper orientation to the job, the facility, and the other employees can reduce dissatisfaction and turnover. It is also a time to explain policies, procedures, rules, and regulations; to reduce fears of the unknown and anxiety about the job; and to outline specific expectations that the facility has for the employee.

The dietary manager must carefully plan the orientation; the use of a checklist as in Figure 9.3 is helpful. Since it serves as a reminder of the required orientation activities, a checklist helps in supervising the orientation and in evaluating and improving the process. Before beginning the orientation, review materials to be covered, assemble all needed materials, and plan for evaluation and follow-up.

On the first day the new employee is in the department the immediate supervisor should sit down with the employee in a quiet place and talk about the department, the facility, regulations, the job description and so on.

The supervisor should be systematic in the process and cover at least the following:

- Hours of duty, when to report to work, lunch time (how long), and breaks;
- Time clocks—location and how to use;
- Uniforms, good personal hygiene, hand washing, name tags;
- Fire, disaster, safety;
- Infection control, employee health, open lesions;
- Confidentiality, patients' rights and responsibilities;
- Line of authority, organizational chart;
- Job description;
- Job performance.

Human resource department personnel generally cover employee handbook, policies, and paycheck information, listed below:

- Payday—when and where to pick up check, etc.;
- Leave policy for illness, holidays, and annual leave;
- Smoking policy.

It is important to secure the signature of the employee and supervisor when the orientation is completed.

The dietary manager plays a major role in the orientation process. The supervisor is responsible for:

- Implementing the orientation process;
- Informing other staff about new staff members;

NEW SUPERVISOR'S ORIENTATION GUIDE FOR ______________________
(Name)

Advancing from wage roll ranks to salary supervisor is a major step. This "Guide" is provided as a checklist to cover the more essential aspects of the new supervisor's position which may or may not have been developed while detailing. Please review the following subjects with your new supervisor in the minimum period of time but consistent with good understanding, initial each broad subject when discussed and return to the issuing department.

Subject	Discussed (Initials)
1. Salary Administration A. Specific salary which can be expected during discussion of promotion. B. General administration policies—see written statement. C. New supervisor "progression."	
2. Change Associated with New Assignment A. Management attitude 1. Show, by personal example, attitude toward: a. Safety and housekeeping b. Time keeping for supervisors c. Attendance d. Honesty and fairness 2. Community image	
B. Responsibility and Authority 1. Use attached "Supervisory Responsibilities" (Suggest this be discussed by immediate supvr.)	
2. Support which can be expected from: —Upper supervision —Various staff groups	
3. Emergency and Disaster Procedures	
C. P.I.P. (Proprietary Information Protection)	
D. Area Goals and Objectives	
E. Factors Specific to the Area 1. Planning—Scheduling 2. Routines a. Work Time —Reporting and Quitting —Extra Hours —Overtime —Excused Absence —Availability —On Call	
b. Privileges	
c. Selection of Personal Vacation	
d. Reports—injury—safety—public liabilities—guest problems	
F. Measurement of Performances 1. Criteria by which a supervisor is measured [discuss (see JPR forms)]	
2. Criteria used to measure and discuss subordinate's performance. a. Personal contacts as situation requires b. Annual performance reviews (1) Purpose (2) Procedure	

FIGURE 9.3 NEW ORIENTATION CHECKLIST *(Continued on next page)*

Subject	Discussed (Initials)
G. Improve Existing Business (See item "Q"—"Costs" in attached "Supervisory Responsibilities")	
H. Labor Relations (See item "E" in "Supervisory Responsibilities" att.) 1. Importance of: a. Being aware of people's concerns.	
2. Correct, guide and train problem employee to develop improvements in performance	
3. Disciplinary action methods and procedures.	
4. Know policies and procedures relating to most common problems. (Ref.: "Supervisory Guide") a. Poor overall performance b. Attendance c. Timekeeping d. Thievery e. Alcohol abuse f. Insubordination g. Fighting h. Other	
3. Communications A. Up and Down (how and why) B. Committee Assignments C. Meetings to attend —Routine —Special	
4. Sources of Information and Assistance A. References (Readily available key items?) 1. "Supervisory Guide" 2. "Safety How" 3. Personnel Manual 4. Area Rules 5. Staffing Guide 6. Standards Quality 7. Sanitation Manual	
B. Contacts 1. Safety 2. Medical 3. Industrial Relations—Personal 4. Accounting 5. Support Team member (Training) 6. Sources of supplies and services needed to run operations on a day-to-day basis 7. Other	
C. What to Do if Don't Know or Don't Understand	

FIGURE 9.3 *Continued*

SUPERVISORY RESPONSIBILITIES **Responsibility & Authority**	DEGREE OF AUTHORITY Should handle on own (unless help is wanted) I	Should handle on own and advise superior after-the-fact II	Should discuss with superior before taking action III	Remarks
A. JOB ASSIGNMENT	—	—	—	
1. Assign employee to job				
2. Assign non-routine tasks to employee				
3. Acquaint with facilities and co-workers				
4. Explain regulations and practices				
B. JOB INSTRUCTION	—	—	—	
1. Describe job				
2. Tell how job is done				
3. Show how it is done				
4. Supervise during "try-out" by employee				
5. Reinstruct when needed				
6. Explain what is expected of employee				
C. PAY	—	—	—	
1. Explain wage to new employee				
2. Recommend wage/progression increases				
3. Recommend overtime work				
4. Assign employee overtime work				
5. Recommends advance vacation payment of wages				
6. Correct pay errors				
7. Approve weekly time reports				
8. Keep time records				
D. WORK PERFORMANCE	—	—	—	
1. Appraise performance of employee				
2. Discuss appraisal with employee				
3. Upgrade employee within group				
4. Suggest promotions and transfers				
E. MAINTAIN DISCIPLINE	—	—	—	
1. Acquaint employee with rules and practices				
2. Sell employee on compliance				
3. Observe for deviations				
4. Determine corrective action —minor offenses				
5. Determine corrective action —major offenses				
6. Make corrective interviews				
7. Make reprimands				
8. Obtain specialized help in unusual cases				
F. HANDLING COMPLAINTS	—	—	—	
1. Accept complaints from employees				
2. Make decisions on complaints that do not affect other groups				
3. Make decision on complaints that do affect other groups				
4. Advise employee of decision				
5. Anticipate complaints				
6. Handle complaints from clients				

FIGURE 9.3 *(Continued on next page)*

SUPERVISORY RESPONSIBILITIES Responsibility & Authority	DEGREE OF AUTHORITY Should handle on own (unless help is wanted) I	Should handle on own and advise superior after-the-fact II	Should discuss with superior before taking action III	Remarks
G. HANDLE REQUESTS	—	—	—	
1. Accept requests from employee				
2. Make decisions on requests that do not require deviation from rules or practices				
3. Make decisions on requests that do require deviations				
4. Advise employee of decision				
5. Handle requests from clients				
H. SAFETY	—	—	—	
1. Train employee to be safety conscious				
2. Change written safety rules				
3. Change unwritten safety rules				
4. Take unsafe tools out of service				
5. Shut down unsafe equipment				
6. Maintain "spic and span" housekeeping standards				
7. Eliminate unsafe conditions involving minor expenditures.				
8. Eliminate unsafe conditions involving major expenditures				
9. Enforce safety rules				
10. Train employees to use medical facilities				
11. Prepare injury reports				
12. Make investigation of injuries				
13. Conduct safety meetings				
I. ABSENCES	—	—	—	
1. Report absentees				
2. Follow-up on absentees				
3. Request medical follow-up				
4. Request medical interview for chronic absentees				
5. Give excused absences a—portion of day b—1 or 2 days c—2 to 16 days				
6. Initiate leave of absence				
7. Plan and initiate vacations				
J. TERMINATIONS AND LAYOFFS	—	—	—	
1. Initiate termination form				
2. Talk with quitting employee				
3. Advise employee of layoff				
4. Clear separating employee (retrieve facility property)				

FIGURE 9.3 *Continued*

SUPERVISORY RESPONSIBILITIES **Responsibility & Authority**	DEGREE OF AUTHORITY Should handle on own (unless help is wanted) I	Should handle on own and advise superior after-the-fact II	Should discuss with superior before taking action III	Remarks
K. INDUSTRIAL RELATIONS PLANS	—	—	—	
1. Acquaint employee with benefits				
2. Acquaint employee with obligations				
3. Schedule vacations (with managerial guidance)				
4. Distribute accident, health, and group policies				
5. Review plans as employee becomes eligible				
L. FLOW OF INFORMATION	—	—	—	
1. Explain policy changes				
2. Accept suggestions				
3. Maintain bulletin boards				
4. Conduct employee meetings				
5. Keep superior informed of employee's feelings				
6. Newsletter				
M. CONTACTS WITH OTHER EMPLOYEES OR OUTSIDERS	—	—	—	
1. Take advantage of specialized assistance —Engineering/Maintenance (minor) —Personnel/Industrial relations —Control/Accounting —Medical				
2. Keep interest groups informed				
Selecting wage roll employees interviewing—follow-up on hired date—schedule for medical				
N. QUALITY	—	—	—	
1. Meet quality standards				
2. Re-do to meet standards				
3. Accept or reject materials or supplies				
4. Recommend changes in specifications				
5. Find and implement new methods that will improve quality and consistency				
6. Try out suggested changes				
7. Evaluate new methods				
8. Make changes in methods				
9. Furnish information to other groups a—to people of same level b—to people of higher level				
10. Make salvage decisions				
O. WORK SCHEDULES	—	—	—	
1. Accept requests for work				
2. Make up work schedules/weekly labor budgets				
3. Meet established schedules/budgets				
4. Requisition necessary supplies—material				
5. Requisition necessary equipment				
6. Schedule use and maintenance of equipment				
7. Replan work schedules in emergency				
8. Hold quality/service meetings with employees				

FIGURE 9.3 *(Continued on next page)*

SUPERVISORY RESPONSIBILITIES Responsibility & Authority	DEGREE OF AUTHORITY Should handle on own (unless help is wanted) I	Should handle on own and advise superior after-the-fact II	Should discuss with superior before taking action III	Remarks
P. MAINTENANCE	—	—	—	
1. Accept employee's reports of bad equipment or conditions				
2. Check to determine what is wrong				
3. Request repairs (minor)				
4. Follow-up to see that repairs are completed				
5. Accept or reject complete repairs				
6. Request additional repairs until satisfactory				
7. Encourage careful use of equipment				
Q. COST	—	—	—	
1. Estimate cost budget				
2. Meet budget figures				
3. Determine time required to do job				
4. Assist employees in increasing output				
5. Find new methods to reduce time or eliminate work				
6. Solicit employees' suggestions				
7. Try out new methods				
8. Evaluate new methods				
9. Make changes in methods				

FIGURE 9.3 *Continued*

- Introducing new employees to peers and others;
- Providing a tour;
- Providing details of the job.

Orientation of new employees will vary in length of time and complexity depending on the job duties and the facility. Orientation will vary depending on their prior experience. The employee needs the assurance of the supervisor that help, coaching, and answers to questions are available at all times during the orientation.

The dietary manager is the key to effective orientation, as the manager sets the stage for the employee's first impression. Effective orientation programs affect the employee's attitude and relationship with the supervisor, peers, and others. It eliminates confusion and heightens enthusiasm.

EMPLOYEE TRAINING PROGRAMS

All dietary services employees, those new on the job and those with years of experience, can benefit from effective training programs. Done properly, training can be used to help employees learn and/or improve job skills, and gain knowledge.

Everyone probably agrees that training is important; however, frequently it is not done correctly. If, for example, training means placing a new staff member in a department, letting him or her "observe what is going on," and then placing him or her in a workstation with little or no supervision, it is easy to see how training can be "blamed" for problems really caused by ineffective management and supervision.

The Joint Commission for the Accreditation of Healthcare Organizations (JCAHO) and most state licensing laws require specific employee training programs, which generally include:

- Orientation for all employees;
- Inservice for all employees;
- Continuing education for managers and registered dietitians;
- Performance evaluation for all employees.

In some states the requirements are very specific and include such topics as:

- Infection control and personal hygiene to include at least four hours of AIDS instruction;
- Safety (fire, disaster planning);
- Therapeutic diets;
- Proper cleaning and safe operation of equipment;
- Right to know . . . handling hazardous materials;
- General sanitation and safety;
- Proper food handling;
- Risk management.
- Sexual harassment.

Check your state's regulations for specific guidelines.

The inservices must be documented, provided to all employees from all shifts, and be planned and conducted for all dietetic personnel.

Developing and implementing effective training programs is not difficult, but it does take time and requires the dietary manager (or other trainer) to develop a plan and procedures to ensure that effective training can take place. Time, of course, is money, and training is initially more expensive than is the option of not training. However, since trained employees are more productive, are better able to meet quality requirements, and also feel better about the work that they do, it is relatively easy to justify training. With its impact on cost, high turnover, and low morale levels, training has many benefits if it is done correctly.

It is obvious that new employees need to be trained. What about experienced staff members? As new procedures are implemented and new equipment is purchased, there is a need for ongoing inservice training. One can see that everyone benefits from training activities. Many dietary managers assume responsibility for professional growth and continuing education activities for all staff members, and training is at the heart of these responsibilities.

Characteristics of Good Trainers

Can anyone train? The answer to this question is "no." The trainer must have an ability to teach, and be willing to commit the time necessary for training activities. Since the person selected to train is so critical to the ultimate success of the program, the characteristics of effective trainers must be well known and must be applied to the selection of a trainer within the dietary department.

Among the attributes of a good trainer are (a) an interest in training, (b) extensive knowledge of job requirements, (c) an ability to communicate effectively, (d) the need for objectivity and patience, (e) a sense of humor, (f) adequate time for training, (g) the respect of trainees, and (h) an enthusiasm for the training assignment.

Adult Learning Theory

Several principles of learning should be incorporated into training programs. Each is relevant to the training of adults and can be very influential in the ultimate success or failure of training activities.

First of all, trainees must have a desire to learn. There must be an internal motivating force which leads the trainee to desire additional job knowledge and/or new job-related skills. It is not possible for the dietary manager to force employees to accept and learn from training. Trainees must see the benefits in training and must recognize how their own wants, needs, and goals can be better met through training.

Dietary employees want to take an active part in training activities. Everyone learns best by doing, not by passively reading or listening. The more that staff members can be involved in training, the more effective it will be.

Training must focus on real-world problems which employees do or will face on the jobs. Trainees, then, must be shown how the training activities will apply directly to the specific work tasks which they must do.

Dietary managers must recognize that a trainee's prior experiences impact on the learning which can take place. This concept must be recognized especially in group training, where each employee brings a different background to the training. Trainees learn at different rates and will react differently to specific training experiences. For this reason, individualized training is frequently more beneficial than group training methods.

Early efforts to understand how adults learn were done by psychologists who studied learning in general; adult educators then joined in. A number of theories, models, or sets of principles have been proposed, each of which purports to capture the nature and the uniqueness of adult learning. However, no single explanation has emerged as a rallying point by which adult educators can define and explain just what goes on when a learner enters the classroom, apprentices himself or herself to an expert, or checks out a videotape to learn a new skill.

For the purposes of this chapter, training (or the transfer of learning) will be the focus of discussion, although it is necessary to mention that business psychology and organizational behavior has developed into fields of their own and should be researched by those interested in a more detailed study of learning, memory, and motivation.

Many educational programs are built on the assumption that people have the ability to transfer what they have learned in one situation to another. If transfer was not possible, there would be little justification for formal education; every element of knowledge, skill, and capacity would have to be taught separately.

Lateral Transfer

Lateral transfer involves performance at the same level of complexity as the initial learning, but in a different context.

Sequential Transfer

Sequential transfer occurs when we build on a learning foundation. A fact learned today in a subject may have some relationship to a fact or idea learned tomorrow.

Vertical Transfer

Vertical transfer occurs when there is a transfer from the simpler components of a task to the more complex ones.

Positive Transfer

When training or performance in one task can be transferred to another, positive transfer is said to occur (for example, mastering the skill of driving a car results in positive transfer to truck driving).

Negative Transfer

Negative transfer is said to occur when previous learning in a particular task hinders learning in another task (for example, a worker with experience using one type of sanitizing equipment has to learn to use a new model with different controls).

A variety of training techniques, methods, and procedures are available. These include lectures, films, video tapes, computer-assisted instruction, case studies, conferences, simulation, behavior modeling, coaching and mentoring.

A number of questions can be asked about the various techniques. Does the technique emphasize content (information), process (behaviors), or both? Where does the training occur—on-site or off-site? Does the training emphasize psychomotor skills, cognitive skills, social skills, or a combination of all three? How is the trainee actively involved? Does the method used facilitate transfer of learning? In the final analysis, what we must try to achieve is to ensure that the technique or techniques chosen are appropriate in the light of the identified training needs.

One-way Communication

Lectures, video tapes, and films, are examples of a one-way flow of information from the trainer to the trainees. Although these methods are efficient in the use of time and money, they require the recipients of information to be passive, with no opportunity to assess how well or how badly they are absorbing the message or information.

Computer-assisted Instruction

Computer-assisted instruction adopts the principles of programmed instruction and adds the power and flexibility we associate with rapidly expanding computer technology. It utilizes two important learning principles—motivation and feedback. The motivation of trainees is normally high because of their interest in the process, and they are allowed to progress through the material at their own pace with the benefit of immediate feedback. However, transfer of learning is not always assured, except where, for example, the computer is used to enhance the realism through use of simulator training.

Conferences

A conference could be described as a carefully planned meeting with a specific purpose. The proceedings rely heavily on verbal communication among trainees, which can help them understand concepts and influence attitudes.

Case Studies

This method relies on presenting a written report describing an organizational problem to trainees. On an individual basis, the trainee analyzes the problem, makes certain assumptions about a number of events, and puts forward a set of solutions.

A consistent criticism of lectures, conferences, and case studies rests on the issue of transfer of learning. Information obtained from a conference or lecture may have limited effect if the trainee returns to an organizational setting that does not support the application of such information. With regard to case studies, the outcome of these exercises may involve embracing principles that cannot easily be applied in the trainee's real-time situation.

Simulations

The purpose of simulation is to reproduce an actual work situation under the control of a trainer, whereby the latter is able to provide trainees with useful and rapid feedback, and influence their motivational disposition. Other types of interpersonal simulations include business games, as well as the case studies referred to earlier. With business games, trainees are required to make decisions in conditions that approximate circumstances found in the normal business environment.

Today, business games are operated using sophisticated computer packages that may have participants managing a fictitious company, for example. These games can be used as a diagnostic tool for identifying management training and development needs in an assessment center, and for assessing team interaction as part of team-building programs.

Behavioral Role Modeling

Apart from learning from one's direct experience, people may learn from observing the behavior of others. This is referred to as vicarious (second-hand) learning. In the last couple of decades, behavior modeling has been applied to industry:

- Modeling: the trainee observes another person engaging in desired behavior for which he or she receives a reward. The trainee receives vicarious reinforcement by observing the role model receive the reward.
- Retention Processes: the trainee encodes (stores) the observations for later recall.
- Rehearsal: the trainee goes through the motions where the actual observed behavior is rehearsed or practiced.
- Social Reinforcement: the trainer and the other trainees reward the trainee for imitating the previously observed role model.
- Transfer of Training: the trainee tries out the newly learned behaviors in his or her job and reports successes or failures back to the training group.

Behavioral role modeling is concerned with the trainee's motivation, provision of feedback, and the transfer of learning. It also emphasizes the importance of observation and vicarious reinforcement to learning, in addition to actual practice and direct reinforcement.

Steps in the Training Process

There are a series of steps which generally can be followed as training programs are designed, implemented, and evaluated. These steps include:

Step 1: *Define Training Needs.* Dietary managers may notice many problems which might be resolved through training. Low levels of employee morale, high levels of product waste, low productivity, excessive number of accidents, inconsistency in work methods, etc. are typical examples of problems which might be resolved through training. In addition to observation, complaints from other departments and/or from residents, guests, and others, feedback from employees, results from formal and informal instruction programs, etc. may also identify training needs;

Step 2: *Establish Training Priorities.* Since expenses are involved in developing and implementing training programs, the dietary manager must consider the regulatory agencies' requirements for inservices as well as the cost effectiveness of training being considered. Those efforts which are most important relative to costs incurred as well as those that must meet the standards must be given priority as training efforts evolve. Typically, performance-related problems which are most highly visible, which occur most frequently, which create the most additional expense and are required by surveying agencies and/or which otherwise most significantly impact upon dietary services are given priority;

Step 3: *Select Trainees.* Training can be used for both new and experienced staff members. It is true that newly hired employees must be taught many job skills and must be informed about many things as they begin work. However, experienced staff members may also need training or retraining as operating problems evolve and/or as standard operating procedures change. Dietary managers must provide training for all employees who can benefit from it, not just those whose length of service with the facility is relatively short.

Step 4: *Evaluate Current Level of Performance.* In order to determine what has been learned as a result of training, the dietary manager must first assess the level of knowledge and performance exhibited by trainees before training begins. Establishing productivity levels provides a base or foundation of adequate performance against which current performance can be measured;

Step 5: *Develop a Job List.* This training tool notes each task that an employee occupying a specific position must perform. In effect, then, it records each activity that the employee must be able to do as a result of training. Figure 9.4 (Sample Job List for Dishwasher) shows the format for a job list;

Step 6: *Develop a Job Break-Down.* A job break-down should be developed for each task in the job list. This training tool simply specifies how each task should be done. It tells what is necessary to do the task and lists required steps and procedures. This information will be used as the foundation for developing training program content;

Step 7: *Define Goals of Training.* Typically, dietary services training focuses on an ability to "do," not an ability to "know." For example, a training goal might focus on the ability of a trainee to properly perform all tasks indicated on the job list for a specific position. (The proper procedures will have been identified in the job break-downs.);

Step 8: *Establish Specific Performance Objectives.* In contrast to training goals, performance objectives are specific statements of exact outcomes expected from training. Each task, which has been identified in the job list (Figure 9.4) and outlined in a detailed job break-down, should have performance objectives to indicate the skill level a trainee must demonstrate after completing the training. For example, a training objective may be as follows: "As a result of the training, the trainee will be able to wash service-ware according to each of the six steps specified in job break-down #84";

Step 9: *Develop the Training Program.* The actual design of the training program requires that subject matter be arranged in a logical sequence. Necessary materials must be prepared and/or assembled. Procedures for a demonstration, if applicable, must be considered. Training activities must be organized. Tools utilized for this purpose include training plans (Figure 9.5) and training lessons (Figure 9.6). The training plan provides an overview of a series of more specific training lessons. It provides an outline of the entire training program. By contrast, a

Position: Dishwasher — Date Developed: 0/00/00

Tasks: The employee in this position must be able to:	Job Break-down # ______
1. Select proper cleaning chemicals	17
2. Operate dish machine	19
3. Arrange soiled-dish counter	20
4. Manually wash pots and pans	21
5. Clean ventilation filters	23
6. Sort cleaned flatware	27
7. Mop floors	34
8. Assist on tray assembly line	38
9. Properly wash serviceware	84
10. Other	

FIGURE 9.4 SAMPLE JOB LIST FOR DISHWASHER
This is a partial job list; each facility must develop a detailed list for its own use.

1. General Training Goal: ______					
2. Specific Training Objectives: ______					
3. Performance Standards Required: ______					
4. Employees To Be Trained: ______					
5. Other Information	Session #				
	1	2	3	4	5
(a) Date of Training					
(b) Time of Training					
(c) Location					
(d) Instruction Method(s)					
(e) Equipment Needed					
(f) Room Set-Up					
(g) A-V Requirements					
(h) Method of Evaluation					
(i) Special Notes					
6. Other Special Instructions:					

FIGURE 9.5 FORMAT FOR TRAINING PLAN

Topic: ______

Objective(s): ______

______

Type of Training: ______

Activity	Training Techniques	Personnel Involved	Time Required

FIGURE 9.6 FORMAT FOR TRAINING LESSON

training lesson indicates specific training activities which will be undertaken during a specific session;

Step 10: *Select Training Methods.* At the time training lessons are developed the specific type of training method must be selected. There are several types, including individual methods. On-the-job training is an example and will be reviewed below. Group training methods are also possible and include alternatives such as lecture, demonstration, seminar, conference, panel, role-playing, and case studies;

Step 11: *Prepare Trainees.* The trainees desire to know what is expected of them before the training begins. Information about the program's length, its purposes, and specific activities to be used should be announced. Plans must be made for the performance of work which is otherwise the responsibility of the trainee. All too frequently, dietary managers try to squeeze training in with other ongoing activities. If training is important, then the time for training activities must be provided;

Step 12: *Implement Training.* A wide range of training procedures involving either individual or group methods can be used. These will impact the way actual training activities evolve;

Step 13: *Evaluate Training.* It is important to evaluate training to assess its success, that is, to learn how well training objectives have been met. The dietary manager will also be interested in learning whether employees can perform their jobs better as a result of the training experiences. Both the training methods which have been used and the actual results of the training itself should be evaluated;

Step 14: *Undertake Follow-up Activities.* Many dietary managers believe that training evaluation is the final step in the training process. In fact, coaching (reminding trainees about what has been learned) and counseling (emphasizing feelings that an employee may have about the job or other matters) are also necessary as final steps in the training activity.

On-the-Job Training Procedures

On-the-job training (OJT) is common in many dietary departments. It is one type of individual training method. Since it is used so frequently in dietary services, some discussion of it is important.

There are four basic elements in professionally developed on-the-job training programs. The first step is *preparation.* Techniques and strategies for developing OJT programs are basically the same as those required for any other training activity.

A second step in OJT programs is *presentation.* As with any training effort, the job break-down should be used as a foundation for presenting the training information. Training, then, should illustrate and emphasize the correct ways to do things. These are clearly delineated in the job break-down. It is often useful to give applicable job break-downs to trainees at the beginning of training. In effect, the trainer is saying: "Here are the procedures. The objective of the training is to show you how to do the work and to develop the skills necessary to follow the procedures outlined in the job break-down."

After the trainer has reviewed job break-down information, he or she can demonstrate the correct way to do the procedure. As this is done, all of the characteristics of an effective trainer which were noted earlier in this chapter become important. Demonstration should include repetition as necessary to ensure that the trainee understands how each activity fits into work tasks outlined in the job break-down.

The third step in on-the-job training is *practice.* After the trainer has reviewed the basic procedures, the trainee should be allowed to perform the task alone. Repetition is important both to make sure that the trainee knows how to do the work and to provide him/her with an opportunity to build the speed necessary to work efficiently.

Coaching, an integral part of training, is also important while the trainee practices. It is necessary for the trainer to observe and to make suggestions about better ways to do the work. The trainer should frequently compliment the trainee for performance which meets quality standards.

The final step in on-the-job training is *follow-up*. After the training has been completed, the trainee should be able to do work without constant supervision. However, the trainer should continue to observe the trainee to assure that no problems arise. At this time, reinforcement (emphasizing the proper way to do the work) and feedback (indicating the trainer's reactions to the trainee's activities) become important. Coaching is also important at this stage.

Checklist for Effective Training

One has learned that training is very important and that a number of steps are necessary to ensure that it is undertaken correctly. Figure 9.7 provides a checklist of steps important in training. It can be used to help develop training programs in specific dietary services departments.

Employee Performance Evaluations

A dietary manager must be involved in the process used to evaluate the performance of employees. One type of evaluation occurs informally almost continuously as one makes decisions about and judgments regarding the work performed by staff members. Is the employee working correctly? Is the quality and quantity of output meeting expectations? Does the employee seem to catch on? Has training helped to resolve problems? As the manager considers answers to these and related questions, performance appraisal is occurring.

It is also necessary to more formally evaluate employees. Staff members want to know how their "boss" feels about their work performance. Wage and salary decisions, promotion/transfer, and many other matters are affected by the evaluation of employees' work.

The role of the dietary manager in personnel evaluation depends upon the facility. In small departments, all staff members may be evaluated by the director of the department. In very large dietary departments, the role of the dietary manager may be more direct since he/she may have immediate supervisory responsibility for some subordinates.

The role of the dietary manager in performance evaluation, then, depends upon the size (number of employees) of the department. The procedures specified by the facility may also impact on the dietary manager's role. Consider, for example, the facility which requires supervisory input as contrasted with another institution where supervisory input is optional. The responsibility for employee appraisal may, by policy, be the responsibility of the department head alone in many facilities.

In those operations where the dietary manager's role is less direct, he or she must still assume responsibility to (a) respond to employee questions about the process, (b) provide information to the official undertaking the evaluation, and (c) interpret and utilize results of the performance review.

Employee performance review programs can benefit the employee, the dietary manager, and the facility itself. For example, as the dietary manager recognizes the individual staff members through a formal review process, he or she may obtain ideas from the employee about how work procedures can be improved. As strengths and weaknesses of each employee are identified, action plans to improve performance can be developed.

The "ground work" for motivation programs can be laid during performance appraisal. This occurs when employees understand that the dietary manager is

PART I: RECRUIT, SELECT AND ORIENT "TRAINABLE EMPLOYEES

- ☐ 1. Responsibilities for recruitment and selection are clearly separated between personnel (staff) and the user (line) department.
- ☐ 2. Final selection decisions are made by the user department.
- ☐ 3. Personnel needs are planned for when possible; an active file of potentially acceptable candidates is maintained.
- ☐ 4. All company policies regarding hiring are closely followed.
- ☐ 5. Job descriptions—which list major job duties and personal qualities needed by employees to successfully perform the job—are used as part of the selection process.
- ☐ 6. Applicants are recruited from all possible sources.
- ☐ 7. All applicants are required to complete an application form.
- ☐ 8. An initial applicant interview is used to screen potential employees.
- ☐ 9. All managers and supervisors are trained in effective selection and interviewing techniques.
- ☐ 10. The manager/supervisor who will be responsible for the new employee is involved in the selection decision.
- ☐ 11. All references are checked.
- ☐ 12. Selection tests (written and/or performance) are used, where applicable, as part of the screening process and selection decision.
- ☐ 13. All new employees are given a thorough orientation to their new jobs:
    - ☐ information about the company is provided
    - ☐ benefits, pay, etc. are explained
    - ☐ the organization of the company—and where the employee "fits in" is explained
    - ☐ working conditions—breaks, meal periods, training schedules, etc.—are outlined
    - ☐ company rules and regulations are discussed
    - ☐ the new employee is introduced to the work group
    - ☐ uniforms, lockers, special equipment, etc. are provided
    - ☐ an employee handbook is given to the new employee

PART II: PLANNING FOR TRAINING

- ☐ 14. Job-related training is presented to every employee.
- ☐ 15. A job list is developed for each position. It indicates all skills and abilities which an employee must perform as part of the job.
- ☐ 16. Employees who perform the job are involved in preparation of the job list for their position.
- ☐ 17. Job breakdowns are used to break down each task on the job list. Each task is defined in terms of:
    - ☐ a performance-based statement to describe the task
    - ☐ tools and materials needed to do the task
    - ☐ steps in performing the task
    - ☐ how each task step is to be performed
    - ☐ any additional information which is needed
- ☐ 18. Experienced management, supervisors, and employees are involved in developing job breakdowns.
- ☐ 19. Job descriptions are written around the job breakdown information.
- ☐ 20. Job performance standards which indicate quality and quantity requirements for each task identified in the job breakdowns are specified.
- ☐ 21. Work simplification procedures are utilized to ensure that work being analyzed is being performed as efficiently as possible.

PART III: BASIC PRINCIPLES OF LEARNING ARE INCORPORATED INTO TRAINING

- ☐ 22. Learning activities are planned to involve the trainee's sense of hearing, seeing, tasting, smelling, and touching.
- ☐ 23. Trainees are shown the personal benefits of training and learning.

FIGURE 9.7 CHECKLIST FOR EFFECTIVE TRAINING *(continued on next page)*

Source: Lewis Forrest, *Training for the Hospitality Industry.* Educational Institute of American Hotel and Motel Association, East Lansing, Mich., 1982, pp. 334–340.

- ☐ 24. Training maximizes trainee participation in accordance with performance objectives.
- ☐ 25. The training must relate to the trainees' experience.
- ☐ 26. An informal training environment is utilized.
- ☐ 27. A variety of training methods is utilized.
- ☐ 28. Trainees are objectively informed of their training progress.
- ☐ 29. Training periods do not exceed the trainees' attention span.
- ☐ 30. Training sessions are spaced over time rather than concentrated into long sessions.
- ☐ 31. Training takes into account the learning speed of the trainees.
- ☐ 32. Training stresses the right way to do things in a step-by-step approach and incorporates repetition into the process.
- ☐ 33. Cooperation—*not* competition—between trainees is built into the training process.
- ☐ 34. Trainees know exactly what is expected of them when training begins.
- ☐ 35. Trainers are qualified to conduct the training.
- ☐ 36. Training is adapted to the needs of the individual trainee.
- ☐ 37. Trainees are able to practice what has been learned.

PART IV: INDIVIDUAL TRAINING IS EFFECTIVELY DESIGNED AND IMPLEMENTED

- ☐ 38. On-the-job training is properly planned.
- ☐ 39. The trainer is selected, based on skills and interest, and is prepared for the training:
  - ☐ training objectives are written
  - ☐ training methods are determined
  - ☐ training timetables are established
  - ☐ training locations are selected for effective results
  - ☐ necessary materials and tools are collected
- ☐ 40. The trainee is prepared for training:
  - ☐ reasons for training are explained
  - ☐ the knowledge and experience of the trainee are assessed
- ☐ 41. The training is presented in an effective manner:
  - ☐ procedures are explained and demonstrated
  - ☐ the trainer speaks in simple terms, takes adequate time, is patient, and recognizes and utilizes principles of learning (see Part III)
  - ☐ the trainee repeats the training to demonstrate learning
- ☐ 42. The following are used where applicable:
  - ☐ audio-visual aids
  - ☐ individualized instruction techniques
  - ☐ learner-controlled instruction (LCI) techniques
  - ☐ correspondence courses
- ☐ 43. The trainee is coached as necessary after training to ensure that proper procedures are learned and utilized.

PART V: GROUP TRAINING METHODS ARE EFFECTIVELY DESIGNED AND IMPLEMENTED

- ☐ 44. The group trainer is prepared and qualified to train. He/she:
  - ☐ knows how to lead the group
  - ☐ asks and answers questions
  - ☐ uses props and training aids to facilitate the training
  - ☐ practices techniques to build confidence within the individual trainees
- ☐ 45. Group training is properly planned; the four-step training method is used to facilitate planning.
- ☐ 46. Various group training techniques are used where applicable. The following methods are used as appropriate:
  - ☐ lecture method is limited to use when retention of details is not essential
  - ☐ demonstration method is widely used for basic skills training
  - ☐ conference method is used when the training objective involves problem solving

FIGURE 9.7 Continued

- ☐ seminar method is used for upgrading the knowledge and skills of experienced employees
- ☐ panel methods are used for presentations by in-house and outside resource people
- ☐ role playing is used for interpersonal skills training
- ☐ case study method is used to teach situational analysis techniques
- ☐ simulation method is used to develop and refine skills
- ☐ project method is used with experienced employees for upgrading systems

☐ 47. The group is properly oriented to the training which will take place.

☐ 48. Techniques to control the group—and the learning which is to take place—are utilized.

☐ 49. Handouts are used where applicable.

PART VI: DEVELOPING THE TRAINING PROGRAM

☐ 50. Training needs are assessed.

☐ 51. Broad training goals are defined.

☐ 52. Specific and measurable training objectives are defined.

☐ 53. A training plan is developed for the department. It determines;

- ☐ what must be learned and by whom
- ☐ how much is to be learned
- ☐ when it should be learned
- ☐ where the training will take place
- ☐ what training methods will be used
- ☐ what evaluation methods will be used

☐ 54. Training lessons are developed based upon the training plan. They tell:

- ☐ the objective (outcome) for each lesson
- ☐ what the trainer must do
- ☐ how the trainer should do it
- ☐ other information of help to the trainer

PART VII: EVALUATING THE TRAINING PROGRAM

☐ 55. Methods used to undertake training are evaluated.

☐ 56. Training results are evaluated.

☐ 57. Measurable information is collected as part of the evaluation process.

☐ 58. Evaluation information collected is properly interpreted.

☐ 59. Evaluation information is used by the manager/trainer responsible for training.

☐ 60. Training evaluation focuses upon the learning process. It includes:

- ☐ what you want to know
- ☐ where and how information will be obtained
- ☐ by whom the information will be collected
- ☐ how information will be analyzed
- ☐ what the information means

☐ 61. Information collected as part of the evaluation process is accurate, measurable, and objective.

☐ 62. Evaluation occurs before, during, and after training.

☐ 63. Training evaluation is undertaken using a variety of methods. In use are:

☐ questionnaires	☐ case studies	☐ study of records
☐ interviews	☐ planned observations	☐ tests

☐ 64. Tools used to evaluate must be:

- ☐ valid—the tools measure what needs to be evaluated
- ☐ reliable—the tools adequately measure all subject matter or trainees
- ☐ objective—the tools provide a tangible basis for evaluation
- ☐ practical—the tools recognize time, cost, and convenience
- ☐ simple—the tools are simple to use and easy to understand, administer, and summarize

☐ 65. Evaluation generally makes use of simple, numerical counts, percentages, and averages to summarize and interpret the information in understandable terms.

FIGURE 9.7 Continued on next page

PART VIII: TRAINER GUIDELINES FOR SPEAKING AND WRITING

- ☐ 66. Trainers know exactly what is to be said.
- ☐ 67. Trainers look at the person(s) to whom they are speaking when possible.
- ☐ 68. Trainers ask trainees if they understand what was said.
- ☐ 69. Trainers listen to and hear trainees in order to evaluate understanding of what is said.
- ☐ 70. Trainers recall educational backgrounds of listeners/readers when developing training materials.
- ☐ 71. Trainer use short sentences; written statements are precise.
- ☐ 72. Trainers recognize that physical obstacles (noise, lighting, temperature, etc.) can be barriers to learning.
- ☐ 73. Trainers control the training and do not let trainees' actions/responses interfere with the training.
- ☐ 74. Trainers adequately defend, justify, and explain concepts taught in order to overcome resistance to change.
- ☐ 75. Trainers think as they speak to avoid losing their thoughts and their audience.
- ☐ 76. Trainers avoid jumping to conclusions, hearing what they want to hear, or acting with prejudice.
- ☐ 77. Trainers are well organized.

PART IX: COACHING AND COUNSELING PROCEDURES

- ☐ 78. Coaching procedures are used to provide feedback to trainees as an extended part of the training.
- ☐ 79. Counseling procedures are used to help employees with one-on-one problem solving, encouraging them to seek solutions on their own.
- ☐ 80. Employees are encouraged to get involved in appraising problems and outlining possible alternative solutions.
- ☐ 81. Employees are encouraged to take an active role in coaching and counseling sessions.
- ☐ 82. Managers do more listening than speaking while coaching and counseling.
- ☐ 83. Procedures for effective use of directed (focused) and nondirective (allowing employees to explain what is meant) interviews are well known and properly utilized.

PART X: TRAINING RESOURCES

- ☐ 84. Trainers make maximum use of a wide variety of resources as training is planned and implemented, including:
  - ☐ colleges and universities
  - ☐ vocational and technical schools
  - ☐ continuing education and extension programs
  - ☐ externship work programs
  - ☐ trade associations
  - ☐ sales representatives
  - ☐ equipment manufacturers
  - ☐ Chambers of Commerce/other civic groups
  - ☐ Small Business Administration/Small Business Institute
  - ☐ libraries
  - ☐ professional training societies
  - ☐ labor unions
  - ☐ apprentice programs
  - ☐ competitors
  - ☐ special counseling services
  - ☐ community service organizations
  - ☐ general training programs
  - ☐ outside consultants
  - ☐ governmental agencies
  - ☐ packaged training programs

FIGURE 9.7 Continued

concerned about them and is interested in learning about their needs. Coaching, counseling, training, orientation, and many other ongoing programs can be strengthened as the result of information learned during performance appraisal. It also becomes easier to justify job actions such as demotions and transfers when formalized evaluation sessions have been utilized. If the dietary manager can show that performance is consistently inadequate and if the employee has agreed that a problem exists and that improvements will be made, failure to make these improvements may provide justification for actions which are taken.

Performance evaluation can also improve basic management techniques and can help improve the relationship between the dietary manager and employee. Dietary managers can consider the implication of reviews. If employee performance is judged adequate, it may provide support for the type of leadership style being used. If problems are consistently observed with several employees, supervisors may conclude that management styles and procedures are less adequate. As the dietary manager and employees work together as partners in the performance review process, a relationship can be built which helps each to gain a mutual understanding and respect for each other.

The performance review process is affected by established performance standards. The dietary manager's efforts to design training programs will be helpful in yielding quality of work requirements to be evaluated as the performance review process evolves. The process should consider how the quality and quantity of an employee's work compares with the performance standards which have already been established for the job (and for which the employees have received the proper training, tools, supervision, etc.).

Types of Performance Reviews

There are several basic types of performance reviews available to evaluate work. Some of the more common types include:

1. *Comparative types.* Comparative reviews require the evaluator to compare employees against each other. Each employee may be listed in order from "best" to "worst." Alternatively, the best employee may be listed at the top of a list, the worst employee at the bottom of a list, and the process continued until all employees have been ranked. Other comparative types of performance reviews rank each employee from "best" to "worst" in terms of a specific factor (such as quality of work, attitude toward work, etc.). It is also possible to rank employees according to categories. (For example, perhaps only 10 percent of employees can be rated superior and the remaining employees must be "forced" into categories such as "average," "below average," "unsatisfactory," etc.).

An obvious disadvantage of comparative methods of employee appraisal is that it is necessary to compare employees against each other. Since staff members may perform different tasks, it becomes hard to use these methods in a consistent and objective manner. Many people believe that the evaluation should focus on the individual employee and how well he or she works rather than comparing work performance between employees;

2. *Absolute standards type.* When this type of performance review is used, work performance of an individual staff member is considered without regard to other employees. One popular example of the absolute standard type of performance review is the critical incident method. When this technique is used, the dietary manager keeps a "diary" of incidents that represent "good" and "bad" job performance. The diary is then used to measure employee performance. Figure 9.8 illustrates a critical incident evaluation form. The evaluator lists job activities judged important to effective job performance. The date on which "good" or "bad" job performance is noted, this information is recorded. It is also possible to indicate other activities which are noted, in addition to predetermined elements utilized for all employees.

Name of Employee: ______________________ Evaluation Period: ______

JOB ACTIVITY	DATE	OBSERVED ACTIVITY

Signature of Evaluator: ______________________ Date: __________

FIGURE 9.8 CRITICAL INCIDENT EVALUATION FORM

A second example of this basic performance review approach involves use of a checklist developed by the supervisor. A sample checklist evaluation is shown in Figure 9.9. The desirable activities can be evaluated on a scale from positive to negative. Then, as a specific employee is considered, it will be possible to develop a "score." Activities considered most important for effective job performance will be given a larger weight than would other elements. All activities judged most important might be given a point value of "5;" other less important activities would be given a lower weighted point value.

Another example of the absolute standards approach is a forced-choice plan which requires a dietary manager to select a statement judged most accurate in describing how an employee performs on a job. A sample is shown in Figure 9.10. The dietary manager first lists factors judged important to successful job performance in the left-hand column. Then he or she must indicate, for each factor, how the work performance of the employee "meets" each factor.

A final example of an absolute standard evaluation requires the manager to complete an open-ended summary of selected factors judged important in successful job performance (see Figure 9.11).

3. Management by objectives. A management by objectives (MBO) performance evaluation plan is developed from input from both the dietary manager and the employee. First, a mutually defined set of job-related goals is developed. A subsequent evaluation session assesses the extent to which these goals were attained and, simultaneously, defines future goals for the supervisor.

SUPERVISORY EVALUATION

NAME OF SUPERVISOR ____________________ DEPARTMENT __________ DATE __________

CIRCLE ONE FOR EACH ITEM:

ADMINISTRATION	POSITIVE		←		→		NEGATIVE
Knows and utilizes proper forms and procedures	7	6	5	4	3	2	1
Meets deadlines	7	6	5	4	3	2	1
Organizes personal workload	7	6	5	4	3	2	1
Organizes work of those supervised	7	6	5	4	3	2	1
Apprises immediate superior of all current developments	7	6	5	4	3	2	1
Works from well designed calendar of responsibilities & projects	7	6	5	4	3	2	1

Explain where improvement is needed: ____________________

SUPERVISION	POSITIVE		←		→		NEGATIVE
Gives continuous orientation and on the job training to employees supervised	7	6	5	4	3	2	1
Explains orders whenever possible	7	6	5	4	3	2	1
Answers questions fully or obtains answers for employees supervised	7	6	5	4	3	2	1
Administers and supports proper policy	7	6	5	4	3	2	1
Listens to and attempts to correct employee complaints	7	6	5	4	3	2	1
Holds periodic meetings with employees to pass on information	7	6	5	4	3	2	1
Administers discipline when necessary	7	6	5	4	3	2	1

Explain where improvement is needed: ____________________

LEADERSHIP	POSITIVE		←		→		NEGATIVE
Sets goals and objectives for self	7	6	5	4	3	2	1
Sets goals and objectives for employees supervised	7	6	5	4	3	2	1
Meets goals and objectives for self	7	6	5	4	3	2	1
Helps employees meet goals and objectives	7	6	5	4	3	2	1
Supports employees supervised within the limits of proper subordination	7	6	5	4	3	2	1
Supports hospital policies and procedures	7	6	5	4	3	2	1
Helps develop employee potential for advancement	7	6	5	4	3	2	1

Explain where improvement is needed: ____________________

FIGURE 9.9 SAMPLE CHECKLIST EVALUATION *(continued on next page)*

MOTIVATION	POSITIVE		←		→		NEGATIVE
High propensity to accomplish and achieve	7	6	5	4	3	2	1
Identifies with goals of hospital	7	6	5	4	3	2	1
Feels part of hospital team	7	6	5	4	3	2	1
Attempts to help others understand the importance of their work	7	6	5	4	3	2	1
Urges others to excel	7	6	5	4	3	2	1
Gives competent professional image	7	6	5	4	3	2	1

Explain where improvement is needed: ______

ATTITUDE	POSITIVE		←		→		NEGATIVE
Positive toward hospital policy and procedures	7	6	5	4	3	2	1
Feels administration is aware of employee problems	7	6	5	4	3	2	1
Feels hospital changes are for the better	7	6	5	4	3	2	1
Is receptive to constructive criticism	7	6	5	4	3	2	1
Openly supports action of superiors	7	6	5	4	3	2	1
Avoids any negative comments to employees or visitors	7	6	5	4	3	2	1
Takes criticisms up with immediate superior	7	6	5	4	3	2	1
Passes on positive and negtive feedback quickly and accurately	7	6	5	4	3	2	1

Explain where improvement is needed: ______

Comments: Describe the supervisor specifically in terms of the following:

Technical Competence: ______

Creative ability: ______

Motivation and drive: ______

Human Relations: ______

Overall Performance: ______

Additional comments: ______

Signature and title of individual completing evaluation:

______ Signature ______ Title

Signature of supervisor being evaluated: ______

Supervisor's comments: ______

FIGURE 9.9 Continued

License or Registration No. ____________
Date Issued ____________
Expiration Date ____________
Sighted By ____________

Employee Name ______________________________ Job Title ____________
Dept. Name ______________________ No. ________ For Period ______ through ______

REASON FOR EVALUATION

end of probation ______ wage increase ______ annual evaluation ______ termination ______
transfer ______ promotion ______ other ______

The purpose of this evaluation is to aid employees and their supervisors in determining the employee's strong points and shortcomings, if any, on the job. The standard or norm should be the performance of other employees of the same classification and with similar training and experience. Asterisked (*) entries must be justified in the remarks section. All pre-written statements may be modified by adding or deleting words. Use additional paper if needed and indicate the total number of pages for this evaluation at the bottom of this page.

QUALITY (The accuracy or completeness of each unit of work or assigned task. Don't confuse with Quantity.)	* Superior, virtually every procedure is accomplished error-free. ( )	* Careless, needs constant supervision and follow up. ( )	Sometimes inadequate, usually meets minimum standards. ( )	Above average, each procedure is above standards normally expected. ( )	Does job completely and thoroughly. ( )
QUANTITY (Volume of work produced in terms of assigned units or tasks)	* Needs prodding, consistently produces less than is expected. ( )	Completes assignments on time. ( )	Very fast worker, produces more than expected. ( )	* Top producer, exceptionally fast. ( )	Marginal producer, sometimes falls behind. ( )
INITIATIVE (Desire to perform the job properly. Adherence to hospital rules and regulations.)	Meets the requirements of the job. ( )	* Lacks initiative, seems to be lazy and/or uninterested. ( )	Completes work and seeks additional tasks. ( )	* Outstanding, demonstrates drive and ability for increased responsibility. ( )	Sometimes fails to apply self, half-hearted approach to assigned task. ( )
PERSONAL GROOMING (Personal hygiene, grooming, usie of make up, appropriateness of dress.)	* Exceptionally well groomed, demonstrates good taste in dress. ( )	Meets requirements of the job. ( )	* Frequently careless in appearance. ( )	* Wears inappropriate clothing, disregrds departmental standards ( )	Better than average appearance. ( )
ATTENDANCE (Punctuality, absenteeism, tardiness.)	Always dependable and on time. ( )	*Chronically absent or late. ( )	Demonstrates responsibility toward job requirements. Occasionally absent or tardy. ( )	Needs improvement; is tardy or absent several times per month. ( )	Above average, seldom absent or tardy. ( )
DEPENDABILITY (Judgment demonstrated in conserving confidential information, performing on the job, following instructions.)	Inconsistent, requires follow up and/or monitoring. ( )	Efficient, demonstrates discretion, good professional attitude. ( )	* Violates hospital policy, fails to follow instructions. ( )	Usually reliable, carries out instructions with normal supervision ( )	* Demonstrates exceptional judgment; learns quickly, needs little supervision. ( )
RELATIONSHIP WITH OTHERS (Patients, co-workers, public. General courtesies and attitudes.)	Gets along well with others, good attitude. ( )	Goes out of way to promote good will. ( )	* Antagonistic toward others, inconsiderate. ( )	Satisfactory relationship with others, generally adapts to persons and situations, pleasant. ( )	* Defensive, sometimes rigid to change, not awlays cooperative. ( )

Date of Evaluation ________________

Evaluator ______________________ Page 1 of ____________
(Print) (Total # Pages)

FIGURE 9.10 SAMPLE OF A FORCED-CHOICE EVALUATION *(continued on next page)*

Evaluator's (supervisor's) Remarks: ____
____
____
____
____
____
____
____
____

____
Evaluator's Signature

Employee's Remarks: ____
____
____
____
____

____
Employee's Signature

Note: The employee's signature in no way shows that he or she agrees with this evaluation. It merely indicates that the employee has seen the evaluation and understands the contents.

FIGURE 9.10 Continued

Employee's Name: ______________________________ Assignment: ____________________
Date: ____________________

List areas of strength:

List areas of weakness:

List help provided:

List suggestions for strengthening areas of weakness with time limits:

List disciplinary action if no improvement is shown:

General comments:

Comments by employee:

______________________________ ______________________________
Signature of Employee Signature of Evaluator

Date: ______________________________ Date: ______________________________

FIGURE 9.11 ABSOLUTE STANDARD EVALUATION: OPEN-ENDED EMPLOYEE SUMMARY

Basic steps in an MBO evaluation plan include:

a. The manager and employee set measurable behavioral goals which the employee must attain by the time of the next appraisal;

b. The employee is given assistance on the job through training, coaching, and/or other developmental activities;

c. At the time of the performance review, the actual level of performance is measured against the level defined by the goals (both the dietary manager and the employee react at this point.);

d. The supervisor and staff member work together to develop new goals and plan strategies for attaining them before the next performance review session.

The Use of Job Descriptions with Performance Reviews

Job descriptions can be used in the performance review. Since they identify tasks to be done, they provide the foundation for subsequent evaluation. The dietary manager must assure that the employee is properly trained to perform all tasks defined by the job description. Then, as part of the performance review process, he or she can assess the extent to which each job task has been performed correctly.

Possible Problems with Performance Review Programs

Several common problems can confront improperly designed and/or executed employee performance review programs. Some include:

1. Using incorrect procedures. "Shortcuts" found by "creative" supervisors often undercut the objective analysis of employees;
2. Using for disciplinary action only. Sometimes performance reviews are used only to "punish" employees rather than to assess where, if at all, employees can improve;
3. Using ineffective review forms. If review forms do not correctly summarize factors important for effective job performance, the evaluation process will be less than adequate;
4. Failing to use performance reviews. Some dietary managers may not evaluate employees so advantages of performance reviews are lost;
5. Failing to apply basic principles. Sometimes dietary managers may not have the knowledge or skill necessary to effectively evaluate employees;
6. Using overly complicated procedures. When procedures for implementing performance review programs are too complex, difficulties are likely to occur and there will be resistance among some personnel about using them at all;
7. Conducting reviews irregularly. Performance reviews must be conducted on a routine and prescribed basis—not "when time permits";
8. Offending employees. Some dietary managers are unwilling to evaluate employees for fear of offending them;
9. Comparing employees. The objective of performance reviews should be to compare worker performance with expected performance—not with that of other employees;
10. Failing to use performance review information. Some dietary managers may perform appraisal reviews but then fail to make use of information gained;
11. Overemphasizing possible errors in judgment. Some dietary managers may have an overriding concern that errors on their part will hurt employees and, therefore, fail to implement programs;
12. Influencing personnel records. Some dietary managers may be overly concerned that information from performance reviews will become part of an employee's permanent personnel record and may be detrimental to him or her.

In conclusion, the institution should develop a basic set of procedures which should be utilized with modification as necessary to administer the performance review process. Basic elements to be included in the formalized employee appraisal program are shown in Figure 9.12. One may wish to assess whether each of the procedures is used in the process in his or her own facility.

It is very important that dietary managers practice effective principles of employee performance appraisal. The objectives to be gained from this program make it highly cost-effective in every dietary operation.

Employee Corrective Action

Dietary managers must know how to correct employees effectively. Reasonable rules must be established by the human resources department with input from all departments and must be approved by the chief financial officer (or other appropriate officer) and the governing board. Staff members must then follow them. Most employees will understand this and will make a sincere effort to meet reasonable performance requirements. There are, unfortunately, a small number of staff members who may not be interested in cooperating as dietary goals are attained. Corrective action procedures may be necessary to modify behaviors of these staff members and to assure that all reasonable rules and policies are consistently followed. In effect, the task of employee corrective action is really just an extension of motivation efforts.

Corrective action is an effort to modify employee behavior. It does not need to be negative—involving punishment. In a positive sense, the dietary manager should respectively undertake activities to correct, strengthen or improve employee performance.

Check if used in existing review program	Required Procedure
○	1. Objectives for performance reviews are defined.
○	2. Factors used to judge performance are developed.
○	3. It is clearly understood who will conduct the performance reviews.
○	4. The frequency of performance reviews has been determined, and they are conducted on this regular basis.
○	5. Ways to generate employee participation in the performance review process have been developed.
○	6. Procedures for appeal of the performance review finding have been established.
○	7. Follow-up plans, which indicate what the dietary manager must do after the evaluation is completed, have been determined.
○	8. Employees are well aware of all details of the performance review process.
○	9. Effective interviewing techniques are used during the performance review process.

Figure 9.12 Checklist of Elements in Formalized Employee Appraisal Program

It is important for supervisors to be involved in efforts to improve the performance of subordinates. It is, first, necessary to hire the most qualified employees. Second, effective orientation and training programs must be implemented, followed by coaching, communication, and motivation efforts. Positive action can be helpful in keeping employees on course and working correctly. As such, it is an effective tool for a dietary manager.

Corrective Action Process

Designing a corrective action program to reduce labor hours is important. Variations between standards and actual labor hours should be identified and explained by the position supervisor as the weekly labor hour report is completed (see Figure 9.13). This form should be analyzed by the supervisor's manager, and the two offi-

Weekly Section Labor Hour Report

Week of: *7/14/00* **Section:** *Food Service* **Supervisor:** *Sandra*
Shift: *PM*

Actual Labor Hours Worked

Position/ Employee	7/14 Mon	7/15 Tues	7/16 Wed	7/17 Thurs	7/18 Fri	7/19 Sat	7/20 Sun	Total Labor Hours Actual	Total Labor Hours Standard
DINING ROOM									
Jennifer	7	—	7	6.5	7	6	—	33.5	31.0
Brenda	—	7	6.5	7	6.5	6.5	5	38.5	38.5
Sally	—	5	8	7	8	10	—	38.0	36.0
Patty	8	6	6	4.5	—	—	6	30.5	31.0
Anna	4	4	6.5	—	4.5	—	5	24.0	22.0
Thelma	6	5	5	5	5	—	—	26.0	24.0
Elsie	6	—	—	6	6	8	8	34.0	34.0
								224.5	216.5
COOK									
Peggy	4	4	4	4	4	—	—	20.0	20.0
Kathy	4	4	4	—	—	4	4	20.0	20.0
Tilly	4	—	—	4	4	4	4	20.0	18.0
Gert	—	4	4	4	4	4	—	20.0	20.0
Sam	4	4	—	—	—	—	4	12.0	12.0
								92.0	90.0
DISHWASHING									
Terry	—	—	6	6	6	—	—	18.0	18.0
Andrew	6	6	—	—	8	5	5	30.0	30.0
Robert	8	8	8	8	—	—	6	38.0	38.0
Carl	5	—	5	5	5	6	—	26.0	26.0
								112.0	112.0
Total (all personnel)								428.5	418.5
Difference								+10.00	

Remarks: *7/19 – Sally stayed 2 hours–special cleaning*
7/18 – Jennifer, Sally and Elsie given extra hours to learn tableside flaming
7/20 – Tilly stayed 2 hours – clean storeroom shelves

Figure 9.13 Weekly Labor Hour Report

Source: Jack Ninemeier, *Planning and Control for Food and Beverage Operations.* Third Edition. East Lansing, Mich., Educational Institue of American Hotel and Motel Asociation, 1991

cials should meet to discuss the problem. An agreement about corrective action should be made. The agreement should include a time limit within which labor efficiency/costs should be normalized.

Corrective action procedures, once agreed upon, should be implemented. Both the supervisor and the dietary manager can monitor whether the corrective action procedures are effective. At an agreed-upon time, the officials should meet to review effectiveness of corrective action procedures. Then any findings applicable to other positions/sections can be noted. Any need for an updated position-productivity analysis can be reviewed. Deciding the type of corrective action which will be most helpful is an important task. One must *know* exactly what the problem is, *consider* ideas about the effective management of work, *supervise* work as it is performed, and *evaluate* the success of corrective action plans.

Who should be involved in the corrective action process? Factors to be considered include:

1. Is the problem important? As potentially lower operating costs become possible, higher administrative levels become concerned. As proposed solutions impact upon more than one department, other administrative staff will probably become involved;
2. How specific is the problem? If, for example, the problem relates to a storeroom clerk position, the clerk himself or herself may need to be consulted as corrective action plans are developed. If these personnel have an interest in the process (which they often will), they should be consulted. Often, affected employees who have to perform the work daily are familiar with ways to resolve the problems which are occurring;
3. Who is responsible? Clearly, the supervisor who is responsible must be involved in the corrective action plans.

Depending upon the factors above, corrective action plans can include assistance from top and intermediate levels of management, the position supervisor(s), the affected staff, and external consultants (who may be necessary if the knowledge and experience of currently employed staff are not sufficient to resolve problems).

Specific Corrective Action Procedures

Comparison of standard operating procedures with actual work procedures and discussions about observed problems with administrators, affected staff, and others will often identify possible alternatives to resolve labor problems. These options must be analyzed to assess (a) where the problem actually is occurring, and (b) which alternative is most likely to resolve the problem. Concerns about selecting the corrective action plan include:

1. Probability for success (reduction of variance between labor plans and actual operating results) with each alternative;
2. Estimates of costs to be incurred with implementation of each alternative;
3. Knowledge of what has and has not helped to resolve similar past problems;
4. Feasibility of alternative chosen (capable of being implemented). While this may be obvious, some dietary managers waste a lot of time thinking "if only we could do this . . . ," instead of accepting the current situation and attempting to work within its restraints;
5. Compromise between two (or more) possible solutions is often the best plan to resolve a labor control problem;
6. Possible alternative might be tested (one employee or one shift might use changed procedures to see if the proposed solution is likely to be effective);

7. Study of similar facilities, review of books and trade publications, conversations with other dietary managers, and similar activities may help to identify possible ways to reduce labor control problems.

After a corrective action plan is defined, it must be implemented. Dietary managers should be aware that employees affected by corrective action procedures often resist change; they want to "defend the status quo" (comments such as "We have never—or have always—done this" often are heard). This problem often occurs when affected employees have not been involved in the process leading to the corrective action plan. As employee-related concerns arise, dietary managers might best resolve them by explaining and defending the need for change and telling employees how the changes will be best for them (work will be easier or faster, employees will not get as tired, etc.).

Employees must be trained in the new procedures. Too often dietary managers get in a hurry, show employees how to do something one time, and then forget about the procedures necessary to make training successful. Employees must understand clearly what they are expected to do. Dietary managers must communicate carefully their expectations to the staff and must provide all necessary tools and equipment required to perform the work.

After corrective action plans have been formulated and implemented, they must be evaluated. The dietary manager will want to determine whether the variance between standard and actual labor hours has been reduced. If it has, the corrective action plan has been effective; if it has not, another plan or procedure will need to be implemented and evaluated.

Dietary managers will also need to be sure that the corrective action procedures have not created "spin-off" problems in other areas. For example, a labor problem in the dishwashing area might be reduced if revised dish handling procedures are used. However, these procedures might affect the way soiled dishes are brought to, and clean dishes are removed from, the dishwashing area. Systems within the dietary operation are closely related. Be sure that focused attention upon one area does not create problems in another area.

There are several concerns when corrective action efforts are evaluated:

1. If corrective action plans significantly "tighten up" the labor control program, the staffing guides may need to be revised;
2. Evaluation cannot be undertaken too early; some time is necessary for staff to "learn what they are supposed to do." While the new ways are being learned, variance levels may continue to be high;
3. Evaluation should continue over several fiscal periods; often, a change may show a temporary positive or negative impact and then, for some reason, problems might recur;
4. The evaluation and control process is continuous. Dietary managers should not think that problems will not recur. A continual process of labor control, beginning with the review of differences, if any, between standard and actual results, taking corrective action, and concluding with evaluation, is necessary.

Negative Action

A more common definition of corrective action is that it is a negative process which involves punishing employees for wrongdoing. It is, of course, sometimes necessary for dietary managers to punish staff members. As this is done, other employees should know about the actions so that there is less likelihood that others will fail to follow required rules and procedures.

Dietary managers must be extremely careful in discussing corrective action taken against an employee as this may be construed as violating an employee's privacy or confidentiality of information.

Some dietary managers seem to easily acquire the ability to correct staff members. Others do not seem to have this ability. They must often resort to punishment or other negative actions to encourage employees to follow rules and policies. There is a third type of dietary manager who does nothing when rules are broken, and still another who rules with an iron hand. One should understand that the type of leadership practiced by dietary managers can affect their desire and ability to correct employees.

Today many dietary managers place a great emphasis on positive action. In other words, the "big stick" approach to corrective action does not always work. In unionized facilities, dietary managers obviously have less freedom to deal arbitrarily with the corrective action process. The type of dietary employee coming to the job also suggests a way of thinking about the most effective efforts to supervise him or her. The dietary manager who looks at things from an employee's perspective may gain additional ideas about positive, rather than negative, action efforts.

One major problem with negative action is that it encourages employees to do only the minimal amount of work necessary to avoid punishment. The goal of avoiding punishment is, of course, different from a positive attitude which focuses on how to do required work in the best possible way. Many employees who get into trouble are concerned about meeting immediate rather than long-range needs. Therefore, fear of punishment may not deter those who are thinking of immediate concerns only.

Unfortunately, it is true that some staff members may only respond to negative action. However, the dietary manager should make an effort to ensure that attempts are made to focus on the staff member's needs and to react to them with the most appropriate supervisory strategy.

In order for a corrective action program to be effective, staff members must know all job requirements. They should learn these through orientation, training, coaching, and so on. Rules and other requirements must be fair and reasonable. Positive action programs can and must be an integral part of supervisors' work efforts, and only then should negative corrective action efforts be implemented.

Causes of Corrective Action Problems

Major problems which require corrective action include:

- absenteeism and/or tardiness;
- insubordination;
- falsification of records, especially time records;
- honesty-related issues (often involving the theft of hospital/department supplies);
- lack of productivity and/or poor work habits;
- miscellaneous rules.

Corrective action problems can be classified by origin as follows:

- Inadequate aptitudes and/or abilities;
- Inadequate knowledge and/or skills;
- Problems relating to one's personality and/or motivation;
- Problems in the work environment itself.

To reduce problems which otherwise will require negative action, the dietary manager must be an effective communicator. There is always the need to carefully discuss matters and listen to staff members. Many problems, once discovered, can be resolved so that negative action will not be necessary.

There are two basic types of improper behavior: that which results from a purposeful decision made by the employee (examples include stealing, lying and willfully damaging equipment); and that which stems from conditions beyond the employee's control (examples include lack of training, unavailability of proper tools and equipment, inadequate supervision, etc.).

Unacceptable behavior within the staff member's control might best be handled through effective corrective action. Behavior beyond the employee's control really becomes the problem of the dietary manager; employee correction is not appropriate. Therefore, when behavior problems arise, the dietary manager must first look at his or her own actions, the organization of the dietary department and the entire institutional facility to be sure that causes for employee behavior are in fact within the staff member's control.

Classification of Corrective Action Problems

Corrective action is classified as:

- minor infractions;
- major violations;
- unacceptable offenses.*

Minor infractions do little harm and do not result in major problems (unless the infraction happens frequently or in connection with another infraction). Usually oral and/or written warnings correct the action.

Examples of these types of infractions are:

- absenteeism/tardiness;
- clocking in too early, leaving early, not clocking out for lunch;
- failure to meet work standards;
- failure to clean up work area.

Major violations are infractions that interfere with work performance. These violations usually begin with a written corrective action or suspension and require careful, methodical investigation.

Examples of major infractions are:

- stealing;
- refusing to obey work orders;
- sleeping on duty;
- falsifying time records, punching someone else's time card;
- horseplay—violating safety rules;
- threatening, intimidating, coercing or interfering with employees or supervisors at any time;
- poor or careless work.

Unacceptable offenses are infractions that are so drastic that immediate action must be taken. The offense may be criminal in nature, illegal or may endanger other employees. The consequences are serious. Termination is usually the result of these offenses.

Examples of these infractions are:

- stealing private or facility property;
- fighting on facility property;

---

*Each institution/facility has its own specific procedures for taking corrective action. The following information may not apply in your facility.

- using drugs; drinking on duty;
- sexual harassment;
- possession of weapons on facility property;
- immoral, indecent conduct on duty;
- falsification of records;
- punching someone else's time card.

When the dietary manager must take action he or she will need to:

- know the proper corrective action procedure;
- secure input from human resources and/or other officials;
- use that action that fits the offense;
- gather the facts;
- impose action *only* after a fair hearing of all sides and all persons involved.

Principles of Employee Corrective Action Procedures

Basic principles of corrective action should be incorporated into efforts to influence or modify employee behavior. Typically, the staff member's immediate supervisor should be directly involved in corrective action efforts. In some, especially small, dietary departments, the dietary manager—not the supervisor—becomes involved. However, the supervisor should still play some role in the process.

As the level of punishment increases, it is likely that other administrative levels within the facility will become involved. For example, a supervisor may be able to reprimand an employee. He or she may or may not be able to place a written report in the employee's files. In some facilities, this must be done by the department head. It is unlikely that a supervisor will have authority to discharge a staff member, at least without approval from higher-level administrators.

Principles to be incorporated into an effective employee corrective action program are as follows:

- Policies, rules, and procedures must be developed for all areas in the facility. Both administrators and subordinate staff members must be involved in decisions leading to these policies, rules and procedures;
- Rules and policies must be written down. For example, they can be included in employee handbooks and can be explained during orientation, training, and other activities;
- What is true in law is also true in corrective action cases: An employee is assumed innocent until he or she is proven guilty. The burden to prove guilt should rest with the dietary manager, not with the employee;
- Policies, rules, and procedures must be reasonable, fair, and just from the perspective of both the employee and the dietary manager;
- Policies, rules, and procedures must be enforced on a consistent, fair, and honest basis;
- Specific situations must be taken into account. The supervisor must determine whether observed problems were within or beyond the employee's control;
- Investigate what happened and why;
- The affected staff member must be able to tell his or her side of the story as the situation is assessed;
- Do not lose control or let emotions compromise fair and objective judgment;
- Progressive penalties should be used for employee corrective action. For example, a first penalty may be a spoken warning. This may be followed by a written warning. A third occurrence may result in the written notice being placed

in the personnel record. Demotion and/or transfer and discharge may result if problems continue;

- Appeal procedures should be incorporated into the corrective action program;
- Supervisors must prepare for corrective action. A quick "bawling out" is unlikely to yield improved behavior. The supervisor who carefully considers all aspects of the situation and subsequent discipline is more likely to develop plans which will be effective;
- The timing of corrective action must be considered. When practical, punishment should be given as soon as possible after a problem has occurred;
- Affected employees must be informed of any changes in policies, rules, and procedures before they are implemented;
- Corrective action programs should be objectively administered without personal or other bias;
- Once the dietary manager is sure the actions are correct and defensible, the corrective action programs should be undertaken;
- Reprimands should be done in private. The supervisor should not threaten, argue, and/or display anger. The purpose of action is to correct the employee's behavior, not the employee himself or herself;
- After corrective actions have occurred, follow-up is needed to be sure that problems are resolved. The dietary manager should attempt to reestablish a friendly professional relationship with affected employees;
- Corrective activities can be incorporated into the performance review process;
- Dietary managers new on the job should not start off easy by ignoring rules so the staff members will like them. Some employees will test new dietary managers. It is, therefore, important that rules, regulations, policies, and so on be consistently enforced;
- It is important for dietary managers to keep records of all actions involving employee discipline. Figure 9.14 illustrates a form which might be used for this purpose;
- Keep all actions taken confidential;
- Do not discuss actions taken with employees, friends, or others. Employees have rights to privacy.

SUMMARY

Motivation comes from within people. The goal of the dietary manager is to create a delicate set of conditions wherein individuals can somehow meet their needs while doing what management wants them to do. There are numerous theories of motivation that address the question of why people do things.

The best-known motivation theory is Abraham Maslow's hierarchy of needs. These needs are:

- physiological needs;
- safety ;
- social needs;
- ego;
- self-fulfillment.

Creative supervisors can become aware of specific employee concerns and address these as his or her relationship with the staff member evolves.

Fredrick Herzberg and others have considered two sets of factors necessary in a work environment to promote motivation. One set, called maintenance factors, include wages, salaries and other economic concerns, seniority privileges, the ability

In all cases involving disciplinary action or discharge, representation shall be made available prior to such action, except in cases involving probationary employees.

EMPLOYEE'S NAME ____
(last) (first) (middle)

SOCIAL SECURITY NUMBER ______________________________________

DEPARTMENT ____

POSITION ____

It is recognized by Administration and the Union that the Immediate Supervisor, as designated by Administration, may issue written warnings and reprimands to employees.

Accumulation of such reports may lead to dismissal.

Copies of warnings and reprimands will be distributed to the affected Employee and the Union. Serious breaches of conduct or failure to meet responsibilities may lead to instant suspension leading to dismissal. Less serious offenses, incidents of which may accumulate within a given period of time, may lead to suspension and dismissal.

This form is official notice that you are hereby issued a (underline appropriate) WARNING, REPRIMAND or SUSPENSION notice.

Serious offenses shall include, but not be limited to, the following:

________ Leaving job assignment during working hours without permission

________ Absence of (3) continuous working days without properly notifying supervisory personnel

________ Falsification of personnel or other records

________ Possessing concealed, unauthorized weapons or explosives on the job site

________ Theft

________ Sleeping on the job during working hours

________ Fighting on the job site at any time

________ Immoral conduct or indecency

________ Insubordination (except in instances where safety is involved in carrying out an assignment)

________ Making false, vicious or malicious statements about any employee or supervisor

________ Failure to report from approved leaves of absence on or before the appointed time, including recall from layoff

________ Accepting other employment during leaves of absence

________ Reporting for work under the influence of alcohol or drugs

________ Falsification of pertinent information on application for employment or other employment records, where settlement with the employee has been made for total disability

________ Other (explain) ____

Less serious offenses shall include but not be limited to:

________ Contributing to unsanitary conditions or poor housekeeping

________ Engaging in horseplay, running, scuffling or carelessly throwing things

________ Unauthorized distribution of literature, written or printed matter of any description

________ Reporting late for work

________ Abuse, misuse or deliberate destruction of property, equipment, or personal property of any employee in any manner

________ Deliberate violation of an established safety practice or rule

________ Failure to call in reason for not reporting to work prior to starting time

________ Unprofessional appearance

________ Other (explain) ____

FIGURE 9.14 WARNING, REPRIMAND, OR SUSPENSION NOTICE *(Continued on next page)*

Reprimand and warning reports issued for less serious offenses will remain in effect for a period of six (6) months unless the Employee has received more than one (1) report within the six (6) month period. In the latter case, all such reports shall remain in effect for a period of six (6) months from the date of issue of the last report. At the end of any six (6) month period during which the Employee has had a record clear of any other reports, all reports for less serious offenses shall be removed from the Employee's Personnel Record and returned to the Employee at his/her request. Reprimand reports issued for serious offenses will remain in effect for a period of eighteen (18) months unless the Employee has received more than two (2) such reports within the eighteen (18) month period. If more than two (2) such reports have been issued, the Administration may proceed to suspend the Employee and/or process dismissal. At the end of any eighteen (18) month period during which the Employee has had a record clear of any other reports, all reports for serious offenses shall be removed from the Employee's record and returned to the Employee at his/her request.

It is understood, however, that nothing herein is intended to prevent the Administrative Representatives from taking immediate disciplinary action for serious offenses, subject to the grievance procedure.

____
SIGNATURE OF SUPERVISOR

______________ ______________
TITLE DATE

I acknowledge that I have been informed of the reason for my (underline appropriate) WARNING, REPRIMAND or SUSPENSION notice.

____
SIGNATURE OF EMPLOYEE

____
DATE

____
NAME OF UNION REPRESENTATIVE PRESENT (if appropriate)

FIGURE 9.14 Continued

to interact with one's peers, adequate working conditions, and so on, and they will not cause motivation. The second basic set of factors, called motivation factors, provide conditions necessary to motivate employees. Examples of motivation factors include work which is challenging, feelings of personal accomplishment, a recognition for work well done, the ability to perform work of increasing responsibility, and so on. The goal of dietary managers should be to include elements in the job which commonly prevent dissatisfaction (maintenance factors) and which generate job commitment (motivation factors).

David McClelland's work on achievement motivation resulted in the development of a technique with which to measure an individual's achievement motivation and determine how behavior varies in a number of situations as a function of the level of the "need for achievement."

McClelland concluded that people with high achievement needs will, in their everyday activities (and particularly in their work) seek situations that will allow them to satisfy these achievement needs. They will set certain achievement standards for themselves and then work hard to reach those standards.

When employees have been employed and before they actually begin work, they should be oriented to the facility and the department. Proper orientation of new employees is one of the most important first steps in introducing the new employee to the job. Proper orientation to the job, the facility, and the other employees can reduce dissatisfaction and turnover. The dietary manager is the key to effective orientation, as the manager sets the stage for the employee's first impression. Effective orientation programs affect the employee's attitude, relationship with the supervisor, peers, and others. It eliminates confusion and heightens enthusiasm.

The Joint Commission for the Accreditation of Healthcare Organizations (JCAHO) and most state licensing laws require specific employee training programs. Since trained employees are more productive, are better able to meet quality requirements and also feel better about the work that they do, it is relatively easy to justify the cost of training. As new procedures are implemented and new equipment is purchased, there is a need for ongoing inservice training through continuing education activities for all staff members.

Since the person selected to train is so critical to the ultimate success of the program, the characteristics of effective trainers must be well known and must be applied to the selection of a trainer within the dietary department. Among the attributes of a good trainer are the following:

- an interest in training;
- extensive knowledge of job requirements;
- an ability to communicate effectively;
- the need for objectivity and patience;
- a sense of humor;
- adequate time for training;
- the respect of trainees;
- an enthusiasm for the training assignment.

Many educational programs are built on the assumption that people have the ability to transfer what they have learned in one situation to another. Learning transfers include:

- Lateral transfer;
- Sequential transfer;
- Vertical transfer;
- Positive transfer;
- Negative transfer.

There are several training techniques, methods, and procedures available. These include lectures, films, video tapes, computer-assisted instruction, case studies, conferences, simulation, behavior modeling, coaching, and mentoring.

There are a series of steps which generally can be followed as training programs are designed, implemented, and evaluated. These steps include:

1. Define training needs;
2. Establish training priorities;
3. Select trainees;
4. Evaluate current level of performance;
5. Develop a job list;
6. Develop a job break-down;
7. Define goals of training;
8. Establish specific performance objectives;
9. Develop the training program;
10. Select training methods;
11. Prepare trainees;
12. Implement training;
13. Evaluate training;
14. Undertake follow-up.

A summary of steps can be created in a checklist form and then used to help develop training programs in specific dietary services departments.

A dietary manager must be involved in the process used to evaluate the performance of employees. One type of evaluation occurs informally almost continuously as one makes decisions about and judgments regarding the work performed by staff members. It is also necessary to more formally evaluate employees.

Employee performance review programs can benefit the employee, the dietary manager, and the facility itself. As strengths and weaknesses of each employee are identified, action plans to improve performance can be developed.

There are several basic types of performance reviews. Some of the more common types include:

- Comparative types;
- Absolute standards type;
- Management by objectives (MBO).

The dietary manager must assure that the employee is trained to properly perform all tasks defined by the job description. Then, as part of the performance review process, he or she can assess the extent to which each job task has been performed correctly.

Several common problems can confront improperly designed, and/or executed employee performance review programs. Some include:

- Using incorrect procedures ("Shortcuts");
- Using for disciplinary action only;
- Using ineffective review forms;
- Failing to use performance reviews;
- Failing to apply basic principles;
- Using overly complicated procedures;
- Conducting reviews irregularly;
- Offending employees;
- Comparing employees;
- Failing to use performance review information;
- Overemphasizing possible errors in judgment;
- Influencing personnel records.

Dietary managers must know how to effectively correct employees. Corrective action procedures may be necessary to modify behaviors in the dietary department. In a positive sense, the dietary manager should respectively undertake activities to correct, strengthen, or improve employee performance.

Designing a corrective action program to reduce labor hours is also important. After analyzing the weekly labor hour report, the dietary manager and the supervisor should meet to discuss the problem, and then agree about corrective action.

After a corrective action plan is defined, it must be implemented; the employee must be trained in the new procedures; then the corrective action plans must be evaluated to determine its success.

Some dietary managers seem to easily acquire the ability to correct staff members. Others do not seem to have this ability. They must often resort to punishment or other negative actions to encourage employees to follow rules and policies. One major problem with negative action is that it encourages employees to do only the minimal amount of work necessary to avoid punishment. The dietary manager should make an effort to ensure that attempts are made to focus on the staff member's needs and to react to them with the most appropriate supervisory strategy.

There are two basic types of improper behavior: that which results from a purposeful decision made by the employee (examples include stealing, lying, and willfully damaging equipment); and that which stems from conditions beyond the employee's control (examples include lack of training, unavailability of proper tools and equipment, inadequate supervision, etc.). Therefore, when behavior problems arise, the dietary manager must first look at his or her own actions, the organization of the dietary department, and the entire institutional facility to be sure that causes for employee behavior are in fact within the staff member's control.

Corrective action is classified as:

- minor infractions (example: absenteeism / tardiness);
- major violations (example: stealing);
- unacceptable offenses (example: sexual harassment).

Basic principles of corrective action should be incorporated into efforts to influence or modify employee behavior. As the level of punishment increases, it is likely that other administrative levels within the facility will become involved.

KEY TERMS

- Motivation
- Hierarchy of Needs Theory
- Physiological needs
- Safety
- Social needs
- Esteem
- Self-fulfillment (self-actualization)
- Maintenance-Motivation Theory
- Maintenance factors
- Motivation factors
- McClelland's Achievement, Power, Affiliation Theory
- Orientation
- Training programs
- One-way communication
- Computer-assisted instruction
- Conferences
- Case studies
- Simulations
- Behavioral role modeling
- On-the-Job training procedures
- Coaching
- Employee performance evaluations
- Comparative type of performance review
- Absolute standards type of performance review
- Management by Objectives (MBO) performance
- Corrective action

QUESTIONS/PROBLEMS/CASES

1. Explain Maslow's hierarchy of needs. How can it relate to human resource management?

2. You are a dietary manager who desires to promote motivation in your work environment. In reference to Herzberg's maintenance-motivation theory, which factors will you enlist to achieve your goal?

3. According to McClelland's Achievement, Power, Affiliation theory, motivation can be "taught." What are the guidelines necessary to induce a change in the level of "need achievement?"

4. What is the difference between orientation and training?

5. Which learning technique(s) would be most practical in a dietary department? Why?

6. Summarize the "steps" in the training process.

7. Describe the four basic elements in on-the-job training.

8. Joe is the dietary manager of a nursing home with 20 individuals on the payroll. The administrator, Marge, has Joe working very hard as he does the ordering and receiving, figures the payroll and completes special assignments handed to him by Marge. Today he is extremely busy as Marge approaches him with the following.

   "Joe," she says, "I do not know where we are going wrong, but food costs are up, employee turnover has never been higher and the residents seem to be complaining more and more. While I know it is not your expertise, do you think that our employees could use more training?"

   With that question, she left Joe with one final thought suggesting that they might both work together to improve the situation through better training. In fact, she dropped it on him that a new prep cook would be in early morning tomorrow and that a dishwasher was to report at the same time for orientation. Job training would begin immediately for all employees.

   Joe was frustrated as the term orientation had been discussed previously and now a full training program had been suggested by Marge.

   a. What could Joe do to orient the new employees?

   b. What might be the best training to organize in such a short time period?

   c. As far as prioritizing his work, who should Joe train first within the nursing home?

   d. Should Joe involve the other employees in the training process or act as the sole trainer?

   e. Comment on the best time to train and the hours that should be devoted to it.

   f. In light of Joe's present responsibilities, should he recommend to Marge that she do the training or would an outside agency be a better choice? Why or why not?

   g. Describe briefly how to develop the ideal training program that you would recommend for the staff and who would do it.

   h. How soon can you expect results from training?

9. Give two examples of each classification of corrective action. What action corrects it?

10. Which of the three types of performance reviews discussed in this chapter would you prefer to evaluate your own performance?

11. List possible problems with performance review programs.

10

SUPERVISOR AS MANAGER OF CHANGE

Chapter Outline

- Implementing Changes in the Dietary Facility
- Organizational Change
  - Resistance to Change
  - Sources of Resistance
  - Controlling Resistance to Change
  - The Dietary Manager and Change
- Diversity in the Workplace
- Employee Unions
  - Why Employees Join Unions
  - Administrators' View of Unions
  - Unions' View of Administrators
  - Employee Dislike of Unions
  - Structure of Unions
  - Impact of Unions on the Administration
  - The Collective Bargaining Process
  - The Dietary Manager and the Union

Implementing Changes in the Dietary Facility

Dietary managers are change agents. Sometimes change is made voluntarily, as when ideas about performing work more effectively are generated within the dietary department. At other times, change may be forced upon the department from higher levels in the organization. Dietary managers must accept as an integral part of their job the responsibility to consider whether change is necessary and, if so, how it can be most effectively implemented.

Change is really a continuing process; it is not an activity with a distinct start and finish. The facility in general and the dietary department specifically are evolving at all times.

What is change? It results from an alteration, substitution, or new development or process. In other words, change occurs when there is a difference in the way things are done.*

All elements in the dietary department and within the facility itself are closely related. Therefore, a change made in one area of the facility is likely to have an impact on other areas as well.

*This definition is suggested in: Robert M. Fulmer, *Supervision: Principles of Professional Management.* Glencoe Press, Beverly Hills, CA., 1976, p. 352.

For change to be effective, the dietary manager must first show employees why—from their perspective—there is a problem with the existing situation. He or she can justify a change by explaining how it will benefit the employee as well as the dietary department and facility.

When working toward a desired change, it is important for the dietary manager to attempt to modify behaviors of the subordinates. Using rewards and punishments, practicing motivation principles, using effective communication tools, and so on are some approaches that can be used.

Dietary managers are more likely to implement change effectively when they have the respect of the employees.

ORGANIZATIONAL CHANGE

All elements in an organization—its people, structure, and technology—are related; each can be changed. Typically, as the amount of change being considered increases, there is a greater likelihood that other aspects of the facility will also be affected. For example, a change in the philosophy of a hospital which emphasizes community service / outreach programs is likely to have an impact on every department within it. By contrast, a change in an equipment item in the kitchen is likely to affect only the dietary department.

Employees should, when possible, be involved in change being considered. Dietary managers can attempt to modify their attitudes, change skills necessary to work within the changed situation and utilize participative management approaches to involve employees in planning for the change. As employees are trained, coached, and counseled about changes being proposed, their involvement will, ideally, reduce their resistance to the changes.

It is possible to change the organizational structure itself, for example, when the chain of command and / or the flow of communication through the organization is revised. As responsibilities of departments and / or personnel within them are expanded or decreased, structural change is likely to occur. Organizational structure sometimes changes as the philosophy of the facility changes. As external pressures (such as today's emphasis on Diagnostic Related Groups [DRGs] and cost containment efforts) evolve, organizational change is more likely to occur. Re-engineering or restructuring may occur with a merger or simply to increase effectiveness.

New technologies affect the organization and often create a need for organizational change. Consider, for example, the ways that the computer and highly sophisticated food production equipment have changed the organizational structure of many dietary departments.

RESISTANCE TO CHANGE

Often it is difficult for dietary managers to implement change. Why is this? Frequently, it is because affected personnel resist the change. It is probably human nature to be anxious and / or nervous about changes in the way things are done.

Reasons for staff members resisting change can include the following:

- *Economic concerns.* Sometimes changes have a negative economic impact upon employees;
- *Inconvenience.* Some changes will require employees to learn new operating procedures, become responsible for extra duties, etc.;
- *Anxiety.* Employees are frequently threatened by the unknown;
- *Changing relationships.* Changes in the work environment can modify working relationships which some employees enjoy;
- *Increased control.* Changes often require that employees be more closely supervised during transitional periods;

- *Mistrust in supervisors.* If employees have not had successful experiences with change, mistrust can create problems as additional changes are proposed.

Change creates uncertainty as to what the future holds, and as a consequence can lead to personal insecurity. Therefore, it is not surprising to encounter resistance to change within organizations.

An organizational change, such as a move to a better office, can be warmly accepted, simply because it is seen to have obvious advantages. But not all changes fit into this category. Where changes create ambiguity and uncertainty, then resistance to change is likely to emerge. In essence, the resistance is not to change as such—rather it is to the personal loss (or possibility of personal loss) that people believe will accompany the change.

Sources of Resistance

Six sources of resistance to change can be observed at the organizational level. Most of these sources are people-centered and are connected with people being fearful of loss in one form or another (loss of power, or resources, or the loss of the security of a predictable routine). These six sources, which do not necessarily reside in all situations of organizational change, are:

Over-determination. The structure of the organization is designed to maintain stability by resorting to an elaborate process regulating such activities as recruitment, selection, training, rewards and performance appraisal. The organizational system is over-determined in the sense that lesser control or safeguards could achieve the same outcome. As a result, the elaborate structure could become an impediment to change.

Narrow focus of change. On many occasions efforts to introduce change in organizations take a rather narrow focus, instead of considering the likely knock-on effects arising from the existence of normal interdependencies between tasks, structure and people found in organizations.

Group inertia. The norms of the group constrain attempts by individuals to change their behavior. In fact the group is obstructive. This could arise when the group refuses to engage in complementary behavior in order to reinforce the position of the individual.

Threatened expertise. A change to a job may result in an alteration to, for example, the skills requirement of that job. Such an eventuality may pose a threat to people's expertise developed over many years, with the inevitable consequence of resistance to change.

Threatened power. A reorganization may lead to changing the existing pattern of decision making for individuals who benefited in the past from exercising the power to make decisions, but now stand to lose a significant part of their power base, the reorganization may trigger resistance to change.

Resource allocation. Individuals could be quite content with the way resources are currently allocated to them. A change that heralds less than satisfactory arrangements for individuals previously satisfied with the status quo, is likely to be resisted.

Moving away from the organizational level, a number of specific individual factors have been identified as sources of resistance to change:

- Habit;
- Security;

- Economic considerations;
- Fear of the unknown;
- Lack of awareness;
- Social considerations;
- Self-interest;
- Misunderstandings and lack of trust;
- Contradictory assessments; and
- Low tolerance of change.

Controlling Resistance to Change

Resistance can be constructive if it forces managers to interact more frequently with subordinates, to review the decision to introduce change and perhaps to explore alternative ways to meet the desired objective. The action taken by management to review the proposed change that is the cause of resistance may be perceived by employees as a desirable symbolic gesture, conveying the impression that management cares about them and has respect for their viewpoint.

Six approaches have been put forward as ways of controlling resistance to change and are detailed in Figure 10.1.

- Education and communication;
- Participation;

Approach	Commonly Used in These Situations	Advantages	Drawbacks
Education & Communication	Where there is a lack of information or inaccurate information and analysis	Once persuaded, people will often help with the implementation of the change	Can be very time-consuming if lots of people are involved
Participation & involvement	Where the initiators do not have all the information they need to design the change, and where others have considerable power to resist	People who participate will be committed to implementing change, and any relevant information they have will be integrated into the change plan	Can be very time-consuming if participators design an inappropriate change
Facilitation & support	Where people are resisting because of adjustment problems	No other approach works as well with adjustment problems	Can be time-consuming, expensive, and still fail
Negotiation & agreement	Where someone or some group will clearly lose out in a change, and where that group has considerable power to resist	Sometimes it is a relatively easy way to avoid major resistance	Can be too expensive in many cases if it alerts others to negotiate for compliance
Manipulation & co-optation	Where other tactics will not work, or are too expensive	It can be relatively quick and inexpensive solution to resistance problems	Can lead to future problems if people feel manipulated
Explicit & implicit coercion	Where speed is essential, and the change initiators possess considerable power	It is speedy, and can overcome any kind of resistance	Can be risky if it leaves people mad at the initiators

FIGURE 10.1 APPROACHES FOR CONTROLLING RESISTANCE TO CHANGE

Source: Kotter, J.P. & Schlesinger, L.A. (1979). Choosing strategies for change. *Harvard Business Review,* March/April, 106–114.

- Facilitation and support;
- Negotiation and agreement;
- Manipulation and co-option; and
- Coercion.

The Dietary Manager and Change

Change is easier to implement when the dietary manager has developed a relationship of trust and respect with the employees. In fact, some staff members may favor a change simply because they trust the judgment of the dietary manager. Other staff members may not believe the dietary manager, or at least will need time to evaluate the proposed impacts of the change.

The relationship between the dietary manager and employees evolves from a history of honesty, fair play, and a concern for the welfare of staff members. The dietary manager must interact with employees as change is implemented. He or she must share reasons for change and, as noted throughout this chapter, must solicit employees' input whenever possible.

Involving employees in change begins long before it is implemented. Employees' views should be solicited from the time changes are first contemplated, through the process of actual decision making. Employees can also provide help in generating alternatives, in conducting studies and tests if applicable, and in developing the final procedures to be used after change is implemented.

Dietary managers should address any economic concerns employees may have. This can be done by communicating effectively and by analyzing the true impact of change on the employees.

If a dietary manager has strong position power, he or she may use authority as a tool in implementing change. In fact, if he or she has a poor relationship with employees, there may be few alternatives other than formal authority. However, persuasion (discussed further in Chapter 12) can also be a useful tool in implementing change.

Training programs are often necessary as changes are implemented. Employees must be informed about new work procedures, and complementing training by other techniques can be very useful in overcoming resistance to change. One such technique is to involve both formal and informal employee groups and their leaders in the change process. To the extent that leaders can assist dietary managers with defending the need for change, the tactic can be very useful.

After change has been implemented, it must be evaluated. It is important to see whether the change has been beneficial and whether any additional changes are needed to further improve the effectiveness of the dietary department. The dietary manager should also assess whether there have been any spin-off effects of the change. Since the dietary department is comprised of a number of closely related subsystems, the spin-off problem is always of potential concern.

It is difficult to evaluate change effectively. Frequently, information required for evaluation is unavailable or inaccurate. It is also frequently difficult to state the exact results of change in measurable terms. However, even though evaluation is difficult, it is necessary. One approach is to consider how the situation will differ after change has been effectively implemented. Then, as part of the evaluation, the existing situation can be studied in comparison with the planned situation.

Figure 10.2 provides a review of strategies which can be helpful if each of these factors is addressed as change is considered, implemented, and evaluated.

Diversity in the Workplace

The meaning of diversity has changed in recent years. Not long ago, diversity referred simply to a person's gender or ethnic group. Diversity today encompasses differences in age, tenure in an organization, educational background, sexual pref-

	YES	NO
1. Is change necessary?	○	○
2. Do you completely understand—from your perspective as a supervisor—why the change is necessary—and what exactly it is supposed to do?	○	○
3. Do you think about possible reasons why employees might resist the change—and develop effective counter arguments for these reasons?	○	○
4. Do you use an individual counseling technique to discuss the change and its implication with each affected employee?	○	○
5. Do you use a persuasive technique to discover employee perceptions of disadvantages—and to counter these with information which will help employees see advantages to change?	○	○
6. Do you involve group leaders—both formal and informal—and request their help in gaining acceptance to change?	○	○
7. Do you use a trial approach (test the proposed change and then modify it as necessary) rather than implement it on an "all or nothing" basis?	○	○
8. Do you make sure that affected employees know what must be done differently before changes are implemented?	○	○
9. Do you carefully supervise employees during the awkward transitional period when changes are being implemented?	○	○
10. Do you provide carefully designed training experiences before changes are implemented?	○	○
11. Do you develop indicators of effective change that measurably describe what the situation should be after the changes are made?	○	○
12. Do you evaluate the results of the change based upon the extent to which indicators of effective change are seen in the network situation?	○	○
13. Do you try to recognize any benefits that may result from employee resistance to change?	○	○
14. Do you know how to generate a need for change?	○	○
15. Do you have the respect of the employees who must change?	○	○
16. Do you have a good track record for implementing change with few surprises for employees?	○	○
17. Do you know what other changes are occurring in the organization at this time?	○	○
18. Do you know the impact of the proposed change on other departments?	○	○
19. Do you have necessary training programs already planned and in place?	○	○
20. Do you know whether existing work flows will be improved as a result of the change?	○	○
21. Do you know whether the situation requiring change is of continuing importance to the organization?	○	○
22. Are all employees permitted, to the extent possible, to participate in all activities relating to the change	○	○
23. Do you know what you can and should do to increase pressure for change?	○	○
24. Do you have all the information you need to make the change?	○	○

FIGURE 10.2 CHECKLIST FOR IMPLEMENTATION OF CHANGE

erence, physical abilities or qualities, social status, economic status, lifestyle, religion, ethnicity, and gender, among many other characteristics.

Diversity has multiple dimensions. A **primary dimension** is defined as one that is immutable or inborn and that exerts a profound and constant impact throughout a person's entire life or a substantial portion of it. Under this definition, primary dimensions include age, ethnicity, gender, physical abilities, or qualities. **Secondary dimensions** are attributes that can be acquired, discarded, or modified. This category includes education, geographic location, income, marital status, religion, and work experience. Many organizations include both types of diversity in their definitions.

According to Ann Morrison, author of *The New Leaders: Guidelines on Leadership Diversity in America,* organizations that manage their diverse work forces effectively can benefit in the following ways:

Increased market share. A customer is more likely to buy from someone with whom she or he readily identifies than from someone with whom there is no affiliation.

Reduced costs. Encouraging diversity saves the costs of unwanted turnover by providing non-monetary reasons to stay with an organization, by reducing recruitment costs because companies with diversity policies and programs are sought out by those who value such policies, and by reducing discrimination lawsuits. A company that makes employees of all stripes feel welcome could offset the decline in organizational loyalty noted by some observers.

Increased productivity. People who enjoy coming to work generally produce more, as will workers who believe that their work will be valued or lead to advancement. Research also indicates that heterogeneous groups are generally more creative and innovative than homogeneous groups.

Improved management quality. Including all employees in consideration for managerial positions improves the pool of applicants. It also may unblock some highly qualified individuals who may have been unable to advance due to spoken or unspoken policies that discriminated against them for one reason or another. Moreover, exposure to diverse colleagues can help managers develop depth in their ability to solve workplace problems.

Improved recruiting efforts. Spot shortages in labor appear from time to time. Recruitment of a diverse population can offset shortages because many workers are drawn to companies that embrace diversity.

Fostering diversity requires a comprehensive and carefully planned approach, there is no such thing as a quick fix. Approaches to addressing diversity have evolved in recent years:

Golden-rule. The concept of treating others as you would wish them to treat you appears in a number of religions and philosophies, but a common codification is the "golden-rule." According to this approach, everyone is unique and the only important differences are individual differences. The golden-rule approach suggests that everyone should be appreciated and treated evenhandedly. Individuality and morality make diversity successful.

Assimilation. The idea of this approach is that all people are expected to shape themselves to fit an organization's dominant style and thus to be assimilated. Under this theory, the best approach to instilling diversity in the work force is to suggest that persons in minority groups abandon their preferred dress style, cultural values and such when they are working so that they can be assimilated into the preferred style of the organization's dominant coalition. The "dress for success" concept is an offshoot of this theory.

Righting the wrongs. This approach emphasizes correction of past wrongs in the workplace. Much like affirmative action, this plan calls for targeting specific groups to ensure that they receive fair representation in the workplace. Although past wrongs need to be addressed, the weakness in this approach is that it can create a "we versus they" mentality.

Culture-specific approach. Education in various cultural norms allows different groups to coexist more or less comfortably. That is the principle underlying the culture-specific approach, which resembles preparing workers for assignment in a foreign country. A training program that uses this approach for diverse employees has the intention of hastening adjustment to the "foreign country."

Multicultural approach. The multicultural approach involves increasing the awareness, consciousness and appreciation of differences among people. Because this approach emphasizes differences, it takes into account diversity issues that the other approaches do not, including sexual orientation, religion, and personal values. This approach suggests that it is the organization, not the individuals within it, that must change to make diversity work, although it is time-consuming and costly to implement.

A facility could adopt portions of each of the five approaches to ensure a successful diverse workplace. Unlike the five individual approaches, the combined approach emphasizes sharing power and control in the workplace among people who are different, rather than simply asking the dominant group to design programs for others.

Employee Unions

Dietary managers may need to interact with employee unions. This section provides basic helpful information.

Why Employees Join Unions

Reasons for an employee desiring to join a union include:

Problems with dietary managers. Managers (especially first-line supervisors) often fail to provide, to some minimal degree, what employees want from their jobs. In many instances, employees vote "for or against" their immediate supervisor when they assess their interests in a union.

Implementation of procedures to address employee concerns can be helpful in eliminating many of the reasons for affiliating with a union. Dietary managers will do well to continually assess each employee's needs and wants. Some techniques used to do this include a suggestion box, employee survey(s), "employee relations rounds" conducted by the personnel department (or by the dietary manager in small facilities), employee meetings and effectively conducted employee appraisal programs.

Whenever these or other techniques are utilized to assess employee concerns, there must be a subsequent real attempt to resolve matters identified by employees.

Improved benefits and working conditions. Many employees desire the attractive benefits which unions promise. These may include higher pay rates, security/tenure provisions, grievance and arbitration processes, and so on. Unresponsive administrators and the absence of desired benefits and work conditions often drive employees into unions.

Group/social pressures. Many employees join unions for social reasons. Some employees (who otherwise might be apathetic) may join "because their friends and/or peers joined." Social and group pressure can be a strong motivating force for the union movement.

Other reasons. Among these are "a desire to be heard," a formal means to express themselves to administrators, and a feeling that group attachment brings security: a formal group of workers is stronger than an informal group.

Administrators' View of Unions

Administrative personnel and employee unions often view the world of work (and each other) differently. Unions, as seen from the perspective of administrators, often cause problems:

1. They interfere with the administrators' rights and prerogatives to operate the facility as they wish;
2. They affect productivity: (1) unions assume that all (most) productivity increases arise from increased worker efficiency (which discounts productivity increases from revised work methods, new equipment, etc.); (b) unions often negotiate "make-work" provisions or are able to tie output to pre-established maximums. These plans eliminate other possibilities to increase productivity;
3. Unions can cause strikes which affect the best interests of the facility;
4. Unions cause significant, detrimental changes in the supervisor-worker relationship. Administrative decisions may be challenged, personnel policies may be frequently reviewed/criticized, and rules may become rigid (and often must be developed at a centralized level to provide necessary consistency);
5. "Outsiders" from non-internal branches of the union become involved in the administrator-employee relationship.

Unions' View of Administrators

Administrators, as viewed by the unions, likewise cause problems:

1. The organization places its needs, rather than the employees' concerns, first. This lack of caring for employees is a very important and frequently-held view of union advocates;
2. Administrators frequently fail to give unions "credit" for the contributions which they have made to society and to improving the life of the "average" worker;
3. The facility's emphasis is on making money or minimizing expenses rather than meeting the workers' needs on the job.

It appears that there are often wide differences between the goals of administrators and unions. Administrators strive to reduce labor costs and increase efficiency, to retain authority over the dietary operation, and to maintain a nonunion operation. In contrast, the union desires greater wages, benefits, and working conditions for employees, and greater opportunities to bargain for the employees.

Employee Dislike of Unions

The majority of all dietary employees are not union members. One reason is that unions do not generally want to organize small facilities with relatively few staff members. Additional reasons include:

1. Cultural and social reasons. Some staff members may dislike unions because of previous experiences. Others want to be "in control of their own future" without union assistance. Still others believe that "professionals should not join unions";
2. Individual reasons. Some staff members desire to represent themselves to facility administrators and want to "work things out" without external assistance;

3. Desire to affiliate with the administration. Many staff members in administration, and those who aspire to these positions, want to identify with top-level administrators and may develop "anti-union views";
4. Fear of punishment. Even though employees are protected by various laws, some fear punishment if they promote and/or affiliate with a union.

Structure of Unions

The local union is the basic unit of organization. It may represent, for example, all unionized dietary staff members in a single community. Conversely, it may only represent members within a specific facility. Local unions elect officers by a democratic vote of their members.

Full-time officers are generally found in large unions. In contrast, small employee unions have a president who may devote part of his or her time at work to union duties.

Union members elect shop stewards who represent all the unionized staff in a specific department. Both the president and shop stewards have a regular job, are paid by the employer, and use some time from the job—in addition to personal time—for required union activities.

Some unions have regional organizations to coordinate the activities of the local unions. Some unions are affiliated with a national or international union whose purpose is to establish basic policies, provide necessary services, collect information, and administer strike and retirement funds as necessary.

Impact of Unions on the Administration

Once employees are represented by a union, the administration will probably have to alter operations in several ways. It will no longer be able to make decisions or deal with individual employees on a specific basis. Rather, it will need to follow all requirements imposed by the union agreement. Regardless of an employee's ability or skills, each must be treated equally if he or she is in the same (or similar) job classification. Frequently, seniority rather than other factors which might separate "good" from "bad" employees may become the most important factor in matters affecting dietary services.

There can be advantages to unionization. It will be necessary to develop and/or improve policies or procedures which affect relationships with employees. Facilities not having these personnel management tools are likely to benefit. Facility administrators will also be able to deal with only one representative of unionized employees rather than with individual staff members. Finally, top levels of administration may need to recover much decision-making responsibility which had previously been delegated to supervisors, since the actions of a single supervisor may have facility-wide implications in a unionized facility. To the extent that centralized decision making is good (and many administrators believe this), it is another advantage to union affiliation.

The Collective Bargaining Process

Many dietary managers define collective bargaining as negotiations between union and facility representatives leading to a contract. More generally, however, the term applies to routine interactions between administrators and the unions. In reality, collective bargaining involves aspects of organizing staff members, negotiating and administering agreements, interpreting contract clauses, and resolving disputes (grievances) between union and administrative officials.

A great deal of time can be spent in negotiating a union agreement. It is common for union contracts to extend for three or more years. To prepare for the negotiation, facility officials must obtain information about prevailing wage and salary rates and fringe benefit provisions, as well as its own economic position. They must also analyze existing contracts and consider probable union concerns.

At the same time that administrators are preparing for contract negotiations, union officials must collect their own information, survey membership about concerns, and develop strategies for collective bargaining.

1. Union recognition
2. Union security
3. Management security
4. Dues check off procedures
5. Union representation
6. Duties/responsibilities of stewards
7. Grievance procedures
8. Seniority rights
9. Probationary periods
10. Promotions and job openings
11. Leaves of absence, vacations, and sick leave
12. Discipline and discharge procedures
13. Hours of work, scheduling, and overtime
14. Discrimination prohibition
15. Safety concerns
16. Meals, uniforms, and dressing rooms
17. Wages and benefits
18. General provisions (discipline, breaks, lay-offs, posting of jobs, etc.)
19. Successors
20. Strikes/lockouts
21. Conflict of laws
22. Duration of agreement

FIGURE 10.3 TYPICAL CONCERNS ADDRESSED IN COLLECTIVE BARGAINING AGREEMENTS

A wide range of topics can be addressed in collective bargaining agreements; many of these are listed in Figure 10.3.

THE DIETARY MANAGER AND THE UNION

The dietary manager is an important element in the employee's decision about whether or not to support the union. He or she may also be the one staff member most affected by a union. There are basic actions which a dietary manager can and cannot undertake during an organizing campaign. It is obvious that a facility must seek qualified legal counsel as it faces possible unionization efforts. The following information cannot, then, substitute for this advice, but is presented only to show basic supervisory principles as they apply to the unionization process.

The administration, including dietary managers, can attempt to assess the union's strength as the organizing effort evolves. Dietary managers in close contact with their subordinates may have reasonable estimates about this information. Studying a union's campaign strategy can help assess strength; for example, if a union takes extreme positions, it may be concerned about its potential for success. If broad issues are cited, the union may be "searching" for ways to generate interest among employees.

If the facility is unionized, the relationship between the dietary manager and the employees will obviously be affected. He or she must continue to treat all employees fairly and consistently, but will probably find that some authority has been reduced. Since the dietary manager must comply with all contract provisions, he or she will have less ability to deal directly with employees on matters covered by the union bargaining agreement. The union steward will become involved.

Both the dietary manager and the union steward are in unique positions. The manager ranks between employees and higher levels of administration. The union steward plays two roles simultaneously—as an employee and a union representative. These officials share many responsibilities and must understand, interpret, and enforce the contract while acting as representatives for others.

If a union steward agrees, a union employee may file a formal grievance when he/she is not satisfied with the way a complaint has been settled. While the specific grievance process will be outlined in the union contract, certain components are typical. The dietary manager may first meet with the union steward and the employee in an attempt to resolve the problem. If this is not possible, the dietary manager's boss or another administrative official may meet with the union's grievance committee. If this is not successful, top administrative officials may meet with the grievance committee; if necessary, top administrative officials may need to meet further with top-level officials of the local, national, or international union. If resolution is still impossible, the matter may go to mediation (in which advice is given to both parties) or to arbitration (in which a third party makes a binding decision).

SUMMARY

Dietary managers, as change agents, must accept as an integral part of their job the responsibility to consider whether change is necessary and, if so, how it can be most effectively implemented. When working toward a desired change, it is important for the dietary manager to attempt to modify behaviors of the subordinates by the following approaches: reward and punishment, practicing motivation principles, and using effective communication tools.

Employees should, when possible, be involved in change being considered. As employees are trained, coached, and counseled about changes being proposed, their involvement will, ideally, reduce their resistance to the changes. Where changes create ambiguity and uncertainty, then resistance to change is likely to emerge.

Six sources of resistance to change can be observed at the organizational level:

1. Over-determination;
2. Narrow focus of change;
3. Group inertia;
4. Threatened expertise;
5. Threatened power; and
6. Resource allocation.

In addition, a number of specific individual factors have been identified as sources of resistance to change: habit, security, economic considerations, fear of the unknown, lack of awareness, social considerations, self-interest, misunderstandings, lack of trust, contradictory assessments, and low tolerance of change, among others.

Resistance can be constructive if it forces managers to interact more frequently with subordinates, to review the decision to introduce change, and perhaps to explore alternative ways to meet the desired objective. Six approaches have been put forward as ways of controlling resistance to change:

1. Education and communication;
2. Participation;
3. Facilitation and support;
4. Negotiation and agreement;
5. Manipulation and co-option; and
6. Coercion.

Change is easier to implement when the dietary manager has developed a relationship of trust and respect with the employees. Employees' views should be solicited from the time changes are first contemplated through the process of actual decision making. And after change has been implemented, it must be evaluated. It is important to see whether the change has been beneficial and whether any additional changes are needed to further improve the effectiveness of the dietary department.

The meaning of diversity has changed in recent years. Diversity today encompasses differences in age, tenure in an organization, educational background, sexual preference, physical abilities or qualities, social status, economic status, lifestyle, religion, ethnicity, and gender, among many other characteristics.

Organizations benefit from diversity in many ways:

1 Increased market share;
2. Reduced costs;
3. Increased productivity;
4. Improved management quality; and
5. Improved recruiting efforts.

Approaches to addressing diversity have evolved in recent years:

1. Golden-rule approach;
2. Assimilation approach;
3. Righting the wrongs approach;
4. Culture-specific approach; and
5. Multicultural approach.

Dietary managers may need to interact with employee unions. There are several reasons why an employee may desire to join a union:

1. Problems with dietary managers.
2. Improved benefits and working conditions.
3. Group/social pressures.
4. A desire "to be heard."

From the perspective of administrators, however, unions often cause problems:

1. They interfere with the administrators' rights and prerogatives to operate the facility as they wish;
2. They affect productivity;
3. Unions can cause strikes which affect the best interests of the facility;
4. Unions cause significant, detrimental changes in the supervisor-worker relationship;
5. "Outsiders" from non-internal branches of the union become involved in the administrator-employee relationship.

Administrators, as viewed by the unions, likewise cause problems:

1. The organization places its needs, rather that the employees' concern first;
2. Administrators frequently fail to give unions "credit" for the contributions which they have made;
3. The facility's emphasis is on making money or minimizing expenses rather than meeting the workers' needs on the job.

The majority of all dietary employees are not union members. Reasons include:

1. Cultural and social reasons;
2. Individual reasons;
3. Desire to affiliate with the administration; and
4. Fear of punishment.

The local union is the basic unit of organization. It may only represent members within a specific facility and officers are elected by a democratic vote of their members. Some unions have regional organizations to coordinate the activities of the local union. Some unions are affiliated with a national or international union whose purpose is to establish basic policies, provide necessary services, collect information, and administer strike and retirement funds as necessary.

Once employees are represented by a union, the administration will probably have to alter operations in several ways. It will need to follow all requirements imposed by the union agreement. Advantages include dealing with only one representative of unionized employees rather than with individual staff members, and centralizing the decision-making responsibilities to just the top administrators. Many dietary managers define collective bargaining as negotiations between union and facility representatives leading to a contract. More generally, however, the term applies to routine interactions between administrators and the unions. Collective bargaining involves aspects of organizing staff members, negotiating and administering agreements, interpreting contract clauses, and resolving disputes (grievances) between union and administrative officials.

The dietary manager is an important element in the employee's decision about whether or not to support the union. There are basic actions which a dietary manager can and cannot undertake during an organizing campaign:

1. The administration, including dietary managers, can attempt to assess the union's strength as the organizing effort evolves;
2. If the facility is unionized, the relationship between the dietary manager and the employees will obviously be affected. He/she must continue to treat all employees both fairly and consistently, but will probably find that some authority has been reduced;
3. Both the dietary manager and the union steward are in unique positions. They share many responsibilities and must understand, interpret, and enforce the contract while acting as representatives for others.

If a union employee files a formal grievance, the dietary manager may first meet with the union steward and the employee in an attempt to resolve the problem. If this is not possible, the dietary manager's boss or another administrative official may meet with the union's grievance committee. If this is not successful, top administrative officials may meet with the grievance committee; if necessary, top administrative officials may need to meet further with top-level officials of the local, national, or international union. If resolution is still impossible, the matter may go to mediation or to arbitration.

KEY TERMS

Organizational change	Assimilation approach
Resistance to change	Righting-the-wrongs approach
Over-determination	Culture-specific approach
Narrow focus of change	Multicultural approach
Group inertia	Union
Threatened expertise	Shop stewards
Threatened power	Collective bargaining
Resource allocation	Formal grievance
Diversity	Mediation
Golden-rule approach	Arbitration

QUESTIONS/PROBLEMS/CASES

1. Most resistance to change is connected with people being fearful of loss in one form or another (loss of power, resources, or the security of a predictable routine). Cite a personal experience that you've had with one of the "six sources of resistance" in this chapter. Can you now define what your sense of loss was? Was it real or imagined? If imagined, which "individual" factors might have contributed to your resistance to change? What could management have done differently to make the transition a smooth one?

2. As dietary manager in a moderate facility, you've initiated some changes in training procedures. You've spoken personally with a few of your employees and your impression is that the changes will be well received. You are surprised to find, however, resistance to your plan every step of the way, including those you've spoken with. How might you explain this phenomenon and what is your plan to correct it?

3. Refer to the approaches for controlling resistance to change in Figure 10.1. Listing each approach, cite an example from your own life where this approach was used. Then analyze whether or not the approach was successful by reviewing the advantages and drawbacks listed in the figure.

4. How can a dietary manager make change easier to implement?

5. Compare primary and secondary dimensions of diversity. Why might attributes of the secondary dimension be harder to accept than attributes of the primary dimension?

6. Jill is the dietary manager of a small nursing home and was about to quit due to the heavy workload she carried without support. She had felt this way for weeks and was thinking of writing a letter of resignation when Dale knocked on her door. Being one of her best employees, Dale never took too much time and usually came right to the point, so she invited him into her office.

   To her surprise, Dale was on the verge of quitting. Having been thinking the same herself, Jill asked Dale what was wrong. His response was simply for personal reasons. This got Jill all the more interested and she began to pursue every possible avenue for the answer as to why such a fine employee would wish to quit. Was he, too, feeling overworked and not appreciated?

   After some discussion, Dale confessed that he had been working with a new employee, Bill, and found out today that he was gay. Dale said, "I do not appreciate his sexual orientation and will not take the time to understand him. Besides I am very uncomfortable working with him."

   Jill had met Bill at another nursing home and had hired him recently knowing of the quality of his work. She had never heard that he had made advances to anyone and knew that he was a fine individual. She asked Dale if he had been approached by Bill or had any inappropriate conversation with him. Dale said he had not but that he would not work with such an individual.

   Jill then decided to take a different approach by asking Dale if there might be another option, besides quitting, that would be appropriate for Dale to take. She noted the quality of Bill's work and that the nursing home values all types of diversity. She suggested that Dale remove his thoughts of one's personal life from the workplace and accept Bill for the fine job he had been doing.

   She did not feel she was making any headway, when the thought came to her that Dale and Bill might work different shifts. She suggested this to Dale and he said that could probably work. On the other hand, Jill countered with the fact that they both would still meet one with another at meetings now and then and there could be no disagreements between the two based on lifestyle choices. Dale said he would reconsider and get back to her. Jill said she would look at schedules to determine if shift changes would work.

   1. What is the real problem at this nursing home whether Dale stays or not?

2. Should Jill have Bill and Dale discuss this situation openly? Why of why not?

3. How would you have handled Dale and was Jill's handling of the situation sending the correct message to Dale?

7. Based on the advantages and disadvantages of unions, and the differing views of unions from an employee point of view and administrator point of view, are you of the opinion that unions are necessary in a given administration? Does union activity prevent a facility from "working out" democratic activity (the ability to negotiate and reach agreement) between employees and administrators? Is it possible that unions have served their purpose and are no longer needed in society?

11

LEADERSHIP

CHAPTER OUTLINE

- Types of Leadership
  - Autocratic Leaders
  - Bureaucratic Leaders
  - Democratic Leaders
  - Laissez-faire Leaders
- Which Leadership Style is Best?
- Situational Leadership
- Leadership Qualities and Skills
- A Balanced View of Power
- Employee Participation Programs
- The Setting of Goals and Priorities by Dietary Managers
- Decision Making
- Time Management

TYPES OF LEADERSHIP

Leaders have the ability to get a lot done, they know where they want to go and how to get there. Dietary managers must also direct the work of personnel—and this activity is the topic of this chapter. Dietary managers must be skilled in dealing effectively with people at all organizational levels. Much of their time and attention is focused on the supervision of their employees. The dietary manager, therefore, must be an effective leader.

What is a leader? A common definition is a person who can guide or direct the attitudes, behaviors, and opinions of other people. Therefore, anyone who supervises people must possess leadership skills.

In the old days, many supervisors could simply tell a staff member what to do. When the directions were carried out, the supervisor was "a good leader." Today, this strategy is less useful. The ability of the supervisor to dictate what must be done has been replaced with the need to influence and request employees to do required work. Said another way, then, today's dietary manager must be able to facilitate the conduct of work. He or she cannot simply tell employees what to do. The role of the dietary manager is changing from that of dictatorial taskmaster to one of a leader who provides necessary resources, guidance, and direction.

Many dietary managers consistently relate the same way to all employees; that is, they use the same leadership style with everyone. Some supervisors may do this purposefully; others use this approach because it is easy; still other dietary managers are not aware that other strategies are possible. Effective supervisors realize the advantages of using different leadership styles, when possible, to meet the specific needs of individual staff members.

TYPE	OVERVIEW OF LEADERSHIP TYPE	TARGET EMPLOYEE FOR LEADERSHIP TYPE
Autocratic Manager	Manager retains as much power and decision-making authority as possible. He/she makes decisions without consulting employees. Orders are given and must be obeyed without employee input.	New employees who must quickly learn work tasks; difficult-to-supervise employees who do not respond to other styles; temporary employees.
Bureaucratic Manager	Manager "manages by the book." Emphasis is on doing things specified by rules, policies, regulations, and standard operating procedures. Manager relies on higher levels to resolve problems not addressed "by the rules."	Employees who must follow set procedures; employees working with dangerous equipment or under special conditions.
Democratic Manager	Manager involves employees in aspects of the job which affect them. Their input is solicited; they participate in the decision-making process and are delegated authority.	Employees with high levels of skill and/or extensive experience; employees who will need to make significant changes in work assignments; employees who want to voice complaints; employee groups with common problems
Laissez-Faire Manager	Manager maintains a "hands off" policy and "delegates by default" much discretion and decision-making authority. The manager gives little direction and allows extensive levels of freedom.	Highly motivated employees such as staff technical specialists; consultants.

FIGURE 11.1 TYPES OF LEADERSHIP STYLES

What is a leadership style? It is simply the mix of attitudes and/or behaviors that a dietary manager can use to direct the work of the employees. Figure 11.1 presents a basic description of four common styles, and indicates the type of employees with which each style might be used. They are presented as follows:

AUTOCRATIC LEADERS

An autocratic leader likes to make decisions and solve problems without getting information from affected employees. Instructions are generally given unilaterally—and they must be followed. A structured set of awards (used to encourage employees to follow orders) and punishments (used to discipline employees when orders are not followed) are used.

Employees can easily become dependent upon dietary managers who are autocratic. They act only under his or her supervision and have relatively little opportunity to make decisions as work is undertaken. The autocratic leader emphasizes the task and getting work done. There is more concern about the facility and less concern about the employees. Because of the leader's strong control over the group and the group's dependence on the leader, the group is lost when the leader is absent.

Many autocratic managers believe in McGregor's Theory X leadership approach.[1] They think that employees do not like to work and view work as a "necessary evil." Autocratic managers believe that employees avoid work whenever possible and that they must be forced to work, and must be controlled and closely directed.

[1]See Douglas McGregor, *The Human Side of Enterprise.* McGraw Hill Publishing Company, N.Y., New York, 1960.

Bureaucratic Leaders

Dietary managers using this approach manage by the book. There is an emphasis on enforcing rules. Problems not addressed by the rules must be referred to higher levels of administration.

The bureaucratic manager is more of a policeman than a leader. Since the emphasis is on rules, not cooperation with people, the rules become more important than the outcomes of work.

Democratic Leaders

The democratic (participative) dietary manager desires to include employees in decision-making activities that affect them. A democratic manager focuses on the subordinates and the role that they should play in the facility. He or she searches for the means to help employees find satisfaction in their jobs.

There are some potential disadvantages to this leadership approach. For example, it is likely to take longer to make decisions, and mistakes are more likely to occur. Also, once this leadership style has been used, it is difficult to switch to another approach (as when a new supervisor is brought into the work section).

The democratic style of leadership incorporates many of the factors noted by McGregor's Theory Y[2]. This view holds that employees do not dislike work nor want to avoid responsibility. Rather, employees find work to be natural, and they respond favorably to procedures which allow them to help plan for work which must be done. The position of leader is usually assumed by an assistant or an employee who is well liked by the group.

Laissez-Faire Leaders

This manager uses a hands-off approach and really does as little supervising as possible. Employees are allowed to make decisions in almost total absence of supervisory input. Since employees really, then, have no leader, this approach can only be used with highly motivated and experienced employees; the approach has little utility in most dietary operations.

Which Leadership Style is Best?

Which of the four basic leadership styles should be used—and when? First of all, it is doubtful whether any dietary manager uses any one of the four basic leadership styles. In an ideal situation the dietary manager would know each employee and be able to adopt the leadership style appropriate to the specific employee in the specific job situation. What is best for one situation may not work in another. It depends on the manager, the group of employees being supervised, and the activities in which everyone is involved. In most work situations the dietary manager has to choose the style or a combination of styles.

Several factors influence the type of leadership styles used:

- The dietary manager's personal background. Everyone brings unique knowledge, experience and common sense to the job situation. These will influence one's feelings about employees and the job to be done;
- Characteristics of employees. Some employees desire decision-making responsibility; others do not. Some employees agree with the facility's goals; others may not. The point is that the employees, with differing backgrounds and attitudes, should be considered as leadership approaches are determined;
- Relationship between dietary manager and employees. The degree of confidence which a dietary manager has in employees will affect leadership style. If there is a large element of trust and acceptance, a democratic approach may be

[2]See Douglas McGregor, *The Human Side of Enterprise.* McGraw Hill Publishing Company, N.Y., New York, 1960.

useful. In contrast, when these elements are lacking, an autocratic approach resulting in a battle between the dietary manager and the employees may be more likely;

- The job situation itself. The organizational climate of the facility, the makeup of employee groups, the type of work to be done, and so on also affect choice and effectiveness of varying leadership styles. Even the tradition of leadership in the facility is an important factor. Consider the institution that, through prior action and policies, has stressed use of autocratic leadership styles. Contrast this with another facility which has a long-standing commitment to the employee. To be effective in either institution, the supervisor must consider, and probably accept, the prevailing philosophy of his or her employer.

Many other situational elements affect leadership style considerations. For example, the size of the work group must be considered; it becomes more difficult to use a group decision-making approach as the size of the group increases. What about the effectiveness of communication and cooperation among departments? If these are not satisfactory, the supervisor may be uncertain of goals and may need to use less participative approaches as decisions are made. Consider also the type of work and the magnitude and type of problems which must be resolved. There are situations where employee input will be helpful and others where, for many reasons, this input cannot be used.

As you can see, then, the situation itself has a dramatic impact upon the utility of the leadership style.

SITUATIONAL LEADERSHIP

How can one use information about leadership styles when so many elements in the situation itself must be considered? Two writers have suggested concepts of situational leadership which can help dietary managers understand the situation and the leadership style which can be used.[3] They suggest that the supervisor should consider both the amount of direction which must be provided as a task is undertaken and the amount of social/emotional support necessary in this situation as the direction is given. They make a distinction between task and relationship behavior:

- Task behavior is the amount of direct supervision that must be provided as a task is done;
- Relationship behavior is the amount of social/emotional support and two-way communication provided by the supervisor in efforts to maintain a personal and professional relationship with the employee.

A dietary manager focusing on the task is likely to closely supervise employees to assure that work is done correctly. He or she puts emphasis on getting the job done correctly, not on interacting effectively with employees. The relationship-centered dietary manager, on the other hand, will place emphasis on motivating rather than on controlling subordinates.

What does this all mean? Is it best to direct activities by focusing on tasks to be done or by providing social/emotional support or a combination of both? The answer is that "it all depends on the situation."

Let's review Figure 11.2. It shows four extremes in the relationship between task behavior and social/emotional support which might be used by the dietary manager:

[3]Paul Hersey and Kenneth H. Blanchard, *Management of Organizational Behavior: Utilizing Human Resources* (3rd ed.). Prentice-Hall, Englewood Cliffs, N.J., 1977.

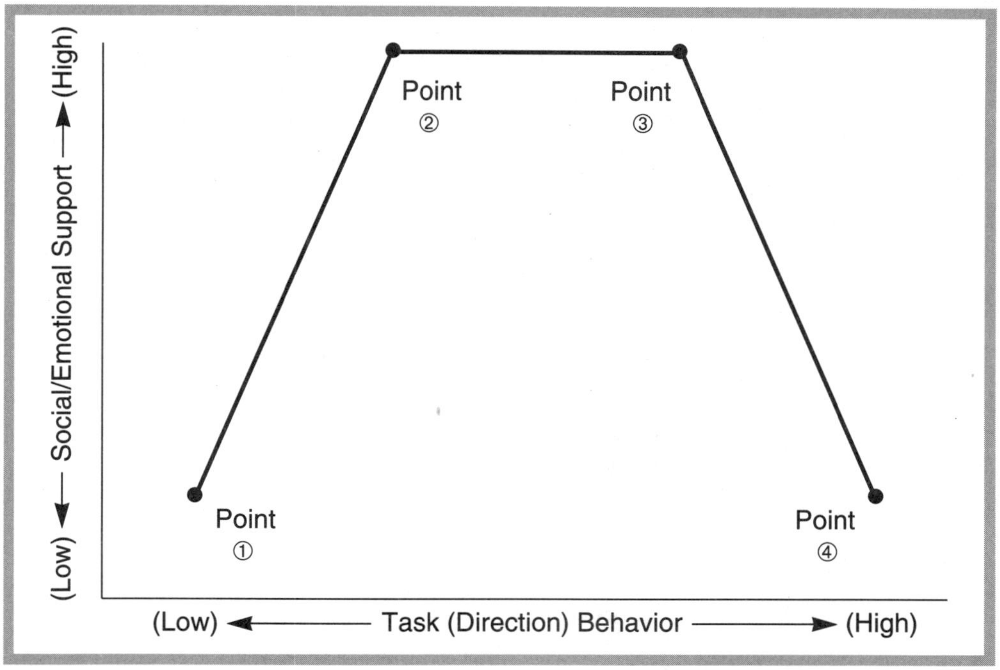

FIGURE 11.2 BASIC LEADERSHIP BEHAVIOR STYLES

Adapted from concepts presented in Paul Hersey and Kenneth H. Blanchard, *Management of Organizational Behavior: Utilizing Human Resources* [3rd ed.]. Prentice-Hall, Inc., Englewood Cliffs, N.J., 1977, p. 167

1. At point number one, the supervisory style is one of almost no social/emotional support and, simultaneously, little task direction;
2. At point number two, a high level of social/emotional support is given, but a relatively lower level of task direction is provided;
3. At point number three, the dietary manager exhibits high levels of both direction and social/emotional support;
4. At point number four, the dietary manager exerts much direction and relatively little social/emotional support.

In order to use this information in developing leadership styles, one must be familiar with one more concept—maturity. Simply stated, this term refers to an employee's ability to set high but realistic and attainable goals. Maturity concerns the employee's level of motivation and willingness and ability to accept responsibility. Once an employee's maturity level is known, it is possible to develop an appropriate leadership style. Simply stated, the dietary manager must assess the employee's level of maturity. As this level rises, there is less emphasis placed on the task and more emphasis placed on the social/emotional relationship. As the maturity level is judged to rise still further, emphasis can be reduced not only on the task but also on the relationship. Figure 11.3 puts together the concepts of social/emotional support, task (direction) behavior, and perceived maturity levels. It can help us determine the most appropriate leadership style to be used in a specific situation.

For example, assume that a dietary manager perceives an employee's maturity level for setting up a foodservice line to be low; in other words, the employee lacks the motivation, ability, or training and experience required to do the work correctly. The dietary manager should use a high task, low social/emotional support style to direct work as the serving line is set up (Point Four in Figure 11.3—high task, low social/emotional support—is the most appropriate style).

In contrast, if the dietary manager judges the employee to be at a high maturity level, then leadership style number one (low task, low social/emotional support)

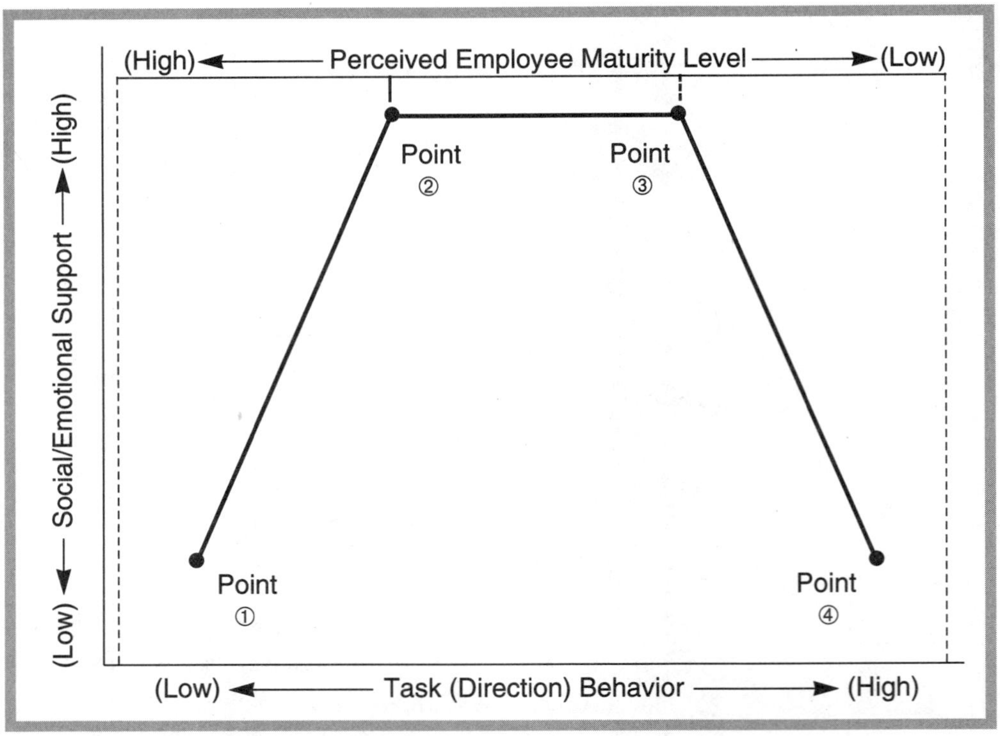

FIGURE 11.3 BASIC LEADERSHIP BEHAVIOR STYLES
Adapted from concepts presented in Paul Hersey and Kenneth H. Blanchard, *Management of Organizational Behavior: Utilizing Human Resources* [3rd ed.]. Prentice-Hall, Inc., Englewood Cliffs, N.J., 177, p. 167

could be effective. [*Note:* Low social/emotional support does not mean that the supervisor should be impersonal or unfriendly. Rather, it means that there is little need for the supervisor to demonstrate emotional support or reinforcement since the employee is willing and able to do the work without direct supervision.]

Each of the four leadership styles illustrated in Figure 11.2 and 11.3 can be summarized as follows:

POINT 1: Low task (direction) and low social/emotional support. The dietary manager can *allow* the employee to perform work with little or no direction;

POINT 2: High social/emotional support and low task direction. Both the manager and the employee will need to *share* in decision-making about how work is to be done;

POINT 3: High task (direction) and high social/emotional support. The supervisor must attempt to *sell* the employee on what must be done;

POINT 4: High task (direction) and low social/emotional support. The supervisor must *tell* the employee what to do.

The first, directive behavior, is the autocratic, authoritative way of commanding that an employee does something. In this case, the dietary manager tells the employee exactly what needs to be done and where, when and how to do it. This behavior is best used with new employees or those uncertain as to how a task is to be done.

The second, supportive behavior, is more of a participative assistance on the part of the dietary manager as he or she is listening to and working with the employee to offer suggestions, support, encouragement, etc. Together, management and the employee accomplish the task at hand in this situation. This behavior is suited to an employee who has demonstrated that he or she can do the job, but is either unwilling to do it correctly or with enthusiasm. In other words, the employee lacks commitment.

By using a simple illustration of an adult teaching a teenager how to drive, the four possible leadership styles of combining directive and supportive behavior can be easily understood. These styles are directing, coaching, supporting, delegating.

The illustration has an enthusiastic teen backing out of the garage on her first day of driving with her father in the passenger's seat. Like any new employee, the teen believes that she is able to do the job at hand. In fact, she may have so much confidence that to give her any directions at all might insult her. But, both father and daughter recognize that this is the first day of driving, and that while she may have confidence, she has no competence. (Realizing the relationship between an employee's confidence and competence will help in understanding the leadership styles to be used).

The first style, directing, has the manager, or father in this case, stating very clearly to his daughter that she is to release the brake, put the car in reverse, turn around and look over her right shoulder and slowly press the accelerator to proceed out of the driveway. Now the employee, or daughter in this case, who is new to her position and anxious to do well, listens carefully to the instruction as her manager closely supervises her. Communication is very direct and the result is a car correctly driven in reverse onto the road. If the father were in the car with his wife, who has been driving as long as he has, and he starts to tell her how to back out of the driveway, there are going to be problems because the wife is not only confident in her driving, but she is also competent. Dietary managers who use a directing style with more experienced employees are only going to find themselves in trouble as they insult the employees, yet poor managers seem to do this all the time. While the directing style is good to train the beginner, it is also appropriate when risk is involved and immediate attention to a situation must be communicated, i.e. years later, as the daughter, who is now both confident and competent in her driving, travels down the road, her father sees a car pulling out suddenly in front of her and he commands, "Watch out on the left"! Such as statement is making the decision, solving the problem and closely supervising an experienced driver, much as a manager would do with an employee who needs immediate instruction to avoid making a mistake. Such instruction is appreciated by the experienced employee and is appropriate for the manager to use.

The second style, coaching, is used as the daughter becomes more competent and retains her initial level of confidence. The father does not wish to be as directive as he recognizes his daughter's increased level of performance, yet he knows he must continue to train and assist Lessons are now not how to proceed slowly in reverse, but how to center the car in the lane as it proceeds down the highway at 70 miles per hour. The employee at this stage is interested in building skills, refining technique and increasing commitment, as the manager listens, encourages and consults with the employee.

The next style, supporting, sees the employee competent on the job, but demonstrating commitment that wavers between enthusiasm and uncertainty. Feedback on results is the number one motivator is this case and the daughter wants to know that she is doing well as her father supports her. The supporting style is using less directive behavior and sees the father congratulating her for coming to a complete stop before turning right on a red light. It is at this stage that many managers remain silent rather than taking advantage of the opportunity to build an employee's commitment to the job.

The last style, delegating, has the father comfortable with the level of confidence and competence demonstrated by his daughter. The workplace employee is trained and ready to do the job on his or her own. It is this style, for example, that the father would use with his wife, unless he wanted to get into real trouble.

Unfortunately, managers sometimes feel that they must continue to use the other style with employees who really should be left alone to make the day-to-day decisions about their jobs. They do not need much instructions or directions any longer and provide their own support.

While the four leadership styles are now easily understood, one can understand why the father would be wrong to allow his confident and enthusiastic daughter to back out of the driveway without any instruction, just as the manager should give complete detailed directions to employees who need it. Dietary managers must correctly identify the level of confidence and competence that each employee has as well as his or her level of commitment and enthusiasm. By judging correctly, the dietary manager will be better able to apply the appropriate leadership behavior for the task to be done.

Leadership Qualities and Skills

There are no two leaders who lead exactly alike. Each may emphasize different aspects of leadership. Each has different capacities to accomplish results, and each has to work at being a leader. There is no magic characteristic that will make a dietary manager a better leader. There are, however, some common traits found among all leaders. They include personal skills as well as skills derived from experience. The major traits are:

- *Trustworthiness.* These leaders feel comfortable with their employees. They accept different views, opinions and abilities of others as well as accept the influence of others over their decisions;
- *Intelligence.* A leader is usually more intelligent than the average person. Leaders are not "know-it-alls." Leaders know where to get the answers when they don't know;
- *Empathy.* A leader understands and feels for another. A leader is sensitive to the values, perceptions, and needs of the group, as well as each individual;
- *Inspiration and Sharing the Same Vision.* Leaders look to the future. They dream, inspire, and set goals, both personal and work-related. They have a desire to see that something unique happens. They enlist the aid of others to help them meet their vision;
- *Role Models, Mentors, Coaches.* They lead by example; they help others achieve by helping them climb the ladder of opportunity; they possess high ethical standards;
- *Communicators.* Leaders help employees understand directions and ideas, and give messages that are clear;
- *Encouragement.* Leaders get others to follow the vision willingly. Leaders depend on employees for support; employees depend on leaders for encouragement and caring;
- *Giving Credit.* Leaders give credit when a job is well done and improve the process when the job is poorly done. Leaders don't take credit for something they did not do;
- *Self-Confidence.* Leaders must have self-confidence in their abilities to lead, and have the respect and confidence of their followers;
- *Delegation, Empowerment.* Leaders delegate both authority and responsibility to the work group. They empower employees to make decisions. They motivate, influence, counsel, develop, and encourage teamwork. They create new goals and opportunities for employees to succeed. Leaders will take risks.

A Balanced View of Power

Many authorities argue that the effective use of power is the most critical element of management. Effective leaders share one significant characteristic: they make others feel powerful. These leaders are powerful because they have learned how to build a strong power base in their organizations or institutions. They are influential because they use their power to help peers and subordinates accomplish exceptional tasks.

Many people feel uncomfortable discussing power because it conjures up images of vindictive, domineering bosses and manipulative, cunning subordinates. However, this is a very narrow view of power. The use of influence is in itself not bad, but in fact can often lead to a great good. Like any powerful force—from potent medicine to nuclear power—it is the morality with which influence is used that makes all the difference. Power need not be associated with aggression, brute force, craftiness, or deceit. Power can also be viewed as a sign of personal efficacy. People with power shape their environment, whereas the powerless are molded by theirs. In fact, those who are unwilling to exercise power and influence are condemned to experience unhappiness throughout their lives.

There is nothing more demoralizing than feeling you have a creative new idea or a unique insight into a significant organizational problem and then coming face-to-face with your lack of organizational power. Young college graduates, energetic, optimistic, and supremely confident that their "awesome" ability and state-of-the-art training will rocket them up the career ladder when they discover that the organization is not open to new ideas. They blame the "old guard" for protecting their turf, and go looking for greener pastures.

In the long run, no one benefits from lopsided distributions of power. One seasoned veteran of organizational power games summarized his experience: "Powerless members of an organization either get angry and try to tear down the system, or become apathetic and withdraw. Either way, everyone loses."

Powerful managers not only can accomplish more personally, but can also pass on more information and make more resources available to subordinates. For this reason, people tend to prefer bosses with "clout." Subordinates tend to feel that they have higher status in an organization and their morale is higher when they perceive that their boss has considerable upward influence. In contrast, powerlessness tends to foster bossiness and petty, rules-minded managerial styles, rather than true leadership. Figure 11.4 identifies several indicators of a manager's upward and outward power in an organization which serves as a set of behavioral objectives for a discussion of power and influence.

But what about Lord Acton's well-known dictum, "Power corrupts, and absolute power corrupts absolutely"? This certainly appears to be an ageless lesson of

Powerful managers can

- intercede favorably on behalf of someone in trouble.
- get a desirable placement for a talented subordinate.
- get approval for expenditures beyond the budget.
- get items on and off the agenda at policy meetings.
- get fast access to top decision makers.
- maintain regular, frequent contact with top decision makers.
- acquire early information about decisions and policy shifts.

Figure 11.4 Indicators of a Manager's Upward and Outward Power

history. Support for the modern-day relevance of this warning is reflected in the observing of successful and unsuccessful managers. The unsuccessful managers demonstrated careers that had become "derailed" by the personal inadequacies shown in Figure 11.5. Note how many of these problems relate to the ineffective use of power in interpersonal relationships. It seems that they were given a little authority, and they failed the test of worthy stewardship.

The successful managers use their power to empower others and accomplish exceptional organizational objectives. As they applied their influence in positive ways, they gained more power and formal organizational authority, creating a positive, upward spiral that carried them up the organizational career ladder.

The relationship between power and personal effectiveness is depicted in Figure 11.6. Both lack of power and the abuse of power are equally debilitating and counterproductive. The goal, of course, is to stay on top of the "power curve." This is accomplished with the aid of two specific management skills. The first focuses on how to gain power (overcome feelings of powerlessness); the second examines how to convert power effectively into interpersonal influence in ways that avoid the abuse of power. The latter will be covered in Chapter 12 in the discussion on persuasion.

- Insensitive to others; abrasive and intimidating
- Cold, aloof, and arrogant
- Betraying others' trust
- Overly ambitious; playing politics and always trying to move up
- Unable to delegate to others or to build a team
- Overdependent on others (e.g., a mentor)

FIGURE 11.5 CHARACTERISTICS THAT DERAIL MANAGERS' CAREERS

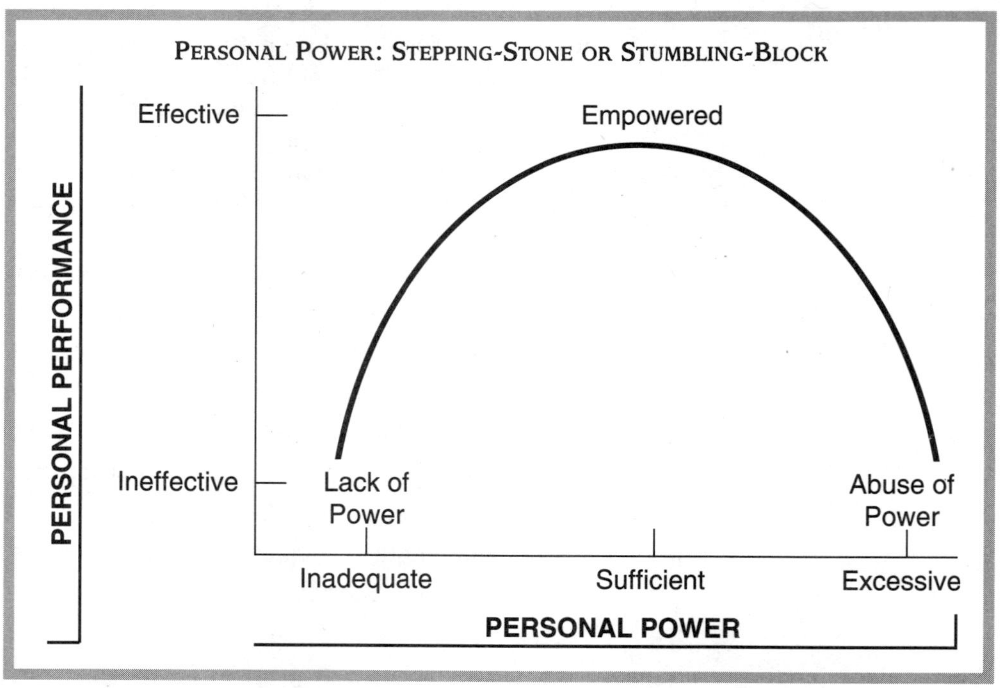

FIGURE 11.6 POWER AND PERSONAL EFFECTIVENESS

CHARACTERISTICS	DESCRIPTION
Expertise	Task-relevant knowledge or experience
Personal attraction	Desirable characteristics associated with friendship
Effort	Higher-than-expected commitment of time
Legitimacy	Behavior consistent with key organizational values

FIGURE 11.7 DETERMINANTS OF PERSONAL POWER

Four personal characteristics are important sources of power as seen in Figure 11.7. **Expertise** reflects cognitive abilities, **personal attraction** involves affective appeal, **effort** suggests personal commitment, and **legitimacy** conveys credibility.

Expertise is "knowledge-ability." It provides a strong base of power in large, technologically sophisticated, rapidly changing organizations. In this environment the specialist is especially powerful because top management is so far removed from the core work activities of the organization.

Personal attraction is manifested in a variety of ways: "When she makes a presentation in a management meeting, her presence is powerful and her message sounds good"; "His magnetic personality enables him to attract the most qualified and dedicated people to his department—everyone wants to work for him." These are two sources of personal attraction: agreeable behavior and attractive physical appearance.

Individuals with agreeable personalities become more influential than those with disagreeable personalities. Attractive people are more likely to feel good about themselves and to have a higher self-confidence than unattractive people. However, if one suspects that he or she does not measure up very well in this category, despite best efforts at "accentuating the positive," it is a good idea to compensate by emphasizing other sources of power. If indeed self-confidence is the primary mechanism for transforming personal attractiveness into organizational power, then other personal and positional characteristics can contribute in a similar manner to one's self-confidence.

A high level of personal effort can result in increased responsibility and opportunity through a process known as **cognitive dissonance reduction.** A fundamental principle of psychology is that individuals strive to reduce inconsistencies between their own personal beliefs and personal behavior, and between their expectations of others and the behavior of others. When individuals exert more effort to perform their jobs than is expected, according to organizational policy or office norms, an inconsistency exists. Since the person's rewards are based on completion of the amount of work normally expected, the inconsistency can be eliminated only by reduced effort or increased responsibility.

At the managerial level, extraordinary effort is viewed as a sign of commitment and dedication, and should be encouraged and rewarded. Extraordinary effort by a manager, therefore, is likely to be interpreted positively if it is focused on enhancing the organization's goals rather than on personal self-aggrandizement. Power accrues, in other words, when individuals are viewed as contributors to the good of the group. On the other hand, if their efforts are seen as costly to others personally, or detrimental to the general welfare of the group, dissonance occurs, which leads to resistance.

Values play an important role in organizations. Organizational leaders are vigilant in defending core organizational values and in socializing newcomers to proper modes of thinking and acting. Managers strive to create a distinctiveness that merits attention from the financial community, potential employees, and customers. This may involve placing a premium on quality, economy, value, service, loyalty to employees, or civic involvement. This uniqueness is the basis for internal organizational pride and external projections of excellence. It is often referred to as the organization's **distinctive competence** (vision).

Actions that are congruent with the prevailing value system are deemed credible, or legitimate, by other organizational members. They are taken for granted, rather than challenged or scrutinized. Therefore, legitimacy increases acceptance, and acceptance is a key to personal influence. However, this doesn't mean that strict conformity is necessarily in the best long-term interests of the firm. In fact, there is evidence that highly inbred, rigid companies have a high rate of failure. Successful organizations have members who are both capable of gaining power by fitting in and of using that power to challenge the prevailing belief system that, in some sense, has been responsible for their gaining power.

Furthermore, unchallenged organizational beliefs often interfere with a company's necessary adaptation to changing competitive and regulatory conditions. However, challenges are most successful when mounted by members whose commitment to the organization has been the most loyal. So, "paying your dues" creates legitimacy, and legitimacy is a prerequisite for effective criticism.

Employee Participation Programs

There is frequently a wide difference of opinion between supervisors and employees about what staff members desire from their jobs. Thousands of workers around the country were asked to consider the factors which they thought most impacted upon employee morale (feelings about the job). Supervisors were also asked to give their opinion on this question. The three most important items suggested by employees were the last three items cited by supervisors. Many supervisors do not actually know what their employees want from the job. Also, the factors judged most important by employees (appreciation for work done, a feeling of "being in on things," and help with personal problems) are very often within the control of supervisors. Contrast that with the supervisor's view that an employee's concerns commonly center on such factors as higher wages, job security, and job promotion. How is it possible that supervisors, working so closely with employees for long time periods, don't have a better idea about the needs and desires of their employees?

You have learned that many employees desire to participate in job-related matters which affect them. You also know that at least one leadership style (democratic) emphasizes employee participation. How should the dietary manager decide when a decision should be made alone, when to involve others, and when to delegate authority for the decision entirely to other personnel?

Some studies have shown that solutions to problems are often better when input from more than one individual is utilized. Advantages to employee participation programs include the increased possibility that errors will be noted when decisions are reviewed, and that employee input will provide additional alternatives to be considered. Employees are also less likely to resist change since their participation allows *their decisions* rather than *their supervisor's decisions* to be made.

Other advantages to allowing employee input in the decision-making process include:

- Increased productivity;
- Improved work quality;
- Higher levels of employee motivation and morale;
- Increased commitment to attaining dietary department goals;
- Establishment of improved channels of communication.

The above advantages can be summarized by stating that generally employee participation programs enable the dietary department to better meet its goals. There is a difference between the dietary manager who really desires employee participation and one who only wants to manipulate employees into "doing what I want them to do."

There are at least two types of formal group participation programs. The first type, use of task groups, involves the establishment of special committees to work on special problems. These committees may be short term or ongoing total quality management teams. A second type, employee suggestion programs, ranges from use of a suggestion box to letters to the editor in the facility's newsletter.

In order for employee participation programs to be effective, the employees must make a purposeful effort to participate. They must really believe that their interests and goals will be best met on the job by participating in those areas where participation is permitted. Also, employers must then accept the responsibility to implement decisions which reflect employee participation.

Figure 11.8 reviews some conditions which must be present for participation programs to be successful. Factors shown to influence the effectiveness of the employee participation activity include:

- The interests and abilities of staff members;
- Personal factors within each staff member;
- The availability of adequate time;
- The extent to which benefits exceed costs;

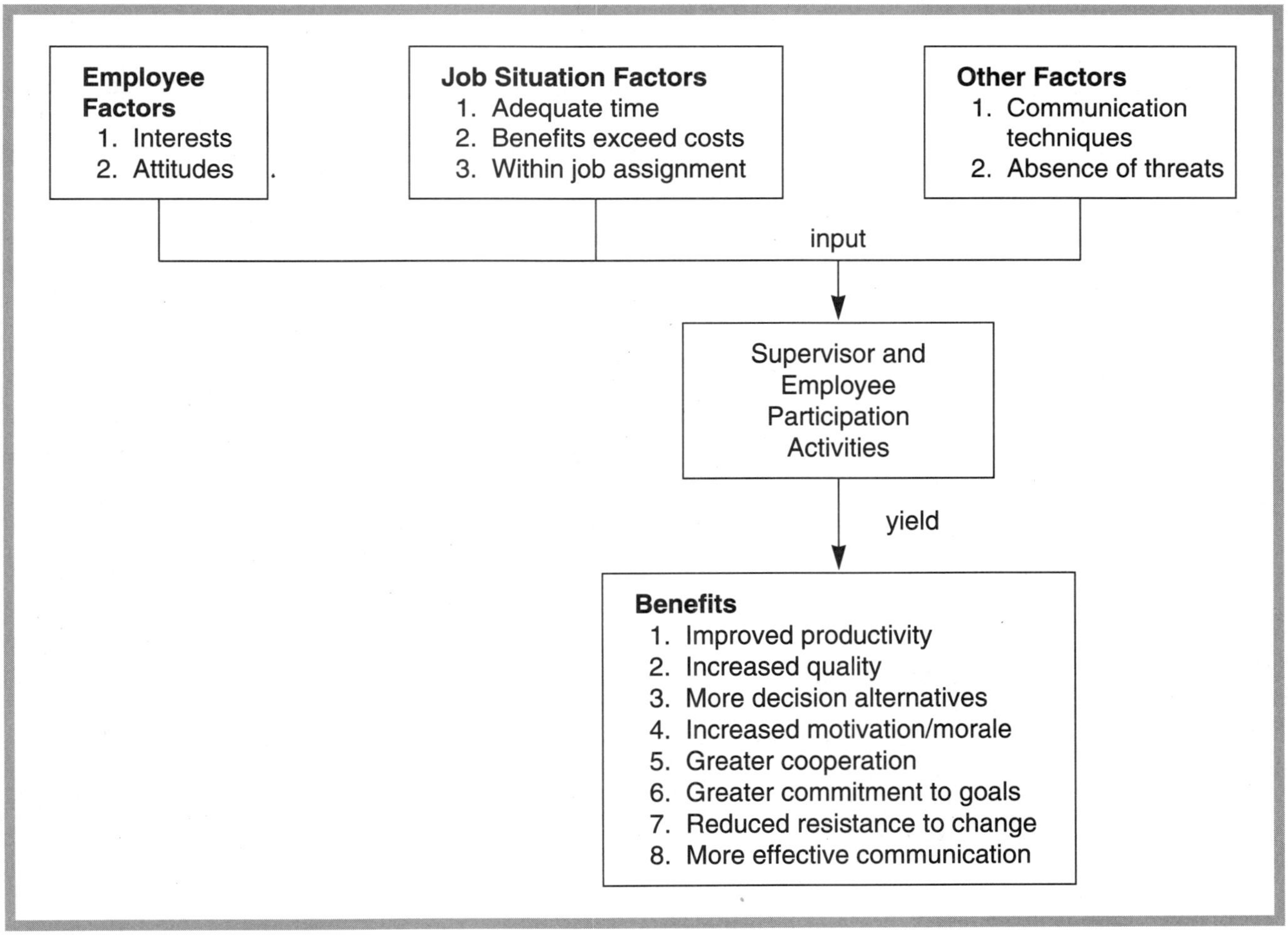

FIGURE 11.8 FACTORS INFLUENCING SUCCESS OF EMPLOYEE PARTICIPATION PROGRAM

Source: John Daschler and Jack Ninemeier, *Supervision in the Hospitality Industry.* Educational Institute of the American Hotel and Motel Association, East Lansing, Mich., 1984, p. 257

- Participation outside the job assignment;
- Job situation factors;
- Other factors such as the use of communication and persuasion techniques, absence of threat, etc.

It is very unlikely that a dietary manager could—or would—allow the same amount of staff input for every decision which must be made. Employees could be allowed significant input, for example, on decisions about work schedules and/or vacation times, but might be permitted less input on decisions relating to job assignments and evaluations of work quality. At the other extreme, there are likely to be situations where employees may be given no (or almost no) input on decisions (development of an operating budget, for example).

Frequently there are barriers which must be overcome for employee participation programs to be effective. First of all, the factors noted in Figure 11.8 which must be present within both the employee and the job situation itself must be considered. Some staff members may lack ego/esteem needs, which limit their interests in employee participation activities. Some, for example, may feel very comfortable working in an authoritarian job environment where little discretion is allowed. Still other staff may not have the knowledge, interest, or access to information necessary to make effective participative decisions. Finally, the organizational environment itself must be conducive to participation. For example, if only one dietary manager recognized the benefits of employee participation, subsequent actions might be considered negative. A top-level manager in this facility might view participation activities to be unnecessary delegation, or dietary employees might believe these actions to be suggestive of a weak and/or inexperienced supervisor.

Contrast this situation with another facility where employee participation is commonly used. In this facility the dietary manager who did not encourage participation would probably be viewed as weak from the level of top administration and as authoritative from the employees' view.

There are many informal methods of employee participation which can be used in many dietary departments. For example, let's assume that a decision must be made. As part of this process, a dietary manager might consider all possible ways to resolve a problem. Employees could be requested to give their ideas as well. This information could be gained by talking with each employee affected by the problem, only those employees believed to have special ideas, only influential employees, only experienced employees, or only staff members who work effectively. After the dietary manager discussed the problem with any or all of these groups, other alternatives would probably have been generated. The dietary manager could then discuss advantages and disadvantages of each alternative with any or all of the groups of employees just identified and ask them for ideas about how to implement or evaluate the alternatives. From this brief discussion, one can see that there is a wide range of informal methods which can be used to encourage employee participation in matters affecting them.

Dietary managers must manage groups of employees as well as individual staff members. Some of these groups will be formal, established by and for the benefit of the facility. Other groups will be informal, evolving because of the mutual interests of participating employees. Informal groups may or may not benefit the facility. The effective dietary manager must know how to manage both formal and informal groups, and be able to direct them in efforts to assist the dietary department in meeting goals.

A group is comprised of two or more individuals. It is important to recall that the group is, first of all, a collection of individuals. Many of the principles used to supervise employees in groups will be the same as those used to manage specific persons.

At its most general level, the institution is comprised of a formal group of employees. Subsections of this broad group are developed so that an organizational chart will represent the relationships among all formal groups. One should understand that the dietary department is a formal work group established by the facility to provide the food and nutrition services required for its patients/residents and others. Within the dietary department, work is divided into other groups (dining services, tray assembly, food production, dish and pot washing, etc.). Different work shifts may further separate work units within the facility. Each formal group has a formal supervisor who is responsible for coordinating, directing, and controlling the group's work.

In addition to formal work groups, informal groups may develop within the dietary department for many reasons, some of which are:

- Common interests of group members;
- The desire to be close to other employees in a similar situation;
- Economic concerns;
- A desire to satisfy personal—but common—needs.

One can see, then, that there are obvious personal advantages in belonging to a group, whether it is formal or informal. Groups can provide companionship, understanding, help in resolving problems and protection of interests for group members.

How does an individual become a member of a group? Consider a new staff member joining the dietary department. When a staff member is hired, he or she becomes a member of several formal groups such as the facility itself, the dietary services department, and perhaps an individual work section or shift. If the new-employee orientation program is effective, the new staff member will be comfortable with the formal group. However, if the process is ineffective, there is likely to be an awkward transitional period during which the new staff member does not feel like an integral part of the formal work groups.

At the same time that the new staff member becomes affiliated with the formal work group, he or she reacts with informal groups. For example, the new staff member will probably seek out those with common interests and will be looking for "someone friendly" to answer basic job-related questions.

While new on the job, the employee will analyze the work situation and attempt to size up fellow employees. At the same time, other staff members attempt to learn something about the new employee. An initial period of neutrality toward specific individuals in groups may turn to positive feelings (if these individuals and groups are friendly and/or cooperative), or to negative feelings (if people and/or groups did or said things which were offensive to the new staff member).

Over time, the new employee will learn what can or cannot be done. He or she will also begin to interact with those staff members with whom he or she feels most comfortable. At the same time, the new staff member may begin to avoid other individuals and groups. In effect, then, one's attitudes and behavior become modified to meet the needs of the new situation.

Later, the new staff member will begin to accept or reject ideas of specific individuals. He or she is apt to be more influenced by those individuals and groups with whom he or she can most identify. Still later, the staff member will become an accepted member of a group. As an accepted member of a group, one is likely to become concerned about the group's reaction as well as one's own reaction to a given situation. As this occurs, the group can really begin to represent the employee. Behavior exhibited by members in the group will become similar to that of the individual.

Groups develop in stages similar to those by which a new employee becomes accepted into a group. For example, as a group first develops, members may mistrust each other. A process of gradual acceptance becomes necessary. A second stage in the evolution of a group occurs as individual members begin to communicate frankly with each other. This communication process will develop into the structure by which effective group decisions can be made. As members become involved in mutual activities and begin to cooperate, they find satisfaction and become more committed to working toward the group's success.

As the group evolves, group members will probably be more concerned about attaining group goals and more motivated to help each other. The group will become stronger as each stage in its development evolves. For example, groups in the early stage of formation may not resolve some problems; mature groups faced with the same problems are much more likely to generate and implement creative and effective solutions to the problem.

When the dietary manager believes informal group members desire to attain organizational goals, he or she should attempt to work with the informal group. This principle violates the common practice of many dietary managers of ignoring informal groups—whether they support or oppose organizational goals. Friendly groups can be strengthened by increasing their status, reacting favorably toward group members, and/or insuring that no obstacles hinder the continuation of the informal group.

On the other hand, if the dietary manager believes the informal group is working against the facility's goals, he or she can make an effort to reduce the cohesiveness of group members. The dietary manager might limit the status of a group and/or design obstacles to discourage its cohesiveness. For example, scheduling breaks, hours of work, and so on can sometimes lead to reduced group cohesiveness.

The dietary manager must be aware that conflicts can arise if efforts to discourage membership in informal groups are not successful. The attitudes group members hold toward the organization and the job are likely to affect the quality and quantity of work output. Attitudes of group members obviously affect the group's behavior. Therefore, the dietary manager confronted with an informal group working against the facility's goals must attempt to (a) modify the attitudes of group members, (b) redirect the group toward more useful goals, and/or (c) confront those factors which are causing negative attitudes of group members.

Dietary managers must pay special attention to interactions with group leaders. Recall that employees leading formal groups have been retained by the facility for this purpose. In contrast, informal leaders generally emerge through the interaction of informal group members. Many factors important to success in dietary management (such as the ability to respond differently to different people, being aware of an individual's special needs, an interest in initiating action, etc.) are also important to an individual's ability to serve as an informal group leader. Likewise, the knowledge, skill, abilities, and benefits which a group derives from the leader will impact upon a group member's opportunity to become an informal group leader.

Effective dietary managers recognize the need to interact with formal and informal group leaders and to request their support and assistance as activities are undertaken. Typically, however, this principle is violated: dietary managers frequently believe that they should not recognize or interact with informal group leaders nor solicit their assistance. It is important to realize, however, that informal groups can help the dietary department to attain goals.

The Setting of Goals and Priorities by Dietary Managers

The dietary manager, as an official in the dietary department, should provide a great deal of input to planning activities for the department. Those dietary managers serving as department heads will likewise be involved in planning meetings which impact the future of the facility as a whole. A great deal of coordination is necessary in either instance to develop action plans that do, in fact, best use limited resources to maximize the attainment of facility goals.

Frequently, goals are developed for a short time period. For example, economic, personal, and professional goals may be formulated on a one-year basis. A one-year, short-range operating budget serves as an example of economic goals of the dietary department. As the time frame for goal development becomes longer, the goal statements themselves frequently become broader and less specific. For example, some facilities may develop three- or five-year operating budgets to identify their long-term economic goals. In practice, the operating budget may spell out weekly economic figures for the first year, monthly economic statistics for the second year, and yearly figures only for the third through fifth years. The point is that the dietary manager must make time to plan for short and long range. Time must be set aside from the day-to-day operation to establish plans, read, network, and develop studies and programs that will enhance the future of the department.

Communication is obviously important as the planning process evolves. How does the dietary manager learn about the facility's short- and long-range goals? How does he or she know about the economic resources potentially available to the dietary department? Both of these and related other questions can only be properly answered if there is an effective and free-flowing channel of communication down through the organizational levels. The need for communication to flow up the organizational chart is also important so that a give-and-take system of goal setting and planning is possible.

To plan effectively, the dietary manager must have available a wide range of information. In fact, the control of information is a strategy which enables some administrators to become more powerful, to the detriment of the facility as a whole.

A related communication problem occurs when there is an inadequate means of interpreting and explaining plans to personnel at lower levels of the organization. Frequently, an assessment of external pressures, an analysis of future needs and services, and so on require detailed explanations in addition to the numbers found in reports submitted to dietary managers and others.

Dietary managers must recognize the need for flexibility as plans are developed. No one has a crystal ball to see the future. Therefore, plans must be based upon the best estimates of the future, while at the same time recognizing that alternative plans may be necessary. For example, many facilities develop operating budgets based upon a specified level of occupancy, participation, or other factors. Based upon this estimate, expense categories for the operating budget can be developed. However, in view of the uncertainty of budget estimates, a variable budget, which lists expenses according to various levels of business volume, is also helpful. With increased availability of automated budget systems, variable operating budgets are becoming more commonplace. The same concern about the uncertainty of the future creates a similar need for variable planning for other aspects of the facility's operation. What are the future needs for professional staff in the dietary department? What are the implications of the use of a frozen food production/delivery system? While no one can know for sure, planning which estimates the impact of personnel, economics and technology on the future is still very important.

As has already been suggested, a number of limiting/strategic factors must be considered. It is, for example, difficult to accurately plan for the future. The rapid change confronting the dietary department is also difficult to quantify. Internal organizational changes, the impact of legislation, and changes in the facility's philosophy and mission are among the variables that make planning difficult. At the same time, each of these factors also makes planning an important priority.

It is important that long-range planning start at the top of the organization. It must be well organized, and action steps must be developed from the plans adopted. It is necessary to integrate short-range efforts with long-range planning, being constantly aware of the problems associated with planning. Each plan developed must contribute in some way to accomplishing group goals and must also make efficient use of limited resources. The planning activity must take precedence over other management functions such as organizing, directing, and so on.

The activity of planning, while important, is frequently overlooked or insufficiently addressed by management. In fact, dietary managers must place a high priority on planning, incorporate their planning with that undertaken by higher levels of the organization, and constantly consider how fast-paced changes in dietary services will affect the dietary department in the future. To do otherwise forces the dietary manager to become a *victim* of change rather than an active element in it. The dietary manager who does plan is much more likely to attain facility and dietary department goals than is his or her counterpart who recognizes the need to plan but who plans only when time permits.

Decision Making

Making objective and fair decisions based on facts is one of the most difficult tasks the dietary manager will encounter. Decision making is the process of choosing a course of action among alternatives to solve a particular problem. Once the decision has been made, action needs to be taken.

There are two general types of decisions; programmed and non-programmed.

Programmed decisions are decisions that must be made when problems are repetitive, routine, or frequent. This type of decision making is the most common and occurs on a day-to-day basis. Policies, procedures, standards, methods and rules are frequently used in programmed decisions.

Non-programmed decisions occur when the dietary manager is confronted with a decision that is one of a kind, may never recur, or is new and unusual. These decisions are complex and difficult to make since the problems are rare, unique, and unstructured. As a result of non-programmed decisions, the standards, rules, policies, and procedures may be changed.

Supervisory decisions derive from the role and responsibility of being a manager. A manager's decision should be a conscious choice among alternative courses of action directed toward a specific purpose. There are three key phrases in this definition that describe the elements in the decision-making process.

1. Choice among alternatives. If there is no alternative, if there is only one option, there is no decision to make: you do the only thing you can do. Choice is the primary essential in decision making. Furthermore, you deliberately choose one course of action over the others. You are not influenced by events, habit or others. You are making it happen, not just letting it happen.
2. Specific purpose. The decision has a goal or objective: to solve a specific problem, to accomplish a specific result.
3. Course of action. The decision is to do something or have something done in a particular way. Making a decision includes seeing that the decision is feasible and is implemented.

When considered in total, effective decision-making results in the best benefits being achieved with the least amount of risk. Some managers use a scientific method in decision-making moving through a series of logical steps. Time is involved, lists are developed, alternatives are considered and the best possible choice is made. On the other hand, some managers use an intuitive method, relying on their experience, intellect and gut reaction, and live with the results whether it is the best choice or not. Working with such individuals can be frustrating and even confusing.

In considering all of this, most dietary managers use intuition when solving problems since many problems are based on past experience. However, dietary managers need to learn a more precise scientific method in solving problems. The basic steps, as seen in Figure 11.9, are:

- Define problem;
- Analyze problem and gather data;

1 **IDENTIFY THE PROBLEM**

- **a. State the problem precisely. Be specific.**
- **b. Set objectives**
  What is the purpose of this decision?
  Rules-policies-requirements-limitations?

2 **ANALYZE THE PROBLEM**

- **a. Gather the facts**
  Who-what-where-when-how-why-how much?
  What else?
- **b. Analyze the facts**
  How do they apply?

3 **DEVELOP ALTERNATIVE SOLUTIONS**

- **a. Brainstorm**
- **b. Evaluate alternatives:** pros and cons
- **c. Rank alternatives**

4 **CHOOSE THE BEST ALTERNATIVE**

- **a. Analyze the top-rated alternatives**
  Risk versus benefit
  Economy: cost versus results
  Feasibility: do you have what it takes?
  Acceptability: will workers accept?
  Objectives: which meets them best?
- **b. Weigh and compare**

5 **IMPLEMENT THE DECISION**

- **a. Inform**
- **b. Secure acceptance and commitment**
- **c. Carry out**

6 **FOLLOW UP**

- **a. Evaluate progress**
  Everything OK? Yes? Praise
  No? Coach and support
  Try another alternative
- **b. Evaluate your decision**

FIGURE 11.9 POSSIBLE SCIENTIFIC METHOD IN SOLVING PROBLEMS

Source: Supervision in the Hospitality Industry by Jack Miller, Mary Potter, Karen Eich Drummond, John Wiley & Sons, Inc. 1992, p. 322

- Develop alternatives;
- Choose the best alternative;
- Implement action;
- Follow-up;
- Evaluate.

Identify the real *problem,* often the most difficult step in problem-solving. Symptoms of the problem may be identified as the problem; therefore it is important to start over and get a clear picture of the problem. Defining what the problem really is can be a time-consuming task, but worth the effort when the *real* problem is defined.

Analyze the problem and gather facts. Gather the facts, talk to employees, review policies, procedures and reports. Conduct a thorough investigation. Observe situations. In analyzing the problem look at all the factors, both tangible and intangible—which can play a role in the solution. Know the employees or situation of the problem; look at reputation, discipline, prejudices, biases.

Develop various alternatives. The dietary manager needs to develop as many alternatives as possible even though some may not be desirable or feasible, too risky or expensive. Provide a choice.

Choose the best alternative. The dietary manager will need to consider carefully, evaluate all the alternatives, and select the best one. Recognize the good features of each. Think of the impact and consequences on the operation, the employees, and you as dietary manager. After a careful evaluation of each solution, choose the one that will cause the least friction and has the most good to offer, with the least negative consequences.

Implement the decision. Once the decision has been made, implement the solution. Consider the timing.

Follow-up, evaluate. Follow-up and evaluation of the decision and its effect on the operation must be done in a timely, objective manner. If the decision was a good one the dietary manager may need to only monitor its results on a random basis. If the follow-up indicates that the expected results are not forthcoming, the dietary manager may need to start the problem-solving process all over.

In making day-to-day decisions dietary managers will need to:

- Avoid snap decisions—get the facts and analyze them carefully;
- Use policies, procedures and standards to find answers to problems;
- Know the process and evaluate it before judging the employee or the employee's action;
- Seek help when in doubt. Discuss problems with an administrator, consultant, or others who are well informed or expert in their field;
- Decide if the decision is big or small. If it is a big problem, study it and follow the steps in problem solving. If the problem is little, spend only the time needed to solve;
- Avoid fire-fighting or crises. Stop and consider the situation. Does a decision need to be made at that moment? When it is necessary, such as the case of a fire or other crisis, the manager has the responsibility to make decisions that will protect the life and property of the employee;
- Not brood over a decision. If a mistake was made, rectify it and move on.

There are times when decisions may be made by a group. Participation in group decisions may have advantages, especially when it deals with cross-functional duties.

Time Management

Dietary managers have to plan their time effectively to meet the goals and priorities of the facility and department. Many dietary managers work long hours but fail to accomplish or stay on top of their jobs. Long hours may not be the same thing as effectiveness. The key to time management is to be in control of your time and plan how to use your time effectively.

Before a manager can get control of time, he or she must know how time is currently being spent. Time analysis can be done a number of ways, such as breaking the duties of the job into:

- Routine duties (minor things that have to be done daily, but have little direct contributions to meeting the goals/priorities of the job);
- Regular duties (management/supervisory duties that are directly related to meeting the objectives of the departmental guide);
- Special duties (meetings, committees, and special projects assigned by others that may not relate to department objectives but to overall facility objectives);
- Creative duties (time needed to evaluate new ways of accomplishing goals).

Other ways to assess how one might spend his or her time include:

- Use daily, weekly, and monthly logs where every activity is logged by activity and time spent on activity, and then evaluated to determine its effectiveness;
- Evaluate planned time versus unplanned time. Determine how much time is lost in telephone conversations, drop-ins, and talking to others about non-work activities;
- Evaluate productivity. Review each task and determine how long it takes to do each. How long did it take to do the activity? You need to do it, or can it be delegated or deleted?
- Count all the meetings attended in a month. How many hours were spent? Were the meetings effective, productive, organized? Did they meet the goals set?

Use a desk calendar and/or weekly planning sheet. Note on the calendar those meetings that must be attended; report due dates and time needed to accomplish the task. A weekly planning sheet can be used to list those duties which will need to be accomplished. The log should be prepared a week in advance. Break the days down to mornings and afternoons, and add those tasks that must be completed that week. Divide morning and afternoon equally. As each task is completed, mark it off and go on to the next task.

"To do" lists are important but can be overwhelming if everything you do in a day is listed. You may find yourself spending more time on the list and less time doing. When developing a "to do" list, prioritize the list. If you have several supervisors reporting to you, you may want to do a "Tickler List." Figures 11.10 and 11.11 are exhibits of such lists.

TO DO: WEEK 2/3–2/10	PRIORITY
Attend safety meeting (2/6)	1
Rewrite job description (due 2/11)	1
Work on budget (due 3/10)	2
Go to Sally's luncheon	3
Review CQI (due 2/17)	2
Attend staff meeting (2/5)	1
Call John in New Orleans	3
Answer mail	2
Meeting with the "Boss" (2/4)	1

FIGURE 11.10 To Do List

Supervisor Name	Supervisor Name	Supervisor Name
Review patient survey results (2/3)	Meet with nursing to finalize: 1. Nourishment Request 2. Isolation Procedure (3/12)	Review policies and procedures for ingredients (3/1)
Finish productivity report (2/5)	Finalize modified diet menu (3/8)	Evaluate new meat product (3/2)
Write letter to employee about leave (3/3)		Follow up on safety report (3/10)
Discuss proposed price increase (3/8)		

FIGURE 11.11 TICKLER LIST FOR FOLLOW-UP OF SUPERVISORS

After evaluating how you spend your time, and having the tools needed to plan that time, the next step is to implement and evaluate the outcome. In implementing the plan you should follow these suggestions:

- Handle a piece of paper as few times as possible; file, discard, or write a note on it and forward it;
- Reduce telephone time and telephone tag. Have information needed before returning calls. Return all calls at a set time;
- Reduce the time you are interrupted. Set appointments, close the door, stand up to talk when people enter the office uninvited;
- Set time limits for tasks. Avoid over commitment. Set up blocks of quiet time to accomplish tasks. Learn to say "No";
- Stay focused. Write down goals and objectives. Use a planner;
- Conquer the biggest time-waster: procrastination. Don't put it off; do it now. Work on only one thing at a time. Keep priorities in mind;
- Get things ready *before* beginning the task. Have paper, pen, notes, planners, and other needed items at hand. Maintain an orderly work area;
- Delegate, delegate, delegate! Give assignments to the secretary; give to the supervisor with a clear deadline when due.

Evaluate successes and failures. Continually upgrade the "to do" list and priorities. Review, adjust, and change as needed.

SUMMARY

The role of the dietary manager is changing from that of dictatorial taskmaster to one of a leader who provides necessary resources, guidance, and direction. Effective supervisors realize the advantages of using different leadership styles, when possible, to meet the specific needs of individual staff members.

A leadership style is the mix of attitudes and/or behaviors that a dietary manager can use to direct the work of the employees. There are four common styles of leadership:

- **Autocratic Manager:** An autocratic leader likes to make decisions and solve problems without getting information from affected employees. Because of the leader's strong control over the group and the group's dependence on the leader, the group is lost when the leader is absent;
- **Bureaucratic Manager:** Dietary managers using this approach manage by the book. There is an emphasis on enforcing rules.

- **Democratic Manager:** The democratic (participative) dietary manager desires to include employees in decision-making activities that affect them.
- **Laissez-faire Manager:** This manager uses a hands-off approach and really does as little supervising as possible.

Several factors influence the type of leadership styles used:

- The dietary manager's personal background;
- Characteristics of employees;
- Relationship between dietary manager and employees;
- The job situation itself;

The situation itself has a dramatic impact upon the utility of the leadership style.

Situational leadership makes a distinction between task and relationship behavior. By putting together the concepts of social/emotional support, task (direction) behavior, and perceived maturity levels, the most appropriate leadership style can be determined and then used in a specific situation.

The four leadership styles can be summarized as follows:

1. Low task (direction) and low social/emotional support;
2. High social/emotional support and low task (direction);
3. High task (direction) and high social/emotional support;
4. High task (direction) and low social/emotional support.

There are no two leaders who lead exactly alike. There are however, some common traits found among all leaders: trustworthiness; intelligence; empathy; inspiration and sharing the same vision; role models, mentors, coaches; communicators; encouragement; giving credit; self-confidence; delegation; and empowerment.

Effective leaders make others feel powerful. The use of influence is in itself not bad, but in fact can often lead to a great good. It is the morality with which influence is used that makes all the difference. Both the lack of power and the abuse of power are equally debilitating and counterproductive.

Four personal characteristics are important sources of power. Expertise reflects cognitive abilities, personal attraction involves affective appeal, effort suggests personal commitment, and legitimacy conveys credibility.

Expertise is "knowledge-ability." It provides a strong base of power in large, technologically sophisticated, rapidly changing organizations.

There are two sources of personal attraction: agreeable behavior and attractive physical appearance. If one does not measure up in this category, it is possible to compensate by emphasizing other sources of power.

A fundamental principle of psychology is that individuals strive to reduce inconsistencies between their own personal beliefs and personal behavior, and between their expectations of others and the behavior of others (cognitive dissonance reduction). Since the person's rewards are based on completion of the amount of work normally expected, the inconsistency can be eliminated only by reduced effort or increased responsibility.

Actions that are congruent with the prevailing value system are deemed credible, or legitimate, by other organizational members. Legitimacy increases acceptance, and acceptance is a key to personal influence. Successful organizations have members who are both capable of gaining power by fitting in and of using that power to challenge the prevailing belief system. Legitimacy is a prerequisite for effective criticism.

Some studies have shown that solutions to problems are often better when input from more than one individual is utilized. Advantages to employee participation programs include the increased possibility that errors will be noted when decisions are reviewed, and that employee input will provide additional alternatives to be considered.

There are at least two types of formal group participation programs: (1) task groups focused on special problems, or total quality management teams; and (2) employee suggestion programs.

Factors shown to influence the effectiveness of the employee participation activity include:

- The interests and abilities of staff members;
- Personal factors within each staff member;
- The availability of adequate time;
- The extent to which benefits exceed costs;
- Participation outside the job assignment;
- Job situation factors;
- Other factors such as the use of communication and persuasion techniques, absence of threat, etc.

Dietary managers must manage groups of employees as well as individual staff members. Some of these groups will be formal, established by and for the benefit of the facility. Other groups will be informal, evolving because of the mutual interests of participating employees. The effective dietary manager must know how to manage both formal and informal groups and be able to direct them in efforts to assist the dietary department in meeting goals.

Several basic techniques should be used to manage groups. Many of the basic principles of supervision can be helpful in working with groups.

The dietary manager must be aware that conflicts can arise if efforts to discourage membership in informal groups are not successful. The attitudes which group members hold toward the organization and the job are likely to affect the quality and quantity of work output. Therefore, the dietary manager confronted with an informal group working against the facility's goals must attempt to (a) modify the attitudes of group members, (b) redirect the group toward more useful goals, and/or (c) confront those factors which are causing negative attitudes of group members.

The dietary manager, as an official in the dietary department, should provide a great deal of input to planning activities for the department. A great deal of coordination is necessary in either instance to develop action plans which do, in fact, best use limited resources to maximize the attainment of facility goals.

Frequently, goals are developed for a short time period. As the time frame for goal development becomes longer, the goal statements themselves frequently become broader and less specific. The dietary manager must make time to plan for short and long range. Time must be set aside from the day-to-day operation to establish plans, read, network, and develop studies and programs that will enhance the future of the department.

Dietary managers must recognize the need for flexibility as plans are developed. Plans must be based upon the best estimates of the future, while at the same time recognizing that alternative plans may be necessary. The rapid change confronting the dietary department is also difficult to quantify. Internal organizational changes, the impact of legislation, and changes in the facility's philosophy and mission are among the variables that make planning difficult. At the same time, each of these factors also makes planning an important priority.

Making objective and fair decisions based on facts is one of the most difficult tasks the dietary manager will encounter. Decision making is the process of choosing a course of action among alternatives to solve a particular problem. Once the decision has been made, action needs to be taken. Programmed decisions are decisions that must be made when problems are repetitive, routine, or frequent. Non-programmed decisions occur when the dietary manager is confronted with a decision that is one of a kind, may never recur, or is new and unusual. These decisions are complex and difficult to make, since the problems are rare, unique, and unstructured. As a result of non-programmed decisions standards, rules, policies and procedures may be changed.

Different people approach decision making in different ways. The logical approach of deliberately going through a series of steps is recommended, although it takes a great deal of time. At the opposite extreme is the intuitive approach. People who take this approach to decisions tend to be creative, intelligent people with strong egos and high aspirations.

The scientific method in solving problems involves seven steps:

- Define problem;
- Analyze problem and gather data;
- Develop alternatives;
- Choose the best alternative;
- Implement action;
- Follow-up;
- Evaluate.

As dietary managers make day-to-day decisions, they will need to:

- Avoid snap decisions;
- Use policies, procedures and standards;
- Know the process and evaluate it before judging the action;
- Seek help when in doubt;
- Decide if the decision is big or small;
- Avoid "fire fighting" or crises;
- Not brood over a decision.

Many dietary managers work long hours but fail to accomplish or stay on top of their jobs. Long hours may not be the same thing as effectiveness. Before a manager can get control of time he or she must know how time is currently being spent. Time analysis can be done a number of ways, such as sorting the duties of the job by type, or by using time management tools such as activity logs.

A calendar and/or weekly planning sheet can be used to control the use of time. After evaluating how time is spent, the next step is to implement and evaluate the outcome. Evaluate success and failure, upgrade "to do" lists, review priorities, and change as needed.

KEY TERMS

- Leader
- Leadership style
- Autocratic
- Bureaucratic
- Democratic
- Laissez-faire
- Situational leadership
- Task behavior
- Relationship behavior
- Maturity
- Directive behavior
- Supportive behavior
- Directing style of leadership
- Coaching style of leadership
- Supporting style of leadership
- Delegating style of leadership
- Formal leader
- Informal leader
- Expertise
- Personal attraction
- Effort
- Legitimacy
- Cognitive dissonance reduction
- Distinctive competence
- Task group
- Employee suggestion program
- Short-range goals
- Long-range planning
- Logical approach
- Intuitive approach
- Indecisive approach
- Impulsive approach
- Time management

QUESTIONS/PROBLEMS/CASES

1. Describe a work situation suited to each of the four leadership styles.

2. What are the negative aspects of each of the four leadership styles?

3. What is the distinction between "directive" leadership behaviors and "supportive" leadership behaviors? Why is it a good idea to combine these two behaviors?

4. Ed is a 27-year-old server responsible for the dining room in a medium-sized healthcare facility where outside guests also dine regularly. Ed is dedicated to his profession and is determined to do a good job meeting the needs of clients and their guests. Unfortunately, he is often faced with frustrating situations, such as the following description of a single day.

   It is Saturday afternoon and there is a private party planned for one of the clients at the facility that evening. The healthcare facility has everything ready for a wonderful evening for the client and his guests. The host of the event is the client's son who has asked for additional bottles of non-alchoholic sparkling grape juice to be served throughout the evening rather than just at the reception. That seems to be no problem for Ed.

   However, Ed has only a limited number of bottles of non-alchoholic sparkling grape juice, which were delivered earlier that day. Ed had ordered enough for only one to one-and-a-half glasses per guest, due to the projected arrival time of the guests at the reception. Even though there is more non-alchoholic sparkling grape juice in the beverage storeroom, only the store clerk and dietary manager have keys. The store clerk seldom works on weekends, so Ed first tries to call the dietary manager to ask her to drive to the facility and get more bottles out of the storeroom. The dietary manager lives less than ten minutes by car from the facility, and this is the plan for dealing with this type of situation.

   The dietary manager is not at home, so Ed goes to the dining room and collects all the bottles of non-alchoholic sparkling grape juice that he can find. He then tells the host of the event that he has to change to a different type of non-alchoholic sparkling grape juice for the extra servings. The host says he thinks it is strange that they cannot get more non-alchoholic sparkling grape juice, which was originally ordered. Ed can do nothing and the host is unhappy.

Ed tried several strategies to prevent this incident from happening. On prior occasions, he tried to change the system so that he or someone else had keys to the storeroom in the evenings. The dietary manager refused to discuss this issue at all and would not give a key to anyone. When this strategy did not work, Ed started calling the manager each time they needed anything from the storeroom; he hoped that the manager would get tired of being called and realize that she had to do something about this situation. The manager usually came down and took out of the storeroom whatever the staff needed and then returned home. The dietary manager did not seem to be bothered that she was called quite often.

Ed has become very tired of fighting the management and the storage clerk to satisfy clients and their guests. In the beginning he was committed to giving clients what they wanted. Currently, Ed has resigned himself to giving less than excellent service, often telling clients or their guests that what they want is locked in the storeroom and it cannot be taken out. Although it discourages Ed that the clients do not perceive him as being helpful, he rationalizes that management obviously does not want him to be helpful to the clients and their guests.

a. Who do you think is right in this situation?

b. Why do you think the dietary manager has this policy?

c. What messages are being sent by the dietary manager?

d. What do you think Ed might do in the future?

5. List the four sources of personal power. Have you experienced in your own life a time when you were given power in one of these ways? What is meant by "Paying your dues creates legitimacy, and legitimacy is a prerequisite for effective criticism"?

6. Summarize how an employee goes about becoming a member of a group.

7. What kind of problem might one face if decision making is intuitive, indecisive or impulsive?

8. Margaret has been head cook at a cafeteria for 25 years. Up until a year ago, the cafeteria has always been crowded with customers who came back to enjoy the same fresh pasta dishes they remember from years before. In the past year, however, there has been a noticeable drop in walk-in customers, owing to competition from several new restaurants that feature gourmet foods, diet menus, and other fads and fashions.

   Margaret's boss, Raymond, the manager, is an eager young man fresh out of a college program. He sees what is happening and wants Margaret to change the menu, but Margaret flatly refuses. She says that the food is as good as it ever was, and that Raymond simply isn't promoting it properly and is probably making other mistakes, too.

   Margaret makes it clear that she has no respect for college graduates who haven't paid their dues. She also objects to new sanitation practices that Raymond requires.

   The other employees are aware of this ongoing situation between Margaret and Raymond, and are beginning to take sides. Raymond is aware that he must do something quickly, but what?

   Raymond sees that increased competition has decreased the cafeteria's share of the market. He thinks new menu items will put it out front where it has always been. He can see only the following alternatives:

   a. Fire Margaret and train a new person to his liking. But Margaret is an excellent cook and no one on Raymond's staff can duplicate her pasta sauces, as well as other dishes for which there are no recipes. Also, many loyal customers might leave as well.

b. Try it Margaret's way—a marketing program emphasizing an old-time image—the good old days, tradition. Raymond can't believe Margaret is right. He also thinks that giving in to Margaret will put her in charge—and will make it difficult for Raymond to maintain his authority with his other employees;

c. Discuss the problem with his boss, the owner of the facility. However, Raymond doesn't want to admit to her that he has this problem;

d. Get some expert advice on market trends and how to conduct a market study; by hiring a consultant or paying a visit to his favorite management professor at the university.

Raymond has made a preliminary decision. He visits his former teacher and comes back with a new perspective. He still has not made his decision but he is making headway.

a. Which alternative would you recommend he use and why?

b. Who is at fault in this situation? What is the problem?

c. Are there any other solutions besides those Raymond has listed? Suggest as many as you can, and give pros and cons for each.

d. Who do you think is right about the menu—Margaret or Raymond? How would you change the menu?

e. How can Raymond increase effectiveness in working with Margaret?

9. Describe you own decision-making style. Do you make impulsive decisions or gather all the facts and take time to make an appropriate decision? Do you avoid making decisions? Do you let someone else make your decisions?

10. Describe two time management skills you use at work or at home to more effectively utilize your time.

12

COMMUNICATION: INTERNAL AND EXTERNAL RELATIONS

Chapter Outline

- The Dietary Manager and the Communication Process
  - Communication Process
  - Basic Communication Skills
  - Barriers to Effective Communication
  - Overcoming Barriers to Communication
  - Common Communication Myths
  - Channels of Communication
- Methods of Communicating
  - Effective Speaking
  - Effective Listening
  - Effective Writing
  - Effective Nonverbal Communication
- Preparing, Planning, and Conducting Facility Meetings
  - Techniques for Effective Meetings
  - Persuasion Techniques
- Preparing for Internal/External Communication
  - Presenting the Message
  - Purposes of Presentations
  - Types of Presentations
- The Dietary Manager Representing the Dietary Department Internally
- Task Forces and Committees
- Coordinating Facility Services and Plans with Outside Groups
- The Dietary Manager and the Client's Rights and Responsibilities

The Dietary Manager and the Communication Process

The dietary manager must be able to effectively communicate. Speaking, writing, and listening are important activities which consume a large amount of a manager's time. He or she must be able to prepare, plan, and conduct meetings according to basic management principles. Training is another very important activity of dietary managers. A structured set of procedures for training, coaching, and counseling is very important in the labor-intensive dietary department. A dietary manager must know how to persuade personnel at all organizational levels, serving as a salesperson and spokesperson for the needs of dietary services. He or she must also know how to establish goals and priorities for dietary services since there are not resources available to do everything that is "best" for the dietary department.

Communication, an exchange of information, plays a major role in how efficiently and effectively employees will work together to finish a task or meet an objective. Even when we do not say anything we are still communicating by our actions. Most people talk; few people communicate. Lack of communication is the basis of most problems in life. The communication process is complex. As a dietary manager it is vital that you become knowledgeable in the process and techniques of good communication, and apply this knowledge as you interact with administrators, physicians, clients, employees, and families. Miscommunication leads to dissatisfaction, misunderstanding, misinterpretation, and, in some cases, to anger and resentment. You should understand that there are basic principles of communication which can help every dietary manager be more effective.

Communication Process

Communication is the exchange of an idea between two people. There must be an idea, a sender, a receiver, a message, and feedback.

The sender has an idea that he or she wishes to transmit. He or she must think about the receiver's perspective as the message is put together. However, the sender is also influenced by his or her own perception of the message and the situation. Your perception is influenced by the skills, abilities, attitudes, and experiences which make up your background.

After proper consideration the message, verbal and/or nonverbal, is transmitted through formal and/or informal channels of communication. Examples of formal channels are meetings, memos, and rules. Informal communication channels include the grapevine, rumors, and general conversations. Finally, the message is received, and the receiver attempts to understand it based upon his or her own perceptions.

Feedback is the reaction which the receiver has to the sender's message. Feedback can be positive or negative. Positive feedback lets the sender know how well he is doing, while negative feedback may identify areas where improvement may be needed. Feedback may take many forms, including oral, written, electronic mail, and body actions such as a shrug of the shoulders. Feedback should be given as soon as possible. When feedback is high quality it builds trust, fosters problem-solving, and provides useful outcomes. Constructive feedback is not personal; it is problem-oriented rather than people-centered.

The process of feedback can occur formally or informally and, regardless of the type, the sender's message will be most effectively received when he or she attempts to evaluate how well the receiver has understood the message transmitted.

The communication process is rather complex. Although you should understand the basic process, it is more important to recognize the need to consider the receiver as you develop the message, and to be aware that perceptions will influence your ability to send and receive the message. Feedback is essential to an effective communication process.

Communication may be one-way or two-way. In one-way communication, the sender does not expect a reply from the receiver. In two-way communication the sender expects a reply from the receiver. One-way communication is less accurate and less time-consuming. Two-way communication allows for feedback, as the sender and receiver are face-to-face. Dietary managers most often use oral two-way communication in their job. This type of communication gives the other person an opportunity to question and speak freely. A good dietary manager will promote open, face-to-face communications encouraging employees to ask questions and openly express ideas.

Basic Communication Skills

Effective communicators know about the need to:

Analyze the receiver. The sender must know how to consider "where the receiver is coming from." If, for example, the sender can anticipate how the receiver will act, what might influence him or her to be more receptive, and/or how to send the right message, the communication is likely to be more effective;

Use feedback. The need to generate effective feedback is difficult but necessary. Asking questions such as "Do you understand?" or "Do you have any questions?" and so on is generally not effective. Asking specific questions that require the receiver to make use of information just learned can be a helpful technique;

Make messages meaningful. It is important to consider the perceptions of the receiver as the message is developed. Would you give instructions to both a new and an experienced staff member in exactly the same manner? Of course not. You must think about the receiver as he or she formulates and sends the message.

Barriers to Effective Communication

You have learned that the communication process is complex and important. The dietary manager who can overcome the following barriers will be a more effective communicator:

Barrier 1: Differences in perception. The sender must consider the receiver's perceptions and develop messages in a way which will make them more clearly understood;

Barrier 2: Lack of knowledge. The communication process cannot be effective when the sender and/or the receiver do not have knowledge adequate to develop and/or understand the message;

Barrier 3: Role of emotions. Sometimes emotions, either obvious or subconscious, can cause communication problems. Said another way, the communication process must also consider irrational concerns of both the receiver and the sender;

Barrier 4: Lack of interest. It is difficult to communicate effectively if the receiver and/or sender does not have an interest in the message being conveyed;

Barrier 5: Personality problems. Personality clashes between the receiver and sender can cause communication problems. Have you ever rejected the message offered by someone whom you believed to have a "bad" personality? Likewise, have you ever "blindly" accepted communication from a sender with a "charismatic" personality?

Barrier 6: Appearance. Just as your personality and emotions may get in the way of effective communication, your appearance may detract from communication effectiveness. When we are upset about or pleased with another's appearance, it can have an impact on our acceptance of the message;

Barrier 7: Prejudice. We can be biased for or against an individual for very irrational reasons. If you don't like a person because of his or her race, sex, or color, there is negative prejudice. Defending the "status quo," or liking things as they are may be a positive prejudice. Prejudicial concerns of any type can be a barrier to effective communication;

Barrier 8: Distractions. Noise, other conversation, temperature, and other environmental influences often make it difficult for communication to take place effectively;

Barrier 9: Disorganization. If the sender or receiver is disorganized or uncertain about the exact message to be sent, communication problems arise. The receiver may also be disorganized because he or she is not aware of proper procedures for listening or reading;

Barrier 10: Language. There may be a lack of common understanding among a group when slang, jargon, or technical languages are used;

Barrier 11: Status. Differences in rank, education, socioeconomic, or prestige may detract from the process. Either the sender or receiver may face the pressure of the difference in status;

Barrier 12: Size of the Organization. In a small facility, such as a long-term care facility, everyone knows everyone on a first-name basis. There are few levels of organization. In larger organizations there are more layers and the opportunity for distortion is greater.

Overcoming Barriers to Communication

Overcoming barriers to communication can be simple common sense. The best methods to employ in overcoming barriers are:

- Use face-to-face communications. Talk directly to the person; seek clarification and feedback;
- Observe body language for clues;
- Use simple, clear, precise wording;
- Repeat the message several times using different words. Be aware of symbolic meanings of words;
- Be empathetic. Seek to understand and respect the receiver's opinions, ideas, attitudes, perceptions;
- Have a genuine concern for the receiver and the effect of the message on him or her;
- Use proper timing for messages (end of day is often best, but not on Friday afternoons, and never when an employee is visibly upset or emotionally stressed). Communicate when everyone is calm;
- Choose a location that will enhance the process;
- Be an effective listener.

Common Communication Myths

There are several misunderstandings about communication which should be resolved:

MYTH 1: People only communicate when they want to. We can't really control every aspect of communication. For example, if a dietary manager ignores a situation or does not respond to it promptly, these actions express low priority or lack of interest just as clearly as do words;

MYTH 2: Words mean the same to everyone. We understand words based upon our experience with them. What does the following mean: "Jane, please come to work early tomorrow." Does this mean Jane should report to the "early" shift, before the early shift, or earlier than she usually reports to work—or is there another meaning?

MYTH 3: Words are the primary vehicle by which we communicate. In reality, we also communicate nonverbally. The way we look and act as we speak or listen are also very effective indicators of our responses;

MYTH 4: Communication is a one-way activity: the sender tells the receiver. In fact, communication is most effective when it is a two-way activity. Effective communicators talk *with* rather than *at* or *to* others;

MYTH 5: There is no such thing as too much communication. Too little information is not good; however, too much information can also be a problem.

Channels of Communication

There are two distinct channels of communication found in an organization: formal, or official channels; and informal channels, usually called the grapevine and/or gossip. Both carry a message from one person or a group to another person or group. The formal channels are downward, upward, and horizontal communications.

Downward Communication

Downward communication is the flow of information from individuals at a higher level to a lower level, such as the administrator to the dietary manager. This type of communication is frequently used in large organizations to communicate policies, procedures, directives, objectives, and other information to subordinate personnel. When a dietary manager uses downward communication it is to give instructions, explain information or procedures, train employees, and communicate other activities that may have a bearing on the employee's job.

Downward communication is important in an organization; it may be the only contact subordinates have with upper management. As a result, administration must:

- Be honest, accurate, and factual, whether the information is good or bad news;
- Use words and phrases that subordinates can understand;
- Make the message specific; explain what effect it will have on the employee.

Upward Communication

In upward communication the dietary manager is responsible for keeping the administrator informed. Employees also will communicate ideas, requests, and opinions to their supervisor.

Upward communication is usually reporting and questioning. In many organizations upward communication is a problem as subordinates know the supervisor has the authority to fire, block promotions and salary increases, and give unpleasant assignments. The supervisor must find ways to work with the subordinates to maintain face-to-face communication that is free flowing, open, honest, and respectful of differences in opinions.

Horizontal Communication

Horizontal communication is "lateral," which means communicating with people who are at the same level but doing different functions among different departments. Horizontal communication usually involves discussions and meetings to solve problems and accomplish tasks that cross department or functional lines. Without horizontal communications much of the coordination of care for the patient would go lacking; common goals and free flow of information would be practically impossible.

Informal Communication

Informal communication is commonly called the grapevine, rumor mill, gossip, or scuttlebutt. It exists in all organizations and comes about due to curiosity, insecurity, and lack of formal communications.

The grapevine can offer an insight into what employees think and feel. The grapevine may carry some factual information, but often it is half truths, rumors, and suspicions. The grapevine provides a channel for employees to express their fears, desires, and apprehensions in the form of rumors. In most cases the grapevine is unreliable, unconfirmed, and unauthorized. Dietary managers need to learn how to use the grapevine to their advantage and realize that it fills a need of the employees. Ignoring rumors can cause problems, as a rumor may have some elements of truth.

METHODS OF COMMUNICATING

EFFECTIVE SPEAKING

The dietary manager must know how to speak effectively. Figure 12.1 lists some of the traits and qualities necessary for effective speech. As one can see, the list is long; the "art of speaking" is not easily learned.

You can improve speaking skills by following these suggestions:

- Know what is going to be said and develop a plan to use when speaking;
- Identify the most important points of the message and organize what is going to be said around these points;
- When talking, keep in mind what is to be said; don't digress and introduce things not critical to the message;
- When speaking, concentrate on the listener. Remember that the objective of speaking is to communicate, not to create "a good image" of oneself;
- Speak enthusiastically, be committed to the purpose of the message, and show interest by the way that words are spoken;
- Be able to back up all information which is provided. A well-documented talk allows the listener to concentrate on what is being said, not on questioning whether statements are accurate;
- Always consider the background and perceptions of the listener;
- Use simple language that will be easily understood by the listener.

EFFECTIVE LISTENING

Many dietary managers spend more time listening than they spend writing or speaking. If you listen carefully, you will have a better idea about employee attitudes and morale, and will be able to reduce problems caused by management inattention. A manager who is a good listener can obtain work-related information, be more effective in interpersonal relationships, and generate information necessary to make good decisions.

There are several basic principles helpful in effective listening:

1. Confidence	15. Understanding
2. Knowledge	16. Humility
3. Organization	17. Concern about listener
4. Pleasing voice	18. Responsiveness
5. Concern	19. Awareness of situation
6. Control of emotion	20. Humor
7. Language command	21. Forcefulness
8. Friendliness	22. Sensitivity
9. Objectivity	23. Charisma
10. Empathy	24. Concentration
11. Open-mindedness	25. Spontaneity
12. Trustfulness	26. Tact
13. Acceptable appearance	27. Intelligence
14. Honesty	28. Enthusiasm

FIGURE 12.1 ELEMENTS IN EFFECTIVE SPEAKING

- Think about the central idea the speaker is trying to convey;
- Focus attention on what the speaker is saying; don't be distracted;
- Don't let emotions influence. Try to listen objectively to what is being said;
- Don't "tune out" a speaker just because the message seems familiar, strange, or unimportant;
- Don't listen just for specific facts. There may be a "hidden agenda," which is a subtle but important part of the message;
- Understand the speaker's basic ideas before discussing, defending, or arguing against him or her;
- Don't be distracted by an uncomfortable physical environment;
- Search for special meaning in the speaker's message. Some parts of the message are likely to be more important than others;
- Be sure to notice the speaker's nonverbal communications;
- Don't avoid listening to complicated information. Rather, use feedback to express potential misunderstanding;
- Concentrate on the message and its content, not on its delivery;
- Allow the speaker to finish and then react fairly and sensibly to what has been said;
- Don't take notes unless the information is too detailed or specific, or unless it will be needed in the future.

Effective Writing

Most dietary managers must write formal and informal reports. They will also need to keep written records and will be expected to send written replies to memos and instructions.

When writing, always consider the reader. The message will be understood according to the receiver's perceptions and his or her ability to understand written words.

The written message must be clear and accurate. A simple message is best; big words, special jargon, and so on are generally unnecessary and often hurt communication. Follow the "KISS" principle: Keep it simple and short.

Be sure that the writing expresses a clear and concise central idea. The reader should not have to search for a hidden element in the message. Always emphasize the *who, what, where, when,* and *why* of the situation. Memos indicate the central idea in a subject line.

Writing will not generally permit immediate feedback. Therefore, the writer must consider how the effectiveness of the communication will be judged. Sometimes a preliminary outline or rough draft document can be sent to solicit input from the reader before developing a final written message. A written message can also be delivered in person, so that conversation can help provide necessary feedback.

Writers should be tactful and should focus on the reader's concerns rather than on their own. Written messages should contain no obvious grammar and presentation problems. Sentences and paragraphs should not be overloaded with too many ideas. Finally, the writer should be positive, not negative, when writing.

Effective Nonverbal Communications

"Actions speak louder than words." "Lead by Example." Employees observe the actions of their supervisor as a form of communicating whether intended or not. Smiles, gestures, shrugs of shoulders, hands on hip, handshakes, and silence all convey messages. Some people may communicate by a look. Some of this behavior may be a planned, conscious effort to get the attention of another person and/or to add emphasis to a message.

Many employees and supervisors try to analyze these actions and put labels on the meanings of the actions. Nevertheless, the actions convey information to another. Gestures appear to be universal and appear to have the same meaning regardless of the difference in the spoken language. However, some gestures do have different meanings, and it is for this reason that an analysis of body language must be done cautiously.

PREPARING, PLANNING, AND CONDUCTING FACILITY MEETINGS

The dietary manager will be called upon to develop, conduct and/or attend meetings with employees, higher-level officials, and others. Following some basic principles can make meetings more effective.

You have learned about advantages to and basic procedures for employee participation. Using meetings to gain this participation is a common practice of many dietary managers. Both the quality of the decisions made and the commitment of those who must carry them out will be enhanced if group discussion has preceded the decision-making process. Meetings are the most popular way to accomplish these objectives.

There are many purposes for meetings. The dietary manager might, for example, wish to inform, to discover, to decide, to clarify, to sell, to consult, to seek participation, to problem-solve, to brainstorm, or to seek opinions.

While each situation must be considered separately, the dietary manager should decide the amount of group involvement, if any, which will be most helpful in handling problems, making decisions, and carrying on the general business of the dietary department.

When conducting a meeting, the dietary manager must do four things:

Stimulate group discussion. This is best done by providing information at the beginning of the meeting. The objective(s) and the exact purpose(s) of the meeting should be discussed at its beginning. Stimulation occurs as the dietary manager asks questions and explores ideas during the meeting. He or she also stimulates meetings by showing excitement and enthusiasm, and by asking open-ended questions which allow several people to present a broad range of ideas.

Control group members. It is important to make sure that time is used effectively and that the discussion does not digress. The dietary manager exerts control by keeping the discussion moving, by redirecting group members straying from the topic, and by periodically summarizing progress made in the meeting. The group leader also controls as he/she notes the time allowed for the meeting at its beginning and provides a count-down of time remaining;

Support each group member. Each individual should be allowed to state his or her opinion; the group leader should make sure that all points made are considered objectively, and that ideas—not personalities—are examined. The dietary manager also supports members in meetings as he or she draws in non-contributing members and praises those with creative and potentially useful ideas;

Observe group members. He or she must know what is going on, must be aware of the atmosphere of the meeting, and must be able to identify and resolve any resistance or conflicts which might occur. It is also important for the group leader to be aware of his or her own behavior, and to recognize and dismiss any emotional reactions which arise as ideas are expressed counter to his or her own. In doing these things, the dietary manager will be able to explore underlying conflicts or resistance levels of group members, so that consensus can be obtained.

Techniques for Effective Meetings

Much planning must be done for effective meetings. For example, the dietary manager must identify the specific purpose of the meeting. Necessary facts and commonly held opinions about the topic must be gathered and understood. Problems must be given priority, since time for meetings is generally limited. The group leader must also decide the extent and type of group discussion needed.

As the meeting is planned, it is necessary to consider (a) who should attend, (b) what topics are to be discussed, (c) specific objectives for the discussion, and (d) the best approach to involve group members in the discussion.

Select a time and day for the meeting that is most convenient for everyone. List the materials needed such as chalk board, audio-visuals and handouts. Choose a place for the meeting that is quiet, comfortable, well lighted, and large enough to provide ample space for all attendees. Notify all participants at least one to two weeks in advance. For most meetings, sending an agenda with the notice helps the attendees be prepared to participate. At the beginning of the meeting the dietary manager must clearly state the objective(s) of the meeting. Determine what is the expected outcome. He or she should also present all relative facts and opinions, tell why the matter must be resolved, and encourage all attendees to participate actively in the meeting.

At the beginning of the meeting it is helpful for the group leader to show how each member will benefit from the meeting. Generally, formality is not necessary; a first-name basis can be used. If attendees do not know each other, introductions are very important. Finally, the leader should encourage a friendly team spirit as the meeting evolves, and should amply discuss the meeting's importance.

The group leader has several activities as the meeting evolves. For example, he or she must guide the group to keep it on track, keep the discussion moving forward, and draw in unresponsive persons. Asking the views and experiences of all attendees and ensuring that the discussion is not overpowered by one or a few speakers is very important. If disagreement arises between group members, the leader should explore the reason for the disagreement and try to seek consensus. He or she must also make certain that all comments by all attendees are understood by everyone. Summarizing progress and ensuring that time is spent effectively are other activities of the leader as the meeting evolves.

At the end of the meeting, the group leader can summarize the progress made and check to be sure that all relevant aspects of the topic have been considered. He or she can review the extent to which the meeting's objectives have been attained, clarify the next actions to be taken, and see that everyone understands the action and the need for it.

Sometimes, members of a group need special attention as a meeting evolves. Figure 12.2 indicates some basic strategies which can be used in different situations.

The agenda for the meeting should be distributed to each member invited to the meeting. The agenda needs to be planned carefully with a list of topics to be discussed and in the sequence they will be discussed. A time limit should be established for each topic, but this limit should not be so rigid that it cannot be adjusted. The agenda serves as an outline for the meeting and can assist in keeping the meeting on track.

A recorder should be appointed to maintain a record of the meeting. This record should include at least:

- Name of meeting;
- Date, time started and ended;
- Name of the leader and recorder;
- Names of those present;
- Key points and discussion topics (brief);

The Group Member Who:	Strategy to Use:
1. Wants to argue.	1. The group leader should not get involved. The member's ideas should be stated and summarized and the group should decide upon their value, if any.
2. Wants to help.	2. The group leader should encourage the member to give ideas, especially when the discussion is veering "off course."
3. Wants to discuss details.	3. The group leader should acknowledge the member's points but should also remind him/her of the meeting's objective and the time limit which has been set.
4. Will not stop talking.	4. The group leader should interrupt the member tactfully and then ask a question to bring him/her back to the topic of conversation.
5. Is afraid to speak.	5. This group member can be asked easy questions, recognized for earlier contributions, and made to feel important.
6. Wants to be recognized.	6. The group leader can recognize the individual, can note his/her interest in the topic of conversation, and can ask the group member about creative or unique solutions to the problems at hand.
7. Is not interested.	7. The group member can be asked about his/her own concerns and how the discussion can help him/her with them. If there is no way that this group member can be brought into the conversation, he/she might be asked to leave.
8. Acts superior.	8. This group member can be recognized for his/her ability and can be asked the most difficult and challenging questions.
9. Wants to show cleverness.	9. Trick questions should be identified and should be given to the group for answering.

Figure 12.2 Strategies to Handle Types of Group Members

- Action to take;
- Who is responsible to take the action.

All participants should be provided a copy of the minutes. Corrections if needed, should occur at the next meeting.

Persuasion Techniques

Dietary managers are frequently the experts in their facility in matters pertaining to dietary services. The "art and science" of persuasion is still often necessary to tell one's story to top-level administrators and others. Resources available to the facility are limited. There are always several departments with conflicting views on what's best for the facility. The dietary manager in his or her role as spokesperson for dietary services must be able to compete with others for limited resources; use of persuasive strategies can often be effective in efforts to obtain dietary goals while simultaneously helping the facility to accomplish its mission.

The term **persuasion** can be defined as any effort which the dietary manager uses to influence and/or to change the beliefs, feelings, or attitudes of someone else. When the dietary manager persuades, he or she is attempting to gain the consent of another person. Persuasion strategies range from subtle suggestions to the use of force. In the context of dietary services, persuasion generally is limited to supplementing knowledge and facts with arguments which favor the position of the dietary manager when justifying a need.

Basic principles of persuasion a dietary manager can use include the following:

- Recall that it is easier to persuade when you have credibility;
- Use concepts and facts which are familiar to the other person;
- Show that the desired outcome will benefit the other party;
- Repeat direct and indirect suggestions most critical to the point.

When attempting to persuade, start with material on which both parties will agree. Complimenting the listener and emphasizing how he or she will benefit from the improvement can be helpful. The persuader should continually solicit questions and comments, and should be prepared to restate and respond to the basic issues in positive terms.

The dietary manager should allow the listener time to absorb information, and to analyze and consider all points which are made. The persuader should encourage others to agree with him or her and should remember to thank the listeners for time spent involved in the conversation.

While many of the above points are really just common sense, one should recall the need to arouse the other party's interest by promising him or her some benefit. Be ready to show definite examples of how that benefit will impact the other party and the facility itself. When concluding a persuasive conversation, always present a suggestion for the next specific action to be taken.

Preparing for Internal/External Communication

Can a dietary manager "automatically" practice basic principles of external relations? No, these must be learned, and they are very important. Examples of concepts important in external relations activities include:

- The dietary manager must recognize the important role of dietary services in the mission of the facility and be able to explain, defend, and justify both the purpose of the facility and the role of dietary services within it;
- The dietary manager must be familiar with all policies, rules, and procedures of the facility and department. For example, what should be done if a nursing home is offered food products by church or civic groups or others? The dietary manager must know and consistently apply policies which have been developed on this topic. He or she must know the conditions for accepting products for use in the facility and be able to graciously accept or reject foods, while at the same time showing appreciation for the group's actions;
- When in doubt about the appropriate role, the dietary manager should talk with his or her own supervisor. There could be a long history of experiences and previous actions which could impact upon new policies. How can the dietary manager know about these precedents unless he or she asks?
- The dietary manager must be acutely aware of his or her exact role in the facility. Can he or she make binding commitments upon the facility? Under what

specific conditions? Serious problems can be avoided if the dietary manager is aware of, and does not exceed, his or her limits of authority;

- It is important to recognize the need to gather information for later decisions. For example, as the dietary manager learns something that might benefit other decision makers in the facility, he or she can share this information. The dietary manager must know, when asked for an opinion, whether a response will be taken as a personal opinion or as an "official position" of the facility.

Many dietary managers do not feel comfortable in the role of external spokesperson. However, they must recognize that "all of the action" in dietary services does not take place within the facility itself. In fact, many important actions and decisions which will have long-lasting impact upon dietary services take place outside the walls of the facility itself. The concerned dietary manager must, then, "get involved" in the process of external relations.

Presenting the Message

How does the dietary manager communicate effectively with external groups? What should the dietary manager do when he or she is asked to speak to church and civic organizations, or to groups of other health professionals? An important first step is to be very familiar with the topic to be presented. It is always better to say "no" and refer the group to another individual than to take the chance of providing inaccurate information and embarrassing the department and/or facility, or otherwise failing in the role as external relations specialist.

In making internal/external presentations it is important to know the objective of the presentation. Is it to inform a group about the facility or department? Is it to seek volunteers or donations to the facilities? Knowing the objective leads to the audience. Is the audience teenagers, children, adults, retired persons, males, or females? Understand the expectations of the audience. Know where to obtain the information needed to make the presentation more meaningful and useful to the attendees.

Sources of information include current trade journals and library reference materials (many facilities have internal research/study libraries with useful information). Interviews with others, recollections of one's own experiences, and conversations with professionals in other facilities and with professional associations provide additional examples of "where to go" for information.

When a dietary manager must make a public presentation, he or she usually develops an outline of the talk. Considerable effort is needed to develop an effective outline and to adequately prepare for the presentation. Several basic outline styles can be used:

Topical outline. Subjects that are similar to each other are placed together. For example, if the dietary manager is giving a talk on nutrition, perhaps all points to be made about Vitamin A can be discussed at one time.

Step outline. This approach is used when a sequence of steps must be taken to do something, for example, procedures required to develop a diet history.

Chronological outline. With this style, events are placed in a time dimension, with earlier activities before later events, for example, a history of the local Dietary Managers Association chapter.

Problem-solution outline. This presentation style involves addressing a series of problems by proposing alternatives/solutions for each problem in turn. For example, several factors leading to high dietary costs might be discussed, with alternatives for reducing costs given.

Advantages and disadvantages format. With this approach, the dietary manager may cite a situation and then discuss its advantages and disadvantages, for example, the concept of charging for nutrition education materials.

After the main part of the presentation has been outlined, an introduction and a conclusion should be developed. The introduction provides the setting for the rest of the presentation and should meet the following criteria:

- It should relate to the topic of the presentation;
- The audience should be able to identify with the introduction;
- The introduction should establish a common ground between the speaker and audience;
- It should be a preview of the remainder of the presentation;
- It should help to establish a good relationship between the speaker and the audience;
- It should tactfully lead into the main points being presented.

The conclusion to the public presentation is also very important and accomplishes several purposes:

- It provides the opportunity to summarize what the speaker hopes the audience will do, or remember;
- It provides an effective way to terminate the presentation;
- It helps to maintain the rapport and relationship necessary for the maintenance of the public relations image being established.

The effective presenter knows the importance of using audio-visual aids. For example, many times it is much easier to transmit information if it can be seen *and* heard. Visual aids can help to keep the audience's attention and can provide much more information than can be presented orally by the speaker. If done well, visual aids can make the difference between a very effective and just a "good" speech. Visual aids range from videos, charts, graphs, pictures, and models, to handouts. Although it takes time and experience to learn effective use of audio-visual aids, they can help make the dietary manager a real public relations expert and effective trainer.

After the presentation has been developed, the dietary manager must practice its delivery. A good way to practice the presentation is to record it, play it back, and note where words may have been mispronounced or if the speed was not appropri-

1. Remember your objective—to "sell" the audience on your ideas.
2. Make sure that you're well prepared. (Write out what you want to say, at least an outline, but don't read it.)
3. Take your time, don't rush.
4. Don't *appear* nervous. (It's okay—and natural—to *be* nervous!)
5. Maintain good eye contact to all areas of the room.
6. Don't repeat the same point too many times.
7. Defend each major point with reasons for its importance.
8. Dress appropriately.
9. Be in control of your actions.
10. Use humor appropriately.
11. Use audio-visual aids when appropriate.
12. Be careful about your hand and body movements.
13. Be sure that you know how to use each piece of required equipment and be sure that it works.
14. Speak at appropriate speed (not too fast or too slow).
15. Speak normally.
16. Don't use terms, jargon, etc. which are unfamiliar to the audience.
17. Use handouts if appropriate.
18. Practice your presentation.
19. Be sure that you are organized, and stay on track.
20. Give credit for use of guides and copyright material.

FIGURE 12.3 IMPROVE YOUR PUBLIC SPEAKING

ate. Another way is by a private practice followed by a rehearsal with a member of the dietary department. At other times, this activity is not required. The dietary manager who is thoroughly familiar with the topic and who knows how it is to be delivered will be a much more effective presenter than will his or her counterpart who has not invested the time necessary for proper development and practice.

Figure 12.3 presents a list of basic principles important in making an effective public speaking presentation.

Purposes of Presentations

Many objectives can be addressed by external presentations. For example, the goal may be simply to inform or instruct attendees about a specific topic. Lectures supplemented with audio-visual aids are an excellent device for this purpose.

Unfortunately, many presentations which are educational in nature cannot hold the attention of the audience. For this reason, many professional speakers interject humor or stories when appropriate. For example, a joke which illustrates a person's losing sight of objectives can be very helpful in emphasizing the need for the facility to be constantly aware of its objectives, or for the audience to know the objectives of the speakers.

Still other presentations have as an objective a desire to persuade an audience to do something. Providing additional budgetary funds, recognizing the increased importance of nutrition and nutrition education, and the presentation of health concerns about diet are all examples of topics which may benefit from helpful persuasion. One of the keys to persuasive techniques is to show, from the perspective of the audience, why revised actions are better. If the dietary manager can show this difference quantitatively, the effort is likely to be more successful.

The dietary manager can represent the facility in many other ways besides presenting a speech. Examples include publishing bulletins; writing letters, handbooks and manuals; and developing bulletin boards, posters, and billboards. Creative dietary managers can think of many ways to generate interest among their audiences. Many commercial companies or associations have printed and audio-visual materials covering a wide range of topics, which can also be helpful in the presentation.

Dietary managers are being asked with increasing frequency to make presentations at meetings of their peers or allied professionals. When one must speak to these groups, he/she obviously needs very careful study and preparation. The professional recognition and challenge which this opportunity provides should be an incentive for the dietary manager to place a high priority on developing the presentation. Maintaining objectivity, providing information which might be transferable to another situation, and "telling it like it is" are all examples of techniques which can be helpful in an association presentation. Timing is very important, and practice prior to the presentation will be helpful in measuring allowable time.

Types of Presentations

There are a wide variety of presentations other than lectures which a dietary manager can use in his/her role as an external public relations specialist. Several of these include:

Demonstration. The dietary manager might show people how to do something. For example, he or she may demonstrate methods for garnishing meals in ward/galley kitchens. Community service group members might observe the dietary manager as he or she demonstrates how to prepare a favorite recipe at the facility. Demonstrations, followed by attendees applying what they have seen, can be a very effective external public relations method.

Seminar. This is a planned approach which utilizes several procedures such as lectures, discussions, and conferences. The seminar method utilizes group participation. For example, the dietary manager may present basic information to a group and then permit the exchange of information through discussion. Frequently, dietary managers will be part of a seminar presentation, stressing points and then participating in subsequent discussion.

Conference. Dietary managers may participate in conferences designed to generate ideas about possible alternatives to resolving a problem. For example, a conference dealing with alternative food production/delivery systems may involve the dietary manager in a presentation of systems utilized at his or her facility, followed by a discussion of ways to improve and/or modify the operation.

Panel presentation. With this method, the dietary manager may serve as a member of a small group who shares in the preparation of a presentation and follow-up on a topic. Frequently, panel members make a presentation, share discussion with each other, and then open up for questions and further discussion from the audience.

Role-playing. While role-playing is typically used as a training tool, dietary managers may also use it to explain problems and propose solutions to external groups. For example, the dietary manager may use this technique to teach a patient/resident about basic principles of nutrition.

Case studies. A case study is a description of a specific situation—either real or imaginary. Events are reported without explanation, and attendees then use the experiences illustrated in the case as a basis for subsequent discussion. Dietary managers may use the case-study approach to point out the need for additional space for preparation facilities, to discuss the need for a specific capital equipment item, or for other purposes.

Interactive ad hoc groups. Dietary managers may serve as part of a project team which crosses departmental lines to work on general problems relative to the facility. As he or she performs this role, the dietary manager is practicing principles of interaction with members and departments in the facility external to the dietary department.

As the dietary manager represents the department, he or she must utilize basic procedures necessary to deal with an external group. For example, the dietary manager must know the subject matter, act in a professional and businesslike manner, and otherwise adequately represent the dietary department. Can you imagine problems caused if the dietary manager makes careless errors, performs in an unprofessional manner, and/or otherwise gives the impression that dietary personnel are not competent and/or do not care about the facility? The need to be concerned about adequate representation of the dietary department must begin with interaction within the facility, and must then extend to activities external to the facility.

The Dietary Manager Representing the Dietary Department Internally

Who wants to know about the dietary department? Sources of internal concern range from the facility's board of directors (or other governing body) and the top levels of administration to business-office personnel with fiscal concerns about the department. Each of the departments/areas within the facility with which dietary personnel must interact (and, at one time or another, this represents almost every functioning unit) likewise has a concern. After all, each administrative unit, including dietary services, must work toward attaining the goals of the facility. A great deal of close cooperation/interaction is necessary for this to occur.

In many facilities, healthcare teams are made up of personnel who have specialized training in some aspect of patient care. For example, there may be a healthcare team for the renal, cardiovascular, diabetic, and/or pediatric division. This team is usually headed by a physician. Other members of the healthcare team may include registered nurses and licensed practical nurses, physicians, medical records administrator, physical and occupational therapists, recreational therapist, social worker, pharmacist, x-ray and laboratory technicians, dietitians, dietetic technicians, and/or dietary managers. The number of professionals involved in the care will depend on the needs of the clients, their significant others, and the faculty. This team works in unison to develop care plans as well as discharge plans for clients. A cooperative effort and shared goals on the part of all team members are necessary to provide continuous quality improvement of care, and to meet the needs of the clients and their significant others.

The team is usually stable and client-oriented. The team may include family members who have input into the long-term care of their significant other. This approach may increase the client's and their significant other's capability and desire to assume the responsibility for their own care.

Size and complexity of a facility will dictate the education, experience, and skill levels needed by each practitioner. For example, a long-term facility will usually employ a certified dietary manager as the department manager and a consultant dietitian to advise, observe, evaluate, instruct, and recommend. In a large university teaching hospital, clinical, teaching, research, and administrative dietitians, dietetic technicians, and dietary managers may be employed. All categories of professionals will work together to plan, coordinate, develop, coach, counsel, assess, evaluate, direct, control, and communicate the goals and objectives of the nutritional care of the clients.

In large institutions there may be a dietetic-team approach to the care of the client. In smaller facilities the team may be composed of a dietary manager and a consultant dietitian. Regardless of the size of the facility, the authority and responsibility of the dietetic team is granted by the facility's board of directors and chief executive officer. Other regulatory agencies, such as the Joint Commission on Accreditation of Healthcare Organizations (JCAHO) and state licensing agencies, also issue guidelines for the dietetic services. (The JCAHO standards include more leadership participation as a major component of the director of the service.)

The dietetic team may include:

- Director of the service;
- Clinical, research, education personnel;
- Community consultant dietitian, management dietitians;
- Dietetic technician;
- Dietary managers;
- Other dietetic personnel.

Each member of the team plays a role in the translation of physician's orders into foods that meet the body's needs as well as the social, emotional, and psychological needs of the patient and their significant other. Quality nutritious food is essential for the well-being of clients, for prevention and treatment of disease and for rehabilitation and restoration of health.

The role of the members of the dietetic team have been defined by the American Dietetic Association (ADA) through its Role Delineation Studies and the Dietary Managers Association and its Role Delineation Studies. The ADA and the DMA are responsible for setting educational requirements, program approvals, and continuing education for their members.

Task Forces and Committees

The dietary manager may be asked to represent the dietary department on a number of facility committees and task forces. Committees and task forces are established to coordinate activities within the facility and to problem-solve, especially when the problem is multi-departmental.

Committees and task forces are formal units chaired by an appointed chairperson. Meetings are regularly scheduled. Attendance and minutes are recorded and dispensed to all members.

A committee is a group of persons within the organization who work together to mutually solve problems and to perform some of the administrative activities. This group has been granted specific authority. Committees may be temporary or permanent. Committees are usually appointed for ongoing activities and may be mandated by regulatory agencies.

Task forces are usually appointed to deal with specific problems. Task forces analyze the problem, complete the research, and make recommendations which may become a plan of action. Once the problem is solved the task force is disbanded. Task force members are chosen on the basis of technical competence and specialized training, not as representatives of a specific group of employees or group interest. When dietary managers are appointed to committees or task forces they should:

- Attend scheduled meetings;
- Be on time;
- Participate as appropriate in the discussion;
- Keep to the point of the discussion;
- Review the assignment as important;
- Know the scope, function, and authority of the group;
- Maintain confidentiality as required;
- Share information and seek others' opinions;
- Be flexible, a team player;
- Support the recommendations and outcomes;
- Be prepared and meet the time limit if assigned a project.

Foodservice departments may also appoint committees within the department. For example, there may be need for a menu committee to review menus and make suggestions for improvements; safety committees that oversee the safety aspects of the department; and quality assessment and improvement committees that review, evaluate, and recommend opportunities for improvement.

Dietary managers may be asked to serve on facility-wide committees such as:

Infection Control. This committee's purpose is to develop policies and procedures for sanitation techniques, for isolation procedures, for reporting of infectious diseases, and for educating and training all personnel.

Safety Committee. The purpose of this committee is to review all unsafe acts within the facility, both for clients and others, and to establish fire safety and disaster preparedness, to implement OSHA and other regulatory standards, and provide education and training for all personnel.

Budget Committee. The purpose of this committee is to provide involvement for the manager in the budgeting and cost-effectiveness process.

Quality Assessment and Improvement. The purpose of this committee is to monitor, evaluate, and document actions for the provision of quality service and products for all clients.

There may be other committees to which the dietary manager may belong. These include such clinical committees as:

- Discharge planning;
- Nurse/nutrition;
- Renal service committee.

The number and types of institutional committees will vary from institution to institution.

A wide range of external publics must also be served. Consider, for example, the various governmental units concerned with licensing, sanitation, safety, taxation, and other requirements. Non-governmental certification bodies, such as the Joint Commission of Accreditation of Healthcare Organizations (JCAHO), also have concerns which must be addressed by the dietary manager in his or her role as an external relations "expert." The consumers of dietary services—the client and others—are an obvious market whose wants, needs, and concerns must be addressed by the dietary manager. What about the suppliers, consultants, various community groups, and other organizations participating in cooperative programs? Professional association involvement, membership in community service and other clubs, and service on advisory boards provide still additional examples. While our list can be expanded, the point is that the dietary manager must have a wide range of knowledge, skills, and abilities which extend beyond the dietary department.

The implications of this external role are significant. The way the dietary manager dresses, talks, acts, and looks will have at least a subconscious—if not overt—impact upon the external community and will shape their attitudes toward the facility and the dietary department itself. The old saying "First impressions are lasting impressions" is correct. The professional dietary manager must represent the department and facility in the most professional and businesslike manner possible. This applies to all activities by which the dietary manager represents the facility, whether formally or informally.

Skilled nursing facilities carry out utilization reviews of the services provided in the facility to in-patients entitled to benefits under federal programs. The purpose of utilization reviews is to ensure high-quality client care and appropriate and efficient utilization of facility services. There are two elements to utilization reviews: medical care evaluation studies and review of extended-duration cases.

Medical care evaluation studies are systematic studies which relate directly to client care. Their purpose is to seek out any problem area(s), determine appropriate methods to improve the situation, and ultimately to improve overall client care. A dietitian may be involved in these studies, that is, those designed to determine problems related to dietary intake of clients, effectiveness of specific dietary regimens, and so on.

The composition of this committee includes two physicians (committees reviewing intermediate care clients may require only one physician). The committee may also include any appropriate ancillary personnel such as nurse, medical records administrator, pharmacist, dietitian, and so on. These members serve in a role supportive to the physician to offer information relative to their professional disciplines.

Coordinating Facility Services and Plans with Outside Groups

There are many examples of how the dietary manager coordinates activities within the facility with those of outside groups. Examples within the dietary profession include cooperation in shared consulting services, cooperative purchasing systems, and cooperative employee training programs. As community resources available for healthcare and other programs are carefully analyzed, a wide range of possible shared services can be suggested. For example, production and delivery of meals for external groups (see below) is relatively common. In some areas, the dietary manager or other professional in charge of foodservices may have responsibilities which extend beyond a specific facility. In effect, this professional then represents several health care or other facilities to the external public.

The dietary manager must have knowledge of how other healthcare facilities operate. The need to avoid duplication, be cost-effective, and provide quality products and service is a must. The dietary manager needs to have a pulse on the market and know the competition and capabilities of other facilities within the area.

Dietary managers must know how to develop a service plan for a facility which can help meet community needs. For example, should the dietary department offer satellite meals for external groups? What should be the role of the dietary department in an emergency/disaster program within the community? How should the dietary department relate to education programs in dietary services within the high school, junior college, or other educational institutions within the community?

Basic procedures for developing a plan to analyze alternatives include:

- Assess current needs. This activity is called market research and involves determining whether there are unmet needs within the community. Surveys, questionnaires, interviews, personal observation, and analysis of written information—such as community newspapers and Chamber of Commerce annual reports—can all provide insight to assist the dietary manager;
- After needs are known, the dietary manager must determine the extent to which these needs are currently met. For example, are other facilities providing meals for shut-in elderly? If so, are they providing services to persons in the same area that would be served by the dietary manager's facility? Much assistance can often be provided by governmental agencies such as the Department of Health and Social Services, the Department of Community Nutrition, agencies focusing on the elderly, and so on;
- The dietary manager must assess his or her department's capability for expanded production and division of services. Are all of the department's facilities and other resources being utilized to capacity? How would the menu need to be changed? Will more labor be required? What about using convenience foods? Is storage space available to house added quantities of raw products? How would production and assembly of meals for transport affect the ongoing operation?;
- A budget must be developed. Frequently, all direct costs and a prorated share of indirect, fixed costs can be assessed as the provision of additional meals/services is analyzed. If this is the case, there may be a real economic incentive for program expansion. Again, the dietary manager faced with cost containment and DRG pressures must consider these alternatives in order to remain competitive with other healthcare facilities.
- After all operational, economic, public relations, and other matters have been assessed from the perspective of dietary services, the dietary manager should discuss the matter with his or her own supervisor. Frequently, matters involving relationships with external groups will need clearance from top-level administration—if not the board of directors. It is at this point that the salesmanship of the dietary manager must really be perfected. Top-level administrators are likely to ask, "What will this proposal cost?" The dietary manager must be able to "turn this analysis around" to review "how much it will save," "how we can quantify the goodwill to be generated," and so on.

The Dietary Manager and the Client's Rights and Responsibilities

Applicable federal and state regulations require that clients be advised of their rights. Each facility must maintain records which certify that both clients and all staff members are familiar with the rights and responsibilities of the persons served by the facility. Institutions, including dietary service departments, would be wise to include this basic information in the orientation programs of all new personnel. Basic information should also be placed in a public area within the foodservice operation.

Some basic client rights relate to food. For example:

- A client has the right to be served food according to his or her ethnic, cultural, and/or religious beliefs. This means that the dietary manager must make efforts to provide Kosher/Jewish, Mexican, Oriental and other ethnic foods when prior notice has been given to the department of a client desiring these foods;
- The client has a right to be served food according to his or her individual food preferences. For example, many people develop food preferences based upon regional eating practices. If a client is on a special diet, he or she should be provided, to the extent possible, with his or her preferences within the restrictions imposed by the diet;
- The client has the right to be served attractive, tasty food at the proper temperature in a pleasing environment by a pleasant dietary staff member. This client right involves almost all departments. For example, the administration must provide funds sufficient to purchase a variety of quality foods. The dietary department must also be responsible for preparing and serving food which is appetizing and nutritious. The housekeeping department must provide a clean and pleasant environment in both the dining facilities, private rooms, and other client areas. Nursing services must prepare the client to receive the tray. For example, the client's hands may need to be washed, the bed and adjacent areas may need to be prepared, and so on. These activities should be performed in a pleasant and appropriate manner;
- The client has the right to participate, as much as possible, in the serving of traditional holiday meals. These meals are meaningful and greatly appreciated by the client and his/her relatives and friends. Such meals are an integral part of the backgrounds of many people, and help remind clients of celebrations they have had with their own families;
- The client has the right to expect the right interpretation of his or her diet order as it is translated into food and meals being served. For example, the physician must write the order and nursing service personnel must transfer the information to the dietary department, which must then implement orders by means of food production and meal service;
- The client has a right to consultation about normal nutrition needs and diet modification practices. After a diet order has been entered on a person's chart, a dietitian is obligated to meet with the client and/or the immediate family to provide information about these orders.

As one can see from the above list, there is a basic structure of client rights which helps to determine procedures used by the dietary manager to communicate and interact with the client. What to many people may be "common sense" is, to the professional dietary manager, both a charge of responsibility and a benchmark against which the subsequent performance of his/her own actions and those of the dietary department can be evaluated.

The basic rights which clients have that pertain to foodservice have just been reviewed. Now, let's take a look at responsibilities which the clients have to dietary services:

- A client has the responsibility to follow the nutritional care plan which is recommended as a result of the client-care planning meeting;
- The client has the responsibility to seek more nutritional information and/or clarification of information which has been given. When questions remain after instructions or consultations have been given to the client and/or his family, the client has the responsibility to ask for clarification and to request follow-up;
- The client is responsible for his or her own actions if diet instructions are not followed. A client should be instructed in diet and other special concerns upon discharge. Once the diet has been explained, it is then the responsibility of the patient to follow it.

As you review the above client responsibilities, you can see many situations in which there is a need for the dietary manager to function as an external relations specialist. For example, nutritional aspects of client care plans must be explained, the need for adherence to dietary requirements must be defended, and nutrition and nutrition education activities must be undertaken. Therefore, as the dietary manager and other dietary department staff interact with the client, external public relations principles must be followed.

SUMMARY

Communication, an exchange of information, plays a major role in how efficiently and effectively employees will work together to finish a task or meet an objective. Miscommunication leads to dissatisfaction, misunderstanding, misinterpretation, and in some cases anger and resentment.

Communication is the exchange of ideas between people. There must be an idea, a sender, a receiver, a message, and feedback. After proper consideration the message, verbal and/or nonverbal, is transmitted through formal and informal channels of communication. Examples of formal channels are meetings, memos, rules, and so on. Informal communication channels include the grapevine, rumors, general conversations, and the like.

When the message is received, the receiver attempts to understand it based upon his or her own perceptions. Feedback is the reaction which the receiver has to the sender's message. Feedback can be positive or negative. It may take many forms including oral, written, electronic mail, and body actions such as a shrug of the shoulders. When feedback is high-quality it builds trust, fosters problem-solving, and provides useful outcomes. Constructive feedback is not personal; it is problem-oriented rather than people-centered.

Communication may be one-way or two-way. In one-way communication, the sender does not expect a reply from the receiver. In two-way communication the sender expects a reply from the receiver. A good manager will promote open, face-to-face communications encouraging employees to ask questions and openly express ideas.

The manager who can overcome the following barriers will be a more effective communicator:

- Differences in perception;
- Lack of knowledge;
- Role of emotions;
- Lack of interest;

- Personality problems;
- Appearance;
- Prejudice;
- Distractions;
- Disorganization;
- Language;
- Status;
- Size of the organization.

There are five common communication myths which also hinder communications.

Formal channels of communication are: downward, upward, and horizontal or lateral.

Informal communication is commonly called the grapevine, rumor mill, gossip, or scuttlebutt. It provides a channel for employees to express their fears, desires, and apprehensions in the form of rumors.

The dietary manager must know how to speak effectively. Ways that one can improve speaking skills are listed below:

- Know what you're going to say; develop plan;
- Identify the most important points of the message and organize around these points;
- Keep in mind what you want to say;
- Concentrate on the listener;
- Speak enthusiastically;
- Be able to back up all information;
- Always consider the background and perceptions of the listener;
- Use simple language.

A manager who is a good listener can obtain work-related information, be more effective in interpersonal relationships, and generate information necessary to make good decisions. Basic principles of listening include:

- Think about the central idea the speaker is trying to convey;
- Focus attention on what the speaker is saying;
- Don't let your emotions influence you—be objective;
- Don't tune out a speaker;
- Don't listen just for specific facts;
- Understand the speaker's basic ideas before discussing, defending, or arguing;
- Don't be distracted by an uncomfortable physical environment;
- Search for special meaning in the message;
- Be sure to notice the speaker's nonverbal communications;
- Don't avoid listening to information that is complicated;
- Concentrate on the message and its content;
- Allow the speaker to finish and then react fairly and sensibly;
- Don't take notes unless the information is too detailed or specific, or unless it will be needed in the future.

Most dietary managers must write formal and informal reports. When writing, always consider the reader. The written message must be clear and accurate, concise and tactful. There should be no obvious grammar and presentation problems.

Sentences and paragraphs should not be overloaded with too many ideas. Additionally, the writer should be positive, not negative, when writing.

Employees observe the actions of their supervisor as a form of communicating, whether intended or not. Smiles, gestures, shrugs of shoulders, hands on hip, handshakes, and silence all convey messages. Gestures appear to be universal and appear to have the same meaning regardless of the difference in the spoken language. However, some do have different meaning, so it is important that an analysis of body language be done cautiously.

Dietary managers will be called upon to develop, conduct, and/or attend meetings with employees, higher-level managers, and others. There are many purposes for meetings. The dietary manager might, for example, wish to inform, to discover, to decide, to clarify, to sell, to consult, to seek participation, to problem-solve, to brainstorm, or to seek opinions. When conducting a meeting, the manager must do four things: stimulate, control, support, and observe.

Much planning must be done for effective meetings. The manager must identify the specific purpose of the meeting. Necessary facts and commonly held opinions about the topic must be gathered and understood. Problems must be given priority since time for meetings is generally limited. As the meeting is planned, it is necessary to consider: attendees, discussion topics, objectives, and participation methods.

At the close of the meeting, the group leader can summarize the progress made and check to be sure that all relevant aspects of the topic have been considered. He or she can review the extent to which the meeting's objectives have been attained, clarify the next actions to be taken, and see that everyone understands the action and the need for it.

The agenda for the meeting should be distributed to each member invited to the meeting. It needs to be carefully planned, with a list of topics to be discussed and in the sequence they will be discussed. The agenda serves as an outline for the meeting and can assist in keeping the meeting on track.

A recorder should be appointed to maintain a record of the meeting. This record should include meeting description, attendees, key points, and follow-up actions.

All participants should be provided a copy of the minutes. Corrections, if needed should occur at the next meeting.

The term **persuasion** can be defined as any effort which the dietary manager uses to influence and/or to change the beliefs, feelings, or attitudes of someone else. Basic principles of persuasion which a dietary manager can use include the following:

- Recall that it is easier to persuade when one has credibility;
- Use concepts and facts which are familiar to the other person;
- Show benefits of the desired outcome;
- Repeat direct and indirect suggestions most critical to the point.

There are many important concepts in good external relations. Many actions and decisions which will have long-lasting impact upon dietary services take place outside the walls of the facility itself. In making presentations it is important to know the objective of the presentation and the expectations of the audience. Know where to obtain the information needed to make the presentation more meaningful.

Considerable effort is needed to develop an effective outline and to adequately prepare for the presentation. Several basic outline styles can be used: topical, step, chronological, problem-solution, and advantages/disadvantages.

After the main part of the presentation has been outlined, an introduction and a conclusion should be developed. Additionally, visual aids provide much more information than can be presented orally by the speaker. Visual aids range from videotapes to handouts.

There is a wide variety of presentations other than lectures which a dietary manager can use in his or her role as an external public relations specialist.

Sources of internal concern range from the facility's board of directors and the top levels of administration to business office personnel with fiscal concerns about the department. Utilization reviews are carried out by skilled nursing facilities to ensure high-quality client care and appropriate and efficient utilization of facility services. There are two elements to utilization reviews: medical care evaluation studies and review of extended duration cases.

The role of the members of the dietetic team have been defined by the American Dietetic Association (ADA) through its Role Delineation Studies and the Dietary Managers Association and its Role Delineation Studies. The ADA and the DMA are responsible for setting educational requirements, program approvals, and continuing education for their members.

Committees and task forces are established to coordinate activities within the facility and to problem-solve, especially when the problem is multi-departmental. Committees and task forces are formal units that are chaired by an appointed chairperson. Dietary managers may be asked to serve on facility-wide committees such as:

- Infection control;
- Safety committee;
- Budget committee;
- Quality assessment and improvement;

and clinical committees such as:

- Discharge Planning;
- Nurse/Nutrition;
- Renal Service Committee.

A wide range of external publics must also be served. There are various governmental units concerned with licensing, sanitation, safety, taxation, and other requirements, as well as professional association involvement, membership in community service and other clubs, service on advisory boards, and so on. The dietary manager must have a wide range of knowledge, skills, and abilities which extend beyond the dietary department.

There are many examples of how the dietary manager coordinates activities within the facility with those of outside groups. Examples within the dietary profession include cooperation in shared consulting services, cooperative purchasing systems, and cooperative employee training programs. Dietary managers must know how to develop a service plan for a facility which can help meet community needs. Basic procedures for developing a plan to analyze alternatives include:

- Assess current needs;
- Determine the extent to which these needs are currently met;
- Assess department's capability for expanded production and division of services;
- Develop a budget;
- After all operational, economic, public relations, and other matters have been assessed from the perspective of dietary services, a supervisor should be consulted.

Applicable federal and state regulations require that clients be advised of their rights. Institutions would be wise to include information in the orientation programs of all new personnel. Basic information should also be placed in a public area within the foodservice operation. Some basic client rights relate to food. For example:

- A client has the right to be served food according to his or her ethnic, cultural, and/or religious beliefs;

- The client has a right to be served food according to his or her individual food preferences;
- The client has the right to be served attractive, tasty food at the proper temperature in a pleasing environment by a pleasant dietary staff member;
- The client has the right to participate in the serving of traditional holiday meals;

KEY TERMS

Communication	Problem-Solution outline
Feedback	Advantages and disadvantages format
One-way communication	Demonstration
Two-way communication	Seminar
Communication barriers	Conference
Communication myth	Panel presentation
Downward communication	Role-playing
Upward communication	Case Studies
Horizontal communication	Projects and ad hoc groups
Informal communication	Healthcare team
Nonverbal communication	Multi-discipline team
Persuasion	Dietetic team
Topical outline	Basic client rights
Step outline	Basic client responsibilities
Chronological outline	

- The client has the right to expect the right interpretation of his or her diet order as it is translated into food and meals being served;
- The client has a right to consultation about normal nutrition needs and diet modification practices.

Not only do clients have rights, but they also have responsibilities to dietary services. Among these responsibilities are following the recommended nutritional plan, seeking more nutritional information and/or clarification of information given, and being responsible for his or her own actions if diet instructions are not followed.

Questions/Problems/Cases

1. Explain why two people describing the same object or the same situation may give different accounts of it. How does this interfere with communication?

2. Comment on the statement, "When emotions are involved, the emotions become the message." Do you agree? Give examples from your own experiences to back up your answer. How does emotion block communication on the job?

3. Do words mean the same to everyone? Look at the words "fun," "soon," "a little," "pretty." Pick two or three examples and describe what each means to you. Compare your meanings with other classmates and discuss how the differences could complicate communication.

4. Identify which type of communication each of the following situations represents.

    a. The dishwashers are asking their supervisor about changing the schedule.

    b. The dietary manager informs department employees about a new dental insurance program.

    c. Employees are discussing what the chef and dietary manager are planning in the main office.

    d. A cook asks another cook about a recipe.

5. Discuss the "basic principles helpful in effective listening" presented in the text. Do you know people who practice all of them? Some of them? None of them? Which do you find the most difficult to practice? Do you think a dietary manager would be able to learn and practice them? What is the best way to learn them?

6. What are the four things a dietary manager must do when conducting a meeting? What is the purpose of each?

7. What should be included in the "minutes" of a meeting? Why?

8. What are the basic principles of persuasion a dietary manager can use.

9. What's the difference between a committee and a task force? What types of facility-wide committees might a dietary manager participate in?

10. What are the techniques for communicating with external groups?

11. In helping to meet community needs, dietary managers must know how to develop a service plan. Describe the procedure that you would follow if asked to assist the local Red Cross in a potential disaster program.

12. List basic client rights related to food.

13

FINANCIAL MANAGEMENT

CHAPTER OUTLINE

- Supervising Cash Cafeteria Operations
  - Focus on the Cashier
  - Using the Cash Register
  - Cafeteria Operating Reports
  - Processing of Cash for Deposit
  - Other Cash-Handling Concerns
- Reviewing the Cost of the Menu Against Budget Guidelines
- Implementing Cost-Effective Procedures
- Records Help in Financial Management
- Calculating Costs and Setting Prices for Catered Events
- Recommending Salary/Wage Adjustments
  - Factors Affecting Levels of Wages and Salaries Paid
  - Concerns in Salary/Wage Administration
  - Job Evaluation
  - Determining Salary/Wage Increases
  - Employee Benefit Programs
- Budget Development Process
  - Steps in Budget Development
  - Budget Control Procedures
  - Zero-based Budgeting
- Ideas for Generating Revenue
- Benchmarking
- Doing More with Less

SUPERVISING CASH CAFETERIA OPERATIONS

The dietary manager must be able to manage financial resources. The days of thinking "I'll handle operations; let the business office handle the money and accounting" are gone. The professional dietary manager must design systems to control income generated by cash foodservice operations. Pre-costing principles should be applied as menus are planned. The dietary manager must know how to calculate costs and set prices for catered events, and should have a role in recommending salary and wage adjustments for employees. Finally, today's dietary manager must be able to develop and utilize an operating budget for dietary services.

There are many specific roles the dietary manager must play in the management of the facility's financial resources. Each of these tasks is essential, and the professional dietary manager must be just as competent in financial management as he or she is in the activities of food production, personnel supervision, nutritional assessment, and so on.

The dietary manager has an important role in the control of sales generated from cash cafeteria operations. For effective control, the dietary manager must know (a) the amount of sales which should be collected, (b) the amount of sales which actually is collected, and (c) when corrective action is necessary to reduce the variance between (a) and (b) above.

Let's take a look at each of these control points:

1. Knowledge of sales which should be collected. What is the possibility that cafeteria staff will give away food, charge a smaller than required fee, eat on the job and/or otherwise misuse food products to the detriment of sales? What is the possibility that cafeteria staff will overportion, waste food, make cash register and/or arithmetic errors, and so on? Regardless of whether staff purposely try to cheat or make "human" mistakes, the impact on the dietary operation will be the same: sales which should be collected to reduce the amount of operating expenses to be offset with income from other sources will not be collected. The result will be higher than necessary deficits to be borne by the facility.

How much sales should be collected? The answer relates to the number and cost of menu items which have been sold. Figure 13.1 provides a format which might be used to track the amount of standard (potential) cafeteria food sales which should be collected. (The actual amount of sales will probably need to be adjusted by deducting the value of any "free" or reduced price meals served to employees, physicians, administrative personnel, and others.)

In the example cited in Figure 13.1, mashed potatoes is a menu item featured in the cafeteria line. As the line opened, one half-pan of potatoes was issued to the line. During the meal period, two additional half-pans are sent to the line; a total of three half-pans were issued. At the end of the meal period, one-quarter of a pan remains. Therefore, one and one-quarter pans of mashed potatoes have been used

Date: ______________________ Serving period: ______________________

Item	Quantity issued				Amount Left	Total Used	Sales Income/ Per Pan	Total Income
	#1	#2	#3	Total				
Mashed Potatoes	.50 pan	.50 pan	.50 pan	1.50 pans	.25 pan	1.25 pan	$12.00	$15.00

Total income ______________________

Potential income ______________________

FIGURE 13.1 CAFETERIA FOOD SALES RECORD

(3.00 half-pans equal 1.50 pans – .25 pans = 1.25 pans). If the potential sales per full pan is equal to $12, then the total income which should be generated from the sale of mashed potatoes will approximate $15 (1.25 pans @ $12 per pan = $15). If this procedure is repeated for each item on the serving line, it will be possible to estimate the amount of potential income which should be collected;

2. *Assess actual sales collected.* At the end of the serving period, the amount of sales actually collected can be assessed. To do this, the dietary manager should "X" the cash register with the sales journal tape printing. (The term "X the register" refers to reading the amount of sales which has been rung on the machine since the time of the last reading.) It is important that specific cash register operating procedures be used (see below) to make sure that the reading of a register is accurate. The amount which should be available (from the X reading) should be compared with the amount of cash/charge (if any) available in the cash drawer; overages and shortages should be noted;

3. *Compare standard and actual income.* If the dietary manager knows the standard amount of sales which should be collected (Step 1 above) and the amount of sales which has been collected (Step 2 above), it is possible to make a comparison. Based upon experience, for example, the dietary manager may allow a variance of no more than 1 or 2 percent between standard and actual sales levels before he or she feels further investigation is necessary.

Focus on the Cashier

A cafeteria cashier may have many duties beyond sales collection; however, this section will focus on those applicable to sales control. At the beginning of the work shift, the cashier should count the cash bank assigned to the register to be sure that the amount for which he or she will be responsible is, in fact, available. During the cashier's shift, standard operating procedures for use of the register should be followed. At the end of the shift, the cashier may be required to complete applicable cashier records. The dietary manager should "cash out" the register. During the cafeteria operation, there may be times when the cashier must inform the dietary manager about voids necessitated by over/underringing and/or other problems. Standard operating procedures to address these requirements should be developed.

Using the Cash Register

It is very important that specific operating procedures for the cash register be followed consistently. While the actual procedures will vary by operation, some basic principles are generally applicable. Examples would include keeping the cash drawer closed when not in use, giving each new cashier his or her own bank and keeping procedures for the operation of each register readily available for use by the cashier. Dietary managers should modify these and other procedures as necessary to fit the needs of the specific operation, and should train and consistently supervise the cashiers to ensure that these procedures are followed.

Cafeteria Operating Reports

The type and number of cafeteria operating reports vary according to the needs of the facility and the type of register equipment available. For example, many electronic "data" machines are programmable to provide almost any type of financial/meal countdown information for any desired time period. Use of more traditional mechanical equipment may require a great deal of hand tally work to develop the most basic information. It is obvious that the dietary manager and other managers of the facility must consider the exact needs of the dietary department when purchase decisions for register equipment are made.

There are basically two general types of operating data which can be generated and are most useful to the cafeteria operation: cash sales and number of meals by category. First it is important to confirm that all sales which should have been collected are, in fact, collected. Figure 13.2, a cafeteria cash report, represents the type

Day ______________________ Date ______________________

	Time	Reading	Count	Cash	Instruction	Deposit	Audit
A	9 a.m.	Ending					Cshr
B	6:30 a.m.	– Beginning					Cshr
C		= Breakfast sales					Spvr
D	11 a.m.	Ending			Cash		Cshr
E	9 a.m.	– Beginning			– Bank		Cshr
F		= A.M. snack sales			= Deposit		Spvr
G		C & F = Subtotal			Over/(short)		Reset
H	2 p.m.	Ending			Cash		Cshr
I	11 a.m.	– Beginning			– Bank		Cshr
J		= Lunch sales			= Deposit		Spvr
K		J = Subtotal			Over/(short)		Reset
L	5 p.m.	Ending					Cshr
M	2 p.m.	– Beginning					Cshr
N		= P.M. snack sales					Spvr
O	6:30 p.m.	Ending			Cash		Cshr
P		– Beginning			– Bank		Cshr
Q	5 p.m.	= Dinner sales			= Deposit		Spvr
R		N & Q = Subtotal			Over/(short)		Reset
S	G + K + R = Total sales				F + J + Q =		Total deposit

	$	11:00 a.m.		2:00 p.m.		6:30 p.m.	
U	Bills						
V	Q						
W	D						
X	N						
Y	P						
Z	Total						

Comments:

Figure 13.2 Cafeteria Cash Report

Source: Faisal A. Kaud et al., *Cafeteria Management for Hospitals.* American Hospital Association. Chicago, Ill., 1982, p. 72

of form needed and the kind of financial information collected. As one will note from study of the form, the sales day is divided into five periods (breakfast, A.M. snack sales, lunch, P.M. snack sales, and dinner). For each of these serving periods, the amount of sales which has been generated is assessed. This is done by reading the cash register (as noted above, this should be done by the dietary manager). The difference between the reading of sales income at the end of the last service period and that at the end of the present service period equals the amount of income generated for the sale period. For example, if the cash register sales reading at the end of breakfast is $300 and the reading at the end of "A.M. snack time" is $400, then the difference ($100) equals the amount of sales income generated during the A.M. snack sales period.

The total amount of funds which should be in the cash register at the end of the shift is represented by the total amount of sales rung on the register (ending sales less beginning sales plus the amount of the cash bank). In some facilities monies may be removed from the drawer during the shift for security or other reasons. This amount, if any, would also need to be considered as the cash amount is reconciled.

Daily cash sales information should be tallied on a cumulative monthly summary of cafeteria sales report (see Figure 13.3). This form is used to recap gross sales figures for each meal period. Since a basic sales control principle requires that all income should be deposited intact daily, it is possible to "track" the total amount of sales collected into the deposit made in the facility's bank account. (The total sales col-

Month ____
Year _____
Totals
Breakfast
$ ________
# ________
A.M. snack
$ ________
# ________
Lunch
$ ________
# ________
P.M. snack
$ ________
# ________
Dinner
$ ________
# ________
Sales
$ ________
Customer
____
Deposit
$ ________
Charge
$ ________

Date	Brkf.	#	A.M. snk.	#	Lunch	#	P.M. snk.	#	Dinner	#	Total	#	Deposit	O/S	Charge
Total															

FIGURE 13.3 MONTHLY SUMMARY OF CAFETERIA SALES REPORT
Source: Faisal A. Kaud et al., *Cafeteria Management for Hospitals.* American Hospital Association. Chicago, Ill., 1982, p. 73

lected per register reading would need to be adjusted by the amount of any overages and shortages which are also recapped in Figure 13.3.) If any sales have not been collected (for example, some employees, administrators, physicians and others may be allowed to charge their meals), this will also result in a necessary adjustment.

A second basic type of operating information collected by many cafeteria operations refers to income by specified category; Figure 13.4 a cashier's report by category, illustrates a format which can be utilized. In the sample cafeteria, income is categorized as follows: patient meals, cash (public) meals, doctors, employee meals, interns, administration, auxiliary, and "other." This type of information is relatively easy to generate if specific "clerk" keys are available on the register. (The register operator need only depress a specified clerk key as the transaction is rung.) Information from Figure 13.4 can be tallied into a cumulative report (see Figure 13.5, a public feeding weekly revenue report and meal count summary).

At the end of the week, total dollars generated in sales by each classification can be converted into a meal count (equivalent). Typically, this is done by assessing the average sales per meal (often at lunch) and dividing this into the total number of sales dollars collected. For example, in Figure 13.5, if the meal equivalent has been estimated at $2.50, the total sales dollars generated can be divided by $2.50 to estimate the number of meals which have been served.

Hospital:	*Memorial*
Date:	*1/20/76*
Shift:	*2*
Area:	*Cafeteria*
Cashier:	*Mrs. Smith*

Readings		Cash	Charge	Total
Patient meals	(1)	0	0	0
Cash meals	(2)	358		358
Doctors	(3)		15	15
Employee meals	(4)		53	53
Interns	(5)		—	—
Administration	(6)		8	8
Auxiliary	(7)		—	—
Other	(8)		—	—
Total	(9)	338	76	414

Beginning transaction number	(10)	105
Ending transaction number	(11)	625
Total transactions	(12)	520
Cash in drawer	(13)	437
Less bank	(14)	100
Net cash	(15)	337
Less reading	(16)	338
Cash over (short)	(17)	(1)
Voids	(18)	0

Prepared by: *Mrs. Smith* (19)
Verified by: *Joan Jones* (20)

FIGURE 13.4 CASHIER'S REPORT BY CATEGORY
Source: *Determination and Allocation of Food Service Costs.* American Society for Hospital Food Service Administrators, undated

An alternative meal count recap sheet is shown in Figure 13.6. Note that meal counts are tallied by various classifications for an entire month.

PROCESSING OF CASH FOR DEPOSIT

The dietary manager, not the register operator, should determine the amount of sales rung on the register during the work shift, and make sure this amount is available. Typically, this amount can be transferred to the business office with a transmittal copy of the daily cashier's report. With this plan, one copy would be retained by the dietary manager; the second copy would be provided to the business office.

In many facilities, personnel in the business office are responsible for preparing the bank deposit. However, a procedure should be set up to help the dietary manager assure that all sales generated were, in fact, deposited, and that the amount was credited to the appropriate dietary services account.

OTHER CASH-HANDLING CONCERNS

There is a wide range of methods dishonest register operators can use to steal. One common method involves "no ringing." With this scheme a register operator "no rings" a sale item and keeps a record of the amount of sales collected and deposited in the register drawer but not entered into sales journal tapes within the register. (The register operator will then know the amount of income which he or she can safely remove at the end of the shift.) Use of basic register operating procedures which require that all sales be rung on the machine, and constant supervision to ensure that these requirements are followed, are a good start at minimizing the potential for this problem. Spot checks of the amount of sales income in the register drawer can also be helpful. For example, on a routine but random basis, the dietary manager can read the register, withdraw the cash drawer, and count the money in the drawer. The total should equal the amount rung on the machine plus the amount of the beginning cash bank. Any excess funds in the register may represent income deposited by the register operator but not rung onto the register. Other common theft methods include giving away free food, undercharging friends and/or others for meals served, and so on.

Hospital: ______________ Account number: __________

Week ending: __________ Area: ______________

Prepared by: ______________________________

	Shift	Sunday	Monday	Tuesday	Wednesday	Thursday	Friday	Saturday	Total dollars	Divided by	Meal count
	1										
	2										
	3										
Patient meals (1)	Total										
	1										
	2										
	3										
Cash meals (2)	Total										
	1										
	2										
	3										
Doctors (3)	Total										
	1										
	2										
Free dietary	3										
employee meals (4)	Total										
	1										
	2										
	3										
Interns (5)	Total										
	1										
	2										
	3										
Administration (6)	Total										
	1										
	2										
	3										
Auxiliary (7)	Total										
	1										
	2										
	3										
Other (8)	Total										
							Total	(9)			

Figure 13.5 Public Feeding Weekly Revenue Report and Meal Count Summary

Source: *Determination and Allocation of Food Service Costs.* American Society for Hospital Food Service Administrators, undated

	Breakfast	Lunch	Dinner	NPO	CCU	ICU	Psych	Staff	Extras	Total
1	100	108	119	2	12	3	55	20		417
2	100	109	120	4	14	4	59	24	3	433
3	101	114	116	3	12	6	60	23		432
4	98	108	113	4	12	3	58	22		414
5	99	109	114	5	13	5	57	24		421
6	101	115	118	7	9	4	54	18	1	420
7	99	108	110	4	8	3	53	19		400
8	101	108	112	3	9	6	54	23		413
9	98	117	119	6	15	4	60	26	2	441
10	99	112	117	4	14	4	59	25		430
11	102	114	118	8	12	5	59	25	4	439
12	103	114	117	4	12	3	58	24		431
13	101	115	115	4	15	3	57	23	2	431
14	90	118	118	3	10	2	60	24	1	423
15	92	108	110	2	11	2	56	13	3	395
16	99	112	113	5	14	4	58	26		426
					•••••••••					
27	99	100	108	5	10	4	59	24		404
28	97	102	104	3	6	3	56	16		384
29	90	110	112	3	5	2	56	17	3	395
30	95	115	116	6	9	3	58	23	4	423
31										
	2951	3297	3414		356	113	1735	654	28	12548

FIGURE 13.6 MEAL COUNT RECAP SHEET
Used by permission of North Charles General Hospital, Baltimore, Md., courtesy of Pat Parker

It is possible for register operators and/or cafeteria guests to steal by failing to make change correctly. For example, if the register operator can confuse the guest, funds can be diverted from the guest. A dishonest guest can practice the same fraudulent scheme to the disadvantage of the cashier (and the facility).

When cashiers make change, they should always "count up" from the amount of the sale. For example, if a lunch bill is $3.68 and a $5 bill is given to the register the operator should, first, select two pennies (to make the equivalent of $3.70), then, in sequence, count out a nickel and a quarter (to represent $4) and, finally, withdraw a $1 bill from the register. Then, this amount can be "counted back" to the cafeteria guest to make sure that no mistakes in change-making have occurred. It is important that the register operator keep the currency tendered by the guest in plain view (the cash register ledge is a good place) until the guest is satisfied with the accuracy of the transaction.

Cash Register Tape Helps

It is generally best to utilize a system which generates a sales tape for each purchase. (A sample is shown in Figure 13.7.) The guest receives a summary of the transaction, information is recorded in machine's financial data system and it is easier to observe that the cashier is following required cash register operating procedures.

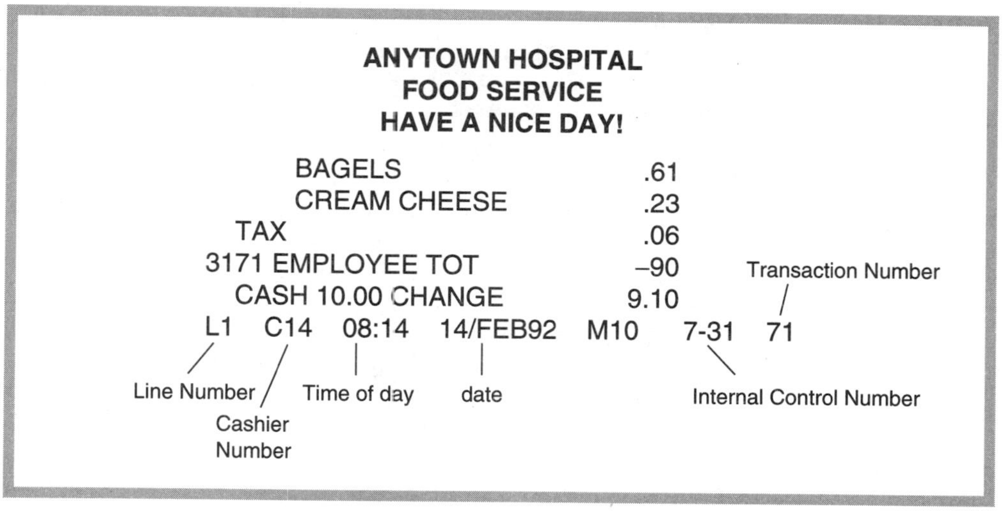

FIGURE 13.7 CASH REGISTER SALES TAPE (ENLARGED)

Need for Audit Trail

The concept of an "audit trail" refers to the ability of an analyst of the accounting system to trace the sales from the point of entry into the system (entry onto the sales journal tape) through to the point of deposit. Use of the procedures outlined above will help to "track" all income, minimizing the possibility of theft and/or error.

Facilities in which No Money Changes Hands

There are long-term care, upscale, continuous-care facilites in which no money changes hands. The residents purchase "points" on a monthly basis and according to the number of meals per day that they wish to receive—it's primarily an honors system. Employees purchase tickets to eat in the cafeteria from the business office. The dietary department handles no money. Tickets for the guests of residents may be handled in a similar fashion. Debit cards, a relatively new "no cash" system to healthcare facilities, offer another alternative to traditional cash handling techniques. The dietary manager should be aware of these diverse systems and recommend their use where appropriate.

REVIEWING THE COST OF MENU AGAINST BUDGET GUIDELINES

It is obvious that the dietary manager must control food costs. There are many procedures outlined throughout this book that can be helpful in minimizing costs without reducing quality requirements at the control points of purchasing, receiving, storing, issuing, producing, and serving. However, another important step in the food control plan involves pre-costing to ensure that menus which are planned will be within budgeted guidelines.

Many facilities utilize the operating budget as a source of standard costs. The operating budget provides a "road map" of agreement between the dietary manager and the finance manager about the expected level of income and expense for the dietary operation. If the operating budget specifies that no more than $300,000 can be spent for food during the year, this amount must be incorporated into the menu planning process.

How can this be done? Wise dietary managers consider the allowable food costs in the operating budget. If menus are planned on a weekly basis, the annual allowable food cost (from the operating budget) may be divided by 52 weeks to determine the amount of expense which can be incurred for food during the week. If using a 3-week cycle menu, multiply the weekly amount by 3. If menus are planned on a daily basis, the budgeted food costs can be divided by 365 days to assess the allowable daily food cost figure. As a third example, if food costs are to be based on cost per client day, the total budgeted food cost for the year can be divided by the number of client days (forecasted number of clients times 365 days).

Several forms make the pre-costing process easier to understand and use. You should understand, however, that the use of computers (either personal computers, systems available to the facility on a total or shared time basis, and programs made available through suppliers) have made the pre-costing procedure much faster.

Let's see how pre-costing procedures work:

Step 1: Determine allowable food cost from budget. Using the approved operating budget as a base, the menu planner must first determine the amount of food costs which can be allowed as the menu is planned. Let's assume that the operating budget permits food costs of approximately $600 per day. This is a 200-bed nursing home; approximately $3 per day per client can be spent for food; for an upscale retirement community the approved cost per day per client may be $6.

Step 2: Pre-cost proposed menus. Figure 13.8 provides a form which can be used to plan and to estimate the per-portion cost for a menu. (Some worksheets provide for the planning of an entire week's menu on one worksheet.) However, information required for calculations must consider each of the factors in Figure 13.8. Notice that the total estimated food cost per client day is $3.25; to offer the menu planned in the portion sizes suggested will cost approximately 25¢ per client day more than the budget allows. What can be done?

Date/Day: ____________________

Meal period	Menu item	Portion size	Per portion cost
Breakfast			
	Oatmeal	½ cup	.08
	Orange juice	½ cup	.14
Lunch			
Dinner			

Total Food Cost/ Patient Day $3.25

FIGURE 13.8 MENU PRE-COST SHEET

Alternatives include revising the menu to include different items, reducing the portion size of one or more items, and/or serving the menu as planned. If the latter alternative is chosen, it would then be necessary to reduce the total food cost per patient day on another day to keep within the budgeted allowable cost of $3 daily.

Step 3: Make necessary adjustments. The menu planner considering the menu being planned in Figure 13.8 would need to make necessary adjustments, given the several alternatives listed. A cumulative tally of the amount of money spent for food to date in the menu period can be very helpful in selecting the "right" alternative for the situation.

Step 4: Finalize menu. After the menu planner has planned the menu for the appropriate time period and confirmed that the planned food cost will not exceed the budgeted allowable cost, the menu can be finalized and posted, necessary quantities of required food products purchased, personnel and equipment scheduled, and each of the other required subsystems in the dietary department activated to produce the required menu.

One should note that one critical element in the above pre-costing system is the per-portion cost. Obviously, this cost will change as prices fluctuate. Facilities receiving U.S. Department of Agriculture donated commodities will have an additional variable to be considered. One can begin to see how a computerized system (which can update per portion cost almost "at the touch of a button") can be much more helpful than the manual counterpart.

Implementing Cost-Effective Procedures

Procedures used to determine what food costs should be have been discussed. How does a dietary manager determine what food costs actually are? The basic process involves calculating "net cost of goods used." Figure 13.9 illustrates the elements to be considered in the process of calculating net cost of goods used. Note that the value of beginning inventory must first be assessed. What is inventory? Is it just the products in central dry and refrigerated/frozen areas? Does it also include the value of products in broken case and/or ingredient rooms? What about products in process and/or in workstation areas? The point is that the dietary manager must consider locations in which "inventory" products are stored and must then consistently assess the cost of products in these areas.

What is cost? Is it the purchase cost? Replacement cost? An average cost? Again, the dietary manager must know. Since there can be serious accounting, man-

Value of beginning inventory	$44,500	
Add value of purchases	+$26,300	
Cost of goods available		$70,800
Less value of ending inventory		–$45,600
Gross cost of goods used		$35,200
Less adjustments:		
nourishments	($800)	
employee meals	($1100)	
other "free" meals	($200)	– $2,100
Net cost of goods used		$33,100

FIGURE 13.9 CALCULATION OF COST OF NET GOODS USED (SAMPLE)

Source: *Cafeteria Management for Hospitals*, by Kaud et al., published by American Hospital Publishing, Inc., copyright 1982

agement, tax, and other implications to the assignment of value to inventory, this decision to adjust value of inventory should generally be delegated to a manager in the business office.

How does one assess the value of purchases? Typically, the value of purchases is the sum of all delivery invoices received during the month, adjusted by the credit memos which have been issued.

The value of ending inventory must be assessed according to the same concerns we identified for values of beginning inventory. The value of ending inventory for one month becomes the value of beginning inventory for the subsequent month. By adding values of beginning inventory and purchases and by reducing this sum by the value of ending inventory, the gross cost of goods used can be calculated.

Many dietary facilities may end their food cost calculations at this point. Others desiring a more accurate assessment of actual costs incurred make adjustments for the cost of nourishments, employee meals, other "free" meals, and other incidental food-related concerns which decrease or increase food costs. By reducing the gross cost of goods used by the sum of these adjustments, the net cost of goods used can be assessed. In Figure 13.9, for example, the cost is calculated to be $33,100.

It is possible to determine the food cost per client day (or for any other period) by making simple calculations. For example, if there are 300 patients in a 30-day month, the actual food cost per client day can be calculated as follows:

300 clients × 30 days = 9,000 client days
$33,100 ÷ 9,000 client days = $3.68 food cost per client day

The dietary manager will be interested to learn what the food cost per client day is. More important, however, is the question of what *should* the food cost per patient day be? How much variance is there between the actual and expected food costs per client day?

Records Help in Financial Management

Dietary managers can keep better track of actual costs when effectively designed forms are used. For example, Figure 13.10 is a weekly dietary report that illustrates a form which can track actual food costs on a cash accounting basis. As items are delivered during the week, information about the date (column 1), name of supplier (column 2), cost of food product by category (columns 3–9), total food cost (column 10), nonfood item (column 11), and total expense per day (column 12) are entered. The total costs for each food category and nonfood item and total expenses for the week can then be tallied. (In Figure 13.10 the total weekly cost is shown to be $1,673.61.)

Allowable costs per client day for each category, total allowable costs per patient day ($2.50 in Figure 13.10), and the amount budgeted weekly for each category are also shown. (In Figure 13.10, $1,715 was budgeted for the week. Only $1,673.61 was spent; the dietary operation is under the budget by $41.39 for the week.)

Figure 13.10 also provides recap information about per-client-day food expenses for the current week and three previous weeks, and enables the dietary manager to effectively assess whether budget goals are being attained.

A weekly food cost report is very helpful. It helps the dietary manager adjust food costs to keep within budget guidelines. If the department stays within budget limits, only total cost information (such as columns 10–12 in Figure 13.10) need be completed. If there are problems, however, analysis of food costs on a by-category basis can help to determine where costs are excessive so that corrective actions can be taken.

MONTH January 1984 FACILITY Willowbrook Manor WEEK: FROM 1/9 Through 1/15 AVERAGE CENSUS PER DAY 98 (100 beds)

DATE	SUPPLIER	MEAT/FISH POULTRY	DAIRY PRODUCT	PRODUCE	EGGS	COFFEE/ TEA	BREAD PASTRY	GEN. GROC FROZ FOOD	TOTAL FOOD EX	NON-FOOD ITEM	TOTAL EXPENSE
(1)	(2)	(3)	(4)	(5)	(6)	(7)	(8)	(9)	(10)	(11)	(12)
1-11	Feldbro	462.26							462.26		462.26
1-9	Creamline		234.17						234.17		234.17
1-13	Sun Valley			31.56					31.56		31.56
1-10	Musel					15.81			15.81		15.81
1-12	Albrecht				45.05				45.05		45.05
1-10	Taystee						28.89		28.89		28.89
1-13	Gordons							803.24	803.24		803.24
1-13	Gordons									52.63	52.63
TOTAL		462.26	234.17	31.56	45.05	15.81	28.89	803.24	1620.98	52.63	1673.61
PPD Allowance		.60	.35	.03	.06	.03	.04	1.29	2.40	.10	2.50
BUDGET Weekly Amt.		411.60	240.10	20.58	41.16	20.58	27.44	884.94	1646.40	68.60	1715.00
DIFFERENCE		–50.66	+5.93	–10.98	–3.89	+4.77	–1.45	–81.70	+25.42	+15.97	+41.39

AVERAGE PER FOOD EXPENSE FOR PAST FOUR WEEKS

THIS WEEK'S FOOD EXPENSE PPD:	2.36	.08
LAST WEEK'S FOD EXPENSE PPD:	2.03	.06
PREVIOUS WEEK'S FOOD EXPENSE PPD:	2.08	.08
PREVIOUS WEEK'S FOOD EXPENSE PPD:	2.50	.04
TOTAL OF ABOVE	8.97	.26
DIVIDED BY 4	2.24	.07

		NON-FOOD	LESS DISCOUNTS
	0	0	0
LESS MEALS SOLD	0	0	0
NET EXP. THIS WK	1620.98	52.63	1673.61
÷ DIV. BY TOT. PT DAYS	686	686	686
EXP. PPD THIS WK	2.36	.08	2.44
DAILY GOAL ESTABLISHED	2.40	.10	2.50

Administrator

Dietary Supervisor

FIGURE 13.10 WEEKLY DIETARY REPORT

Figure 13.11 is a dietary department operating statement which illustrates a computerized printout of revenue (sales) and cost information applicable to a large hospital dietary department. The dietary department operating statement is a critical report that provides a financial "picture" of the dietary department. In Figure 13.11 note that actual, plan (budget), and variance are shown for the current period (December), and the applicable figure for December (last year) is shown on the left side of the page. Year-to-date information for each revenue and expense item are also shown for actual and plan (budget) along with the variance and the cumulative amounts for the same time period "last year" as well. Revenue is derived from in-patient and out-patient sources and, as well, from 20 additional "other operating revenue" centers such as cafeteria, sandwich shops, physicians cafeteria, and so on which are summarized.

Let's see how the dietary manager reads this information: The first source of operating revenue is in-patient revenue. Note that (left side of page) $45,756 was generated from this source which is $4,278 (variance) more than that budgeted under the current plan ($41,478). The actual amount for this December compares favorably with the revenue generated during December of last year ($39,018). Now you know

Period–December 19XX

CURRENT PERIOD ACTUAL	CURRENT PERIOD PLAN	CURRENT PERIOD VARIANCE	CURRENT PERIOD LAST YEAR		YEAR TO DATE ACTUAL	YEAR TO DATE PLAN	YEAR TO DATE VARIANCE	YEAR TO DATE LAST YEAR
				REVENUE				
				OPERATING REVENUE				
45,756	41,478	4,278**	39,018	INPATIENT REVENUE	230,549	258,742	28,193–	230,896
11,271	5,303	5,968**	3,075	OUTPATIENT REVENUE	63,993	31,933	32,060**	19,979
57,027	46,781	10,246**	42,093	TOTAL OPERATING REVENUE	294,541	290,675	3,866	250,775
				OTHER OPERATING REVENUE				
				CAFETERIA				
				SANDWICH SHOP				
				PHYSICIAN CAFETERIA				
				GUEST TRAY				
				DIET MANUALS				
				CASH CATERING				
				NON-PAT KITCHEN REV				
				NON-PAT CAFE REV				
				VENDING MACHINE REV				
				GREASE SALES				
				VENDING, CANCER CENTER				
				BURGERS & SUCH				
				BAKE SHOPPE				
				ICE CREAM PARLOR				
				STOREFRONT				
				VENDING AREA				
				PIZZA PARLOR				
				FACULTY DINING ROOM				
				CARRY-OUT SERVICE				
				OTHER NON-PAT REVENUE				
255,581	248,881	6,700	184,632	TOTAL OTHER OPER REVENUE	1,582,689	1,618,654	35,965–	1,196,827
				NON OPERATING REVENUE				
0	0	0	0	TOTAL NON OPERATING REVENUE	0	0	0	0
312,609	295,662	16,947	226,725	TOTAL REVENUE	1,877,231	1,909,329	32,099–	1,447,602
				DEDUCTIONS FROM REVENUE				
0	0	0	0	TOTAL DEDUCTIONS FROM REV	0	0	0	0
312,609	295,662	16,947	226,725	TOTAL ADJUSTED REVENUE	1,877,231	1,909,329	32,099–	1,447,602
				EXPENSES				
				SALARIES AND WAGES				
				MNGMT/SUPR PERMANENT				
				MNGMT/SUPR-OT				
				MNGMT/SUPR-SHIFT				
				MNGMT/SUPR-ON-CALL				
				TECH/SPECL PERMANENT				
				TECH/SPECL-OT				
				TECH/SPECL-SHIFT				
				TECH/SPECL-ON-CALL				
				AIDES, ORD, ATT PERM				
				NA/SA-OT				
				NA/SA-SHIFT				
				ENV/FOOD SRVCS PERM				
				ENV/FOOD SVCS-OT				
				ENV/FOOD SVCS-SHIFT				
				CLER/OTHER ADM PERM				
				CLERICAL-OT				
				CLERICAL-SHIFT				
				CLERICAL-ON-CALL				
				OVERTIME				
				SHIFT PAY				
				ON-CALL PAY				
				RECOVERED SAL EXP-HC				
237,504	246,209	8,705–	210,700	TOTAL NET SALARIES/ WAGES	1,381,151	1,453,086	71,935–	1,267,944
				EMPLOYEE BENEFITS				
				FICA				
				GROUP HEALTH INSUR				
				GROUP LIFE INSURANCE				
				LONG-TERM DISABILITY				
				OTHER EMP BENEFITS				
				RECOVERED BENEFITS				
40,214	40,955	741–	32,700	TOTAL NET EMP BENEFITS	235,613	245,603	9,990–	197,043

FIGURE 13.11 DIETARY DEPARTMENT OPERATING STATEMENT *(continued on next page)*

277,718	287,164	9,446–	243,399	TOTAL NET SAL/WAGE/ BENEFITS	1,616,764	1,698,689	81,925–	1,464,987
				PROFESSIONAL FEES				
				CONSULT/MANAGEMENT 603301				
0	0	0	0	TOTAL PROFESSIONAL FEES	0	0	0	0
				MEDICAL AND SURGICAL SUPPLIES				
				DRUGS				
				OTHER MED SUPPLIES				
				OTH MED SUP-CHG-CDC				
405	447	42–	466	TOTAL MEDICAL/SURGICAL SUP	2,890	2,707	183	2,378
				NON-MEDICAL/SURGICAL SUPPLIES				
				MEATS FISH POULTRY				
				DAIRY PRODUCTS				
				STAPLES				
				FRUITS VEGETABLES				
				SNACKS SPECIALTY				
				DIET BABY FOOD FRMLA				
				FOOD PURCHASES-INV				
				SEASONINGS SPICES				
				CEREALS BREADS				
				TABLEWARE KIT UTENSL				
				DISPOSABLE TEXTILES				
				DISP TEXTILES-CHG-CDC				
				DISP TEX-NONCHG-CDC				
				CLEANING SUPP-CHEM				
				OFFICE & ADMIN SUPP				
				EMP WEARING APPAREL				
				MINOR EQUIPMENT				
				COMPUTER SUPP/EQUIP				
				P.O. PRICE VARIANCE				
				LOSS/GAIN-INV ADJ				
				OTHER NON MED SUPPL				
224,623	210,090	14,533	213,337	TOTAL NON-MED/SURG SUPPLIES	1,362,774	1,289,031	73,743	1,428,985
				UTILITIES				
				TELE-ADD/MOVES/CHGS				
				SUNCOM/TOLL CALLS				
				TELE-SERVICES				
77	274	197–	89	TOTAL UTILITIES	544	1,638	1,094–	874
				PURCHASED SERVICES				
				REPAIRS & MAINTENANCE				
				MAINTENANCE CONTRACTS				
				PUR DATA PROC SERVICES				
				PUR ADVERTISING				
				PUR MAT-PRINT/COPIED				
				OTHER PUR SERVICES				
8,807	10,801	1,994–	7,699	TOTAL PURCHASED SERVICES	37,577	65,961	28,384–	56,418
				OTHER DIRECT EXPENSES				
				BUSINESS LICENSE				
				DUES & MEMBERSHIPS				
				BOOKS, SUBSCRIPTIONS				
				REGISTRATION FEES				
				TRAVEL EXPENSE				
				PUB SERVICES-PRINTING				
				POSTAGE/SHIPPING COST				
				COPY MACH FEES/SUPPLY				
				COURT COSTS/JUDGMENTS				
				CASH OVER/SHORT				
				FOOD-CATERING (CONTRA)				
				DIETARY REQ/FOOD PURC				
				OTHER DIRECT EXPENSE				
22,458	8,687–	13,771–**	33,920–	TOTAL DIRECT EXPENSE	114,476–	51,728–	62,748–**	119,809–
				DEPRECIATION/RENT				
				LEASE/RENTAL OTHER				
35	166	131–	3,949	TOTAL DEPRECIATION/RENT	1,000	997	3	14,115
211,490	213,091	1,601–	191,620	TOTAL OTHER EXPENSES	1,290,308	1,308,606	18,298–	1,382,960
				NON-OPERATING EXPENSE				
0	0	0	0	TOTAL NON OPERATING EXPENSE	0	0	0	0
176,598–	204,593–	27,995	208,294–	NET GAIN/LOSS	1,029,842–	1,097,966–	68,125	1,400,345–

FIGURE 13.11 Continued

about December; what has happened to in-patient revenue during the entire year? Looking at the right side of the page, you can note that the actual revenue ($230,549) is $28,193 (variance) less than that which has been budgeted ($258,742), and is almost the same as for last year ($230,896).

Continuing on with our analysis, you can see that out-patient revenue (line 2) was substantially above the plan (budget) both for the month and for the year. Skipping to the "bottom line" (total revenue) you note that more has been generated than what was budgeted for the month ($16,947 positive variance) and almost to the budget for the year ($32,000 under budget on a total operating budget of $1.9 million).

The remainder of this statement details the types and amounts of expenses allocated to this dietary department. Note specific accounts for salaries and wages, employee benefits, professional fees, medical and surgical supplies, nonmedical and surgical supplies, purchased services, other direct expenses, and depreciation/rent. (The dollar amounts for these expenses have been omitted to make the operating statement more readable for the figure.) Finally, note the true "bottom line": the amount of expenses over revenue which must be carried in the general operating budget of the facility. (The dietary department's loss for the month and for the year are, respectively, $27,995 and $68,125 *less* than planned.)

With detailed information such as that shown in Figure 13.11, the dietary manager will know, first, what sales and costs should be, and, second, what sales and costs actually are. With this information at hand, he or she can take corrective action as necessary to ensure that costs are managed and financial goals are met.

In summary, the expected food cost is based upon the operating budget, and the actual food cost is calculated according to procedures above. The process of comparing actual with expected cost becomes, then, an integral part of the control process which a professional dietary manager uses to control sales and costs. This also ensures that it is not necessary to reduce quality requirements in order to compensate for lower sales and/or higher costs.

The comparison process may indicate, for example, that costs are too high. Why is this? Are there justifiable and/or explainable reasons for the variance? For example, did the purchase unit cost of a product increase significantly beyond its level at the time the operating budget was developed? Have changes in operating plans been implemented since the time the budget was developed? For example, is a higher level of convenience-food products being used? The "clue" to the need for corrective action appears when the dietary manager cannot explain and/or justify the reason for variance between the budgeted and actual sales and cost levels. The job of dietary manager involves the making of creative decisions to resolve nonroutine problems such as these unexplained variances.

Calculating Costs and Setting Prices for Catered Events

The dietary manager should recognize that special catered events can be a significant source of revenue to a dietary department, while at the same time enhancing its reputation and prestige within the facility and the community. How are prices for these events set? The dietary manager, perhaps working with the business office, should typically make this decision.

The operating budget can be a source of information for catered event pricing decisions. Generally, the pricing plan should not be for the event to be "sold" at cost. Rather, it should be planned to generate its "fair share" or more of the required revenues which accrue to dietary services. For example, assume that food is sold in the cash cafeteria operation at a 30-percent cost (of all the sales generated, approximately 30 percent are "spent" for purchase of food necessary to generate the sales). The wise dietary manager will expect a lower food cost percentage (higher contribution margin: sales minus food cost) from catered events than from the cash cafeteria operation. In the above example the dietary manager may establish a base selling price for catered events based upon 25-percent food cost. In other words, the dietary manager will determine the food cost for the catered event being planned and multiply this cost by four (1.00 ÷ .25 = 4.00). This base selling price can then be adjusted to arrive at an actual selling price. This plan allows the dietary manager to work from budget requirements and to incorporate these concerns into the pricing structure established for catered events.

Recommending Salary/Wage Adjustments

Everyone from the highest-level facility manager to subordinate staff within the dietary department is concerned about the wage/salary which he or she receives. All staff members, including the dietary manager and his or her employees, must know something about procedures for establishing and administering wage and salary programs in the facility.

What should be the role of the dietary manager in the facility's compensation program? Typically, he or she will not be involved in determining rates, at least originally. This is defensible since the great amount of time required and the necessity to know a great deal about many positions in many departments represent time which should otherwise be spent in managing the dietary department.

The dietary manager should know about proposed changes and plans in basic compensation systems so that he or she can provide information about their perceived impact on dietary departments. The dietary manager will probably need to explain and justify compensation programs to subordinate staff. Since the dietary manager represents all employees in the department to the facility's administration, it is important that he or she know how the plans will impact upon the department so this information can be relayed to higher-level management or administration.

What are goals of effective wage/salary programs? First, if developed correctly, wage and salary programs help in recruitment efforts. Institutions must offer competitive pay programs to recruit the most qualified personnel. This concern applies to dietary services just as much as to all other areas within the facility.

Second, the level of wages and salaries paid has a dramatic impact upon the institution's operating budget. Labor costs are one of the most significant expenses incurred, obviously the result of wages/salaries paid.

Many employee-related problems can be traced to perceived problems in the wage and salary program; therefore, reasonable programs (from the perspective of the employees) can help to reduce these problems.

Wage and salary adjustments can also be used to reward staff members for good performance. To the extent that this plan increases the quality of work performance and decreases operating problems, another goal of effective salary/wage programs has been identified.

Factors Affecting Levels of Wages and Salaries Paid

Several factors impact on the level of wages and salaries paid. First, it is necessary to consider pay levels of other facilities competing for the same personnel. Many dietary managers routinely compare salaries paid for their position with those offered by other facilities.

The economic status of the facility affects its ability to pay. In this age of cost containment and diagnostic related groups (DRGs), facilities can literally go out of business, so economic concerns are always important.

Cost-of-living factors also affect rates. Many facilities with union contracts or other pay plans related to cost of living changes are dramatically affected by an inflationary spiral.

Performance and productivity levels also must be considered. As the level of output rises (higher productivity), the facility is able to pay higher wage/salary rates.

The employees' bargaining ability must also be considered. This is important not only when individuals "bargain" as specific staff members but when an employee union represents a large number of staff members.

Job requirements themselves affect wage/salary rates. Those jobs which require greater skill levels, efforts, and/or responsibility typically reward position incumbents more than do jobs which require lesser amounts of these attributes.

Applicable labor laws also have impact upon wage/salary rates. There are minimum-wage requirements which must be addressed. "Equal pay" laws require equal pay for equal work, prohibiting discrimination against minorities, women, and others.

Concerns in Salary/Wage Administration

It is important that salary/wage plans be consistent. When applicable, the same basic elements should be used to administer the program in every department within the facility. It is also important to consider pay rates for the position first, and then for the specific employee within the position.

Existing pay rates are an important factor. Facilities do not "throw out" existing pay structures and "start over" as new plans are implemented. Rather, wage/salary increases are changed and, in the process, have an impact upon the existing pay structure.

Dietary and other facility administrators must communicate basic rules, policies and provisions of the wage/salary plan to all affected employees. This matter is of dramatic concern to staff members. They cannot be "left in the dark" about wage/salary procedures or determinations.

Job Evaluation

Job evaluation involves analysis of specific jobs to assess pay rates. The job evaluation process answers the question "What should a specific job be worth to the facility?" When done properly, job evaluation can be a complex, time-consuming process. Simplified systems can be used, however, with some accuracy. Job descriptions and job specifications provide information important for job evaluation. Job pay rates are developed as an output of the job evaluation process. A final step is to classify employees according to the pay rates which have been established.

As noted above, it is important to emphasize that the job itself, not the employees doing the work, should be evaluated.

If practical, advice and counsel from several people can be helpful in the evaluation.

There are several basic methods of job evaluation. Let's look at each:

Method 1: Simple ranking. When a simple ranking plan is used, job descriptions and specifications are studied and decisions are made about job requirements. Positions are then ranked in order from "low" to "high." The "dietary manager" position may be rated very high in the dietary department when a scale from high to low is developed in terms of job requirements. By contrast, the position "tray line attendant" will be rated relatively low.

The ranking system as described helps the facility to assess whether rates are fair since those positions with higher skill and other requirements should typically receive higher pay rates.

While the simple ranking method is easy, it has several disadvantages: it is subjective; judgments are made on the basis of existing wage rates, rather than on what rates should be; the job evaluation process will not tell which positions have more or fewer job requirements; and difficulty is encountered when a large number of jobs must be considered.

Method 2: Grade description. This plan involves dividing various positions into different pay rates (grades). Job definitions are then written for each grade so that jobs can be classified by a specific grade. Information necessary to separate positions into grades is taken from the current job description.

It may be possible for a facility to use a grade description method for all jobs. However, special attention must be addressed to each factor helping to distinguish between jobs. These factors will include assigned duties, abilities, responsibilities, and so on. Descriptions of factors important in each grade can be written and then used as the basis for assigning jobs to specific pay grades.

Advantages of this method include the fact that a written scale will be developed against which jobs can be measured. However, the content of jobs can change over time. It will be necessary to continually review new job requirements against written grade standards to confirm that the existing wage/salary program is current.

An obvious disadvantage to the grade description method is that descriptions for each job grade must be general in order to review a wide range of jobs. There is no way that specific factors can be compared. For example, how do you assess the worth of a job with high skill requirements but low job hazard (such as a dietary manager) compared to another job involving low skill but higher levels of hazards (such as a food preparation employee working with potentially dangerous equipment)?

Method 3: Point system. When a point system method of job evaluation is used, a wide range of job characteristics that relate to skill, effort, responsibility, and job conditions is developed. It is possible to divide each factor into degrees so that its weight can be assessed. If experience is judged important, an experience factor can be divided into time intervals such as (a) zero to four months experience, (b) five to eight months experience, and so on. Points can be assigned to each degree, and can be allocated and summed to assess a job score, which can then be the basis for assigning a specific wage/salary grade.

Determining Salary/Wage Increases

After a basic pay structure has been established, procedures to assess periodic salary/wage increases must be developed. Several possibilities include:

1. *Flat rate plan.* Each employee assigned to a job receives the same basic pay increase regardless of seniority or performance;
2. *Step rate plan.* Fixed pay levels based upon job seniority are established. An employee can then progress from one step to another within the pay range based upon seniority, unless performance is not satisfactory;
3. *Cost-of-living allowance.* In some facilities, wage/salary increases are tied (all or in part) to cost of living increases. These plans typically use a recognized index of living costs; as costs rise (or decrease), wages/salaries are adjusted accordingly;
4. *Merit performance plans.* Compensation is based on the extent to which an employee is judged to meet or exceed performance standards. These plans are generally very acceptable if employees know about the process to be used and consider it to be objective.

There is a wide range of other types of wage/salary increase plans which combine concerns about performance and seniority, allocate predetermined amounts of salary increase funds to various positions, and so on. In each case the dietary manager must know the procedures used and be able to easily communicate this information to staff members within the dietary department.

Employee Benefit Programs

Employee benefits (fringe benefits) are a large operating expense for most dietary operations. It is possible for the expenses to approximate one-third or more of the total payroll. Employee benefit programs have been expanded significantly beyond the traditional uniform allowance, meal provisions, and perhaps vacation and sick leave. Today, pension, medical and life insurance plans are popular. Vacation, holidays, and sick leave can also present attractive packages, as can special cash rewards for significant work efforts, suggestion programs, and so on.

Employee benefits can really be of three types:

1. *No-cost benefits.* Use of flexible working schedules, job rotation, and/or job enrichment activities are examples of programs that cost little, if anything, for the facility to implement but which, from the employee's perspective, may make the job more attractive. To the extent they do, there may be fewer needs for other types of wage/salary increases;
2. *Low-cost benefits.* Employee meals, uniform allowances, and child care services provide examples of these benefits;
3. *High-cost benefits.* Facility-financed insurance and pension plans are examples.

Employees must be informed about the compensation program—including benefit provisions—which the facility uses. This information should be shared with new staff members at the time of initial orientation. (Oral discussions and review of applicable pages of the employee handbooks are two techniques which can be used.) Updates about benefit programs can be an integral part of ongoing staff meetings.

Budget Development Process

Dietary managers must know how to develop and use an operating budget. This financial management tool is a plan which specifies the economic goals of the dietary department and indicates how much income and expenses are expected as the plan evolves. Its importance in the comparison, analysis, and corrective action processes was illustrated earlier in this chapter when the dietary department's operating statement was reviewed.

Unfortunately, some dietary managers view the operating budget as a "necessary evil." They resign themselves to developing the budget "because the business office demands it." With this view, they don't develop statistical information and undertake strategic planning necessary to really develop a "fine-tuned" budget. After the budget is developed, it is filed away until this "historic" information is needed to develop the subsequent year's budget.

By contrast, the wise dietary manager realizes that the operating budget is a significant help in managing many aspects of dietary service. First, it is a tool for communication between the dietary department and the business office; it expresses the best views of both parties about the volume of meals to be produced, the estimate of sales to be generated, and costs to be incurred. The budget also provides planning help as menus are developed; budgeted food costs should not be exceeded as the year evolves (recall the discussion about pre-costing earlier in the chapter) and the menu dictates the amount of funds to be spent.

The operating budget also helps with pricing decisions. For example, if food costs for the catering function are 30 percent of the sales to be generated from catering, a standard or "benchmark" pricing plan can be developed. Benchmarking will be discussed later in this chapter. The standard food cost for the catered event can be multiplied times 3.3 ($1.00 \div .30 = 3.3$) in order to establish a base selling price for the catered event.

In this age of cost containment, it is simply not possible for the dietary manager to "play it by ear" or to "operate so that costs are not excessive." A detailed and accurate operating budget must be developed. It must be discussed with and agreed upon by the business office. From this point, the operating budget becomes the financial plan for the dietary department.

The development of an operating budget for the dietary department can be time-consuming and complex (although it need not be). The overall responsibility for the budget rests with the business office. However, the dietary manager, as the "expert" in dietary services for the facility, should have a great deal of input into its development.

A basic problem, often beyond the control of the dietary manager, involves the allocation of costs between dietary and other facility departments. There is a need to determine direct expenses incurred by dietary services and to allocate these to dietary (in other words, to require dietary to be responsible for these costs). Unfortunately, it is difficult to allocate many expenses. Consider the custodian who spends several hours daily cleaning the dining room, which is used for food service but also for other functions. How should these cleaning costs be allocated? What about the facility with only one utility meter? How should energy costs applicable to dietary service be allocated? As a final example, how are costs for the purchasing agent, who purchases food products but also a wide range of other products and supplies needed for the facility, to be allocated?

The process of determining and allocating foodservice costs is beyond the scope of this chapter.* However, it is necessary for the dietary manager to work closely with the business office as procedures for allocation are developed. The dietary manager must provide input and understand exactly what and how costs are allocated.

The dietary manager should also be responsible for developing initial versions of the operating budget and for making modifications as a result of meetings with business and other officials.

Let's take a look at the actual budget development process.

Steps in Budget Development

The easiest and most common budget to develop is a fixed departmental operating budget. A document of this kind is fixed to one level of sales and typically reviews expected income, expense and, perhaps, operating surplus levels for the dietary department for one year. It is also possible to develop variable budgets, which look at anticipated expenses across a range of varying meal production. Variable budgets are relatively easy to develop when computerized budget development systems are utilized. In contrast, developing budgets manually is time-consuming but often necessary and helpful.

Some dietary facilities develop separate operating budgets for client and non-client meal operations and for many other revenue or cost centers (See our example in Figure 13.11.) An advantage of this approach is that more specific information can be used to assess costs for each operation. Some facilities also develop "profit" (operating surplus) requirements into operating budgets for non-client operations. Excess revenues received can then be used to purchase equipment, supplies, and other necessities for dietary services.

Figure 13.12 briefly illustrates the process used to develop an annual budget. First, the dietary manager must estimate client days, average meals per client day, total department meals as a ratio to client meals, equivalent non-client meals and their value, and estimates of increases for categories of expenses.

Notice how the food expenses are estimated in Figure 13.12. First, the current per meal food cost is multiplied by the estimated increase in food cost. This product is multiplied by an estimate of the total meals to be served [$1.52 + ($1.52 × 8 percent)] × 539,200. The resulting estimated food cost ($885,151) is reduced by the percentage of cash receipts historically applicable to food costs. Note the separation of operating budget information for clients and cash meals noted above. In the example shown in Figure 13.12, approximately 30 percent of cash receipts are estimated

*Interested readers are referred to: American Society for Hospital Food Service Administrators, *Determination and Allocation of Food Service Costs.* American Hospital Association, Chicago, Ill., undated.

Assume: Patient days = 100,000
Meals per patient day = 2.74
Total department meals/patient meals = 5.392
Nonpatient meal equivalent = 260,000;
an increase of 2% is estimated.

Nonpatient meal equivalent value = $3.00; an increase of 10% is projected.
Estimated cost increases: food 8% labor 9%, supply 7%, and other costs 6%.

1. Total meals

100,000 patient days × 2.74 meals	=	274,000	51%
260,000 nonpatient meals × 1.02	=	265,200	49%
Total		539,200	100%

2. Projected nonpatient cash receipts
$3.00 meal value × 1.10 increase × 265,200 meals = $875,160

3. Preparation of an annual budget

Description	Current Cost		Estimated Increase %		Total Meals		Operating Expenses	% of Cost*	Cash Receipts	Net Operating Expenses
Food	$1.52	×	8	×	539,200	=	$885,151	less	(30 × 875,160) =	$622,603
Labor	3.15	×	9	×	539,200	=	1,851,343	less	(61 × 875,160) =	1,317,495
Supply	0.35	×	7	×	539,200	=	201,930	less	(7 × 875,160) =	140,669
Other costs	0.10	×	2	×	539,200	=	57,155	less	(2 × 875,160) =	39,652
Total	$5.12						$2,995,579			
								less 100		$2,120,419

*Distribution based on historical usage by category

FIGURE 13.12 ANNUAL BUDGET PREPARATION
Source: Faisal A. Kaud, *Budgeting: A Comparative Analysis of Techniques and Systems.* In James C. Rose, *Handbook for Health Care Food Service Management.* Aspen Publishers, Frederick, Md., 1984, pp. 118–119. Reprinted with permisison of Aspen Publishers, Inc.

to be for food costs. This is deducted from the total operating expenses for food to yield the net operating expenses for food costs ($622,603).

The budget estimates for food and for all other categories of expenses become very important for the dietary manager, since they represent the "benchmark" for estimated expenses. The dietary manager will not be doing his or her job correctly if net operating expenses exceed those specified by the budget—unless there is an acceptable, explainable, and justifiable reason for any variance.

Information from the operating budget can be used to establish a base selling price for menu items sold in cash cafeteria operations. A formula to do this is:

$$\frac{\text{BUDGETED FOOD SALES (CASH CAFETERIA OPERATIONS)}}{\text{BUDGETED FOOD COSTS (CASH CAFETERIA OPERATIONS)}}$$

ASSUME: Budgeted Food Sales $900,000
Budgeted Food Costs $350,000

The cost markup derived above can be multiplied by the standard food cost per portion to yield the base selling price.

$$2.57 \times .78 = \$2.00$$
$$\text{Cost markup} \times \text{standard portion cost} = \text{Base Selling Price}$$

After this calculation is made the actual selling price can be determined based upon other factors such as "competitors" prices (if any), physiological pricing (what the guest may be willing to pay), and other factors specific to the facility.

Some facilities re-forecast budgets as the year evolves. For example, as the client census changes, expenses increase (or decrease) and / or as sales levels from cash operations change dramatically, there will be an obvious impact on the budget. To counter this and to assure the continued usefulness of the budget as a planning tool, some facilities modify operating budgets on a monthly or other basis to reflect changes in actual operating conditions. The use of a computer for budget re-forecasting simplifies the task. It is, however, possible to do under manual systems, and it should be considered when there are significant variations between expected and actual cost and / or sales levels.

Budget Control Procedures

Once the operating budget is developed, it becomes an important control tool for the dietary services. For example, it specifies the percentage of net operating expenses which should apply to each category of expense. In Figure 13.12, food costs are estimated to be 29 percent of total operating expenses. ($622,603 [food costs] ÷ $2,120,419 [total operating expenses] = 29 percent.)

The dietary manager should carefully study each month's departmental operating expenses. What is the actual food-cost percentage? (Procedures to calculate actual food costs were noted earlier in this chapter.) Why, if at all, is it different from the budget plan? If the variance between standard costs (expressed in the operating budget) and the actual cost (expressed in the departmental operating statement) becomes excessive, the dietary manager must investigate reasons, take corrective action, and make sure that revised procedures have reduced the problem.

Budget control becomes much easier when a monthly operating budget is utilized. For example, the annual budget (illustrated in Figure 13.12) can be expressed in monthly terms. Facilities without changes in client meal counts can frequently use the annual budget, divide by 12 months and make necessary adjustments to develop a monthly budget. In contrast, facilities with variances in monthly operations will need to first develop the annual budget (Figure 13.12) by developing monthly budgets and "putting these together" to form the annual budget. Figure 13.13 shows one month of the annual budget shown in Figure 13.12.

Zero-Based Budgeting

An interesting variation in budget development uses a zero-based budgeting plan. Note in the budget development process above that operating information from the previous year was used as a base for developing the budget. Then, estimates of increases / decreases to historic operating statistics were used to develop the budget. In contrast, a zero-based budget, while making use of historic information, requires the dietary manager to justify every dollar of expense to be budgeted for each category of cost—not just the increase in cost from the base expressed by actual expenses from the previous year. Few commercial facilities use zero-based budgeting. It is practiced in some institutional operations and can be relevant to dietary ser-

Description	% of Cost	Operating Expenses		Nonpatient Cash Receipts		Net Cost	Cost per Meal
Food	30	$73,763	less	$21,879	=	$51,884	$1.15
Labor	61	154,278	less	44,487	=	109,791	2.44
Supply	7	16,827	less	5,105	=	11,722	0.26
Other costs	2	4,763	less	1,459	=	3,304	0.08
	100	$249,631		$72,930		$176,701	$3.93

Figure 13.13 Monthly Budget

Source: Faisal A. Kaud, *Budgeting: A Comparative Analysis of Techniques and Systems.* In James C. Rose, *Handbook for Health Care Food Service Management.* Aspen Publishers, Frederick, Md., 1984, pp. 119.

vices. It can help counter a common problem occurring when the budget is developed: using last year's "numbers" as a base for developing a new budget can, in fact, perpetuate an inefficient operation if the expense levels incurred during the previous years were higher than necessary. Obvious disadvantages are the greater difficulty of preparation and the longer amount of development time required in the budget calendar.

The dietary manager must conform to the procedures for developing budgets required by the facility. The relationship between the business office and the dietary manager will affect the ease with which the dietary budget is developed. If the facility requires a zero-based or other type of budget, the dietary manager must obviously comply with these desires. However, it is also expected that the business office will provide the dietary manager with technical and/or other assistance necessary.

Ideas for Generating Revenue

Today's dietary manager must be creative in generating sales and controlling costs. A "first step" is to generate revenues from sources which were previously a cost center. Charging clients for dietary counseling and selling nutrition brochures and information are two examples.

Increasingly, facilities look to sources outside of the facility for ways to generate income. Some facilities provide meals to social agency clientele; "meals on wheels" and congregate site feeding programs for the elderly are examples. The provision of foodservices in neighborhood centers in low social-economic neighborhoods is another example.

Generally, everyone "wins" from these arrangements. The recipients of the foodservice enjoy what often is the only nutritional dietary intake of the day. The facility "wins" when its reputation in the community is enhanced. Dietary services also gain; cost recovery structures can include allocated overhead expenses which otherwise must be borne by the dietary operation.

There is increasing interest in using available dietary facilities to generate income from nontraditional sources. Catering special functions in the facility such as wedding receptions, retirement parties, and a wide range of other special events is an example. Offering a "take-home" meal program for hungry employees can be beneficial; dietary services can generate revenues and busy employees do not have to stop for "fast food" on their way home.

Increasingly, financial objectives of dietary operations emphasize lower levels of support from the facility. As this occurs, the need to find new sources of income as well as new ways to reduce operating expenses becomes increasingly important.

Benchmarking

Decisions about staffing levels and overall service quality are based on intense comparative analyses of performance to determine appropriate levels of quality, productivity and speed of service. This process, known as **benchmarking,** is beginning to be used to improve services in the healthcare industry.

The healthcare industry is in the midst of a paradigm shift. Regardless of the outcome of healthcare reform, competition among all providers is going to become more fierce as employers seek the best value for their money. As managed care alternatives continue to grow, healthcare organizations that fail to provide low-cost, high-quality healthcare will not survive. Being a "best performer" is the key to surviving this paradigm shift.

Benchmarking begins as a targeting process. A large volume of information about potential benchmarking partners is obtained and processed for the purpose of targeting the initial research on possible comparisons. Next, target areas with comparable performance data are identified, enabling performance comparisons to get underway.

The initial comparisons of data from an organization and its benchmarking peers offer a primary gap analysis, which identifies the difference in performance levels that exist between the benchmarking partners' operational methods and processes. From this comparison, the potential for performance improvement can be determined.

Once a real potential for and practices leading to improved performance are identified, a short study can be launched. Short studies generally take three to four months and begin to identify improvement opportunities. As the depth of analysis in the study increases, the length, cost, and duration of the study increases as well. A full study can be a six- to nine-month process involving a number of organizations. Efforts in that situation are designed to identify detailed information about processes and methods.

For most healthcare organizations, benchmarking is best understood as both a product and a process, with most of the value derived during the data gathering. The benchmarking organization's staff learns about itself and begins to look for new and more effective ways of delivering products and services. Well structured programs will involve front-line management in a step-by-step methodology that forces managers to explore their organizations. These steps usually incorporate:

- Identify what is to be benchmarked. It could be something tangible—such as food costs per meal, bad-debt accounts, staff training time—or something intangible—such as client satisfaction;
- Identify potential benchmarking partners. Spend time researching other successful organizations, including those outside the heathcare industry;
- Determine data collection methods and collect data;
- Analyze the data collected and determine current performance levels. Measure the facility's performance and compare it with the performance of benchmarked facilities;
- Project future performance levels;
- Communicate benchmarking findings. Present findings and recommendations to senior managers and other employees;
- Establish functional goals by writing objectives;
- Develop action plans to reach objectives;
- Implement the plans and monitor progress. If objectives are not being met, teams should be formed to monitor progress and make additional recommendations;
- Recalibrate measurements. Are the organizations chosen to benchmark against still barometers of excellence? If not, find others and set new goals.

Doing More With Less

Organizations are still downsizing and still expecting employees to do more with less. Trainers are learning what works and what doesn't in the way of effective training on budgets stingy in comparison to times past.

Re-engineering may combine new job tasks in one position, thus requiring additional training. It's been called "power training." Instead of the leisurely eight-hour program of yesterday, training today is more likely to be punctuated into a quartet of 90-minute segments tightly focused on what trainees need to know right now, on skills they can take back to their jobs today to apply and practice at once.

Training demand is outpacing training budgets. Corporate downsizing remains ubiquitous, and slimmed-down organizations require more training. With fewer workers to do the work, almost certainly those fewer workers are going to need to learn to do additional tasks or to work more effectively or both.

In many cases the training department itself has been downsized and placed under the same edict: find ways to do as much, or more, with less in staff and resources. Trainers are being forced to work harder or smarter or both.

Here is what some organizations are trying to meet the training needs challenge:

- *Standardization.* Programs are much more focused, much more standardized so that they can be repeated by different instructors;
- *Pack the training room.* Taking advantage of professional trainers, including more team leaders than would normally be trained at one time;
- *Computer-based training.* For example, a course on a particular program might cost $300 per trainee with classroom training, but only $60 per trainee with computer-based training;
- *Use in-house experts.* By inviting other department heads into the training process, each "expert" shares only his expertise, then goes back to working his job;
- *Do-it-yourself.* By producing training booklets and videos for employees, training is effective, but perhaps not as professionally accomplished, producing some savings depending on the time expended to develop;
- *Leverage.* Choosing respected leaders, at the director or vice president level, and then training them to train others also saves in cost because there is no need for external consultants;
- *Collaboration.* For example, "team-building" training with another facility and sharing the cost of training is a creative way to cut training costs.

The result is that trainers no longer do those 12-classes-in-three-days teaching assignments. But they are finding that if they *show* somebody else how to be effective as a leader, as a trainer, they're going to gain from it and the trainer gains from it also because he or she is heading up the intervention. In this way, the trainer tells trainees only what they need to know at the moment. But then the trainee can draw on that vast hidden store of know-how when he or she asks a question in the classroom or on the job. This is sometimes referred to as "iceberg training," because an iceberg can be an inspiring vision as well as a hazard to navigation. Only time will tell which it will be in the coming years for trainers and their organizations.

SUMMARY

The professional dietary manager must be just as competent in financial management as he or she is in the activities of food production, personnel supervision, nutritional assessment, and so on. The manager has an important role in the control of sales generated from cash cafeteria operations. For effective control, the dietary manager must know (a) the amount of sales which should be collected, (b) the amount of sales which actually is collected, and (c) when corrective action is necessary to reduce the variance between (a) and (b) above.

It is important that specific operating procedures for the cash register be followed consistently. While the actual procedures will vary by operation, some basic principles are generally applicable. Dietary managers should modify these procedures as necessary to fit needs of the specific operation, and should train and consistently supervise the cashiers to ensure that these procedures are followed.

The type and number of cafeteria operating reports vary according to the needs of the facility and the type of register equipment available. Each facility must consider the exact needs of the dietary department when purchase decisions for register equipment are made.

There are basically two general types of operating data which can be generated by and are most useful to the cafeteria operation. One deals with money *(Cafeteria Cash Report);* it is important to confirm that all sales which should have been collected are, in fact, collected. Daily cash sales information should be tallied on a cumulative *Monthly Summary of Cafeteria Sales Report.* This form is used to recap gross sales figures for each meal period.

A second basic type of operating information collected by many cafeteria operations refers to income by specified category. This type of information is easy to generate if specific "clerk" keys are available on the register. Information from the *Cashiers Report* can then be tallied into a *Cumulative Report.* At the end of the week, total dollars generated in sales by each classification can be converted into a meal count (equivalent). Typically, this is done by assessing the average sales dollars collected.

The dietary manager, not the cashier, should determine the amount of sales rung on the register during the work shift, and make sure this amount is available. A procedure should be set up to help the manager assure that all sales generated were, in fact, deposited, and that the amount was credited to the appropriate dietary services account. There is a wide range of methods which dishonest register operators can use to steal.

It is generally best to utilize a system which generates a sales tape for each purchase. Additionally, the concept of an "audit trail" refers to the ability of an analyst of the accounting system to trace the sales from the point of entry into the system through to the point of deposit. The dietary manager should be aware of "no cash" systems and recommend their use where appropriate.

An important step in the food control plan involves pre-costing to ensure that menus which are planned will be within budgeted guidelines. The operating budget is a result of agreement between the dietary manager and higher-level managers about the expected level of income and expense for the dietary operation. Wise managers consider the allowable food costs in the operating budget.

Several forms make the pre-costing process easier to understand and to use. There are four steps in pre-costing:

- *Determine allowable food cost from budget;*
- *Precost proposed menus;*
- *Make necessary adjustments;*
- *Finalize menu.*

The dietary manager will calculate to learn what the food cost per client day is. More important, however, is the question of what the food cost per patient day *should* be. How much variance is there between the actual and expected food costs per client day? Managers can keep better track of actual costs when effectively designed forms are used. *Weekly dietary reports* and *weekly food cost reports* help the dietary manager adjust food costs to keep within budget guidelines. If there are problems, analysis of food costs on a by-category basis can help to determine where costs are excessive so that corrective actions can be taken, or information can be shared with the finance manager.

A *dietary department operating statement* is a critical report that provides a financial "picture" of the dietary department. Current periods and year-to-date information for each revenue and expense item are shown for actual and plan (budget) along with variance and the cumulative amounts for the same time period "last year." With this detailed information, the dietary manager will know, first, what sales and costs should be and, second, what sales and costs actually are.

The process of comparing actual with expected cost becomes, then, an integral part of the control process a professional dietary manager uses to control sales and costs, and to ensure that it is not necessary to reduce quality requirements in order to compensate for lower sales and/or higher costs. The "clue" to the need for corrective action appears when the dietary manager cannot explain and/or justify the reason for variance between the budgeted and actual sales and cost levels.

Managers should recognize that special catered events can be a significant source of revenue to a dietary department, while at the same time enhancing its reputation and prestige within the facility and the community. The dietary manager, perhaps working with the business office managers, should typically make the decision on how to set prices for these events.

All staff members, including the dietary manager and his or her employees, must know something about procedures for establishing and administering wage and salary programs in the facility. Typically, the dietary manager will not be involved in determining rates, at least originally. But he or she will probably need to explain and justify compensation programs to subordinate staff.

It is important that salary/wage plans be consistent. When applicable, the same basic elements should be used to administer the program in every department within the facility. Dietary and other facility administrators must communicate basic rules, policies, and provisions of the wage/salary plan to all affected employees.

Job evaluation involves analysis of specific jobs to assess pay rates. Job pay rates are developed as an output of the job evaluation process. A final step is to classify employees according to the pay rates which have been established. There are several basic methods of job evaluation: simple ranking, grade description, or point system.

After a basic pay structure has been established, procedures to assess periodic wage/salary increases must be developed. Several possibilities include a flat rate plan, a step rate plan, a cost-of-living allowance, and a merit performance plan.

Employee benefits are a large operating expense for most dietary operations. Pension, medical, and life insurance plans, as well as vacation, holidays, and sick leave can present attractive packages, as can special cash rewards for significant work efforts, suggestion programs, and sabbatical leaves. Employee benefits can really be of three types: no-cost, low-cost, or high-cost benefits.

Dietary managers must know how to develop and use an operating budget. This financial management tool is a plan which specifies the economic goals of the dietary department and indicates how much income and expenses are expected as the plan evolves. Wise managers realize that the operating budget is a significant help in managing many aspects of dietary service. It expresses the agreement about the volume of meals to be produced, the estimate of sales to be generated, and costs to be incurred. The operating budget also helps with pricing decisions and becomes the financial plan for the dietary department.

The development of an operating budget for the dietary department can be time-consuming and complex. The overall responsibility for the budget rests with the business office, although the dietary manager should have a great deal of input into its development.

Once the operating budget is developed, it becomes an important control tool for the dietary services. For example, it specifies the percentage of net operating expenses which should apply to each category of expense. If the variance between standard costs and the actual cost becomes excessive, the dietary manager must investigate reasons and take corrective action to reduce the problem. Budget control becomes much easier when a monthly operating budget is utilized.

An interesting variation in budget development uses a zero-based budgeting plan. While making use of historic information, zero-based budgeting requires the dietary administrator to justify every dollar of expense to be budgeted for each category of cost—not just the increase in cost from the base expressed by actual expenses from the previous year. It can help counter perpetuation of an inefficient operation if the expense levels incurred during the previous years were higher than necessary. Obvious disadvantages are the greater difficulty of preparation and the longer amount of development time required in the budget calendar.

Today's dietary manager must be creative in generating sales and in controlling costs. A "first step" is to generate revenues from sources which were previously a cost center. Increasingly, facilities look to creative sources of the facility for ways to generate income. Examples include providing meals to social agency clientele, catering special functions in the facility, and offering a "take-home" meal program for hungry employees.

The healthcare industry is in the midst of a paradigm shift. Regardless of the outcome of healthcare reform, competition among all providers results in employers seeking the best value for their money. Decisions about staffing levels and overall service quality are based on intense comparative analyses of performance to determine appropriate levels of quality, productivity, and speed of service. This process, known as **benchmarking**, is beginning to be used to improve services in the healthcare industry.

Organizations are still downsizing and expecting employees to do more with less. Restructuring requires more frequent training. Trainers are learning what works and what doesn't in the way of effective training on smaller budgets. Many times, the training department itself has been downsized and placed in a position of finding ways to do as much, or more, with less in the way of staff and resources. Trainers are being forced to work harder or smarter or both.

KEY TERMS

- "X" reading
- Cafeteria cash report
- Monthly summary
- "No ringing"
- Audit trail
- Operating budget
- Net cost of goods used
- Weekly dietary report
- Dietary department operating statement
- Variance analysis
- Job evaluation
- Simple ranking
- Grade description
- Point system
- Flat rate plan
- Step rate plan
- Cost-of-living allowance
- Merit performance plans
- Employee benefits
- Operating budget
- Zero-based budget
- Benchmarking
- "Doing more with less"

QUESTIONS/PROBLEMS/CASES

1. You are managing a hospital cafeteria and suspect that one of the cash register operators is stealing, using the "no ringing" scheme. What might you implement in order to minimize the potential for this problem?

2. If the net cost of goods used totals $ 44,600, and there are 159 clients in a 30-day month, is it possible to determine the food cost per client day? If not, why not? If so, what is it?

3. With the detailed information provided by the operating statement, the dietary manager will be able to know what sales and costs should be, and what sales and costs actually are. Using variance analysis, what questions would you ask yourself if there is a variance between the budgeted and actual sales and cost levels?

4. Which method of job evaluation would you use to assess pay rates? Give your reasons.

5. If food costs for a catering function are 39% of the sales to be generated from catering (according to the operating budget), how can this knowledge help with pricing decisions?

6. If the budgeted food sales for a particular item (in a cash cafeteria operation) = $ 750,000, and the budgeted food costs = $ 225,000, and the standard food cost per portion is .93, what would be the base selling price for that menu item sold in the cafeteria?

7. What are the advantages and disadvantages of using zero-based budgeting in dietary services?

8. What is your opinion concerning "benchmarking?" Does it make a facility more effective? Why or why not? Do you see any disadvantages of implementing this strategy? Discuss your views with your classmates.

9. Why is "doing more with less" sometimes referred to as *power training?* Why is it sometimes referred to as *iceberg training?*

10. In "doing more with less," which of the methods of training discussed in the chapter would you consider best to use in a dietary department? Explain.

14

MARKETING MANAGEMENT

Chapter Outline

- Distinguishing between Marketing and Advertising
- Methods to Determine the Market
  - Market Research
  - Focused Group Study
  - Life-style Analysis
  - Determining the Wants and Needs of Residents
- Developing a Marketing Plan
- Merchandising
  - Training Employees
  - Planning Special Promotions
  - Promotion of Services

Distinguishing between Marketing and Advertising

Every foodservice operation makes decisions concerning the packaging of products and services in a manner that is most pleasing to customers. The first step is to determine who the customers are and what they want. The process of answering these questions and devising a program to meet the identified needs is called **marketing.**

Marketing is not the same as advertising. Advertising programs are only one aspect of a marketing plan. Marketing involves building in customers' minds the business image that management would like them to perceive, while advertising is simply one method of conveying that image to customers.

When many people think of marketing, they automatically think of advertising and personal selling. Of course, advertising and sales are important parts of the overall marketing process, but they are not the only parts. There are controllable variables that a facility manipulates in order to achieve its overall objectives. Traditionally, marketing has been characterized as being composed of four parts: product, promotion, price, and place.

Product. The product is the actual good or service being offered for sale. It could include all of the features of the good or service as well as the packaging and brand name of the good or service. The term **product** does not necessarily refer to a tangible or physical thing; rather, it is the total goods/service package that is being sold. In many industries such as the baking industry, the physical product dominates the sale. However, in the sale of retirement community living, the service product dominates the sale.

Promotion. This part of marketing is concerned primarily with communication. How do you communicate with customers about what there is to sell? How do you convince them that what is being sold is what they want to buy? The promotional part of marketing, what you normally refer to when thinking of advertising and personal selling, will be covered later in this chapter.

Price. The price of a product or service is one of the main considerations customers have when buying products or services. When you set prices, you have to consider whether the customers will think the price is fair, too high, or too low. Will all customers think the same way? Would a dinner priced at $100 affect sales to a millionaire in the same way that it would to a typical college student? These are the kinds of issues that make pricing very difficult to do.

There are a number of factors that influence how prices are set. These fall under the realm of strategic, cost, and market demand considerations. First, consider the strategic objectives of a company. Survival of the company could be the main objective. Market leadership might be another objective. One way to become a market leader is to lower prices to get more business. Product/service quality leadership is another strategy. In this strategy, a company seeks to be seen as having the highest-quality product or service in the market; charging high prices contributes to the image.

Facilities have costs of their own that affect the minimum prices they must charge for their products and services. These would include all of the costs for producing, marketing, and distributing their products or services. The lower a facility's costs are in relation to the competition's, the lower price it can charge and still make a profit.

While costs will set the minimum price that a facility must charge, market demand will set the maximum price. One very good way of creating market segments is on the basis of price sensitivity, or how much each segment is willing to pay.

Place. Place refers to distribution: how one goes about getting the product or service to the customer. A good coffee shop will fail if customers are not available. A nice cafeteria will fail if no one likes the location. Ironically, a mediocre dining facility might be successful simply because it is in the right place at the right time. The operator must plan to position the business in the market. Since the market in which a foodservice is located probably offers a variety of dining options to choose from, the foodservice operator should pinpoint the segment of the market for which it will compete. The public is likely to associate the operation with a few salient features such as price, type of foods sold, and ambiance; therefore, the operator should determine how to present these features before entering the market. This is at the heart of positioning a business.

The dietary manager must consider his or her product, promotion, price, and place if he or she is to be successful in marketing. While it is one matter to serve food to clients which is hot, nutritious, and correctly portioned, it is a far different challenge to make it eye-appealing with proper garnish, color contrast, and diversity of shape and texture. The former takes attention to detail, but the latter requires the manager to go the extra step in making the meal picture perfect. This is the essence of marketing.

Methods To Determine The Market

Unless the right market is identified and reached, the dietary manager will be running in circles attempting to please an audience which cannot be satisfied. Such is the case when sophisticated gourmet foods are served to a group wishing meat and potatoes. The reaction is that portion sizes are too small, the food is too fancy, and prices are too high. The balance of correctly distributing (placing) the right product at the right price through the right promotion to the right people is why you spend so much time determining the right market.

Market Research

Determining the likely customers of a foodservice operation can be accomplished in several different ways. The most common is through a market research survey. To make good decisions, a marketing department must have good information at its disposal. Good-quality information is essential, and collecting demographic information concerning the operation's locale is a great place to start. From this information, the dietary manager can determine such critical factors as the educational levels of potential clientele, food taste preferences, age, income, number of persons per household, and average amount of money spent dining out. On the basis of this information, a marketing plan can be built.

For example, before a dietary facility would implement an elderly feeding program, a market research survey should assess the need for the program. Each of the other steps noted earlier (Chapter 13) for assessing the cost/benefit of a proposed project is also necessary. The government is continually willing to support dietary managers willing to identify and assist markets needing special attention.

Title XII of the Older Americans Act (1965) established authority for providing federal funds to provide nutrition services for the elderly. The Act has subsequently been amended (Title IIIC of the Older Americans Act [1972]). Basically, federal legislators have recognized that elderly citizens as a group are nutritionally at risk, and that proper nutrition can help to reduce medical and other problems which affect many members of this age group. Federal funds are made available for congregate (group) site-feeding, and also for the production and transportation of meals to elderly citizens in their homes.

While there are a vast number of regulations (many of which frequently change), dietary managers should recognize that:

- healthcare and other facilities are a natural site for the production of these meals;
- programs can be sponsored (or co-sponsored) by healthcare facilities, or other state or local agencies administering services to the elderly can sponsor these programs and then sub-contract meal production and/or delivery to institutions such as healthcare facilities;
- within limitations, funds can be used to reimburse the institution for direct and indirect (pro-rated) costs incurred for the management, production, service and/or delivery of meals. Supplies (such as disposable units used for prepackaged meals) can also be reimbursed;
- in addition to providing nutritious meals, many programs incorporate nutrition education elements. Other services, such as shopping assistance and recreation and hobby facilities, can also be provided.

In some institutions, congregate site-feeding operations are provided at the facility itself. In other operations, meals are prepared at the institution and transported to another site for service. A simple needs survey can be developed to collect the type of information which must be assessed, and then mailed to community residents. Alternatively, a telephone survey could be completed, or information could be distributed in a church, shopping center, grocery store, or other retail sales business. Doctors, public service agencies, state departments of aging, the healthcare facility itself, and other sources should be contacted for input into the needs survey. Some questions appearing on a simple needs survey might be:

Q1: Do you feel there is a need for a home-delivered meals program in this community?
____Yes ____No

Q2: Do you think people will use this program if available?
____Yes ____No

Q3: How many citizens aged 55 or above do you know would participate in this type of program? _____

Q4: Would you be willing to volunteer your time to assist in this program?
____Yes ____No

Q5: Number of hours per week you would be willing to help: _________

Most elderly feeding programs are funded through a sponsoring state agency. Dietary managers can contact the state, county, or local commissions on aging, departments of health and social services, elderly citizens advocacy groups, or other facilities offering similar programs, to obtain more specific information applicable to the area.

A contract with the sponsoring agency will need to be signed. This will specify details about finances, nutrition, compliance with sanitation codes, and so on. Some federally donated commodities (foodstuffs) can frequently be made available for facilities participating in this program.

The facility will usually bill the sponsoring agency on a weekly or other basis for the number of meals served. Generally, a flat rate per meal is assessed and, as noted above, charges can be for indirect as well as direct operating expenses.

The healthcare or other institution which participates in an elderly nutrition or other community service program becomes much more visible in the local area as a helping institution. The amount of goodwill accruing to the facility, as well as personal, professional, and societal satisfaction derived, frequently makes these types of programs worth expending the effort to implement and carry out.

Focused Group Study

In addition to the basic market research survey, more involved methods can be used to determine the market for a foodservice. One such method used for foodservices is a focused group study, in which meetings are conducted with the potential patrons to identify specific likes and dislikes about an existing or planned foodservice. This is especially beneficial in determining the attitudes and spending habits of members of the prospective market.

Life-style Analysis

Life-style analysis is another method of market research. It is based on the assumption that, by studying the life style of the market, amounts of time spent on various leisure activities, preferences for life style, and so on, an operator can better determine how to tailor the operation to fit those with that life style.

Determining the Wants and Needs of Residents

Other research which may be appropriate for any facility is that which determines the wants and needs of the resident population in a captive clientele situation, like a nursing home or long-term care, continuous-care community. Often the residents of such communities are of a higher economic status and demand better service and elite, higher-costing meals. The food is a large marketing tool of such a facility, and the dietary manager who caters to the likes and dislikes of his or her clients is going to be more successful in the long run.

Focused group studies and life-style analysis are both excellent formal methods to conduct such research. On the other hand, informal discussions with clients while they are dining can accomplish much toward the collection of data, as long as such information is recorded accurately and reviewed frequently.

Developing a Marketing Plan

Just as individuals have long-term objectives (such as having a good job, making a good living, etc.), foodservice operations have long-term goals. The planning process that a student of *managing foodservice operations* goes through, and will continue to go through, is nothing more than an example of strategic planning. In business terms this can be defined as the process of developing and maintaining a close fit between a company's goals and its present situation.

The first task in the strategic marketing process is to consider what *objectives* a business has. These objectives can be short-term, such as making sure there are enough food supplies on hand for next week's banquets, or long-term, such as determining how many new facilities to open in the next five years. When objectives are created, they need to be clearly stated, and also need to be realistic. It is easy to make the statement "we will be the largest dietary department in the world in ten years." It is a lot harder to reach that objective.

The next task is to perform a **situation analysis.** A situation analysis is a critical look at where the facility is now. One method is to analyze the strengths, weaknesses, opportunities and threats of the facility. It is important to analyze what the strengths and weaknesses are compared to those of the competition. For example, a facility may have better foodservice or a better location than the competition, but perhaps the building is older and does not look as nice as the competitor's. When dealing with strengths or weaknesses, it is important to be realistic. Sometimes it is easier to point to the strengths than to notice the weaknesses.

It is also important to analyze what *opportunities* for success a facility has and weigh them against possible *threats* to success. Is business booming in a certain area? Is the elderly nutrition program one that people like? Alternatively, does the economy look bad in the future, or is the nutrition program conflicting with the advice of the medical community? Again, a critical assessment is necessary.

After the objectives have been identified (where the facility wants to be in the future) and the situation analysis has been completed (where the facility is now), it is time to figure out how to accomplish those objectives. *Strategies* and *tactics* are the precise methods used to achieve objectives. Developing marketing strategies may seem simple, but it actually isn't. Predicting the future is always difficult. There are too many variables that can influence events. Who, for example, really predicted the rapid changes that occurred in the former USSR in the early 1990s? Who foresaw the sweeping behavioral changes brought about by the AIDS epidemic? Obviously, planning for the future requires a lot of time and thought; the methods mentioned earlier in determining the market certainly help in developing these essential marketing strategies.

Merchandising

Once the market and the positioning of the business in the customers' minds are established, the operator can begin to promote the business, *externally*, through a marketing plan, and *internally*, through merchandising. If an operation is to succeed in pleasing customers and building sales, merchandising must occur. One example: use of known brands such Pizza Hut or Taco Bell have increased sales in cafeterias. This is true not only for commercial operations that must attract customers, but also for institutions that serve a captive audience.

Many operations fail to realize the importance of good merchandising, and as a result have poor merchandising systems. The operation that does a little extra in merchandising often beats out the competition, even when the quality of its food and service may be slightly inferior. The areas of chief importance to merchandising are the training of employees, the planning of special promotions, and making presentations.

Training Employees

The term **merchandising** may be narrowly defined as the selling of merchandise, but in a broader sense it is the presentation of factors that entice people to buy. Many operations could sell more product if they used better merchandising techniques. Employees can be invaluable in getting people to buy. Training is supposed to narrow the gap between actual performance and desired performance. If training is effective, sales people will use those skills or behaviors to improve results. Most training is not realized in the classroom. Training takes place in the field with continuous practice and feedback. The classroom is just useful for presenting the concepts and getting people familiar enough with them to practice in the field. Effective training programs recognize and use the following key points:

- Effective training focuses on understanding the customers' perspective and their reasons for buying;
- Adults resist change and do not wish to take risks;
- Any trainer should have worked in the foodservice industry or know it very well;
- Traditional sales approaches that are product-based will not reliably work in the foodservice industry. Marketing—not selling—is the key to foodservice programs;
- People retain perhaps 10 percent of what they hear. Hence, ongoing training that focuses on incremental improvements in what people already know will likely yield better retention than intensive seminars;
- Appropriate motivation goes a long way.

Consumers have a personal perspective about products before they begin the process of purchasing. You are likely to have a well-formed frame of reference for each of these: BMW, IBM, Days Inns, The Plaza. Customers have a frame of reference that is personal and subjective. The salesperson who can explore what that perspective is will be in a favorable position. The basic tenet of the art of persuasion is to tell people what they need to hear. Training should address potential customer reasons for buying: prestige, security, and so on. It is safer, for example, to book a well-known name than an independent. It may not be the best facility, but it's a *safe* choice. Branding (use of brand name foods) is popular for the same reason.

Many adults tend to keep doing things the way they've always done them. The reason is that doing so is relatively safe—probably nobody will call their judgment into question if they just keep doing what has always been done. Training and subsequent follow-up must relieve the risk of trying something new. The participants must know they will be applauded for the attempt, not the outcome. Progress must be encouraged slowly, letting those being trained know that it's okay to be one percent better every day.

Principles being presented must relate to actual foodservice situations. If it's the facilitator's personal experience, so much the better. If not, the facilitator needs to be able to demonstrate clearly that he or she understands the foodservice world.

Most training programs are product-oriented, not customer-oriented. Define what the customer wants, and meet those expectations by training staff to fulfill those identified needs.

Some studies show that the brain can process data at a rate of up to 1,000 words a minute—but most people speak at a rate of about 100 words a minute, so the mind wanders while it waits. Moreover, people retain as little as 15 to 20 percent of what they hear. Build on marketing concepts slowly and continuously rather than all at once. The result will be retained information rather than lost concepts.

Create an environment that allows people to motivate themselves. Treat every person as an individual, learn what excites them, and use that knowledge to help them improve. Some people are motivated by recognition, some by prestige, some by money, and some by challenge. If people don't want to improve or be more productive, they could attend a training program every week and it wouldn't matter. One must help them find their motivational trigger.

Investing in the facility's greatest resource, the employees, can be gratifying and rewarding. But most everyone is afraid of change because it involves risk. Trying to completely make over employees is folly at best, wasteful at worst. Minimize the risk by developing people's natural tendencies; look for small, incremental improvements, and results will be seen.

Planning Special Promotions

Many people consider promotion to be the single most critical element in the entire marketing process. The complex nature of promotion makes it a very interesting element to evaluate. It is the one area where the producer and consumer are completely intertwined.

The two-part goal of promotion is to inform and persuade. Information means knowledge. It's important to know about a product or service before ever considering to buy it. Persuasion means convincing people to buy the product or service. After knowing about it, it is necessary to be convinced that the product or service is worth buying. If the elements of informing and persuading are present, then the promotion has a good chance of being successful.

Business in a foodservice may fluctuate, and low-volume periods may cause a major loss of profit. Building business at these times can take up some of the slack and help meet overhead and labor costs that exist whether or not there is business. Three methods are used to build foodservice business with special promotions: personalizing service to include special events in customers' lives, developing special promotions around holidays, or capitalizing on local events that lend themselves to special promotions.

All customers have especially important days in their lives—birthdays, anniversaries, graduation days, or visits from friends or relatives. Some operations offer patrons cards to fill out identifying such special days. These cards are then filed and used to remind the customers to come in to celebrate; some type of arrangement in keeping with the occasion is offered to make the proposal more attractive. Even if the guest does not come in, the reminder is good public relations.

Holiday promotions can be quite successful. Mother's Day, New Year's, Thanksgiving, and other holidays are special days on which many people want to eat out. Special menus can be printed and sent to customers or shown around the operation; they also can be put into newspapers or otherwise advertised.

Additionally, special promotions can also be productive when combined with local events. A football game, a convention, or a community project may provide the occasion. For example, a "winning-team special" can be used to feature the first event, and a "convention caper dinner" can be used to feature the second. Special theme events with an international flavor or nutritional focus are also appreciated by clients.

Promotion of Services

The dietary manager will most likely be involved in making presentations of the facility to external sources. This is the step where the manager actually presents the benefits of the facility's supply and demonstrates how these benefits satisfy the community demand or needs. Due to the time involved, promotion activity requires administrative support. Most often, the interested party visits the facility so that they have the opportunity to sample the product and get a true picture of the efficiency of the facility. While this is the ideal method to make a presentation, it cannot always be arranged. Presentations by telephone, supported by sales brochures and videos or in the prospect's office, are alternative methods.

During this step of the sales process, the manager will invariably encounter objections to points that are made in the presentation. Answering and overcoming these objections is an art and comes with experience. Additionally, the manager must "ask for the order" or attempt to close the sale by obtaining a signed contract. Since this is a big moment, it sometimes makes managers anxious, but obviously it is an imperative action.

The dietary manager is encouraged to market his or her property by becoming involved within the operation as well as outside the operation. Advertising, merchandising, and marketing each have their place, but the manager who is constantly searching to build business through creative and new techniques will, in the end, be the one with the unique competitive advantage, winning over the others in the marketplace.

SUMMARY

Every foodservice operation makes decisions concerning the packaging of products and services in a manner that is most pleasing to customers. The process of researching and making these decisions and then devising a program to meet the identified needs is called *marketing.*

Marketing is not the same as advertising. Advertising and sales are parts of a marketing plan. And although advertising and sales are important parts of the overall marketing process, they are not the *only* parts.

Traditionally, the 4 P's of marketing are: product, promotion, price, and place/location.

This chapter covers three methods to determine the market:

- *Market Research.* To make good decisions, a marketing department must have good information at its disposal. Collecting demographic information concerning the operation's locale is a great place to start. From this information, the foodservice operator can determine such critical factors as the educational levels of potential clientele, food taste preferences, age, income, number of persons per household, and average amount of money spent dining out. On the basis of this information, a marketing plan can be built. A simple needs survey can be developed to collect the type of information which must be assessed.
- *Focused Group Study.* Meetings are conducted with the potential patrons to identify specific likes and dislikes about an existing or planned foodservice.
- *Life-style Analysis.* Based on the assumption that, by studying the life style of the market, amounts of time spent on various leisure activities, preferences for life style, and so on, an operator can better determine how to tailor the operation to fit those with that life-style.

Developing a marketing plan is the process of developing and maintaining a close fit between a company's goals and its present situation. The first task in the strategic marketing process is to consider what objectives a business has. These objectives can be short-term or long-term. When objectives are created, they need to be clearly stated and also need to be realistic.

The next task is to perform a situation analysis, a critical look at where the facility is now. It is important to analyze what the strengths and weaknesses are compared to those of the competition. It is important to be realistic because it is easier to point to the strengths than to notice the weaknesses.

It is also important to analyze what opportunities for success a facility has and weigh them against possible threats to success; a critical assessment of these opportunities and threats is necessary.

After the objectives have been identified and the situation analysis has been completed, it is time to figure out how to accomplish those objectives. Strategies and tactics are the precise methods used to achieve objectives. Planning for the future, however, requires a lot of time and thought.

Once the market and the positioning of the business in the customers' minds are established, the operator can begin to promote the business, externally, through a marketing plan, and internally, through merchandising. Many operations fail to realize the importance of good merchandising, and as a result have poor merchandising systems. The operation that does a little extra in merchandising often beats out the competition, even when the quality of its food and service may be slightly inferior.

The areas of chief importance to merchandising are:

Training Employees. Training takes place in the field with continuous practice and feedback. The classroom is useful for presenting the concepts and getting people familiar enough with them to practice in the field. Effective training programs recognize and use the following key points:

1. The customer's frame of reference.
2. Adults are inherently resistant to change and are risk-averse.
3. The trainer should have actual experience in the foodservice industry.
4. Traditional sales approaches that are product-based will not reliably work in the foodservice industry.
5. People retain perhaps 10 percent of what they hear.
6. Appropriate motivation goes a long way.

Planning Special Promotions. The complex nature of promotion makes it a very interesting element to evaluate. It is the one area where the producer and consumer are completely intertwined. The two-part goal of promotion is to inform and persuade. If these two elements are present, then the promotion has a good chance of being successful. Three methods are used to build foodservice business with special promotions: personalizing service to include special events in customers' lives, developing special promotions around holidays, or capitalizing on local events that lend themselves to special promotions or theme events.

Making Presentations. The dietary manager will most likely be involved in making presentations to external sources. This is the step where the manager actually presents the benefits of the facility's supply and demonstrates how these benefits satisfy the community demand or needs. While the ideal method is for the interested party to visit the facility for this presentation, it cannot always be arranged. Presentations by telephone, supported by sales brochures and videos or in the prospect's office, are alternative methods. Answering and overcoming any objections that a prospect may have is an art and comes with experience. The manager must "ask for the order" or attempt to close the sale by obtaining a signed contract.

KEY TERMS

Marketing
Advertising
Product
Promotion
Price
Place
Market research
Title XII of the Older Americans Act
Needs survey
Life-style analysis
Focused group study
Marketing plan
Objectives
Situation analysis
Merchandising

This is a big moment and sometimes makes managers anxious, but obviously, it is the goal of the presentation.

15

PROFESSIONAL DEVELOPMENT

CHAPTER OUTLINE

- Professional Ethics
- Confidentiality
- Benefits of Professional Associations
- Career Opportunities in Management
- Continuing Professional Education

PROFESSIONAL ETHICS

The concept of ethics relates to views and attitudes about what is "right" and "wrong." Words like integrity, fairness, honesty, and trust are used to describe an ethical person. Obviously, views about ethics vary between individuals.

The dietary manager must know about and consistently practice the highest possible standards of ethics in all work and non-work related activities. The dietary manager must possess the skills and knowledge required to serve the client. This can be translated to mean that the dietary manager must practice in such a manner as to provide the best service with the least harm to the client.

The dietary manager should have a knowledge of legal and ethical principles of the federal, state, and local governments, as well as the ethics committee's guidelines within the facility. The dietary manager needs to:

- Avoid discrimination against any individual or group because of age, sex, religion, disability, origin, or creed;
- Maintain confidentiality of information;
- Provide service to all clients within their rights;
- Avoid conflict of interest;
- Conduct his/her duties with loyalty, integrity, and honesty;
- Assist clients in making their own decision by providing accurate information concerning diet, nutrition, foodservices, etc.;
- Use only the credentials possessed (CDM if certified; DM if not certified);
- Be loyal to his or her profession, institution, and professional organizations;
- Provide support, help, and empathy in a meaningful, sincere way;

- Be accountable for his or her competency;
- Comply with rules, regulations, and laws;
- Adhere to the facility's ethical committee decisions.

The Certifying Board for Dietary Managers (CBDM) has developed and recommended a Code of Ethics for Certified Dietary Managers; see Appendix 1.

CONFIDENTIALITY

Confidentiality means that the knowledge one has concerning a client must not be discussed with others. Clients and employees have a right to privacy. The condition of a client is a private matter between the client and the physician. Maintaining confidentiality of information is part of ethical behavior.

The dietary manager has responsibility for the quality of products and services provided by the facility's dietary department. In recognizing this responsibility, he or she must set a good example for employees and staff, consistently evaluate the quality of the operation against pre-determined standards of performance, and make effective use of input from all internal and external sources to the end that dietary services will be administered in the most professional manner possible.

As suggested in this section, the terms "ethics" and "professionalism" are similar in many ways. The professional dietary manager who is dedicated to the client, the dietary department, and the facility within which he or she works will have a genuine concern to do "what is right." As a healthcare provider, the manager recognizes that ethics is the foundation for excellence in client satisfaction.

There can frequently be honest differences of opinion about correct actions to take. The dietary manager with a proper sense of ethics who is willing to seek advice and counsel from higher levels of administration at the first potential concern about a problem will be practicing the highest standards of ethics in institutional dietary services.

In a recent survey of 4,000 U.S. employees by the Ethics Resource Center in Washington, nearly a third said they felt their companies put pressure on them to violate company policy in order to achieve business objectives. On the positive side, the existence of an ethics code and accompanying training and monitoring program led employees to take a more positive view of how the company behaved toward customers, suppliers, and others.

Most interestingly, where the company had an ethics code and had no training program, employee perceptions of their company's behavior tended to be even worse than in companies without any code. This is presumably explained by the widening credibility gap between expectations and actions, which might occur if a code was adopted and not observed.

However, ethics codes are not useful without a program of training and communication to back them up. Every company has an ethics code; it's just that most are unwritten. The burden is therefore on the company to write its code down and ensure that it is used and understood by the whole workforce, through training and modeling.

Modeling of a Code of Ethics by the dietary manager could include the following:

- Under pressures of a changing healthcare environment, you maintain ethical standards;
- As a manager, you work cooperatively across department boundaries and avoid turf conflicts;
- Assume personal responsibility for the success of the organization;
- Recognize and praise employees who demonstrate ethics, integrity, honesty, or client-service excellence;
- Take personal responsibility for improving your job performance.

The *Institute of Business Ethics* provides a model statement and code which it sees as a framework from which companies can develop their own.

The code summarizes ethical standards expected of employees. The institute stresses it should be short, and written in simple language to help employees deal with likely problems. In the model, these include conflicts of interest, the giving and receiving of gifts, confidentiality, environmental pollution, health and safety, equal opportunities, sexual harassment, moonlighting, and political activity.

Codes of conduct can be outlined in booklet form, outlining the facility's group vision and priorities, the code itself, general guidance on conduct, and sections on "implementing our code" and "achieving our goals." However, many codes are much less specific. They state broad principles and leave it to employees to work out how to apply them. These are usually broad statements about quality and customer focus ("What we stand for"), rather than specific guidance on how to deal with potential problems.

Benefits of Professional Associations

Professional associations can be of great help to the dietary manager and his or her facility. The common interests of association members dealing with governmental representation, education/training, availability of insurance programs, etc., all point to benefits derived from active involvement with associations. Figure 15.1, a partial list of trade associations, will assist the dietary manager in his or her professional memberships.

At the most professional level, many dietary managers believe that they owe something to their profession. After all, they have learned from others, both as students and in early years of practice within their industry. At some point, many dietary managers want to help improve the profession and provide assistance to younger persons entering the industry. These managers serve as mentors, role models, and coaches for the newest members. They network and share ideas.

There is a great deal of "spin-off" benefit to the facility as the dietary manager becomes active in professional associations. For example, the dietary manager will be among the first to know and be able to apply new information in the improvement of dietary services. Surely the facility benefits as this occurs. Active dietary managers will also "make the news" in trade publications, community newspapers, and so on. Their affiliation with a specific facility can be part of the public relations activities of the institution. Dietary managers active in professional associations meet new people, make professional acquaintances, and gain allies in solving problems and recruiting staff for vacant positions.

Not only should the dietary manager invest in oneself, but he or she should use information gained for in-service training programs for staff. With this approach, all members of the dietary department can benefit from the dietary manager's active involvement in professional associations. Giving a written report along with a copy of a program attended to the administrator of the facility will let him or her know about one's professional interests and concern for the benefit of the facility.

Furthermore, if considering further professional education, it is helpful to contact professional organizations. Every area of specialization has a professional organization designed to inform members of current trends and to monitor or establish industry standards of professionalism. Membership in an organization will expose you to specialized areas of interest, and put you in a position to collect solid information from both the association and its practicing members. These members will often become one's first networking contacts—and sometimes role models. An additional incentive for joining professional organizations is that many offer students reduced membership fees.

American Association of Homes and Services for the Aging
901 E. St. NW #500
Washington, DC 20004-2037
202-783-2242

American College of Health Care Administrators
325 S. Patrick St.
Alexandria, VA 22314-3580
703-549-5822

American Correctional Food Service Association
Management Excellence Incorporated
11 W. Monument
PO Box 2307
Dayton, OH 45401-2307
513-223-8008

American Culinary Federation
10 San Bartola Rd.
St. Augustine, FL 32085
904-824-4468

American Dietetic Association
216 W. Jackson Blvd., Suite 800
Chicago, IL 60606-6995
1-800-877-1600

American Health Care Association
1201 L St. NW
Washington, DC 20005-4024
202-842-4444

American Hospital Association
One N. Franklin
Chicago, IL 60606
312-422-3000

American Meat Institute
1700 N. Moore St. #1600
Arlington, VA 22209-1903
703-841-2400

American School Food Service Association
1600 Duke St. 7th Floor
Alexandria, VA 22314-3421
703-739-3900

American Society of Hospital Food Service Administrators
840 N. Lake Shore Drive
Chicago, IL 60611-2431
312-280-6416

CHRIE (Council on Hotel, Restaurant, and Institutional Educ.)
1200 17th St. NW
Washington, DC 20036-3097
202-331-5990

Club Managers Association of America
1733 King St.
Alexandria, VA 22314-2720
703-739-9500

Dietary Managers Association
One Pierce Place, #1220W
Itasca, IL 60143-3111
630-775-9200

Educational Foundation of the NRA
250 S. Wacker Dr., #1400
Chicago, IL 60606
312-715-1010

Educational Institute of the American Hotel & Motel Association (AH&MA)
1407 S. Harrison Rd.
E. Lansing, MI 48826
517-353-5500

Food Equipment Manufacturers Association
401 N. Michigan Ave.
Chicago, IL 60611-4267
312-644-6610

Food Processing Machinery & Suppliers Association
200 Daingerfield Rd.
Alexandria, VA 22314-2884
703-684-1080

Foodservice Coalition for a Better Environment
304 W. Liberty St., #201
Louisville, KY 40202-3011
502-583-3783

Foodservice Consultants Society International
304 W. Liberty St. #201
Louisville, KY 40202
502-583-3783

Foodservice Equipment Distributors Association
332 S. Michigan Ave. Suite 1840
Chicago, IL 60604
312-427-9605

Health Industry Group Purchasing Association (HIGPA)
1350 New York Ave NW #200
Washington, DC 20005
202-393-7306

Hospitality Sales & Marketing Association
1300 L. St. NW #800
Washington, DC 20005
202-789-0089

Institute of Food Technologists
221 N. LaSalle St., Suite 300
Chicago, IL 60601
312-782-8424

International Association of Culinary Professionals
304 W. Liberty St., Suite 201
Louisville, KY 40202-3011
502-581-9786

Figure 15.1 Partial List of Trade Associations *(continued on next page)*

International Food Information Council Association
1100 Connecticut Ave NW #430
Washington, DC 20036-4101
202-296-6540

International Food Service Executives Association
1100 S. State Rd 7 #103
Margate, FL 33068-4033
305-977-0767

International FoodService Manufacturers Association
180 N. Stetson #4400
Chicago, IL 60601
312-540-4400

National Association of Catering Executives
60 Revere Drie #500
Northbrook, IL 60062
708-480-9080

National Assoc. of College and University Food Services
1405 S. Harrison Rd. #303
Manly Miles Bldg. MSU
East Lansing, MI 48824-5243
517-332-6400

National Association of County Health Officials
440 First St. NW #500
Washington, DC 20001-2028
202-783-5550

National Association of Food Equipment Manufacturers
Smith Bucklin & Associates Incorporated
401 N. Michigan Ave.
Chicago, IL 60611-4267
312-644-6610

National Association of Meal Programs
101 N. Alfred St. #202
Alexandria, VA 22314
703-548-5558

National Assoc. of Nutrition and Aging Services Program
2675 44th St. SW, Suite 05
Grand Rapids, MI 49509-4191
1-800-999-6262
616-531-9909

National Association of State Units on Aging
1225 I St. NW #725
Washington, DC 20005-3914
202-898-2578

National Fisheries Institute
1525 Wilson Blvd., Suite 500
Arlington, VA 22209-2411
703-524-8880

National Food Processors Association
1401 NY Ave. NW #400
Washington, DC 20005-2102
202-639-5900

National Frozen Food Association Incorporated
4775 Linglestown Rd. #300
P O Box 6069
Harrisburg, PA 17112-6069
717-657-8601

National Nutritional Foods Association
150 E. Paularino Ave., Suite 285
Costa Mesa, CA 92626-3302
714-966-6632

National Executive Housekeepers Association
1001 Eastwind Dr., #301
Westerville, OH 43081
614-895-7166

National Restaurant Association (NRA)
1200 17th St. NW
Washington, DC 20036-3097
202-331-5900

National Society for Healthcare Foodservice Management
204 E. Street NE
Washington, DC 20002-4923
202-546-7236

National Soft Drink Association
1011 16th St. NW 7th Fl
Washington, DC 20036-4803
202-463-6732

National Yogurt Association
2000 Corporate Ridge, #1000
McLean, VA 22102
703-821-0770

Potato Chip/Snack Food Association
1711 King St., #1
Alexandria, VA 22314
703-836-4500

Retailers Bakery Association
14239 Park Center Dr.
Laurel, MD 20707
301-725-2149
800-638-0924

Salad Manufacturers Association
2971 Flowers Rd. S., Suite 266
Atlanta, GA 30341
770-452-0660

Society for Foodservice Management
304 W. Liberty St., Suite 201
Louisville, KY 40202-3011
502-583-3783

Society for Foodservice Systems
HITM, 830 Transfer Rd.
St. Paul, MN 55114
612-646-7077

FIGURE 15.1 Continued

Career Opportunities in Management

The structure of the healthcare industry is changing so rapidly that past predictions of employment trends are not appropriate for future professional roles. Similarly, as healthcare organizations continue to incorporate business strategies, such as strategic planning and cost-benefit analysis, into new organizational structures, job requirements for all health professionals will be substantially altered. The assumption that there will be only one job or one profession throughout a career is no longer valid. All indicators point to a new workplace for dietary managers.

A growing number of forces and trends will dramatically reshape the healthcare industry and the practice of dietetic food services. Understanding and responding to these trends will determine how the profession will change in the future and how practitioners will compete in this new healthcare environment. Five major forces will reshape career opportunities in the ongoing battle to manage change and to deal successfully with healthcare reform: restructuring, emergence of mergers and coalitions, shift toward managed care and managed competition, formation of integrated networks, and alterations in referral patterns.

The impact of healthcare reform on dietetics is mixed. Healthcare reform and growth in managed care and other integrated systems have positive implications for both prevention and medical nutrition therapies. New opportunities for management responsibilities may develop. On the other hand, nutrition services could be cut if managers do not document the cost-effectiveness of services. Regardless of the positive or negative effects of healthcare reform, dietary managers must be accountable for providing quality care. They must commit to use outcome information to change their practice behaviors, and they must be client focused. Practitioners must become more proactive, integrate more services into the community, and form alliances or networks that will place them in a strong position for change. In many cases, dietetics professionals will have to realign their services from nutrition specialties to primary care. Additionally, they must become more business-oriented. As managed care exerts greater influences on the profession, it will become more important to know how to position services in these new systems.

According to Sara C. Parks, MBA, RD, (past president of the American Dietetic Association), the following tactics should be seriously considered to take advantage of every opportunity, and to position dietetics practitioners as cost-effective providers: develop a vision and remain flexible; strengthen alliances with other providers; stay on the leading edge of the profession; document cost-effectiveness of services; keep all options open; understand; network, network, network! Additionally, for the profession to succeed in the information age, new relationships outside the traditional boundaries must be developed, for example, with business and industry, government agencies, and other allied health professionals.

Continuing Professional Education

Today's employers indicate that they want well-rounded individuals with a willingness to work hard, a sense of focus and a wide variety of skills. There are two areas critical to one's success in the foodservice industry: technical and management skills.

Technical Skills. The technical skills area includes all those skills needed to master the hands-on details of the job. All jobs have a technical component to them. The sooner you learn what is required of you technically, the faster you will be able to master a position and prepare for future challenges. The best way to improve any skill level is to practice and be persistent. Some commonly required technical skills essential to foodservice are the ability to:

- Operate computers (computer literacy);
- Perform financial analysis;
- Calculate statistics (cost-to-revenue ratios);
- Take and extend inventory;
- Staff planning and scheduling.

Management Skills. The foodservice industry is a service industry. Developing management skills that enables one to deal with people will save time and energy and will help reduce turnover. The following skills are well regarded in the industry:

- Effective communication (listening, as well as speaking and writing);
- Innovation and creativity;
- Leadership;
- Critical thinking and decision making;
- Customer relations;
- Negotiation and conflict management;
- Staff training and supervision.

It is important to find a balance between technical and managerial skills; neither should be undervalued. Managers who focus their energy only on the technical aspects of their operation and disregard people-management skills may find themselves alienating their employees and customers. On the other hand, managers who focus solely on people management skills, without attending to technical competencies, may fail to recognize trends or anticipate problem areas.

Professional development can take many forms: from degree programs, to hands-on learning, to management theory, to culinary appreciation. As a manager it will be helpful to understand the different types of training available. This may help in the selection of employees, or perhaps more importantly, help to suggest avenues through which existing staff can grow professionally and personally.

Professional Certifications. The Certified Dietary Manager (CDM) credential is offered by the Certifying Board for Dietary Managers. Eligibility to take this national examination requires completion of a 1- or 2-year program in dietetic foodservice management. Programs such as those offered by the National Restaurant Association's Educational foundation (EF) provides training, testing and certifying in critical food safety practices (including HACCP principles) as well as a diploma in management development and certification in a variety of other courses. Among the Educational Institute of the American Hotel & Motel Association (EI) certifications is the certified human resources executive (CHRE) designation.

Technical Programs. Technical or vocational programs, whether private or public, usually involve two years of full-time study (or equivalent coursework spread over a longer term for part-time students). Classes are tightly focused, and there are usually no requirements for competencies in English or exposure to the liberal arts courses. Such programs are often attractive to students who have already taken some college coursework and opted not to pursue a degree. Other candidates for such a concentrated approach are career changers anxious to gain expertise quickly en route to new employment. Students in such programs are given some exposure to management issues, but are not usually asked to demonstrate critical or abstract thinking skills.

Community College Programs. Community college programs usually are two-pronged. They offer practical training in a short time period but may also expect students to pursue a broader general education. Students who opt for a community college degree or certificate are required to demonstrate competencies in English, math, and general knowledge across the liberal arts. Community colleges have an advantage over most technical schools in the transferability of their credit hours toward a four-year university degree. This gives students the potential for "extra mileage" from their two years of coursework, should they decide to pursue a bachelor's degree.

Associate and Four-Year Programs. This extra-mileage advantage is shared by associate programs, a format offered by some four-year colleges. These, too, are usually two-year programs allowing the option of further work toward a bachelor's degree. Advantages include a degree or certification from a university (which some perceive as more prestigious than the equivalent from a community college). Disadvantages include a greater expense on average in enrollment costs per credit hour.

Four-year degrees from colleges and universities continue to be the most popular and perhaps financially viable degrees in the industry. Many fast-food chains now require college degrees for management recruits, as do many major lodging companies. Four-year programs offer the advantage of extended contact with the same faculty throughout the student's academic career.

Graduate Programs. Those who plan to pursue collegiate teaching and research, or who aspire to executive positions in national and multinational corporations and agencies may continue their education with master's and/or doctoral degrees. CHRIE (the Council on Hotel, Restaurant, and Institutional Education) lists more than 30 member schools here and abroad that offer graduate degrees in hospitality management; hotel, restaurant and/or institutional management; recreation and leisure; international tourism management; urban and regional planning; human nutrition and food systems; travel industry management, and so on.

Internships. One popular means of getting work experience while going to school is through internships. *Dun's Employment Opportunity Directory* provides listings (organized by industrial classification code) of companies that offer specialized training programs and internships. These are supervised, structured learning experiences. As an intern, one is given the opportunity to gain hands-on experience in an organization or company.

The intern will gain knowledge about the host organization. Progress and development will be monitored by a designated individual. Supervisors are also encouraged to include interns in a variety of meetings where they can observe decision-making and managerial styles—and offer input, if appropriate. It's not unusual for companies to implement changes in their policies or procedures based on interns' input.

An internship can be an excellent opportunity for an organization and a student to "test" each other. It can be a win-win experience for both parties. Students get a chance to find out if their expectations about the industry are well founded and whether or not they would consider the organization as a place of permanent employment after graduation. The company has the opportunity to find out whether or not the intern has the qualities, skills, and characteristics it desires in its employees.

Most internships in the dietary industry fall under one of three categories:

- Some corporations and larger operations have well-established, specially designed *structured internship programs.* Interns are provided with formal training in the form of seminars, meetings, and one-to-one supervision;
- Sometimes, operations offer students the opportunity to get involved in specific projects from beginning to end. These could include planning a promotion, launching an in-house employee program, converting departmental systems, or planning and helping execute a special event. Such *project-based in-*

ternships are invaluable, since interns become part of a team and see the results of their efforts by finishing a project;

- Most internships in a foodservice operation fall into the category of *rotational internships*. Interns are exposed to two or more aspects of an operation, either by rotating between departments or by rotating responsibilities within a single department.

SUMMARY

The concept of ethics relates to views and attitudes about what is "right" and "wrong." The dietary manager must know about and consistently practice the highest possible standards of ethics in all work and non-work related activities. This can be translated to mean that the dietary manager must practice in such a manner as to provide the most good for the least harm to the client.

The dietary manager should have a knowledge of legal and ethical principles of the federal, state, and local governments, as well as the ethics committee's guidelines within the facility. The dietary manager needs to: develop their personal code of ethics or adopt the code of ethics recommended by the Certifying Board for Dietary Managers.

Confidentiality means that the knowledge one has concerning a client must not be discussed with others. Clients and employees have a right to privacy. Maintaining confidentiality of information is part of ethical behavior.

The terms "ethics" and "professionalism" mean the same thing in many ways. The professional dietary manager who is dedicated to the client, the dietary department, and the facility within which he or she works will have a genuine concern to do "what is right." Additionally, the manager with a proper sense of ethics who is willing to seek advice and counsel from higher levels of administration at the first potential concern about a problem will be practicing the highest standards of ethics in institutional dietary services.

A recent survey by the Ethics Resource Center in Washington revealed that the existence of an ethics code and accompanying training and monitoring program led employees to take a more positive view of how the company behaves towards customers, suppliers and others. But where the company had an ethics code and no program, employee perceptions of their company's behavior tended to be even worse than in companies without any code. This can be explained by the widening gap between expectations and actions, which might occur if a code was adopted and not observed.

Ethics codes are not useful without a program of training and communication to back them up. The *Institute of Business Ethics* stresses that a code that is short and written in simple language to help employees deal with likely problems can be outlined in booklet form outlining the facility's group vision and priorities.

Professional associations at the local, regional, state, and/or national levels are an external public with which dietary managers must interact. The common interests of association members dealing with governmental representation, education/training, availability of insurance programs, and so on, all point to benefits derived from active involvement with associations. Every area of specialization has a professional organization designed to inform members of current trends and to monitor or establish industry standards of professionalism.

The structure of the healthcare industry is changing so rapidly that past predictions of employment trends are not appropriate for future professional roles. A growing number of forces and trends will dramatically reshape the healthcare industry and the practice of dietetics. Understanding and responding to these trends will determine how the profession will survive in the future and how dietetics practitioner will compete in this new healthcare environment. Five major forces will reshape career opportunities in the ongoing battle to mange change and to deal successfully with healthcare reform:

- Downsizing in hospitals;
- Emergence of mergers and coalitions;
- Shift toward managed care and managed competition;
- Formation of integrated networks;
- Alterations in referral patterns.

The impact of healthcare reform on dietetics is mixed. Healthcare reform and growth in managed care and other integrated systems have positive implications for both prevention and medical nutrition therapies. Dietetic professionals must be accountable for providing quality care, they must commit to using outcome information to change their practice behaviors, and they must be client focused. Practitioners must become more proactive, integrate more services into the community, and form alliances or networks that will place them in a strong position for change. As managed care exerts greater influences on the profession, it will become more important to know how to position services in these new systems.

According to Sara C. Parks, MBA, RD, (past president of American Dietetic Association), to take advantage of every opportunity and to position dietetics practitioners as cost-effective providers, the following tactics should be considered:

- Develop a vision and remain flexible;
- Strengthen alliances with other providers;
- Stay on the leading edge of the profession;
- Document cost-effectiveness of services;
- Keep all options open;
- Understand;
- Network, network, network.

Today's employers say they want well-rounded individuals with a willingness to work hard, a sense of focus, and a wide variety of skills. The two areas critical to success in the foodservice industry are *technical* and *management* skills.

Professional development can take many forms. As a manager it will be helpful to understand the different types of training available. They are:

- Professional certifications;
- Technical programs;
- Community college programs;
- Associate and four-year programs;
- Graduate programs;
- Internships.

KEY TERMS

Ethics
Confidentiality
Ethics code
Professional association
Continuing professional education
Educational Foundation (EF)
Educational Institute (EI)
The International Association of Convention and Visitor Bureau (IACVB)
Technical programs
Community-college programs
Associate and four-year programs
Graduate programs
Dun's Employment Opportunity Directory
Internship

QUESTIONS/PROBLEMS/CASES

1. As dietary manager of a small foodservice operation, you are responsible for purchasing several thousand dollars' worth of perishable and nonperishable items for your facility. In order to get your business, a supplier offers you a substantial bargain on a house. You can live in the house, which will be under another person's name, for as long as you continue to buy from this supplier. The quality of this supplier's products and services are equal to the others. What should you do with the offer?

2. As dietary manager, it is your responsibility to explain and interpret the facility code of conduct to employees. Using a copy of a facility code of conduct, evaluate the code for inclusion of the facility vision and priorities, guidance on conduct, and achievement of goals. Does it give direction on conflict of interest, giving or receiving gifts, confidentiality, environmental pollution, health and safety, equal opportunities, sexual harassment, moonlighting, and political activity? Is the code short, and written in simple language?

3. Locate a magazine published by a professional association in your field of interest. Clip an article providing new information in the improvement of dietary services; an advertisement for an upcoming seminar; an article in which the member is able to promote his/her specific facility simply by being affiliated with it. What other benefits do you see in being a member in a professional association?

4. Refer to the *five major forces* that will reshape career opportunities in the ongoing battle to manage change and to deal successfully with heathcare reform listed in the chapter. List each force, and include your own prediction on how each one might affect your own chosen career.

5. Read the Code of Ethics for Certified Dietary Managers. Summarize its points.

6. Why is it important to find a balance between technical and managerial skills in management today?

7. You are the dietary manager of a small facility and your employees ask your professional opinion concerning professional development. What would you tell the employee who:

   a) would like to obtain an executive position in national or multinational corporations and agencies?

   b) isn't interested in obtaining a degree, but is anxious to gain expertise quickly?

   c) would like hands-on experience in a supervised setting while going to school?

   d) is interested in management eventually?

   e) is satisfied working in a reputable facility?

APPENDIX

- A. Code of Ethics
- B. Food Guide Pyramid
- C. Dietary Manager References
  Articles
  Journals
  Reference Books
- D. Dietary Manager Resources
  Healthcare Information Organizations
  Food Resource Organizations
  Government Agencies

A

Code of Ethics

Governing Conduct of Certified Dietary Managers from Certifying Board For Dietary Managers

The Certified Dietary Manager

1. Provides professional services with the objectivity and respect for the unique needs and values of individuals.
2. Avoids discrimination against individuals on the basis of race, creed, religion, gender, age and national origin.
3. Fulfills professional commitments in good faith.
4. Conducts himself/herself with honesty, integrity and fairness.
5. Remains free of conflict of interest while fulfilling the objectives and maintaining the integrity of the Certified Dietary Manager profession.
6. Practices dietary management based on professional principles and current information.
7. Assumes responsibility and accountability for personal and professional competence and practice in the foodservice industry.
8. Maintains confidentiality of information obtained in the performance of his/her duties.
9. Recognizes and exercises professional judgment within the limits of his/her qualifications and seeks counsel or makes referrals as appropriate.
10. Provides sufficient information to enable clients to make personal, informed decisions.
11. Utilizes products in a manner that is neither false nor misleading.
12. Permits use of his/her name for the purpose of certifying that dietary services have been rendered only if he/she has supervised or assisted in the provisions of those services.
13. Accurately presents professional qualifications and credentials.
    a. The Certified Dietary Manager uses eithers the full title, Certified Dietary Manager, or its abbreviation, "CDM", and maintains current certification authorized by the Certifying Board for Dietary Managers.
    b. The Certified Dietary Manager provides accurate information and complies with all requirements of the Certifying Board's certification program in which he/she is seeking initial or continued credentialing from the Certifying Board for Dietary Managers.

c. The Certified Dietary Manager shall not aid another person in violating any Certifying Board certification requirements nor aiding another person in misrepresenting that third party as a Certified Dietary Manager.

14. Presents information generally accepted within the foodservice industry and interprets experimental information without personal bias, recognizing that legitimate differences of opinion may exist.

15. Makes all reasonable efforts to avoid bias in professional evaluations in the foodservice industry. The CDM provides objective evaluation of candidates for professional association memberships, awards, scholarships or job advancement.

16. Accepts the obligation to protect society and the profession by upholding the Code of Ethics and by reporting alleged violations of the Code to the Certifiying Board for Dietary Managers.

B

Food Guide Pyramid
A Guide to Daily Food Choices

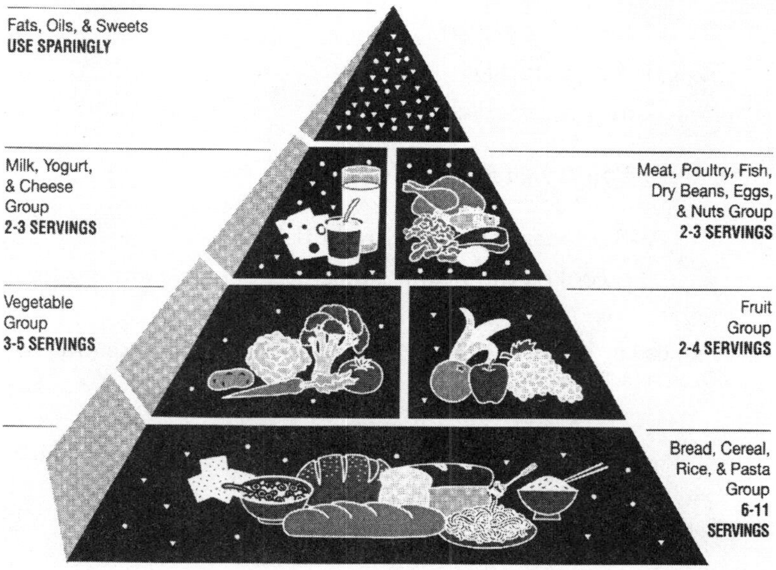

Source: USDA/HNIS, 1992.

How Many Servings Do You Need?

(Guidelines apply to ages 2 and older.)

	Sedentary Women, Older Adults	Children, Teenage Girls, Active Women Sedentary Men	Teenage Boys, Active Men, Very Active Women
Grains	6	9	11
Vegetables	3	4	5
Fruit	2	3	4
Milk	2–3	2–3	2–3
Meat (oz.)	5	6	7
Fat (g.)	53	73	93

What Counts as a Serving?

Bread, Cereals, Rice, Pasta
See checklist opposite side.

Vegetables

- 1 c. raw leafy vegetables
- ½ c. cooked or chopped vegetables
- ¾ c. juice

Fruit

- 1 medium apple, banana, orange
- ½ c. chopped, cooked, canned
- ¾ c. juice

Milk, Yogurt, Cheese

- 1 c. milk or yogurt
- 1-½ oz. natural cheese
- 2 oz. processed cheese

Meats, Poultry, Fish, Dry Beans, Eggs, Nuts

- 2–3 oz. lean meat, poultry or fish
- ½ c. cooked dry beans, 1 egg, or 2 Tbsp. peanut butter count as 1 oz. lean meat.

Provided by the Kansas LEAN Food Professionals Task Force (316) 838-6755 and the Wheat Foods Council (303) 694-5828.

C

Dietary Manager References

Articles

Allinson, Robert Elliott, "A Call for Ethically-Centered Management," *Academy of Management Executive*, Feb. 1995.

Alperin, Diane E. and Nicholas Richie, "Continuing/Life Care Facilities and the Continuum of Care," *Journal of Housing for the Elderly*, 1990.

Anderson-Miles, Eleanor, "Benchmarking in Healthcare Organizations: An Introduction," *Healthcare Financial Management*, Sept. 1994.

Anonymous, "Challenge: How to Manage Food Purchasing Costs Better," *Food Management*, Aug. 1994.

Anonymous, "Food for Thought," *Nation's Restaurant News*, Jan. 1994, p. 9.

Bartlett, Michael, "Restaurants & Institutions' 1996 Annual Forecast," *Restaurant & Institutions*, Jan. 1996.

Bauman, Howard, "HACCP: Concept, Development and Application," *Food Technology*, May 1990.

Benitez, Ben, "Reinvention Battle Must Continue and Must be Won," *Public Manager*, 1995.

Bliesmer, Mary and Pat Earle, "Research Consideration: Nursing Home Quality Perceptions," *Journal of Gerontological Nursing*, June 1993.

Boss, Donna and Mitchell Schechter, "Visions: Today's Trends, Tomorrow's Possibilities," *Food Management*, Sept. 1994.

Boss, Donna, Mitchell Schechter and Gerald White, "A Meeting of the Minds," *Food Management*, Sept. 1995.

Brent, Nancy J., "Risk Management and Legal Issues in Home Care: The Utilization of Nursing Staff, *JOGNN*, Oct. 1994.

Bruno, Ronald, "Policy for the People: One Facility's Introduction to Restraint Reduction," *Journal of Gerontological Social Work*, 1994.

Capozzalo, Gayle, John Hlywak Jr., Barbara Kenny and Charles Krivenko, "Experts Discuss How Benchmarking Improves the Healthcare Industry," *Healthcare Financial Management*, Sept. 1994.

Caudron, Shari, "Diversity Ignites Effective Work Teams," *Personnel Journal*, Sept. 1994.

Chellis, Robert, Margaret Kelly and Michael Steininger, "Assistance in Living Assures Aging in Place," *Caring Magazine*, Oct. 1994.

Cofer, Jennifer, Hugh Greeley and Jay Coburn, *Information Management: A Guide to the JCAHO Standards*, Opus Communications, Marblehead, MA.

Cohen, Camille, Richard Neufeld, Joan Dunbar, Linda Pflug and Brenda Breuer, "Old Problem, Different Approach: Alternatives to Physical Restraints," *Journal of Gerontological Nursing*, Feb. 1996.

Corlett, Jr., Donald A., "Regulatory Verification of Industrial HACCP Systems," *Food Technology*, April 1991.

Couchman, MSc, BA, CSS, Wendy, "Joint Education for Mental Health Teams," *Nursing Standard*, Vol. 10, Nov. 1995.

Cornyn, John, Joyce Coons-Fasano and Mitchell Schechter, *Noncommercial Foodservice: An Administrator's Handbook*, John Wiley & Sons, Inc., New York.

Curry-Baggett Patricia, "Long-Term Care: Resolution of a Dilemma?" *Nursing Management*, March 1996.

De Marzo, Denise Liotta, "Policies and Procedures: Protection or Peril?" *RN*, July 1993.

DeYoung, Sandra, Gloria Just and Robert Van Dyk, "Assisted Living: Policy Implications for Nursing," *Nursing & Health Care*, Dec. 1994.

Editors, "The Non-Commercial Operator as Brand Manager," *Food Management*, March 1996.

Funk, Kristine and Celeste Ayton, "Improving Malnutrition Documentation Enhances Reimbursement," *Journal of the Dietetic Association*, April 1995.

Gift, Robert, Tom Stoddart and Kirk Wilson, "Collaborative Benchmarking in a Healthcare System," *Healthcare Financial Management*, Sept. 1994.

Ginsberg, Michele, "Foodhandlers and the Need to Test for AIDS," *Journal of Environmental Health*, 51:378.

HCFA RULINGS, U. S. Government 1996-404-792/43463, Dept. of Health and Human Services, March 1996.

Hensel, Terry, "OBRA Regulations," *Topics in Geriatric Rehabilitation*, Sept. 1995.

Just, Gloria, Sandra DeYoung and Robert Van Dyk, "Assisted Living: Challenges for Nursing Practice," *Geriatric Nursing*, Jul./Aug. 1995.

Kasavana, Michael, "Computers and Multiunit Food-Service Operations," *The Cornell Quarterly*, June 1994, pp. 72–79.

Keegan, Peter, "Sullivan: Training for Change and the Future," *Nation's Restaurant News*, Oct. 1994.

Klevans, Deborah R. and Joan Parrett, "Continuing Professional Education Needs of Clinical Dietitians in Pennsylvania," *Journal of the American Dietetic Association*, Feb. 1990.

Knight, John B. and Lendal H. Kotschevar, *Quantity Food Production, Planning and Management*, Van Nostrand Reinhold, New York, 1989.

Knox, Margaret, Janie Heath, Janet Nussbaum and Rachel Franklin, "Acute Care Advanced Practice Nurse: A New Program in Response to Health Care Reform," *The South Carolina Nurse*, July-Aug.-Sept. 1994.

Krasker, Glenn and Lucy Balogun, "(1995) JCAHO Standards: Development and Relevance to Dietetics Practice," *Journal of the American Dietetic Association*, Feb. 1995.

Kushner, Robert, Elizabeth Ayello, Peter Beyer, Annalynn Skipper, Charles Van Way III, Eleanor Young and Lucy Balogun, "National Coordinating Committee Clinical Indicators of Nutrition Care," *Journal of the American Dietetic Association*, Oct. 1994.

Letort, Nancy and Jane Boudreaux, "Incorporation of Continuous Quality Improvement in a Hospital Dietary Department's Quality Management Program," *Journal of the American Dietetic Association*, Dec. 1994, Vol. 94, Number 12, pp. 1404–1408.

Lorenzini, Beth, "A Trio of Trends to Bank On," *Restaurants & Institutions*, Feb. 1996.

Mayfield, Barbara K., "Line-Item Versus Prime Vendor Purchasing," *Journal of the American Dietetic Association*, June 1984.

McCormack, James, "Good Ethics, Smart Tactics-Avoiding the Top 10 Grievance-Prone Mistakes," *Law Practice Management*, Sept. 1995.

McWilliams, Brian, "What's Wrong with Benchmarking," *CFO*, May 1995.

Miller, Jack E., Mary Porter and Karen Eich Drummond, *Supervision in the Hospitality Industry*, John Wiley & Sons, Inc., 1992.

Moore, Shirley, Marilee Kuhrik, Nancy Kuhrik and Barry Katz, "Coping with Downsizing: Stress, Self-Esteem & Social Intimacy," *Nursing Management*, March 1996.

Orta, John, "Training Food Service Supervisors Using Hand-Held Computers to Conduct Nutritional Screening of Institutional Elderly Patients," *Journal of Nutrition for the Elderly*, Vol. 14, 1995.

Parks, Sara C., "President's Page: Creating Your Future-Career Opportunities in an Era of Change," *Journal of the American Dietetic Association*, April 1994.

Partlow, Charles, "How Ritz-Carlton Applies 'TQM,'" *The Cornell Quarterly*, Aug. 1993, pp. 16–24.

Pickard, Jane, "Prepare to Make a Moral Judgment," People Magazine, May 1995.

Rosenblum, Robert, "Medicare Revisited: A Look through the Past to the Future," *Journal of Health Politics, Policy and Law*, Vol. 9, 1985.

Scarlett, Thomas, "An HACCP Approach to Product Liability," *Food Technology*, June 1991.

Schultz, Barry, Jan Blustein, Mark Kator and James Knickman, "Improving Access to Long-Term Care for Persons with AIDS: Contrasting the Need for Acute Care with the Need for Functional Assistance," *AIDS & Public Policy Journal*, Vol. 9, Spr. 1994.

Shechter, Mitchell, "Five Legal Pitfalls Every Operator Needs to Avoid," *Food Management*, April 1996.

Spath, Margaret and Lois Buttlar, "Information and Research Needs of Acute-Care Clinical Nurses," *Bulletin of the Medical Library Association*, Jan. 1996.

Sperber, William H., "The Modern HACCP System," *Food Technology*, June 1991.

Steele, Shirley, "Deinstitutionalization of Persons with Mental Retardation/Developmental Disabilities," *Issues in Comprehensive Pediatric Nursing*, Vol. 10, 1987.

Stephenson, Susie, "Baby Boomers Do Health," *Restaurants & Institutions*, Feb. 1996.

Stepp, Judy, "OBRA Provides Guidelines for Quality Assurance Programs," *Provider*, March 1990.

Stevenson, K. E., "Implementing HACCP in the Food Industry," *Food Technology*, May 1990.

Tisler, John M., "The Food and Drug Administration's Perspective on HACCP," *Food Technology*, June 1991.

Van Hoop, Hubert, Marilyn McDonald, Lawrence Yu and Gary Vallen, "A Host of Opportunities: An Introduction to Hospitality Management," IRWIN, 1996.

Virani, T., "Making Policy and Procedure Systems Work Effectively," *Canadian Journal of Nursing Administration*, Jan. 1996.

Woods, Robert and Michael Sciarini, "Diversity Programs in Chain Restaurants," *The Cornell Quarterly*, June 1995.

Zimmer, James, Gerald Eggert, Anne Treat and Belinda Brodows, "Nursing Homes as Acute Care Providers-A Pilot Study of Incentives to Reduce Hospitalizations," *Journal of the American Geriatrics Society*, Vol. 36, Feb. 1988.

JOURNALS

American Journal of Nursing
American Journal of Nursing Co.
555 West 57th Street
New York, New York 10019

Chef Institutional
Talcott Communication Corp.
20 N. Wacker Dr. #3230
Chicago, Illinois 60606

Cooking for Profit
Post Office Box 267
Fond du Lac, Wisconsin 54935

Dietary Manager Magazine
Dietary Managers Association
One Pierce Place #1220W
Itasca, Illinois 60143

Dietetic Currents
Ross Laboratories
625 Cleveland Avenue
Columbus, Ohio 43216

Food Management
Advanstar Communications
270 Madison Avenue
New York, New York 10017

Foodservice Director
Bill Communications, Inc.
633 Third Avenue
New York, New York 10017

Geriatric Nursing
American Journal of Nursing
555 West 57th Street
New York, New York 10019

Hospital Food & Nutrition Focus
Apsen Publishes, Inc.
7201 McKinney Circle
Frederick Maryland 21701

Journal of the American Dietetic Association
American Dietetic Association
216 W. Jackson Boulevard, Suite 800
Chicago, Illinois 60606-6995

Journal of Nutrition for the Elderly
Haworth Press, Inc.
28 East 22nd Street
New York, New York 10010

Nursing Homes
Centaur and Company
5 Willowbrook Court
Potomacton, Maryland 20854

Nutrition and the MD
PM, Inc
14349 Victory Boulevard #204
Van Nuys, California 91401

Restaurants and Institutions
Cahners Publishing Company
1350 East Touhy Avenue
Des Plaines, Illinois 60017-5080

The Stokes Report
Judy Ford Stokes and Associates, Inc.
2041 West Wesley Road NW
Atlanta, Georgia 30327

Topics in Clinical Nutrition
Aspen Publishers, Inc.
7201 McKinney Circle
Frederick, Maryland 21701

REFERENCE BOOKS

Covey, S.R., 1990
The 7 Habits of Effective People
Simon Schuster, New York

Deming, W.E., 1986
Out of Crisis
Massachusetts Institute of Technology
Center for Advanced Engineering Study, Cambridge, Massachusetts

Drummond, K., 1997
Diet Therapy for the Dietary Manager
Dietary Managers Association, Itasca, Illinois

Gabor, A., 1990
The Man Who Discovered Quality
Random House, New York

Hilgert, C. and Harmann T., 1991
Supervision: Concepts and Practices of Management, 5th edition
South-Western Publishing, Cincinnati, Ohio

Inservice Manual, 1991
Consultant Dietitians in Healthcare Facilities, Pensacola, Florida

Ninemeier, J., 1990
Professional Procurement Practices
Dietary Managers Association, Itasca, Illinois

Beyers, B., Hoover, L., and Shanklin, C., 1994
Foodservice Manual for Healthcare Institutions, 2nd edition
American Hospital Association Publishing, Chicago

Puckett, R. and Brown, S., 1992
Shands Hospital at the University of Florida Guide to Clinical Dietetics
Kendall/Hunt Publishing Company, Dubuque, Iowa

Rinke, W., 1990
The Winning Foodservice Manager
Dietary Managers Association, Itasca, Illinois

Rinke, W., 1997.
Winning Management: Six Failsafe Strategies for Building High Performance Organizations
Dietary Managers Association, Itasca, Illinois

Robinson, C. H. and Weigley, E. S., 1989
Basic Nutrition and Diet Therapy, 6th edition
Macmillen Publishing, New York

Sullivan, C., 1990
Management of Medical Foodservice, 2nd edition
Van Nostrand Reinhold, New York

Walton, M., 1990
The Deming Management
Putnam Publishing Group, New York

Zaccarelli, H., 1991
Food Service Management by Checklist
John Wiley, New York

D

Dietary Manager Resources

Healthcare Information Organizations

American College of Healthcare Executives
1 North Franklin St. #1700
Chicago, IL 60606
Telephone: 312/424-2800
- Publishers of the *Healthcare Forum Journal*

American Health Information Management Association (AHIMA)
919 North Michigan, Suite 1400
Chicago, IL 60611
Telephone: 312/787-2672
- Publishers of the *Journal of the American Health Information Management Association*
- Offers seminars on information management

Center for Healthcare Information Management (CHIM)
3800 Packard Rd #150
Ann Arbor, MI 48108
Telephone: 313/973-6116
Fax: 313/973-6996

College of Healthcare Information Management Executives (CHIME)
3300 Washenaw Ave. #225
Ann Arbor, MI 48104
Telephone: 313/665-0000
Fax: 313/665-4922

Hospitals: The Magazine for Health Care Executives
American Hospital Publishing, Inc.
737 N. Michigan Avenue
Chicago, IL 60611
Telephone: 312/440-6800

Information Week: The Newsmagazine for Information Management
CMP Media, Inc.
600 Community Drive
Manhasset, NY 11030
Telephone: 516/562-5000

Inside Healthcare Computing
3600 South Harbor Blvd., Suite 220
Oxnard, CA 93035
Telephone: 805/984-8500

M.D. Computing
Springer-Verlag New York, Inc.
175 Fifth Avenue
New York, NY 10010
Telephone: 800/777-4643

Modern Healthcare
Crain Communications, Inc.
740 N. Rush Street
Chicago, IL 60611-2590
Telephone: 312/649-5200

Opus Communications
P.O. Box 1168
Marblehead, MA 01945
Telephone: 617/639-1872
Fax: 617/639-2982

- Publishers of the following newsletters, books, and manuals:
  Briefings on Hospital Safety (monthly)
  Briefings on JCAHO (monthly)
  Briefings on Long-Term Care Regulations (monthly)
  Briefings on Practice Management (monthly)
  Briefings on Subacute Care (monthly)
  Effective Survey Preparation Workbook and Guide, Volume I
  Effective Survey Preparation Guide for the Medical Staff, Volume II
  Health Information Management: Challenges and Solutions
  Quality Improvement Techniques for Hospital Society
  Quality Improvement Techniques for Long-Term Care
  Quality Improvement Techniques for Medical Records

The Quality Letter for Healthcare Leaders
Bader & Associates
P.O. Box 2106
Rockville, MD 20847-2106
Telephone: 301/468-1610
Fax: 301/770-4919

Quality Progress
American Society for Quality Control
611 East Wisconsin Avenue
Milwaukee, WI 53202
Telephone: 414/272-8575
Fax: 414/272-1734

Quality Review Bulletin
Joint Commission on Accreditation of Healthcare Organizations
One Renaissance Blvd.
Oakbrook Terrace, IL 60181
Telephone: 630/792-5000

QRC Advisor
Topics in Health Information Management
Topics in Health Record Management
Aspen Publishers, Inc.
7201 McKinney Circle
Frederick, MD 21701
Telephone: 800/234-1660

Food Resource Organizations

ORGANIZATION & ADDRESS	SUBJECT
American Egg Board 1460 Renaissance Drive Park Ridge, IL 60068 847-296-7043	Diet-Wise Tips. Egg nutrition and cholesterol. Egg handling, preparation tips, cookery problems, food safety, specifications, purchasing and menus. Salmonella and egg safety and special risk audiences.
American Heart Association 7320 Greenville Avenue Dallas, TX 75231 214-750-5362	Creative Cuisine Recipes
American Sheep Industry Asso. 6911 South Yosemite St. Englewood, CO 80112-1414 303-771-3500	Recipes, various cuts and charts. Cooking methods. Video tapes and slide sets. Posters and brochures.
American Spice Trade Association Box 1267 Englewood Cliffs, NJ 07632 201-568-2163	Information and recipes using spices.
Beef Foodservice Dept. **National Cattlemen's Beef Assoc.** 444 N Michigan Ave. Chicago, IL 60611 312-467-5520	Safety Guidelines on storage, handling and preparation. Beef Recipes, Rubs and Marinades.
Beans of the West **California Dried Bean Advisory Board** P O Box 943 531-D North Alta Dinuba, CA 93618 209-591-4866	Recipes.
California Apricot Advis. Board Department APB 1280 Boulevard Way Walnut Creek, CA 94595	Nutrition Guide. Fruit Nutrition Calculator.
California Avocados 1251 E. Dyer, Ste. 200 Santa Ana, CA 92705 714-558-6761	Recipes. Health benefits. Storage and handling.
California Fig Advisory Board 3425 N. First Street, Suite 109 Fresno, CA 93726	Nutrients and health benefits. Recipes.

California Fresh Carrot Advisory Board
15 Willow Street
Salinas, CA 93901
408-753-2354 (Phone & Fax)

Recipes. Storage and handling. Nutrition. Recommended Daily Allowances. Disease Preventions. Nutrient profile. Posters. Fact Sheet. Industry Video. Grades K–6 Activity Sheets (reproducible).

California Olive Industry
1903 North Fine, #102
Fresno, CA 93727

Salad recipes. Olive facts on calories and fat.

California Prune Board
P O Box 10157
Pleasanton, CA 94588-0157
510-734-0150
510-734-0525 FAX

Nutrients. Fiber facts for a healthier you. Recipes. Poster. Ways to Prune the Fat.

California Strawberry Comm.
P O Box 269
Watsonville, CA 95077
408-724-1301
408-724-5973 FAX

Posters, Recipe cards. Handling fresh and frozen strawberries. Nutrition facts. Tips on fresh and frozen. Thawing, and food cost analysis.

Canned Fruit Promotion Service
P O Box 7111
San Francisco, CA 94120

Nutritional information. Syrup designation and brix measurement. Adult and Healthcare (Posters, diets, recipe cards, brochures, clip art, Menu special sheets. Healthcare kit (Heart-healthy with canned fruit, recipes, food guide pyramid, buying guide, and merchandising tips brochure.) Videos.

The Culinary Institute of America
433 Albany Post Road
Hyde Park, NY 12538-1499
800-285-8280
914-451-1078 FAX

Baking bread. Nutritional cuisine, table and wine service, basic culinary skills and sanitation. Videotapes and software. Knife skill videos and recipe costing videos.

Dairy Management Inc/ American Dairy Association
P O Box 2018
Brownsdale, MN 55918
800-454-COWS

Recipes. Tips for proper storage and handling on butter. Cheese board tips.

Egg Nutrition Center
1819 H. St.,
N W Suite 520
Washington, DC 20006
202-833-8850

Healthy habits, prevention, weight control hints, benefits of exercise, heart disease links, fat limit. Fiber facts and healthy strategies for healthier bones. Vitamin supplement and good nutrition. Ways to cut fat.

General Foods
250 North Street
White Plains, NY 10625
914-335-3381

Recipes using sugar-free Jello-O and puddings.

Idaho Bean Commission P O Box 9433 Boise, ID 83707 208-334-3520	Recipes.
Idaho Potato Commission P O Box 1068 Boise, ID 83701 800-824-4605 208-334-2350	Recipes & Toppings. Storage & Preparation. Times & Preparation. Set Up & Production. Nutrition & Menu Ideas. Spa Series calorie-controlled quantity recipes.
Malaysian Palm Oil Council of America, Inc. John Hancock Center, Suite 2644 875 N. Michigan Ave. Chicago, IL 60611 312-944-3180/3296 312-944-1272 Fax 102533.3535@compuserve.com (E-Mail)	Facts on Natural Palm Oil vs Partially Hydrogenated Fat.
Maine Potato Board 744 Main Street Presque Isle, ME 04769 207-769-5061	Recipes
Moore's Food Products (appetizers) 1221 Broadway Oakland, CA 94612 800-556-1234	Recipes.
Nabisco Brands **Foodservice Division** **Marketing Department** 100 DeForest Avenue East Hanover, NJ 07936	Recipes using Egg Beater, Cholesterol-free 99% Real Egg Product.
National Association of Meat Purveyors 1920 Association Drive Suite 400 Reston, VA 22091-1547 703-758-1900	Meat Buyers Guide (Meat purchase specifications).
National Cherry Foundation 190 Queen Ann N. Seattle, WA 98109 206-285-7082	Recipes.
National Dairy Council 10255 W. Higgins Rd., Suite 900 Rosemont, IL 60018-5616 847-803-2000, x 220 800-974-6455 FAX	Calorie catalog. Women's guide to health and nutrition. Poster. Food and activity record. Getting along with milk. Pregnancy calendar. Growth record leaflet. Videotape with teachers guide. Charts

National Fisheries Ind. Inc. 1525 Wilson Blvd. Suite 500 Arlington, VA 22209	Nutrition Chart. Guidelines for purchasing, storage and preparation. Benefits.
National Fisheries Institute Inc. 2000 M. Street, NW., Suite 580 Washington, DC 20036 202-296-3428	Recipes using nutritious fish.
National Live Stock & Meat Board 444 N Michigan Ave. Chicago, IL 60611 312-467-5520	Foodservice cuts of beef and veal.
National Pasta Association 2101 Wilson Blvd., Suite 920 Arlington, VA 22201 703-841-0818	Nutrients. Recipes.
National Peanut Council 1500 King Street Suite 301 Alexandria, VA 22314-2737 703-838-9500	Nutrition (Fat calories, saturated fats, cholesterol sodium and dietary fiber). Recipes.
National Pork Producers Council PO Box 10383 Des Moines, IA 50306 515-223-2600 515-223-2646 FAX	Recipes. Audio Visual Aids. Breading and Genetics. Nutrition and quality. Health and safety. Posters and Videotapes.
National Sunflower Association 4023 North State Street P O Box 2533 Bismarck, ND 58502	Recipes.
National Turkey Federation 11319 Sunset Hills Road Reston, VA 22090	Recipes
North American Blueberry Council P O Box 166 Marmora, NJ 08223 609-399-1559	Recipes.
Ocean Spray Cranberry Water St. Plymouth, MA 02360 617-747-1000	Recipes.
Pacific Coast Canned Pear Serv. P O Box 7111 San Francisco, CA 94120	Nutrition kit (Grades 4–6). (Food guide pyramid, worksheets, posters, certificate, coloring book and game cards.) Cafeteria kit (posters, recipes).

Peanut Advisory Board 1133 Avenue of the Americas New York, NY 10036 212-536-8787	Recipes.
Potato Board 1385 South Colorado Blvd., #512 Denver, CO 80222 303-399-8130	Recipes.
Produce for Better Health Foundation 1500 Casho Mill Rd P O Box 6035 Newark, DE 19714-6035 302-738-7100 302-738-4825 Fax	Five Servings of fruits and vegetables a day. Low and non-fat sauces or dressings. Low fat menu items.
Product Marketing Association 700 Barksdale Plaza Newark, DE 19711	Food For You Series includes nutritious recipes.
Retailer's Bakery Association 14239 Park Center Drive Laurel, Maryland 20707 301-725-2149 800-638-0924 301-725-2187 FAX	How to get started. Job opportunities and Pay. Working conditions. Education and Certification. Owning your own baking business.
Rice Council of America P O Box 740121 Houston, TX 72274 713-270-6699	Recipes.
Soyfoods Association of America P O Box 3179 Walnut Creek, CA 94598	Top 10 benefits of soyfood. Soyfoods and Cancer. Soyfoods and Your Heart.
Sugar Association, Inc. 1101 15th St., NW Washington, DC 20005 202-785-1122	Leaflets (Low Fat, Fiber, Calories, Diabetes, Snacking, Picky Eaters, Heart-healthy Eating, Tips on Weight Measurement, Nutrition and Aging, Sports Nutrition and Weight Management). Nutrition and Fitness brochure for children ages 4–8. Recipes. Handbooks provide guidelines for evaluation of nutrition and food studies. Videos (Fat and Nutrition VNR, B-Roll Tape).
Tea Council of the USA 230 Park Avenue New York, NY 10169 212-986-6998	Health benefits. Types of tea.

Uncle Ben's Inc. P O Box 1752 Houston, TX 77251-1752 713-674-9484	Recipes.
USA Dry Pea & Lentil Council 5071 Hwy 8 West Moscow, Idaho 83843-4023 208-882-3023	Recipes for split peas, lentils and chickpeas.
USA Rice Council P O Box 740123 Houston, TX 77274 USA 713-270-6699 713-270-9021 FAX	Nutrition. Recipes. Food Guide Pyramid.
The Vegetarian Resource Group P O Box 1463 Baltimore, MD 21203 410-366-VEGE	Vegetarian nutrition for teenagers. Vegan diets. Heart healthy eating tips. The Vegetarian Res. Group. Handy Foodservice tips for vegetarian cooking. Product listing. Tips for introducing vegetarian food into institutions. Vegetarian Journal (Vegan diet during pregnancy, lactation and childhood. Position of The American Dietetic Association Vegetarian diets.Vegetarianism in a nutshell (Making the change to a vegetarian diet). What's in your Cheese (Why wouldn't cheese be Vegetarian). I love animals and broccoli shopping basket. The Vegetarian Resource Group's Annual Essay Contest. Vegetarian Journal Health Ecology Ethics. Books, pamphlets, posters, bumer stickers and post cards.
Walnut Marketing Board 55 Union Street San Francisco, CA 94111 415-984-6240	Recipes.
Washington Apple Commission P O Box 18 Wenatchee, WA 98807 590-663-9600 509-662-5824 FAX	Recommended uses for apples. Nutrition Facts. Storage and handling. Grade size.
Washington State Potato Commission 108 Interlake Road Moses Lake, WA 98837 509-765-8845	Recipes.
Welchs Grape Juice 100 Main St. Concord, MA 01742 617-371-1000	Recipes.

Wheat Foods Council
5500 S Quebec, Suite 111
Englewood, CO 80111
303-694-5828
303-694-5807 FAX

What are Wheat Foods. Why Eat Wheat. Dietary Guidelines.

Wild Blueberry Assoc. of North America
59 Cottage Street
PO Box 180
Bar Harbor, ME 04609-0180
207-288-2655
800-ADD-WILD
207-288-2656 Fax

Nutrition facts. Recipes. Poster.

Government Agencies

Center for Food Safety & Applied Nutrition
200 C Street SW, Rm. 6815
Washington, D.C. 20204-0001
Information & Assistance (202) 205-4850

Office of Food Labeling: Division of Programs & Enforcement Policy (202) 205-5229

Division of Pesticides & Industrial Chemicals (202) 205-4036

Division of HACCP Programs (202) 205-4231

Environmental Protections Agency
401 M Street SW
Washington, D.C. 20460
Information & Assistance (202) 260-2090

Food & Drug Administration
5600 Fishers Lane
Rockville, MD 20857
Information & Assistance (301) 443-1544
Office of Public Affairs (301) 443-1130

Occupational Safety & Health Administration (OSHA)
U.S. Department of Labor
200 Constitution Avenue NW, Rm. N 3647
Washington, D.C. 20210
Information & Assistance (202) 219-8148
Emergency Hotline (800) 321-OSHA

U.S. Department of Agriculture
12th St. & Jefferson Drive SW
Washington, D.C. 20250
Information & Assistance (202) 720-2791

The Food & Nutrition Service (703) 305-2062

Food Safety & Inspection Services (202) 720-7025

Meat & Poultry Hotline (202) 720-3333

Agriculture & Agri-Food Canada
Headquarters:
930 Carling Avenue
Ottawa, Ontario, CAN K1A 0C5
(613) 759-1000

INDEX

A

A la carte menu, 46, 47
ABC analysis, 157–58
Absolute standard evaluation (Figure), 366
Absolute standards performance review, 361–62
Accidents, causes and prevention of, 93–98. *See also* Hazards *and* Safety
  burns, 93–94
  choppers, 98
  cuts, 95
  deck ovens, 96
  electrical, 95–96
  falls, 94
  fryers, 97–98
  kettles, 97
  mixers, 98
  pans, 97
  ranges, 96
  slicers, 98
  steamers, 97
Accounting, 128–39
  large operations, 130–34
  payment policies, 136
  price reduction, 134–36
  small operations, 129
  supplier selection, 136–39
Administrative management, 277–501
AIDS, 34, 90
All-purpose oven (Figure), 182
American Dietetic Association (ADA), 442
American Gas Association, 176
American Hotel & Motel Association, 499
American service, 222
Americans with Disabilities Act (ADA), 306, 326–328
Anxiety, 384
Appearance, and communication, 429
Appetizer soups, 211
Applicant references, check of, 305
"As purchased" (AP), 123, 219
Assimilation, and diversity, 389
Associate programs, 500
Audit trail, 461
Authority, 16–17
  and communication (Figure), 22
  defined, 16
  formal vs. informal, 17
Automatic mixers, and cleaning supplies, 193
Automatic sprinkler system, 107
Average cost, 463

B

Backshelf broiler (Figure), 183
Bacteria, 74
  overview (Figure), 75–81
Bain marie pot (Figure), 188
Barriers to change, 385
  group inertia, 385
  threatened expertise, 385
  threatened power, 385
  resource allocation, 385
Behavioral role modeling, 352
Belt conveyor dishwashing equipment (Figure), 190
Benchmarking, 476–77
Bidding,141–42
  competitive, 141–42
  formal, 142
  informal, 142
Biological hazards, 85
Blast chill, 172
Bona fide occupational qualifications (BFOQ), 326
Bookkeeper, duties of, 129
Botulism, 83
Box lunch, 222
Braising pans, 97
Brand names, 488
Bread, 213–14
  and facility layout, 168–69
Broiler (Figure), 183
Budget committees, 443
Budget development, 472–76
Budget guidelines vs. menu cost, 461–63
Budget preparation, annual (Figure), 474
Buffalo Choppers (Figure), 180
Buffet, 222
Buffet service (Figure), 223
Bulk food transport (Figure), 224
Burns, prevention of, 93–94
Buying/ordering, defined, 116

C

Cafeteria cash report (Figure), 456
Cafeteria food sales record (Figure), 454
Cafeteria operations, 453–61
  cash processing for deposit, 458
  cash register use, 455
  cash-handling concerns, 458–61
  cashier, 455
  operating reports, 455–58
  sales report, 456–57
  serving lines, and design, 170
Cakes, 217
Campylobacter jejuni, 75
Campylobacteria, 74
Canned vegetables, 206
Capital equipment purchases, 173–75
Carriers, defined, 86
Carts, 229
Case studies, 351
Cash register, 455, 458
Cash register sales tape, 460, 461
Cashier, 455
Cashier's report (Figure), 458
Catered events, 468–69
Cereals, 214–15
Certified Dietary Manager (CDM), 499, 507–8
Certified human resources executive (CHRE), 499
Certifying Board of Dietary Managers, 501
Checklists
  employee appraisal program (Figure), 368
  evaluation, 245
  implementing change (Figure), 388
  menu planning (Figure), 48
  product quality, 236
  safety (Figure), 99–103

Cheese, 204–5
Chemical hazards, 85
Chicken stew, 54–56
Chicken stew critical control points (Figure), 55–56
Chief financial officer, job description (Figure), 287
Chilling, 87
Chopper (Figure), 181
Choppers, and accidents, 98
Chronically ill, 34–35
Civil Rights Act of 1964, 325
Cleaning supplies, and cost control, 193
Cleanliness habits, personal (Figure), 86
Cleanup, 189–90
Cleanup duties, and sanitation, 88
Client, visiting with for product quality, 239
Client's rights review, 446
Clinical committees, 443
Clinical dietitian, 291
Clostridium perfringens, 76, 83
Coaching, as leadership style, 405
Code of Ethics, 494, 507–8
Collander (Figure), 187
Collective bargaining, concerns in (Figure), 393
Color, food, 45, 51
Color and product quality, 236
Color-coded utensils, 85
Commercial foodservices, 4
Committees, 442–44
  budget, 443
  infection control, 443
  quality assessment, 443
  safety, 443
Communication, 427–41
  barriers to, 429–30
  basic skills, 428–29
  channels, 431
  communication methods, 432–41
  communication myths, 430–31
  communication preparation, 437–41
  and dietary manager, 427–31
  facility meetings, 434–37
  overcoming barriers to, 430
  process, 428
Communication, and authority (Figure), 22
Communication, barriers to, 429–30
  appearance, 429
  disorganization, 429
  distractions, 429
  emotions, 429
  interest, 429
  knowledge, 429
  language, 430
  organization size, 430
  perception, 429
  personality, 429
  prejudice, 429
  status, 430
Communication, methods of, 432–33
  listening,432–33
  nonverbal, 433
  speaking, 432
  writing, 433
Communication flow, 21–23
Communication skills, basic, 428–29
Communicators, and leadership, 406
Community college programs, 499–500
Community service, 11
Comparative performance review, 361
Competitive bidding, 141–42
Computer-assisted instruction, 351
Computer printout, of standard recipe (Figure), 62
Computers
  and food preparation, 66–69
  and food production equipment, 384
  and food storage, 159
  and interviewing, 312
  and time clocks, 323
  and tray service, 227
Conferences, 351
Consistency, of food, 45
Contamination, defined, 85
Continuity of supply, 119
Continuous Quality Improvement (CQI), 251–53
Controller, 287
Convection ovens, 182, 229
Convection steamer (Figure), 184
Convenience-food products, 145–46
Cook-chill process technology, 171–72
  blast chill, 172
  sous vide, 172
  tumble chillers, 172
Cookies, 217
Cost, of food, 45–46
Cost comparison calculation, in make/buy analysis, 147
Cost control points, 454–55
Cost-of-living allowance, 471
Costs, and diversity, 389
Costs per client day, 464
Council on Hotel, Restaurant, and Institutional Education (CHRIE), 500
Cream pie fillings, 218
Credit memo (Figure), 151
Credit memo problems, and theft, 140
Critical control points (CCP), 49–50, 88–92. *See also* Hazard Analysis *and* Critical Control Point
Critical control points decision tree (Figure), 57
Cryptosporidium, 82
Culture-specific approach, to diversity, 390
Customer satisfaction, and forecasting, 128
Cuts, prevention of, 95
Cycle menu, 43–46
  color, 45
  consistency, 45
  cost, 45–46
  flavor, 45
  form and shape, 45
  preparation method, 45
  temperature, 45
  texture, 45

D

Daily cashier's report, 458
Deck oven, 96, 182
Delegating, as leadership style, 405
Delegation, 18
  and leadership, 406
  problems, 25
Delivery invoice errors, 140
Department of Agriculture food code, 88
Dessert preparation, 216–18
Detection systems, 106
Diarrhea, 83
Dietary department goals, 244–45
Dietary department statement (Figure), 17, 466–67
Dietary Guidelines, for Americans (Figure), 44
Dietary management, and medical records, 254
Dietary management, office design of, 171
Dietary manager, as part of healthcare team, 31–33
Dietary manager references, 511–13
Dietary manager resources, 517–25
  food resource organizations, 519–25
  government agencies, 525
  healthcare information organizations, 517–18
Dietary report, weekly (Figure), 465
Dietary services, organizing, 24–31
  basic principles, 26–29
  common mistakes in, 24–26
  systems approach, 29–31
Dietary staff, specifications for, 120
Dietary survey, preliminary tasks for (Figure), 269
Dietary survey (Figure), 266–67, 269
Directing, as leadership style, 405
Disabilities, and employees, 326
Discrimination, defined, 325
Discrimination in Employment Act of 1967, 326
Dishwasher, job list (Figure), 353
Dishwashing equipment (Figure), 189–90
Disorganization, and communication, 429
Distractions, and communication, 429
Distribution of power, 407
Diversity in the workplace, 387–390
Dollies, 176
Door model dishwashing equipment (Figure), 189
Doors, and hazards, 103
Double oven (Figure), 183
Downsizing, 477
Downward communication, 431
Draw-plate oven (Figure), 182
Dress codes, 326
Dried whole eggs, 203

Drug testing, and position applicants, 306
Dry heat, 201
Dry-pipe sprinkler system, 106
Du jour menu, 46, 47

E

E. coli, 77
Economics, 10
Edible portion (EP), 123, 219
Edible yield (EY), 123
Education, 10
Egg preparation, 203–4
Eggs, frozen, 203
Electrical equipment, and accidents, 95–96
Emotions, and communication, 429
Empathy, and leadership, 406
Employee appraisal, formalized (Figure), 368
Employee corrective action, 368–75
  causes of problems, 372–73
  classification of problems, 373–74
  negative action, 371–72
  principles of procedures, 374–75
  process, 369–70
  specific procedures, 370–71
Employee input, in decision making process, 410–11
Employee labor control, 313–25
  controlling overtime, 319–20
  determining labor hours, 321–22
  employee turnover, 320–21
  informing employees, 319
  payroll information systems, 322–23
  performance standards, 313–16
  salaried personnel scheduling, 319
  schedule writing, 318
  scheduling hours, 316–18
  standard vs. actual labor hours, 323–25
  work performance objectives, 316
Employee participation program, success of (Figure), 411
Employee policies, and eating/drinking, 199
Employee procedures, developing (Figure), 317
Employee recruitment, 298–99
  employers sources, 299
  interview process, 307–12
  obtaining information, 299–306
  selection decision, 312–13
Employee turnover, 320–21
Employee unions, 390–94
  administrators' view, 391
  collective bargaining process, 392–93
  and dietary manager, 393–94
  employee dislike of, 391–92
  impact on administration, 392
  reasons for joining, 390–91
  structure, 392
  unions' view of administrators, 391
Employer's basic report of injury, 104
Encouragement, and leadership, 406
English service, 222
Environmental hazards, defined, 85
Environmental Protection Agency (EPA), 220
Equal Employment Opportunity Commission (EEOC), 302, 307, 328
Equal employment opportunity laws (Figure), 304
Equipment, and planning, 199
Equipment, capital purchases, 173–75
  factors in selection, 174
  financing, 174
  suppliers of, 174
  used equipment, 174–75
Equipment, selection factors in purchasing, 175–76
  compatibility, 176
  construction concerns, 175–76
  cost, 175
  durability, 175
  ease of operation, 175
  sanitation/safety concerns, 176
  suitability, 175
Equipment, transport, 223–26
Equipment cleaning procedures (Figure), 178
Equipment maintenance, 191–92
Ethics, 139–42, 493–95
  competitive bidding, 141–42
  confidentiality, 494–95
  prime vendor, 142
  professional development, 493–95
  in purchasing, 139–42
  security concerns, 139–41
Evaluation checklist (Figure), 363–64
Evaluation of food service, 235–75
  external quality control, 247–71
  internal quality control, 235–47
Evaluation process overview (Figure), 244
Experience, with supplier, 137
Expert power, 23
External quality control, 247–71
  CQI, 251–53
  governmental agencies, 253–63
  JCAHO, 247–53
  licensure, 265–68
  OBRA, 264
  surveys, 268–71
Extinguishers, 104–6

F

Facility design, 167–71
  design principles, 168–70
  food preparation area design, 170–71
  food service area design, 170–71
  storage area design, 170
  work flow, 167–68
Facility equipment, 175–94
Facility layout, 167
Family style serving, 221–22
Falls, prevention of, 94
Federal Right of Privacy Act, 326
Fictitious companies, and theft, 140
Financial management, 453–82
  benchmarking, 476–77
  budget development, 472–76
  budget guidelines vs. menu cost, 461–63
  cash cafeteria operations, 453–61
  catered events, 468–69
  cost-effective procedures, 463–64
  efficiency, 477–78
  record-keeping, 464–68
  revenue generating, 476
  salary/wage adjustments, 469–72
Fire detection systems, 106
Fire exits, 103
Fire extinguishers, portable, 104
Fire safety, 104–7
  detection systems, 106
  fire extinguishers, 104–6
  sprinkler systems, 106–7
First-in, first-out (FIFO), 158
Fish preparation, 203
Flat rate plan, for salary increases, 471
Flavor, of food, 45, 53
Food acceptance evaluation, 238–40
Food cutters, 180
Food Guide Pyramid, 509–10
Food-borne infections, 83
Food mixers (Figure), 179
Food preparation, 47–69
  computers and, 66–69
  procedures for, 56–69
  standardized recipes, 56–66
  standards for, 47–56
Food preparation, equipment (Figure), 181
Food preparation, standards for, 47–56
  characteristics of high-quality foods, 51–56
  HACCP format, 51
  HACCP principles, 49–50
  hazard characteristics, 50
Food procurement, production, and service, 41–275
Food production planning and leftover report, 200
Food production, 197–229
  control, 199–200
  identifying service type, 221–22
  planning, 197–99
  principles, 200–218
  solid waste monitoring, 219–21
  transport equipment, 223–26
  tray line systems, 227–29
  waste monitoring, 219–21
Food quantity, and purchasing, 122
Food requisition form, 157
Food service evaluation, 235–75
Food slicer, 98, 180, 181
Food standards, defining, 235
Food storage practices, 153–61
  assigning values to inventory, 158
  computerized systems, 159
  issuing practices, 159–61
  perpetual-inventory system, 154–58
  record-keeping, 154
  reduction of inventory costs, 158
  storage security concerns, 158–59

Food-borne illness, 82–83, 85
Food-borne illness, investigating procedures (Figure), 89
Food-holding times, 87
Foodservice
contracted, 8–10
equipment, 175–94
non-commercial, 12–38
operations, 3–7
organization of, 16–24
overview, 1–3
Foodservice, organization of, 16–24
communication flow, 21–23
institutional foodservices, 16
organizing concepts, 16–18
power in, 23–24
process steps, 18–21
Foodservice, self–operated, 8–10
Foodservice equipment, 175–94
chilling, 178
cleanup, 189–90
cooking, 180
holding, 189
preparation, 178–80
receiving, 176
refrigeration, 178
selection, 175–76
serving, 189
Foodservice growth (Figure), 6
Foodservice operations, categories (Figure), 4
Foodservice sales, healthcare market overview (Figure), 5
Foodservice sales, overview of student market (Figure), 5
Forced-choice evaluation, 365–66
Form and shape, of food, 45
French hot plates (Figure), 183
French service, 222
Fresh vs. thawed, in received products, 140
Fringe benefits, 471–72
Frozen eggs, 203
Fruit cleaning, equipment for, 178
Fruit pie fillings, 218
Fruits, 206–7
canned, 207
fresh, 206
fried, 207
frozen, 207
Fryers, and accidents, 97–98
Fryers, deep, 97

G

Garnish, salad, 210
Garnishes, 46, 47
Gas burners (Figure), 183
Gelatins, 216–218
Goals, procurement, 117–18
delivery schedule, 118
quality, 117
quantity, 117
price, 117–18
supplier selection, 118
Goals of institutional foodservices, 10–12
community service, 11
economic, 10–11
educational, 10
nutritional, 10
personal, 11
professional, 11
social/personal, 10
societal, 11–12
Golden rule, and diversity in workforce, 389
Governmental agencies, 253–63
Governmental facilities, 7–8
Graduate programs, 500
Griddle (Figure), 183
Group, defined, 412
Group discussion, 434
Group inertia, 385
Groupwork, and leadership, 412–14

H

Halo effect, and interviewing, 311
Hazard analysis, 88–92
Hazard Analysis and Critical Control Point (HACCP), 49–54, 88, 153, 499
cooking process (Figure), 53
corrective action table (Figure), 58
holding process (Figure), 53
preparation process (Figure), 52
receiving process (Figure), 51
recipe worksheet, 54
storage process (Figure), 52
Hazard analysis and risk assessment, 49
Hazard Communication Standard (HazComm), 107–8
Hazards, 99–102. *See also* Accidents *and* Safety
in dining areas, 101
in food preparation area, 102
in pots and pans room, 101
in receiving area, 99
in serving area, 100
in soiled dish process area, 101
in storage area, 100
in walk-in coolers and freezers, 102
Health Care Financing Administration (HCFA), 264
Healthcare, and client needs, 241
Healthcare market sales (Figure), 5
Healthcare reform, impact on dietetics, 498
Healthcare team, and dietary manager, 31–33
Heat detectors, 106
Herzberg's maintenance-motivation theory, 340–41
High-compression compartment steam unit (Figure), 184
High-cost benefits, 472
High-cost items, 134
Holiday promotions, 489
Home-delivered meals, 485–86
Horizontal communication, 431
Hospital, organizational chart (Figure), 30
Hospital cook, 293
Hospital dietary services (Figure), 28
Hospital foodservice worker, 294
Hospitality industry, overview (Figure), 2
Human resource development, 337–75
employee corrective action, 368–75
employee training programs, 348–56
motivation, 337–41
orientation and training, 342–48
performance evaluations, 356–68
Human resource management, 277. *See also* Staffing
Human resource planning, 280–82
objectives of, 280
process (Figure), 281
steps in, 281–82

I

Immediate use, vs. inventory purchasing, 123–24
Implementation of change, checklist for (Figure), 388
Importance ratings (Figure), 285
Improper planning, 24
Incineration, and environment, 221
Infection control committees, 443
Informal communication, 431
Infrared radiation system, 228
Injury, report form (Figure), 105
Institute of Business Ethics, 495, 501
Institutional foodservice, 4, 10, 16
Insulated tray (Figure), 228
Insurance, and food purchase, 122
Intelligence, and leadership, 406
Interest, and communication, 429
Intermediate care facilities, 33
Internal communication, 437–41
Internal quality control, 235–47
defining food standards, 235
developing procedures, 243
dietary department goals, 244–45
evaluating strategies, 244
food acceptance evaluation, 238–40
food evaluation, 240–41
implementing checks, 236–38
improving dietary services, 246–47
operating procedures, 243–44
self-review procedures, 245–46
special nourishments, 241–42
supplemental feedings, 241–42
testing, 236
training employees, 235–36
Internships, 500–501
Interviews, 307–12
atmosphere for, 310
computer-assisted, 312
directive (Figure), 310
follow-up after, 311
questions (Figure), 308–10
techniques, 311
tips (Figure), 309

Inventory, cost reduction methods, 158
Inventory, and food quantity determination, 122
Inventory, physical, 154

J

Job applicant, reference check (Figure), 306
Job application form, 299–301
Job breakdown (Figure), 283
Job breakdown procedures, 282–98
  description, 284–97
  service-ware washer (Figure), 283
  specifications, 297
Job descriptions, 284–97
  assistant administrator, dietary services, 286
  assistant administrator, financial services, 287
  chief clinical dietitian, 290
  clinical dietitian, 291
  controller, 287
  dietary manager, 292
  food production manager, 289
  foodservice director, 288
  hospital cook, 293
  hospital foodservice worker, 294
  nursing home cook, 295
  nursing home foodservice worker, 296
Job evaluation, methods of, 470–71
  grade description, 470–71
  point system, 471
  simple ranking, 470
Job satisfaction, and forecasting, 128
Job specification, cook (Figure), 298
Joint Commission for the Accreditation of Healthcare Organizations (JCAHO), 247–53, 349, 442, 444
  standards (Figure), 249
Journals, professional, 514–15

K

Kettles, and accidents, 97
Kettles, steam jacketed, 97, 184
Kickbacks, and theft, 139
KISS (keep it simple and short), 433
Kitchen design, types of, 171–72
  cook-chill, 171–72
  cook-serve, 171
  no-cook, 171
Knives (Figure), 185–86
Knowledge, and communication, 429

L

Labor, and planning, 199
Labor costs, vs. quality, 313
Labor hour report (Figure), 369
Landfills, 221
Language, and communication, 430
Last-in, First-out (LIFO), 158
Lateral transfer, 350
Lawful vs. unlawful pre-employment inquiries (Figure), 302–3
Layout, factors in, 167–170
  amount of food used, 168
  funds, 168
  menu, 167–70
  necessary equipment, 168
  production systems, 168
  quantity to prepare, 168
  space, 168
Lead time, defined, 125–26
Leadership, 399–420
  balanced view of power, 407–10
  decision making, 416–18
  defined, 399
  employee participaton programs, 410–14
  goals and priorities by dietary managers, 414–16
  qualities and skills, 406
  situational, 402–6
  style of, 400–402
  time management, 418–20
  types of, 399–401
Leadership style, defined, 400
Leadership styles (Figure), 400, 403, 404
Leadership types, 399–401
  autocratic, 400
  bureaucratic, 401
  democratic, 401
  laissez-faire, 401
Leftovers, handling of, 87
Legal power, 23
Licensure, 265–68
Lighting, 102
Limited menu, 46, 47
Line and staff relationships, 118
Listeria monocytogenes, 78
Listeriosis bacteria, 78, 83
Long-term care facilities, guidelines for (Figure), 255–60
Low-compression compartment steam unit (Figure), 184
Low-cost benefits, 472

M

Mailing brochures, 138
Main dish soup, 211
Maintenance log, for equipment (Figure), 177
Make/buy analysis, 142–149
  convenience-food products, 145–46
  decision making, 143–44
  important factors in, 144
  necessity of study, 143–44
  on-site production, 144–45
  procedures, 146–49
Malnutrition diagnosis form (Figure), 252
Management By Objectives (MBO), 362–63
Management company, considerations in use of (Figure), 8
Management loop, 13–16
  controlling, 15
  coordinating, 14–15
  directing, 15
  evaluation, 15–16
  organizing, 14
  planning, 13–14
  staffing, 15
Management loop (Figure), 14
Management principles in non-commercial foodservices, 12–40
  definition of, 12–13
  dietary manager, 31–33
  dietary services, 24–31
  management loop, 13–16
  nursing care, 33–37
  old vs new, 13
  organization of, 16–24
Management quality, and diversity, 389
Management skills, 499
Manager confidence, and forecasting, 128
Manager's role in recruitment and selection, 297–313
Managerial obsolescence, defined, 280
Managerial power (Figure), 407
Market share, and diversity, 389
Marketing, 483–90
  vs. advertising, 483–84
  determining the market, 484–87
  group study, 486
  life-style analysis, 486
  management, 483–90
  marketing plan development, 487
  merchandising, 487–90
  place, 484
  price, 484
  product, 483–84
  promotion, 484
  research, 485–86
  resident needs, 486
Maslow's hierarchy of needs (Figure), 339
Material safety data sheet (MSDS), 107–9
Material safety data sheet (Figure), 109
Maximum level, defined, 126
McClelland's theory of motivation, 341
McGregor's Theory X/Y leadership, 400–401
Meal count recap sheet (Figure), 460
Meal survey (Figure), 238
Meat, and moist heat, 201
Meat preparation, 200–201
Meat thermometer, 201
Meat trimming, equipment for, 178
Meat-processing equipment, 180
Medicaid, 35–37
Medical center, dietary department chart (Figure), 27
Medical exams, and applicants, 305
Medical records analysis worksheet, 249–250
Medicare, 35–37
  sources of funds (Figure), 36

Menu, example of (Figure), 226
Menu planning, 43–72
checklist for, 47–48
cycle menu, 43–46
Menu pre-cost sheet (Figure), 462
Menu types (Figure), 46–47
a la carte menu, 47
du jour menu, 47
limited menu, 47
table d'hote menu, 47
Menus, and computer, 66–69
analysis, 68
forecasting, 68
ingredient filing, 67
menu planning, 67–68
nutrient analysis, 68–69
recipe filing, 67
Merchandising, 487–90
employee training, 488–89
promoting services, 489–90
special promotions, 489
Meringue, 218
Merit performance plan, for salary increases, 471
Metal pellet system, 227
Microorganisms, classification of, 74, 82
Microwave oven, 229
Military foodservice, 4
Military reserve obligations, and employees, 326
Minimum/maximum purchasing system, 124–27
Mission statement, 18
Mixers, 98, 179
Mixers, and accidents, 98
Modeling, and training, 352
Moist heat, and meat, 201
Moist heat, and poultry, 202
Molds, 82
Monthly budget (Figure), 475
Morale, and motivation, 338
Motivation, 337–341
importance of, 338
maintenance/motivation theory, 340–41
Maslow's human needs theory, 338–40
McClelland's theory, 341
Multicultural approach, and diversity, 390
Muscle strains, 94

N

National Advisory Committee on Microbiological Criteria for Foods (NACMCF), 49
National Restaurant Association, 499
National Sanitation Foundation International, 175–76
National Social Security Act, 253
Negative transfer, 350
Negotiation, 135–36
Net goods cost (Figure), 463
No-cost benefits, 472
No-money facilities, 461
No-touch hand-washing stations, 85
Non-commercial foodservices,12–38
Nourishment centers, design of, 171
Nourishment intake record (Figure), 242, 243
Nursing care, types of, 33–37
acute care, 33
assisted living, 34
institutional living, 34
long-term care, 34–35
mental health care, 34
rehabilitation care, 34
skilled care, 33
subacute care, 33
Nursing home cook, 295
Nursing home foodservice worker, 296
Nutrition, 10
Nutrition assessment form (Figure), 252
Nutrition care process (Figure), 248

O

Occupational Safety and Health Administration (OSHA), 104, 107
Office design, of dietary management, 171
Older Americans Act, 485
Omnibus Budget Reconciliation Act (OBRA), 264
On-the-job concerns, 325–29
ADA, 326–28
EEOC, 325–26
sexual harassment, 328–29
On-the-job training (OJT), steps in, 355–56
coaching, 356
follow-up, 356
practice, 355–56
preparation, 355
presentation, 355
On-site production, 144–45
One-way communication, 351
Open-ended employee summary, 366
Operating reports, 455–58
Operational accuracy, and forecasting, 128
Order point, defined, 126
Order quantity, calculating, 127–28
Organization, vs. overorganization, 25
Organization size, and communication, 430
Organizational changes, 384–87
and the dietary manager, 387
resistance to, 384–87
Organizational charts (Figure), 27
hospital (Figure), 30
medical center dietary department (Figure), 27
retirement community dietary services (Figure), 28
small hospital dietary services (Figure), 28
university food service (Figure), 29
Organizing concepts (Figure), 19
Organizing process, steps in (Figure), 20
Orientation and training, 342–48
checklist (Figure), 343–48
Outline, types of, 438
advantages and disadvantages format, 438
chronological, 438
problem-solution, 438
step, 438
topical, 438
Ovens (Figure), 182–83
Ovens, and accidents, 96
Ovenfrying, and poultry, 202
Overtime, 319–20
Overview, hospitality industry (Figure), 2

P

Padding the invoice, and theft, 139–40
Pans, and accidents, 97
Paperwork flow, 129
Parasites, 82
Pasta cooker (Figure), 188
Pastries, 218
Patient questionnaire (Figure), 239
Payment method, and theft, 141
Payment policies, 136
Payroll, manual processing of, 322
Payroll information systems, 322–23
Peeler, vegetable (Figure), 181
Pellet system equipment (Figure), 227
Perception, and communication, 429
Performance review, types of, 361–63
absolute standards, 361–62
comparative, 361
management by objectives, 362–63
Performance standard system, for employees, 313–16
flow chart (Figure), 315
Perishable product call sheet (Figure), 125
Perpetual inventory form (Figure), 156
Perpetual inventory system, 154–58
Personal cleanliness habits (Figure), 86
Personality, and communication, 429
Personnel pride, and forecasting, 128
Persuasion, defined, 436
Philanthropic facilities, 7–8
Physical inventory form (Figure), 155
Pies, 218
Pilferage, 122
Plan of correction (POC), 268
Plate waste information (Figure), 240
Plate waste sampling, 240
Poisons, 82–83
Portions, and planning, 198
Positive transfer, 350
Poultry preparation, 201–2
Power, determinants of (Figure), 409
Power, in interpersonal relationships, 408
Power, sources of (Figure), 23
Power and personal effectiveness (Figure), 408

Pre-action sprinkler system, 106
Pre-costing procedures, 462
Pre-employment inquiries, lawful vs. unlawful (Figure), 302–3
Pre-employment inquiry guide (Figure), 302–3
Pre-production planning, 197–99
  equipment, 199
  labor, 199
  portions, 198–99
Prejudice, and communication, 429
Preparation method, of food, 45
Presentations, 438–41
  case studies, 441
  conference, 440
  demonstration, 440
  interactive ad hoc groups, 441
  panel, 441
  role-playing, 441
  seminar, 440
Prevention of food-borne illnesses, 83
Preventive-maintenance program, 191
Preventive-maintenance schedule (Figure), 192
Price, determination of, 134
Price, negotiation with seller, 134
Price quotation request (Figure), 132
Prime vendor purchasing, 142
Principles, food production, 200–218
  bread, 213–14
  cereals, 214–15
  cheese preparation, 204–5
  dessert preparation, 216–18
  egg preparation, 203–4
  fish preparation, 203
  fruits, 206–7
  meat preparation, 200–201
  poultry preparation, 201–2
  salad preparation, 207–10
  sandwich production, 215–16
  sauce preparation, 211–13
  soup, 211
  stock preparation, 210–11
  thawing, 202–3
  vegetables, 205–6
Problem solving, scientific method of (Figure), 417
Procurement, defined, 116–17
Procurement process, 117–19
  importance, 118
  objectives, 117–18
  staff functions, 118–19
Product flow, 54
Product score sheet (Figure), 237
Production control, 199–200
Production-planning records, 200
Productivity, and diversity, 389
Professional associations, 495
Professional certifications, 499
Professional development, 493–495
  career opportunities, 498
  continuing professional education, 498–501
  ethics, 493–95
  professional associations, 495–97
Professional education, continuing, 498–501
  associate programs, 500
  community college programs, 499–500
  four-year programs, 500
  graduate programs, 500
  internships, 500–501
  management skills, 499
  professional certifications, 499
  technical progams, 499
  technical skills, 498–99
Professionalism, defined, 494
Proprietary facilities, 7–8
Public accommodations, and employees, 327
Pulper (Figure), 189
Punitive power, 23
Purchase cost, 463
Purchase order (Figure), 133
Purchase price, procedures to reduce, 134–35
Purchase requisition (Figure), 131
Purchase specifications, 119–22
  advantages of, 120–22
  developing, 120
  disadvantages of, 121
  factors of (Figure), 122
  format for (Figure), 121
  minimum requirements, 120
Purchase unit, defined, 125
Purchasing, 115–65
  accounting records, 128–39
  definition of terms, 116–17
  determining quantity, 122–28
  ethics, 139–42
  make/buy analysis, 142–49
  process, 117–19
  and profits, 119
  specifications, 119–22
Purchasing staff, specifications for, 120

Q

Quality assessment committees, 443
Quality control, 235–71
  external, 247–71
  internal, 235–47
Quality deterioration, and food purchase, 122
Quality substitutions, and theft, 140
Quantity, in purchasing, 122–28, 134
  assessing of needs, 123–24
  EP/AP conversions, 123
  forecasting, 127–28
  immediate use, 124
  minimum/maximum systems, 124–26
Quantity recipe, sample (Figure), 61

R

Rack conveyor dishwashing equipment (Figure), 190
Ranges, and accidents, 96
Rate-of-rise detectors, 106
Receiving clerk's report (Figure), 152
Receiving equipment, 176
Receiving procedures, 150–53
  accepting products, 151–52
  checking against purchase records, 150
  completing receiving report, 152
  inspecting against delivery invoice, 151
  inspecting against specifications, 150–51
  monitoring hazard analysis, 153
  removing to storage, 153
Receiving process, 149–53
  components of system, 149–50
  procedural steps, 150–53
Receiving security, 140
Recipe form, standardized (Figure), 60
Recipes, 43–72
  increasing or decreasing (Figure), 64
  standard (Figure), 62
  standard score card (Figure), 65
  yield, 60
Record-keeping, 154, 464–68. *See also* Accounting
Recruiting, and diversity, 389
Recruitment procedures, 298–99
Recycling, 221
Reel oven (Figure), 182
Re-engineering, 477
Reference books, 515–16
Reference check (Figure), 306
Referent power, 23
Refrigeration, 178. *See also* Temperature
Refrigeration equipment (Figure), 179
Rehearsal, and training, 352
Relationships, not clearly defined, 25
Religious discrimination, 326
Replacement cost, 463
Report forms, injury (Figure), 105
Residential care facilities, 33
Resistance to change, 384–85
  anxiety, 384
  changing relationships, 384
  economic concerns, 384
  inconvenience, 384
  increased control, 384
  mistrust in supervisors, 385
  sources of, 385
Responsibility vs. authority, 25
Restaurant style menu, 46, 47
Retention, and training, 352
Rethermalization center, and design, 171
Rethermalization kitchens, 160
Retirement community dietary chart (Figure), 28
Revenue report, public feeding (Figure), 459
Reward power, 23
Rice, cooking, 215
Roasting, of poultry, 202
Role models, and leadership, 406
Rotational internships, 501
Russian service, 222

S

Safe food-handling guidelines, 86–88
Safety, 92–113. *See also* Hazards *and* Accidents
  accident investigation programs, 104
  checklist (Figure), 99–103
  fire safety, 104–7
  foodservice accidents, 93–98
  HazComm, 107–8
  management in work areas, 92–93
  OSHA, 104
Safety checklist (Figure), 99–103
Safety committees, 443
Safety inspection programs, 99–103
Safety level, defined, 126
Salad dressing, 209–10
Salads, 207–10
  equipment for, 178
  garnish, 210
  ingredients, 207–8
  parts of, 209
  preparation, 207–10
Salaried personnel scheduling, 319
Salaries, factors affecting, 469–70
Salary / wage adjustments, 469–71
  administration, 470
  employee benefit programs, 471–72
  factors affecting wage levels, 469–70
  job evaluation, 470–71
Salary / wage increases, determining, 471
Salespeople, and supplier, 138
Salmonellosis, 79, 83
Sandwich production, 215–16
  assembly, 216
  precautions for, 216
  preparation, 216
  variation in bread, 215
  variation in fillings, 215–16
Sanitary food-handling practices (Figure), 84
Sanitary terminology (Figure), 85
Sanitation, 73–113
  critical control point system, 88–92
  defined, 85
  food-borne illnesses, 82–83
  hazard analysis, 88–92
  microorganisms, 74, 82
  personal cleanliness and sanitation, 86
  prevention of food-borne illnesses, 83
  safe food-handling guidelines, 86–88
Sauces, preparation, 211–13
Sauces, types of, 211
Scales, as preparation equipment, 178
Scales, and receiving equipment, 176, 179
Scheduling hours, 316–18
Security principles, in storage, 158–59
Selection, defined, 116
Selection tests, and applicants, 305
Self-confidence, and leadership, 406
Self-review procedures, 245–46
Semi a la carte menu, 46, 47
Sequential transfer, 350
Service types, 221–22
  American service, 222
  box lunch, 222
  buffet, 222
  English service, 222
  family style, 221–22
  French service, 222
  Russian service, 222
  waiter / waitress, 222
Sex discrimination, 326
Sexual harassment, 328–29
Shigellosis, 80, 83
Short weight, 140
Situational interview questions, 309–10
Simulations, 351–52
Skilled nursing facilities, 33
Slicer (Figure), 181
Slicers, and accidents, 98
Smoke detectors, 106
Social reinforcement, and training, 352
Solid waste monitoring, 219–21
Soup, 211
Source document, defined, 129
Source document flow (Figure), 129–30
Source reduction, and environment, 220–21
Sous vide, 172
Special promotions, 489
Spoilage, 85
Spoiled food, and production control, 199–200
Sprinkler systems, 106–7
Staff specialists, 25
Staffing, 279–329
  employee recruitment and selection, 297–313
  human resource planning procedures, 279–82
  job breakdown procedures, 282–97
  labor control, 313–25
  management tools, 282
  on-the-job concerns, 325–29
Stairways, and safety, 103
Standard vs. actual labor hours, 323–25
Standardized recipes, 59–66
  alternate method for developing, 66
  developing, 60–66
  evaluating, 60–66
Staphylococcal poisoning, 83
Status, and communication, 430
Steam cooking, 205
Steam unit (Figure), 184
Steam-jacketed kettle (Figure), 184
Steamer (Figure), 97, 184
Steamers, and accidents, 97
Steaming, of poultry, 202
Step rate plan, for salary increases, 471
Stew, chicken, 54
Stock pot (Figure), 188
Stock preparation, 210–11
Storage. *See* Food storage
Storage security concerns, 158–59
Structured internship programs, 500
Student market, foodservice sales (Figure), 5
Stuffing, for poultry, 202
Subrecipes, 67
Supervisor, as manager of change, 383–94
  diversity in the workplace, 387–90
  employee unions, 390–94
  implementing changes, 383–84
  organizational change, 384–87
Supplemental feedings, 241–42
Supplier, 136–39
  catalogs, 138
  characteristics of (Figure), 137
  financial stability, 138
  honesty of, 139
  information about, 137–38
  and local purchasing, 139
  location of, 138
  selection process, 136–39
  specifications for, 120
  technical ability of, 138
  visit to facility, 138
Supply, continuity of, 119
Supply, managing cost of, 192–94
Supply of purchasing information, 119
Supporting, as leadership style, 405
Surveys, 255–60
  challenging results of, 270–71
  guidelines for (Figure), 255–60
Sweet dough, 213
System worksheets (Figure), 261–63

T

Table d'hote menu, 46, 47
Task analysis information, 282
Task force, defined, 442
Taste panel, 236
Technical progams, 499
Technical skills, 498–99
Temperature
  basic rule of, 88
  chart (Figure), 91
  of food, 45
  and meats, 236
  and poultry, 236
  and product quality, 240
  and sanitation concerns (Figure), 91
Tenderizer (Figure), 181
Terminal heat process, 50
Testing instrument, and product quality, 236
Texture, of food, 45, 52
Texture, and product quality, 236
Thawing meats, 201–3
Thawing poultry, 202–3
Theft, 122
Theft, types of, 139–40
  credit memo problems, 140
  delivery invoice errors, 140
  fictitious companies, 140
  kickbacks, 139
  padding the invoice, 139–40
  processing thefts, 140
  quality substitutions, 140
  receiving security, 140
Thermometer, calibration, 87

Thermometers, recording, 85
Thermostatically controlled dishes, 228
Tickler list (Figure), 420
Time clocks, 322, 323
  computerized, 323
Time management, 418–20
Time / temperature relationships (Figure), 241
Title VII (Civil Rights Act), 325, 328
To-do list (Figure), 419
Tools, for cooking areas (Figure), 185–88
Trade associations (Figure), 496–97
Trade journals, 138
Trade shows, 138
Training, checklist (Figure), 357–60
Training employees, 235–36
Training lesson format (Figure), 354
Training programs, 348–56
  adult learning theory, 349–52
  characteristics of good trainers, 349
  need for, 478
  on-the-job training, 355–56
  training process steps, 352–55
Training techniques, 351
Transfer, of training, 352
Transfers, types of, 350
Transport equipment, 223–26
Transport racks (Figure), 224–25
Tray line systems, 227–29
Trustworthiness, and leadership, 406
Tumble chillers, 172
Turkey, roasting, 202
Turnover, factors leading to, 321

U

Undercounter dishwashing equipment (Figure), 189
Underwriters Laboratories, 176
Unions. *See* Employee unions
University food service, organizational chart (Figure), 29
Upward communication, 431
Usage rate, defined, 125
Used equipment, 174–75

V

Vegetables, 205–6
  cleaning equipment, 178
  color of, 206
  cooking in steam, 205
  cooking in water, 205
  fresh, 206
  frozen, 206
  peelers, 180
  preparation of, 205–6
Vegetable peeler (Figure), 181
Ventilation, and safety, 103
Vertical cutter and mixer (VCM), 180
Vertical transfer, 350
Virus, 74
Viscosity of food, 52
Visual inventory, 129

W

Waiter / waitress, 222
Ward kitchen, design of, 171
"Warm-body syndrome," and human resource planning, 279
Warning notice (Figure), 376–77
Waste monitoring, 219–21
Waste report (Figure), 220
Weight, and theft, 140
Weighted average, and inventory, 158
Wet-pipe sprinkler system, 106
Whisk, wire (Figure), 187
Work performance objectives, 316

X

X-ray services, and medicare, 36

Y

Yeast breads, 213
Yeasts, 82
Yellow pages, 138
Yersinia enterocolitica, 81